Exploring Evolutionary Biology

Readings from *American Scientist*

EDITED BY
MONTGOMERY SLATKIN
UNIVERSITY OF CALIFORNIA, BERKELEY

Sinauer Associates, Inc. Publishers
Sunderland, Massachusetts

The Cover

A partial skull of a vervet monkey resting on leaf litter in the woodlands of Amboseli Park, Kenya. This is all that remains of the monkey's skeleton after predation and scavenging. The specimen is weathered and fragile, indicating that it has been exposed to the elements for several years. Most bones are destroyed by the same natural processes that affected the remains of this monkey. Taphonomy is the study of these processes and how they control what is preserved in the fossil record (see Chapter 6). Photograph by Anna K. Behrensmeyer, National Museum of Natural History, Smithsonian Institution.

Library of Congress Cataloging-in-Publication Data

Exploring evolutionary biology: readings from American Scientist / edited by Montgomery Slatkin
p.   cm.
Includes bibliographical references.
ISBN 0-87893-764-1 (paper)
1. Evolution (Biology)   I. Slatkin, Montgomery. II. American Scientist.
QH366.2.E96 1995   94-45568
575—dc20   CIP

Printed in Hong Kong
5 4 3 2 1

Contents

Preface

Evolutionary biology is a subject with a long tradition. Many of its most important questions were asked before Charles Darwin's *On the Origin of Species* was published in 1859. In the twentieth century, the evolutionary perspective became an essential component of biology. The subject is still full of excitement, with new discoveries of every type being made nearly every day. We have new techniques for finding and interpreting fossils. We have new methods, borrowed from molecular biology, that give us novel perspectives on the genetic basis of evolution. And we have new conceptual theories that challenge the most deeply held and comfortable views of the past. Those of us who teach evolutionary biology try to convey this novelty and excitement to our students. We are not just cleaning up after Darwin—we are continuing the job he and others only started. We try to teach our students not only how much we know but how much we do not know. This book is intended to help.

Exploring Evolutionary Biology is not a comprehensive review of the subject; there are several excellent textbooks that serve that need. Instead, it is a collection of articles by people who have tried to make their specialty accessible to a wide audience. It is intended to be a supplement for a course on evolution, even one taught to nonbiology majors, and it could also introduce a curious reader to some of the most interesting areas of research in evolutionary biology and provide a guide to the more specialized literature.

Acknowledgments

This is the second time Sigma Xi and Sinauer Associates have cooperated to produce a volume of readings collected from *American Scientist*. As with the earlier collection (*Exploring Animal Behavior*, 1993, edited by Paul W. Sherman and John Alcock), the project would not have been possible without the goodwill of the authors who agreed to have their work reprinted and the cooperation of the photographers and artists whose work illustrates the book. I take this opportunity to thank them all.

The idea for *Exploring Evolutionary Biology* originated with *American Scientist*'s editor, Rosalind Reid. Her preliminary groundwork and hard work in bringing the book to reality were keys to its success. Lil Chappell and Hui Hu of the editorial and production staff at *American Scientist* also did yeoman service. At Sinauer Associates, Andy Sinauer shepherded the project as the editorial and production staff, including Christopher Small, Janice Holabird, Carol Wigg, and Kathaleen Emerson, chased down the details and put the book together.

Montgomery Slatkin
Berkeley, California

Part I
Decoding the Fossil Record

An evolutionary biologist must be concerned with both pattern and process. The *pattern* is the actual record of events in the history of life, and the *process* is what made those events and not others occur. Until we can relive the past, our knowledge of the pattern comes from fossils and from the diversity of organisms alive today.

The fossil record has always been a problem. In *On the Origin of Species,* Darwin began his discussion of the subject under the heading "On the Imperfection of the Geological Record," conceding that the fossil record rarely showed the continuous series of intermediates that Darwin argued must have existed. Many more fossils have been found since 1859—including many from Precambrian rocks that Darwin and his contemporaries thought were devoid of fossils—so we now have a much clearer idea about many details of the pattern.

This section, then, covers the pattern of evolution as we currently interpret it from the fossil record. The first three papers focus on major transitions in the history of life. Gray and Shear review what is known about the earliest inhabitants of land, who had to solve the manifold problems created by living in air rather than water. Although information is still sketchy, the recent discovery of microfossils has revealed that the first colonists of land arrived earlier than had been thought. Gensel and Andrews describe the earliest terrestrial plants in more detail, illustrating how plants dealt with both air and gravity. Forey and Janvier describe the fishes that were the earliest vertebrates. They show how a detailed analysis of seemingly minor characteristics of fossils can show us the evolutionary relationships of early species. Thomson provides a commentary on recent fossils that provide more details about the transition from early vertebrates to the first tetrapods (four-limbed vertebrates). These articles taken together show that, despite the limitations of the fossil record, we can learn some of the details of major transitions that have occurred long in the past. Unfortunately, they also reveal how much remains to be learned.

The article by Briggs and the one by Behrensmeyer discuss the fossil record in quite a different way. They discuss the conditions under which fossils form and the ways in which that process might bias our understanding of the pattern of evolution. Briggs focuses on the very rare fossil remains of soft body parts and fragile bones. These "extraordinary fossils" give us a glimpse not only of how much we must be missing but also of what we have to learn from the lucky accidents that formed these rare specimens.

Behrensmeyer's paper shows us how contemporary studies of the degradation of remains reveals the ways that some fossils must have been distorted and modified.

The next two readings deal with extinction. Extinctions, and in particular mass extinctions, have recently taken a prominent place in evolutionary thinking. According to many evolutionary biologists, mass extinctions create new opportunities for evolutionary changes that might not have been possible otherwise. For example, the explosive evolution of mammals at the beginning of the Tertiary* might not have occurred without the mass extinction at the end of the Mesozoic, and in particular the extinction of the dinosaurs. That is a very different view than the more traditional scenario, in which the rise of the mammals was an inevitable consequence of their homeothermy (ability to regulate their own body temperatures) and their intelligence.

Glen discusses the controversial evidence surrounding the mass extinction at the end of the Mesozoic and the evidence that other mass extinctions were caused by the impact of extraterrestrial objects such as asteroids. Since the publication of Glen's article in 1987, there is evidence that the "smoking gun" he refers to may have been found in Mexico, in the form of the impact crater from a meteorite that fell some time around the end of the Cretaceous. Controversy remains, however, about whether—and how—such an event could cause the pattern of mass extinction observed at the end of the Cretaceous and whether there were other contributing factors. The paper by Burney examines another cause of extinction: humans. Today it is distressingly clear that humans are causing a mass extinction comparable to the major mass extinctions of the past. The evidence comes from archaeological and fossil records and from contemporary ecological studies.

The last paper in this section, by Marshall, describes what happened when North America and South America were first connected by a land bridge, thus initiating an experiment of staggering proportions. The mammals of North America and the mammals and large flightless birds of South America encountered each other for the first time. This exchange took place so recently and the organisms involved were so readily fossilized that we have an excellent record of what happened.

The table on inside back cover defines the eras, periods, and epochs of the geological time scale.

Early Life on Land

Minute fossils offer evidence that life invaded the land millions of years earlier than previously thought

Jane Gray and William Shear

Life originated in the early seas less than a billion years after the earth was formed. Yet another three billion years were to pass before the first plants and animals appeared on the continents. Life's transition from the sea to the land was perhaps as much of an evolutionary challenge as genesis.

What forms of life were able to make such a drastic change in lifestyle? The traditional view of the first terrestrial organisms is based on megafossils—relatively large specimens of essentially whole plants and animals. Vascular plants, related to modern seed plants and ferns, left the first comprehensive megafossil record. Because of this it has been commonly assumed that the sequence of terrestrialization reflected the evolution of modern terrestrial ecosystems. In this view primitive vascular plants first colonized the margins of continental waters, followed by animals that fed on the plants, and lastly by animals that preyed on the plant-eaters. More-

Jane Gray is professor of biology and adjunct professor of geology at the University of Oregon. She received her Ph.D. in paleontology from the University of California, Berkeley. Her research interests in early land plants and paleoecology have taken her to many parts of the globe, including China, Africa, South America and northern Canada. William Shear is Charles Patterson Distinguished Professor of Biology at Hampden-Sydney College, and a Research Associate in the Department of Entomology of the American Museum of Natural History. He received his Ph.D. in evolutionary biology from Harvard University in 1971. His current research is on the systematics and evolution of arachnids and myriapods, and the fossil evidence for early terrestrial ecosystems. Gray's address: Department of Biology, University of Oregon, Eugene, OR 97403. Shear's address: Department of Biology, Hampden-Sydney College, Hampden-Sydney, VA 23943

over, the megafossils suggest that terrestrial life appeared and diversified almost explosively near the boundary between the Silurian and the Devonian periods, a little more than 400 million years ago.

Recently, however, paleontologists have been taking a closer look at the sediments below this boundary. It turns out that some fossils can be extracted from these sediments by digesting the rocks in an acid bath. The technique has uncovered new evidence from sediments that were deposited near the shores of the ancient oceans—plant microfossils and microscopic pieces of small animals. In many instances the specimens are less than one-tenth of a millimeter in diameter. Although they were entombed in the rocks for hundreds of millions of years, many of the fossils consist of the chemically altered organic remains of the organism.

These newly discovered fossils have not only revealed the existence of previously unknown organisms, but have also pushed back the dates for the invasion of land by multicellular organisms. Our views on the nature of the early plant and animal communities are now being revised. And with those revisions are new speculations about the first colonists.

Landed Immigrants

What form of life was the first to colonize the continents? Unfortunately the fossil record provides little direct evidence about these migrants—their forms left no impression in the rocks. Although their identity and the nature of their transition to land may never be known for sure, circumstantial evidence does provide some clues about the first settlers.

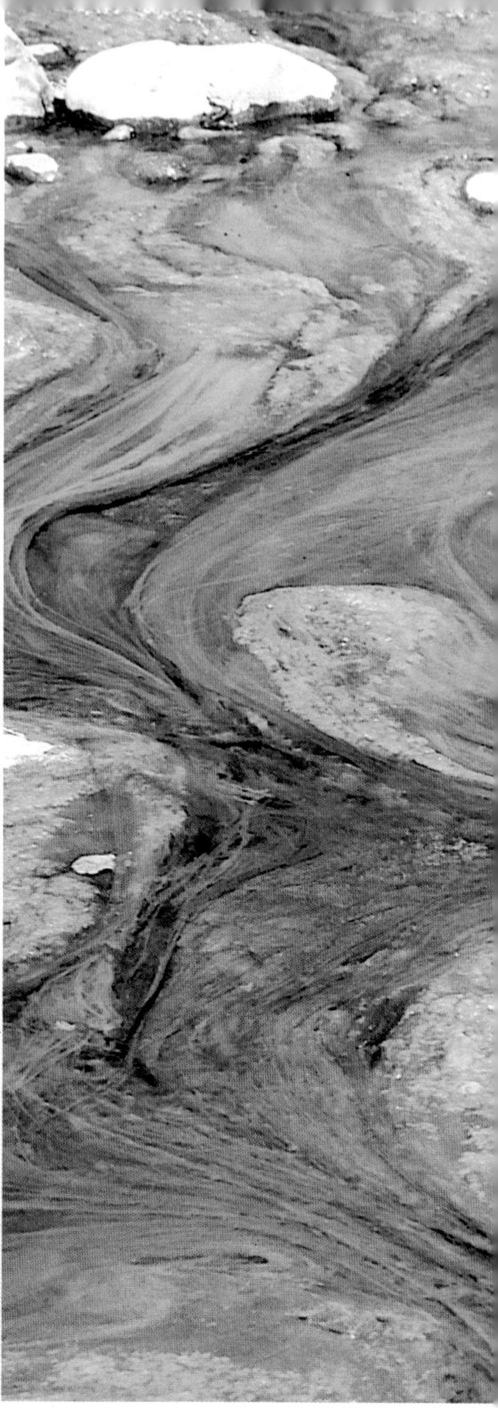

Figure 1. Green algae are hypothesized to be among the earliest forms of life on the

Cyanobacteria, formerly called blue-green algae, are among the most likely candidates. Cyanobacteria were common in the ancient seas during much of the Precambrian, from about 3,500 million to 1,400 million years ago. Fossils of their communities, called stromatolites, are abundant in sedimentary rocks up until the evolution of marine animals that preyed on them. Stromatolites are still found in warm, shallow waters in the Persian Gulf and along the western coasts of Australia and Mexico, where their predators are limited.

Some species of modern cyanobacteria are found in fresh water and on dry

Pat and Tom Leeson (Photo Researchers, Inc.)

continents. Along with cyanobacteria, green algae are thought to have invaded fresh waters and the surface of the land more than 600 million years ago in the Precambrian era. Here an algae-filled stream evokes a scene suggestive of the first life on the continents.

land, where they have invaded a variety of habitats. Most remarkably, cyanobacteria have the ability to survive in some of the world's most inhospitable settings. Large masses of cyanobacteria frequently form crusts on hot desert soils, which may contain little other organic material (Campbell 1979).

As it happens, some of these crust-forming organisms are similar to the cyanobacteria that were present in the Precambrian oceans, particularly in the intertidal zone. Life on the shores of the ancient oceans would have exposed the cyanobacteria to a wide range of salinity, and to daily desiccation. Survival in

such harsh conditions suggests that some cyanobacteria may have possessed characteristics that predisposed them for the invasion of dry land (Campbell 1979). Indeed there is growing evidence that freshwater stromatolites have existed throughout geological time at least since the late Precambrian (Awramik 1984). The structure and chemistry of Precambrian fossil soils also suggest the presence of some forms of life (Retallack 1992).

What other organisms might have been among the first to colonize the continents? It seems likely that green algae (chlorophytes) were also early

migrants to land. The argument is partly based on the evolutionary relationships of the green algae. The cellular structure and biochemistry of these organisms strongly suggests that some ancient chlorophyte was the progenitor of all land plants. Moreover, modern green algae are extremely successful inhabitants of fresh waters and land surfaces.

In this hypothetical scenario, the green algae were joined by fungi soon after they moved to land. As is the case today, the algae and the fungi could have combined in a symbiotic union to form lichens. The presence of modern

3

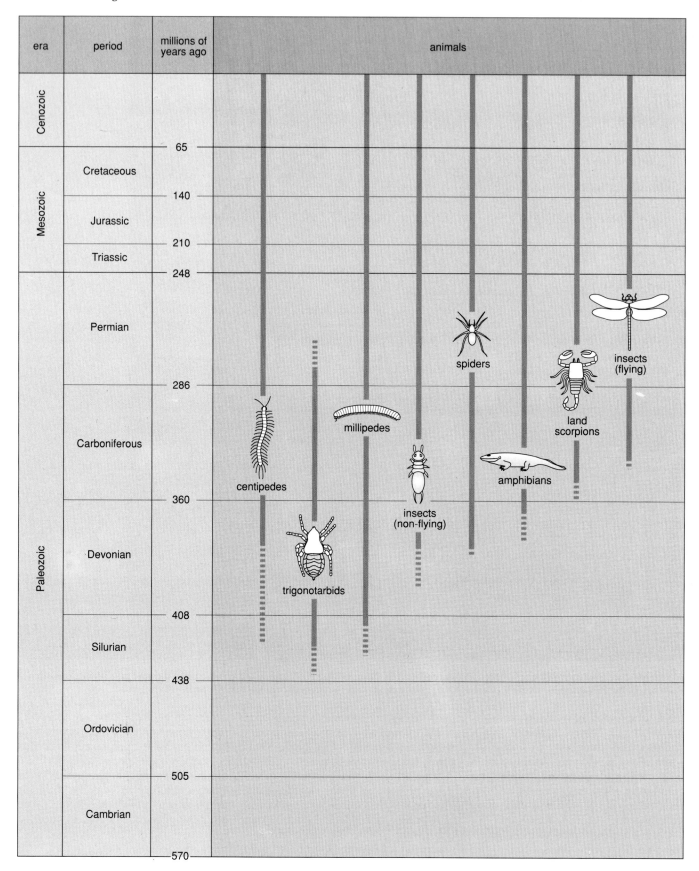

Figure 2. Fossil evidence for some major groups of terrestrial plants and animals dates back to the Paleozoic era, more than 400 million years ago. Microscopic fossil spores from ancient plants offer the earliest evidence of terrestrial life, about 470 million years ago. Small fragments of extinct plants (cuticles and tubes) appear in sediments that were deposited about 440 million years ago. The oldest known tracheophyte-like megafossil, *Cooksonia*, dates to about 420 million years ago. The oldest indisputable evidence for tracheophytes (vascular plants) dates back to a plant called *Baragwanathia* that lived in the Late Silurian, about 410 million years ago. Centipedes, millipedes and spider-like animals called

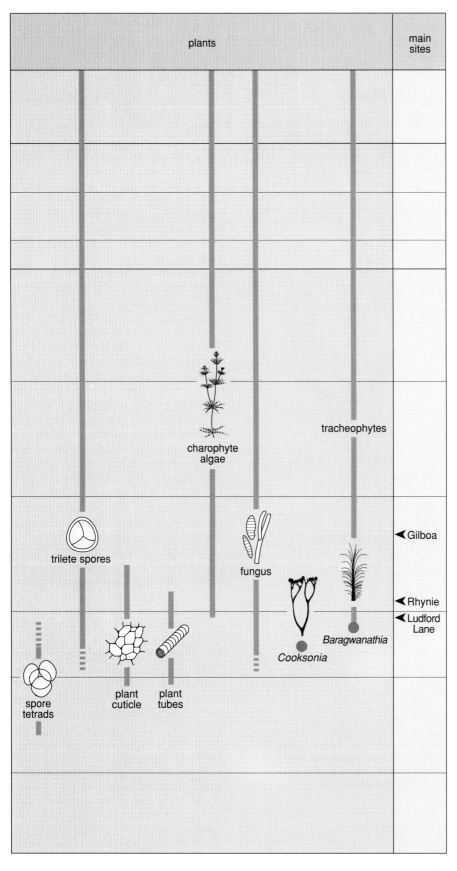

plants	main sites

trilete spores

charophyte algae

tracheophytes

◄ Gilboa

fungus

◄ Rhynie

◄ Ludford Lane

Baragwanathia

Cooksonia

spore tetrads

plant cuticle

plant tubes

trigonotarbids provide the oldest identifiable fossils of land animals. Recent discoveries of fossil burrows and minute fragments of small arthropods dating to about 430 million years ago suggest that some animals may have been on the continents at an earlier time. Much of the fossil evidence for early terrestrial animal life is derived from three sites: Gilboa in New York State, Rhynie in Scotland and Ludford Lane, Ludlow, in the Welsh Borderland.

lichens in arid and otherwise lifeless parts of the world also suggests that this kind of symbiotic union could have thrived on the early continents. The succession of organisms observed today on newly exposed rock faces—cyanobacteria, lichens, and then mosses—is also suggestive of a land invasion that involved lichens (Gray and Boucot 1977).

Though lacking fossil evidence, we can reconstruct a plausible scenario for the first life on the continents. It is easy to imagine mats of cyanobacteria and algae invading fresh water and dry land, perhaps some time in the Precambrian. Followed soon after by fungi and lichens, the microbial and algal sludge would have provided the basis for the development of more complex soils. As in the succession of organisms on newly exposed rock, the death and decay of the first life on land would release mineral nutrients absorbed from the rocks. In this way the inorganic soils were enriched, and the stage was set for new immigrants.

Early Land Plants
The cyanobacterial and algal mats probably dominated life on land in the Precambrian and Early Paleozoic for many millions of years. The next step, the evolution of land plants, was evidently a difficult transition. This should be apparent when one considers the physical challenges faced by a terrestrial organism compared to an aquatic form. Water is a protective medium, surrounding an organism with dissolved nutrients and gases while buffering it against extreme changes in temperature. On land, plants not only need the means to acquire and retain water but must also protect themselves against large doses of ultraviolet radiation.

What type of plant was the first to adapt to life on land? Again, the fossil record does not help us. It is, however, widely believed that some form of aquatic or terrestrial green alga was the progenitor of the two great classes of modern land plants, the bryophytes and the tracheophytes. Interestingly, a modern group of green algae called charophytes share a number of structural and biochemical similarities with bryophytes and tracheophytes. It may be that some ancient group of charophycean algae is ancestral to both modern charophytes and some modern land plants.

Modern bryophytes, which include

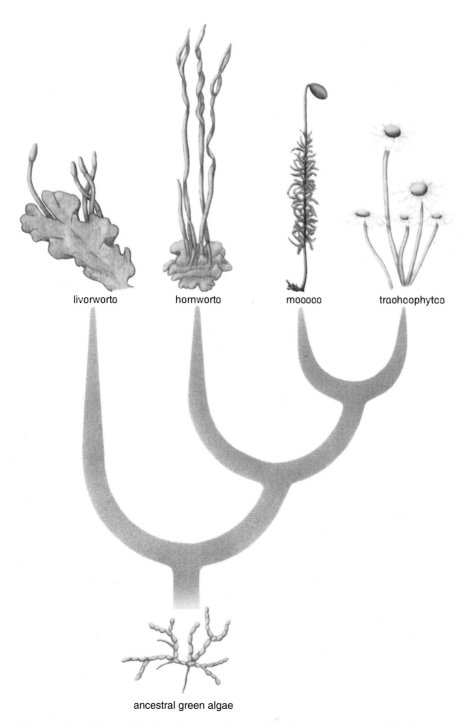

livorworto   hornworto   mooooo   traohoophytoo

ancestral green algae

Figure 3. Bryophytes and tracheophytes may have evolved from green algae that lived more than 600 million years ago. The ancestral alga was probably a filamentous form related to modern charophycean green algae. Three lineages—liverworts, hornworts and mosses—comprise the bryophytes, commonly referred to as "nonvascular" plants. Tracheophytes, commonly referred to as "vascular" plants include lycopods, horsetails, ferns and seed plants.

the mosses, hornworts and liverworts, are typically limited to moist habitats. Nonetheless some species are able to survive in desert-like conditions, on bare rocks and even in the extreme Antarctic. Remarkably, bryophytes have been able to adapt to these conditions despite the lack of highly developed tissues to conduct fluids and nutrients.

In contrast, modern tracheophytes—lycopods, horsetails, ferns and seed plants—have developed vascular tissues called xylem and phloem for the transport of water and nutrients. Xylem contains lignin, an organic compound that serves to strengthen and support the erect plant. The development of these features has allowed vas-

cular plants to survive in widely different habitats, including some of the driest regions of the planet.

Bryophytes and tracheophytes share some developmental features that suggest they evolved from a common ancestor. These land plants have an alternating life cycle, consisting of two distinct phases. One phase of the cycle, the sporophyte, contains two sets of chromosomes and, in spore-producing tracheophytes and bryophytes, releases spores, which are distributed in the plant's environment. When the spore germinates, it produces a plant with only one set of chromosomes. This phase of the cycle, the gametophyte, produces the plant's eggs and sperm. When the eggs of the gametophyte are fertilized by sperm, they produce an embryo that ultimately develops into the sporophyte, and the cycle repeats. Because they both form an embryo, bryophytes and tracheophytes are collectively called embryophytes.

Embryophytes also have certain qualities that distinguish them from charophycean green algae. The walls of embryophytic spores are made of a durable organic substance called sporopollenin, which resists physical and chemical assaults in the environment. The development of these nonmotile spores is also typically characterized by a tetrahedral association of four spores, called a tetrad.

In contrast to embryophytes, charophycean green algae have only one distinct phase in their life cycle, which has only one set of chromosomes. A single-celled zygote is the only structure with two sets of chromosomes; a multicellular embryo is never formed. The spores of these algae lack sporopollenin walls, and typically they have a flagellum (which propels the spore in water), a structure distinctly lacking in embryophyte spores. And significantly, charophyte spores never have an embryophyte-like tetrad stage in their development.

It seems likely that the qualities that distinguish embryophytes from charophytes were evolutionary developments that appeared after the two groups diverged from their common ancestor. Consequently, spore tetrads with sporopollenin are considered to be a development that characterizes the ancestral embryophyte. This is consistent with the observation that some modern liverworts, which are thought to be similar to the ancestral embryophytes (Mishler

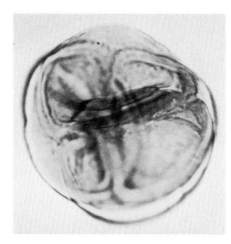

Figure 4. Fossil spores—less than 50 micrometers in diameter—from ancient plants provide the earliest evidence for life on land. A tetrahedral association of four spores *(top)* forms a spore tetrad, the oldest of which are found in sediments deposited more than 470 million years ago. Younger sediments (beginning about 425 million years ago) contain individual spores *(bottom)* with a Y-shaped, or trilete, mark. The spore tetrads are believed to be reproductive and dispersal devices of plants that were ancestral to modern bryophytes and tracheophytes. Trilete spores, on the other hand, may be representative of the tracheophyte lineage or perhaps some of the bryophyte lineages. (Unless otherwise noted, all photographs courtesy of the authors.)

and Churchill 1985), also have spores that are permanently associated in a quartet (Gray 1985).

The recent discovery of fossil spores (less than 50 micrometers in diameter) is consistent with the theory that spore tetrads were an early development of embryophytes (Gray 1985, 1991). Spore tetrads have been found in Middle Ordovician and Early Silurian deposits (470 to 430 million years ago) in many parts of the world, including Australia, the Americas, Europe, Saudi Arabia and Africa (Gray 1985, 1988b; Burgess

1991). We have yet to discover any fossils that would reveal the appearance of these plants. There is some speculation, however, that these ancient plants may have been comparable to some modern liverworts, especially since the fossil spores are similar to some liverwort spores (Gray 1985).

The oldest fossil spores from Saudi Arabia (about 470 million years ago) are now being studied by one of us (Gray) and Harold McClure and Arthur Boucot at the University of Oregon. The Arabian spores provide the first direct evidence of land plants, pushing back the traditional date for higher life forms on the continents about 50 to 60 million years. These early embryophytes may have been the first to follow the cyanobacterial and algal communities as the dominant life on land.

About 425 million years ago in the Early Silurian a remarkable change occurred in the spore assemblages. Instead of remaining intact, most mature tetrads came apart into four individual spores. Each single spore is characterized by a Y-shaped scar, or trilete suture, which indicates that it was attached to three others to form a tetrahedral tetrad. Although spore tetrads persisted into the Late Silurian, they never dominate spore assemblages after the Early Silurian. Single trilete spores became the dominant type in the fossil record.

What kinds of plants produced the trilete spores? It is not clear whether the plants evolved from those that were producing the mature spore tetrads in the Ordovician and Early Silurian, or whether a new lineage entered the evolutionary picture. We do know, however, that the first primitive tracheophytes and tracheophyte-like plants in the fossil record had trilete spores. Most modern spore-producing tracheophytes, including primitive ferns, also produce trilete spores. The appearance of trilete spores in the Early Silurian suggests that the tracheophytes and perhaps some of the bryophyte lineages had their origins about 425 million years ago (Gray 1989, 1991).

Although no plant megafossils accompany the change in spore assemblages, tracheophyte-like fossils appear about 420 million years ago in Ireland (Edwards and Feehan 1980), and the oldest known tracheophytes appear about 415 million years ago in Australia (Garratt et al. 1984). Such a close

link in time between the appearance of trilete spores and the appearance of these megafossils is suggestive. It is tempting to see the change in spore type as an indicator of the first major adaptive radiation of tracheophytes or their immediate predecessors.

Why did it take so long for land plants to appear as megafossils when their spores were around for such a long time? Why are tracheophytes the first plant megafossils to be preserved, rather than some bryophyte-like ancestor? The answer may lie in the evolution of lignin. This organic substance is highly resistant to biological and geological degradation, and probably allows some tissues of tracheophytes to survive the ravages of geologic time. Modern bryophytes do not produce lignin, and it may be that the earliest spore-producing (bryophyte-like) plants were not preserved because they also did not produce the substance. The only record that remains of them is their spores, whose survival was assured by the presence of sporopollenin.

From the mid-Silurian through the Early Devonian a variety of plant megafossils appear that complement the increasing diversity of trilete spore assemblages. Many of these earliest plants were superficially similar to tracheophytes but seem to lack vascular

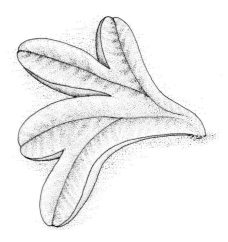

Figure 5. Hypothetical primitive embryophyte—ancestral to bryophytes and tracheophytes—may have resembled a primitive liverwort. The ancestor was probably a small, ground-hugging plant that is thought to have lived about 470 million years ago in the Ordovician period. The spore-producing bodies of these plants were probably embedded in their upper surfaces. Although no fossils reveal the form of these early plants, a few modern liverworts bear some primitive traits, including the formation of spore tetrads.

Figure 6. Megafossil of *Baragwanathia* provides the oldest definitive evidence of tracheophytes. Laid down in deposits from the Late Silurian (about 410 million years ago), *Baragwanathia* was remarkably advanced compared to other plants of the period. Some Devonian specimens stood up to a meter high, towering over their contemporaries, which were no more than a few centimeters tall.

tissues. In a few, Dianne Edwards and her colleagues at Cardiff University have found vascular elements (Edwards, Davies and Axe 1992). In some instances the anatomy is more like that of a bryophyte than that of a tracheo-

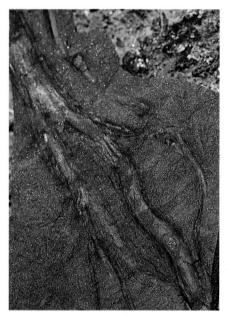

Figure 7. Burrows in the fossil soils of Pennsylvania may be the first traces of animal life on land. The soil appears to have been disturbed by a burrowing creature more than 430 million years ago near an ancient shoreline. The identity of the burrower is unknown. (Courtesy of Greg Retallack, University of Oregon.)

phyte. Some of these plants may indeed be bryophytes, whereas others appear to be evolutionary experiments that became extinct in the Devonian, perhaps unable to compete with the tracheophytes.

During the early part of the Devonian, the number of verifiable tracheophyte fossils increases. This period saw the beginning of the major structural and reproductive changes associated with the present diversity of tracheophytes. By the end of the Devonian most major lineages of tracheophytes had appeared, including spore-producing lycopods, horsetails, ferns and early seed plants. Many of these plants were structurally modern: They bore leaves, some had woody growth and seeds and many were as tall as modern trees (Gensel and Andrews 1987).

Such a diversity of plant life was an important antecedent to the invasion of land by animals. The early plants played an important role in ameliorating the terrestrial environment. The roots of the plants provided stability for the soil and prevented erosion, whereas transpiration from the leaves raised the local humidity. In life their masses provide shelter, and in death they contribute organic matter while forming a litter layer. And, of course, they may have been a source of food for the early land animals.

Early Land Animals

The remnants of the earliest known land animals consist of various odds and ends, small scraps of what remains of their bodies. Some of the pieces are mysterious, not clearly attributable to a particular part of the body or even to a known animal group. In other cases, the animal's carcass has long since disappeared—all that is left are traces of its actions, such as tracks or burrows. In only a very few instances do we have relatively intact remains of the early forms.

The recovery of microscopic animal fragments is a relatively rare and recent event. The acid bath that is used to retrieve the fragments was originally developed by paleobotanists to uncover organic plant remains in the 1950s. One of the most commonly used baths, hydrofluoric acid, works because the fluoride ion attacks the silicates of the shale and sandstone rocks, without harming the organic matter within. The technique was not used for the recovery of animal remains until the early 1970s, when some paleobotanists accidentally discovered animal cuticles in deposits containing fossil plant matter. Indeed most of the animal fossils found by the acid-bath technique turn up in the search for fossil spores or plant parts.

Whether the fossils consist of intact

remains or small fragments, it does seem clear that the earliest fossilized land animals were arthropods (segmented animals related to insects, spiders and crustaceans). As with the investigations of the first terrestrial plants, the traditional view holds that these animals arrived on land during the end of the Silurian and the beginning of the Devonian, a little over 400 million years ago. Recent fossil evidence suggests that animals may have been on land more than 30 million years earlier.

In this context it is important to note that the algal and lichen mats of the Early Paleozoic could probably have supported a small community of arthropods, worms and other soil-dwelling animals. The mats would have served as hospitable oases where these early settlers could feed on the microorganisms, their decomposition products and each other. The absence of fossil evidence need not indicate the absence of animals in such an environment.

Potential evidence for such a community does appear late in the Ordovician (over 430 million years ago), in deposits of central Pennsylvania. Here Retallack and Feakes (1987) discovered fossil soils that contain burrows, apparently made by a small animal. What kind of beast disturbed this soil 430 million years ago? There is some

chance that the creature was actually a marine animal; the deposits themselves are close to a former shoreline. Such animal burrows in marine deposits are common in Ordovician sediments. Ultimately, there is no easy way to determine the identity of the burrower without its corpse.

Slightly younger sediments of the Early Silurian (about 430 million years ago) do contain small, occasionally identifiable bits of animals. Close to the beds that contain the animal burrows in Pennsylvania, one of us (Gray) and Arthur Boucot discovered remains that appear to be cuticle and bristles from arthropod-like creatures. Although the deposits are close to a former shoreline, the sediments are unequivocally nonmarine; the animal remains are also associated with the spores of land plants. It seems possible that the remains are those of riverine and even terrestrial animals.

Late Silurian deposits (about 415 million years old) on the Baltic Sea island of Gotland, Sweden, contain another type of remnant that may be indicative of animal life (Sherwood-Pike and Gray 1985). Small enigmatic pellets have been found in shale deposits that also contain the spores of land plants. The nature of the pellets was obscure until we realized that they are composed of microscopic fungal fila-

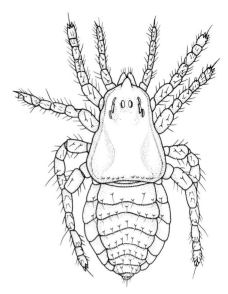

Figure 9. Spider-like trigonotarbid, shown here in a reconstruction, was among the most common and fearsome arthropods living 400 million years ago. Trigonotarbids were small (1 to 14 millimeters long) predatory animals that were encased in heavy armor and bore distinctive fangs. Unlike modern spiders, trigonotarbids did not have any specialized structures for spinning silk to make webs. Trigonotarbids became extinct more than 250 million years ago.

ments (hyphae). It turns out that some modern soil-dwelling arthropods, living on a diet of fungus, produce fecal matter that is similar to the fossil pellets. Perhaps an ancient relative of a modern arthropod was feeding on a similar diet in the Late Silurian.

By the end of the Silurian and the beginning of the Devonian the land appears to have been colonized by a wide range of arthropods. The oldest indisputable terrestrial arthropods are found in Late Silurian deposits (about 415 million years old) at Ludford Lane in the Welsh Borderland (Jeram et al. 1990). Here Paul Selden of the University of Manchester and his colleagues Andrew Jeram of the Belfast Museum and Dianne Edwards have discovered what may be the oldest fossil centipedes. The appearance of some of the arthropods suggests that they are the result of a long period of terrestrial adaptation. Slightly younger deposits at another site in Britain contain fossils of large millipede-like animals. Although there is no evidence that these animals were terrestrial, they bear a striking resemblance to modern land-dwelling millipedes.

Most of what we know about Devonian terrestrial arthropods, however, is based on two other sites. Near

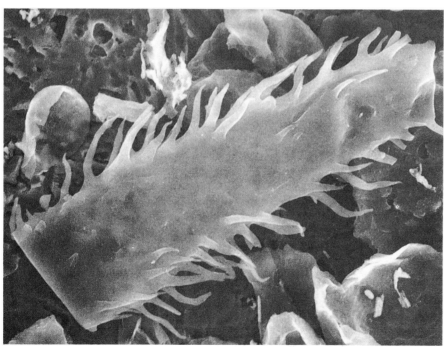

Figure 8. Microscopic fragment of an animal's bristle provides evidence that the continents were inhabited 430 million years ago. Bristles and cuticles removed from rocks deposited in the Early Silurian period suggest that some arthropod-like animals may have lived on the continents about 30 million years earlier than previously thought. The fragment of bristle shown here is about 70 micrometers long.

Rhynie in Scotland is a site that is most famous for the remains of 400-million-year-old plants, discovered in the early part of this century (Kidston and Lang 1917). However, the site also contains animals preserved in silicified rock, or chert. The remains, some of whole animals, have been studied from transparent, thin sections of rock, and chips from the chert (Hirst 1922).

The second site, near the little village of Gilboa in upstate New York, is one of the richest fossil deposits of early terrestrial animal life in the world. The site contains a remarkable diversity of life forms from a period near the middle of the Devonian, about 380 million to 375 million years ago (Shear et al. 1984). In contrast to the fossils at Rhynie, the animal remains at Gilboa are recovered with the acid extraction technique.

These Devonian deposits are limited to sediments of wet lowlands. Former lowland sediments tend to contain fossils because they are optimal sites for the preservation of plants and animals. Such basins also tend to accumulate plant and animal remains that wash in from other environments. Despite the apparent bias toward wet lowlands in the fossil record, it seems likely that many other regions of the continents were inhabited, especially since the land was probably covered with vegetation by the Early Devonian.

The most common arthropod at Gilboa and Rhynie is an extinct spider-like creature called a trigonotarbid. Five species of trigonotarbid have been found at Gilboa, and three more at Rhynie (Shear et al. 1987). Another nearly complete fossil trigonotarbid was found at Ludford Lane, the Late Silurian site in the Welsh Borderland. The similarity of the trigonotarbids in Britain and New York state is not as surprising as one might initially assume. In the Silurian and Devonian, these two sites were geographically much closer to each other than they are today.

What kind of animal was a trigonotarbid? Like a spider, a trigonotarbid had a body divided into an abdomen and a cephalothorax, which carried six pairs of appendages. The lungs of the trigonotarbids are also much like those of modern spiders. Despite these similarities, trigonotarbids were cousins, rather than ancestors, of modern spiders. Unlike spiders, trigonotarbids were encased in a heavy, segmented armor. Some extremely well-preserved fossils also reveal that trigonotarbids did not have spinnerets, the silk-producing appendages of spiders. Trigonotarbids could not spin a web. The fangs of trigonotarbids show no trace of poison ducts, so they probably lacked the venom that modern spiders use to subdue their prey.

The discovery of trigonotarbid fossils among the fossilized spore cases of plants at Rhynie suggested to some that these animals may have been eating the spores (Kevan et al. 1975). But the absence of poison ducts does not mean that trigonotarbids were herbivorous. The trigonotarbids' fangs and jaws are clearly those of a predator, one that chewed and dissolved its prey the way modern spiders do. A spore-eating animal would not bear the specialized structures for food processing found on the trigonotarbids. Some well-chewed lumps of cuticle from an arthropod discovered at Gilboa may be the leftovers of a trigonotarbid meal.

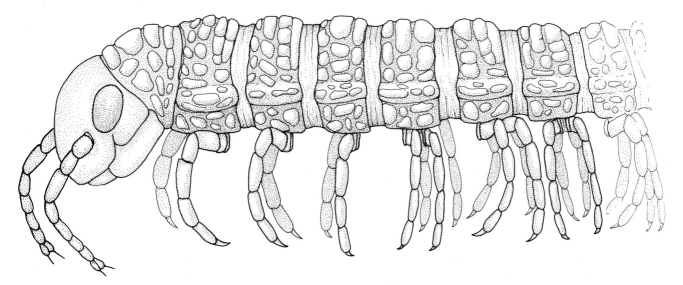

Figure 10. Millipede fossil (left) appears in the Devonian deposits of Scotland about 390 to 400 million years ago. Earlier millipedes (about 420 million years ago) provide the oldest known body fossils of an animal that probably lived on the land. Millipedes appear to have been abundant in the Late Silurian and Early Devonian. Curiously millipedes are largely absent from Middle and Late Devonian deposits but become abundant again in the Carboniferous. An artist's reconstruction (above) shows how the animal may have appeared in life. (Photograph courtesy of Ian Rolfe of the National Museums of Scotland.)

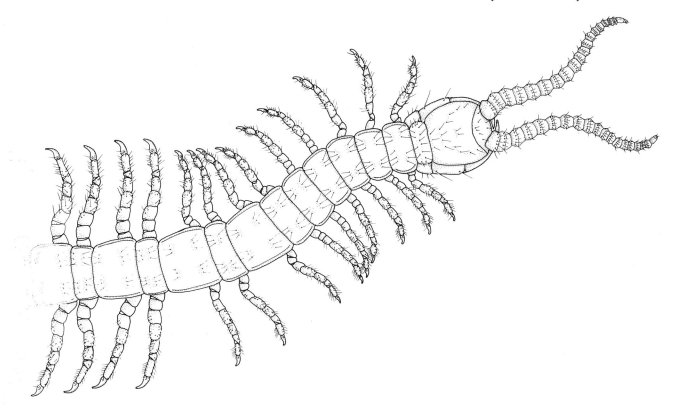

What other animals lived during this period? The Gilboa site offers evidence of the earliest spiders, centipedes and pseudoscorpions. The Gilboa spider was originally considered to be a trigonotarbid, but Paul Selden of the University of Manchester matched the patterning on its cuticle to that of a spider's spinneret found close to the cuticle. A few pieces of true scorpions have also been found. The oldest known scorpions were marine or brackish-water animals in the Silurian. They appear to have entered freshwater habitats by the Early Devonian. The oldest known air-breathing scorpion dates to the Early Carboniferous, about 335 million years ago (Jeram 1990). As yet we have been unable to determine whether some scorpion remains—jaws, pincers and stingers—from Gilboa were those of an aquatic or a terrestrial animal.

Some of the oldest known mites have also been found at Rhynie and Gilboa. One modern group of mites, the oribatids, appears to be represented in the deposits of Gilboa. Modern oribatids play important roles in soil ecosystems, feeding mostly on fungi and detritus. The oribatids from Gilboa may have been equally significant to the ecosystems of the Devonian soils, where they appear to have been detritus-eaters. Another group of mites, the alicorhagiids, are also represented in

Figure 11. Head and poison claws are preserved fragments of the earliest known centipede, which lived about 375 million years ago. The original organic remains of the animal *(bottom)* were found in mudstone sediments of the Devonian in Gilboa, New York. A reconstruction *(top)* shows how the head and claws could have been attached to a segmented body about 10 millimeters long.

Figure 12. Silk-producing spinnerets provide the earliest evidence for spiders (about 375 million years old). Many remains of spiders, including jaws and legs, have been unearthed from the Devonian sediments of Gilboa. It is not clear whether the spider produced an aerial web with the silk or used it for some other purpose, such as lining the opening to a tunnel.

the Gilboa deposits. Similarities between these mites and modern alicorhagiids that prey on nematode worms suggest that the ancient mites may also have been predatory (Norton et al. 1988, Kethley et al. 1989).

The extraction of fossils from the rocks of Gilboa by one of us (Shear) and Patricia Bonamo of the State University of New York at Binghamton continues to uncover the remains of previously unknown animals and the earliest representatives of modern taxa. We have, for example, recently discovered a group of enigmatic animals that resemble millipedes. Although unrelated to modern millipedes, the animals may belong to an extinct group of arthropods, the arthropleurids. Giant arthropleurids that lived during the Carboniferous period are known to have been detritus-eaters. We have also determined that some scraps of cuticle belong to archaeognaths, a group of primitive wing-

less insects that includes modern bristle-tails. Although older remains of bristle-tails have been found in Early Devonian deposits in Canada (Labandeira, Beall and Hueber 1989), there is some possibility that the specimens are modern contaminants (Jeram et al. 1991).

It is important to note here that the abruptness of the invasion of land by these arthropods near the Silurian-Devonian boundary may be more apparent than real. The study of fossil spores has shown us that the sudden abundance of terrestrial plant megafossils in the Late Silurian and Early Devonian does not represent the true evolutionary picture. There is no reason to think that the sudden appearance of terrestrial animals during this period accurately reflects the history of their migration to land, rather than an accident of the collection or fossilization process.

Finally, the tetrapod vertebrates, which along with insects dominate today's terrestrial communities, appear only late in the Devonian, about 365 million years ago. Recent evidence suggests that some of these early vertebrate colonists remained primarily aquatic and fed mostly on fish (Ahlberg 1991).

Early Ecosystems

We have only a rudimentary picture of the early continental ecosystems (Gray 1988, Shear 1991, Behrensmeyer et al. 1992). The fossil record does not allow us to integrate the plant and animal communities that existed on land before the middle of the Paleozoic era. Despite what must have been interdependent evolutionary histories, the first indications of terrestrial plants and animals are divorced by tens of millions of years.

The first community of prevascular embryophytes that followed the hypothesized algal mats of the late Precambrian and Early Paleozoic appears to have had a lone hold on the land for much of the Ordovician and Early Silurian. Assemblages of spore tetrads from these plants are quite similar over a span of 50 to 60 million years, suggesting a long period of evolutionary stasis. About 420 million years ago, near the end of the Early Silurian, the fossil spores document a rapid change in the plant community. Tracheophytes or their immediate precursors began to transform the landscape (Gray 1991).

Throughout this period, however, there is little direct evidence for the animals that may have accompanied the land plants. Traces of animal burrows

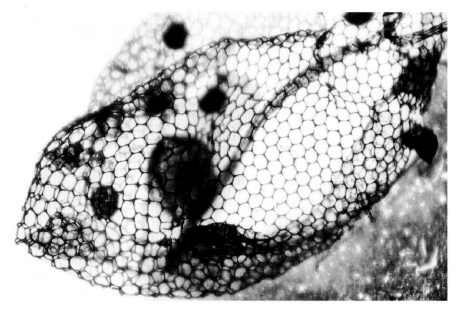

Figure 13. Scaffolding from a compound eye is the oldest indisputable evidence for the existence of terrestrial insects. Consisting of the original organic matter, the scaffolding and some scraps of cuticle were discovered in Gilboa deposits that are about 375 million years old. Although a few other insect remains have been found in this period, there is little other evidence of insects in the fossil record for the next 50 million years.

in Ordovician deposits and scraps of arthropod cuticle in the Early Silurian offer hints that the first plants may have been joined by some animals. If so, the first arthropod steps onto land may have been taken even before the arrival of vascular plants—by tiny forms colonizing the microbial mats. These miniature colonists would have been in a good position to exploit the altered habitat provided by the first land plants. Such a scenario would allow sufficient time for the evolution of the refined terrestrial adaptations seen in the fossil arthropods at Ludford Lane, Rhynie and Gilboa. The presence of similar forms at these sites, spanning a period of at least 40 million years, suggests that terrestrial arthropods may also have undergone a period of evolutionary stasis.

What sort of environment did these plants and animals form? The current fossil evidence suggests that the arthropods of the Devonian were organized in a community not unlike the soil and litter ecosystems of today. Such ecosystems are dominated by arthropods and worms that eat detritus and prey upon other animals.

The presence of a community based on soil and detritus offers a puzzle to the paleontologist. During most periods of geologic time, soil- and litter-dwelling organisms are poorly represented compared to ecosystems above the ground. Were there many arthropods or other invertebrates living above the soil and litter layer? Why were so few of these surface-dwelling animals preserved? It is true that the plants of the Early and Middle Devonian were quite small—perhaps too small to shelter and support animal life. But the end of the Devonian saw the evolution of plant communities that would have rivaled some modern forests. And yet there is a surprising dearth of evidence for arthropods that would have lived on the surface.

Particularly vexing is the paucity of insect remains in the Devonian. The primitive bristletails (flightless archeognaths) discovered in the Canadian Devonian deposits and at Gilboa are the only potential insects known from this period. Remarkably, insects do not appear in the fossil record again for another 35 million years, in the Late Carboniferous period, about 315 million years ago. By that time flying insects were abundant and had diversified into many forms (Shear and Kukalová-Peck 1990).

Late Carboniferous sediments also contain the first evidence of insects that ate living vascular plants. Not only do the fossils of some Carboniferous plants bear the marks of an insect's bite, but in addition the structure of some insects' mouthparts and the contents of their gut reveal their predilection for plants (Labandeira and Beall 1990). Although it was formerly thought that the absence of herbivores in the Silurian and Devonian was an artifact of preservation, it now seems possible that plant-eating arthropods were not part of the early food chains. The lag in the appearance of plant-eaters may be attributable to the low nutritive value of the early vascular plants or the presence of unappetizing toxins.

Vertebrates were even slower to turn to living land plants as a source of food. Vertebrates remained dependent on insects, fish and each other for sustenance almost up to the end of the Carboniferous period, about 280 million years ago. At that time a few reptiles and amphibians show adaptations—peg-like teeth and barrel-shaped bodies—suggestive of a plant diet. The critical adaptation, however, was probably the formation of symbiotic relationships with microorganisms that could digest and detoxify vascular plant matter (Shear and Kukalová-Peck 1991).

It is evident that there are many gaps and puzzles in the fossil record of early terrestrial life. Paleontologists must often use modern analogues to deduce the habits and strategies of primitive organisms that are long extinct. Although this method is often inescapable, the best evidence for former plant and animal communities comes from well-preserved fossil specimens. There is an urgent need for more fossils of the Early and Middle Paleozoic. All hypotheses about the ecology and the evolutionary history of terrestrial life must be tested by the evidence in the rocks.

Bibliography

Ahlberg, P. E. 1991. Tetrapod or near-tetrapod fossils from the Upper Devonian of Scotland. *Nature* 354:298–301.

Almond, J. E. 1985. The Silurian-Devonian fossil record of the Myriapoda. In Evolution and Environment in the Late Silurian and Early Devonian, ed. W. G. Chaloner and J. D. Lawson, pp. 227–237. *Philosophical Transactions of the Royal Society of London* B309.

Awramik, S. M. 1984. Ancient stromatolites and microbial mats. In *Microbial Mats: Stromatolites*, ed. Y. Cohen, R. W. Castenholz, H. O. Halvorson, pp. 1–22. New York: A. R. Liss.

Behrensmeyer, A. K., J. D. Damuth, W. A. DiMichele, R. Potts, H.-D. Sues and S. L. Wing. 1992. *Terrestrial Ecosystems Through Time*. Chicago: University of Chicago Press.

Burgess, N. D. 1991. Silurian cryptospores and miospores from the type Llandovery area, south-west Wales. *Palaeontology* 34:575–599.

Campbell, S. E. 1979. Soil stabilization by a prokaryotic desert crust: implications for Pre-Cambrian land biota. *Origins of Life* 9:335–348.

Dubinin, V. B. 1991. Class Acaromorpha. In *Fundamentals of Paleontology*, volume 9, ed. B. B. Rodendorf, translated by D. R. Davis, pp. 681–722. Washington: Smithsonian Institution Press.

Edwards, D. and J. Feehan. 1980. Records of *Cooksonia*-type sporangia from late Wenlock strata in Ireland. *Nature* 287:41-42.

Edwards, D., K. L. Davies and L. Axe. 1992. A vascular conducting strand in the early land plant *Cooksonia*. *Nature* 357:683–685.

Garratt, M. J., J. D. Tims, R. B. Rickards, T. C. Chambers, J. G. Douglas. 1984. The appearance of *Baragwanathia* (Lycophytina) in the Silurian. *Botanical Journal of the Linnean Society* 89:355–358.

Gensel, P. G. and H. N. Andrews. 1987. The evolution of early land plants. *American Scientist* 75:478–489.

Gray, J. 1984. Ordovician-Silurian land plants: The interdependence of ecology and evolution. *The Palaeontological Association, Special Papers in Palaeontology* no. 32:281–295.

Gray, J. 1985. The microfossil record of early land plants: advances in understanding of early terrestrialization, 1970–1984. In Evolution and Environment in the Late Silurian and Early Devonian, ed. W. G. Chaloner and J. D. Lawson, pp. 167–195. *Philosophical Transactions of the Royal Society of London* B309.

Gray, J. 1988a. Evolution of the freshwater ecosystem: the fossil record. In *Paleolimnology: Aspects of Freshwater Paleoecology and Biogeography*, ed. J. Gray, pp. 1–214. Amsterdam: Elsevier.

Gray, J. 1988b. Land plant spores and the Ordovician-Silurian Boundary. *Bulletin of the British Museum (Natural History), Geology* 43:351–358.

Gray, J. 1989. The adaptive radiation of early land plants. *28th International Geological Congress*.

Gray, J. 1991. Tetrahedraletes, Nodospora, and the 'cross' tetrad: an accretion of myth. In *Pollen and Spores, Systematics Association Special Volume No. 44*, ed. S. Blackmore and S. H. Barnes, pp. 49–87. Oxford: Clarendon Press.

Gray, J. and A. J. Boucot. 1972. Palynological evidence hearing on the Ordovician-Silurian paraconformity of Ohio. *Geological Society of America Bulletin* 83:1299–1314.

Gray, J. and A. J. Boucot. 1971. Early Silurian spore tetrads from New York: Earliest New World evidence for vascular plants? *Science* 173:918–921.

Gray, J. and A. J. Boucot. 1977. Early vascular plants: proof and conjecture. *Lethaia* 10:145–174.

Gray, J., D. Massa, and A. J. Boucot. 1982. Caradocian land plant microfossils from Libya. *Geology* 10:197–201.

Gray, J., J. N. Theron and A. J. Boucot. 1986. Age of the Cedarberg Formation, South Africa and early land plant evolution. *Geological Magazine* 123:445–454.

Gray, J., G. K. Colbath, A. deFaria, A. J. Boucot and D. M. Rohr. 1985. Silurian age fossils from the Paleozoic Parana Basin, southern Brazil. *Geology* 13:521–525.

Hirst, S. 1922. On some arachnid remains from the Old Red Sandstone (Rhynie Chert Bed, Aberdeenshire). *Annals and Magazine of Natural History* 9:455–474.

Jeram, A. 1990. Book-lungs in a Lower Carboniferous scorpion. *Nature* 343:360–361.

Jeram, A. J., P. A. Selden and D. Edwards. 1990. Land animals in the Silurian: Arachnids and Myriapods from Shropshire, England. *Science* 250:658–661.

Kethley, J. B., R. A. Norton, P. M. Bonamo, and W. A. Shear. 1989. A terrestrial alicorhagiid mite (Acari: acariformes) from the Devonian of New York. *Micropaleontology* 35(4):367–373.

Kevan, P. G., W. G. Chaloner and D. B. O. Savile. 1975. Interrelationships of early terrestrial arthropods and plants. *Palaeontology* 18:391–417.

Kidston, R. and W. H. Lang. 1917. On Old Red Sandstone plants showing structure, from the Rhynie Chert Bed, Aberdeenshire, part 1: *Rhynia gwynne-vaughani*, Kidston and Lang. *Transactions of the Royal Society of Edinburgh* 51:761–784.

Labandeira, C. and B. S. Beall. 1990. Arthropod terrestrialization. In *Short Courses in Paleontology, No. 3: Arthropod Paleobiology*, ed. D. Mikulic and S. J. Culver, pp. 214–232. Knoxville, Tennessee: The Paleontological Society.

Labandeira, C. C., B. S. Beall and F. M. Hueber. 1989. Early insect diversification: evidence from Lower Devonian bristletail from Quebec. *Science* 242:913–916.

Little, C. 1990. *The Terrestrial Invasion*. Cambridge: Cambridge University Press.

Mishler, B. D. and S. P. Churchill. 1985. Transition to a land flora: Phylogentic relationships of the green algae and bryophytes. *Cladistics* 1:305–338.

Norton, R. A., P. M. Bonamo, J. D. Grierson and W. A. Shear. 1988. Oribatid mite fossils from a terrestrial Devonian deposits near Gilboa, New York. *Journal of Paleontology* 62(2):259–269.

Retallack, G. J. 1992. How to find a Precambrian paleosol. In *Early Organic Evolution: Implications for Mineral and Energy Resources*, ed. M. Schidlowski et al., pp. 16–30. Berlin: Springer-Verlag.

Retallack, G. and C. Feakes. 1987. Trace fossil evidence for Late Ordovician animals on land. *Science* 235:61–63.

Rolfe, W. D. Ian. 1980. Early invertebrate terrestrial faunas, In *The Terrestrial Environment and the Origin of Land Vertebrates*, ed. A. L. Panchen, pp. 117–157. *Systematics Association Special Volume* No. 15. London: Academic Press.

Rolfe, W. D. Ian. 1985. Early terrestrial arthropods: a fragmentary record. In *Evolution and Environment in the Late Silurian and Early Devonian*, ed. Chaloner and Lawson, pp. 207–218. *Philosophical Transactions of the Royal Society of London* B309.

Scott, A. C. and T. N. Taylor. 1983. Plant/animal interactions during the Upper Carboniferous. *Botanical Review* 49(3):259–307.

Selden, P. A., W. A. Shear and P. M. Bonamo. 1991. A spider and other arachnids from the Devonian of New York, and reinterpretations of Devonian Araneae. *Paleontology* 34:241–281.

Shear, W. A. 1990. Silurian-Devonian terrestrial arthropods. In *Short Courses in Paleontology, No. 3: Arthropod Paleobiology*, ed. D. Mikulic and S. J. Culver, pp. 197–213. Knoxville, Tennessee: The Paleontological Society.

Shear, W. A. 1991. The early development of terrestrial ecosystems. *Nature* 351:283–289.

Shear, W. A., and P. M. Bonamo. 1988. Devonobiomorpha, a new order of centipeds (Chilopoda) from the Middle Devonian of Gilboa, New York State, U.S.A., and the phylogeny of centiped orders. *American Museum Novitates* 2927:1–30.

Shear, W. A. and J. Kukalova-Peck. 1990. The ecology of Paleozoic terrestrial arthropods: The fossil evidence. *Canadian Journal of Zoology* 68:1807–1834.

Shear, W. A., W. Schawaller and P. M. Bonamo. 1989. Record of Palaeozoic pseudoscorpions. *Nature* 341:527–529.

Shear, W. A., P. M. Bonamo, J. D. Grierson, W. D. . Rolfe, E. L. Smith and R. A. Norton. 1984. Early land animals in North America: evidence from Devonian age arthropods from Gilboa, New York. *Science* 224:492–494.

Shear, W. A., P. A. Selden, W. D. Ian Rolfe, P. M. Bonamo and J. D. Grierson. 1987. New terrestrial arachnids from the Devonian of Gilboa, New York (Arachnida, Trigonotarbida). *American Museum Novitates* 2901:1–74.

Shear, W. A., J. M. Palmer, J. A. Coddington and P. M. Bonamo. 1989. A Devonian spinneret: Early evidence of spiders and silk use. *Science* 246:479–481.

Sherwood-Pike, M. A. and J. Gray. 1985. Silurian fungal remains; oldest records of the Class Ascomycetes? *Lethaia* 18:1–20.

The Evolution of Early Land Plants

Patricia G. Gensel
Henry N. Andrews

During this century, and particularly in the last decade and a half, a tremendous amount of information extracted from fossil plants has opened a window on several critical stages in the development of the earth's vegetation. An abundance of recent data confirms that simple forms of plant life existed at least two and probably as long as three billion years ago. Diverse assemblages of algae and invertebrate animals then evolved over a period of many hundreds of millions of years. It was not until the Silurian period, 400 to 450 million years ago, that plants and some animals adapted to a land environment and became well established there.

Vascular land plants—that is, plants with distinctive water-conducting tissues, as opposed to nonvascular plants such as mosses—became established by mid-Silurian times and diversified relatively rapidly in the early Devonian period. By the end of that period, about 50 million years later, they apparently outnumbered the nonvascular plants, which eventually included algae, bryophytes (still extant as mosses, liverworts, and hornworts), and other, now extinct forms, and were well on their way to becoming the dominant form of land plant life (Fig. 1). The land was clothed with a great variety of vascular plants, including the first seed plants as well as forest trees that rivaled modern species in size. Probably more crucial steps in plant evolution took place in the Devonian period than in any other comparable span of time (Fig. 2).

Since land plants did not evolve for at least 1.5 billion years after the appearance of the first recognizable

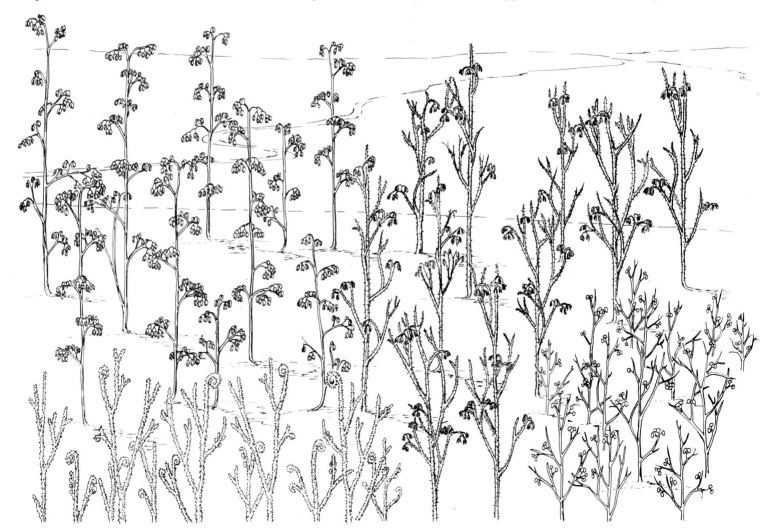

algae, it seems clear that this transition was an extremely difficult one. What did it involve? Several structural adaptations are apparent among all land plants, particularly vascular ones. Plants developed a waxy outer coating, or cuticle, to prevent loss of water, pores called stomates to allow gas exchange, reproductive structures and strategies that could function on land, and a system (quite complex in most vascular plants) to circulate water and food. In addition, there was a progressive differentiation during the Devonian into specialized parts—stems, leaves, and roots—that served different functions. These were responses to problems of no small magnitude, and they were fundamental to all the diverse phases of plant evolution that took place in the Siluro-Devonian and thereafter.

Fossil plants are preserved for the most part as compressed or mummified remains; occasionally portions are petrified, or permineralized, with silica, iron hydroxides, or calcium carbonate. In still other cases only the imprint or impression is preserved in the rock, providing information about size and form. Depending on the type of preservation, a variety of techniques can be used to extract maximum information from plant fossils. Compressed fragments and impressions may be uncovered by removing rock particles with fine needles under a dissecting microscope. Compressions may also be subjected to maceration, a process in which the rock matrix is digested by strong acids, freeing the organic remains. These remains are then oxidized and mounted on slides or stubs for examination with light or scanning electron microscopy. Permineralized specimens can be cut and prepared as thin sections, allowing the study of

Figure 1. A reconstruction of a late Lower Devonian landscape reveals a varied assemblage of plants in a setting resembling a modern salt marsh. Species ranged in height from the ground-hugging *Sciadophyton steinmannii* to the more highly evolved *Pertica* (*both far right*), which attained heights of 2 to 3 m. Fossil evidence from the Gaspé coast in Canada documents a great abundance of *Psilophyton* (*upper row, left*), which was rivaled in numbers only by *Sawdonia* (*right of center*). Smaller pockets of the other species shown would have been interspersed among large stands of these plants.

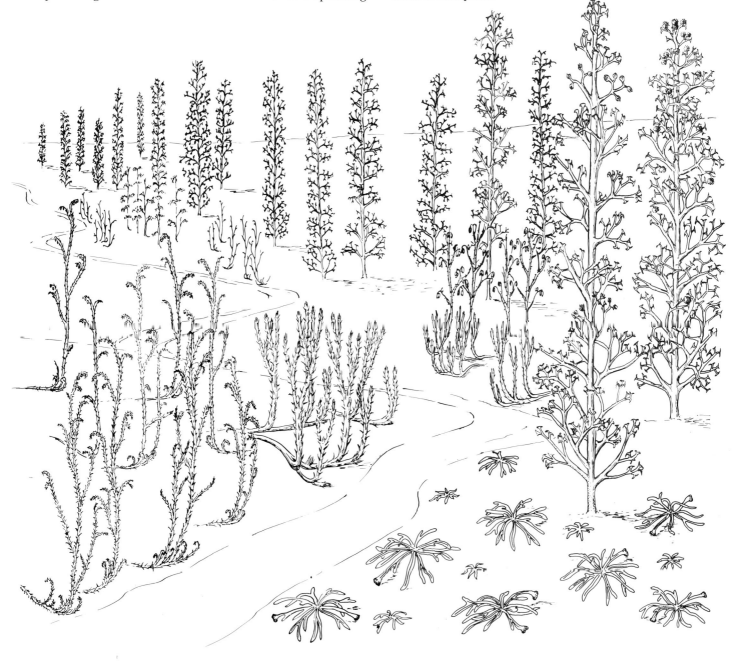

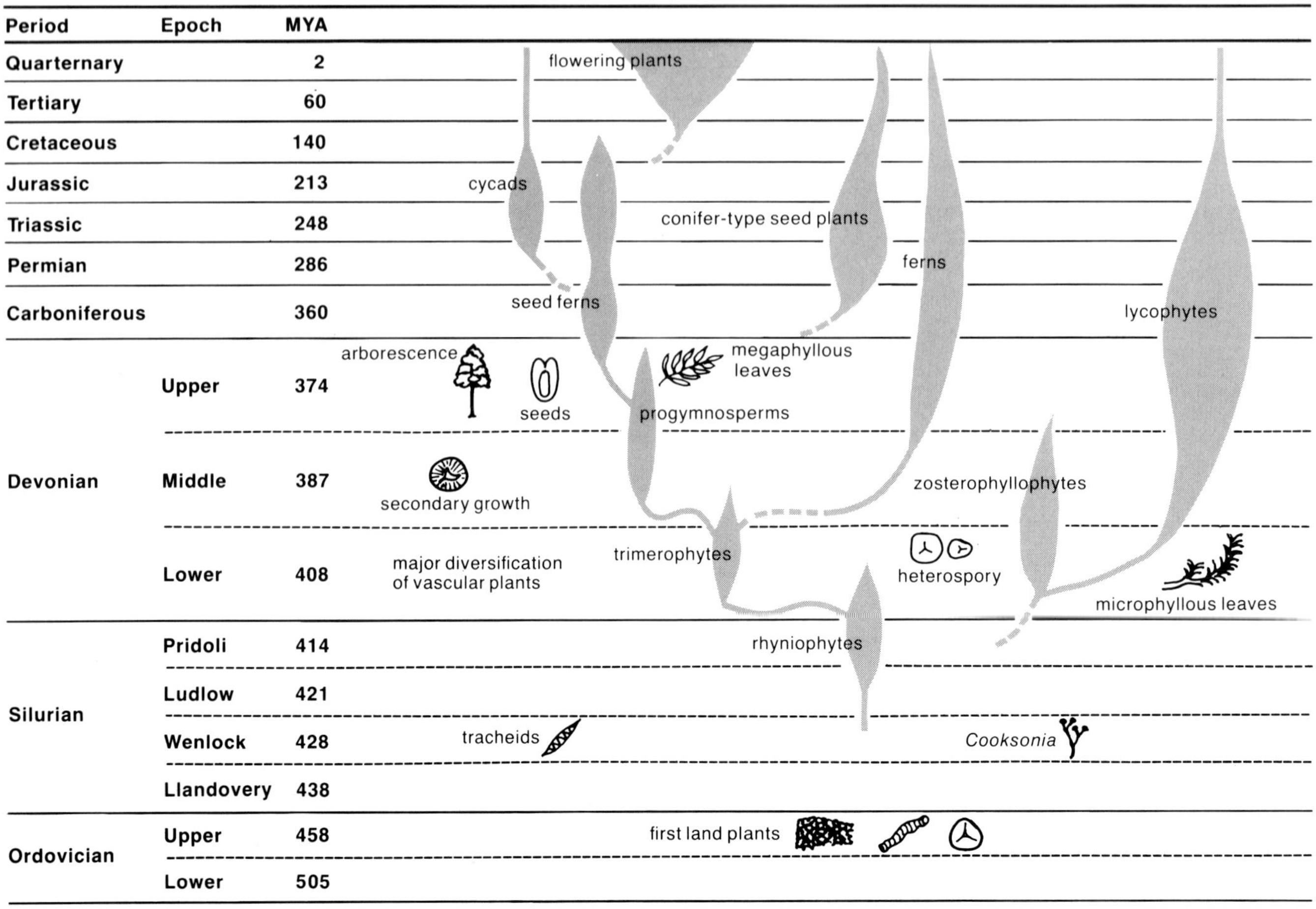

Period	Epoch	MYA
Quarternary		2
Tertiary		60
Cretaceous		140
Jurassic		213
Triassic		248
Permian		286
Carboniferous		360
Devonian	Upper	374
Devonian	Middle	387
Devonian	Lower	408
Silurian	Pridoli	414
Silurian	Ludlow	421
Silurian	Wenlock	428
Silurian	Llandovery	438
Ordovician	Upper	458
Ordovician	Lower	505

Labels within diagram: flowering plants; cycads; conifer-type seed plants; ferns; seed ferns; lycophytes; arborescence; seeds; megaphyllous leaves; progymnosperms; secondary growth; zosterophyllophytes; major diversification of vascular plants; trimerophytes; heterospory; microphyllous leaves; rhyniophytes; tracheids; *Cooksonia*; first land plants

Figure 2. During the Devonian period a remarkable burst of evolution took place among land plants. Major events of the early Devonian include the rapid spread of the rhyniophytes and the emergence of two other lineages, the zosterophyllophytes and the trimerophytes. Other important Devonian developments were the appearance of leaves, heterospory, and secondary growth, or the ability to increase girth, and finally the emergence of arborescence and seeds. In this graph, the time scale for the Silurian and Devonian periods has been expanded.

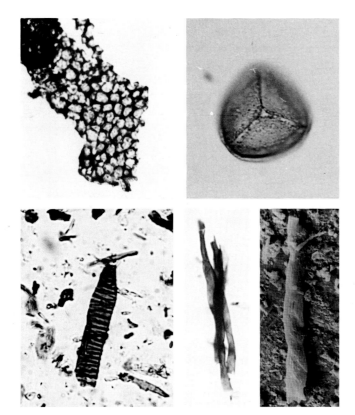

cell organization. All evidence obtained by these means is brought together in the reconstruction of plant parts or, more rarely, whole plants.

In 1859—the same year as the appearance of Darwin's *Origin of Species*—the Canadian geologist Sir John William Dawson published a pioneering study of early land plants with his report of *Psilophyton princeps*, based on the rich fossil evidence of the Gaspé coast of Quebec. His publications, which appeared between 1850 and 1890, reported plants so primitive and different from anything that now lives that they were for the most part ignored, or regarded with considerable skepticism, by nineteenth-century botanists. Interest in his findings revived with the discovery in 1912 of beautifully preserved permineralized plants in Lower Devonian chert in Rhynie, Scotland, described by two British botanists,

Figure 3. Remains of possible land plants from the Lower Silurian of Virginia include (*clockwise from upper left*) a fragment of cuticle resembling the outer waxy coating of vascular plants, lacking in most aquatic plants; a spore with resistant wall and trilete mark, both characteristic of land-plant spores; and three tube-shaped forms, two smooth and one banded with a regular pattern of lignin-like material. The presence of tubes strongly suggests a plant that lived on land. Magnifications are × 270, 687, 250, 400, and 420, respectively. (Photos courtesy of L. Pratt; unless otherwise noted, all other photos are by the authors.)

Kidston and Lang. Work in Germany, Belgium, and America in the decades that followed resulted in an emerging picture of an early land flora of simple plants. Another major advance occurred in 1968, when Banks proposed replacing the single order Psilophytales with the three lineages discussed below: Rhyniophytina, Zosterophyllophytina, and Trimerophytina. This new system of classification allowed a clearer delineation of the relationships among early land plants as well as between early and extant forms, paving the way for a more precise analysis of this remarkable assemblage of plants.

Progress in understanding the evolution of early land plants has been enhanced by the great strides made in the past decade or so in determining the exact age of the various sediments in which plant fossils are found, so that changes occurring over relatively short periods of a few million years are more easily identified. Studies of both the environments in which the fossils were formed and the positions of the continents in the Paleozoic have also advanced to the point where these lines of evidence can be incorporated. It now seems probable that most early land plants were buried in low-lying freshwater or marginal marine environments such as floodplains or coastal marshes, probably after being transported a relatively short distance. Fossil-bearing Silurian and Devonian rocks occur along the Appalachians from Tennessee to southeastern Canada as well as in parts of western North America and as far north as Ellesmere Island, within the Arctic Circle. They also are found in Great Britain, Ireland, Europe, the USSR, China, Africa, and Australia. In the Paleozoic, most of these landmasses were located between 30° and 60° of the paleoequator, implying a warm or even hot climate. Conditions were probably harsh, with abundant sunlight, frequent dry periods, and poor soil formation.

Primitive land plants

We still lack any precise information concerning the presumed aquatic ancestors from which land plants evolved, and the search for evidence of these precursors and of probable transitional stages continues. Based on similarities of many aspects of life history and on biochemistry, however, certain green algae in the charophycean line seem to be the most likely ancestors of land plants (see Graham 1985). Some researchers suggest that charophyceans with a predominantly haploid life cycle constitute the probable antecedents (Graham 1985; Mishler and Churchill 1985), while others favor extinct, predominantly diploid terrestrial forms (Stebbins and Hill 1980). Further fossil evidence is needed to test these ideas and to determine whether the transition was sudden or gradual.

The first appearance of land plants is located by most researchers in the early Silurian, with the oldest known vascular plants occurring in mid-Silurian times. However, Gray (1985) and others have argued that some microfossil assemblages of spores dating from the late Ordovician may represent early phases of land plant life. Other fossils have been interpreted as possible early Silurian land plants (Fig. 3). These fragments of reticulate-patterned cuticles and tubes tend to resemble vascular plant cuticle and tracheids, a type of water-conducting cell typical of primitive vascular plants, although

Figure 4. The extreme simplicity of *Cooksonia*, the first accepted vascular land plant, is seen in this fossil from the Upper Silurian of New York state and in the reconstruction of *C. caledonica* at the right. The first plant to exhibit upright, branched stems terminating in sporangia, *Cooksonia* also had a resistant cuticle and produced spores typical of a vascular plant. Specimens range from pin-sized to a few centimeters in height. These tiny plants probably lived in moist environments such as mud flats. About eight species are now known. (Photo courtesy of H. P. Banks.)

they are distinctive enough not to be included with that group (see Edwards 1982; Gensel and Andrews 1984).

Rocks dating from the mid-Silurian to early Devonian do contain undoubted land plants, including some structurally simple vascular plants, some algae, and a few possible bryophytes. There also occur some unique, problematic plants which may be allied to algae or bryophytes or which may represent totally separate and now extinct lineages.

The fossil record most widely accepted as representing the earliest known vascular plant reveals Y-shaped axes, or stems, lacking any appendages and terminating in a round or elliptical sporangium, or spore-producing structure (Fig. 4). Assigned to several species of the genus *Cooksonia*, a rhyniophyte, these plants seem to have attained a height of only a few centimeters. *Cooksonia* was first described from Lower Devonian rocks by Lang in 1937, but new fossil specimens discovered within the last decade in Wales and Ireland push its occurrence back to the Middle Silurian (Edwards 1979; Edwards et al. 1983). Although *Cooksonia* exhibits several

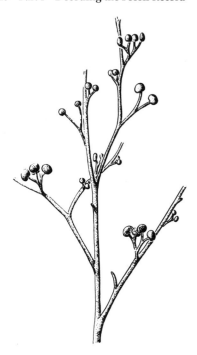

Figure 5. The transitional plant *Renalia*, shown in the reconstruction at the left, represents an elaboration of the branched, three-dimensional form of *Cooksonia*. The specimen at the right was buried in sediment and preserved as a compression; oxidizing agents were used to remove the carbon, leaving behind resistant tissues such as cuticle, tracheids, and spore walls. The kidney-shaped sporangia attached to the stem can be seen in more detail in the photograph at upper center. In this single sporangium the spores appear as black dots; the sporangium opens like a clam to release its contents. Two spores are shown magnified × 430 at lower center.

features of vascular plants, tracheids have never been found in its stems. This may be simply because they were not preserved, an occurrence common in coalified compressions; or the Silurian *Cooksonias* may instead be nonvascular plants with an exterior structure similar to later vascular plants. Tracheids have been found in as yet unidentified sterile stems associated with Devonian and Silurian *Cooksonias,* the earliest record of these being in the Wenlock of Ireland (Edwards and Davies

1979). *Cooksonia* is widely distributed, and is known from the Silurian-Devonian horizons of New York state, Wales, Britain, Czechoslovakia, and the USSR.

An early plant that combines features of the rhyniophytes with those of a second major lineage, the zosterophylls, is *Renalia hueberi*, a late Lower Devonian plant discovered on the Gaspé coast (Gensel 1976). The superbly preserved specimens are found in large quantities in a gray shale, suggesting that they represent

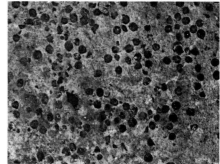

Figure 6. Fossilized plants lacking vascular tissue are varied, ranging from the branched, spiny stems found associated with *Tortilicaulis* in Wales (*upper right*) to the 2 to 3 mm filamentous balls of *Pacytheca* (*lower right*), believed to be algal. The fossil of *Prototaxites* from Gaspé shown in the center measures about 15 cm in diameter. A longitudinal section of *Prototaxites* (*upper left*) shows large tubes paralleling the plant's axis intermingled with smaller tubes of various orientations. (Photo at upper right courtesy of D. Edwards.)

a pure stand of plants buried close to the point at which they grew. *Renalia* plants are larger than *Cooksonia*, measuring from 20 to 30 cm in height, and are distinguished by a main axis with lateral branches bearing kidney-shaped sporangia (Fig. 5)—hence the name *Renalia*. In contrast to *Cooksonia*, in *Renalia* the sporangia split open along a special row of cells to shed spores. After chemical treatment, a dark central strand of tissue in the stems reveals the presence of tracheids. The only part of the plant not known is the underground system, as is commonly the case with early Devonian plants. When underground axes are present on such plants, they tend to have a structure similar to the parts above ground, and are thus probably not true roots.

Cooksonia and *Renalia* exhibit many of the features characteristic of primitive vascular plants: small size, a lack of differentiation into stems and leaves, the absence of true roots, the presence of a simple vascular system in the form of a small strand of tracheids, and a rather simple branching pattern. Like many early vascular plants they produced a large number of spores per sporangium, a feature which may have increased the chances of finding suitable places to germinate and develop in the inhospitable environments in which these plants lived. Several other genera of early plants have been described which are equally simple, differing mainly in the size and shape of the sporangia, the details of branching, or other features. A number of these have also been classified as rhyniophytes.

From the Middle Silurian on, macrofossils of presumed nonvascular plants are often found intermixed with *Cooksonia*. Specimens discovered in Wales (Edwards 1979) show the presence of erect land plants with branched, sometimes spiny axes lacking vascular tissue and reproductive structures (Fig. 6). These and other, more completely preserved plants from the late Silurian and early Devonian probably represent an unknown lineage, or possibly some may be early bryophytes. For example, *Tortilicaulis*, a late Silurian plant, has a twisted stem and elongate sporangium that strongly resemble the spore-bearing region of some modern mosses.

Still other presumed nonvascular fossils, collectively referred to as nematophytes, are more consistently allied to algae or to lines other than the three described here. *Nematothallus* exhibits small pads of tissue a few centimeters in diameter with an outer cuticle and possibly an inner region of randomly arranged cells and tubes, *Nematoplexus* consists of small clusters of tubes, and *Prototaxites* appears as large logs, up to a meter in diameter, composed of tubes of various sizes and orientations. Two other macrofossils, *Parka* and *Pachytheca*, are of equally problematical lineage. Niklas (1976) has suggested that they may be related to green algae of the genus *Coleochaete*, considered to be in the vascular plant line. Many of these nonvascular forms extend into the Devonian, and others appear during that time.

Diversification of vascular plants

Other, apparently distinct vascular lines were also initiated in the late Lower and early Middle Devonian, indicating the burst of diversification that took place once the basic problems of the transition from an aquatic to a land environment were solved. Analysis of both macrofossils

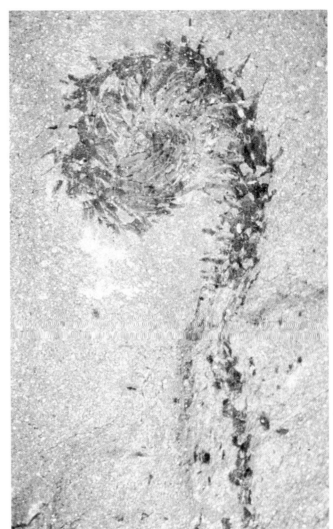

Figure 7. A fossil of *Sawdonia ornata* from New Brunswick is distinguished by a crozier, or unfurling tip, and numerous spiny emergences along the stem. *S. ornata* reached a height of about 50 cm, and was the second most abundant plant after *Psilophyton* in some regions. Plants found preserved in great numbers in the siltstone of Gaspé were probably buried at or close to the site at which they grew. The reconstruction at the right shows the distinctive zosterophyll structure, which is characterized by both creeping and upright stems, with rounded sporangia borne along the sides. As in the case of *Renalia*, the sporangia of *Sawdonia* contain a line of cells along which the structure splits open to release spores. At present only two species of *Sawdonia* are known.

and microfossils shows that a major taxonomic and morphological radiation of vascular plants occurred from the late Silurian to the end of the Lower Devonian (Chaloner and Sheerin 1979). The number of known vascular plant genera increases from one in the late Silurian to approximately 28 at the end of the Lower Devonian; from then until the end of the Devonian the numbers remain about the same, with earlier genera becoming extinct and new ones appearing. In addition, many of the major structural features typical of modern

Figure 8. *Baragwanathia longifolia*, the oldest lycophyte, exhibits a robust stem 1 to 2 cm in diameter thickly covered with long, slender leaves (*right*). The stems reached lengths of up to a meter and were probably rhizomatous, creeping along the ground. Shown at the left is a stand of shining club moss (*Lycopodium lucidulum*) from the mountains of North Carolina. This smaller living lycophyte closely resembles *B. longifolia*, demonstrating the longevity of the lineage. (Photo of *B. longifolia* from Lang and Cookson 1935.)

Of all living plants, lycophytes are most similar in their appearance to some early vascular plants. They have the longest and most completely known history of any vascular plant, starting in the late Lower or early Middle Devonian and continuing into the present as epiphytes and trailing evergreens widely distributed in tropical and temperate forests. In essence, the ?Silurian-Devonian genus *Baragwanathia* is simply a very large version of shining club moss (*Lycopodium lucidulum*), a living lycopod (Fig. 8). The lycophytes are characterized by the presence of abundant microphyllous leaves—that is, leaves that are usually small in size, exhibiting one unbranched vein—and sporangia which are borne either on the leaves or in their axils.

Some early Devonian plants may represent stages in the evolution of these lycophyte features, and seem to provide a link between putative zosterophyll ancestors and true lycopods. *Asteroxylon mackiei*, identified from the Rhynie chert by Kidston and Lang in 1920, bears lateral sporangia located on the ends of short stalks interspersed among "leaves." The latter are unique in that while they appear leaflike externally, they are not vascularized. Instead, a vascular strand extends only to their base. *Kaulangiophyton akantha*, first found in northern Maine in rocks probably dating from the late Lower Devonian (Gensel et al. 1969), is known from impressions which show axes with thornlike, fully vascularized leaves and sporangia on the ends of short stalks interspersed among leaves. These plants suggest that microphyllous leaves evolved through the enlargement and progressive vascularization of thorns or other emergences, and point to the early appearance of the lycophytes as a distinct group.

Baragwanathia longifolia, first reported by Lang and Cookson from well-preserved specimens found in Australia in 1935, is the oldest undoubted lycophyte. The age of the rocks, then regarded as Late Silurian, was later revised to early Devonian based on the presence of graptolites, a unique group of extinct invertebrates. However, Tims and Chambers's recent find (1984) of remains apparently identical to *Baragwanathia* with other very simple plants in older Australian rocks tentatively dated as late Silurian raises the intriguing possibility of the Silurian occurrence of vascular plants much more complex than *Cooksonia* or *Renalia*. Although the dating is problematical, other finds in Libya may support this possibility (Klitszch et al. 1973; Boureau et al. 1978). *Baragwanathia* was a large and complex plant, seemingly rather out of place among the predominantly small, primitive plants of the late Silurian and early Devonian. The fossil specimens show robust stems up to a meter long bearing slender, closely arranged leaves 4 cm long. The sporangia are found along the stem, although it is

plants were established during this time: leaves, roots, particular reproductive syndromes, and secondary growth. Knoll and his colleagues (1984) have pointed out that different plant parts apparently evolved at different rates—that is, that plants exhibit mosaic evolution, which may be a direct result of the way they develop and grow.

A few million years after the establishment in the Silurian of the rhyniophytes, a second major group of plants, the zosterophylls, appeared. These were plants up to several centimeters high with both crawling and erect stems, a robust vascular strand, a fairly resistant cuticle, and sporangia attached laterally to the stems. Stems may be smooth, as in *Zosterophyllum,* or the stems and sometimes the sporangia may be covered with spines or teeth, as in *Sawdonia* or *Crenaticaulis* (Fig. 7). The genus *Zosterophyllum* was first described in 1892 by Penhallow, who thought the stems of Scottish specimens resembled those of the modern aquatic eelgrass *Zostera*. It was nearly seventy years before sufficient evidence was obtained to establish the distinctive features of the group. Since Banks's characterization of the lineage in 1968, nine other genera have been described, based on specimens from North America, Great Britain, Europe, Australia, and the USSR. Although these genera were closely related, they were also rapidly diversifying during the early Devonian. It is interesting that some genera, such as *Sawdonia*, were relatively persistent, occurring over a span of about 25 million years. The zosterophylls clearly differ from *Cooksonia* and allied plants, and may have been directly ancestral to an important group known as the lycophytes.

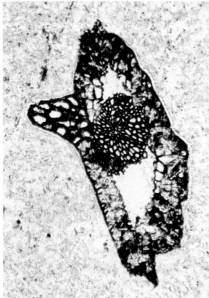

Figure 9. The ultimate ancestors of the seed plants are the trimerophytes, an important lineage that appeared in the middle of the Lower Devonian. Representative of this group is the abundant genus *Psilophyton*. *P. forbesii* (*upper left*), shown also at the upper left of Figure 1, bears paired sporangia at the tips of drooping lateral branches. A cross-section of a stem of *P. coniculum* (*lower left*) reveals vascular tissue visible as a central cluster of water-conducting cells occupying about a third of the stem. *Pertica varia*, another trimerophyte (*upper right*), exhibits a more sophisticated external structure, with a central stem bearing branches arranged in a regular pattern. A reconstruction of *Pertica* at lower right shows this structure in more detail. Clusters of up to 200 sporangia are located at the tips of some branches.

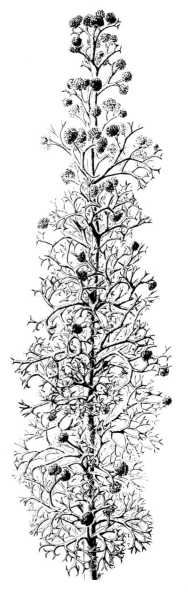

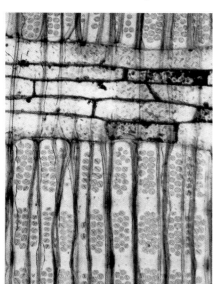

Figure 10. A fossil of the progymnosperm *Archaeopteris macilenta* from West Virginia displays some of the earliest megaphyllous leaves (*right*). The small patches of pink pigment on the surface of the fossil were produced by the needles used to split away rock particles in uncovering the compressed remains. A longitudinal section of a stem of *Archaeopteris* at lower left shows the further evolution of vascular tissue, which now fills most of the stem. The bricklike structures are unspecialized cells allowing lateral movement of materials; the dots are thin areas in the walls of tracheids which permit water to pass between adjacent cells. The reconstruction at the upper left shows the dramatic increase in both girth and height. *Archaeopteris* plants reached diameters of approximately 1 m and heights of about 25 m. (Photo and reconstruction at left courtesy of C. Beck.)

uncertain whether they were attached to the stem itself or to the base of the leaf.

By Middle Devonian times several other kinds of lycophytes are known, and some interesting variations appear. *Leclercqia complexa*, discovered in the Middle Devonian rocks of New York state (Banks et al. 1972), consists of abundantly branching axes covered with microphyllous leaves divided toward their distal end into five units. Other lycophytes of middle and late Devonian age exhibit two- or three-forked leaves. It has

recently been suggested that lycopods with forked leaves represent a different line within the group, and that their leaves evolved through changes in branches rather than from emergences (Stewart 1983).

The lycopods continued to evolve at a rapid rate throughout the Devonian. By the end of this period some members of the group had become arborescent, with trunks of up to a half meter in diameter and heights of eight to ten meters. Leaves became correspondingly larger in some species, although remaining anatomically

similar to those of the earlier herbaceous forms. Interestingly, the
forked leaf appears to have died
out relatively quickly. During the
Carboniferous, some lycophytes
achieved heights well in excess of 30
m, and such specimens became a
dominant element in the great Upper
Carboniferous coal swamps. These
types declined rapidly toward the
end of the Carboniferous, while the
smaller, herbaceous forms continued
on to the present time.

Trimerophytes as precursors

The third major line, the trimerophytes, is important for its possible
role in the evolution of megaphyllous
leaves, seen in modern ferns, and as
the probable ancestor of ferns and
seed plants. First appearing in the
middle of the early Devonian and
extending just into the Middle Devonian, trimerophytes are best characterized by the genus *Psilophyton*, of
which at least eight species are now
recognized (Fig. 9). A wide variety of
fossil plant types was originally included in *Psilophyton*; the genus was

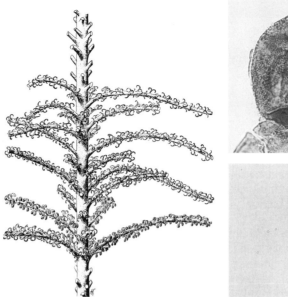

Figure 11. The earliest fossil evidence of heterospory, thought to be an important step in the evolution of seeds, occurs in *Chaleuria cirrosa*, a late Lower Devonian plant shown in the reconstruction at the left. The megaspore and microspore seen magnified at upper and lower right, respectively, were produced by different sporangia on the same plant. Although *C. cirrosa* has a central stem and lateral branches similar to those of *Pertica*, its branches are unique in being covered with densely spiraled, twice-bifurcated, curled appendages resembling those of some Middle Devonian plants.

redescribed and clarified in 1967 by Hueber and Banks.
Several new species have been added in the past dozen
years, together with new information about the anatomy
of previously known species (Banks et al. 1975; Gensel
1979; Trant and Gensel 1985). *Psilophyton crenulatum*, an
exceptionally well-preserved species recorded by Doran
(1980), shows the characteristically varied branching
patterns of the slender, mostly erect stems. The plants
were probably up to 30 cm high, with many branches
terminating in masses of paired sporangia producing
large numbers of spores, and with needlelike, spinelike,
or forked emergences.

Certain larger species of *Psilophyton* seem to merge
into a more advanced type, *Pertica quadrifaria*, which has
been found in abundance in northern Maine (Kasper
and Andrews 1972). The fossil evidence shows that *P.
quadrifaria* had a strong central axis with side branches
arranged in four clearly defined rows. The branches are
three-dimensional, some being sterile and probably photosynthetic, while others terminate in compact, densely
divided branchlets bearing a mass of sporangia. This
differentiation into main stem and side branches probably represents an initial stage in the evolution of fernlike
megaphyllous leaves, which are characterized by broad,
flat surfaces with branched veins. Some Middle and
Upper Devonian plants such as *Archaeopteris* have distinctly two-dimensional branch systems or branches plus
leaves which may be variously webbed or laminated
(Fig. 10). Thus leaves originated in the Early Devonian in
at least two different ways in vascular plants and perhaps several times in different lineages. Most microphyllous leaves may have arisen from emergences such as
spines or needles, while megaphyllous leaves (and pos-

sibly some microphyllous leaves) arose from modifications in branches.

The trimerophytes also lead, via the progymnosperms—Middle and Upper Devonian plants with fernlike reproductive habits and a gymnosperm anatomy—
to the first seed plants, which are now known from the
uppermost Devonian horizons (Pettitt and Beck 1968;
Chaloner et al. 1977; Gillespie et al. 1981). All groups
mentioned so far are homosporous—that is, they exhibit
sporangia with spores which are all essentially the same
size. These would presumably develop into the small,
sex-bearing plants referred to as gametophytes. The life
cycle is complete when an egg in the female organ is
fertilized and the resulting zygote grows to form a new
sporophyte, or spore producing plant. In many distinct
lines of vascular plants, including the progymnosperms,
it is now clear that a differentiation of spores into two
kinds, microspores and megaspores, took place. Microspores develop into male gametophytes, whereas megaspores, which are usually much larger, become female
gametophytes. This phenomenon, known as heterospory, is found in several different groups of living plants,
and is believed to represent an intermediate stage in the
evolution of seed plants.

The earliest appearance of heterospory is in *Chaleuria cirrosa*, a late Lower Devonian plant found on the
northern coast of New Brunswick (Andrews et al. 1974).
Specimens reveal a main stem about one centimeter in
diameter with spirally arranged side branches (Fig. 11).
When the sporangia were analyzed, some were found to
contain megaspores measuring 60 to 156 μm in diameter, while others yielded microspores of 30 to 48 μm.
Heterospory is now known in several distinct lines of

later Devonian plants, including not only the progymnosperms but the lycopods. In one extinct line, represented by *Barinophyton*, a very different form of heterospory occurs: it is the only known plant, living or fossil, which produces both microspores and megaspores in the same sporangium (Brauer 1980).

Converging adaptations

The growing fossil record now documents in some detail the establishment of a varied assemblage of vascular and nonvascular land plants during the Silurian and early Devonian. What has been revealed is a landscape first of very tiny plants, some erect and some prostrate, which changed in a matter of 20 million years or so to a very diverse array of erect plants 0.5 to 9 m high, most of which show a combination of creeping stems and upright branches. At a distance the Devonian landscape must have resembled a modern salt marsh, seemingly offering to the eye a large expanse of fairly uniform vegetation, but closer inspection would reveal that stands of *Psilophyton*, for example, were interspersed with smaller pockets of plants dominated by one or more of several types of zosterophylls, perhaps ringed by a group of *Renalia* or shaded by some of the taller *Pertica*, which ranged up to 3 m in height. Wetter areas might have supported the nonvascular types, some zosterophylls, or lycophytes (Gensel and Andrews 1984).

Early vascular plants were small and probably short-lived, partly reflecting the fact that their capability was limited to primary growth. Collectively they exhibit numerous adaptations for terrestrial existence, including increasingly greater amounts of vascular tissue. Some middle and late Devonian plants show the further development of leaves and the initiation of a vascular cambium, allowing plants to increase in girth and thus in overall size and longevity. The appearance of heterospory in the late Lower Devonian was followed a few million years later by the emergence of seed plants—the ultimate adaptation for reproduction in the absence of water.

Evidence is mounting that plants of various affinities exhibit conducting cells which, while not all showing secondary walls patterned like tracheids, seem to converge on a tracheid morphology and function (Hueber 1982; Fairon-Demaret 1985; Edwards 1986). Although this makes the recognition of undoubted vascular plants more difficult, it is interesting in that it suggests the existence of convergent adaptations to life on land in several plant groups.

Patricia G. Gensel is associate professor of botany at the University of North Carolina, where she has taught since 1975. She received her Ph.D. in botany from the University of Connecticut. Her research focuses on the morphology, systematics, and evolutionary significance of early vascular plants, and has included extensive study of fossil plants in southeastern Canada and the eastern US, as well as in Great Britain and Europe. Henry N. Andrews received his degrees from MIT and Washington University, and has taught at Washington University, the University of Connecticut, Poona University in India, and the University of Aarhus, Denmark. In addition to explorations of fossil evidence in northern Maine and on the coasts of New Brunswick and Quebec, he has carried out paleobotanical investigations in the Canadian Arctic, Sweden, and Belgium. Address for Dr. Gensel: Department of Biology, Coker Hall 010 A, University of North Carolina, Chapel Hill, NC 27514.

One major aspect of early vascular plants that remains relatively unstudied concerns their gametophytic phase of life. Most of the fossils represent parts of the spore-bearing, or sporophyte, phase of the plant's life cycle, whereas the sexual, or gamete-producing, structures remain unknown. Based on extant plants, botanists have long proposed two possible alternatives for these unknown gametophyte plants: they may have been branched axes superficially similar to the sporophyte but instead producing gametangia, or gamete-bearing structures; or they may have been thalloid in form, as in some modern liverworts. A few gametophytic plants such as *Lyonophyton* and (possibly) *Sciadophyton* have been described (Remy and Remy 1980; Remy et al. 1980; Schweitzer 1983). Whether these represent bryophytes or the gametophyte phase of some vascular plants is unclear, although we suspect the former.

In addition, we are only beginning to learn about the possible factors that might have influenced the geographical and local distribution of these plants, and to piece together the information needed to answer some crucial questions. Which plants grew together? What kind of ecological niches were available in the Silurian and Devonian, and how variable were the plant communities? What effect did the appearance of arborescent forms have on the survival of other plants? Similarly, clearer assessments of evolutionary rates and modes are now coming within reach. The next few decades promise to bring significant additions to the emerging picture of the rise of plant forms on land.

References

Andrews, H. N., P. G. Gensel, and W. H. Forbes. 1974. An apparently heterosporous plant from the Middle Devonian of New Brunswick. *Palaeontology* 17:387–408.

Banks, H. P. 1968. The early history of land plants. In *Evolution and Environment*, ed. E. T. Drake, pp. 73–107. Yale Univ. Press.

Banks, H. P., P. M. Bonamo, and J. D. Grierson. 1972. *Leclercqia complexa* gen. et sp. nov., a new lycopod from the late Middle Devonian of eastern New York. *Rev. Palaeobot. Palynol.* 14:19–40.

Banks, H. P., S. Leclercq, and F. M. Hueber. 1975. Anatomy and morphology of *Psilophyton dawsonii*, sp. n. from the late Lower Devonian of Quebec (Gaspé), and Ontario, Canada. *Palaeontographica Am.* 8:77–127.

Boureau, E., A. Lejal-Nicol, and D. Massa. 1978. À propos du Silurien et du Dévonien en Libye. *C. R. Hèbdomadaire des Séances de l'Acad. des Sci.* 186D:1567–71.

Brauer, D. 1980. *Barinophyton citrulliforme* (Barinophytales incertae sedis, Barinophytaceae) from Upper Devonian of Pennsylvania. *Am. J. Bot.* 67:1186–1206.

Chaloner, W. G., and A. Sheerin. 1979. Devonian macrofloras. In *The Devonian System*, ed. M. R. House, C. T. Scrutton, and M. G. Bassett. *Special Papers in Palaeontology* 23:145–61.

Chaloner, W. G., A. J. Hill, and W. S. Lacey. 1977. First Devonian platyspermic seed and its implications in gymnosperm evolution. *Nature* 265:233–35.

Doran, J. B. 1980. A new species of *Psilophyton* from the Lower Devonian of northern New Brunswick, Canada. *Can. J. Bot.* 58:2241–62.

Edwards, D. 1979. A late Silurian flora from the Lower Old Red Sandstone of Southwest Dyfed. *Palaeontology* 22:23–52.

———. 1982. Fragmentary non-vascular plant microfossils from the Late Silurian of Wales. *Bot. J. Linn. Soc.* 84:223–56.

Edwards, D., and E. C. W. Davies. 1979. Oldest recorded *in situ* tracheids. *Nature* 263:494–95.

Edwards, D., J. Feehan, and D. G. Smith. 1983. A late Wenlock flora from Co. Tipperary, Ireland. *Bot. J. Linn. Soc.* 86:19–36.

Edwards, D. S. 1986. *Aglaophyton major*, a nonvascular land-plant from the Devonian Rhynie Chert. *Bot. J. Linn. Soc.* 93:173–204.

Fairon-Demaret, M. 1985. Les plantes fossiles de l'Emsien du Sart Tilman, Belgique. I. *Stockmansia langii* (Stockmans) comb. nov. *Rev. Palaeobot. Palynol.* 44:243–60.

Gensel, P. G. 1976. *Renalia hueberi*, a new plant from the Lower Devonian of Gaspé. *Rev. Palaeobot. Palynol.* 22:19–27.

————. 1979. Two *Psilophyton* species from the Lower Devonian of eastern Canada with a discussion of morphological variation within the genus. *Palaeontographica* 168B:81–99.

Gensel, P. G., and H. N. Andrews. 1984. *Plant Life in the Devonian.* Praeger.

Gensel, P. G., A. E. Kasper, and H. N. Andrews. 1969. *Kaulangiophyton*, a new genus of plants from the Devonian of Maine. *Torrey Bot. Club Bull.* 96:265–76.

Gillespie, W. H., G. W. Rothwell, and S. E. Scheckler. 1981. The earliest seeds. *Nature* 293:462–64.

Graham, L. 1985. The origin of the life cycle of land plants. *Am. Sci.* 73:178–86.

Gray, J. 1985. The microfossil record of early land plants: Advances in understanding early terrestrialization, 1970–1984. *Phil. Trans. Roy. Soc. London* B309:167–95.

Hueber, F. M. 1982. *Taeniocrada dubia* Kr. and W.: Its conducting strand of helically strengthened tubes. *Bot. Soc. Am. Misc. Ser.* 162:58–59.

Heuber, F. M., and H. P. Banks. 1967. *Psilophyton princeps*: The search for organic connection. *Taxon* 16:81–85.

Kasper, A. E., and H. N. Andrews. 1972. *Pertica*, a new genus of Devonian plants from northern Maine. *Am. J. Bot.* 59:897–911.

Klitzsch, E., A. Lejal-Nicol, and D. Massa. 1973. Le Siluro-Dévonien à Psilophytes et Lycophytes du bassin de Mourzouk (Libye). *C. R. Acad. Sci. Paris, Ser. D* 277:2465–67.

Knoll, A. H., K. J. Niklas, P. G. Gensel, and B. Tiffney. 1984. Character diversification and patterns of evolution in early vascular plants. *Paleobiology* 10:34–47.

Lang, W. H., and I. C. Cookson. 1935. On a flora, including vascular land plants, associated with *Monograptus*, in rocks of Silurian age, from Victoria, Australia. *Phil. Trans. Roy. Soc. London* 224B:421–49.

Mishler, B. D., and S. P. Churchill. 1985. Transition to a land flora: Phylogenetic relationships of the green algae and bryophytes. *Cladistics* 1:305–38.

Niklas, K. J. 1976. Morphological and ontogenetic reconstruction of *Parka decipiens* Fleming and *Pachytheca* Hooker from the Lower Old Red Sandstone, Scotland. *Trans. Roy. Soc. Edin.* 69:483–99.

Pettitt, J. M., and C. B. Beck. 1968. *Archaeosperma arnoldii*—A cupulate seed from the Upper Devonian of North America. *Contrib. Mus. Palaeontol. Univ. Mich.* 22:139–54.

Remy, W., and R. Remy. 1980. *Lyonophyton rhyniensis* nov. gen. et nov. spec., ein gametophyt aus dem chert von Rhynie (Unterdevon, Schottland). *Argumenta Palaeobot.* 6:37–72.

Remy, W., R. Remy, S. Schultka, and F. Franzmeyer. 1980. *Sciadophyton* Steinmann—Ein gametophyt aus dem Siegen. *Argumenta Palaeobot.* 6:73–94.

Schweitzer, H. J. 1983. Dei Unterdevonflora des Rheinlandes. *Palaeontographica* 189B:1-138.

Stebbins, G. L., and G. J. C. Hill. 1980. Did multicellular plants invade the land? *Am. Nat.* 115:342–53.

Stewart, W. N. 1983. *Paleobotany and the Evolution of Plants.* Cambridge Univ. Press.

Tims, J. D., and T. C. Chambers. 1984. Rhyniophytina and Trimerophytina from the early land flora of Victoria, Australia. *Palaeontology* 27: 265–79.

Trant, C. A., and P. G. Gensel. 1985. Branching in *Psilophyton*: A new species from the Lower Devonian of New Brunswick, Canada. *Am. J. Bot.* 72:1256–73.

Evolution of the Early Vertebrates

Recent discoveries provide clues to the relationships between early vertebrates and their modern relatives

Peter Forey and Philippe Janvier

The first vertebrate probably arose about 550 million years ago in the Cambrian period, immediately after the great evolutionary explosion that produced most of the major groups of multicellular plants and animals. With one possible exception, however, these animals do not appear to have left their mark in the fossil record. The oldest undeniably vertebrate remains do not appear until the Ordovician period, about 460 million years ago. These animals, collectively and informally known as the "ostracoderms," were relatively small, fishlike creatures that became extinct about 100 million years later. Some among them, however, had a promising future; in fact the ostracoderms gave rise to most of the vertebrates on the earth today, including human beings.

The 100-million-year reign of the ostracoderms was a crucial period in vertebrate history. It was during this time that many of the features we regard as important evolutionary advances arose, including true bone, paired pectoral appendages and jaws. The last feature is

Peter Forey is a principal scientific officer at the Natural History Museum, London. He earned his Ph.D. in 1971 at the University of London based on his work on the fossil relatives of tarpon and bonefish. Before joining the Natural History Museum in 1975, he taught zoology at the University of Alberta. His current research interests include the history of coelacanth fishes and the postcranial skeleton of agnathans. Philippe Janvier is a director of research in the Centre National de la Recherche Scientifique. He earned his Ph.D. in 1980 at the Université Pierre et Marie Curie, based on his work on the internal anatomy of Devonian osteostracans from Spitzbergen. His current research concerns the unusual galeaspids from the Devonian of Vietnam. Forey's address: Department of Palaeontology, The Natural History Museum, Cromwell Road, London SW7 5BD, United Kingdom. Janvier's address: Muséum National d'Histoire Naturelle, 8 rue Buffon, 75005 Paris, France.

especially significant because jaws undoubtedly served as the impetus for many of the sophisticated vertebrate qualities that followed. This is because jaws permit the bearer to increase the intake of energy by biting off large pieces of other organisms.

The significance of the jaw is recognized by the classification of the modern vertebrates into two major groups, the gnathostomes (meaning "jaw-mouths") and the agnathans (meaning "without-jaws"). Modern agnathans are represented by two groups, the lampreys and the hagfishes. These jawless fishes are recognized not only for their unsavory feeding habits (lampreys rasp the flesh and suck the blood of other animals, whereas hagfish literally eat their way through dead or dying fishes), but also for their primitive appearance. The gnathostomes constitute all the other living vertebrates, including the bony and cartilaginous fishes and the tetrapods. The absence of jaws in all of the known ostracoderms assigns these fishes to the agnathan group, yet some share many similarities with the gnathostomes. Herein lies a central puzzle of vertebrate evolution: Who were the ostracoderms, and how are they related to modern vertebrates?

Unraveling these relationships has long plagued paleontologists because of the peculiar anatomy of the ostracoderms, and because their remains have not always been complete. Although ostracoderms have been known since the middle of the 19th century, their anatomy was not carefully appraised until the early part of this century, when the Swedish paleontologist Erik Stensiö analyzed structural details in serial sections of the fossils. Recently, many new discoveries of different kinds of ostracoderms, combined with acid-etching

Figure 1. Fossils of jawless fishes called ostracoderms provide the best evidence for the appearance of the early vertebrates. Fossil ostracoderms are found throughout the world

techniques that remove either the rock or the bone, have dramatically increased our knowledge of these creatures and their relationships to modern vertebrates. Our results are consistent with the notion that hagfishes are the most primitive vertebrates known (living or extinct) and that the lamprey is more closely related to gnathostomes then either is to the hagfishes.

Jawless but Armored

Since they were first discovered, more than 600 species of ostracoderms have been recovered in the fossil record. Like the piscine equivalents of medieval knights, most species were clad in an external bony armor (ostracoderm means "shell-skin"). The diversity of armor types suggests that some as yet unknown selective forces were at work. Some paleontologists have suggested that giant invertebrates, the scorpion-like eurypterids, may have posed a threat. Others suggest that the bony armor may have helped to prevent the loss of water from the body tissues or

in sedimentary deposits that are between 460 and 360 million years old. Ostracoderms were heavily armored and often lacked paired fins. Here the fossil impressions left by the head shield and body scales of a 400-million-year-old osteostracan from Great Britain are about 15 centimeters long and show the location of the eye sockets and specialized sensory fields on the animal's head. (Except where noted, all photographs courtesy of the authors.)

that it served as storage for calcium and phosphate. In any case, the ostracoderms were also experimenting with other aspects of their new found vertebrate body, being modified with various types of bone, shields, tail shapes, gills and nasal openings.

In spite of their diversity, most ostracoderms can be classified into one of nine or ten groups. Distinctions between them are usually based on certain characteristics, such as the presence of a head shield, the location of the eyes, whether one or two nasal openings is present, and such general features as the shape of the head, the body and the tail. Although we may never discover the reason for the ostracoderms' developments, an appreciation of their appearance should provide clues to their evolution.

The osteostracans were a very successful group of ostracoderms with nearly 200 species. These fishes lived during the Silurian and Devonian periods in North America, Europe, Siberia and central Asia. Most osteostracans appear to have had pectoral fins and an

upturned, flexible tail, suggesting that they would have been among the most maneuverable ostracoderms. The dorsal surface of the osteostracan head was encased in a large semicircular shield, while the undersurface was covered with tiny scales or plates surrounding the openings of the mouth and gills. Beneath the head shield, the brain and the gills were encased in a "skull" made of perichondral bone (a type of bone present in many gnathostomes, but not in lampreys and hagfishes). The top of the head had openings for the eyes and the pineal organ and a single combined nasohypophyseal opening (so named because the hypophysis [or pituitary] develops as an outpouching from this duct in modern agnathans). The dorsal nasohypophyseal opening of osteostracans is strikingly similar to that of lampreys, and has been the primary argument that these two groups are immediately related. However, it is now believed that this similarity came about as a result of parallel evolution. The most distinctive features of the os-

teostracans are the "sensory fields," on the lateral margins of the head shield and just behind the eyes. The sensory fields were connected to the inner ear by radiating systems of tubes. It has been suggested that they were some form of electric organ, a special sense organ or, more likely, a specialized part of the lateral line system (a sensory structure over the head and along the sides of some fishes that enables them to detect vibrations in the water).

During the Lower Silurian and Upper Devonian periods, the geographic regions of China and North Vietnam were covered by seas inhabited by ostracoderms known as the galeaspids. The galeaspids have only been known for 30 years, during which time about 60 species have been discovered. Recent work by Liu Yuhai, Pan Jiang and Wang Nienzong in Beijing and Ta Hoa Phuong of Hanoi University has resulted in a number of exciting discoveries of these fishes. The galeaspids superficially resemble the osteostracans in having a single broad shield on the dorsal

Figure 2. Lampreys *(photograph)* are modern smooth-skinned forms of jawless vertebrates (agnathans) that lack paired fins. About 40 species live in fresh water or marine habitats and feed by rasping away the flesh of other fishes. The earliest lamprey, *Mayomyzon* (reconstructed, *top)*, is about five centimeters long and found in deposits of the Carboniferous period about 300 million years old. There is no direct evidence that *Mayomyzon's* life-style was similar to that of modern lampreys.

surface of the head, whereas the mouth and the gill openings are on the underside of the head. The shield is usually semicircular, but may be extended into a long horn or rostrum in some species. Unlike the osteostracans, the galeaspids have a distinctive median opening in front of the eyes, just behind the anterior margin of the head shield. A similar opening is found in modern hagfishes, and it is believed that it was used for the intake of water into the gill chamber.

While the galeaspids were swimming in the ancient seas of China, the anas-pids were living in the brackish and fresh waters of Europe and North America. Anaspids are poorly known but appear to be characterized by small spindle-shaped bodies and downward-turning tails. Alex Ritchie of the Australian Museum in Sydney has provided evidence for ribbon-like paired fins that extended behind the gill openings. One of us (Janvier) has suggested that the fins may have undulated, moving the fish slowly forward or backward.

There appear to be two types of anaspids, both of which are reminiscent of lampreys in having large eyes with the nasohypophyseal and pineal openings on top of the head. One group has enlarged scales along the length of the animal's back and immediately behind the gills. The members of the other group completely lack scales, or have poorly developed scales. The best known genus of these "naked" anaspids is *Jamoytius*, which resembles modern lampreys in having a circular cartilage surrounding the mouth, large eyes and a basket-like skeleton that supported the gills. These similarities have led some workers to suggest that the naked anaspids are immediate relatives of lampreys.

The heterostracans were among the first of the armored agnathans to be discovered. Although their head shields were initially identified as fossil squid shells or crustacean carapaces, in 1858 the British naturalist Thomas Huxley realized that the shields belonged to vertebrate animals. At this writing the group is known to consist of about 300 species that lived during lower Silurian to upper Devonian times in North America, Europe and Siberia. Their remains are so common in coastal, brackish and possibly freshwater deposits from the Devonian that they are used locally for stratigraphic correlations.

All heterostracans had a well-developed dermal skeleton covering the head, body and tail, and a single external gill opening. In most species the head armor was made of dorsal and ventral shields. Each shield was made of a peculiar type of bone, called aspidin, that did not contain bone cells. Aspidin tissue was also present in the scales or shields of some other groups of ostracoderms (including the anaspids and galeaspids). Unfortunately, little is known of the internal anatomy of heterostracans, since they appear to have lacked a bony endoskeleton. Some reconstructions of the brain and the inner

Figure 3. Modern hagfishes *(bottom)*, superficially similar to lampreys, represent the other major living group of jawless vertebrates. All 42 species of hagfish live in marine habitats, and most feed on dead and dying fishes. The earliest known hagfish, *Myxinikela* (reconstructed, *top)*, about 7 centimeters long, appeared about 300 million years ago in the fossil record.

ear are possible because these structures left impressions on the underside of the head shield.

The tissue structure of heterostracan bone is considered to be the primitive vertebrate type. Not only is its structure simpler than true cellular bone, but it is also found in much older groups of ostracoderms dating from the Ordovician. These Ordovician species are the earliest records of animals that are clearly recognizable as vertebrates. They differ from heterostracans in having several separate gill openings. Until the mid-1970s one of these Ordovician groups, the astraspids, was thought to have the primitive form of the vertebrate armor (made of small polygonal plates that could grow). However, some recent discoveries of heterostracan-like fishes from older deposits have changed this view.

In particular, Alex Ritchie and Joyce Gilbert-Tomlinson of the Australian Museum discovered several heterostracan-like fishes in 1977, including the genus *Arandaspis*, in the Middle Ordovician rocks of central Australia. In 1993 Pierre-Yves Gagnier, then of the National Museum of Natural History in Paris, described a very similar fish, *Sacabambaspis*, from Upper Ordovician deposits in Bolivia. More recently, the Australian paleontologist Gavin Young of the Bureau of Mineral Resources in Canberra found similar fragments of these fishes, collectively called the arandaspids, in the oldest rocks of the Australian Ordovician.

Like the heterostracans, arandaspids have large, solid head shields on the bottom and top of the head. The shields are separated by many small branchial plates (which protected the gill openings), and the body is covered with narrow, elongated scales. However, the large dermal plates of the arandaspids were made of minute polygonal units, which themselves could not grow, but were added to the margin of the shields. Being the oldest known vertebrates, the arandaspids call into question the assumption that the original vertebrate armor consisted of relatively large, polygonal plates, or tesserae, that were capable of growth.

About 60 species of thelodonts are known to have lived in the waters of the Silurian and Devonian throughout the world. Although complete bodies are rarely found, the pointed scales that covered their bodies are so abundant they are commonly used for stratigraphic correlations. The remains of

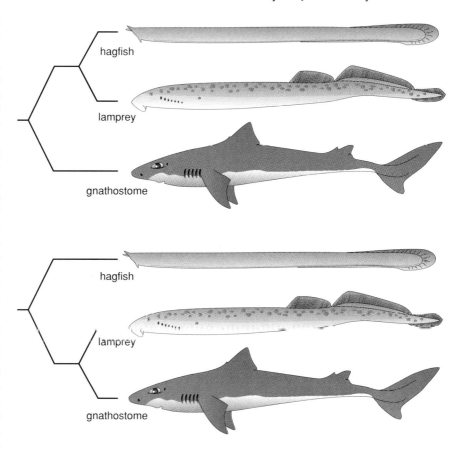

Figure 4. Two phylogenetic trees offer alternative hypotheses about the relatedness of lampreys, hagfishes and jawed vertebrates (gnathostomes). The absence of paired fins and a jaw, as well as similarities in the structure of the gill pouches and the tongue, support the view (top) that hagfishes and lampreys are more closely related to each other than either is to the gnathostomes. In contrast, a number of physiological and anatomical characteristics (including the presence of a cerebellum and optic tectum in the brain, and similarities in the eyes, gills, kidneys and the heart) suggest that lampreys and gnathostomes are more closely related to each other than either group is to the hagfishes (bottom).

complete thelodonts that have been found represent two very different body shapes. Tiiu Märss of the Estonian Academy of Science and Susan Turner of the Queensland Museum in Brisbane, Australia, have described one group with a broad head, flattened from top to bottom, and a downturned tail. Another group of thelodonts found in Silurian deposits in the Canadian arctic have been described by Mark Wilson and Michael Caldwell of the University of Alberta as having very deep bodies. The deep-bodied thelodonts have small, pipette-like mouths, an oblique row of gill openings and very unusual, forked tails. The deep-bodied thelodonts have different shapes of scales on different parts of their bodies suggesting that some isolated scales, originally attributed to different species of thelodonts, may belong to the same animal. Despite their similar scales (with crowns of dentine and bases of aspidin), it may turn

out that the two types of thelodonts are only distantly related to each other.

Perhaps the most unusual of the recently discovered agnathans were described by Gavin Young in 1991. In Lower Devonian deposits in Queensland, Australia, Young discovered a fossil ostracoderm that resembled an osteostracan in the overall shape of the head and the shield and what appear to be pectoral fins. These fishes, the pituriaspids, differed from the osteostracans in lacking a dorsal nasohypophyseal opening, and the site of the nostrils remains a mystery. The pituriaspids have an elongated shield, which is pierced by openings for the eyes and by associated openings of unknown function, as well as a very long rostrum.

At this point the pituriaspids are known from only a few poorly preserved specimens. Unfortunately, they were unearthed in a remote desert of Queensland, and a new expedition does

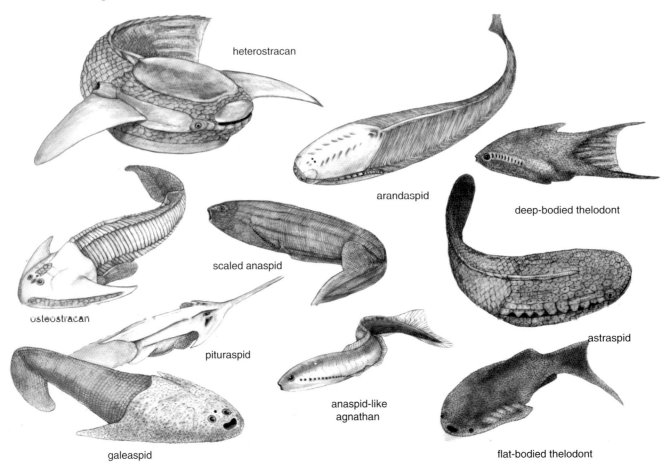

Figure 5. Ostracoderms evolved into a wide variety of shapes and sizes during their 100-million-year reign on the earth. The nearly 600 species of ostracoderms can be classified into one of nine or ten groups.

not appear to be imminent. This is especially frustrating for vertebrate paleontologists because the pituriaspids are probably the most significant discovery of fossil agnathans since the discovery of the galeaspids in the 1960s.

Relationships and Characters
Given the broad range of ostracoderm features, how do we determine which characteristics came first and which were subsequently lost during vertebrate evolution? Surprisingly, there is a reasonable way of assessing the evolution of anatomical traits, or characters, based on the phylogenetic relationships between the groups involved. Here we shall provide a brief review of the phylogenetic schemes that have been proposed in the past and what our own studies suggest.

Up to the first half of this century, lampreys and hagfishes were thought to be each other's closest relatives. Both groups of fishes have smooth, scaleless skins, pouch-like gills, complex tongues and median nostrils. They were also thought to be degenerate in lacking

paired fins and a dermal skeleton; it was assumed that their ancestors had paired fins and armor.

During the 1970s, a considerable amount of evidence cast doubt on this view. It became apparent that the lampreys and gnathostomes share a number of significant features, including the presence of neural arches along the rod-like notochord that supports the body during development, large eyes with associated eye muscles, osmotic regulation of their body fluids, nervous control of the heart, and a brain bearing such structures as a cerebellum, optic tectum and choroid plexus. Interestingly, many of these features appear to be associated with the active life-styles of lampreys and gnathostomes, compared to the relatively lethargic hagfishes. On the basis of these similarities, Søren Løvtrup of Umea University in Sweden proposed in 1977 that the lampreys are more closely related to the gnathostomes than either is to the hagfishes.

In some respects this view has been challenged by the recent work of David Stock of Stanford University and Gre-

gory Whitt of the University of Illinois. Stock and Whitt examined the nucleotide sequences of the 18S ribosomal RNA molecule from various members of the phylum Chordata, which includes the vertebrates, urochordates (tunicates), and cephalochordates (represented by amphioxus). The marine-dwelling and relatively sedentary tunicates and amphioxus are filter-feeders that are considered by many zoologists to be the animals most closely related to vertebrates. In Stock and Whitt's study the vertebrates were represented by lampreys, hagfishes and gnathostomes.

When Stock and Whitt compared the sequence of 1,631 nucleotide bases from the ribosomal RNA of each organism, they found that the resulting phylogenetic relationships depended on *how* the groups were compared. For example, when amphioxus (or amphioxus grouped with the tunicates) was used as the basis for comparing the vertebrate groups, the lampreys and hagfishes were resolved as each being other's closest relatives. In contrast, when the tunicates alone were used as the basis for the comparison, the lampreys and gnathostomes appeared to be most closely related to each other. In other words, the results varied according to whether tunicates or amphioxus are considered to be more closely related to the vertebrates. It seems that more molecular analyses are necessary before we can assess the historical message within the genetic code.

Before we examine what the fossil record has to say about these relationships, we should briefly explain our technique. In recent years there has been a pronounced swing toward cladistic methods of phylogenetic analysis. The method was first introduced in 1950 by the German entomologist Willi Hennig, and later improved by several comparative biologists who employed various computer algorithms. Cladistic classifications express relationships in relative terms; for example, taxon A is more closely related to taxon B than either is to taxon C. A and B are said to be sister groups, and C is the sister group of A + B.

The goal of cladistic analysis is to recognize sister-group relationships by identifying derived characters, unique to the members of the sister-group pair, that are assumed to have arisen in the immediate common ancestor. Primitive characters that are present in taxa other than the putative sister groups have no relevance to establishing the relationship. For example, the absence of paired fins and jaws in both hagfishes and lampreys is irrelevant to determining their cladistic relationship because these traits are absent in invertebrates as well. Finally, in any cladistic analysis, the taxa are grouped so that the number of character changes (across the taxa) is kept to a minimum. The "best" solution is the most parsimonious for a given set of characters.

Using such a cladistic method, we analyzed 56 characters of the living and fossil agnathans to construct a phylogenetic tree. Our results suggest that all of the ostracoderms (except for *Jamoytius*) are more closely related to the gnathostomes than either group is to the lamprey or hagfish. Among the ostracoderms, the osteostracans are most closely related to the gnathostomes, whereas the anaspids are the most distantly related to the gnathostomes. Finally, among the living taxa, the lampreys and the gnathostomes are more closely related to each other than either is to the hagfish. On the basis of these

Figure 6. Osteostracans were among the most successful and diverse groups of ostracoderms. Nearly 200 species have been discovered in deposits throughout North America, Europe, Siberia and central Asia. About a dozen fossil osteostracans were found in this block of sandstone from the lower Devonian period of Great Britain. Most were small fishes, up to 15 centimeters long. (Courtesy of the Natural History Museum, London.)

Figure 7. Internal structures of an osteostracan head—the brain, nerves and blood vessels—can be reconstructed from their cavities within a well-preserved bony braincase. This specimen was unearthed from lower Devonian deposits in Spitsbergen.

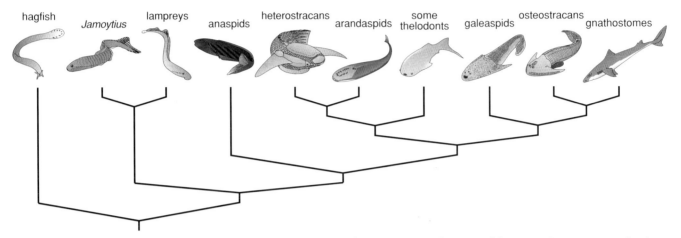

Figure 8. Phylogenetic tree based on a cladistic analysis of 56 anatomical features suggests that most of the ostracoderms are more closely related to modern jawed vertebrates than they are to modern jawless vertebrates. Of the ostracoderms, the osteostracans appear to be the most closely related to the jawed vertebrates. Among the modern groups, the jawed vertebrates are more closely related to the lamprey than either is to the hagfish. The fossil jawless fish, *Jamoytius*, appears to be a close relative of modern lampreys. Hagfishes are the most primitive known living or fossil vertebrates. Such phylogenetic trees allow paleontologists to determine which characteristics are primitive and which are evolutionarily derived.

relationships we can begin to reconstruct the evolution of some vertebrate characteristics, including their earliest habitat, their nasal structures, the brain and the lateral line system.

One of the earliest vertebrate developments is the sense of smell, recognized in both living and fossil forms with the presence of nasal openings. In lampreys and hagfishes the nostrils open into a duct, the prenasal sinus, which itself opens to the outside through the nasohypophyseal opening. In gnathostomes, there is no longer a developmental connection between the nasal sacs and the hypophysis. At one time it was believed that the nasohypophyseal connection signified that lampreys and hagfishes are very close relatives. However, hagfishes differ from lampreys in that the prenasal sinus continues past the nostrils as a nasopharyngeal duct that opens into the roof of the pharynx (allowing for the continuous passage of water). We now know that the fossil agnathans had various forms of nasal apparatus, including those seen in the hagfish and the lamprey. Consequently the nasohypophyseal connection cannot be used to link the modern agnathans.

Among the fossil ostracoderms, paired nasal sacs appear to be present across the groups, including the galeaspids, thelodonts and heterostracans. The presence of paired nasal sacs is probably the primitive condition for most vertebrates, except perhaps the hagfish. The confluence of the nasal sacs, seen in lampreys, osteostracans and hagfishes, appears to be the derived condition.

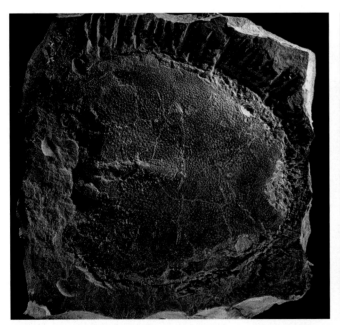 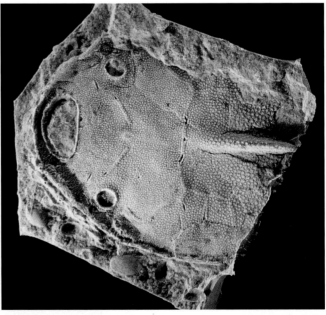

Figure 9. Broad, flat heads of galeaspid ostracoderms superficially resemble those of osteostracans. However, galeaspids lacked paired fins and have a peculiar median opening in front of the eyes. These galeaspids *(Polybranchiaspis)* were discovered in 400-million-year-old deposits in Vietnam. The fossil of one specimen *(left)* shows the dorsal head shield (about 7 centimeters long). A latex cast of another specimen *(right)* was made to reveal the eyes, the lateral-line structure and the median opening. Latex casts are often used to look at details that may have eroded away from the original fossils.

Figure 10. Heterostracan fossils are found in deposits ranging from 420 million to 360 million years old in North America, Europe and Siberia. A complete eight-centimeter-long head shield *(left)* of a *Larnovaspis* specimen from Spitzbergen shows the snout, large dorsal spine and small left eye. A latex cast *(right)* of a complete specimen *(Errivaspis),* about 18 centimeters long, from Great Britain shows the head shield and tail.

The prenasal sinus also seems to be a primitive vertebrate structure, perhaps ultimately leading to the development of the median nasal sac found in lampreys and osteostracans. This is consistent with the view expressed by Hans Bjerring of the Swedish Museum of Natural History, which holds that the prenasal sinus is the remnant of the primary inhalant device in the vertebrate ancestors. Gnathostomes retained the paired nasal sacs, but lost the prenasal sinus, resulting in nostrils that open directly to the outside. In some primitive gnathostome forms, part of the hypophyseal duct is present in the form of a tiny canal that connects the hypophysis to the roof of the mouth.

Some structures appear to be embryologically and phylogenetically related—in particular, the lateral line (which is made of simple sensory buds, or neuromast organs), electroreceptors and the labyrinth of canals in the inner ear (used in the sense of balance). The form and distribution of these systems across the vertebrates suggests these structures arose through a sequence of increasing complexity. Hagfishes appear to have the most primitive complement of these structures, lacking both electroreceptor organs and lateral-line structures. Short grooves on the hagfish head may be rudimentary lateral-line structures, yet they lack typical neuromasts. Lampreys have electroreceptors on the head and sparsely scattered on the body. Lampreys also have short lines of neuromasts on various parts of the head (but not on the body), which represent the lateral-line structure.

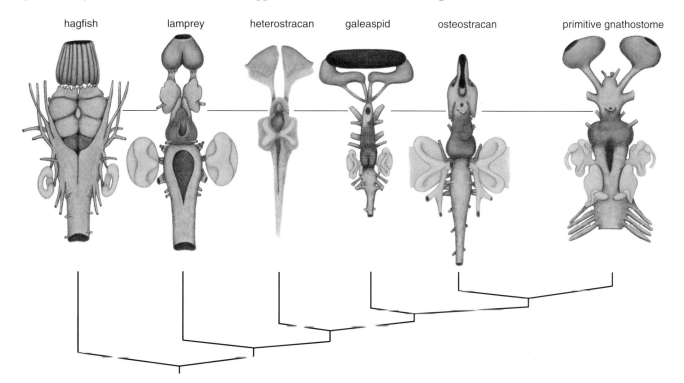

Figure 11. Brains of primitive vertebrates show an evolutionary trend toward increasing complexity of the midbrain and the hind brain, including the cerebellum *(red)*. These changes are associated with the elaboration of certain sensory systems, such as the sense of smell *(nasal capsules, pink)*, the organs of balance *(blue)* and the visual system. The position of the pineal organ *(horizontal bar)* provides a landmark revealing the changes in the relative shapes and sizes of different structures. The shape of the heterostracan brain is inferred from impressions left on the internal surface of the head shield. The primitive gnathostome is a placoderm.

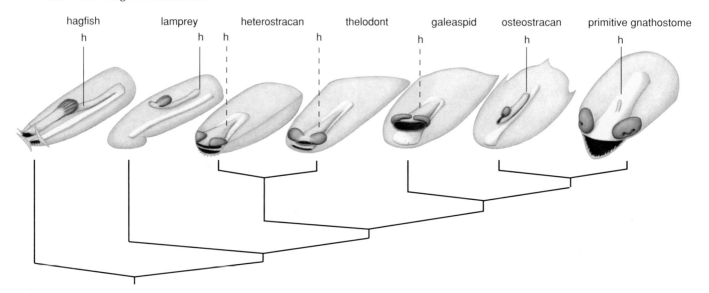

Figure 12. Reconstructed heads of living and fossil vertebrates show the variety of relations between the nasal sacs *(pink)* and their associated ducts. A nasohypophyseal duct *(green)*, which connects the nostrils to an opening on the heads of some vertebrates, is present in all forms except for gnathostomes, which only have a short canal that joins the hypophysis, or pituitary gland *(h)*, to the mouth (pharynx). In certain forms, the pharynx *(yellow)* and the nasohypohyseal duct are directly connected. In lampreys and osteostracans the nasohypophyseal ducts are blind and are no longer involved in the intake of respiratory water. The phylogeny reconstructed by the authors suggests that the connection between the nostrils and a prenasal sinus is the primitive condition for vertebrates. In some instances *(dashed lines)* the hypothesized location of the hypophysis is shown.

The next stage in the evolution of the lateral-line system may be shown by the arandaspids, astraspids and probably the anaspids. The heads of these fishes have a series of discontinuous grooves, which mark the armor and part of the trunk, and may have contained neuromasts. The heterostracans, galeaspids, osteostracans and thelodonts have a well-developed lateral-line system expressed as canals throughout the head and the body that lies deep within the armor and the scales and that opens to the surface through pores. This is very similar to the condition in gnathostomes. Thus the lateral line seems to have evolved from a series of isolated neuromasts, to distinct lines and grooves on the head, to neuromasts embedded within tubes in the armor and scales of the head and the body.

It seems clear that an increase in the complexity of the vertebrate brain is associated with increases in the complexity of the visual, acoustic and lateral-line systems. For example, the hagfish has the simplest kind of vertebrate brain, with well-developed olfactory lobes that match the refined sense of smell in these fishes. However, the midbrain and the hindbrain of the hagfish are very poorly developed. The lack of an optic tectum, a cerebellum and oculomotor nerves is consistent with the presence of a simple eye that lacks muscle attachments, a simple inner ear with only one semicircular canal, and the absence of a lateral line.

The brains of lampreys, osteostracans, galeaspids and possibly the heterostracans, on the other hand, have clearly developed beyond that of the hagfish, although they are not as well developed as in gnathostomes. These fishes have a well-defined optic tectum, which is undoubtedly related to well-developed eyes that can be controlled with extrinsic eye muscles. The cerebellum of the lam-

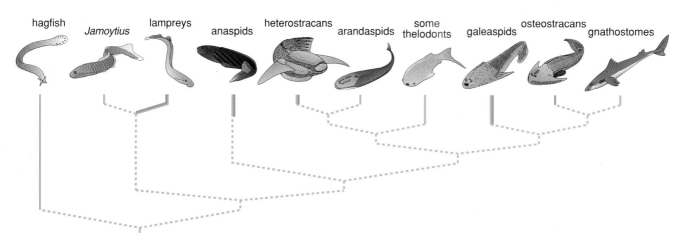

Figure 13. Phylogenetic distribution of habitats strongly suggests that the first vertebrates arose in a marine environment. Most groups lived strictly in the sea *(green)*, whereas only a few groups have members that lived in fresh or brackish water *(blue)*. The habitats of the ancestral forms *(dashed lines)* are reconstructed by inference.

Figure 14. Conodont elements *(left)* are minute toothlike structures that may belong to some early vertebrate forms. The base of the specimen is about 1.3 millimeters long. The recent discovery of soft-tissue impressions associated with conodont elements has allowed a reconstruction of the animal's appearance *(right)*. (Photograph courtesy of Giles Miller, Natural History Museum, London.)

prey is very small, whereas it appears to be prominent in osteostracans, galeaspids and probably the heterostracans. Lampreys, galeaspids and osteostracans have two semicircular canals that are equivalent to the two vertical canals in the gnathostome ear (which also has a horizontal canal). The heterostracans also have at least two semicircular canals. Unfortunately we know nothing about the brains of anaspids, arandaspids, thelodonts and pituriaspids.

Our phylogenetic scheme should also provide clues to the habitats of the early vertebrates. Historically it was thought that vertebrates originated in fresh water and subsequently invaded the seas. The idea was based on the belief that the earliest vertebrates were preserved in oxidized (hence freshwater) sandstone in the Harding deposits of Colorado. Since their remains were highly fragmented, it was believed that the bodies had been broken up after death and washed onto a nearshore deposit. This view was supported by the observation that nearly all modern vertebrates have lower levels of salts in their blood compared to seawater, thus requiring specializations in the kidney and the gills to regulate the osmotic composition of body fluids. The interesting exception to this is the hagfish, whose salt concentrations are nearly identical to those of seawater (not unlike marine invertebrates).

A series of recent investigations now suggest that the early vertebrates probably arose in a marine environment. A study of the Harding sandstone by Nils Spjeldnaes of Oslo University in 1967 revealed that it was deposited in a highly saline (thus possibly marine) environment. In 1982, David Darby of Minnesota University at Duluth provided good evidence that the astraspids lived in a marine environment. Fossils of complete, articulated arandaspids in

marine rocks of Australia and Bolivia preclude the possibility that they lived in fresh water and that their broken remains were washed to sea. The earliest known lamprey (*Hardistiella*) was found in marine rocks of Montana by Richard Lund of Adelphi University. The oldest known hagfish (*Myxinikela*) and the lamprey *Mayomyzon* were recently discovered by David Bardack of the University of Illinois at Chicago in the Upper Carboniferous marine deposits of Mazon Creek in Illinois. It is worth noting that Mazon Creek also contains freshwater deposits; however, no agnathans have been found in them.

The marine origins of the ancestral vertebrates suggest that the hagfishes have primitively retained the marine state, whereas the freshwater habitat of some lampreys is a secondarily acquired niche. This of course does not explain the observation that most vertebrates have lower concentrations of salt compared to seawater. We propose the following possibility. The fossil record of the Silurian and the Carboniferous periods shows that the earliest members of the living fish groups (sharks, lobe-finned fishes and ray-finned fishes) often lived in marginal, brackish environments, comparable to modern mangroves or tidal flats. Although these environments have great variations in the amount of salinity, they tend to have a large food supply for these fishes. It may be that the modern descendants of these early fishes retained the physiological ability to survive in such an environment (having low levels of salt in the blood) even though most now live in the open sea.

Who Were the Conodonts?

The arandaspids from the Lower Ordovician are the oldest known vertebrates. According to our phylogeny, however, arandaspids are relatively de-

rived fishes that must have been preceded by forms resembling thelodonts, anaspids, hagfishes and lampreys. These groups probably had as yet undiscovered representatives in the (earlier) Cambrian period. Curiously, with the possible exception of one group of animals, there appears to be no evidence of vertebrates in the Cambrian period.

The possible exception is the animals that bore the minute toothlike structures known as conodonts. These phosphate-bearing structures are found in marine rocks from the Upper Cambrian to the Upper Triassic and are widely used for stratigraphic zonation and correlation. For many years vertebrate paleontologists disowned conodonts because the teeth of modern agnathans are horny (not phosphatized), and because no animal had been found bearing conodonts in "life position." In 1983, however, Derek Briggs of Bristol University and his colleagues announced the discovery of a soft-bodied worm-like animal (about 6 millimeters long) bearing a conodont feeding apparatus. The animal was preserved in Lower Carboniferous sediments (from about 345 million years ago), which had been laid down in brackish water.

By 1993 sufficient remains had been found to allow Richard Aldridge of Leicester University and his colleagues to reconstruct the conodont animal's appearance. It appears to have been bilaterally symmetrical, with an asymmetric tail-fin fold, large eyes and < -shaped myomeres (muscle blocks). Aldridge and his collaborators also identified traces of a notochord. Although these qualities are hallmarks of a vertebrate, there appears to be nothing that resembles gill openings. Ivan Sansom of the University of Durham in Britain and his colleagues have also examined the hard tissues of the conodont. They note that

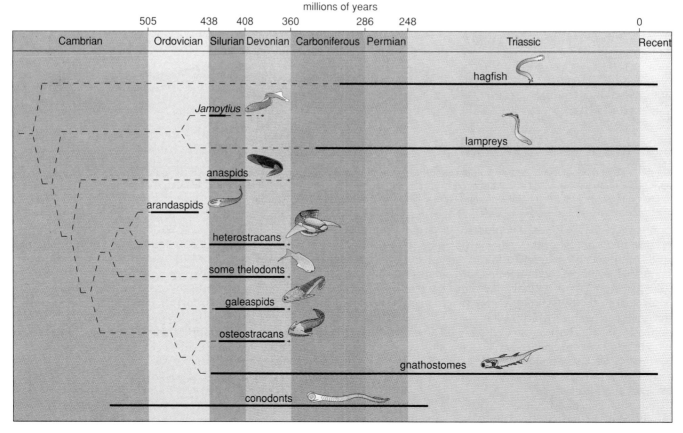

Figure 15. Stratigraphic distribution of living and fossil groups of vertebrates suggests that undiscovered vertebrate ancestors *(dashed lines)* **lived in the Cambrian period, more than 500 million years ago. Conodont elements are found in Cambrian deposits, but their evolutionary relationship to the known vertebrates is not clear. The first jawed vertebrates, here represented by an acanthodian, appeared more than 400 million years ago in the Silurian period.**

the surface layer appears to be an enamel-like tissue that lies atop cellular "bone." As we pointed out in 1993, however, these tissues are very different from the bone and enamel of vertebrates, so it is not at all clear that conodonts are structurally comparable to vertebrate teeth.

Because of these features, it is difficult to assess where the conodont animal fits within the vertebrate phylogeny we propose in this paper. Curiously, the hard tissues of the conodont animal suggest that they have more derived characteristics than either lampreys or hagfishes. There is clearly a need for more studies on the conodonts and the various types of bone and enamel present in fossil agnathans. As has been previously suggested, it may be that the conodont animal is a larval stage of an extinct agnathan. We cannot say.

Vertebrate Mysteries

Although fossil agnathans have helped to resolve some of the questions concerning the evolutionary pathways that led to the origin of gnathostomes, they remain mute on some important issues.

In particular, it is still not clear how jaws arose or how true bone developed.

When jaws first appear in the fossil record (in acanthodian fishes) about 430 million years ago, both the mandibular arch and the associated hyoid arch (behind the jaw) are fully formed. The hyoid already supports the mandibular, and the intervening spiracle is classically regarded as a former gill slit. There are no structures in the gill skeleton of agnathans that are the obvious precursors of gill arches of the gnathostomes. It may be that the gill structures of the agnathans have nothing to do with the gill arches of gnathostomes.

It has been proposed that the velum, a pumping device in agnathans, may have formed the mandibular arch. Indeed, the nerve supply to the agnathan velum suggests that this may be so. Moreover, in lampreys the velum develops from the same embryonic tissue as the jaws do in gnathostomes. Jon Mallat of Washington State University at Pullman has suggested that the earliest vertebrates used the velum to pump in water and food particles, much as do the larvae of lampreys. Modifications of the

velum allowed them to take in larger food particles. Jawlike structures may have permitted these vertebrates to feed on whole prey, perhaps by sucking them into the mouth.

The origin of true cellular bone, present in osteostracans and gnathostomes, poses another puzzle to paleontologists. At various times cellular bone has been regarded as representing either a primitive or an advanced condition. The view that cellular bone is primitive is supported by the embryological development of some modern vertebrates. These species have acellular bone that is derived from a bony matrix in which the cells die and disappear. On the other hand, none of the ostracoderm fossils with acellular bone (all but the osteostracans) has a trace of "dying" cells. Consequently, our phylogeny supports the view that cellular bone is an advanced feature. Even so, the presence of cellular bone in the Ordovician suggests that it is an ancient trait of vertebrates.

Other evolutionary leaps in the history of early vertebrates are also problematic. The appearance of true paired fins (with muscles and skeleton) has long been regarded as arising from a fold of skin devoid of muscles, since this appears to be the way fins develop in embryonic gnathostomes. It is possible to imagine such a gradual evolution, although no supporting evidence has been found in the fossil record. In contrast, the sudden appearance of the horizontal semicircular canal in the inner ear of gnathostomes is more difficult to imagine taking place in a gradual manner. What would be the use of an incipient semicircular canal? There appears to be no trace of a precursor to such a canal in any living or fossil agnathan.

Conclusion

Our phylogenetic analysis of the living and fossil vertebrates allows us to make some general statements about the evolution of vertebrates. Among the living forms, it seems clear that the lampreys are more closely related to gnathostomes than either group is to the hagfishes. The hagfishes are the most primitive vertebrates known, living or extinct. Thus most features of the hagfish that were considered to be degenerate are probably primitively simple, including the lensless eye, the simple hypophysis, the simple ear, the lack of nervous regulation of the heart, the absence of a lateral-line system, electroreceptors and a cerebellum, and an inability to regulate internal ionic concentrations.

It also seems to be the case that the majority of ostracoderms are more derived than either lampreys or hagfishes. This would suggest that the lampreys and hagfishes represent a primitive naked state, and that the dermal skeleton arose after these vertebrates had diverged. At first the dermal skeleton consisted of dentine and acellular bone; and only later was it made of cellular bone. A calcified endoskeleton also appeared in the ancestors of gnathostomes after the lampreys and hagfishes diverged.

Perfected paired fins appear to have arisen first in the common ancestor of the osteostracans, the the pituriaspids and the gnathostomes. Osteostracans and gnathostomes have pectoral fins and cellular bone. The pituriaspids are the only other group of agnathans that might have had pectoral fins. Lampreys probably never had pectoral fins, although they might have had paired fin folds along part of their body length. Hagfishes and their ancestors never developed paired fins.

Some features of modern hagfishes and lampreys—such as the median na-sohypophyseal opening, the prenasal sinus, the pouch-like gills and the complex tongue—belong to the history of gnathostomes. Indeed, these features may have been present in the common ancestor of all known vertebrates but have become modified or lost in gnathostomes. There are other viewpoints on the relationships between modern and fossil agnathans based on other methods. Erik Jarvik of the Swedish Museum of Natural Hisotry considers that hagfishes, lampreys and ostracoderms are more closely related to each other than any are to gnathostomes. He also suggests that the agnathans are more derived than gnathostomes. However, this theory assumes a number of parallel evolutionary paths for which we see no evidence.

Although many questions in the evolution of vertebrate structure remain unanswered, the ostracoderms provide information that no other source could have given. It seems that much could be gained by further excavations in Early Ordovician and Cambrian deposits where ostracoderms should be present. As the recent history of the field shows, new techniques of preparing and observing the fossils may reveal previously unnoticed details.

Acknowledgments

In writing this review we have freely culled and begged information from many of our colleagues who study agnathan fishes. We thank all of them who have discussed their work with us and acknowledge that they may not necessarily agree with our phylogenetic conclusions. Peter Forey would also like to acknowledge financial support from the Robert O. Bass Visiting Scholarship Fund, Field Museum, Chicago.

Bibliography

Aldridge, R. J., D. E. G. Briggs, M. P. Smith, E. N. K. Clarkson and N. D. L. Clark. 1993. The anatomy of conodonts. *Philosophical Transactions of the Royal Society of London*, B 340:405–421.

Forey, P., and P. Janvier. 1993. Agnathans and the origin of jawed vertebrates. *Nature* 361:129–134.

Gagnier, P. Y. 1993. *Sacabambaspis janvieri*, Vertébrés ordovicien de Bolivie. *Annales de Paléontologie*, 79:119–166.

Halstead, L. B. 1973. The heterostracan fishes. *Biological Reviews* 48:279–332.

Hardisty, M. W. 1982. Lampreys and hagfishes: analysis of cyclostome relationships. In *The Biology of Lampreys*, ed. M.W. Hardisty and I. C. Potter, pp. 165–260. London: Academic Press.

Janvier, P., and A. Blieck. 1993. L. B. Halstead and the heterostracan controversy. *Modern Geology* 18:98–105.

Løvtrup, S. 1977. *The Phylogeny of the Vertebrata*. London & New York: Wiley & Sons.

Stock, D.W. and Witt, G.S. 1992. Evidence from 18S ribosomal RNA sequences that lampreys and hagfishes form a natural group. *Science* 257:787–789.

Turner, S. 1991. Monophyly and interrrelationships of the Thelodonti. In *Early Vertebrates and Related Problems of Evolutionary Biology*, ed. M. M. Chang, Y. H. Liu and G. R. Zhang. Beijing: Science Press, pp. 87–120.

Wang, N. Z. 1991. Two new Silurian galeaspids (jawless craniates) from Zhejiang province, China. With a discussion of galeaspid-gnathostome relationships. In *Early Vertebrates and Related Problems of Evolutionary Biology*, ed. M. M. Chang, Y. H. Liu and G. R. Zhang. Beijing: Science Press, pp. 41–66.

Wilson, M. V. H. and M. W. Caldwell. 1993. New Silurian and Devonian fork-tailed 'thelodonts' are jawless vertebrates with stomachs and deep bodies. *Nature* 361:442–444.

Young, G. 1991. The first armoured agnathan vertebrates from the Devonian of Australia. In *Early Vertebrates and Related Problems of Evolutionary Biology*, ed. M. M. Chang, Y. H. Liu and G. R. Zhang. Beijing: Science Press, 67–86.

Where Did Tetrapods Come From?

Keith Stewart Thomson

"In vertebrate paleontology, increasing knowledge leads to triumphant loss of clarity" (1). This was the late Alfred Sherwood Romer's little joke; he certainly did not believe it was true. Romer, director and Alexander Agassiz professor at Harvard's Museum of Comparative Zoology, was a classical paleontologist and no theorist. Working with fossils on his bench made him happiest. Like others of his generation, Romer proceeded as if paleontology consisted principally of finding every fossil, filling in the gaps in the evolution of organisms. Today, paleontology is a rather different field. The gaps are at the same time less important (because they can never be filled precisely) and more important (because they spawn theory). Instead of each new fossil filling in a piece of a pre-existing cosmic jigsaw puzzle, now each discovery reshapes the question. Even with this change of emphasis, however, great excitement surrounds any new fossil that significantly changes the data set and at least partially closes a gap.

Paleontologists face a problem. When tracing the evolutionary transition between two groups of organisms, say fishes and tetrapods (amphibians, reptiles, birds and mammals), how should scientists interpret an incomplete fossil? How can they know if it's a fish or a very early tetrapod? After all, if the fossil comes from a truly transitional form, it should be impossible to tell. This is what Romer meant by "loss of clarity."

Of all paleontological puzzles, Romer best loved this problem of origins: Where did the first amphibians, reptiles or mammals come from? Who were their ancestors and where did they live? Where should we search for the answers? Many of his papers read like detective stories in their search for transitional forms (2). Now, discoveries of early tetrapods seem to be revealing more about Romer's beloved transitional zone and, in the process, both reducing and adding to the confusion.

Thirty years ago, evolutionary biologists thought they had established that the tetrapods had evolved more than 300 million years ago from a group of extinct Devonian lobe-finned fishes. These fishes, with the unlovely name of Osteolepiformes, were part of the equally unattractively named Rhipidistia, which in turn were part of the Crossopterygii, a group that includes coelacanths but not lungfishes. Later, both the Rhipidistia and the Crossopterygii were abolished as formal taxonomic groups, and a great deal of effort has gone into trying to show that lungfishes (Dipnoi) might be the closest relatives of tetrapods. But now we are back where we started 30 years ago, except that we actually have some fossils that bridge the gap between Osteolepiformes and tetrapods.

A key discovery, it turned out, had been made in 1938 when T. Stanley Westoll of the University of Newcastle described a very incomplete skull roof from the Escuminac Formation, a Late Devonian deposit in Quebec (3). The fossil showed what no other fish showed: the presence of paired frontal bones like those found in amphibians. Faced with the problem of deciding whether it was a fish or a tetrapod, most paleontologists discounted it as an aberrant fish. Discoveries made in 1985, however, showed that Westoll's *Elpistostege* was closely related to *Panderichthys*, an osteolepiform fish discovered in Russia, which was also like a tetrapod in certain characters of the skull roof (4).

Osteolepiform fishes appear even closer to tetrapods after detailed studies of the fin skeleton (5). The osteolepiforms, alone among fishes, have the basic tetrapod arrangement of humerus, ulna and radius in the forelimb and femur, tibia and fibula in the hindlimb. This limb pattern, in fact, was discovered way back in 1843 in a Devonian fish called *Sauripterus*, which was discovered in New York State (6).

At this point, the distinction between a fish and an amphibian still remained clear. Although fish might have paired frontal bones after all, amphibians had both frontals and nasals. Other traits sharpened the distinction. Amphibians lacked gills and the gill covering called an operculum and had good limbs with ankle and foot bones and five digits. Amphibians had a middle ear for receiving high-frequency sound; fish did not. And amphibians had the physiological specializations to live out of the water.

All of this, except the actual physiology, was confirmed by the discovery of Late Devonian amphibians in Greenland in the 1930s by Gunnar Save-Soderbergh. These were the famous ichthyostegids, the earliest known amphibians (7). But Save-Soderbergh died very young, and it was not until 1980 that Eric Jarvik published a more-or-less complete description of the best-known form, *Ichthyostega* (8).

Still, the primary question remained unanswered. What would an intermediate between fishes and amphibians look like? Paleontologists looked for a fish with tetrapod-like features—but would a limb with digits have evolved before

Keith Stewart Thomson is president of the Academy of Natural Sciences, 19th Street and the Benjamin Franklin Parkway, Logan Square, Philadelphia, PA 19103.

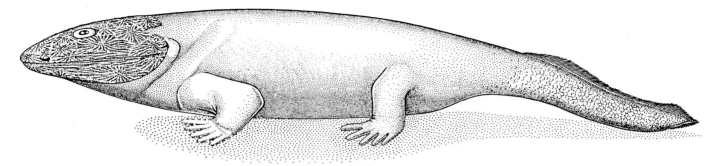

Figure 1. *Ichthyostega*, the earliest known amphibian. (Reproduced from *Basic Structure and Evolution of Vertebrates* by permission of Academic Press.)

or after the gills and operculum were lost? Here entered theory, and its step-children hypothesis and conjecture. The best general construct available to account for the origin of transitional forms was the rather feeble theory associated with the self-contradictory term preadaptation. This theory suggested that major shifts in structure started with gradual morphological changes, followed by a shift in function, then further morphological modifications. Preadaptation provided a useful device to get around the problem of morphology making sudden jumps. According to the theory, the humerus, ulna and radius in an osteolepiform's forelimb were an adaptation for a particular sort of swimming; later, the same adaptation turned out to be useful for moving on land. Digits quickly followed.

Other theories sought to explain how several morphological features might change in unison, with the prediction that the origin of a tetrapod stapes from the first gill arch required loss of gill function and change in jaw mechanics. Part of the problem was that no one had a precise view of the ecological-behavioral shift that divided fishes from tetrapods. In Romer's day, it was possible to argue that the first tetrapods were rather terrestrial organisms capable of really living on dry land (9, 10). The discovery of the Devonian ichthyostegids abolished that idea. These first known tetrapods had a long, fishy tail, and they obviously lived a great deal of the time in water. It now seems apparent that the morphological transition took place not on dry land but in wet environments—in swamps and marshes and pools with dense emergent vegetation. The first amphibians could probably make journeys over land in dry conditions, but not very far.

A particularly fascinating problem is that the forelimbs and hindlimbs of tetrapods, although built on the same *general* pattern, differ significantly. For example, the elbow joint is flexed backward while the knee is pointed forward. Evidence now suggests that these differences developed first on the fishy side of the transition (11). But, did the forelimbs and hindlimbs have significantly different functions in fishes that carried over into the tetrapods? My view is that the forelimbs were used by the transitional fishes to prop up the front part of the body while, at first, only the hindlimbs were used in thrusting backward against the substrate or the water (12).

The middle ear has been the subject of particularly strong debate as various authors have tried to predict the shape of the first true stapes and the presence or absence of a tympanic membrane (ear drum) in the first amphibians (13).

Within the past few years new evidence on transitional forms has started to accumulate. In addition to the Greenland amphibians, there are Devonian tetrapod limb remains

(*Tulerpeton*) from the U.S.S.R., a jaw from Australia (*Metaxygnathus*), and trackways from Brazil and Australia (14, 15, 16). But the most exciting evidence has been found by Jennifer Clack and her associates at the University of Cambridge, who returned to the Greenland sites and unearthed new material of Save-Soderbergh's less well known genus of tetrapod, *Acanthostega*. It turns out to have a perfectly nice-looking, if chunky, stapes that ends, furthermore, in a bony notch that must (although its discoverers deny it) have held a tympanic membrane (17).

The earliest tetrapods are polydactylous. Instead of the expected five fingers, *Acanthostega* had eight and *Tulerpeton* had six; similarly, *Ichthyostega* had seven toes. This would not have been a surprise, however, to anyone who had looked carefully at the *Sauripterus* specimen (18), which has at least 11 rays in the "hand." Once again, then, the forelimbs and hindlimbs differ, and this is reinforced by a recent discovery from the Devonian of Scotland by Per Ahlberg of the University of Oxford (19). He has discovered a humerus that has both fish and tetrapod characters, apparently associated with a tibia that is very strongly tetrapod.

Perhaps the biggest surprise is that *Acanthostega* shows evidence of internal gills (20). There were no gill filaments on the stapes and, although there was no bony operculum, there was a fleshy gill cover. If correct, this is further evidence that the earliest tetrapods lived in and around water, not on dry land, and completely contradicts the old hypothesis that complete aerial respiration was a fishy precursor of the tetrapod condition. (Even modern amphibians have *external* gills in the larvae, of course, as do many fishes.) So theory gets rather a mixed grade.

Vertebrate life in the pools and swamps of the Late Devonian depended on the emergence (literally) of vegetation that supported a whole new set of semi-terrestrial ecosystems. Here there was an abundance of invertebrates and small fishes to feed on. Here was a place for the transitional forms to escape from the huge fishy predators of the rivers and seas and, particularly, a place where they could lay their eggs and their young could grow. In these rich tropical pools and swamps air-breathing was a necessity. But evidently the ancestors of tetrapods spent enough time in open, well-oxygenated water (perhaps foraging for food) for gills to have been useful. The gills may at least have been reduced, as they are in modern lungfishes. These organisims moved by swimming in the open water through undulations of the body and fanning of the fins, probably like *Latimeria*, the modern coelacanth. In the swamps, the transitional creatures moved by a mixture of squirming and pushing backward with the hindlimbs. Only later, on the tetrapod side of the transition, did the forelimbs assume a major role in locomotion. At the beginning, the limbs did not have to be strong enough to lift the whole weight of the body. The forelimbs were first used to prop up the head for breathing and to look around, smell and hear out of the water. If this is correct, there is no basis in theory for a sudden change in function, but rather the evidence suggests a smooth continuum for most structural features.

What was the actual ancestor of the tetrapods? We can only say that *Panderichthys*, the Late Devonian organism discovered in Russia, is the oldest known relative to tetrapods. It would, of course, be exceeding the data tremendously to argue that *Panderichthys* was the ancestor. It just happens to be the closest form to tetrapods that we presently know.

Much of this story recalls the notion of "mosaic" evolution, which was popular many years ago. According to this theory, complex morphologies changed piecemeal, so that any transitional form possessed a mixture of new and old features. Each mosaic condition might be the basis for a modest taxonomic diversification—an adaptive radiation. The trouble with this notion is that, in this case at least, radiations of mosaic forms have not yet been found, and there has not been time for evolution to proceed through the meanderings of mosaic groups. But at the same time, the new discoveries—such as internal gills in *Acanthostega*—show that the evolution of some features that we have considered typical of all tetrapods may have lagged behind, while others, such as the middle ear, proceeded apace.

What then defines a tetrapod? I suggest it is the presence of digits.

Finally, these new discoveries have started to push back the ages of tetrapod fossils and widen their geographical distribution. This, together with changing views as to the ecology of the transition, may mean that we have, all along, been looking for the transitional fossil forms in the wrong place. Probably Romer was both right and wrong: first the confusion and then clarity again, at least for a while.

References

1. Romer, Alfred Sherwood. 1962. *Synapsid Evolution and Dentition*. International Colloquium on the Evolution of Mammals. Brussels.
2. Romer, Alfred Sherwood. 1943. Hunting for grandpa bumps. *Science Monthly* 57:94–96.
3. Westoll, T. S. 1938. Ancestry of the tetrapods. *Nature* 141:127–128.
4. Schultze, H-P., and M. Arsenault. 1985. The panderichthyid fish *Elpistostege*: A close relative of tetrapods? *Palaeontology* 28:292–309.
5. Andrews, S. M., and T. S. Westoll. 1970. The post-cranial skeleton of *Eusthenopteron foordi* Whiteaves. *Transactions of the Royal Society of Edinburgh* 68:207–329.
6. Hall, J. 1843. *Natural History of New York. Geology Comprising the Survey of the Fourth District*. New York.
7. Save-Soderbergh, Gunnar. 1932. Preliminary note on Devonian stegocephalians from east Greenland. *Meddelelser om Gronland* 94(7):1.
8. Jarvik, Eric. 1980. *Basic Structure and Evolution of Vertebrates*. London: Academic Press.
9. Romer, Alfred Sherwood. 1958. Tetrapod limbs and early tetrapod life. *Evolution* 12:361–369.
10. Inger, R. F. 1957. Ecological aspects of the origin of tetrapods. *Evolution* 11:373–376.
11. Rackoff, J. S. 1980. The origin of the tetrapod limb and the ancestry of vertebrates. In *The Terrestrial Environment and the Origin of Land Vertebrates*, ed. A. L. Pachen. London: Academic Press.
12. Thomson, Keith Stewart. 1991. *Living Fossil*. New York: W. W. Norton and Co.
13. Lombard, R. E., and J. R. Bolt. 1979. Evolution of the tetrapod ear: An analysis and reinterpretation. *Biological Journal of the Linnean Society London* 11:12–31.
14. Lebedev, A. O. 1984. The first find of a Devonian vertebrate in the USSR. *Doklady Akademia Nauk SSSR Paleontologie* 278:1470–1473 (in Russian).
15. Campbell, K. S. W., and M. W. Bell. 1977. A primitive amphibian from the Late Devonian of New South Wales. *Alcheringa* 1:369–381.
16. Warren, J. W., and N. A. Wakefield. 1972. Trackways of tetrapod vertebrates from the Upper Devonian of Victoria, Australia. *Nature* 238:469–470.
17. Clack, Jennifer A. 1989. Discovery of the earliest-known tetrapod stapes. *Nature* 342:425–427.
18. Thomson, Keith Stewart. 1968. A critical review of the diphyletic theory of rhipidistian-amphibian relationships. In *Current Problems in Lower Vertebrate Phylogeny*, ed. T. Orvig. Stockholm: Almqvist and Wiksell.
19. Ahlberg, P. E. In press. Tetrapod or near-tetrapod fossils from the Upper Devonian of Scotland. *Nature*.
20. Coates, M. I., and Jennifer A. Clack. 1991. Fish-like gills and breathing in the earliest-known tetrapod. *Nature* 352:234–235.

Extraordinary Fossils

Occasionally circumstances conspire to put flesh on the bones of the skeletal fossil record, thus leaving a vivid snapshot of an ancient world

Derek E. G. Briggs

Etched in the fossil record is nature's chronicle, a history of life on earth. Some of these fossils tell of lives lived and extinguished hundreds of millions of years ago, long before the advent of humankind. But nature is a biased scribe, an unreliable reporter, and nature's chronicle tells only part of the evolutionary tale. The process of fossilization itself inevitably skews the information in the fossil record. Only a fraction of the myriad creatures that have lived on the earth have left behind traces of their existence, and only specific parts of those organisms have been preserved.

Nature relies on recycling. Soft tissues, the fleshy parts of animals' bodies, are a rich source of nutrients and are consumed by predators, scavengers or micro-organisms. The soft parts are thus least likely to be preserved as fossils. More likely to be fossilized are mineralized tissues such as shells, bones and teeth, as well as heavily tanned or sclerotized arthropod skeletons; among plant tissues wood and certain kinds of cuticle are the best candidates for fos-

silization. But a decay-resistant skeleton is no guarantee of preservation, as skeletons too are broken down by physical and biological agents. Occasionally, however, some unusual combination of circumstances brings an extraordinarily clear message from the geologic past: a fossil specimen in which we can see the form of soft tissues.

For years many paleontologists considered extraordinary preservations of soft body parts little more than curiosities. They provided exciting and striking images of fossils, certainly, but their study was somewhat on the fringe of mainstream paleontology. This attitude is changing, however, and extraordinary fossils are moving increasingly to center stage. Soft-bodied fossils are turning out to have just as important a story to tell as the more familiar shells and bones.

When fossils preserve soft tissues, an astonishing amount of additional information becomes available. Extraordinary fossils provide three kinds of data beyond what can be read in the shelly fossil record. They give us insight into the morphology and relationships of organisms otherwise known only from problematic hard parts. They illuminate the nature and distribution of soft-bodied organisms, and they show us the complete diversity of ancient communities. In addition, some extraordinary fossils are a source of preserved biomolecules from which we may be able to glean information on taxonomic relationships and rates of evolution, as well as clues to the environment in which an organism lived.

Quantity vs. Quality

Occurrences of exceptional fossils have been grouped into two main categories: concentration deposits and conservation deposits (Seilacher, Reif and Westphal 1985). Concentration de-

posits are remarkable for the sheer abundance of material preserved, if not for the type of this material. They represent accumulations of skeletal remains over long periods of time where the associated sediment is either winnowed away by currents or deposited in very small quantities in the first place. Examples include ammonite coquinas and oyster beds, as well as bone beds and fissure and cave deposits.

In conservation deposits it is the quality of the preservation of the specimens that is significant. At one end of the spectrum the preservation of a single complete skeleton may be exceptional enough to warrant inclusion in this category, as, for example, the preservation of a complete starfish or crinoid skeleton. The skeletons of these echinoderms consist of large numbers of unfused plates, or ossicles, that are readily scattered after only a few days because the soft tissues decay. Their preservation intact is rare; when it happens, it is often the result of rapid burial by storms. At the other end of the spectrum are conservation deposits that preserve the soft tissues of organisms, the "extraordinary" fossils that are the focus of this article.

Perhaps the best known example of an extraordinary conservation deposit is the Burgess Shale of British Columbia. The Burgess Shale preserves an astonishing range of marine organisms including algae, sponges, various wormlike creatures, arthropods, the earliest chordate, and a variety of peculiar animals with no obvious parallels in today's oceans. Its middle Cambrian age, over 530 million years old, means that it provides an important window on the results of the Cambrian explosion, during which most of the major groups of metazoans evolved. The 300-million-year-old Mazon Creek deposit from southwest of Chicago provides a

Derek E. G. Briggs is Reader in Palaeobiology at the University of Bristol in England. He received his bachelor's degree from Trinity College, Dublin University, and his Ph .D. from the University of Cambridge, where he worked on the Burgess Shale. He is a research associate of the Royal Ontario Museum in Toronto. His major research interest is in the taphonomy and evolutionary significance of exceptionally preserved fossil biotas. This involves a range of approaches, from experimental work on the factors controlling decay and fossilization, through studies of early diagenetic mineralization, to field work on a range of extraordinary fossil occurrences in North American and Europe. He has recently edited Palaeobiology—A Synthesis, *with Peter Crowther. Address: Department of Geology, University of Bristol, Wills Memorial Building, Queen's Road, Bristol BS8 1RJ, England.*

Figure 1. Extraordinary fossils—those in which soft tissues have been preserved—provide striking images of ancient organisms such as the frog *Messelobatrachus*, which lived during the Eocene epoch, some 40 to 50 million years ago. The outline of soft tissue can be seen in this *Messelobatrachus* specimen from the Messel deposits near Frankfurt, Germany. Once valued chiefly as curiosities, soft-bodied fossils have become the source of insights into the nature, distribution, morphology and taxonomy of soft-bodied organisms, the diversity of ancient communities, rates of evolution and the environments in which ancient organisms lived. This specimen has been isolated from a matrix of oil shale by a process that transferred it onto an artificial resin. (Except where noted, all photographs courtesy of the author.)

unique view of life in the late Paleozoic (Pennsylvanian). It includes more than 350 animal and about 100 plant species from a wide range of environments, terrestrial to near-shore marine, preserved in iron carbonate (siderite) nodules. A more recent example is provided by the Eocene Green River Formation, the deposit of large lakes that extended over a wide area of Wyoming, Utah and Colorado about 40 million years ago. These lakes were permanently stratified with cool bottom waters low in oxygen. The spectacularly preserved biota is dominated by fishes, insects and plants.

Making Fossils

The normal fossil record of shells, bones and teeth gives a very incomplete picture of life in the past, particularly in the case of land biotas, where the potential for burial and fossilization is very limited. Even in shallow marine settings, where sediment transport and deposition increase the chances of preservation, the original ancient community is usually represented only by those animals with a mineralized skeleton.

The completeness of shelly fossil assemblages has been assessed in a seminal study by the late Tom Schopf of the University of Chicago, who considered the potential for preservation of the living intertidal fauna (Schopf 1978). He studied macroscopic organisms from three habitats—rock, mud and sand—at Friday Harbor, Washington, and obtained similar results for all

three. About 30 percent of the organisms had a robust mineralized shell or tube, which would be expected to yield many identifiable fossils. Another 40 percent had fragile, largely unmineralized skeletons or hard parts, and therefore had a low preservation potential. The remaining 30 percent lacked any mineralized tissue and would not be expected to fossilize at all under normal conditions. Schopf found that although a full 70 percent of the Friday Harbor genera have some mineralized tissue, only 40 percent are known as fossils. It is clear from such studies that having a skeleton by no means guarantees fossilization.

Relative completeness can also be assessed by comparing extraordinary fos-

eon	era	period	subperiod	epoch	years ago	exceptional fossil occurrences referred to in the text
		(duration in millions of years)			(millions)	
Phanerozoic	Cenozoic (65)	Quaternary (1.64)		Holocene	0.01	
				Pleistocene	1.64	
		Tertiary (64)		Pliocene	5.2	
				Miocene	23.5	
				Oligocene	35.5	
				Eocene	56.5	Messel, Germany Green River, Wyoming
				Paleocene	65	
	Mesozoic (180)	Cretaceous (81)			146	Santana, Brazil
		Jurassic (61)			208	Solnhofen, Bavaria Christian Malford, England
		Triassic (37)			245	Grès à Voltzia, France
	Paleozoic (325)	Permian (45)			290	
		Carboniferous (73)	Pennsylvanian (33)		323	Mazon Creek, Illinois
			Mississippian (40)		363	Granton, Edinburgh, Scotland
		Devonian (46)			409	Gilboa, New York Hunsrück, Germany
		Silurian (31)			439	Waukesha, Wisconsin Lesmahagow, Scotland
		Ordovician (71)			510	Beecher's Bed, New York
		Cambrian (60)			570	House Range, Utah Burgess Shale, British Columbia Kangaroo Island, Australia Lancaster, Pennsylvania Peary Land, Greenland Yunnan Province, China
	Sinian (230)	Vendian (40)			610	Ediacara, Australia

Figure 2. Fossil assemblages that include soft-tissue preservations are more common than is generally realized. They provide evidence for the nature of some of the earliest metazoans in the Precambrian, and examples are known from every geologic period since. Listed here are the sites mentioned in the text. More than 60 major known sites around the world display significant preservation of soft parts.

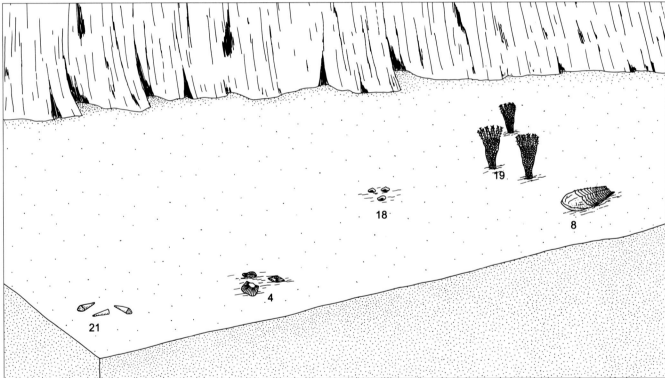

Figure 3. Soft-bodied fossils account for most of the species of the Burgess Shale of British Columbia, a large fossil assemblage that provides an extraordinary window on the results of the Cambrian explosion. No more than 20 percent of the Burgess Shale genera are preserved in shelly fossil assemblages from contemporaneous deposits in the same area. In this restoration can be seen some of the Burgess Shale species living on, above and in the muddy sediments being deposited at the foot of a submarine cliff. Of these species, only the five shown in the lower drawing had mineralized hard parts, and hence only they are preserved in contemporaneous localities where the preservation is not extraordinary. (After Conway Morris and Whittington 1985.)

sponges
1. *Vauxia*
2. *Choia*
3. *Pirania*

brachiopod
4. *Nisusia*

polychaete worm
5. *Burgessochaeta*

priapulid worms
6. *Ottoia*
7. *Louisella*

trilobite
8. *Olenoides*

non-trilobite arthropods
9. *Sidneyia*
10. *Leanchoilia*
11. *Marrella*
12. *Canadaspis*
13. *Molaria*
14. *Burgessia*
15. *Yohoia*
16. *Waptia*
17. *Aysheaia*

mollusc
18. *Scenella*

echinoderm
19. *Echmatocrinus*

chordate
20. *Pikaia*

miscellaneous
21. *Hyolithes*
22. *Opabinia*
23. *Dinomischus*
24. *Wiwaxia*
25. *Anomalocaris*

sil biotas with normal assemblages. One of the best known extraordinary deposits, the Burgess Shale biota, can be regarded as reasonably representative of a moderately deep marine community on the west side of the North American Craton during the middle Cambrian (Conway Morris 1986). It provides as complete a census of a diverse Paleozoic community as is ever likely to be achieved. However, no more than 20 percent of the genera are preserved in shelly fossil assemblages from contemporaneous deposits in the same area.

The likelihood that soft tissues will be fossilized depends on a number of factors, including the sedimentary environment, the sediment chemistry, the nature of individual organisms and the resistance of their tissues to decay.

Soft-bodied organisms must be protected from the attention of scavengers; this usually comes about through a lack of oxygen or by rapid burial. Although anaerobic conditions may eliminate scavengers, they do not prevent decay. Indeed, anaerobic decay is the norm, and can consume soft tissues in a few weeks (Allison 1988a). Even sclerotized arthropod cuticle can disappear within months. Ironically, when soft tissues are preserved, it is often through the agency of the decay bacteria, which under certain circumstances promote the formation of early diagenetic minerals that replicate the soft tissues. The bacteria themselves may even become mineralized, forming an image of the soft tissues (Wuttke 1983, Martill 1988).

The majority of extraordinary fossils are preserved as a result of the precipitation of one of three main mineral groups: pyrite, phosphate or carbonate (Allison 1988b). Silica is more rarely associated with soft-bodied fossils, and its formation in this context is poorly understood. Both silica and calcium carbonate, however, are important in preserving the fine anatomical details (even cells) of plants by the process of permineralization.

Pyrite forms as a result of the activity of sulfate-reducing bacteria, usually in fine-grained marine sediments, but pyritization of soft tissues is rare. It requires the rapid burial of carcasses to form isolated concentrations of organic matter. The two most important examples, Beecher's Bed in rocks of late Ordovician age in New York State, and the Hunsrück Slate of early Devonian age from Germany, both preserve the limbs of trilobites. Only the dorsal skeleton of a trilobite is strengthened by calcium carbonate. Hence we rely on extraordinary preservations for our knowledge of the whole anatomy of the animal. Without the few known examples of preserved limbs, we would have little idea of how trilobites moved about, fed and respired.

Soft-part preservation is most frequently associated with carbonate mineralization, in both marine and fresh-water environments. The Jurassic Lithographic Limestones at Solnhofen in Bavaria, which yielded *Archaeopteryx*, the first bird, are a classic example: The feather impressions are preserved in thinly bedded lime-

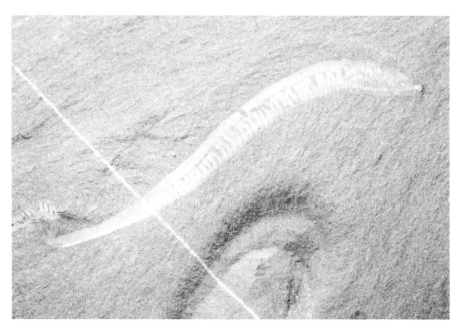

Figure 4. The soft-bodied *Pikaia* from the Burgess Shale is significant as the earliest known chordate, revealing the ancient ancestry of the group that includes ourselves. This specimen gives an impression of *Pikaia*'s elongate swimming form, muscle blocks in the trunk and axial structures.

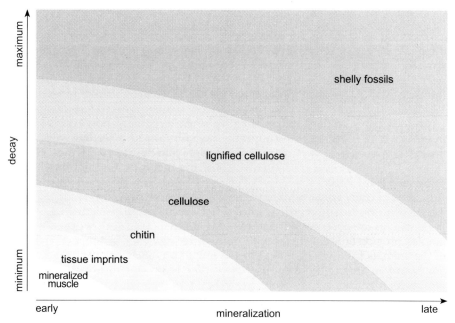

Figure 5. Relative rates of decay and mineralization determine the extent to which many soft tissues are preserved. This conceptual diagram shows the relationship between decay and mineralization in preserving various elements of a biota. Muscle and other volatile soft tissues survive only when decay is inhibited and mineralization is very rapid; this takes place, for example, when carcasses are buried rapidly in a sedimentary environment that promotes rapid diagenetic mineralization. At the other extreme, when the decay of soft tissues continues to completion, only shelly fossils will be preserved. (From Allison 1988b.)

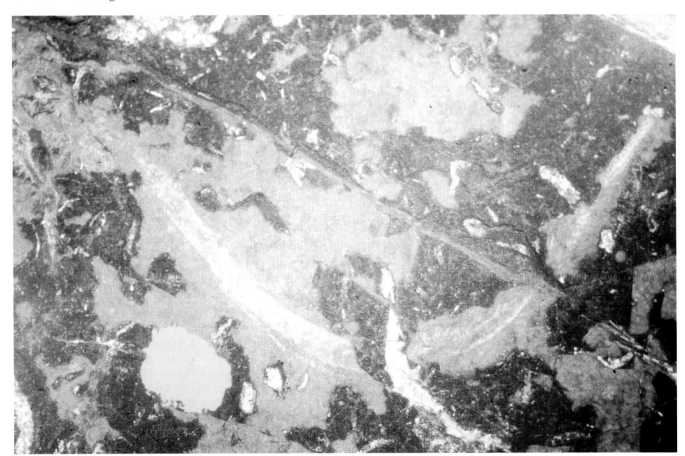

Figure 6. Conodont elements, tiny tooth-like microfossils that can be extracted from sedimentary rocks, are an example of hard parts that, by themselves, provide little information about the animals from which they came. The soft-bodied fossil shown above, found in the Granton Shrimp Bed in Edinburgh, provided the first evidence of the nature of the soft tissues of the conodont animal. The animal turned out to be a primitive chordate from the early Carboniferous period almost 400 million years ago. Some 40 millimeters long and 2 millimeters wide, it had an eel-like trunk, V-shaped muscle blocks and fins, and two lobes flanking the mouth. (Photograph courtesy of J. K. Ingham.)

stones. Rapid burial of large amounts of organic matter may lead to the formation of iron carbonate (siderite) concretions such as those that preserve the remarkably diverse Mazon Creek biota of Illinois.

Some of the most spectacular extraordinary fossils are those preserved in phosphate. These include muscles of squid from the Jurassic of Britain, and some three-dimensional fish with muscle, gills and gut contents from the Cretaceous of Brazil (Allison 1988c, Martill 1988). The decomposition of organisms is the most likely source of the phosphate. The phosphate concentration must exceed the concentration of bicarbonate in order to prevent the precipitation of calcium carbonate. This requires high organic input and very slow sedimentation.

In certain circumstances the organic tissues themselves can survive for geologically significant periods of time (Butterfield 1990). Refractory plant cuticles have the highest preservation potential, but heavily tanned arthropod cuticles also resist decay. For example, there is a diverse assemblage of early terrestrial arthropods from mudstones near Gilboa, New York, which date from the middle Devonian (Shear et al. 1984). The cuticles of trigonotarbids, centipedes, mites, spiders and possible insects are semi-translucent and appear unaltered.

Enigmatic Hard Parts

A number of extinct organisms are represented in the fossil record by hard parts that, in the absence of living examples, provide little clue to the nature of the animals from which they came. For example, among the most useful groups for identifying and dating geologic strata are the tiny tooth-like microfossils known as conodont elements (Sweet 1988). They are acid-resistant and can be extracted readily from most sedimentary rocks. In spite of their quantity, they and their origins have been at the center of controversy since 1856, when they were first discovered in Germany (Aldridge 1987).

Conodont elements come in a variety of shapes, ranging from simple cones to denticulate bars, flattened blades and broad, robust platforms. The discovery in the 1930s that different types of conodont element worked together to form a single apparatus, now considered to have functioned in feeding, yielded no insight into the identity of the soft-bodied organism from which these conodont elements came. As a consequence of this uncertainty, conodont elements have been variously interpreted as parts of plants, assorted worms, arrow worms, molluscs, arthropods and several groups of chordates.

The issue was resolved only as recently as 1983, when my colleagues and I discovered in the Granton Shrimp Bed in Edinburgh, Scotland, soft-bodied fossils from an animal with conodont elements in place (Briggs, Clarkson and Aldridge 1983). The animal, which had an eel-like trunk, was approximately 40 millimeters long and 2 millimeters wide and had V-shaped muscle blocks and fins, and two lobes flanking the mouth.

Figure 7. *Archaeopteryx lithographica (top)*, the world's oldest known bird, could be mistaken for a small dinosaur on the basis of skeletal fossils taken alone; one of the six known skeletons was, in fact, initially confused with the small dinosaur *Compsognathus (bottom)* until feather impressions were recognized. *Archaeopteryx,* which dates from the late Jurassic period, provides critical evidence in the investigation of bird origins; its morphology supports the hypothesis that the first flying vertebrates achieved flight by gliding rather than flapping.

As it turns out, the animal from which these conodont elements came is now thought to be a primitive chordate that lived almost 400 million years ago, early in the Carboniferous period (Aldridge et al. 1986).

A second example of a fossil whose true nature was revealed by extraordinary preservation is *Archaeopteryx lithographica* from the late Jurassic. If identification were to rely solely on skeletal fossils, *Archaeopteryx* could easily be mistaken for a small dinosaur— and indeed it has been. One of the six known skeletons was initially misidentified as a dinosaur until the feather impressions were recognized. Upon reevaluation, the specimen was found to be *Archaeopteryx*. Feathers are not conclusive evidence of an ability to fly, but, in combination with other features, they show that *Archaeopteryx* was at the very least a glider (Rayner 1989). Indeed, *Archaeopteryx* is generally referred to as the first bird, and its fossils provide critical data on bird origins.

Discoveries

Mineralized skeletons are not ubiquitous in the animal kingdom. Two-thirds of existing phyla lack any mineralized hard parts. Many lower-ranking taxa fall into the same category, including most arthropods, because their exoskeletons are very lightly sclerotized. Extraordinary fossils are the only direct source of data on the evolutionary history of soft-bodied animals, including all animals more than about 600 million years old that predate the appearance, in the late Precambrian, of the first mineralized skeletons. Extraordinary fossil remains are important in estimating at least the minimum age of soft-bodied taxa and in assessing the time of their diversification.

The discovery in Waukesha, Wisconsin, of the first significant assemblage of soft-bodied animals from the Silurian period, 400 million years ago, extends the known time range of some taxa back several millions of years (Mikulic, Briggs and Kluessendorf 1985 a, b). For example, among the fossils discovered at Waukesha was a well-preserved centipede-like organism, the earliest known example by 20 million years of a uniramian, a member of the major

group that includes the millipedes, centipedes and insects. A recent finding of the fossil remains of a related organism in Utah may push this date back another 100 million years (Robison 1990). The Waukesha occurrence shows that the ancestors of the modern uniramians were marine and at least as old as the early Silurian period.

Also discovered at Waukesha was a rare large annulate worm with what looks to be a circular structure reminiscent of a leech's sucker. If further material allows the specimen to be confidently identified, the range of the Hirudinea, the class of animal to which the leeches belong, will be extended back by some 280 million years. The earliest leech previously known was only 150 million years old.

The fossil record of the soft-bodied priapulid worms provides important insights into their changing role in marine communities through time. A priapulid worm is known from the

Mazon Creek fauna of the Carboniferous period, about 300 million years old. A number of priapulids occur in the Burgess Shale-type faunas of British Columbia, Utah and China—200 million years earlier (Conway Morris 1977). What is particularly interesting is that in the Burgess Shale communities, priapulids are more abundant than are polychaete worms, and the fossil priapulids are more diverse morphologically than their living descendants. Modern priapulids constitute only a minor element of marine communities; they appear to have been displaced over time by the polychaetes.

Even more significant than fossils that reveal the age and origins of living soft-bodied taxa are extraordinary fossils that reveal the existence of unfamiliar animals—creatures that belong to groups without living representatives, which would otherwise be unknown.

The more bizarre of these forms are termed Problematica, implying that

Figure 8. Faint feather impressions, important in identifying *Archaeopteryx* as a bird, are not immediately evident on this specimen discovered in 1951 at Eichstätt, Germany, but can be detected by close examination.

they do not fall within the description of any known phylum. One of the most widely distributed examples is a creature called *Anomalocaris* (Whittington and Briggs 1985). The animal has been found in rocks of Cambrian age in British Columbia, Utah, California, Pennsylvania, Poland and China. Half a meter long, *Anomalocaris* was one of the largest beasts of its time, and its morphology suggests it must have been a formidable predator. A pair of segmented spiny appendages flanked the mouth, and the jaw comprised a circle of 32 radiating plates armed with inwardly facing spines. This jaw appears to have functioned in a unique way, unknown in any living animal. The plates seem to have swung downward and outward to increase the aperture; then they pulled up again to bite or break the prey. Fossils of the now-extinct trilobites have wounds that may have been inflicted by these jaws, suggesting that the trilobites may have been prey for *Anomalocaris*.

Even in its movements, *Anomalocaris* appears to have developed a unique locomotive mechanism. The animal's trunk bore 11 pairs of closely spaced, overlapping lateral fins that moved in an undulatory fashion to create a propulsive wave. Some modern fish create a similar kind of motion using a single fin, but no creature other than *Anomalocaris* is known to have used an overlapping series of fins.

Other examples of Problematica revealed by extraordinary preservations include *Opabinia* and *Hallucigenia* from the Burgess Shale, *Ainiktozoon* from the Silurian of Lesmahagow in Scotland, and *Tullimonstrum* from the Carboniferous at Mazon Creek.

The head of *Opabinia* had five eyes and a long, flexible proboscis that terminated in opposing bundles of spines, which could presumably be used to grasp food. The 15 trunk divisions each bore a paired lobe. These were presumably used in swimming. On the surface of each lobe was a series of lamellae, probably forming a gill. A series of projections on the tail was used to stabilize the animal during swimming.

A new interpretation of *Hallucigenia* has turned current restorations literally upside down (Ramsköld and Hou in press). The head was poorly defined. It had seven pairs of flexible limbs, each terminating in a claw. It was protected dorsally by seven pairs of long spines. The trunk terminated posteriorly in an extended tube.

The most striking features of *Ainiktozoon* were an ovoid capsule and a segmented tail. The capsule was surrounded by a variety of enigmatic structures, including a compound eye. The organism has been tentatively interpreted as a swimming, filter-feeding protochordate.

Tullimonstrum was an elongate dorsoventrally flattened animal with a paired triangular tail fin. Anteriorly the head, which had a transverse bar-like structure terminating at each end in an eye, projected into a long proboscis-like extension ending in a toothed claw.

Evolutionary Patterns

Even though assemblages of extraordinary fossils provide the most complete chronicle of ancient communities available, until recently they have been largely ignored in considerations of evolutionary patterns, in favor of the much less complete shelly fossil record. This anomaly is the result of two central perceptions regarding ex-

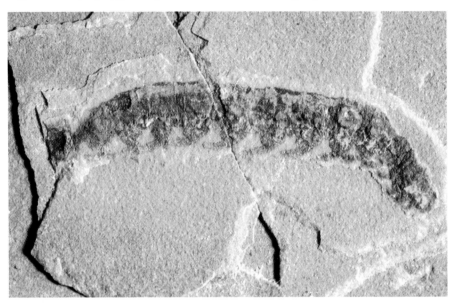

Figure 9. Well-preserved myriapod found at Waukesha, Wisconsin, predates by 20 million years other examples of uniramians, the major group that includes the millipedes, centipedes and insects. The organism was part of the first significant soft-bodied assemblage found from the Silurian period, 400 million years ago. Its occurrence shows that the ancestors of the modern uniramians were marine and appeared much earlier than had been thought.

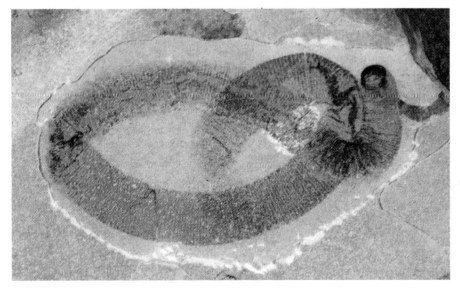

Figure 10. Sucker-like structure seen in a large annulate worm specimen from the Waukesha assemblage of soft-bodied fossils may belong to the first leech. Leeches had been known to exist for only the past 150 million years; this discovery, however, may extend the range of the class Hirudinea back by some 280 million years.

traordinary preservations. First, they are thought to be rare, and therefore they are believed to introduce distortions into analyses of diversity through time. Second, their very nature allows them to be perceived as atypical and consequently unrepresentative.

The fact is, extraordinary fossils *do* introduce distortions into global compilations of diversity through time, but that is because such compilations are necessarily based on the shelly fossil record. Exceptionally preserved fossils can provide a complementary data base that allows equally important questions to be addressed.

Burgess Shale–type preservations are now known from a range of localities, and it is clear that although some of the animals appear bizarre, the fauna is representative of their time and place. About 12 present-day phyla and about 20 genera of Problematica are represented (Briggs and Conway Morris 1986). Problematica are most numerous in the strata corresponding to the Cambrian period, with numbers declining throughout the remainder of the Paleozoic era.

What we learn from the Burgess Shale deposit, and others like it, is that the Cambrian was a period of explosive evolution. The initial radiation of major body plans probably took place largely unhindered by much competition or predation. As later extinctions left ecospace vacant, it was recolonized by new species from existing taxa; there was no potential for evolving new phyla. This suggests that the Cambrian radiation resulted in the rapid evolution of a much larger number of phyla than have survived to the present day (see Gould 1989), and that after the Cambrian the major feature of metazoan evolution was a decrease in the number of major body plans.

The questions before us now concern the number of phyla to have evolved during the Cambrian explosion. It also remains for us to assess the amount of disparity in the morphologies of Cambrian animals versus those of the present day.

Part of the apparent disparity is a reflection of taxonomic practice rather than of actual taxonomic differences. Phyla are defined by their uniqueness. When an organism does not seem to fit into any existing phylum, it is thought to be a part of a phylum of its own. During the hundreds of millions of years since the initial radiation of the metazoan phyla, intermediate forms

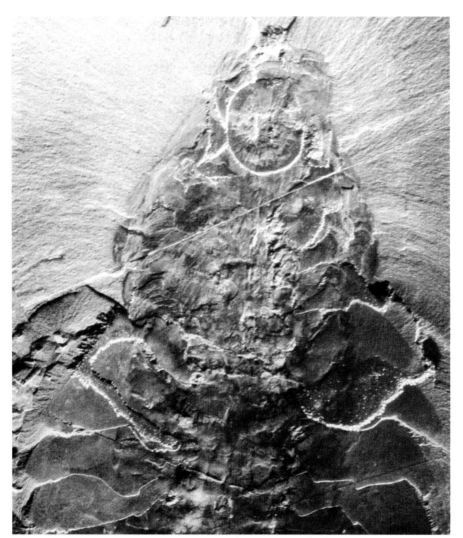

Figure 11. Specimens of *Anomalocaris*, a formidable predator that was likely among the largest of Cambrian beasts, suggest that this Burgess Shale animal developed a unique mechanism for locomotion. The animal had 11 pairs of closely spaced, overlapping lateral fins that undulated to create a propulsive wave. *Anomalocaris*, whose jaw is preserved in the unusual fossil on the cover of this issue of *American Scientist*, is currently classified among the Problematica, indicating that its relationships to other animals are uncertain.

have become extinct. Hence the morphological separation between the survivors has increased, so that the representatives of the living phyla are quite distinct. Thus when we try to insert Cambrian animals into a classification based on living fauna, it is hardly surprising that they cannot be accommodated. A more meaningful interpretation of the Cambrian radiation may be achieved by analyzing the relationships of the Cambrian organisms to each other, without reference to a modern classification.

This approach has already overturned the established theory of evolutionary relationships among arthropods (Briggs and Fortey 1989, Briggs 1990). One possible explanation for the vast diversity of these creatures is that each major group originated independently.

For example, a long-held view was that the trilobites were the first arthropods to evolve, and the crustaceans were believed to have arisen later, independently. Yet the analysis of complete arthropod fossils from extraordinary preservations has suggested that the opposite is true. Based on analyses of a large number of morphological characteristics, we now believe the crustaceans to be the most primitive of the arthropods, whereas the trilobites occupy a more derived position. And it is likely that the arthropods as a whole represent a single radiation, rather than a series of independent originations.

How generally representative are these extraordinary preservations? First, they are not as rare as originally thought. From the beginning of the Cambrian the number of known sites

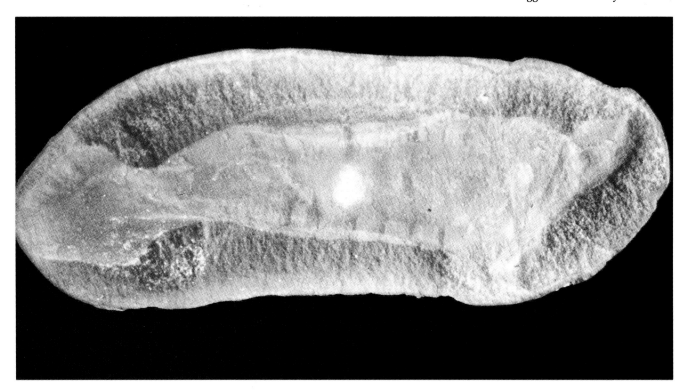

Figure 12. *Tullimonstrum,* the Tully Monster, found in the 300-million-year-old Mazon Creek deposit in Illinois, is another oddball; although it has been interpreted as a bizarre gastropod, it is usually placed in its own phylum. *Tullimonstrum* was an elongate, flattened animal with a paired triangular tail fin (to the left above); its head projected anteriorly into a long proboscis-like extension, ending in a toothed claw.

Figure 13. *Hallucigenia,* from the Burgess Shale, had seven pairs of long, dorsal spines and an equal number of flexible limbs, each terminating in a claw. Like *Anomalocaris* and *Tullimonstrum,* its body plan does not fit readily into any living phylum.

displaying significant soft-part preservation exceeds 60, and for each of these major sites there are many minor ones. For example, major occurrences of extraordinary fossils of Burgess Shale type are found in Yunnan Province, China; Peary Land, Greenland; near Lancaster, Pennsylvania; Kangaroo Island, South Australia; and in the Wellsville Mountains and the House Range in Utah, as well as at the original locality in British Columbia; but at least another 27 sites also yield some Burgess Shale taxa (Conway Morris 1989).

It can be argued that extraordinary fossils are preserved in environments that differ from those represented by the normal shelly fossil record. Nevertheless, the environments that preserve soft-bodied fossils may be equally or even more significant in evolutionary terms. The relative stability of the Burgess Shale fauna over extremely long periods may indicate that life forms established in deeper water are more conservative evolutionarily than were forms living at shallower depths (Conway Morris 1989).

A large number of extraordinary fossil deposits occur in association with broad coastal delta plains in tropical latitudes. In coastal swamps, interdistributary bays, and lagoons, restricted water bodies receive large quantities of organic material and are subject to changes in salinity and rapid influxes of sediment. A comparison of Carboniferous biotas such as Mazon Creek, which are preserved in such transitional environments, with an example from the Triassic of France some 100 million years younger, shows a striking continuity in the types of animal present (Briggs and Gall 1990). This is in contrast to the major changes that affected marine shelly groups in the same interval as a result of the extinction at the end of the Permian, which wiped out 54 percent of marine families. The animals in the fluctuating environments of the coastal plains were much less severely affected by the extinction, probably because of their greater tolerance to habitat variations. They were likely much more resistant to selection pressures than their more narrowly adapted open-marine counterparts.

Understanding the factors contributing to the formation of extraordinary fossils, their ecology and evolutionary significance requires an interdisciplinary approach. Although I have concentrated here on evolutionary aspects, current research ranges from experiments in decay and mineralization, through microbiology, geochemistry, sedimentology, systematic paleontology, functional and paleoecological interpretation, to the compilation and analysis of taxonomic data bases. Extraordinary fossils are no longer perceived as paleontological curiosities preserved in ecological and evolutionary isolation. We now recognize that they are the key to untapped data on patterns in the history of life.

Bibliography

Aldridge, R. J. 1987. Conodont palaeobiology: a historical review. In *Palaeobiology of Conodonts*, ed. R. J. Aldridge, 11–34. Chichester: The British Micropalaeontological Society.

Aldridge, R. J., D. E. G. Briggs, E. N. K. Clarkson and M. P. Smith. 1986. The affinities of conodonts—new evidence from the Carboniferous of Edinburgh, Scotland. *Lethaia* 19:273-291.

Allison, P. A. 1988a. The role of anoxia in the decay and mineralization of proteinaceous macro-fossils. *Paleobiology* 14: 139–154.

Allison, P. A. 1988b. Konservat-Lagerstätten: cause and classification. *Paleobiology* 14:331–344.

Allison, P. A. 1988c. Phosphatized soft-bodied squids from the Jurassic Oxford Clay. *Lethaia* 21:403–410.

Briggs, D. E. G. 1990. Early arthropods: dampening the Cambrian explosion. In *Short Courses in Paleontology 3, pp. 24–43* Knoxville, Tennessee: Paleontological Society.

Briggs, D. E. G., E. N. K. Clarkson and R. L.

Aldridge. 1983. The conodont animal. *Lethaia* 16:1–14.

Briggs, D. E. G., and S. Conway Morris. 1986. Burgess Shale Problematica. In *Problematic Fossil Taxa*, ed. A. Hoffman and M. H. Nitecki, 167–183. New York: Oxford University Press.

Briggs, D. E. G., and J.-C. Gall. 1990. The continuum in soft-bodied biotas from transitional environments: a quantitative comparison of Triassic and Carboniferous Konservat-Lagerstätten. *Paleobiology* 16:204–218.

Briggs, D. E. G., and R. A. Fortey. 1989. The early radiation and relationships of the major arthropod groups. *Science* 246:241–243.

Butterfield, N. J. 1990. Organic preservation of non-mineralizing organisms and the taphonomy of the Burgess Shale. *Paleobiology* 16:272–286.

Conway, Morris S. 1977. Fossil priapulid worms. *Special Papers in Palaeontology* 20.

Conway Morris S. 1986. The community structure of the Middle Cambrian phyllopod bed (Burgess Shale). *Palaeontology* 29:423–467.

Conway Morris S. 1989. The persistence of Burgess Shale–type faunas: implications for the evolution of deeper-water faunas. *Transactions of the Royal Society of Edinburgh: Earth Sciences* 80:271–283.

Conway Morris, S., and H. B. Whittington. 1985. Fossils of the Burgess Shale: A National Treasure in Yoho National Park, British Columbia. *Geological Survey of Canada, Miscellaneous Reports* 43:1-31.

Gould, S. J. 1989. *Wonderful Life—The Burgess Shale and the Nature of History.* New York: Norton.

Martill, D. M. 1988. Preservation of fish in the Cretaceous Santana formation of Brazil. *Palaeontology* 31:1–18.

Mikulic, D. G., D. E. G. Briggs and J. Kluessendorf. 1985a. A new exceptionally preserved biota from the lower Silurian of

Wisconsin, U.S.A. *Philosophical Transactions of the Royal Society of London* B311:75–85.

Mikulic, D. G., D. E. G. Briggs and J. Kluessendorf. 1985b. A Silurian soft-bodied biota. *Science* 228:715–717.

Ramsköld, L., and Hou Xianguang. In press. New Early Cambrian animal and onychophoran affinities of enigmatic metazoans. *Nature.*

Rayner, J. M. V. 1989. Vertebrate flight and the origin of flying vertebrates. In *Evolution and the Fossil Record*, ed. K. C. Allen and D. E. G. Briggs, 188–217. London: Belhaven Press.

Robison, R. A. 1990. Earliest-known uniramous arthropod. *Nature* 343:163–164.

Schopf, R. J. M. 1978. Fossilization potential of an intertidal fauna: Friday Harbor, Washington. *Paleobiology* 4:261–270.

Seilacher, A., W.-E. Reif and F. Westphal. 1985. Sedimentological, ecological and temporal patterns of fossil Lagerstätten. *Philosophical Transactions of the Royal Society of London* B311:5–23.

Shear, W. A., P. M. Bonamo, J. D. Grierson, W. D. I. Rolfe, E. L. Smith and R. A. Norton. 1984. Early land animals in North America; evidence from Devonian age arthropods from Gilboa, New York. *Science* 224:492–494.

Sweet, W. C. 1988. *The Conodonta—Morphology, Taxonomy, Paleoecology, and Evolutionary History of a Long-Extinct Animal Phylum.* New York: Oxford University Press.

Whittington, H. B., and D. E. G. Briggs. 1985. The largest Cambrian animal, *Anomalocaris*, Burgess Shale, British Columbia. *Philosophical Transactions of the Royal Society of London* B309: 569–609.

Wuttke, M. 1983. "Weichteil-Erhaltung" durch lithifizierte Mikroorganismen bei mittel-eozänen Vertebraten aus den Ölschiefern der "Grube-Messel" bei Darmstadt. *Senckenbergiana lethaea* 64:509–527.

Taphonomy and the Fossil Record

Anna K. Behrensmeyer

The complex processes that preserve organic remains in rocks also leave their own traces, adding another dimension of information to fossil samples

There is a great deal to be said
For being dead.
—E. Clerihew Bentley

The death of an organism is the beginning of a creative process of biological and physical transformation. Corporal remains may be immediately recycled into other organisms or gradually reduced to become the raw materials for other biological structures. Some may be removed from this system to be preserved as fossils. Remains that escape recycling through fossilization achieve a certain degree of immortality, and a small portion of these become the fossil record we use as evidence for organic evolution through geologic time.

An accepted fact in paleontology is that most organisms never became fossils, yet paleontologists have also tended to assume that their samples of past life give a reasonable approximation of evolutionary patterns. With increased understanding of the complex effects of preservation, this assumption is now being reexamined. Each fossilized relict of a plant or animal can offer a great deal of information about its evolutionary history and also clues about its environment, its place in the food chain, and its interactions with other species, and even

A graduate of Washington University in St. Louis (B.A. in geology) and of Harvard University (Ph.D. in geological sciences, specializing in paleontology), Anna K. Behrensmeyer is a research curator in the Department of Paleobiology of the National Museum of Natural History. Her research interests include taphonomy, sedimentology, and paleoecology, especially in the realm of Cenozoic mammal evolution. She has also participated in numerous projects involving human evolution. Address: Department of Paleobiology, NHB-E207, M.S. 121, Smithsonian Institution, Washington, DC 20560.

signs that skeletal remains were moved from the place of death to where they were finally interred and later discovered. Such information is coded in a complex way, and in order to read the code correctly we must first understand the processes of preservation.

Problems involving the effects of preservation on the fossil record extend through all the different phyla and span over three billion years, back to the earliest life on Earth. The vagaries of the fossil record have a significant effect on the way we view the history of life. For example, the earliest bird might be mistakenly identified as a reptile, were it not for the fortuitously preserved impressions of feathers in the Solenhofen limestone of Germany. As for life in the early seas, the complexity of fauna before the Cambrian Period, which began 570 million years ago, may today be vastly underestimated simply because the organisms of that time lacked hard shells and other parts that are easily fossilized.

Although we know that many kinds of animals, including the dinosaurs, became extinct 60 million years ago, no signs have yet been found of mass deaths, such as might be expected if a large comet had struck the earth. The absence of evidence could be due to the failure of the fossil record to register this kind of catastrophic event. If so, this bias has fostered an impression of gradual change, even though the past may have been punctuated by many times of great stress for the world's biota.

As the study of natural processes of preservation and destruction, taphonomy directly addresses the problem of how fossils represent past organisms, evolutionary patterns, and important biological events in the history of the earth. The word "taphonomy," derived from Greek terms meaning "the science of the laws of embedding," was coined by the Russian paleontologist I. A. Efremov (1940). In defining the field as "the study of the transition (in all its details) of organic remains from the biosphere into the lithosphere," Efremov intended taphonomy to include plants as well as animals, chemical changes (such as lithification) as well as burial, and the important problem of bias in the fossil record.

Although all the organisms that have lived on Earth have yielded relatively few fossils, fossilization is not always a rare event. There are untold numbers of fossil microorganisms under the floors of the oceans, and billions more all around us in rocks on the continents. In some environments of the past and also today, fossilization is the rule rather than the exception. An organism's chances of becoming fossilized are not randomly distributed in time and space, but follow discernible patterns and measurable probabilities. Thus, fossils can be seen as the products of a "natural sampling" of the original biotas. Once the taphonomic processes responsible for these samples are understood, it is possible to reconstruct the underlying biological patterns with greater accuracy, or to recognize when the samples are not suited to a particular question about evolution or paleoecology.

Taphonomy plays an important role in many different kinds of paleontological problems. It can help to answer the question of why the remains of one type of mollusc are fragmented and incomplete while those of another from the same rock are intact, thereby indicating possible biases in the preservation of different species. Such taphonomic considerations can be very important when the presence

55

or absence of particular species is used to correlate strata and place them in a time sequence. In rock layers with concentrations of bones, shells, or plant remains, taphonomic analysis can help to discriminate between what was buried near the place of death and what was transported from elsewhere: this information is valuable for paleoecologists in reconstructing vanished communities of organisms. In addition, archaeologists use taphonomy to determine whether patterns of bone clustering and breakage were caused by human activity or by other animals such as hyenas or wolves.

Taphonomy is concerned not only with fossils themselves but with all the organic and inorganic processes that affect remains from death to lithification to collection. From a taphonomic perspective, fragmentary skeletons may be more interesting than complete ones, because the nature of the fragmentation can indicate the processes responsible for preservation. As a consequence, taphonomists have much more of a fossil record to study than do researchers who require perfectly preserved remains. The investigation of death, decomposition, and burial in modern environments also is part of taphonomy, since this provides analogs essential for understanding the past.

From the biosphere to the lithosphere

The conceptual framework for taphonomy consists of successive stages of transformation—death, decomposition, burial, fossilization—separated by the processes that take place between each stage. All organisms that become fossils must pass through the major transformations: they die, are consumed or decomposed by exposure to sun, rain, and so on, their remains are moved about or buried where they lie, and finally after permanent burial they are lithified. The resulting sample inevitably bears the mark of the processes it has undergone, but clues for this taphonomic "overprint" may not be readily apparent. Given the complexity of the transformations, it is easy to see why fossil samples cannot be considered, a priori, as equivalent to biological samples taken from modern ecosystems. In order to reconstruct the biological attributes of fossil organisms,

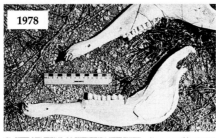

it is necessary to work back through the stages of fossilization, considering possible biasing effects on the fossil sample at each stage.

Although taphonomic processes begin at death, some organisms are much more likely to become fossils than others because of their habits and habitats during life. Aquatic organisms obviously have a great advantage over organisms that live in eroding uplands or other places where their remains have little chance for permanent burial. Organisms inhabiting such environments have undoubtedly been important in evolution, but their record was lost early in the transition from the biosphere to the lithosphere. Some organisms have a head start on fossilization because they are wholly or partly preburied, and for this reason species that live in burrows or that have anchors or roots in the substrate may be overrepresented in fossil assemblages.

The original morphology, population size, life history, and behavior of organisms likewise affect their potential for becoming fossilized. It is no surprise that marine molluscs, with their mineralized, durable shells, form a significant portion of the fossil record, whereas insect remains are rare. Taphonomic study must take into account such overall effects inherited from the living, and questions such as "Was this trilobite species originally abundant, or was it just easily preserved?" are often a major consideration in reconstructing ancient communities.

The best fossils are usually produced by the natural catastrophe of

Figure 1. The disintegration of a bone over a period of seven years illustrates a few of the processes which destroy organic remains but also leave distinctive traces that may allow the processes to be identified. This wildebeest was first photographed a few hours after the animal's death. The jaw (approximately 30 cm long) separated within the first year and is seen undergoing the effects of exposure to sun, rain, dust storms, and trampling on the soil of Amboseli National Park in Kenya. Destruction of the collagen near the bone's surface leads to flaking and splintering, but the chief processes responsible for the final disintegration are trampling and plant growth. The vertebrate remains that escape destruction by these processes, usually through prompt burial, may eventually be recovered as fossils. (Photographs by the author.)

live burial. Many of our most complete specimens have resulted from such events, notably the human remains preserved by volcanic eruptions such as the one at Pompeii, and fossils resulting from the entrapment of living animals in the La Brea tar pits of Los Angeles. The chances for preservation may be enhanced by severe storms, epidemics, or changes in the temperature, availability, or chemistry of water, all of which can leave large numbers of buried and unburied dead at one time. Mass mortality typically swamps the recycling capabilities of local scavengers, allowing time for the burial of more or less complete remains.

Under circumstances of more normal, attritional death due to predation, disease, accident, and old age, organic materials are often consumed or otherwise destroyed, but some types of organisms do leave large numbers of potential fossils. Animals such as ostracods (small crustaceans), and, in the past, trilobites, shed their mineralized parts as they grow and leave many skeletons per individual. Small, prolific organisms such as one-celled Foraminifera and algae produce enormous numbers of mineralized remains that accumulate as the populations undergo normal cycles of birth and death. Many of these remains may even pass through predators without damage.

Because mass mortality or instantaneous death and burial create the optimal initial conditions for fossilization, it is possible that a significant portion of our fossil record is due to such exceptional events. Long-term preservation is of course dependent on many other factors as well, and an episode such as the possible mass extinction of the dinosaurs at the end of the Cretaceous period may simply have failed to unite all the taphonomic conditions required to leave a fossil record.

There is little doubt that the record also includes large attritional samples. The two sources of fossil evidence, catastrophic and attritional, have very different consequences for evolutionary studies. Organisms whose best record may be preserved through mass mortality provide samples of an instant, like snapshots, often with long periods of time intervening between them. Organisms leaving attritional records offer more continuous samples. The amount of time that may be represented within and between samples significantly affects interpretations of evolutionary patterns as "punctuated" or "gradual," because the more continuous samples may appear to show gradual change and the snapshot samples punctuated, sudden change, regardless of their original underlying patterns.

Although paleontologists in general, and paleoecologists in particular, have appreciated the difference between these two types of information in the fossil record, there has been relatively little work on the theoretical implications for evolutionary studies. Only recently has some discussion on the amount of time represented in fossil samples begun to appear in the literature (Schindel 1982; Sadler and Dingus 1982; Behrensmeyer 1982a; Gingerich 1983). Other types of death assemblages—such as those accumulated by predators and scavengers, or those due to repeated smaller-scale events such as minor storms or floods—have different implications for evolutionary and paleoecological studies and require further investigation.

Once an organism dies, whether by attrition or catastrophe, there is usually intense competition among other organisms for the nutrients stored in its body. This combined with physical weathering and the dissolution of hard parts soon leads to destruction (as illustrated in Fig. 1) unless the remains are quickly buried (Behrensmeyer 1978). One mechanism for rapid burial is the churning and mixing of the substrate by burrowing organisms. In marine environments the remains of nonburrowing molluscs, fish, and other organisms may be worked down into the substrate, and on soil surfaces the same process helps to bury bones. Of course, animals that deliberately bury bones or have caches underground or in caves—dogs, hyenas, or even humans—increase the probability of preservation of their chosen food objects. Trampling of soft, muddy ground around water holes or along lake shores can also lead to rapid burial of any object that comes under a heavy foot.

These mechanisms contrast with the popular image of burial as a slow accumulation of sediment through long periods of time, a gentle fallout from air or water that gradually covers organic remains. This mode of burial does occur, especially in the deep oceans, but in many cases preservation by slow burial could not keep up with the rapid rates of destruction and organic recycling.

Remains that are not buried soon after an organism's death are subject to many kinds of processes which may not immediately destroy them but which may add their own story to the fossil record. Shells that lie on the ocean floor for any length of time are typically colonized by encrusting calcarous algae or bryozoans, and the resulting fossil samples allow researchers to assess the likely importance of unburied shell remains, which act as hard substrates and affect the structure of the ancient community (Kidwell and Jablonski 1984). Bones and teeth that are caught up in rivers may acquire traces of abrasion and also pits and holes showing that they served as food or homes for aquatic insect larvae, or that they were partly dissolved in acidic water.

The mixing of different kinds of organic remains indicates a long and complex taphonomic history. Some well known fossil sites, such as Shark Tooth Hill in southern California and the Calvert Cliffs of Maryland, have a combination of land and marine mammal bones, shark teeth, and the remains of birds and marine invertebrates. These sites record the transport and mixing of remains in rivers and estuaries and on beaches, remains accumulated from a large area over perhaps hundreds or thousands of years.

Taphonomic processes often leave distinctive traces on fossils which become an object of study in themselves. If the agent or process responsible for particular characteristics of a fossil assemblage can be identified, then this indicates what taphonomic biases may occur in the assemblage. For example, porcupines in South Africa collect dry bones and take them into caves or burrows to chew, apparently in order to keep their incisors sharp (Brain 1980, 1981). Their tooth marks are distinctive, and paleontologists encountering fossil bones with such marks are thereby alerted to the possibility that the fossil assemblage was created, at least in part, by porcupines. This becomes important in deciding whether the animals represented in the assemblage give a true picture of the original community, and whether the bone-collecting agent might have been a hyena or a human ancestor rather than a porcupine. For remains with simple or complex taphonomic histories, burial is still the most critical step in the process of preservation, and only permanent burial will produce lasting fossils. This is a function of large-scale geological processes; basins that undergo a net accumulation of sedimentary rock through time preserve the organic record, and the intervals of sediment build-up and erosion ultimately determine the times of fossil preservation and the gaps between them.

Fossils are generally regarded as having "turned to stone," by the replacement of original hard parts with secondary minerals. Many fossils retain a large proportion of their original mineral components, however, and in some cases residues of the soft parts as well. The original calcium carbonate in fossil corals and Foraminifera is often well enough preserved to permit isotopic analysis of the water composition that pertained when these animals were alive. Bones may retain enough original calcium phosphate to allow analysis of the living animal's intake of strontium, thus providing information about its diet. Problems with such analyses are often caused by contamination with new minerals deposited in pore spaces, rather than by the loss of original minerals.

The process of mineralization, or diagenesis, is extremely varied and is a function of the original composition of the organism combined with the chemistry of the burial environment. In many chemical settings—highly acidic tropical forest soils, for example—the hard as well as the soft parts of an organism can dissolve completely, leaving a diagenetic bias against the organisms buried there. The loss of a fossil can occur at any time after burial; many survive until they are exposed by uplift and erosion only to be destroyed by soil dissolution before they can be found by collectors. Road cuts and other large-scale human excavations are popular with paleontologists because they expose rocks below this zone of surface dissolution.

Other changes that can take place during diagenesis include the compression, distortion, and even fragmentation of skeletal material by the

Figure 2. An extraordinary Ramapithecine skull from China (*top*), approximately 8.5 million years old, is known as "the perfect one" because it is so nearly complete; however, because it was crushed flat during preservation in a lignite deposit, the morphological features will be difficult to reconstruct. The crushing is apparent particularly in the eye sockets, which in the living creature were more nearly round, and in the braincase, once vaulted to hold the brain but now almost flat.

In contrast, the skull of robust *Australopithcus* (*bottom*), approximately 1.5 million years old, from Kenya, escaped crushing during fossilization because it was filled with sand. The round eye sockets, bony ridges above the eyes, and pointed crest on top of the skull (the anchor for strong jaw muscles) have retained their original structure. (Top photo © Margo Crabtree, Courtesy *Science 84*; bottom photo by the author.)

sheer weight of overlying sediment. Organisms buried in highly compressible mud or peat may preserve less useful information than those buried in sand because of greater distortion in the more compactable sediment. Poor preservation is the bane of many a paleontologist's attempts to recontruct the anatomy of an important fossil. Skulls of the Miocene hominoid *Sivapithecus* from China, for example, are preserved in a lignite (coal) and are so flattened that much of their internal cranial anatomy is inaccessible, at least by existing methods. In particular, the question of cranial capacity, or brain volume, is difficult to address in skulls that have been crushed or flattened (Walker 1980), as is the case with the Ramapithecine skull shown in Figure 2. By comparison, the skull of *Austra lopithecus* has retained much of its original structure, because it was filled with sand during fossilization.

From the lithosphere to our own time

Traditionally, paleontologists have sought only the best-preserved specimens for studies in morphology and evolution, although they have also learned to make the most of fragmentary material if nothing else is available. The search for the most complete fossils has resulted in strong biases toward those individuals, species, and sedimentary situations that offer the best preservation. Most museum collections, although possessing many examples of good preservation, cannot be relied upon to give an accurate census of an ancient community. For instance, often one cannot be sure whether the absence of a species from a particular locality is "real" or is due to conscious or unconscious oversight by the collector.

As new questions have developed in biology of fossil populations and in paleoecology, there has been an effort to collect unbiased samples in which all the fossil material at a new site is recovered, whether small or large, complete or fragmentary. Such careful re-collecting of old fossil sites can help resolve doubts about the presence or absence of a species.

The new type of collection presents a challenge for museums, because its value lies in taphonomic features of the whole assemblage of fos-

sils rather than in identifiable species. Museums usually catalog and store specimens according to what they are rather than what taphonomic features they represent, and thus the new direction in paleontology is likely to bring about some changes in the last resting place of organic remains that have survived the transition from the biosphere to the lithosphere. Museum collections with taphonomic information will allow researchers to build a foundation of solid evidence for processes of preservation and their effects on the fossil record.

Because taphonomy reaches into the modern world for information on processes that transform organic remains into fossils, the study of recent environments and experimental work on problems such as the transport of shells and bones in water form an important part of taphonomic research. This approach has its constraints, however, because not all processes that have affected the fossil record can be found in modern ecosystems or duplicated in experiments. Many biological processes and even some physical ones were different in earlier times and have themselves evolved. The development of bone-crushing teeth in mammals, for instance, clearly had an effect on the completeness of remains left by predators. Part of our understanding of ancient taphonomic processes must come from careful examination of clues left in the fossil record, particularly in the more distant past where recent analogs are of limited value (Olson 1980). In many cases, it is necessary to admit the limitations in fossil samples without being able to decipher the processes that caused their taphonomic biases.

Recurring themes

Various problems in taphonomy are being actively investigated in paleontology and archaeology. Because taphonomy is a relatively new field, and nearly every paleontological investigation has its own set of taphonomic considerations, there is not yet an accepted theoretical synthesis or a set of "typical" taphonomic problems. Several recurring themes, however, cross traditional boundaries between disciplines such as invertebrate and vertebrate paleontology. These themes include the identification of specific

processes that leave marks on organic remains, the circumstances that preserve some species but not others in fossil assemblages, the transport of organic remains, and "time-averaging," or the amount of time represented in single fossil samples. Each can be illustrated by an example from current taphonomic research.

The identification of specific processes, or specific agents, by the marks they leave on fossils is one of the best-known forms of taphonomic research. Such work is important for revealing biases in paleoecological reconstructions, and in addition it can provide evidence about the behavior of extinct organisms—the taphonomic agents that modified the organic remains. In some cases, such as the evenly spaced bite marks of an extinct marine reptile on the shell of a *Nautilus*-like ammonite (Kauffman and Kesling 1960), the identity of the agent is fairly obvious. In many other cases, however, the evidence may be ambiguous: extensive breakage in ammonite shells can be caused by predators, by crushing under sediment loads, or even by implosion due to water pressure. The chief problem in identifying a taphonomic process is to show that particular characteristics of a fossil or fossil assemblage could have been caused only by that one process.

As taphonomic agents, humans or human ancestors have been at work at least since the time that their behavior began to include meat-eating and the use of tools. It seems safe to assume that early hominids would have dealt with meat in ways distinct from other carnivores and scavengers; they should therefore have left definitive marks on the bone debris. Identifying these marks has become a major effort in research on human origins (Gifford 1981), because it may provide some decisive evidence about the behavior of our early ancestors and also perhaps the earliest evidence for a distinctly human trait: the use of tools. (See "Home Bases and Early Hominids," by Richard Potts, in *American Scientist*, July–August 1984.)

For some years anthropologists and popular writers based their hypotheses of violent behavior in early humans on well-known deposits of broken bones in South African caves (e.g., Dart 1949). Recently, however, there have been many studies of bone breakage by agents other than humans, and it is clear that most if not all of the breakage could have been caused by hyenas and other carnivores or scavengers that frequented the caves. The patterns seem to owe as much to the physical properties of different bones as to the agent doing the breaking (Brain 1981). The search for human-specific patterns of breakage goes on, however, and is of particular interest in such questions as when the earliest humans arrived in North America (Haynes 1983).

Cutmarks on bones are now emerging as stronger evidence for human activity than breakage or other patterns of bone damage (Bunn 1981; Potts and Shipman 1981; Shipman and Rose 1983). Many processes leave similar marks on bone, including chewing by carnivores, gnawing by rodents, cutting with stone, bone, or metal tools, trampling, and even the preparation of fossil specimens with dental picks. In an effort to sort out these marks, distinctive grooves found on a small sample of fossil bones from Olduvai Gorge and East Lake Turkana have been examined using light and scanning electron microscopy. To provide a basis for comparison, fresh bones cut with sharp implements of various kinds were also examined. Of all the marks observed, tiny parallel striations in the bottom of grooves appear to be due only to the use

of stone implements by humans, and such features occur on the early Pleistocene fossil bones, as shown in Figure 3. The case for meat-eating by hominids at Olduvai and East Lake Turkana 1.9–1.8 million years ago is strengthened by this work, although research into other processes that might leave microscopic striations will undoubtedly continue.

As a second theme of taphonomic research, the differential preservation of species represents a major concern for paleoecologists, and also for stratigraphers who need to rely on a few fossils in each assemblage for correlation. It is well known that large portions of the original communities of living, interacting organisms are missing from the fossil record; an important paper by Lawrence (1968) compares modern and Oligocene marine oyster communities and estimates that 75% of the information about the species in the Oligocene community has been lost. The portion that is missing would include soft-bodied and planktonic forms that are either completely destroyed or transported away from the site of preservation. Thus, the subset of organisms that form the fossil assemblage is used for paleoecological reconstruction with the understanding that this is only a small portion of the original community.

Certain spectacular examples of preservation throughout the geological

record include the soft-bodied organisms and show us what we are missing in the more typical fossil assemblages containing only mineralized parts. One of the most notable examples is the fauna of the Burgess Shale, an assemblage of soft-bodied and hard-bodied organisms representing marine life of about 530 million years B.P.

The animals include trilobites, brachiopods, worms, sponges, crustaceans, primitive molluscs, jellyfish, the oldest chordate, and numerous arthropods and other organisms with mysterious morphologies. Whole bodies, including delicate parts such as antennae, are preserved as aluminosilicate and carbon films within the shale. Some 150 species have been identified on the basis of this material, about half of them soft-boded organisms (primarily arthropods) unique to this fossil assemblage. The shale occurs along a single rocky slope in British Columbia; the fossil-bearing zone is about 10 m thick, but many of the best-preserved remains occur in a unit less than 1 m thick (Whittington 1971, 1980). Figure 4 shows two fossils and a paleoecological reconstruction of this Cambrian marine community.

The circumstances leading to this preservation have received considerable attention. Although published discussions do not use the word "taphonomy," they are good examples of how paleontologists reconstruct ta-

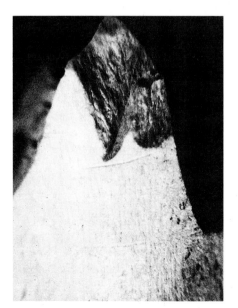
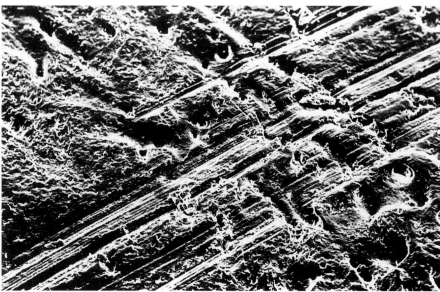

Figure 3. The use of stone tools on bones leaves a characteristic mark: fine parallel striations in the bottom of the groove. The bone at left, from Pleistocene deposits at Olduvai Gorge in Tanzania, bears such marks, which are interpreted as important evidence of meat-eating by hominids at 1.9–1.8 million years B.P. The scanning electron micrograph at the right gives a closer view of such marks, this time on modern bone that has been cut experimentally with a sharp-edged stone implement. (Photographs courtesy of R. Potts.)

phonomic history for a fossil assemblage that lacks a modern analog. It is generally agreed that the deposit formed where the base of a reef merged with submarine fans that delimited pockets of stagnant water poisonous to most aerobic organisms. Between the reef and the anoxic water was a sloping zone of muddy substrate that supported a rich marine fauna. Slumping of the unstable mud carried both live organisms and skeletal material into the anoxic zone, where death and burial probably occurred instantaneously. There was no opportunity for scavengers to work over the remains, and the chemical environment of the mud prevented bacterial action, preserving soft as well as hard parts without disintegration. Subsequent changes primarily involved compression (Morris and Whittington 1979; Whittington 1980).

Reconstruction of the organisms requires careful excavation of the thin films that form the body impressions, followed by microscopic study. The same animal may look very different depending on how its body was oriented during compression. In order to avoid misidentification there have been special methods developed for reconstructing animals "in the round" from their two-dimensional body impressions (Briggs and Williams 1980). Such techniques help to remove a taphonomic bias that might otherwise result in the naming of more species than were actually present in the fauna. Distortion is a recurring problem in all branches of paleontology.

For the Burgess fauna, a different set of taphonomic problems is involved in reconstructing the paleoecology of the original marine community. Because the organisms were transported into the burial environment, rather than being buried where they had lived, it is difficult to recreate their actual life associations and habitats.

The reconstruction shown in Figure 4 in fact combines taxa from different layers of the fossil deposit; their patterns of association in life remain conjectural. Ways of life, whether burrowing, swimming, or actively moving on the bottom surface, must be inferred from morphological attributes rather than from sedimentary context.

An important question for paleontologists is how well the Burgess fauna represents life in the Cambrian seas. In the face of a general tendency to regard it as an unusual, nonrepresentative fauna, Whittington (1980) has argued that it actually may be a good sample of Cambrian marine life. He notes that the fauna includes typical Cambrian organisms with mineralized skeletons and that the plethora of soft-bodied animals can be explained by the unusual circumstances of burial and preservation. Many Cambrian communities were probably dominated by arthropods and worms, but since these

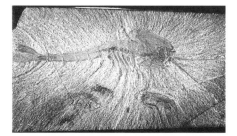

Figure 4. A paleoecological reconstruction of life in the Cambrian sea of 530 million years B.P. is based on the unique record preserved in the Burgess Shale of British Columbia. The two smaller photographs show soft-bodied organisms as they appear in the shale, *Waptia fieldiensis* (*top*) and *Opabinia regalis* (*bottom*). Although these organisms and the others shown in the reconstruction were all buried together, they may not actually have lived in the same place. In life, the various taxa inhabited different niches in the sea, and taphonomic processes carried them into the same burial environment. (Photographs courtesy of C. Clark and the Smithsonian Institution.)

are seldom preserved, the typical samples of organisms with hard parts are biased, like the oyster community mentioned earlier, by the loss of a large part of the original diversity.

The study of transport history—how organic remains may have traveled from the original site of death to their place of final burial—is another theme that recurs in taphonomic research. Durable remains are more likely than delicate ones to go through one or more episodes of movement and survive to become fossils. Shells can be transported by seagulls, waves, or tidal currents; bones may be moved by predators, by stream action, even (for rodent-size bones) by scavenging ants (Shipman and Walker 1980). The more durable the remains, and the longer they remain unburied, the more complex the transport history can become. Thus, scratches on bones due to trampling may be obliterated by a subsequent phase of transport in a sandy stream. Finally the remains may be converted into rounded pebbles of bone or shell, with all evidence for former processes worn away by the strong scouring action of water, wind, and sediment.

For many fossil samples composed of fragmentary remains, some degree of transport appears to be the rule rather than the exception. The more robust vertebrate remains, such as jaws, teeth, and bones of the feet, may survive several stages of transport, first being moved about on a floodplain by sheet wash from rainstorms, then after shallow burial eroding out of a bank and dropping into the river to be carried downstream by the current (Behrensmeyer 1982b). Because fresh bones are full of pore spaces, they are relatively lightweight, and even large bones can be moved by moderate currents of 30 to 50 cm/sec. Thus it can be safely assumed that most bones found in river channels or in beach deposits have been transported and are not buried where the animal died.

Bones are transportable objects, but they can hardly compare with pollen, which is one of the most easily dispersed of all organic remains. Pollen and other plant spores are of major importance for paleoecological reconstructions throughout the Mesozoic and Cenozoic eras, and palynologists continually face the problem of

what their samples mean in terms of original vegetation patterns. The presence, absence, and relative abundance of floral species depend on how well the pollen travels, how much is produced by a species, how far the sample may be from where the species grew, and what the environment of deposition was like.

Perhaps because transport is such an obvious problem for palynologists, considerable effort has gone into testing the relationship between recent vegetation and pollen that is found on soil surfaces, in bogs, and in lakes (e.g., Davis et al. 1975; Webb et al. 1978; Jacobson and Bradshaw 1981; Heide and Bradshaw 1982). Such work has shown that bog samples are faithful to the local vegetation but that lake samples are highly variable, depending primarily on the influence of inflowing rivers. Palynologists work with samples from bogs when they can, and accept limitations on the interpretation of local ecology when forced to use lake sites.

Knowing the transport history of a fossil assemblage, whether of pollen, bones, shells, or other remains, makes it possible to specify the spatial resolution of the sample. Such information is crucial in judging whether bones, for instance, represent animals from an area as small as a local habitat or as large as a whole drainage basin. Sometimes transported remains are added to habitats on the bottom of the sea during a storm, and the resulting mixture of faunas must be separated if the original local community is to be reconstructed accurately.

A fourth recurrent theme in taphonomy is time-averaging, or the problem of how long a time span is represented by a fossil sample. The word "contemporaneous" is used often by paleontologists to describe organisms that lived "at the same time." But in the last decade there has been a gradual realization that the precision of this important statement can vary greatly, depending on the circumstances of death and burial and the degree of time-averaging in the fossil sample. Assemblages that are the product of a catastrophic natural event contain organisms that lived at the same instant of time, but many others combine the remains from years to even hundreds of thousands, or millions, of years. Such assem-

Figure 5. The skull of a bison, with one horn well exposed, erodes out of a bank of the East Fork River in Wyoming. The bison has been extinct in this area for a century, but once in the river, the skull, or the parts of it that have survived the process of erosion, will mingle with the remains of more recent inhabitants of the area. Thus, a fossil sample taken from the river would give a mixture of animals that lived over a time span of a hundred years or more. (Photograph by the author.)

blages pose problems for paleoecologists and morphologists alike, because the samples may include species and individuals that lived over time spans much longer than those that can be observed and measured in modern ecosystems.

Time-averaging can be seen at work in the taphonomic processes affecting the bones of land vertebrates in river systems. Bones found today in the rivers of Wyoming include many that have eroded out of the banks and dropped into the river channel; there they have mixed with other bones derived from skeletons lying on the floodplains (Behrensmeyer 1982b). Specimens eroding from the bank include, for example, the remains of *Bison* (as shown in Fig. 5), a species that has been locally extinct for nearly a century. Thus, in the future, a fossil sample from these rivers would represent at least 100 years of time-averaging and would mix the records of the changing vertebrate community in Wyoming.

As another example, the South Platte River in northeastern Colorado mixes bones from extinct Pleistocene mammals such as camel and ground sloth with the bones of house cats and with soup bones; in this case the degree of time-averaging is at least 10,000 years. The older bones are usually partly mineralized but in very good condition, and in fact, if all the bones were buried and mineralized further, it would probably not be possible to distinguish older components from younger ones. Such examples are a warning that vertebrate remains in the same channel deposit may not represent animals that interacted with one another in the ecosystems of the past (Behrensmeyer 1982a; Behrensmeyer and Schindel 1983).

The four research themes discussed here represent only part of the present activity in taphonomy, but they illustrate how it can provide new evidence about the history of life as well as alerting researchers to information loss and bias in the fossil record. This dual role for the field is rapidly expanding. In addition, as more is learned about taphonomic processes, it is becoming evident that these can also influence the course of evolution itself, since organisms that can efficiently utilize organic remains

have a selective advantage in some evolutionary circumstances (Behrensmeyer and Kidwell, upubl.).

The fossil record gives the long-term history of relatively short-term (biological) processes, and there are many evolutionary questions that can be answered only with fossils. One of the most important contributions taphonomy can make in the future is to encourage more exchange between biologists and paleontologists by providing a perspective on fossils as natural samples, a methodology for deciphering how these samples represent the biology of the past, and new questions that take advantage of the unique information preserved in the fossil record.

References

Behrensmeyer, A. K. 1982a. Time sampling intervals in the vertebrate fossil record. *Proc. Third North Am. Paleontol. Conv.* 1:41–45.

———. 1982b. Time resolution in fluvial vertebrate assemblages. *Paleobiology* 8:211–27.

———. 1978. Taphonomic and ecologic information from bone weathering. *Paleobiology* 4:150–62.

Behrensmeyer, A. K., and S. M. Kidwell. Unpubl. Taphonomy's contributions to paleobiology.

Behrensmeyer. A. K., and D. Schindel. 1983. Resolving time in paleobiology. *Paleobiology* 9:1–8.

Brain, C. K. 1980. Some criteria for the recognition of bone-collecting agencies in African caves. In *Fossils in the Making*, ed. A. K. Behrensmeyer and A. Hill, pp. 108–31.Univ. of Chicago Press.

———. 1981. *The Hunters or the Hunted?* Univ. of Chicago Press.

Briggs, D. E. G., and S. H. Williams. 1980. The restoration of flattened fossils. *Lethaia* 14:157–64.

Bunn, H. T. 1981. Archaeological evidence for meat-eating by Plio-Pleistocene hominids from Koobi Fora and Olduvai Gorge. *Nature* 291:574–77.

Dart, R. A. 1949. The predatory implemental technique of *Australopithecus*. *Am. J. Phys. Anthropol.* 7:1–38.

Davis, R. B., J. E. Bradstreet, R. Stuckenrath, and H. W. Borns, Jr. 1975. Vegetational and associated environments during the past 14,000 years near Moulton Pond, Maine. *Quatern. Res.* 5:435–66.

Efremov, I. A. 1940. Taphonomy: A new branch of paleontology. *Pan-Am. Geol.* 74:81–93.

Gifford, D. P. 1981. Taphonomy and paleoecology: A critical review of archaeology's sister disciplines. In *Advances in Archaeological Method and Theory*, Vol. 4, ed. M. B. Schiffer, pp. 365–438. Academic Press.

Gingerich, P. D. 1983. Rates of evolution: Effects of time and temporal scaling. *Science* 222:159–61.

Haynes, G. 1983. Frequencies of spiral and green-bone fractures on ungulate limb bones in modern surface assemblages. *Am. Antiquity* 48:102–14.

Heide, K., and R. Bradshaw. 1982. The pollen–tree relationship within forests of Wisconsin and Upper Michigan, U.S.A. *Rev. Palaeobot. Palynol.* 36:1–24.

Jacobson, G. L., Jr., and R. H. W. Bradshaw. 1981. The selection of sites for paleovegetational studies. *Quatern. Res.* 16:80–96.

Kauffman, E. G., and R. V. Kesling. 1960. An Upper Cretaceous ammonite bitten by a Mososaur. *Contrib. Mus. Paleontol. Univ. Michigan* 15:193–248.

Kidwell, S. M., and D. Jablonski. 1984. Taphonomic feedback: Ecological consequences of shell accumulation. In *Biotic Interactions in Recent and Fossil Benthic Communities*, ed. M. J. S. Tevesz and P. L. McCall, pp. 195–248. Plenum.

Lawrence, D. R. 1968. Taphonomy and information losses in fossil communities. *Bull. Geol. Soc. Am.* 79:1315–30.

Morris, S. C., and H. B. Whittington. 1979. The animals of the Burgess Shale. *Sci. Am.* 241:122–33.

Olson, E. C. 1980. Taphonomy: Its history and role in community evolution. In *Fossils in the Making*, ed. A. K. Behrensmeyer and A. Hill, pp. 5–19. Univ. of Chicago Press.

Potts, R., and P. Shipman. 1981. Cutmarks made by stone tools on bones from Olduvai Gorge, Tanzania. *Nature* 291:577–80.

Sadler, P. M., and L. W. Dingus. 1982. Expected completeness of sedimentary sections: Estimating a time-scale dependent, limiting factor in the resolution of the fossil record. *Proc. Third North Am. Paleontol. Conv.* 2: 461–64.

Schindel, D. E. 1982. Time resolution in cyclic Pennsylvanian strata: Implications for evolutionary patterns in *Glabrocingulum* (Mollusca: Archaeogastropoda). *Proc. Third North Am. Paleontol. Conv.* 2:482a–482e.

Shipman, P., and J. Rose. 1983. Early hominid hunting, butchering, and carcass-processing behaviors: Approaches to the fossil record. *J. Anthropol. Archaeol.* 2:57–98.

Shipman, P., and A. C. Walker. 1980. Bone collecting by harvesting ants. *Paleobiology* 6:496–502.

Walker, A. C. 1980. Functional anatomy and taphonomy. In *Fossils in the Making*, ed. A. K. Behrensmeyer and A. P. Hill, pp. 182–96. Univ. of Chicago Press.

Webb, T., III, R. A. Laseski, and J. C. Bernabo. 1978. Sensing vegetational patterns with pollen data: Choosing the data. *Ecology* 59:1151–63.

Whittington, H. B. 1971. The Burgess Shale: History of research and preservation of fossils. *Proc. First North Am. Paleontol. Conv.* Part 1:1170–201.

———. 1980. The significance of the fauna of the Burgess Shale, Middle Cambrian, British Columbia. *Proc. Geol. Assoc.* 291:127–48.

What Killed the Dinosaurs?

William Glen

Puzzling mass extinctions punctuate the earth's history. They are the benchmarks of the geological time scale, and they have invited speculation for more than a century. Now two competing ideas have emerged from a decade of controversy to explain how the dinosaurs perished 66 million years ago in the best-known of the mass extinctions. The "impactor" hypothesis pelts the earth with a swarm of meteorites; the "volcanist" alternative calls on volcanic eruptions that dwarfed any seen by man.

The upheaval in earth science was triggered in 1979 by a team of four scientists from the University of California at Berkeley: the geologist Walter Alvarez, his father Luis Alvarez, a physicist, and nuclear chemists Frank Asaro and Helen Michel (1980). The Alvarez team discovered what seemed an unearthly concentration of the element iridium in a distinctive layer of clay in a gorge outside the northern Italian town of Gubbio. The clay bed, only a centimeter thick and sandwiched between much thicker limestone strata, marks the time of the dinosaur extinctions. The boundary is called the K-T; it separates the older Cretaceous Period (geological symbol K), with its reigning dinosaurs and conifer trees, from the Tertiary Period (T), which is dominated by mammals and flowering plants of modern aspect.

It was the unusual abundance of iridium in the Gubbio clay that excited the Alvarezes and their colleagues. The platinum-group element iridium is virtually absent from

William Glen, *Eos* History Editor, is writing a book on the history of the K-T debates. He is the author of *Continental Drift and Plate Tectonics* (Charles E. Merrill Publishing Company) and *The Road to Jaramillo: Critical Years of the Revolution in Earth Science* (Stanford University Press). Address: U. S. Geological Survey, 345 Middlefield Road, Mail Stop 930, Menlo Park, CA 94025.

After a decade of debates, the question remains: Was the earth devastated by meteorites, or were the extinctions caused by cataclysmic volcanism?

the earth's crust; the average abundance is measured in parts per trillion. It is a siderophile (iron-loving) element that was dragged along by iron as it sank into the earth's core early in the planet's history. On the other hand, iridium is relatively abundant in certain kinds of meteorites. When the Gubbio boundary clay was found to have dozens of times as much iridium as ordinary crustal rocks—including the limestones just above and below the clay—the Alvarez team drew a dramatic conclusion. They proposed that the iridium had settled out of a global dust cloud kicked up by the impact of a meteorite 10 kilometers in diameter. The same dust cloud, they suggested, had blocked the sun, chilled the planet and killed the dinosaurs, along with 75 percent of all other species.

It is hard to overstate the impact of the impact hypothesis. In the past decade more than 2,000 papers and books have touched on various aspects of the controversy, and the flood of publications shows no sign of abating. Careers have been redirected, long-quiescent areas of research have been rejuvenated, and workers in formerly isolated fields have been swept into collaborative efforts. The impact hypothesis has led to ingenious experiments, field studies and re-examinations of the evidence. It has also spun off a number of fascinating related ideas, the most notable being the proposal that

mass extinctions are periodic, visiting the earth at regular intervals of 26 million years or so.

Today, out of a host of earlier attempts to explain mass extinctions, only one alternative to the impact hypothesis remains under serious consideration. The alternative volcanist hypothesis suggests that the iridium anomaly, and other evidence claimed for impact, resulted instead from massive volcanic eruptions. Paleontologists, in particular, find volcanism useful in explaining certain puzzling features of the fossil record, such as a pattern of stepped extinctions that appear to precede the great kill at the K-T boundary.

The volcanists propose eruptions on a cataclysmic scale. As a result, they encounter opposition of the same sort that proponents of impact have long faced (French 1990). Both hypotheses raise the specter of catastrophism, a philosophy dislodged during fierce debates in the 19th century by the uniformitarianists, who viewed the workings of the present natural world as the key to the earth's past. A latter-day version of uniformitarianism, more accepting of uncommon events and forces, now serves as the philosophical mainstay of the earth sciences (Gould 1965); nevertheless, quick and violent causes are still not as well received as slow, gradual processes in the interpretation of earth history. But at least volcanism, however great its scale, can be viewed as an enlargement of a familiar earthly process. Articles by volcanists have sometimes closed with the telling sentiment that they find satisfaction in seeking an earthly cause before turning to the sky.

Evidence for an Impact

The hypothesis offered by the Alvarez group was not the first suggestion of a catastrophic origin for mass extinctions. Earlier explanations had included supernovas, solar flares, and

Figure 1. Thin layer of clay marks the boundary between two major periods in the earth's history: the Cretaceous (dominated by dinosaurs and conifers) and the Tertiary (the period in which mammals and flowering plants became dominant). The clay layer, deposited 66 million years ago, is the dark stripe running diagonally across this image, just to the left of the coin. Below the clay are Cretaceous limestones, and above it are darker limestones laid down in the Tertiary. The rocky outcrop is in a gorge near the Italian town of Gubbio. In materials collected at this site in 1979 Walter and Luis Alvarez and their colleagues discovered an overabundance of the rare metal iridium, which led them to propose that the earth was struck by a large meteorite or other astronomical body. It was the aftermath of this impact, they suggested, that caused the extinction of the dinosaurs and of many other species that disappeared at the Cretaceous-Tertiary (K-T) boundary. Another faction argues that purely terrestrial causes—specifically massive volcanism—can account for both the iridium layer and the extinctions. The coin in the photograph is a 50-lira piece, which shows Vulcan at his forge. (Photograph courtesy of Alessandro Montanari, University of California at Berkeley.)

Glen   What Killed the Dinosaurs?   65

Figure 2. Iridium enrichment at the K-T boundary has been detected in sedimentary deposits from almost 100 sites throughout the world, including these rocks from the Raton Basin of Colorado and New Mexico. Whereas the Gubbio sediments accumulated in a marine environment, the Raton area was a coal swamp at the time of the K-T transition. The boundary layer is the white stripe of claystone, which has a thin ribbon of iridium-enriched material at its upper margin. The dark overlying layer is a coal bed. The photograph was made near Trinidad, Colorado, by Glen A. Izett of the U.S. Geological Survey.

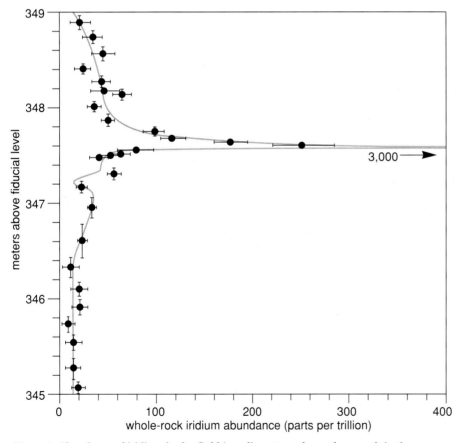

Figure 3. Abundance of iridium in the Gubbio sediments reaches a sharp peak in the Cretaceous-Tertiary boundary clay, but also has "shoulders" of heightened abundance in the limestones that straddle the boundary. The shoulders are composed of about a dozen minor iridium peaks (Asaro et al. 1988, Crockett et al. 1988). The peaks in the Tertiary shoulder tend to be reduced to a smooth curve when the abundance there is compared with that in the clay rather than that elsewhere in the limestone, but the peaks in the Cretaceous rock persist, and so do questions about their cause. The measurements were made by the Alvarez group.

the solar system's passage through the spiral arms of the galaxy. Gradual causes, such as changes in sea level, climate or seawater chemistry, and effects of plate tectonics, had also had their day. There had even been earlier attempts to blame meteoritic impact. Digby McLaren—in his presidential address to the Paleontological Society in 1970—had said that a meteorite caused a mass extinction 365 million years ago, long before the one at the K-T boundary. But McLaren's idea, although based on painstaking analysis of the rock and fossil record, was not compelling.

What made the difference in the reception of the Alvarezes' proposal was the iridium layer. Unlike other hypotheses, this one was based on an empirical finding, from which testable predictions and a program of experiments could be formulated. After discovering the iridium anomaly at Gubbio and postulating a global dust cloud, the Alvarezes predicted that there should be similar concentrations of iridium elsewhere in the world at the K-T boundary. Within a few years, more than 50 such anomalies had been found, all over the globe; now 95 are known (Alvarez and Asaro 1990; Smit and Hertogen 1980; Ganapathy 1980; Kyte, Zhou and Wasson 1980; Orth et al. 1981, Kyte and Wasson 1986). The concentration of iridium in this global layer is typically between 10 and 20 parts per billion, which works out to about half a million tons of iridium spread over the surface of the planet— roughly the amount, according to the Alvarezes, that would be released by the explosion of a meteorite about 10 kilometers across.

In the decade since the Alvarez group introduced its hypothesis, other strands of evidence have emerged to support it. Perhaps the most persuasive evidence of a K-T impact, apart from the iridium itself, consists of signs interpreted as damage done by the meteorite to the rock it struck. A 10-kilometer rock slamming into the earth at a speed of, say, 45,000 miles per hour would deliver a tremendous shock. Bruce Bohor and his colleagues at the U.S. Geological Survey were the first to find grains of quartz in the K-T boundary layer that show the microscopic traces of such a shock: long, parallel planes, called lamellae, along which rows of atoms in the crystal lattice of the quartz have

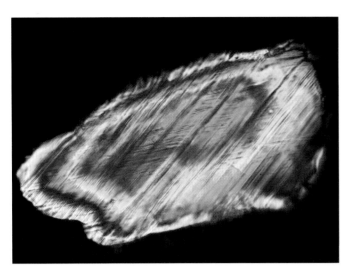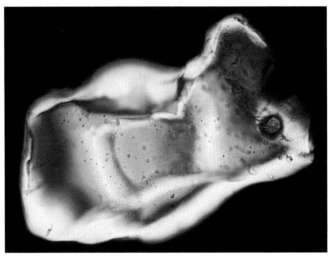

Figure 4. Shocked quartz, a mineral often present at meteorite craters, has been found in several areas of the world at the K-T boundary. The effects of shock on a quartz grain can be seen when a thin section is viewed under a microscope between crossed polarizing filters. The shocked grain (left) has multiple sets of intersecting lamellae, which signal disruption of the crystal lattice. An unshocked grain (right) has no lamellae. Some have argued that shocked quartz can only be generated by an impact, but others suggest that explosive volcanism could also create such lamellae. Shocked quartz was first discovered in K-T sediments by Bruce Bohor and his colleagues at the U.S. Geological Survey. These photographs, made by Izett, show a shocked grain from the K-T boundary stratum at Teapot Dome in Wyoming and an unshocked grain from a Cretaceous sandstone in the Raton Basin.

been disturbed (Bohor et al. 1984, 1987). Old hands in impact studies consider such multiple, intersecting sets of lamellae in quartz to be diagnostic of a meteorite strike. Until Bohor found them at K-T boundary sites, they had been known only from the immediate vicinity of established meteorite craters and in rocks at nuclear explosion sites.

In addition to disrupting the crystal lattice of a quartz grain, an intense shock might change the crystal structure altogether. In quartz, oxygen atoms form a tetrahedron around each atom of silicon, but at extreme pressures (greater than 8.5 gigapascals, or 85 kilobars) the atoms can be rearranged into a denser, octahedral form called stishovite. Stishovite is exceedingly rare in the earth's crust; until recently it had been identified only at a few meteorite craters, and even there it was found only in minute quantities. Last year, however, John F. McHone and his colleagues at Arizona State University reported that they had isolated it from K-T boundary clay at Raton, New Mexico (McHone and Nieman 1989). If their result can be confirmed at other sites, many investigators would consider the argument for a K-T impact strengthened.

Another line of evidence for impact is the presence of small spherical particles that many believe were formed from the rapid cooling of molten droplets of rock splashed into the atmosphere by a meteorite impact.

The mineralogy of the spherules varies considerably. Some regard them as true impact products (tektites) that have been chemically altered after burial (Smit and Kyte 1984; Montanari et al. 1983, 1986; Pollastro and Pillmore 1987). Others believe they were formed within the rock by chemical processes (Naslund et al. 1986; Izett 1987).

Still another way of investigating what happened at the K-T boundary is to examine the distribution of elements other than iridium, as well as the isotopes of various elements. In 1983 Karl Turekian and J. M. Luck at Yale University analyzed two isotopes of osmium (another platinum-group metal) in materials recovered from the K-T boundary layer. But Turekian now thinks the analysis by itself neither ruled out an impact nor proved that the osmium could not have a terrestrial source.

The smoking gun, of course, would be the impact crater. In spite of strenuous efforts, it has not been definitely identified. That is not entirely surprising; most of the earth's surface is ocean, and in the past 66 million years much of the ocean floor has been subducted into the mantle at oceanic trenches. Thus a sea-floor crater may have been obliterated by now. If the meteorite struck a continent, the crater could have been hidden by erosion, destructive movements of the crust, or filling in by sediments or lava flows.

Although the sediment layer at the K-T boundary contains iridium and shocked quartz at a large number of places throughout the world, the layer varies in other ways. The composition at all sites suggests an impact into granitic rocks or quartz-rich sediments, which are typically continental; but at some sites the chemistry of the layer also suggests a basaltic, oceanic target! Such mixed evidence could have been produced by multiple impacts into different kinds of crust or by a single great impact at a site of diverse composition, such as a coastal area.

Some new evidence favors the latter possibility. At a K-T boundary site on Haiti, A. R. Hildebrand and W. V. Boynton (1990) of the University of Arizona have found shocked quartz and a half-meter-thick layer of what they consider to be altered tektites. They propose that a giant meteorite splashed down southwest of Haiti in the Columbian Basin region of the Caribbean, digging a crater 300 kilometers in diameter—twice the size of any known crater. Bohor and Russell Seitz (1990), however, have argued that the Haitian tektites could also have been produced by an impact just south of western Cuba, some 1,350 kilometers northwest of the Columbian Basin site. That part of Cuba is underlain by a geologic unit of K-T age that looks nothing like rocks elsewhere in Cuba. It consists of huge boulders—as much as 12 meters across—compressed in a layer that is as much as 350 meters thick

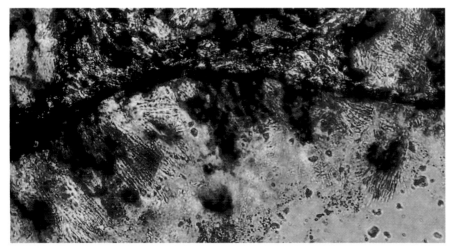

Figure 5. Stishovite, a mineral created by alteration of quartz at extremely high pressure, is considered another telltale marker of impact processes. Whereas ordinary quartz has a tetrahedral crystal structure, in which four oxygen atoms surround each silicon atom, stishovite has a denser, octahedral structure. In this photomicrograph stishovite appears as needlelike crystals, some of which aggregate to form dark purple clusters. The specimen, about 0.3 millimeter across, is from the Vredefort Ring in South Africa, which most workers consider to be the remnant of an impact crater much older than the Cretaceous. John F. McHone and his colleagues at Arizona State University have recently reported evidence of stishovite in K-T clay at Raton, New Mexico. (Photograph courtesy of McHone.)

near the south coast and gets progressively thinner toward the north. Bohor and Seitz suggest that the boulders were hurled onto Cuba by a giant impact, and that the coastline south of Havana may be the rim of the crater.

An impact layer gets thinner away from its crater, just as a layer of volcanic ash gets thinner away from its vent. If Bohor's belief that the impact layer grows thicker south-ward among North American sites is correct (some think not), then both Hildebrand's and Bohor's sites seem plausibly placed in areas to the south of North America.

Another possible impact site is the Manson structure in Iowa. It seems to have formed at K-T time, but it is too small—35 kilometers across—to have produced the postulated K-T catastrophe by itself (Hartung and Anderson 1988). Charles B.

Officer and Charles L. Drake of Dartmouth University (1989) question the age of the Manson structure and do not regard it as an impact crater. Glen A. Izett of the U.S. Geological Survey, however, notes that unpublished seismic profiles across part of the Manson structure indicate it is "a classic impact structure."

If Manson is an impact crater, it may be one of several small K-T craters, with others remaining to be discovered. The fossil record provides some justification for this view—and also for the alternative hypothesis of volcanic cause, to which we shall turn shortly. Erle Kauffman of the University of Colorado (1988) and others have shown that the great terminal kill—marked by the big iridium spike—is preceded by a series of sharply defined smaller extinctions. They occur over a few million years, forming a stair-step pattern. That idea is now also supported by J. F. Mount and Stanley V. Margolis of the University of California at Davis (1985) and others, who find that in some cases spikes of carbon and oxygen isotopes in the rock record coincide almost precisely with the occurrence of the stepwise extinctions.

The seemingly persuasive pattern of evidence for step-wise extinctions has moved the impactors, over the past few years, to all but abandon their idea of a single great terminal Cretaceous impact. Instead they now embrace a revised theory of multiple, serial impacts, perhaps due to a comet swarm. Such a swarm of comets was proposed by S. V. M. Clube and W. M. Napier (1984) to produce "a series of spikes" over a few million years; Piet Hut and others (1985) also found a way to bombard the earth with a dozen or so greater and lesser comets during a period of one to two million years.

The Killing Mechanism

The idea of a comet shower with a series of small, Manson-size impacts spread over a million years or more seems useful in explaining the apparent smaller, stepped extinctions, but it is questionable that the cumulative effects of those impacts could have produced the great kill at the very end of the Cretaceous. Some impactors call for a comet swarm that includes an iridium-rich giant precisely at the K-T boundary.

A new twist on the multiple-

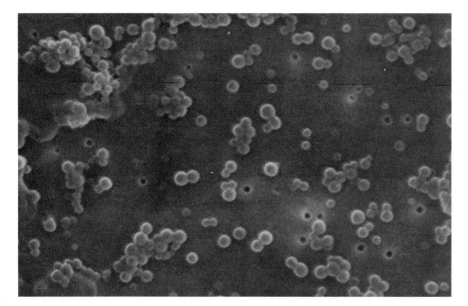

Figure 6. Carbon particles, presumed to be soot, were isolated from a K-T boundary clay in New Zealand. Some workers have attributed such carbon to global wildfires set off in the aftermath of an impact. The carbon particles are the small spheres, which cling together like bunches of grapes. The scanning electron micrograph, which magnifies the image some 20,000 times, was made by Wendy S. Wolbach of the University of Chicago.

Figure 7. Spherules found in certain K-T sediments are thought by some investigators to be microtektites, formed from droplets of molten rock thrown into the atmosphere by an impact. Here two spherules from the Dogie Creek site in central Wyoming are seen in cross section. The wall is composed of gorceixite, an aluminum phosphate mineral that also includes several other metals. The spherule on the left is filled with gypsum; the one on the right is hollow. The spherules found in various areas of the world are quite diverse, and there is controversy about their origin. (Photograph courtesy of Izett.)

impacts idea has recently been proposed by Peter H. Schultz of Brown University. He argues that if a 10-kilometer meteorite were to strike the earth's surface at 45,000 miles per hour and at a low angle (less than 10 degrees from the horizontal), it would break up into a swarm of fragments ranging in size from a tenth of a kilometer to a kilometer in diameter. The fragments would ricochet downrange; one such object might have excavated the Manson crater. Schultz has simulated such an event in the laboratory with a high-velocity gun and has filmed the results. He finds that an oblique impact would eject enough debris into orbit to give the earth a ring like one of Saturn's. Over time (it is not clear how much time) the debris would fall back to earth, but meanwhile it would kill life on the planet by blocking out a significant amount of sunlight. The gradual descent of the impact debris long after the initial cataclysm might explain why some of the chemical evidence for a K-T impact is spread out in the stratigraphic record.

Schultz's work notwithstanding, the climatic effects of a K-T impact, assuming there was one, can best be described as extremely uncertain. The Alvarezes' original idea of a global stratospheric dust cloud that would block out the sun for months or years and choke off photosynthesis is now widely regarded as too simple. But there is no agreement on precisely what to put in its place. Suggestions have run the gamut of contemporary environmental concerns, from nuclear winter (a scenario that was actually inspired by the Alvarez hypothesis) to acid rain to the greenhouse effect.

The acid-rain idea has been advanced since 1981 by Ronald Prinn and his colleagues at the Massachusetts Institute of Technology. In a series of increasingly detailed papers, they have argued that the plume of ejecta kicked up by a giant impact would shock-heat the atmosphere, and that the heat would cause nitrogen and oxygen to combine with water vapor to form nitric acid (Prinn and Fegley 1987). Raining out of the atmosphere in concentrated form, the acid would kill ocean-dwelling organisms, and perhaps others as well. Percolating into the ground, it might also leach away fossilized remains; that, says Gregory Retallack of the University of Oregon and others (1987), might explain the three-meter interval of barren rock that at certain sites separates the youngest (and therefore uppermost) dinosaur fossils from the K-T boundary. The putative three-meter gap (which actually varies from 1 meter to 4.5 meters at North American sites) has often been cited by opponents of the impact hypothesis as evidence that the dinosaurs died out before the postulated impact.

According to H. J. Melosh and his colleagues at the University of Arizona, the plume of vaporized rock ejected by the impact—consisting of roughly equal parts material from the impactor and from the earth's crust—would do much more than cause acid rain. The Arizona workers' calculations suggest that most of the plume would leave the earth's atmosphere, and in the process it would take some of the atmosphere with it; in other words, the earth would be stripped of part of its gaseous blanket. Much of the gas would be permanently lost, but the plume material itself would recondense into solid particles, and those particles would follow ballistic paths around the planet, like microscopic ICBMs. Ballistic trajectories, say Melosh and his coworkers, do a better job than stratospheric winds (the original Alvarez view, but now invoked by those who favor a volcanic cause for the extinctions) in explaining how iridium and shocked quartz from a single impact could have been distributed around the earth. What is more, as the ejected particles re-entered the atmosphere they would heat it even more effectively than the original plume. At the earth's surface, the thermal radiation would be on the order of 10 kilowatts per square meter for as much as several hours after the impact. Such a power level, Melosh and his colleagues note, is "comparable to that obtained in a domestic oven set at 'broil'" (Melosh et al. 1990).

The thermal radiation would ignite wildfires that might surge over most of the globe, even into areas that were shielded from the initial heat blast by thick clouds. Evidence for such fires has been found at several K-T sites by Edward Anders, Wendy Wolbach and their colleagues at the University of Chicago (Wolbach et al. 1985 and 1988). The evidence takes the form of a high concentration of graphitic carbon, presumed to be soot, in the iridium-bearing boundary layer. The concentration of carbon is exceptional, it should be noted, only if one accepts the Alvarez hypothesis as true—that is, only if one believes the K-T boundary layer consists of impact fallout deposited in a few months or years rather than millennia. The carbon itself is not primary evidence for an impact or even for a global wildfire. (Indeed, at a Danish K-T site the carbon seems to have been deposited in pulses, which suggests to some investigators that it could not have originated in a global fire. Still others think the carbon isotope ratios suggest a volcanic source for the carbon.)

Another good way to heat up a planet, of course, is through the greenhouse effect. Enhanced greenhouse warming has been suggested as a killing mechanism almost from the time the impact hypothesis was first put forward. Recently John O'Keefe and Thomas Ahrens of the California Institute of Technology (1989) have provided experimental support for the impact-greenhouse

Figure 8. High-velocity impacts studied in the laboratory offer a glimpse of what might happen in a large-scale earth impact. The photograph at left shows the spray of debris emitted when a high-speed projectile strikes a target of silica sand at a shallow angle. The projectile is an aluminum sphere a quarter inch in diameter, accelerated by high-pressure gases to a speed of 5.5 kilometers per second. (The typical impact velocity of an asteroid, for comparison, is about 20 kilometers per second.) The experiment, conducted by Peter H. Schultz of Brown University and Donald Gault of the NASA Ames Research Center, suggests that a large meteorite or comet striking the earth at a grazing angle would inject a substantial quantity of debris into earth orbit, where it might form a ring like those of Saturn. Material falling back to the earth over a period of years would cause many secondary impacts. The light-gas gun, shown above, is at NASA Ames. The barrel is mounted on the red, Y-shaped frame, which tilts to adjust the impact angle; the target is housed in the blue vacuum chamber.

scenario. They shot steel balls from a cannon into various types of rock at 4,500 miles per hour and measured the amount of carbon dioxide released by the impacts. They calculate that if a 10-kilometer asteroid were to slam into limestone or some other carbon-rich formation, it would increase the atmospheric concentration of CO_2 by a factor of from two to five almost overnight. The resulting heat would have devastated life.

Some of the plants that suffered most during the K-T catastrophe were single-cell marine algae, whose numbers may have dropped by as much as 95 percent. Whether or not the decline was caused by a climatic change, the decline itself may have had an important effect on climate. Michael Rampino and Tyler Volk of New York University (1988) have noted that some of the microalgae that were most affected, notably the chalky coccolithophores, are prodigious emitters of the substance dimethyl sulfide. In the atmosphere dimethyl sulfide is converted into sulfate particles, which serve as the nuclei around which water condenses to form clouds. According to Rampino and Volk, a drastic drop in the population of microalgae would greatly reduce the cloud cover long after the initial catastrophe. With more sunlight streaming in, the earth would heat up to levels lethal for many forms of life.

To summarize, there is no shortage of ideas on how an impact might kill organisms on the earth. Indeed, it sometimes seems as if students of the K-T extinctions, like the nuclear powers, have armed themselves with enough weaponry to extinguish all life on the planet many times over.

The Pattern of Extinctions
The selectivity of the extinctions at the end of the Cretaceous Period has been widely discussed (Clemens

Figure 9. Exceptionally thick layer of K-T boundary sediments has been identified in Haiti by A. R. Hildebrand and W. V. Boynton of the University of Arizona. The layer, indicated by the bracket at right, contains shocked quartz as well as objects that Hildebrand and Boynton identify as tektites. The unusual thickness of the layer—it is about half a meter thick in the outcrop seen here, which is near the village of Beloc—suggests that if the sediments are ejecta from an impact, the site of impact may be nearby. (Photograph courtesy of Hildebrand.)

1982; Emiliani 1982; Hsü 1982; Thierstein 1982; Hallam 1987, 1988; Kauffman 1988). Certain groups of land and ocean organisms seem to have expired gradually in their approach to the K-T boundary; others made it through but then declined shortly afterward (Keller 1989); but many groups, such as the oceanic, limey-shelled, microscopic floaters (foraminifera and coccolithophores) as well as land plants in western North America and eastern Asia, appear to have suffered a catastrophic killing right at the boundary (Tschudy et al. 1984). McLaren (1989) lucidly analyzed such "knife-blade" killing boundaries in the rock record. He focused on the total biomass exterminated rather than on the number of taxa made extinct, since just a few survivors will keep a group off the extinction list, even though almost all of its members have been killed.

The extinction pattern in the oceans shows that tropical groups and those that fed on plant plankton were the most vulnerable. Jennifer Kitchell of the University of Wisconsin at Madison and others (1986) suggest that the oceanic plankton—such as the diatoms and dinoflagellates that make up much of the earth's biomass—survived in greatest numbers because of their resting spore stage of reproduction.

On land the large reptiles (over 50 pounds) suffered much more than their smaller lake- and stream-dwelling relatives. Perhaps big creatures had a harder time finding shelter (Russel 1979). One might guess that land plants that reproduce by seeds, spores, pollen and rhizomes—reproductive bodies that could lay in the soil protected from catastrophe—would have a good chance of survival. That is just what is found; after a short-term crisis right at the boundary, the flowering plants recovered rapidly (Tschudy and Tschudy 1986, Johnson et al. 1989, Wolfe 1990).

David Jablonski (1986) argues that mass extinctions are different from normal or background extinction patterns that hold for most of geologic time. He thinks that the attributes that made for survivorship in normal times did not work during mass extinctions, and that only very widespread geographical distribution of a group seemed to help it survive.

Oceanic organisms that fed on plants were more vulnerable than

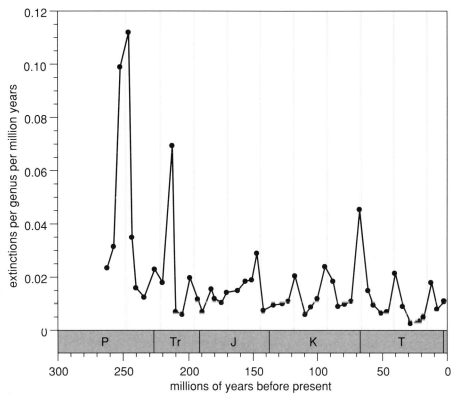

Figure 10. Periodicity in the fossil record of extinctions suggests to some observers that a regular, recurrent event is disrupting the earth's biosphere every 26 million years. The graph is based on an analysis by David Raup and John Sepkoski of the University of Chicago of 11,000 genera of marine organisms. The extinction rate is measured per genus per million years; in other words, a rate of 0.1 signifies there is a one-tenth chance that any given genus will become extinct in a period of a million years. The colored lines represent intervals of 26 million years, which seem to be well aligned with the extinction peaks over the past 150 million years; at earlier times the correlation is not as close. The series of letters at the bottom of the graph designate periods of geologic history: Permian, Triassic, Jurassic, Cretaceous and Tertiary.

scavengers and consumers of detritus—a catastrophe would have produced a long-lasting stockpile of organic waste for those who live on it. On the continents, the doomed herbivorous dinosaurs probably ate living plants, but the small mammals that survived so well likely ate insects. Insects are hardy life-form, and indeed may be why we are here today, evolved from our insect-eating ancestors.

Periodicities

The K-T mass extinction was not the only one in the earth's history, nor even the worst—that distinction goes to the event that marked the transition from the Permian Period to the Triassic, some 250 million years ago, when as many as 96 percent of all species in the ocean vanished. There is evidence in the fossil record for perhaps half a dozen other mass extinctions. One of the most interesting suggestions to grow out of the impact hypothesis is the idea that these mass

dyings have recurred with a regular period of 26 million years.

The proposal was made by David Raup and John Sepkoski of the University of Chicago in 1984. It was based on a statistical analysis of the extinction record of 3,500 families of marine organisms. (Marine families are used because they are most numerous.) Since then the analysis has been extended down to the taxonomic level of genera, of which it now includes 11,000 (Raup and Sepkoski 1986, 1988). According to Sepkoski, the 26-million-year cycle, evident as peaks in the extinction rate, shows up even more strongly than it did in the original data.

Raup and Sepkoski's 1984 results stimulated a rush to find the cause of periodic extinctions. Within a short time three separate mechanisms had been proposed, all of which involved ways of gravitationally knocking comets out of their orbits beyond the outer planets and sending showers of them toward the

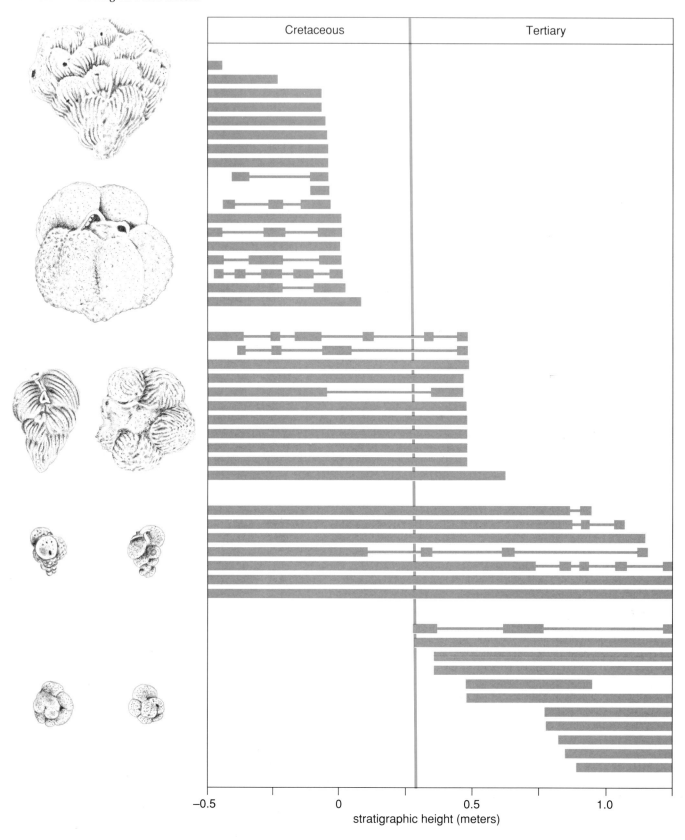

Figure 11. Stairstep pattern of extinctions noted by some observers of the fossil record casts doubt on the idea that a single catastrophic impact could have been responsible for the Cretaceous-Tertiary transition. Gerta Keller of Princeton University has examined the distribution of fossil foraminifera in a section of sediments at the Brazos River in Texas. The iridium layer that marks the K-T boundary in these deposits is shown here as a colored line. At least one major wave of extinctions is found below this layer, and there are two more episodes of loss above it. New species begin to appear at and above the level of the iridium layer. The entire sequence of sediments shown here represents roughly a million years of earth history. It is notable that the first foraminifera to succumb were those with the largest and most elaborate shells; the survivors, and the new Tertiary forms, were small, plain, cosmopolitan species. A few representative specimens are shown here. (Adapted from Keller 1989.)

earth. In the first hypothesis, formulated independently by two different groups, the sun has a faint, dwarf companion—dubbed Nemesis, or the death star, by the Berkeley group—whose eccentric orbit carries it near the solar system every 26 million years (Davis, Hut and Muller 1984; Whitmire and Jackson 1984). In the second hypothesis, a tenth planet that lies beyond Pluto on a highly eccentric orbit passes through a hypothetical trans-Neptunian belt of comets every 26 million years (Whitmire and Matese 1985, 1986). In the third hypothesis, the solar system's vertical oscillations through the plane of the galaxy periodically bring it near dense clouds of interstellar gas that perturb the comets (Rampino and Stothers 1984a).

One problem with this last idea is that it calls for a mass extinction a million years ago that did not happen; another is that interstellar gas clouds exist above and below the galactic plane as well as in it. The main problem with the other two theories is a lack of observational evidence: neither Nemesis nor Planet X has been found. A group led by Richard Muller of the University of California at Berkeley, however, is still looking for the death star.

Quite apart from the question of a causative mechanism, the evidence that impacts recur periodically is not conclusive, at least so far. In 1984 Rampino and Stothers (1984a, 1984b) and independently Alvarez and Muller (1984) suggested that periodic impacting of the earth could be read from crater ages that seemed to be clustered at the times of mass extinctions. But their samples consisted of too few craters, and the results left many workers unconvinced. Nor has an extensive search for iridium anomalies associated with other mass extinctions been particularly fruitful. Apart from the one at the K-T boundary, the only other pronounced and geographically widespread iridium anomaly is at the 34-million-year-old extinction layer of late Eocene age.

Raup and Sepkoski's methods have been criticized on the grounds that the fossil record is too incomplete, and the dating of extinctions is too uncertain, to justify their claims of periodicity. Raup and Sepkoski offer an interesting rebuttal: such uncertainties, they argue, would merely introduce random noise into the

Soames Summerhays (Photo Researchers, Inc.)

Figure 12. Volcanist alternative to the impact hypothesis argues that all the distinctive features of the K-T boundary, including the iridium anomaly, can be explained by purely terrestrial causes. In this photograph volcanic gases spew from a fumarole in the Kilauea volcano on the island of Hawaii. Sulfur dioxide and other substances in such gases might have cooled the planet and later produced lethal acid rain. William H. Zoller of the University of Washington and others have found significant quantities of iridium in volcanic gases; the amount of iridium in the erupting rock, however, is at least two orders of magnitude less than what occurs in the K-T boundary layer. To account for the amount of iridium in the K-T boundary layer, and for the extinctions, the volcanists propose eruptions on a scale never seen in historical times.

Figure 13. Simulation of a plume in the earth's mantle suggests a mechanism that might bring iridium-bearing material from near the core up to the surface. In this physical model of mantle circulation, constructed by David Loper and Kevin McCartney, colored water is overlain by denser corn syrup, much as hot material close to the earth's core is overlain by cooler and denser rock in the upper mantle. The photographs, made over an interval of about six minutes, form a sequence that reads from left to right. Initially, the rising blobs of water transport material only slowly, but once a plume "conduit" is established in the final three frames, the rate of transport increases substantially. (Photographs courtesy of Loper and McCartney.)

data, and if a systematic 26-million-year signal emerges above such a noisy background, there is all the more reason to believe the signal is real. This argument, however, has not won over all the skeptics. In an episode that perhaps epitomizes the polarization of views on periodicity, two members of the statistics department at the same university, after reviewing the Raup and Sepkoski data and analyses, found themselves opposed in the extreme: One said the finding of a periodicity was correct; the other said it was "junk."

Raup's interest in periodicity led him to analyze reversals in the polarity of the earth's magnetic field; he found a 30-million-year signal (1985). Shortly thereafter, however, he abandoned that conclusion when Timothy Lutz of the University of Pennsylvania (1985, 1986) suggested that Raup's periodicity was merely an accident of record length. That was followed by the surmise of R. B. Stothers (1986) that Raup was originally correct, and Lutz's analysis was flawed. Lutz, Antoni Hoffman and others (1985, 1986) as well as Kitchell and Dan Pena (1984) and others have disputed the statistical methodology by which periodicity has been identified in the earth's history. The flood of claims and counterclaims sends the onlooker reeling (Raup and Sepkoski 1988, Stigler and Wagner 1988).

Prompted by Raup's paper on periodic magnetic reversals, Muller teamed with Donald Morris (1986), to propose that reversals of the earth's magnetic field were caused by impact-induced glaciation. They argued that the formation of polar ice would alter the rate of rotation of the crust and mantle, thereby inducing a velocity shear across the earth's liquid core and disturbing the geomagnetic dynamo that produces the magnetic field. A refined version of their hypothesis (1989) has been criticized by David Loper and Kevin McCartney (1990) who do not believe that impacts can cause magnetic reversals and surmise that no viable model yet links impacts with reversals, or with episodes of massive volcanic outpouring that in some cases seem to occur at the times of mass extinction. Still other causes for magnetic reversal have been advanced since the advent of the impact hypothesis in 1979, but they seem not to have evoked much response.

The issue of periodicity was moved to a new arena in 1987 by Herbert Shaw of the U. S. Geological Survey in Menlo Park, California. In a pioneering paper in *Eos*, he used recently evolved methods of nonlinear dynamics, which are different from conventional methods of statistical analysis, to search for patterns in several earth processes that are repeatable, but not necessarily symmetrical or equally spaced. In the case of the mass-extinction debates, he thinks it impossible to demonstrate valid patterns of periodicity because the data sets are too limited for either conventional or nonlinear anal-

yses. He thus put questions of periodicity in a new light, but perhaps further still from resolution.

The Volcanist Alternative

Sulfur dioxide and other substances spewed into the stratosphere by volcanic eruptions would cool the planet for a year or two, extinguishing some species, and would then gradually fall out as acid rain, which would kill off others. Over many thousands of years, carbon dioxide emitted by the volcanoes would warm the planet through the greenhouse effect. The end result would be a series of selective extinctions spread over a considerable length of time. According to many who favor the volcanic hypothesis, such a pattern is similar to what the fossil record shows for latest Cretaceous time.

The test of the volcanist alternative, of course, is its ability to account for the evidence at the boundary that has been used to support the impact hypothesis. Start with the iridium anomaly. Iridium is rare in the earth's crust because it and the other siderophile elements were dragged into the core and the mantle by iron; thus a volcano that coughed up rock from deep in the mantle might also bring up iridium.

Volcanoes that rise up along boundaries where tectonic plates collide—such as those that rim the Pacific—have shallow sources. But "hot-spot" volcanoes, which form in the middle of plates—the Hawaiian volcanoes are good examples—are thought by some geophysicists to be fed by plumes of hot material rising from deep in the mantle, perhaps even from the boundary with the core. In fact, iridium has been detected at hot-spot volcanoes, beginning in 1983 with measurements done at Kilauea in Hawaii by William H. Zoller of the University of Washington. The amount of iridium in the erupting rock is at least two orders of magnitude less than what is observed at the K-T boundary, but the concentration in the volcanic gases, and in sublimates deposited by the gases, is significant.

More recently Zoller and his colleagues have analyzed the Kilauea emissions for the relative abundances of other rare elements, such as selenium and arsenic. They conclude that the elemental signature of the volcanic emissions is closer than that of meteorites to the one typically observed at the K-T boundary. However, Frank Kyte of the University of California at Los Angeles and C. P. Strong and others (1987) seem to reflect an alternative view that the data on volcanic emissions published so far do not necessarily support the volcanist cause.

Of the other volcanoes where iridium has been detected, one is particularly noteworthy. It lies on Réunion Island in the southwest Indian Ocean (Toutain and Meyer 1989). The hot spot that now feeds Réunion is believed to be the same one that created a vast formation of flood basalts called the Deccan Traps in western India. As early as 1972 P. R. Vogt suggested a connection between the Deccan Traps—roughly a million cubic kilometers in volume—and the K-T extinction. The Deccan, one of the largest known continental deposits of volcanic rock, were erupted in just a few great pulses over about a million years. The greatest pulse seems to have encompassed the time of the K-T mass extinction (Courtillot 1990). Not surprisingly, the Deccan Traps have become a touchstone for the volcanists. Paleontologists have also looked to the Deccan for solutions since 1981, when Dewey McLean first proposed that such large-scale volcanism had disturbed the carbon cycle and turned the earth into a lethal greenhouse for many forms of life.

But the volcanic hypothesis must not only explain the iridium at

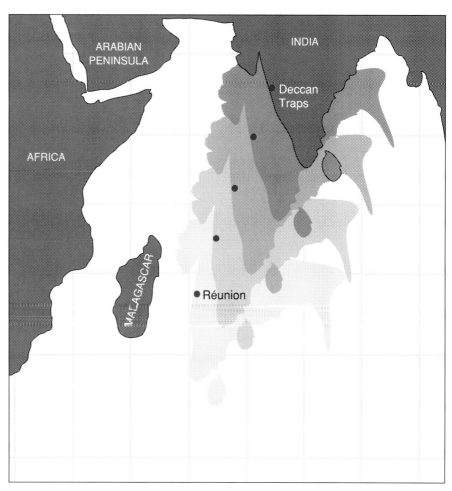

Figure 14. Mantle plume that is now associated with volcanic activity on the island of Réunion in the Indian Ocean may have produced copious outpourings of lava at the end of the Cretaceous. At that time the Indian landmass was located over the plume, and the eruptions formed a vast landscape called the Deccan Traps. Iridium has been detected in emissions from the Réunion volcano; on the other hand, no significant iridium enhancement has been found in the Deccan rocks.

the K-T boundary; it must also explain the shocked quartz. The conventional view is that the pressures needed to produce the characteristic features of shocked quartz—especially multiple sets of intersecting shock lamellae—are found only in impact zones. Volcanists have argued that such pressures might be created in the magma chamber of an exploding volcano (Rice 1987). They also note that little is known about the ways in which a wide range of shock features are produced in quartz, especially at the high temperatures found in volcanic settings. Neville Carter and Alan Huffman of Texas A&M University and others (Carter et al. 1990, Huffman et al. 1990) are currently trying to test this idea in laboratory experiments.

The best hard evidence for the volcanist argument would be the discovery of shocked quartz with multiple lamellae that is clearly volcanic in

origin. Officer, one of the most vocal spokesmen for the volcanic hypothesis (Officer and Drake 1983, 1989), says he now knows of shocked quartz with multiple sets of shock lamellae that has been produced by processes other than impact. His paper, which is in press, is awaited with considerable interest. The response of impact proponents, however, can already be predicted. Even if shocked quartz can be produced by a volcanic explosion, they will say, the Deccan basalts are not of the kind associated with explosive eruptions; the Deccan formation is thought to be the product of more gentle, Kilauea-type flows. They will also argue that only an impact, not volcanism, could propel iridium and shocked quartz into ballistic trajectories around the globe to settle within the same thin sedimentary boundary layer (Alvarez 1986). The volcanists invoke explosive volcanism and giant dust storms

Figure 15. Deccan Traps were created by pulses of volcanic activity that apparently lasted about a million years. Each of the striations visible in the more-distant range of hills represents a separate flood of basalt. The photograph shows the Western Ghats range near Mahabaleshwar, south of Bombay. (Photograph courtesy of John Mahoney, Hawaii Institute of Geophysics.)

to do the same job of transport (Officer and Drake 1989).

The impact proponents will further point out that the iridium level in the Kilauea or Réunion emissions, when extrapolated to the size of the Deccan Traps, falls short by a factor of 10 in the amount of iridium needed to produce the global layer at the K-T boundary. Some volcanists would probably agree that the Deccan eruptions were not by themselves enough to produce the K-T iridium layer or the mass extinctions. Instead, these investigators generally invoke a more loosely defined episode of global volcanism as the cause of the K-T crisis. There is some evidence, for example, that the Walvis Ridge, a submarine mountain range in the southeast Atlantic, was erected by hot-spot eruptions at about the time of the K-T boundary (Officer et al. 1987).

Another type of support for the idea of global volcanism comes from mathematical models and simple physical models. Several volcanists have put forward models that attempt to explain not only mass extinctions but also other geological

phenomena, such as the reversal of the earth's magnetic field and the wandering of its poles, as an effect of plumes rising off the core (Loper and McCartney 1986, 1988; Courtillot and Besse 1987). The key element of the models is a thermal boundary layer, a kind of blanket on the surface of the core, whose presence has been deduced from seismic data and whose thickness increases and decreases episodically.

At a certain thickness in each cycle the boundary becomes unstable and lets loose a covey of hot plumes. Rising to the surface, the plumes trigger bursts of polar motion, volcanic and tectonic activity, and extinctions. Meanwhile plumes of cold iron sink from the core-mantle boundary into the core, disrupting the currents that generate the geomagnetic field and causing the field to flip back and forth. According to David Loper of Florida State University, this sort of thing may happen every 30 million years or so. A recent computer simulation, one of the first to model the mantle as a spherical body in three dimensions, suggests that hot-spot

plumes may indeed rise to the surface from the core-mantle boundary (Bercovici et al. 1989).

Prospects

The debate on the question of what killed the dinosaurs shows no sign of ending soon. A satisfying resolution, of course, would be for everyone to agree that impacts cause extinctions by triggering volcanic eruptions.

That idea has had its proponents. Ever since Ahrens (1983) estimated that the impact of a 10-kilometer body would produce an earthquake of about magnitude 13 on the Richter scale, many have thought that such a quake would have rung the earth like a bell, relaxed an enormous amount of crustal strain, and set off every sleeping volcano on the globe. That idea was finally detailed in 1987 by Rampino and elaborated by D. Alt and others in 1988. Other students of mantle dynamics, however, such as Jason Morgan of Princeton University and G. Schubert of the University of California at Los Angeles, seem skeptical.

On an important subsidiary issue there is some prospect of resolution. One of the key claims made by volcanists is that iridium and shocked quartz are not in fact concentrated in the K-T boundary layer, as impact proponents maintain, but rather are spread over a couple of meters above and below the boundary (Crockett et al. 1988). If that were true, the iridium would have been deposited over hundreds of thousands of years, which would accord with the volcanic alternative. Impact proponents challenge the claim, saying that little is known of how iridium is transported in nature, how long it remains in the sea and in lake waters before it is removed by natural processes, and how far it can move around in the sediment or rock after deposition. Such lack of understanding provides fertile ground for argument.

After several years of disagreement, Officer's Dartmouth group and Alvarez's Berkeley group collaborated in sampling crucial sections around Gubbio. The samples have been split for blind testing at various laboratories, with the effort overseen—with the enthusiastic approval of both sides—by Robert Greenburg of the University of Miami. The results should be in later this year. Whatever the outcome, it is unlikely that it will end these extremely diverse and complicated debates. Furthermore, there is little reason to desire such an end, since the debates have been extraordinarily fruitful.

The issues raised by evidence for the coincidence of an impact, massive volcanic eruptions and the second greatest extinction of life in earth history continue to hold the interest of both the public and the scientific community. They have thrust forward the centuries-old question of how to balance catastrophism against gradualism, and have forced a reexamination of the nature of the fossil record and the role of mass extinctions in evolution. The debates teach us again that the success of a hypothesis, or its service to science, lies not only in its perceived "truth," or power to displace or reduce a predecessor idea, but perhaps more in its ability to promote the research that illuminates suppositions and areas of vagueness that lie hidden in unchallenged canons. By this standard the iridium-backed impact hypothesis, whatever its eventual fate, has already served science well.

Bibliography

Ahrens, T. J., and J. D. O'Keefe. 1983. Impact of an asteroid or comet in the ocean and extinction of terrestrial life. Proceedings of the 13th Lunar and Planetary Science Conference, Part 2, Journal of Geophysical Research 88: Supplement pp. A799–A806.

Alt, D., J. M. Sears and D. W. Hyndman. 1988. Terrestrial maria. The origins of large basalt plateaus, hotspot tracks and spreading ridges. Journal of Geology 96:647–662.

Alvarez, L. W., W. Alvarez, F. Asaro and H. V. Michel. 1980. Extraterrestrial cause for the Cretaceous-Tertiary extinction. Science 208:1095–1108.

Alvarez, W., and F. Asaro. 1990. Progress report on an ancient murder mystery. (In press.)

Alvarez, W., and R. A. Muller. 1984. Evidence from crater ages for periodic impacts on the earth. Nature. 308:718–720.

Asaro, F., H. V. Michel, L. W. Alvarez, W. Alvarez and A. Montanari. 1988. Impacts and multiple iridium anomalies. Eos 69:301–302.

Bercovici, D., G. A. Glatzmaier and G. Schubert. 1989. Three-dimensional modes of convection in an internally heated spherical shell. Eos. 70:1358.

Bohor, B. N., and R. Seitz. 1990. Cuban K/T catastrophe. Nature. 344:593.

Bohor, B. F., E. E. Foord, P. J. Modreski and D. M. Triplehorn. 1984. Mineralogic evidence for an impact event at the Cretaceous-Tertiary boundary. Science. 224:867–869.

Bohor, B. F., P. J. Modreski and E.E. Foord. 1987. Shocked quartz in the Cretaceous-Tertiary boundary clays: Evidence for a global distribution. Science. 236:705–708.

Carter, N. L., C. B. Officer and C. L. Drake. 1990. Dynamic deformation of quartz and feldspar: Clues to causes of some natural crises. Tectonophysics. 171:373–391.

Clemens, W. A. 1982. Patterns of survival of the terrestrial biota during the Cretaceous/Tertiary transition. Geological Society of America Special Paper 190:407–413.

Clube, S. V. M., and W. M. Napier. 1984. The microstructure of terrestrial catastrophism. Monthly Notices of the Royal Astronomical Society 211:953–968.

Courtillot, V. E., and J. Besse. 1987. Magnetic field reversals, polar wander, and core-mantle coupling. Science 237:1140–1147.

Courtillot, V. E. 1990. What caused the last mass extinction. (In press.)

Crockett, J. H., C. B. Officer, F. C. Wezel, and G. D. Johnson. 1988. Distribution of noble metals across the Cretaceous/Tertiary boundary at Gubbio, Italy: Iridium variations as a constraint on the duration and nature of Cretaceous/Tertiary boundary events. Geology 16:77–80.

Davis, M., P. Hut and R. A. Muller. 1984. Extinction of species by periodic comet showers. Nature 308:715–717.

Emiliani, Cesare. 1982. Extinctive evolution: Extinctive and competitive evolution combine into a unified model evolution. Journal of Theoretical Biology. 97:13–33.

French, B. M. 1990. Twenty-five years of the impact-volcanic controversy: is there anything new under the sun? or inside the Earth? Eos. 71:411–414

Ganapathy, R. 1980. A major meteorite impact on earth 65 million years ago: Evidence from the Cretaceous-Tertiary boundary clay. Science. 209:921–923.

Gould, S. J. 1965. Is uniformitarianism necessary? American Journal of Science 263: 223-228.

Hallam, A. 1987. End-Cretaceous mass extinction event: Argument for terrestrial causation. Science. 238:1237–1242.

Hallam, A. 1988. A compound scenario for the end-Cretaceous mass extinctions. Revista Española de Paleontología. No. Extraordinario, Paleontology and Evolution: Extinction Events 7–20.

Hartung, J. B., and R. R. Anderson. 1988. A compilation of information and data on the Manson impact structure. Lunar and Planetary Institute Reports. No. 88–08.

Hildebrand, A. R., and W. V. Boynton. 1990. Proximal Cretaceous-Tertiary boundary impact deposits in the Caribbean. Science 248: 843–847.

Hoffman, A. 1985. Patterns of family extinction depend on definition and geological time scale. Nature. 315:659–662.

Hoffman, Antoni, and Joe Ghiold. 1985. Randomness in the pattern of "mass extinction" and "waves of origination." Geology 122:1–4.

Hsü, K., et al. 1982. Mass mortality and its environmental and evolutional causes. Science. 216:249.

Huffman, A. R., J. M. Brown and N. L. Carter. 1990. Temperature dependence of shock induced microstructures in tectonosilicates. In S. C. Schmidt, J. N. Johnson and L. W. Davison, eds., Proceedings of the American Physical Society Topical Conference on Shock. (In press.)

Hut, P., W. Alvarez, W. Elder, E. G. Kauffman, T. A. Hansen, G. Keller, E. M. Shoemaker and P. Weissman. 1985. Comet showers as possible causes of stepwise mass extinctions. Eos Abstract. 66:813.

Izett, G. A. 1987. Authigenic "spherules" in K-T boundary sediments at Caravaca, Spain, and Raton basin, Colorado, New Mexico, may not be impact derived. Geological Society of America Bulletin. 98:78–86.

Jablonski, D. 1986. Evolutionary consequences of mass extinctions. In D. M. Raup and D. Jablonski, eds., Pattern and Process in the History of Life. Springer-Verlag.

Johnson, K., D. J. Nichols, M. Attrep and C. J. Orth. 1989. High resolution leaf-fossil record spanning the Cretaceous/Tertiary boundary. Nature. 340:708–711.

Kauffman, E. G. 1988. Stepwise mass extinctions. Revista Española de Paleontología. No. Extraordinario, Paleontology and Evolution: Extinction Events 58–71.

Keller, Gerta. 1989. Extended Cretaceous/Tertiary boundary extinctions and delayed population changes in planktonic foraminifera from Brazos River, Texas. Paleonoceanography. 4:287–332.

Kitchell, J. A., and D. Pena. 1984. Periodicity of extinctions in the geologic past: Deterministic versus stochastic explanations. Science. 226:689–656.

Kitchell, J. A., D. L. Clark and A. M. Gombos. 1986. Biological selectivity of extinction: a link between background and mass extinction. Palaios. 1:501–511.

Kyte, F. T., Z. Zhou and J. T. Wasson. 1980. Siderophile-enriched sediments from the Cretaceous-Tertiary boundary. *Nature.* 288: 651–656.

Kyte, F. T., and J. T. Wasson. 1986. Accretion rate of extra-terrestrial matter: Iridium deposited 33 to 67 million years ago. *Science.* 232:1225–1229.

Loper, D. E., and K. McCartney. 1986. Mantle plumes and periodicity of magnetic field reversals. *Geophysical Research Letters.* 13: 1525–1528.

Loper, D. E., and K. McCartney. 1988. Shocked quartz found at the K/T boundary. *Eos.* 69:961,971–972.

Loper, D. E., and K. McCartney. 1990. On impacts as a cause of geomagnetic field reversals or flood basalts. *Geological Society of America Special Paper* 247. (In press.)

Luck, J. M., and K. K. Turekian. 1983. $^{187}Os/^{186}Os$ in manganese nodules and the Cretaceous-Tertiary boundary. *Science* 222: 613–615.

Lutz, Timothy M. 1985. The magnetic reversal record is not periodic. *Nature.* 308:404–407.

Lutz, T. M. 1986. Evaluating periodic, episodic and Poisson models: Reversals and meteorite impacts. *Geological Society of America 99th Annual Meeting Abstracts with Program,* p.677.

Matese J. J., and D. P. Whitmire. 1986. Planet X and the origins of the shower and steady-state flux of short-period comets. *Icarus.* 65: 37–50.

McHone, J. F., and R. L. Nieman. 1989. K/T boundary stishovite: Detection by solid-state nuclear magnetic resonance and powder x-ray diffraction. *Geological Society of America Abstracts,* p. A120.

McLaren, D. J. 1970. Time, life and boundaries. *Journal of Paleontology.* 44:801–815.

McLaren, D. J. 1989. Detection and significance of mass killings. In *Rare Events, Mass Extinction and Evolution, Second Workshop on Rare Events in Geology, Beijing, 1987.* Special issue of *Historical Biology* 2:5–15.

McLean, D. M. 1981. Cretaceous-Tertiary extinctions and possible terrestrial and extraterrestrial causes. Proceedings of a workshop held in Ottawa, Canada, 19–20 May 1981 by the K-TEC group. *Syllogeous* No. 39. National Museums of Canada.

Melosh, H. J., N. M. Schneider, K. J. Zahnle and D. Latham. 1990. Ignition of global wildfires at the Cretaceous/Tertiary boundary. *Nature.* 343:251–254.

Montanari, A., R. L. Hay, W. Alvarez, F. Asaro, H. V. Michel, L. W. Alvarez and J. Smit. 1983. Spheroids at the Cretaceous-Tertiary boundary are altered impact droplets of basaltic composition. *Geology* 11:668–671.

Montanari, Alessandro. 1986. Spherules from the Cretaceous/Tertiary boundary clay at Gubbio, Italy: The problem of outcrop contamination. *Geology.* 14:1024–1026.

Mount, J. F., S. V. Margolis, William Showers, P. Ward and E. Doehne. 1986. Carbon and oxygen isotope stratigraphy of the Upper Maastrichtian, Zumaya, Spain: A record of oceanographic and biologic changes at the end of the Cretaceous Period. *Palaios* 1:87–92.

Muller, R. A., and D. E. Morris. 1986. Geomagnetic reversals from impacts on the Earth. *Geophysical Research Letters.* 13:1177–1180.

Muller, R. A., and D. E. Morris. 1989. Geomagnetic reversals driven by sudden climate changes. *Eos.* 70:276.

Naslund, H. R., C. B. Officer and G. D. Johnson. 1986. Microspherules in Upper Cretaceous and lower Tertiary clay layers at Gubbio, Italy. *Geology* 14:923–926.

Officer, C. B., and C. L. Drake. 1983. The Cretaceous-Tertiary transition. *Science.* 219: 1383–1390.

Officer, C. B., A. Hallam, C. L. Drake and J. C. Devine. 1987. Late Cretaceous and paroxysmal Cretaceous/Tertiary extinctions. *Nature.* 326:143–149.

Officer, C. B., and C. L. Drake. 1989. Cretaceous/Tertiary extinctions: We know the answer, but what is the question? *Eos* 70: 659–660.

O'Keefe, J. D., and J. T. Ahrens 1989. Impact production of CO_2 by the Cretaceous/Tertiary extinction bolide and the resultant heating of the earth. *Nature.* 338:247–249.

Orth, C. J., J. S. Gilmore, J. D. Knight, C. L. Pillmore, R. H. Tschudy and J. E. Fassett. 1981. An iridium abundance anomaly at the palynological Cretaceous-Tertiary boundary in northern New Mexico. *Science.* 214: 1341–1343.

Pollastro, R. M., and C. L. Pillmore. 1987. Mineralogy and petrology of the Cretaceous-Tertiary boundary clay bed and adjacent clay-rich rocks, Raton Basin, New Mexico and Colorado. *Journal of Sedimentary Petrology.* 57:456–466.

Prinn, R. G., and B. F. Fegley, Jr. 1987. Bolide impacts, acid rain, and biospheric traumas at the Cretaceous-Tertiary boundary. *Earth and Planetary Science Letters.* 83:1–15.

Rampino, M. R., and R. B. Stothers. 1984a. Terrestrial mass extinctions, cometary impacts and the sun's motion perpendicular to the galactic plane. *Nature.* 308:709–712.

Rampino, M. R., and R. B. Stothers. 1984b. Geological rhythms and cometary impacts. *Science.* 226:1427.

Rampino, M. R. 1987. Impact cratering and flood basalt volcanism. *Nature.* 327:468.

Rampino, M. R., and T. Volk. 1988. Mass extinctions, atmospheric sulphur and climatic warming at the K/T boundary. *Nature.* 332:63–65.

Raup, David M. 1985. Magnetic reversals and mass extinctions. *Nature.* 314:341–343.

Raup, D. M., and J. J. Sepkoski. 1984. Periodicity of extinctions in the geologic past. *Proceedings of the National Academy of Sciences of the U.S.A.* 81:801–805.

Raup, D. M., and J. J. Sepkoski. 1986. Periodic extinctions of families and genera. *Science.* 231:833–836.

Raup, D. M., and J. J. Sepkoski. 1988. Testing for periodicity of extinction. *Science.* 241: 94–96.

Retallack, G. J., G. D. Leahy and M. D. Spoon. 1987. Evidence from paleosols for ecosystem changes across the Cretaceous/Tertiary boundary in eastern Montana. *Geology.* 15: 1090–1093.

Rice, Alan. 1987. Shocked minerals at the K/T boundary: explosive volcanism as a source. *Physics of Earth and Planetary Interiors.* 48: 167–174.

Russel, D. A. 1979. The enigma of the extinction of the dinosaurs. *Annual Reviews of Earth and Planetary Sciences.* 7:163–182.

Schultz, P. H. Prolonged global catastrophes from oblique objects. *Proceedings of Catastrophes in Earth History.* (In press.)

Shaw, H. R. 1987. The periodic structure of the natural record and nonlinear dynamics. *Eos.* 68:1651–1664.

Smit, J., and J. Hertogen. 1980. An extraterrestrial event at the Cretaceous-Tertiary boundary. *Nature.* 285:198–200.

Smit, Jan, and Frank T. Kyte. 1984. Siderophile-rich magnetic spheroids from the Cretaceous boundary in Umbria, Italy. *Nature.* 310:304–305.

Stigler, S. M., and M. J. Wagner. 1988. Response to Raup, D., and J. J. Sepkoski, Jr., Testing for periodicity of extinction. *Science.* 241:96–98.

Stothers, R. B. 1986. Periodicity of the earth's magnetic field. *Nature.* 322:444–446.

Strong, C. P., R. R. Brooks, S. M. Wilson, R. O. Reeves, C. J. Orth, X.-Y. Mao, L. R. Quintana and E. Anders. 1987. A new Cretaceous-Tertiary boundary site at Flaxbourne River, New Zealand: Biostratigraphy and geochemistry. *Geochemica et Cosmochemica Acta.* 51:2769–2777.

Thierstein, H. R. 1982. Terminal Cretaceous plankton extinctions: a critical assessment. *Geological Society of America Special Paper* 190: 385–399.

Toutain, Jean-Paul, and G. Meyer. 1989. Iridium-bearing sublimates at a hot-spot volcano (Piton de la Fournaise, Indian Ocean). *Geophysical Research Letters.* 16:1391–1394.

Tschudy, R. H., C. L. Pillmore, C. J. Orth, J. S. Gilmore and J. D. Knight. 1984. Disruption of the terrestrial plant ecosystem at the Cretaceous-Tertiary boundary, western interior. *Science.* 225:1030–1032.

Tschudy, R. H., and B. D. Tschudy. 1986. Extinction and survival of plant life following the Cretaceous/Tertiary boundary event, western interior, North America. *Geology.* 14:667–670.

Vogt, P. R. 1972. Evidence for global synchronism in mantle plume convection, and possible significance for geology. *Nature.* 240: 338–342.

Whitmire, D. P., and A. A. Jackson. 1984. Are periodic mass extinctions driven by a distant solar companion? *Nature.* 308:713–715.

Whitmire, D. P., and J. J. Matese. 1985. Periodic comet showers and Comet X. *Nature.* 313:36–38.

Wolbach, W. S., R. S. Lewis and E. Anders. 1985. Cretaceous extinctions: evidence for wildfires and search for meteoritic material. *Science.* 230:167–170.

Wolbach, W. S., I. Gilmour, E. Anders, C. J. Orth and R. R. Brooks. 1988. Global fire at the Cretaceous-Tertiary boundary. *Nature.* 334:665–669.

Wolfe, J. A. 1990. Palaeobotanical evidence for a marked temperature increase following the Cretaceous/Tertiary boundary. *Nature.* 343:153–156.

Zoller, N. H., J. R. Parrington and J. M. Phelan Kotra. 1983. Iridium enrichment in airborne particles from Kilauea volcano. *Science.* 222: 1118.

Recent Animal Extinctions:
Recipes for Disaster

Many late-prehistoric extinctions share ingredients: climate and vegetation change, human hunting, and the arrival of exotic animals

David A. Burney

Figure 1. Thousands of years ago, North America rivaled Africa's Serengeti Plains for big game. A typical scene is depicted in this mural painted in 1919 for the American Museum of Natural History by Charles R. Knight. The reconstruction is based on fossils found in the La Brea tar pits in California. Sabertooth cats, ground sloths, mastodons and dire wolves roamed the plains, as California condors looked on from above. All but the California condor disappeared suddenly about 11,000 years ago at approximately the same time that evidence for human beings and rapid climatic changes appears in the fossil record. (Reproduced with permission by the Department of Library Services, American Museum of Natural History.)

David A. Burney is an associate professor in the Department of Biological Sciences at Fordham University. In the late 1970s, he studied the effects of human activities on cheetahs, earning an M.Sc. degree in conservation biology from the University of Nairobi. He went on to learn sediment coring and pollen analysis with D. A. Livingstone at Duke University, where he received a Ph.D. and participated in a multidisciplinary study of recently extinct animals in Madagascar. This work, supported by the National Science Foundation and the National Geographic Society, has continued for more than a decade, and Burney's research efforts have expanded to include parallel studies in Hawaii, Puerto Rico, Africa and North America. Address: Department of Biological Sciences, Fordham University, Bronx, NY 10458.

Perhaps we are all growing slightly weary of being reminded that we are in the midst of a crisis in species survival, a decline in diversity that may ultimately exceed the greatest catastrophes in the earth's long history of mass extinctions. But whether or not the point has been overstated, the arena of public life is crowded with debates over management decisions concerning species in danger of extinction. It is useful to ask whether these debates can be informed by studying extinctions of the past.

Among the small group of paleo-ecologists, archaeologists, paleontolo-gists and other scientists around the world who have focused their research on multidisciplinary investigations of the extinction record, there are some who have also been looking for ways to bridge the gap between the past that they study and the current public concern over biodiversity. The present period is likely to be viewed in the near future as a time when humanity made, or failed to make, some tough choices between environmental and economic priorities that will decide the fate of much of the planet's remaining biota. There are good practical reasons to know all we can about past extinctions.

Unfortunately, as skeptics would be quick to point out, few extinctions have been well documented. Many of the most interesting, such as the events that claimed many large-animal species or a large portion of regional flora and fauna, took place in prehistoric times. They left only vague stratigraphic clues that may be hard to read, if they can be detected at all. The challenge is to uncover evidence that can be interpreted with sufficient detail and in the proper chronological sequence.

Like detectives on a murder case with only a few stale and murky clues, my colleagues and I have had a frustrating, but always fascinating time. The scarce and sometimes ambiguous details of the lives and deaths of an array of extinct creatures seem to be falling into place now, thanks to dogged persistence and recent scientific advances. The patterns that we see emerging are not only relevant to the present crisis but also, to a chilling extent, remarkably similar. It appears possible that the spread of early human populations interacted with changes in climate and habitat to contribute to a series of extinctions that shaped the biological communities that surround us. Unfortunately, the same factors can be seen at work today in some of the richest of those communities.

Only 12,000 years ago, the landscape from Florida to California provided a spectacle to rival the Serengeti Plains of Africa in large-animal diversity. Extinct Pleistocene animals of North America are the stuff of schoolchild fantasies: woolly mammoths, mastodons, saber-tooth cats, giant ground sloths and the like. In addition to these seemingly exotic animals, the North American fauna also included many forms that have survived elsewhere, such as cheetahs, lions, zebras, yaks, tapirs, capybaras and spectacled bears.

This wildlife spectacle ended with apparent suddenness. Since about 30,000 years ago—as human populations started to expand into previously uninhabited regions, but well before modern technology—most continents and large islands throughout the world lost half or more of their large-animal species. On some oceanic islands, virtually all the larger species, and many smaller ones as well, disappeared, often rapidly.

It stands to reason that the past extinctions most applicable to the present situation are these relatively recent ones. There is much interest in the extinction of the dinosaurs, but the great age of this event and the types of sites and dating methods available dictate that causes and timing are difficult to study, except on a long geological time scale. Fortunately we can date fossils of the past 30,000 years or so reliably enough to know critical details about timing. Ecological events that have taken place in this time frame provide the most direct and concrete information available on which to base predictions concerning future environments and human impacts.

Eurasia: The Art Lives On

Some of the most elegant evidence that early human beings and extinct animals crossed paths can be seen in the caves of southern France and northern Spain. Cave paintings, engravings and sculptures created 10,000 to 30,000 years ago portray a fauna far more diverse than that surviving today in Europe's parks and reserves. Some of these animals, such as the horse, the cow and the reindeer, have survived as domesticated animals. But the woolly mammoth (*Mammuthus primigenius*),

Figure 2. Male human effigy carved about 20,000 years ago in mammoth ivory serves as a reminder that human beings and mammoths did indeed live at the same time. This figure, found in the Czech Republic, was apparently a puppet with movable limbs. A facsimile is on display at the American Museum of Natural History. (All photographs courtesy of the author.)

woolly rhinoceros (*Coelodonta antiquitatis*), cave bear (*Ursus spelaeus*) and giant deer (*Megaloceros gigantea*, also called the Irish elk), among others, survive only as fossils and in the artwork of Cro-Magnon Man.

Since these and some other extinct Eurasian animals were common during the last Ice Age and gradually disappeared about 10,000 to 15,000 years ago (about the time the climate became warmer), early investigators very reasonably suggested that climate change was the probable cause of their extinction. Work in recent decades, however, has cast doubt on such a simple explanation. Paleoclimatological data from deep-sea sediment cores show that while these animals thrived, the climate made more than 20 shifts from glacial to interglacial conditions over the last 2.5 million years. It is quite likely that open-country grazers, as the mammoth and rhinoceros certainly must have been, may have been forced to move far to the north when temperate-zone forests began to recolonize Europe after each thaw. Recent archaeological evidence suggests that it was only within the last 30,000 to 40,000 years that human beings mastered the considerable technical skills needed to colonize the far-northern tundra regions.

Thus, suggests anthropologist Richard Klein of Stanford University, human beings may have triggered these extinctions through a combination of hunting and habitat modification in northern areas that may have served as refuges during earlier periods of warm climate. In a sense, both the climate and humanity were responsible, because they happened to combine effects in a way that was deadly for these species.

Australia: Disaster Down Under

While the northern continents were still under the cold grip of the last Ice Age, Australia and New Guinea were in the midst of a different kind of struggle. During times in the Pleistocene when sea level was more than 100 meters lower than it is now, Australia and New Guinea were joined by a broad land bridge, and the channel separating New Guinea from the Malaysian Archipelago was much narrower. Perhaps some time between 30,000 and 60,000 years ago, the ancestors of the Australian aborigines crossed this water gap and spread southward on the island continent. As-

sessing the age of fossils with radiocarbon dating techniques is difficult in this time period, but it is clear that, by the end of the last Ice Age, Australia and New Guinea had been swept by a wave of large-animal extinctions to rival that of any other continent in the late Pleistocene.

Australia lost 19 genera, totaling more than 50 species. The marsupial fauna associated with the region today is diverse, but it only includes one genus of large animals, the *Macropus* kangaroos. Thirteen other genera of giant marsupials became extinct, including the rhinoceros-like marsupial *Diprotodon*, which weighed perhaps two tons or more. *Thylacoleo* (sometimes called the "giant killer possum," since it may have been a fierce carnivore) was represented by two species the size of a leopard. One giant kangaroo, *Palorchestes*, stood 3–1/2 meters tall. In addition to the extinct giant marsupials, there was a huge lizard (even larger than the Komodo dragon), giant horned tortoises, and an ostrich-like bird similar to the surviving emu.

The Australian case remains puzzling; some of these species are thought

Figure 3. Mauritian dodo, *Raphus cucullatus*, has become a symbol of human-caused extinctions. These approximately turkey-sized, flightless pigeons were hunted to extinction by the 17th century in the Mascarenes not long after Europeans discovered these previously uninhabited Indian Ocean islands. This reconstruction is on display at the American Museum of Natural History.

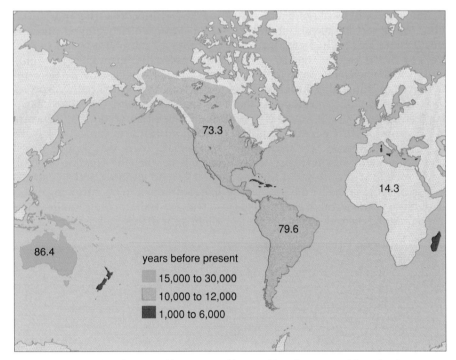

Figure 4. Temporal and geographic pattern of late-prehistoric catastrophic extinction events throughout the world follows the stepwise pattern in which human beings colonized ever more remote regions. Australia and New Guinea suffered major large-animal extinctions some time between 30,000 and 15,000 years ago. North and South America were particularly affected between 10,000 and 12,000 years ago. The Greater Antilles' Mediterranean islands, New Zealand, Madagascar and other oceanic islands experienced major extinctions much more recently, within the past 1,000 to 6,000 years. In contrast, people have inhabited Africa and Eurasia for a much longer time, so those continents have experienced fewer recent extinctions. Numbers indicate percentages of extinct genera during the past 100,000 years.

to have survived more than 10,000 years after the arrival of human beings. Climatic change is often invoked in these extinctions, since there is not much archaeological evidence for large-scale hunting. It has been difficult, however, to visualize how continent-wide climate changes could have been severe enough to do the job. It is tempting to look for an animal that might have been introduced by the prehistoric aborigines that could have proliferated and disrupted native populations. The dingo, Australia's wild dog, might seem a likely candidate, but it appears from the archaeological record that the dingo was introduced long after some of these animals became extinct. It may have played a role in later extinctions, but much work remains to be done in Australia, as there is no entirely convincing theory for the cause of the massive die-offs down under.

The *Blitzkrieg* Hypothesis

The debate over the causes of the late-Pleistocene extinctions has centered in the Americas, perhaps primarily because theories proposed by Paul Mar-

tin and his colleagues at the University of Arizona have sparked a worldwide interest in systematically testing competing ideas with data from multidisciplinary research. The losses in North America are truly staggering to contemplate, dwarfing even many modern environmental catastrophes: 33 genera of large animals, including seven families and one order (elephants and their relatives).

Radiocarbon dates from charcoal associated with mammoth remains in archaeological sites, from protein-rich bones found at the Rancho La Brea tar pits of southern California, and from ground-sloth dung from western caves, all show the same trend: that many of these animals disappeared more or less simultaneously within a few centuries of 11,000 years ago. At the same time or just before, the first solid evidence of human activity appears at many sites in the form of specialized hunting tools, the distinctive Clovis projectile points associated with Paleoindian hunters. Several controversial sites around the continent have been reported to show earlier evidence of Native Americans, but the first

widespread, fully accepted human evidence in North American seems to coincide with this extinction event.

More than two decades ago, this prompted Martin to propose one of the more plausible versions of "Pleistocene overkill" to explain these extinctions. Overkill theories hinge on the notion that it was primarily the hunting activities of the earliest Native Americans that precipitated the faunal crash. These early inhabitants presumably crossed the Bering Land Bridge from Siberia to Alaska when sea level was lower, near the end of the last Ice Age. One of the most serious scientific criticisms of Martin's theory is that these first Americans were probably few in number and were technically incapable of mounting such mass slaughter in so short a time. But in the late 1960s the Russian scientist M. I. Budyko published a series of equations showing that, theoretically at least, such a human-caused faunal crash was possible. He calculated that a small founding population of human beings could multiply fast enough to eventually outstrip the capacity of very large mammals (with their slow birthrate) to replenish their numbers under a steady hunting regime. Then in the mid-1970s James Mosimann of the National Institutes of Health teamed up with Paul Martin to develop a computer model incorporating several key ideas that together came to be known as the *Blitzkrieg* Hypothesis.

In this model, a large human population would not be required to do the job, if the extinctions spread over the Americas as a "front." The early American big-game hunters, they theorized, may have multiplied rapidly (for people) under conditions of unlimited food supply, low incidence of human disease, and an efficient social organization. Beginning in Alaska, where the extinctions and first occurrence of projectile points appear slightly earlier than on the rest of the continent, human hunters encountered a fauna of large animals unfamiliar with the danger they posed. As these animals declined and human beings multiplied, the hunters could have moved like a wave southward and eastward, laying waste to the naive animals as they went. Some support for the idea comes from two kinds of evidence. First, the southern and eastern parts of the continent seem to show progressively later dates for the arrival of the first Native

Americans and the latest occurrences of some of the extinct animals. Second, careful analysis of archaeological sites suggests only a brief period of overlap between the first hunters and the last mammoths.

For a while, it looked as if South America also conformed to the pattern of *Blitzkrieg*. Now this looks less certain, as some sites on that continent seem to be dating to times that are earlier rather than later than dates from the southwestern United States and other areas closer to the Bering Strait. This may not be a definitive test, however, as some Native American groups may have arrived earlier, but may have been less interested in big-game hunting or too few in number to have an effect. Alternatively, the small number of radiocarbon dates that do not agree with the *Blitzkrieg* pattern could simply be wrong.

Other overkill models allow for small human populations in the Americas as much as 20,000 years before their population levels became a threat to the large-mammal prey populations. It is still a matter of debate the extent to which hunting, versus other human activities and natural climatic change, may have played a role. One thing seems fairly certain: North America's ecology was drastically changed, long before European contact, by the loss of so many important faunal elements. The giant beasts that must have modified their environment on the scale of elephants were an especially critical loss. Giant ground sloths, for instance, probably satisfied their dietary need for tree leaves by breaking down large limbs and whole trees. This particular kind of disturbance has been largely absent from the Holocene forests of recent millennia— for the first time in millions of years of American environmental history.

South America has probably suffered from this type of change even more. No other continent lost as many animals in the late Pleistocene. In one article, Dan Janzen of the University of Pennsylvania and Paul Martin speculate reasonably that the structure of many forests in Central and South America may have been fundamentally changed by the loss of large animals that played a major role in the dispersion of large seeds of forest trees and in opening up the forest by breaking down limbs and small trees.

The list of animals that became extinct during this period in South America is staggering: It includes 46 or more genera, more extinctions than are known to have taken place during all of the previous nearly 3 million years on the continent. Among these are four whole families of sloth relatives, one genus of giant rodents, four of large carnivores, four of mastodons, three of horses, and 11 of cloven-hoofed animals including peccaries, camels and deer.

Figure 5. Sabertooth cats were an important top carnivore in the large-mammal ecosystems of the Pleistocene in North America, but they went extinct during the catastrophic decline of large-prey species about 11,000 years ago. This skeleton is found in the Smithsonian Institution.

Losing the Sweepstakes

Perhaps the supreme irony of the global pattern of late-Pleistocene extinctions is that isolated oceanic islands, generally regarded by island biogeographers as particularly extinction-prone ecosystems, were the last places to be affected. On the surface, this fact seems to run contrary to nearly everything that biologists think they know

Figure 6. *Ptaiochen pau*, depicted in this reconstruction by artist Julian Hume, went extinct in the Hawaiin Islands along with the other large waterfowl known as "moa-nalos" after the arrival of the Polynesians about 1,500 years ago. These flightless birds were undoubtedly vulnerable to human predation, which probably contributed to their demise.

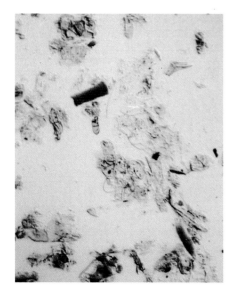
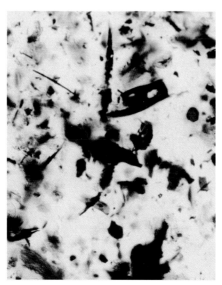

Figure 7. Charcoal levels in sediment cores help trace the history of fires in a region before and after human habitation. Two slices from a core from Madagascar show very little charcoal (*left*) and a great deal of charcoal (*right*) about a century later, following human colonization, indicating many human-caused fires in the area. Fires set by hunters, pastoralists and agriculturalists may rapidly and often dramatically alter an area's vegetation. For example, grasslands might have spread into some previously wooded areas. Such alteration of vegetation may contribute to extinctions.

about evolution. The faunas of oceanic islands (islands not connected to a continent even when sea level is at its lowest during ice ages) are generally regarded as "unbalanced." That is, they are descended from a few founding populations that are not representative of the full array of genetic material

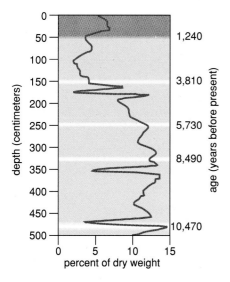

Figure 8. Charcoal diagram from Lake Tritrivakely, Madagascar, shows that fires occurred in this highly seasonal environment prior to the arrival of people. Charcoal concentrations increased above immediately preceding background levels at the presumed time of human arrival in this remote highland locality, 1,200 to 1,300 years ago.

available on the continents. Through a process that the late G. G. Simpson described as a "sweepstakes," the ancestors of animals native to oceanic islands reach the remote land mass by swimming, rafting on floating debris, or some other highly uncertain means. Most native oceanic-island mammal faunas are therefore dominated by animals that can swim well, such as elephants, hippopotami and deer, or that are small enough to cling to debris, such as rodents and insectivores. In addition, especially on the islands that are farthest from the continents, birds and reptiles may occupy a disproportionate share (from the continental viewpoint) of ecological niches. Plants face similar limitations and challenges on remote oceanic islands.

Thanks to the unique genetic configurations and evolutionary pressures posed by isolated islands, however, these founding animals soon become quite different from their continental ancestors who "won" the sweepstakes. Large mammals tend to evolve into dwarf forms, small mammals may get larger, birds may become flightless and reptiles may become huge, lumbering herbivores like the island tortoises, or fierce top carnivores such as the giant monitor lizards of Komodo Island.

For millennia after the late-Pleistocene extinctions, these seemingly fragile and ungainly ecosystems ap-

parently thrived throughout the world. This is one of the soundest pieces of evidence against purely climatic explanations for the passing of Pleistocene faunas. In Europe, for instance, the last members of the elephant family survived climatic warming not on the vast Eurasian land mass, but on small islands in the Mediterranean—an even warmer climate. Radiocarbon dates suggest, for instance, that dwarf elephants persisted on Tilos, a tiny island in the Aegean, until perhaps 4,000 to 7,000 years ago. On Mallorca, in the Balearic Islands, the endemic goat-antelope *Myotragus* survived until 5,000 years ago or less and turns up in some Bronze Age archaeological sites.

But these Mediterranean island megafaunas did eventually become extinct. Thirteen genera of large and small mammals disappeared, along with giant tortoises. Many investigators believe the cause was probably a combination of human activities (hunting and landscape modification) and the introduction of rats, dogs, goats and other animals that came with the people. But a major problem in substantiating this hypothesis has been establishing exactly when people arrived. Only a few archaeological sites have turned up so far that show an overlap between human beings and extinct fauna. I was fortunate a few years ago to visit one of these, Corbeddu Cave on the island of Sardinia. Here, Paul Sondaar of Rijksuniversiteit Utrecht in the Netherlands and his Dutch and Italian colleagues have excavated Late Stone Age artifacts and fragments of human bone in a layer containing many bones, some possibly modified by human beings, of the extinct deer *Megaceros cazioti*. In younger strata above this level, the deer disappears, but the extinct rabbit relative *Prolagus sardus* persists until a later time, then disappears too. Dates from the level containing the earliest human bones are as recent as about 9,000 years.

An even more spectacular example of human interaction with an extinct Mediterranean island megafauna comes from the recent work on Cyprus of A. H. Simmons of the University of Chicago and D. S. Reese of the Field Museum in Chicago. The site of Akrotiri-Aetokremnos provides evidence that, a little over 10,000 years ago, hunter-gatherers camped there and hunted the endemic pig-sized pygmy hippopotamus. More than 240,000 bones representing at least 200 individuals have been found in the archaeological site, some cut and burned. A few pygmy elephants are also represented, along with shellfish and bird bones. In the slightly younger upper strata, the proportion of extinct megafauna in the midden assemblage decreases, implying that these hunters may have been rather efficient at rounding up the unsuspecting hippopotami and depleting this resource. So far, however, sites like this are extremely rare, and detailed chronologies remain to be worked out.

Even less is known about the extinctions on islands of the West Indies. Twenty-one genera of endemic mammals have become extinct since the late Pleistocene, although few dates have been obtained. Among the extinct denizens of Caribbean islands were giant rodents, dwarf ground sloths and large insectivores. Huge birds of prey were probably the top carnivores in some of these peculiar ecosystems. Only a few archaeological sites have been found with bones of extinct animals, but radiocarbon dates from Antigua and the Greater Antilles do show that some of the extinct fauna were present as recently as 4,000 to 7,000 years ago, which is also the time period when the first Native Americans are believed to have reached the islands.

G. K. Pregill at the University of California at San Diego and Storrs Olson of the Smithsonian Institution have suggested that some of the extinctions may have been caused by the combined effects of rising sea level (decreasing the size of some of these islands to less than half) and climatic change. Until more of the extinct animals and the timing of human arrival on these islands are firmly dated, this idea cannot be fully evaluated. Mammalogist Ross MacPhee of the American Museum of Natural History and his colleagues have begun a search for sites in the West Indies containing clues to the fate of the extinct animals. They are now working on some promising sites in Cuba. One interesting clue has turned up from our collaboration in Puerto Rico. MacPhee and I collected a 7,000-year sediment core from Laguna Tortuguero, a freshwater lake on the north coast of the island. Lida Pigott Burney of Fordham University analyzed the core for stratigraphic charcoal particles, a record of past burning in the environment. The charcoal record shows that, about the time Native Americans are thought to have begun

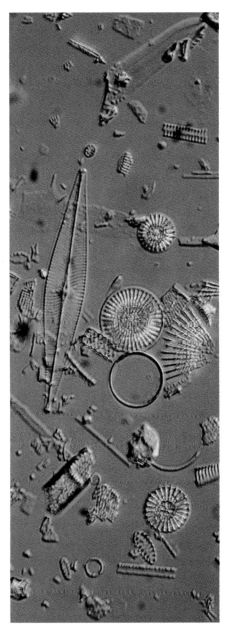

Figure 9. Photomicrographs of sedimentary microfossils help scientists reconstruct prehuman and anthropogenic environments. Different species of microscopic life thrive under different climatic, nutritional and chemical conditions, and scientists can surmise a great deal about local environments from the species present at different levels in the fossil record. For example, these diatom fossils from lake sediments provide information about the pollutants in the lake and help set the date for the arrival of human beings in the area.

colonizing the Greater Antilles, charcoal values make a sudden increase of several orders of magnitude above background (presumably prehuman) values. These fires seem to have predominated in the area from about 5,200 years ago, gradually decreasing to lower levels about three millennia ago.

Perhaps the earliest settlers had a large-scale impact on the islands with a slash-and-burn approach to agriculture, in addition to their other presumed impacts.

Beginning 6,000 years ago or more, prehistoric mariners spread across the South Pacific from west to east, colonizing islands as they went. David Steadman of the New York State Museum and other avian paleontologists have discovered that many islands in the South Pacific had a much richer bird fauna before human arrival, often two times or more as diverse as the modern native fauna. Steadman and his colleagues, archaeologist Pat Kirch of the University of California at Berkeley and palynologist John Flenley of Massey University in New Zealand, believe that, on these relatively small and extremely isolated islands where there are few if any large native animals, human beings may have had their most profound impact not by hunting, but by modifying the environment and introducing rats and domestic animals.

Some of the Last Places on Earth

Among the last major land masses to be reached by prehistoric human beings were the Hawaiian Islands, New Zealand and Madagascar. True to the patterns outlined above, these were also among the last places to record major prehistoric extinction events. Because of the freshness of the subfossil record of these relatively recent events, they have received considerable attention from scientists interested in catastrophic extinctions.

Storrs Olson and Helen James of the Smithsonian Institution continue (literally, up to the present moment) to add new birds to the list of extinctions from Hawaii. One thing is certain now: Their work shows that more native bird species have become extinct in the Hawaiian Islands since the arrival of the Polynesians some 1,500 years ago than now survive. Among them are peculiar flightless relatives of mainland forms, including *Thambetochen* and *Ptaiochen*, giant waterfowl, their "turtle-jawed" relative *Chelychelynechen* on Kauai, and *Apteribus*, an ibis resembling the kiwi of New Zealand in shape and presumed habits.

The list of extinct Hawaiian birds dwarfs the considerable list of bird extinctions that have taken place since European arrival on the islands. Olson and James believe that some of the ex-

Figure 10. Tusks and bones from the woolly mammoth were used by prehistoric people to construct huts like this one in a diorama in the American Museum of Natural History. People may have hunted the animals for meat, but used animal by-products for other purposes.

tinctions may have been precipitated by hunting, and others by introduced rats, pigs and other exotic animals. But a host of small forest birds also became extinct, prompting reasonable speculation that deforestation by prehistoric agriculturalists could have played a major role. I have recently begun a project with Olson and James to use fossil pollen analysis to learn more about past environments and the dietary habits of some of the extinct birds. Perhaps eventually, we will be able to determine more accurately the extent to which various human and natural factors may have played a role in this relatively recent catastrophe.

Lacking terrestrial mammals other than bats, New Zealand's primary large animals were giant birds, known as moas to the Polynesians who arrived about 1,000 years ago. These relatives of ostriches diversified considerably, various authors recognizing between 13 and more than 30 species.

Although the North Island has few archaeological sites with moa bones, the South Island is quite a different matter.

Atholl Anderson of the Australian National University and a host of other investigators have excavated over 100 human sites with moa bones, sometimes in sizable heaps representing many individuals and several species. Radiocarbon dates on these camps of moa hunters are as recent as 300 to 400 years ago, suggesting that it might have taken the native Maoris about 600 years to hunt the moas to extinction. Pollen data from lakes and swamps in New Zealand also show that the Maori probably caused major vegetation changes, perhaps primarily by setting fires.

Madagascar, the world's largest oceanic island, has been separated from the continents for 165 million years or more. It is perhaps not surprising that its late prehistoric fauna was dominated by an array of giant birds and reptiles, pygmy hippopotami, and unique rodents, insectivores and mongoose relatives. The most unusual part of the lineup, however, was the lemurs, including several giant species of these primates as large as chimps and small gorillas.

The first Malagasy people, arriving

between perhaps 1,500 and 2,000 years ago, must have played some role in the extinction of this entire endemic large-animal fauna, including at least 12 genera and more than two dozen species of large and small animals. But as our research group, composed of archaeologists Bob Dewar of the University of Connecticut and Henry Wright of the University of Michigan, primatologist Elwyn Simons at the Duke University Primate Center, paleontologists Ross MacPhee of the American Museum of Natural History and Helen James of the Smithsonian Institution, and other experts in the United States and Madagascar have been learning for over a decade, figuring out exactly how the early settlers of Madagascar contributed to one of the last major prehistoric extinction events on the planet has not been easy. Despite concerted searching, only a handful of bones of extinct animals have turned up in archaeological sites around the island— nothing approaching the hauls from the moa-hunting parties taking place in New Zealand about the same time.

The favorite old theory about the extinctions in Madagascar was that man caused the extinctions less directly, primarily by burning the forests. In recent years, such a simplistic explanation has become less compelling, as fossil pollen and charcoal in my sediment cores from throughout the island have shown that wildfires and vegetation changes were a normal part of many of the highly seasonal environments for 35,000 years or more before the arrival of humankind. The new evidence also shows that many major climatic changes took place prior to human arrival.

Fruitful collaborations with my students and colleagues have documented that major environmental changes took place in prehuman Madagascar. But many kinds of fairly drastic changes occurred more or less simultaneously in the period between about 2,000 and 1,000 years ago, a period when, radiocarbon dating shows, many of the now-extinct creatures went from apparently abundant to essentially absent in the subfossil record. Dates on human-modified hippopotamus bones, the first occurrence in sediment cores of pollen of introduced *Cannabis* and a sudden rise in background levels (which were already fairly high in some sites) of stratigraphic charcoal, all support the notion that people probably arrived in Madagascar about two thousand years ago. Paleolimnological collaborations with Norman Reyes at Fordham University, George Kling of the University of Michigan and Katsumi Matsumoto of Brown University have uncovered evidence in our sediment cores for changes in microscopic diatom floras and lake levels. These stratigraphic records indicate that late-Holocene climates in Madagascar have become increasingly arid, with especially rapid changes taking place about 2,000 years ago.

In an effort to disentangle the various potential causes and their effects, we have increasingly concentrated our multidisciplinary efforts on a very special kind of subfossil site—one where fossil pollen and charcoal, paleolimnological and sedimentological changes, bones of extinct animals, and archaeological materials turn up in the same or nearby (and cross-datable) stratigraphic sequences. Such sites are generally regarded as rare, but we have had some initial successes. A hypersaline pond in the arid southwest known as Andolonomby, for instance, has shown that the region's climate be-

gan to turn drier about 3,000 years ago, with maximum aridity perhaps 1,000 to 2,000 years ago. As the forests were declining, the extinct Malagasy hippopotami, giant tortoises and other large animals become more scarce in the paleontological record for the site. Human-modified hippopotamus bones recovered from the vicinity date to about 2,000 years ago, and no younger hippopotamus bones have been detected here. At the same time, charcoal values peak at about 2,000 years ago, and the pollen of woody plants continues to decline through this hyper-arid phase.

A similar story, showing abundant evidence for the extinct fauna until about 2,000 years ago, then a decline over the next millennium, seems to be emerging from recent work with Helen James and Fred Grady of the Smithsonian and our Malagasy colleagues Jean-Gervais Rafamantanantsoa and Ramily Ramilisonina. We concentrated on another site with many types of evidence in close proximity, the spectacular cavern complex of Anjohibe in the northwestern part of the island. This area, and other northern cave sites excavated by Robert Dewar and Elwyn Simons, show intriguingly late evidence for some of the extinct giant lemurs, including a few radiocarbon dates around the beginning of the present millennium. It is beginning to appear that, whatever happened to the Malagasy fauna, it took well over 1,000 years for the catastrophe to fully develop—a longer time than would have been predicted from the strictest inter-

pretation of the *Blitzkrieg* hypothesis.

The case is not closed in Madagascar, just as in many of the other sites I have mentioned. Because many of our sites show evidence for a combination of simultaneous changes, including natural climate change, activities of the first human hunters, changes in fire regime and vegetation structure, and the arrival of exotic species, I have come to refer to the extinction event in Madagascar about 1,000 years ago as a "recipe for disaster." Instead of finding overwhelming evidence for the actions of a single cause in the extinctions, these four factors, and perhaps others, seem to have been functioning simultaneously on the island. Perhaps none of these agents alone would have wiped out all the extinct animals, but each could have been responsible for some of the extinctions. What I suspect is more likely, though, is that the primary lethal effect was the combination of these factors, acting in a synergistic manner on a fauna unaccustomed to so many disruptions at once.

Cautionary Tales

Late prehistoric extinctions, in my opinion, constitute a series of important cautionary tales for conservation biologists. First, the record shows that the native faunas in most parts of the world today are only damaged fragments of what existed in the recent past. Most ecosystems were first disrupted by people not in recent centuries or decades but thousands of years ago. Most of the "communities" we seek to preserve are not highly integrated entities that have

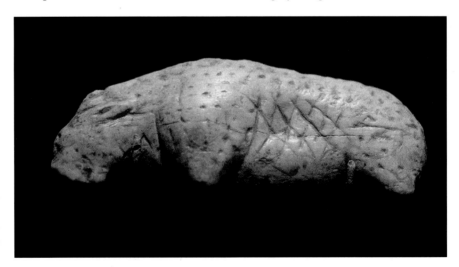

Figure 11. Extinct cave lion carved in mammoth ivory about 30,000 years ago indicates the lion had contact with early people. Although the big lions of Europe and North America are extinct, smaller subspecies survive tenuously in parts of Africa and in one small reserve in India.

Figure 12. Plowshare tortoise, *Geochelone yniphora*, of Madagascar is one of the world's rarest reptiles, with only a few hundred surviving. The larger tortoises of Madagascar disappeared after human colonization. Prospects for the plowshare tortoise's survival in the wild are not good.

reached some long-standing equilibrium. Instead they are primarily of two types: continental biotas with the largest herbivores and the large and medium-sized carnivores "skimmed off," and island biotas lacking many original components of all sizes and heavily invaded by cosmopolitan exotics. This in no way diminishes the value of saving what is left. Instead, the record of recent millennia should serve to remind us of how much has been lost, rather abruptly and without the benefit in most cases of industrial-era lethal capabilities.

Second, environmentalists should be quick to respond to critics who say that "extinction is natural" as justification for allowing a species to go extinct today. Most extinction in recent millennia is fundamentally different from earlier extinction, because it is extinction without replacement, at least on human time scales. Evolution continues to work only if, as the "unfit" become extinct, new species arise to fill their place. On the other hand, the fossil record shows that earlier mass extinctions, such as that of the dinosaurs,

gave rise over the longer geologic time scale to new evolutionary opportunities, such as the great early-Cenozoic radiations of mammals in the apparent vacuum left by the passing of the dinosaurs. This was an evolutionary "recovery" that was apparently millions of years in the making, though.

Third, it is humbling to realize that we still understand very little about extinction, one of biology's most fundamental concepts. When wildlife scientists and managers go through the sad but seemingly unavoidable business of calculating how little habitat or how few individuals are necessary to maintain an endangered population in the face of competing land-use or funding priorities, they should keep in mind the lesson of the mammoths and mastodons: For millions of years, these mighty beasts were abundant and widespread practically throughout the world. Yet, in a relatively short time, a poorly understood combination of circumstances wiped them out. I doubt if anyone around in those days would have believed such a thing possible.

Fourth, studying past extinctions may be leading us to some important new discoveries that relate directly to future conservation efforts. One clear example is a new hypothesis for explaining catastrophic late-Pleistocene continental extinctions put forward by Norman Owen-Smith, which he calls the "Keystone Herbivore Hypothesis." Simply put, he suggests that the apparent suddenness with which virtually whole faunas may disappear without a clear cause is not really surprising, since the fossil record shows that the first animals to go extinct are often the very large, slow-breeding herbivores. These animals play a role in shaping their own environment, creating physical diversity in the habitat and biotic turnover that allows many smaller animals to find niches. If he is correct that the loss of elephants and giant ground sloths in the Americas resulted in a "cascade" of extinctions of the middle-sized grazers and browsers and their predators, what can we expect in Africa in the wake of the decline of the rhino and the elephant?

Which leads to my final point. I have scarcely mentioned Africa, the one place on earth that seems to have virtually escaped the late-prehistoric extinction crisis. Over 80 percent of the late Pleistocene megafauna of Africa is still with us, if somewhat tenuously. However, all the ingredients in the "recipe for disaster" outlined above are now present in Africa in great measure. Human populations are exploding, and lethal technologies (guns, chainsaws and bulldozers) are available as never before. Increasingly confined to parks, many animal species have become naive to the dangers posed by humans with guns instead of cameras. Exotic animals, especially livestock, are having their own population explosion. Fire, although a natural element, has increased in frequency with the help of human beings in many pastoral areas, to the point of degrading much of the soil and vegetation. Finally, climates are certainly changing. Climate change, which for so long has been the major alternative explanation for extinctions otherwise ascribed to humans, may now be rearing its head in an ironic new form: People themselves are changing the climate. The impacts of deforestation, fossil-fuel burning, acid rain, ozone depletion and a host of toxic substances on climates and ecosystems are almost certain to become major factors in species survival. Just as in prehistoric times, the combined effects of all these ingredients may add up to a recipe far more disastrous than each of them taken separately.

Bibliography

Burney, D A. 1987. Late Quaternary stratigraphic charcoal records from Madagascar. *Quaternary Research* 28:274–280.

Burney, D. A. 1987. Pre-settlement vegetation changes at Lake Tritrivakely, Madagascar. *Palaeoecology of Africa* 18:357–381.

Burney, D. A. 1993. Late Holocene environmental changes in arid southwestern Madagascar. *Quaternary Research* 40:98–106.

Burney, D. A., L. P. Burney and R. D. E. MacPhee. In press. Holocene charcoal stratigraphy from Laguna Tortuguero, Puerto Rico, and the timing of human arrival on the island. *Journal of Archaeological Science*.

Diamond J. 1989. Overview of recent extinctions. In *Conservation for the Twenty-first Century*, ed. D. Western and M. Pearl. New York: Oxford University Press, pp. 37–41.

Eldredge, N. 1991. *The Miner's Canary*. New York: Prentice Hall.

James, H. F., T. W. Stafford, Jr., D. W. Steadman, S. L. Olson, P. S. Martin, A. J. T. Jull and P. C. McCoy. 1987. Radiocarbon dates on bones of extinct birds from Hawaii. *Proceedings of the National Academy of Sciences* 84:2350–2354.

Janzen, D. H. and P. S. Martin. 1982. Neotropical anachronisms: The fruits the gomphotheres ate. *Science* 215:19–27.

Kirch, P. V., J. R. Flenley, D. W. Steadman, F. Lamont and S. Dawson. 1992. Ancient environmental degradation. *National Geographic Research and Exploration* 8:166–179.

MacPhee, R. D. E., D. C. Ford and D. A. MacFarlane. 1989. Pre-Wisconsinan mammals from Jamaica and models of late Quaternary extinction in the Greater Antilles. *Quaternary Research* 31:94–106.

Martin, P. S. 1990. 40,000 years of extinctions on the "planet of doom." *Palaeogeography, Palaeoclimatology, Palaeoecology* 82:187–201.

Martin, P. S., and R. G. Klein, eds. 1984. *Quaternary Extinctions: A Prehistoric Revolution*. Tucson: University of Arizona Press.

Mosimann, J., and P. S. Martin. 1975. Simulating overkill by Paleoindians. *American Scientist* 63:304–313.

Olson, S. L. 1989. Extinction on islands: Man as a catastrophe. In *Conservation for the Twenty-first Century*, ed. D. Western and M. Pearl. New York: Oxford University Press, pp. 50–53.

Owen-Smith, N. 1987. Pleistocene extinctions: the pivotal role of megaherbivores. *Paleobiology* 13:351–362.

Steadman, D. W. 1989. Extinction of birds in eastern Polynesia: A review of the record, and comparisons with other Pacific Island groups. *Journal of Archaeological Science* 16:177–205.

Sutcliffe, A. J. 1985. *On the Track of Ice Age Mammals*. Cambridge, Mass.: Harvard University Press.

Land Mammals and the Great American Interchange

Larry G. Marshall

The continents of South America, Africa, Antarctica, Australia, and India were once joined in a large land mass in the southern hemisphere called Gondwana. About 100 million years ago (MYA) South America began to separate from Africa, moving in a primarily westward direction. There is no convincing geological evidence to indicate that South America had a continuous land connection with any other continent until about 3 MYA, when the Bolivar Trough marine barrier disappeared and the Americas were united by the emergence of the Panamanian land bridge. The long-isolated continental biotas of North and South America were brought into contact, resulting in an intermingling that has come to be known as the Great American Interchange (Webb 1976; Fig. 1). The site of the former Bolivar Trough is thus the gateway for this event, denoting the historical boundary between two biotic provinces (Fig. 2). Although many different groups of plants and animals took part in the interchange, I will focus on land mammals, which are the most thoroughly studied of the participants.

The Great American Interchange was first recognized by Wallace (1876), but it has taken another hundred years of intense paleontological study by Ameghino, Matthew, Scott, Patterson, Simpson, Webb, and others to clarify patterns of dispersal (see, for example, Marshall 1981, 1985; Webb 1985; Webb and Marshall 1982). It is only dur-

> *The emergence of the Panamanian land bridge three million years ago permitted the mingling of the long-separated faunas of North and South America.*

ing the last decade, moreover, that greater precision in dating the sediments containing interchange taxa has provided a firm time frame for various aspects of the event. It is now possible to assess the interchange in detail, and to analyze the tempo and mode of dispersal and the rates of extinction and origination in successive faunas through time. As a result, the Great American Interchange represents the best-documented example in the fossil record of the intermingling of two long-separated continental faunas.

By the time of the interchange, the land mammal faunas of North and South America had distinct histories that shaped their character and taxonomic composition. During the Cenozoic (from about 66 MYA to the present), North America was connected at one time with Europe and on multiple occasions with Asia via Beringia, resulting in recurrent additions of Old World taxa (McKenna 1975; Repenning 1980; Russell and Zhai 1987). When the Great American Interchange began, the North American land mammal fauna was part of the vast Holarctic realm, and many families and genera occurred simultaneously in North America, Asia, Europe, and Africa. The taxa present in North America at the start of the interchange were thus the survivors of many earlier exchanges, tested repeatedly by immigrations and attempted immigrations from the Old World.

Megatheriidae

Glyptodontidae

Mylodontidae

Dasypodidae

Myrmecophagidae

Erethizontidae

Didelphidae

Hydrochoeridae

Toxodontidae

Felidae

Soricidae

By contrast, during most of Cenozoic time South America was an island continent, like Australia today. As a result of this isolation, South American land mammals evolved in a world of their own; genera, families, and most orders were autochthonous and endemic to the continent, being found there and nowhere else. When the Great American Interchange began, the land mammals of South America were thus brought into contact with a major influx of potential competitors and predators for the first time in their history. In addition, South American taxa that dispersed to North America were first-time immigrants, entering a fauna that had known numerous earlier invasions. These differences in the histories of the North and South American faunas signal the fact that aspects of the interchange will be different on each continent.

South American land mammals

A brief look at the history of South American land mammals permits the identification of common consequences of the interchange, as opposed to changes that were inevitable or related to trends begun earlier. The constraints imposed on patterns of dispersal by South America's status as an island continent allow us to distinguish three main strata of land mammals (Simpson 1980; Fig. 3).

Stratum 1 consists of groups present in South America at or just before the beginning of the Cenozoic. Included are Marsupialia, Proteutheria, Pantodonta, Condylarthra, and Notoungulata, which are first recorded in rocks of late Cretaceous age, and Xenarthra, Xenungulata, Astrapotheria, Pyrotheria, and Litopterna, which are first found in rocks of middle and late Paleocene age in Argentina and Brazil (Marshall and de Muizon 1988; Marshall 1985). There is much debate as to whether some or all of these groups evolved in South America from long-established Mesozoic stock or whether they arrived there from elsewhere—Africa, North America, or Australia via Antarctica—just before or simultaneous with their first appearance on that continent. The important point here is that the stratum 1 groups were the first to radiate to fill land mammal niches and adaptive zones in South America in early Cenozoic time.

Stratum 2 groups include caviomorph rodents—for example, capybaras and porcupines—and monkeys, both of which are first recorded in rocks of middle Oligocene to early Miocene age. The oldest caviomorph rodents are known from a level dated about 34 MYA in Argentina; monkeys first appear about 26 MYA in Bolivia (Marshall 1985; MacFadden et al. 1985). These groups arrived either from Africa or (more probably) from North America sometime during the late Eocene time or earlier, traveling by the process of waif dispersal across the water barrier which then isolated South America from the other continents (Patterson and Wood 1982). Waif dispersal is thought to occur during times of flooding and high water levels, when rafts of vegetation may break away from the banks of swollen rivers and be carried to sea. Some of these rafts, it is speculated, may contain animals that can subsist on the materials provided by the raft itself. These miniature "Noah's arks" (McKenna 1973) may be carried by prevailing winds and currents to distant shores; upon successful docking, the voyagers disembark to colonize new lands. A prerequisite for successful waif dispersal is the survival of a pregnant female, a female with young, or a male–female pair able to perpetuate the species in a new land. The chances of a successful crossing are clearly low,

Figure 1. The appearance of the Panamanian land bridge set in motion the event now known as the Great American Interchange, which resulted in a major restructuring of the widely differing biotas of North and South America. The land mammals shown on the isthmus and at the left are representative of the 38 South American genera that walked north across the land bridge; at the right are representatives of 47 dispersants from North America that arrived in South America by way of the land bridge. Unlike South American taxa, which showed little diversification after their immigration, North American land mammals experienced an explosive diversification following their arrival on the South American continent.

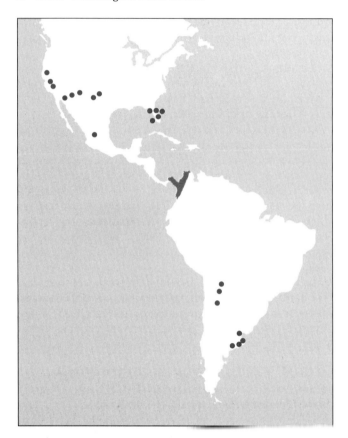

Figure 2. The Panamanian land bridge was formed by the uplift of the earth's crust in the region of the Bolivar Trough marine barrier (*colored area*), which once connected the Caribbean Sea and the Pacific Ocean across what is now southern Panama and northwestern Colombia. Colored dots indicate sites at which interchange fossils of late Miocene to early Pleistocene age have been found in Argentina, the southern and southwestern United States, and Mexico. Virtually nothing is known about the early part of the interchange in Central America and northern South America.

and many voyagers that survived were no doubt unsuccessful in establishing a foothold. Nevertheless, many such Noah's arks probably existed, and some containing rodents and monkeys managed to reach South America.

Stratum 3 includes participants in the Great American Interchange. Two groups are recognized, based on the time and mode of dispersal: taxa that were waif dispersants in the late Miocene, before the emergence of the Panamanian land bridge, and taxa that walked across the land bridge after its final emergence about 3 MYA.

Waifs and walkers

During late Miocene time, a limited interchange of land mammals occurred between the Americas either by rafting across the Bolivar Trough or by island-hopping through the Antilles archipeligoes. South American immigrants of the ground sloth families Megalonychidae (*Pliometanastes*) and Mylodontidae (*Thinobadistes*) are first recorded in North America in rocks of early Hemphillian age, i.e., by 8 MYA (for North and South American ages, see Fig. 5). *Pliometanastes*, which was the size of a modern black bear, makes its first appearance in local faunas of this age in central Florida, New Mexico, and central

California. This family gave rise to *Megalonyx*, a larger and more specialized ground sloth that occurs in rocks of late Hemphillian to Rancholabrean age. *Thinobadistes* is first known from the early Hemphillian of Florida and occurs with *Pliometanastes* in faunas of middle Hemphillian age in Florida and Texas (Webb 1985).

North American immigrants of the raccoon family Procyonidae are first found in South America in Argentinian rocks of Huayquerian age dating from about 7.5 MYA (Butler et al. 1984). The earliest procyonid genus,

---

Miniature "Noah's arks" may be carried by prevailing winds and currents to distant shores

---

Cyonasua, was about the size of a large modern raccoon; by Ensenadan time this genus gave rise to the slightly larger *Brachynasua*, and later to the bear-size *Chapalmalania* (Marshall 1985).

These late Miocene waif dispersants had little impact on the overall diversity of the faunas they joined. However, they did become firmly established and themselves show a low level of diversification. The members of all three families appear to have been adapted to a wide range of habitats; *Thinobadistes* and *Pliometanastes* were large generalized herbivores, whereas *Cyonasua* was a large omnivorous carnivore (Webb 1985). This adaptiveness would have been advantageous on rafts, where food was limited, because these voyagers could have eaten virtually everything available to them. Judging from living relatives, *Cyonasua* may also have had swimming abilities that would have been useful had the raft sunk before docking.

The second group of immigrants was created by the emergence of the Panamanian land bridge, which resulted from a combination of tectonic changes and decreases in the sea level related to ice-cap formation, the separate effects of which are difficult to isolate (Cronin 1981; Savin and Douglas 1985). The first record of South American animals that walked north across the newly emerged land bridge occurs in rocks of late Blancan age that date from about 2.5 MYA. Seven genera of land mammals and one large ground bird appear almost simultaneously in faunas of this age in Florida, Texas, New Mexico, Arizona, and California. These immigrants consisted of two armadillos (*Dasypus* and *Kraglievichia*), a giant armadillo-like glyptodont (*Glyptotherium*), two ground sloths (*Glossotherium* and *Nothrotheriops*), a porcupine (*Erethizon*), a large capybara (*Neochoerus*), and a phororhacoid ground bird (*Titanis*).

The most interesting of these early dispersants is *Titanis*, which is believed to have reached a height of over 3 m (Brodkorb 1963; Fig. 4). Phororhacoids were flightless, carnivorous ground birds that showed marked running specializations in middle and late Tertiary faunas in South America (Patterson and Kraglievich 1960; Marshall 1978). They were the only large terrestrial carnivores on that continent when the land bridge appeared, and *Titanis* was the only large South American carnivore to disperse to North America, where it is recorded in faunas of late Blancan and early Irvingtonian age in Florida (Marshall 1977; Webb 1985). Phororhacoids have one distant living relative in Paraguay, *Cariama*, a long-legged, long-necked bird about 0.7 m tall, capable of running at a speed of 25 miles an hour; it resorts to spurts of short-distance flight only when necessary.

A second major contingent of South American taxa that crossed the land bridge appears in rocks of early Irvingtonian age dating from about 1.9 MYA in northwestern Mexico and numerous localities across the southern United States. These taxa include a giant armadillo (*Holmesina = Pampatherium*), a ground sloth (*Eremotherium = Megatherium*), a giant anteater (*Myrmecophaga*), and a capybara (*Hydrochoerus*). An opossum (*Didelphis*) appears in the late Irvingtonian of Florida, another ground sloth (*Meizonyx*) in the Irvingtonian of El Salvador, and a rhino-like toxodont (*Mixotoxodon*) in the Rancholabrean of southern Central America.

Of these genera, the rhino-like *Mixotoxodon* and the ground sloth *Meizonyx* are known only from southern Central America, and the anteater *Myrmecophaga* only from a single site in northwestern Mexico (Webb and Perrigo 1984; Shaw and McDonald 1987). Records of the latter two have been established only within the last four years, demonstrating that some aspects of the North American part of the interchange are still poorly documented. We now know many of the South American dispersants that reached the southern part of the United States but little of what happened along the way. *Mixotoxodon*, *Meizonyx*, and *Myrmecophaga* did not go to the end of the highway north, and further research in Central America will no doubt reveal that other dispersants also failed to do so. The number of dispersants should decrease as one goes from Panama to the United States, but due to the vagaries of the fossil record and a lack of knowledge of what happened in Central America, the reverse is now true.

The first unequivocal record of the presence of North American land mammals that walked south across the land bridge occurs in Argentinian rocks of Chapadmalalan age, dating from 2.8 to 2.5 MYA. Two taxa are represented: a skunk (*Conepatus*) and a peccary (*Platygonus*). A horse (*Hippidion*) appears at about the same time in faunas of early Uquian age (2.5 MYA) in northwestern Argentina.

Evidence of the main contingent of North American dispersants begins to appear in rocks of late Uquian age (2 MYA) in Argentina. Sixteen genera representing nine families have been found: dogs (*Dusicyon, Protocyon*), cats and saber-tooths (*Felis, Smilodon*), skunks (*Galictis, Stipanicicia*), bears (*Arctodus*), elephant-like gomphotheres (*Cuvieronius*), horses (*Onohippidium*), tapirs (*Tapirus*), camels (*Hemiauchenia, Lama,* and *Palaeolama*), and deer (*Blastocerus, Morenelaphus,* and *Ozotoceros*). Rabbits (*Sylvilagus*) and squirrels (*Sciurus*) appear in the Lujanian; shrews (*Cryptotis*), pocket gophers (*Orthogeomys*), and kangaroo rats (*Heteromys*) are known only in living faunas.

Field mice, found in North America as early as 9 MYA, first appear in South America in Argentinian faunas of late Montehermosan age, dating from 3 to 2.8 MYA. Two genera of these cricetids are represented there (*Auliscomys* and *Bolomys*), and four additional genera

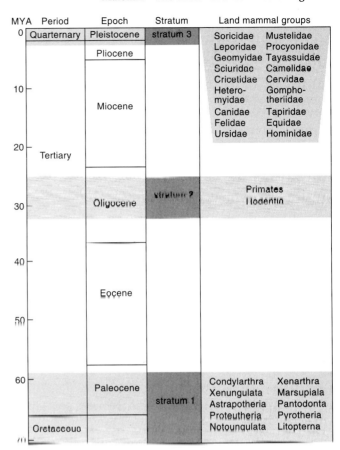

Figure 3. The fact that South America was once an isolated island continent makes it an ideal laboratory for the study of dispersal patterns. The first stratum of South American land mammals consists of early groups, either indigenous or of unknown origins, that radiated to fill niches and adaptive zones within the continent. By contrast, stratum 2 consists of waif dispersants that arrived across water barriers in the Oligocene. Stratum 3 shows the impact of the land bridge, with the appearance of 16 new families. Some Cricetidae and Procyonidae were included among those "walkers," although other Procyonidae, and perhaps other Cricetidae as well, certainly arrived earlier by water.

(*Akodon, Dankomys, Graomys,* and *Reithrodon*) appear in Chapadmalalan faunas (Reig 1978). There are now about 54 living genera of cricetids in South America. This group is not discussed above with the waifs or the walking dispersants because there is a great deal of debate about when and how it arrived in South America. Webb (1985) has admirably summarized two possible scenarios. The first attempts to account for the remarkable present-day diversity of cricetids by hypothesizing that they arrived as waif dispersants earlier than the first documented appearance in Montehermosan time (Hershkovitz 1966; Reig 1978). Reig observes that known fossils strongly suggest a much earlier arrival, probably at the beginning of the Miocene, with the main episodes of development taking place in the northern and central Andes, where fossil deposits are still poorly known. A slightly modified version of this theory holds that cricetids arrived during the period of world-wide low sea levels in the late Miocene, when the Bolivar Trough marine barrier was narrower and conditions for dispersal were optimal (Marshall 1979).

A second scenario accepts the fossil record at face

value, building on the assumption that the first appearance of cricetids in the late Montehermosan marks or approximates their time of arrival (Patterson and Pascual 1972; Jacobs and Lindsay 1984). According to this scenario, cricetids either experienced an as yet undocumented radiation in southern Central America, and were thus taxonomically diverse at the time of their arrival, or they underwent an explosive adaptive radiation following their arrival in South America. If this scenario is correct, cricetids were the first North American group to walk south across the newly emerged Panamanian land bridge.

The total generic diversity of dispersant families in North and South America through time is summarized in Figure 5. In South America there was an exponential increase of genera in families that arrived from North America, whereas in North America the increase of South American immigrants was significantly lower. The possible reasons for this difference will be explored below.

Filter effects of the land bridge

All the "walkers" preserved as fossils represent taxa that were apparently tolerant of or specifically adapted to savanna ecosystems. This indicates the presence of a continuous corridor or, at the very least, a shifting mosaic of open-country habitats through the American tropics (Webb 1978, 1985). Webb points out that the southern part

Figure 4. The flightless phororhacoid ground bird *Titanis* was probably an important predator of small to medium-sized land mammals such as capybaras. *Titanis* was the only large terrestrial carnivore from South America to take part in the interchange, and is found in North America only in Florida. It was comparable in size to *Megatherium*, attaining a height of over 3 m. A human figure is shown at the left for scale.

of the land bridge probably served as a barrier to true steppe biota throughout its existence, because no species adapted to a desert habitat are involved in any phase of the interchange. The shifting distribution of subhumid savanna ecosystems on the land bridge thus influenced the dispersal of the taxa living in them during the time of the interchange.

The history of savanna habitats on the land bridge has been studied in some detail (Raven and Axelrod 1975; Webb 1977, 1978). During glacial advances in temperate regions and at high tropical elevations, low areas in equa-

Man has been credited with being the sole or primary agent in a process of overkill called "blitzkrieg"

torial latitudes became cool and dry, resulting in the shrinking of wet tropical forest habitats to island-like refuges and the expansion of dryer savanna habitats (Haffer 1974; Van der Hammen 1974). The reverse occurred during times of glacial retreat. Several marine regressions occurred in the Caribbean area during times of glacial advance, providing optimal ecological windows for the reciprocal dispersal of savanna biotas between the Americas (Cronin 1981). One such regression is documented at about 3 MYA (± 0.2), another about 2 MYA, and a third about 1.4 MYA. These times approximate those of the major episodes of reciprocal dispersal as recorded in the fossil record: 2.8 to 2.5 MYA, 2 to 1.9 MYA, and 1.4 MYA. These "sister" dispersal events record the existence of savanna corridors, and explain the pulsations of interchange shown in Figure 5.

During times of glacial retreat, such as today, the distribution of savanna consists of disjunct habitats (Fig. 6). In times of glacial advance, however, these habitats would have been united by a corridor along the eastern side of the Andes—Webb's so-called "high road" or "Andean route" (1978). This corridor provided a north–south route that permitted the dispersal of savanna biotas within South America; more important, it continued across the Panamanian land bridge into the southern United States, extending eastward into Florida. In addition to creating this corridor, glacial advances were accompanied by drops of as much as 50 m in sea level, resulting in a widening of the land bridge. During times of glacial advance the savanna habitats of the southern United States and southern South America were thus mutually accessible. The principal obstacles to a complete intermingling of their biotas were distance and competitive exclusion.

Many species in South America today have populations restricted to disjunct savanna habitats, and a similar situation is found in Central America and northern South America, where some species are restricted to savanna habitats now separated by 1,700 km of wet tropical forest (Hershkovitz 1966, 1972; Webb 1985). These disjunct populations testify to the existence of the last savanna corridor between the Americas, which was in operation 12,000 to 10,000 years ago (Bradbury 1982; Markgraf and Bradbury 1982).

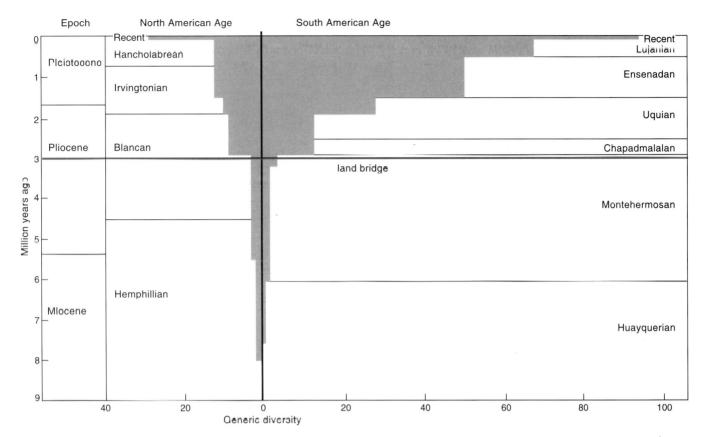

Figure 5. A comparison of the generic diversity of North and South American land mammals over the last 9 million years shows the dramatic effect of the appearance of the land bridge 3 MYA (*color*). In addition, it is apparent that in South America there was an exponential increase in genera that arrived from North America, whereas in North America the increase of South American immigrants was much lower. Four major dispersal events marked by sharp increases in diversity appear to coincide with periods of glacial advance, when the presence of a savanna corridor or a mosaic of open-country habitats may have facilitated immigration.

During the time of the interchange, recurrent glacial events thus produced a filtering effect that determined which types of animals could disperse and when. The expansion of the savanna during glacial advances has its antithesis in the expansion of the tropics in times of glacial retreat such as the present. Taxa in wet tropical forests seldom if ever leave a fossil record, and we therefore know virtually nothing about the dynamics of the interchange during such periods. Many wet tropical forest taxa are present today in both southern North America and northern South America, but we have no record of which taxa went north and which went south during the last three million years. Our understanding of the Great American Interchange is thus biased by the fact that the evidence comes only from times when the savanna habitat was at its maximum.

Faunal dynamics

The success or failure of the dispersants can be investigated by analyzing various aspects of taxonomic evolution—that is, by measuring changes in the total number of taxa or in the number of taxa within clades over time (Marshall et al. 1982; Webb 1984). MacArthur and Wilson's equilibrium theory (1967) predicts that over time a region such as a continent will become saturated with taxa, reaching a level of diversity where rates of turnover are stochastically constant. Equilibrium will then persist until it is disrupted by

the appearance of new taxa, a change in physical environment, or a combination of the two.

Do the taxa involved in the interchange show evidence of turnover induced by immigration? Figure 7 shows that the diversity of stratum 1 families in South America began to decrease steadily in middle Miocene time and slightly more sharply in late Pliocene time, when stratum 3 families began to appear there in large numbers. The decrease in stratum 1 families between the middle Miocene and late Pliocene is offset by an increase in stratum 2 families, suggesting that one was being replaced by the other before the interchange began. The appearance of stratum 3 may have accelerated the decrease of stratum 1 families, but the continued decline of stratum 1 families during late Cenozoic time clearly represents a trend begun before the interchange. It is thus possible to speculate that some or most of the decrease in the diversity of stratum 1 families during the time of the interchange is unrelated to the appearance of stratum 3 groups. Among genera, diversity decreased in strata 1 and 2 in the late Pliocene and Pleistocene but increased markedly in stratum 3 during the same time. The appearance of stratum 3 groups thus resulted in only a minor increase in total family diversity but a significant increase in generic diversity.

It has been suggested that the ungulate-like taxa of stratum 1—litopterns and notoungulates—were actively replaced by immigrating stratum 3 ungulates, which included horses, camels, and deer (Webb 1976). However,

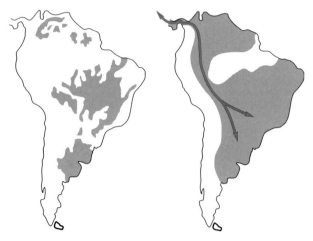

Figure 6. Recurring glacial advances and retreats appear to have played an important part in the rhythm of dispersal. In times of glacial retreat such as the present, savanna habitats contract into disjunct areas, as shown at the left; in periods of glacial advance, however, these habitats were united by a corridor along the eastern side of the Andes (*right*), providing a north–south route that extended into the southern United States and east to Florida. Arrows indicate this route and avenues of dispersal within South America.

much of the extinction of native ungulate-like taxa in South America took place before the interchange, and was thus unrelated to the arrival of stratum 3 groups (Patterson and Pascual 1972). The replacements that occurred during the interchange involved an interplay among the native ungulates, some ungulate-like caviomorph rodents, ground sloths, glyptodonts, and the immigrant North American taxa (Marshall 1981). There is no clear evidence of replacement of any ungulate group during interchange time due to rampant competition

Among the large carnivorous groups, the doglike borhyaenid marsupials were extinct before the time of the interchange. If any competitive interaction with the invading carnivores of stratum 3 occurred, it would have been with the large flightless phororhacoid ground birds, whose extinction in South America coincides with the arrival of this group (Marshall 1977). Among mammals,

the only potential example of competitive replacement is the extinction of the saber-tooth marsupial *Thylacosmilus*, which coincided with the arrival of the true saber-tooth placental, *Smilodon*.

The concept of "prey naivete" has broad implications for the mixing of faunas (Diamond 1984). The introduction of new predators in historic times has repeatedly shown that native species may be naive about predators in general and new predators in particular. The arrival of stratum 3 carnivores, "the likes of which southern ungulates had never before experienced," as Webb points out (1976, p. 225), may explain the fact that a decrease in stratum 1 and 2 ungulate-like forms coincided with an increase in immigrant stratum 3 ungulates. It is possible that the replacement of large stratum 1 and 2 herbivores by stratum 3 ungulates was passive, rather than being due to active competition. The immigrant carnivores may simply have killed off some of the native prey, making room available for immigrant prey.

At the end of the last glaciation, 12,000 to 11,000 years ago, humans migrated out of Asia by way of the Bering land bridge, passing southward through North America and into South America. Within possibly 1,000 years, man apparently occupied most or all of the New World (Martin 1973). Humans were the last stratum 3 dispersants to South America, and their arrival coincides with the extinction of most large-bodied taxa in both North and South America (Marshall et al. 1984). Man has been credited with being the sole or primary agent in this phenomenon through a process of overkill called "blitzkrieg," in which sudden extinctions followed the initial colonization of a land mass inhabited by animals that were especially vulnerable to the new human predator. The disappearance of these large-bodied species in the Americas at the end of the Pleistocene is certainly consistent with such a process, although a model based on climatic change remains a viable alternative (Markgraf 1985).

Whatever the cause, the consequences of this extinction event in South America were dramatic. Of the 37 land mammal families recorded in Lujanian faunas, 8 (21%), were extinct by Holocene time, even though all 8 families included more than one genus. Of the 153 land mammal genera documented in Lujanian faunas, 56 (37%) were

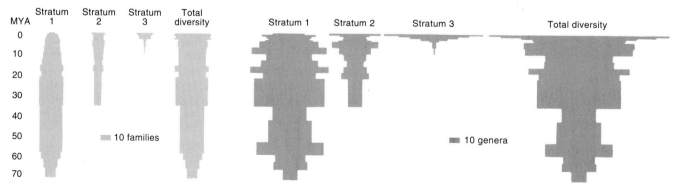

Figure 7. Spindle diagrams of family and generic diversity among South American mammals help to distinguish trends begun before the interchange from the direct effects of the land bridge. The decline of stratum 1 families visible at the far left clearly represents a trend predating the appearance of the land bridge 3 MYA, suggesting that this decrease in diversity is unrelated to the arrival of stratum 3 families. For genera, however, as shown at the right, diversity simultaneously decreased in strata 1 and 2 and increased significantly in stratum 3, demonstrating some replacement between native and immigrant taxa. (After Marshall and Cifelli, in press.)

now extinct, including 35 belonging to those 8 families. Of the extinct genera, 54 (96%) were of large body size, suggesting that this event was selective. The taxa that became extinct were clearly not a random sample of Lujanian land mammal fauna (Marshall and Cifelli, in press).

The success of North American taxa

In evaluating the relative success or failure of North and South American interchange species, two factors must be kept in mind. First, it is necessary to distinguish true dispersants, which are represented by the same or a sister taxon on their native continent, from pseudodispersants, which are derived from true dispersants. Just because a genus belongs to a family that dispersed from another continent, it does not follow that it itself dispersed. For example, the elephant like gomphothere *Cuvieronius*, a true dispersant to South America, is known from pre-interchange faunas in North America. After reaching South America it gave rise to *Haplomastodon* and *Notiomastodon*, which are pseudodispersants; although they belong to a family that dispersed from North America, they themselves evolved in and are endemic to South America (Webb 1985). Such pseudodispersants must be identified and factored out when analyzing dispersal events. Second, the number of potential dispersants is directly related to the size of the source faunas. A larger geographic area will probably have more taxa and hence more dispersants than a smaller area. This, too, must be taken into account.

Of the members of South American families that walked to North America, all 38 may be regarded as true dispersants, indicating that little or no diversification occurred after their immigration. By contrast, of the North American walkers (including cricetids) only 47 can be regarded as true dispersants, whereas 72, from 8 families, represent pseudodispersants. Thus about 60% of the North American genera in South America apparently evolved in situ on that continent, demonstrating that these immigrants experienced considerable diversification after their arrival.

The total surface area of North America and Central America (24 million km^2) is greater than that of South America (18 million km^2). This fact, along with the known fossil record, explains why North America had an average of 60% greater generic diversity and hence more potential dispersants than South America during the time of the interchange (Marshall et al. 1982). When the differences in the size of the source faunas are taken into account and only true dispersants are considered, the interchange can be seen to be balanced, with the number of true dispersants proportional to the size of the source faunas in both continents. More taxa dispersed to South America than to North America simply because there were more potential dispersants in North America.

This aspect of the interchange is predicted by equilibrium theory. However, the later explosive diversification of true dispersants in South America as opposed to North America is unique and asymmetrical. Several theories have been proposed to explain this difference. The classic view during the first half of this century was that the taxa of North America were competitively superior to those of South America. This view was founded on the belief that the taxa existing in North America at the beginning of the interchange were the survivors of numerous earlier invasions and thus tested and "worldly wise," possessing such varied advantages as more rapid reproductive rates, narrower niche selection, and more rapid evolutionary responses to new opportunities (Webb 1985).

A more recent view, compatible with this, sees the North American taxa as "insinuators" able to exploit niches and adaptive zones not occupied by native South American taxa (Patterson and Pascual 1972, Hershkovitz 1972). Thus the North American immigrants would not have competed directly with South American natives, but were able simply to radiate and fill unoccupied space. Another theory holds that ongoing geological activity created new habitats and changed the old ones, resulting in the extinction of some native taxa before and during the time of the interchange. The opening of niches and adaptive zones through the disappearance of prey-naive

---

Nearly half of the families and genera now on the South American continent belong to groups that emigrated from North America during the last three million years

---

natives would have allowed the North American immigrants to disperse into ecological vacuums. These features would have facilitated both the arrival of true dispersants and their radiation into pseudodispersants. This theory implies that the changes which took place in the composition of the South American land mammal fauna were due primarily to passive replacement, and that the North American groups were simply timely invaders.

A fourth theory combines aspects of all these views, suggesting that the two principal evolutionary theaters for the interchange were not South and North America but South America on the one hand and North America and Eurasia on the other (Webb 1985). This theory stresses the imbalance between the area available to northern taxa adapted to temperate conditions and that available to the southern taxa, and holds that the presence of a vast Holarctic staging area rather than any inherent biological superiority explains the greater success of northern taxa after the interchange.

Although the reasons for the success of the North American immigrants remain debatable, the impact on South America is undisputed. When the interchange began about 7.5 MYA, about 60% of the South American

---

Larry G. Marshall is Senior Research Scientist at the Institute of Human Origins, Berkeley. He graduated from Northern Arizona University, and was awarded his M.Sc. from Monash University (Australia) in 1974 and his Ph.D. in 1976 from the University of California, Berkeley. Since 1975 he has been working on the evolutionary history of South American land mammals, and has participated in 17 expeditions to Argentina, Bolivia, Brazil, Chile, Colombia, Mexico, Peru, and Venezuela. Address: Institute of Human Origins, 2453 Ridge Road, Berkeley, CA 94709.

families derived from stratum 1 and 40% from stratum 2; 70% of the genera came from stratum 1 and 30% from stratum 2. Today the composition of South American land mammal fauna is quite different: 19% of the families come from stratum 1, 37% from stratum 2, and 94% from stratum 3; 17% of the genera derive from stratum 1, 29% from stratum 2, and 54% from stratum 3. These data firmly demonstrate that the Great American Interchange resulted in a major restructuring. Nearly half of the families and genera now on the South American continent belong to groups that emigrated from North America during the last 3 million years.

References

Bradbury, J. P. 1982. Holocene chronostratigraphy of Mexico and Central America. In *Chronostratigraphic Subdivision of the Holocene*, ed. J. Mangerud, H. J. B. Birks, and K. D. Jager. *Striae* 16:46–48.

Brodkorb, P. 1963. A giant flightless bird from the Pleistocene of Florida. *Auk* 8:111–15.

Butler, R. F., L. G. Marshall, R. E. Drake, and G. H. Curtis. 1984. Magnetic polarity stratigraphy and 40K–40Ar dating of late Miocene and early Pliocene continental deposits, Catamarca Province, NW Argentina. *J. Geol.* 92:623–36.

Cronin, T. M. 1981. Rates and possible causes of neotectonic vertical crustal movements of the emerged southeastern United States Atlantic Coastal Plain. *Geol. Soc. Am. Bull.* 92:812–33.

Diamond, J. M. 1984. Historic extinctions: A rosetta stone for understanding prehistoric extinctions. In *Quaternary Extinctions: A Prehistoric Revolution*, ed. P. S. Martin and R. G. Klein, pp. 824–62. Univ. of Arizona Press.

Haffer, J. 1974. Avian speciation in tropical South America. *Pub. Nuttall Ornith. Club* 14:1–390.

Hershkovitz, P. 1966. Mice, land bridges and Latin American faunal interchange. In *Parasites of Panama*, ed. R. L. Wenzel and V. J. Tipton, pp. 725–47. Chicago: Field Museum of Natural History.

———. 1972. The recent mammals of the Neotropical Region. In *Evolution, Mammals and Southern Continents*, ed. A. F. Keast, F. C. Erk, and B. Glass, pp. 311–431. State Univ. of New York Press.

Jacobs, L. L., and E. H. Lindsay. 1984. Holarctic radiation of Neogene Muroid rodents and the origin of South American cricetids. *J. Vert. Paleont.* 4:265–72.

MacArthur, R. H., and E. O. Wilson. 1967. *The Theory of Island Biogeography*. Princeton Univ. Press.

MacFadden, B. J., et al. 1985. Magnetic polarity stratigraphy and mammalian biostratigraphy of the Deseadan (Middle Oligocene–Early Miocene) Salla Beds of northern Bolivia. *J. Geol.* 93:223–50.

Markgraf, V. 1985. Late Pleistocene faunal extinctions in southern Patagonia. *Science* 228:1110–12.

Markgraf, V., and J. P. Bradbury. 1982. Holocene climatic history of South America. In *Chronostratigraphic Subdivision of the Holocene*, ed. J. Mangerud, H. J. B. Birks, and K. D. Jager. *Striae* 16:40–45.

Marshall, L. G. 1977. Evolution of the carnivorous adaptive zone in South America. In *Major Patterns in Vertebrate Evolution*, ed. M. K. Hecht, P. C. Goody, and B. M. Hecht, pp. 709–21. Plenum.

———. 1978. The terror bird. *Field Mus. Nat. Hist. Bull.* 49:6–15.

———. 1979. A model for paleobiogeography of South American cricetine rodents. *Paleobiology* 5:126–32.

———. 1981. The Great American Interchange: An invasion induced crisis for South American mammals. In *Biotic Crises in Ecological and Evolutionary Time*, ed. M. Niticki, pp. 133–229. Academic Press.

———. 1985. Geochronology and land-mammal biochronology of the transamerican faunal interchange. In *The Great American Biotic Interchange*, ed. F. G. Stehli and S. D. Webb, pp. 49–81. Plenum.

Marshall, L. G., and R. L. Cifelli. In press. Restructuring of Cenozoic land mammal faunas of South America. In *Long-term Restructuring in Late Cenozoic Terrestrial Ecosystems*, ed. K. Luchterhand. Evanston: Wm Caxton, Ltd.

Marshall, L. G., and C. de Muizon, 1988. The dawn of the Age of Mammals in South America. *Nat. Geog. Res.* 4:23–55.

Marshall, L. G., S. D. Webb, J. J. Sepkoski, and D. M. Raup. 1982. Mammalian evolution and the Great American Interchange. *Science* 215:1351–57.

Marshall, L. G., et al. 1984. Geochronology of the continental mammal-bearing Quaternary of South America. *Palaeovertebrata, Mem. Extr.* 1984:1–76.

Martin, P. S. 1973. The discovery of America. *Science* 179:969–74.

McKenna, M. C. 1973. Sweepstakes, filters, corridors, Noah's arks, and beached Viking funeral ships in paleogeography. In *Implications of Continental Drift to the Earth Sciences*, ed. D. H. Tarling and S. K. Runcorn, pp. 21–46. Academic Press.

———. 1975. Fossil mammals and early Eocene North Atlantic land continuity. *Ann. Miss. Bot. Garden* 62:335–53.

Patterson, B., and J. L. Kraglievich. 1960. Sistematica y nomenclatura de las aves forrorracoideas del Plioceno argentino. *Pub. Mus. Munic. Cienc. Nat., Mar del Plata* 1:1–49.

Patterson, B., and R. Pascual. 1972. The fossil mammal fauna of South America. In *Evolution, Mammals, and Southern Continents*, ed. A. Keast, F. C. Erk, and B. Glass, pp. 247–309. State Univ. of New York Press.

Patterson, B., and A. E. Wood. 1982. Rodents from the Deseadan Oligocene of Bolivia and the relationships of the Caviomorpha. *Bull. Mus. Comp. Zool.* 149:371–543.

Raven, P. H., and D. I. Axelrod. 1975. History of the flora and fauna of Latin America. *Am. Sci.* 63:420–29.

Reig, O. A. 1978. Roedores cricetidos del plioceno superior de la Provincia Buenos Aires (Argentina). *Pub. Mus. Munic. Cienc. Nat., Mar del Plata* 2:164–90.

Repenning, C. A. 1980. Faunal exchange between Siberia and North America. *Can. J. Anthropol.* 1:37–44.

Russell, D. E., and R.-J. Zhai. 1987. The Paleogene of Asia: Mammals and Stratigraphy. *Mem. Mus. Nat. Hist. Natur., Sci. de la Terre* 52:1–488.

Savin, S. M., and R. G. Douglas. 1985. Sea level, climate, and the Central American land bridge. In *The Great American Biotic Interchange*, ed. F. G. Stehli and S. D. Webb, pp. 303–24. Plenum.

Shaw, C. A., and H. G. McDonald. 1987. First record of giant Anteater (Xenarthra, Myromecophagidae) in North America. *Science* 236:186–88.

Simpson, G. G. 1980. *Splendid Isolation: The Curious History of South American Mammals*. Yale Univ. Press.

Van der Hammen, T. 1974. The Pleistocene changes of vegetation and climate in tropical South America. *J. Biogeog.* 1:3–26.

Wallace, A. R. 1876. *The Geographical Distribution of Animals*. Macmillan.

Webb, S. D. 1976. Mammalian faunal dynamics of the Great American Interchange. *Paleobiology* 2:216–34.

———. 1977. A history of savanna vertebrates in the New World. Part I: North America. *Ann. Rev. Ecol. Syst.* 8:355–80.

———. 1978. A history of savanna vertebrates in the New World. Part II: South America and the Great Interchange. *Ann. Rev. Ecol. Syst.* 9:393–426.

———. 1984. On two kinds of rapid faunal turnover. In *Catastrophies and Earth History*, ed. W. A. Berggren and J. A. Van Couvering, pp. 417–36. Princeton Univ. Press.

———. 1985. Late Cenozoic mammal dispersals between the Americas. In *The Great American Biotic Interchange*, ed. F. G. Stehli and S. D. Webb, pp. 357–86. Plenum.

Webb, S. D., and L. G. Marshall. 1982. Historical biogeography of Recent South American land mammals. In *Mammalian Biology in South America*, ed. M. A. Mares and H. H. Genoways, pp. 39–52. Special Pub. Series 6, Pymatuning Laboratory of Ecology, Univ. of Pittsburg.

Webb, S. D., and S. C. Perrigo. 1984. Late Cenozoic vertebrates from Honduras and El Salvador. *J. Vert. Paleont.* 4:237–54.

Part II
Interpreting Patterns

Part of our understanding of the patterns of evolution comes not from fossils but from comparing living species. Underlying the study of organisms alive today is the powerful knowledge given to us by the evolutionary perspective: that *differences* between species must have evolved since the species separately descended from a common ancestor, and that *similarities* between species are probably descended from their common ancestor. The chapters in this section either describe attempts to generalize about patterns or describe in detail some particularly interesting groups of species.

The chapter by Cracraft is similar to the previous chapter by Marshall in that it is also concerned with biogeography. The geographic distributions of both living and extinct organisms often provide important clues to the conditions under which species arose and diversified. Cracraft describes a relatively new aspect of biogeography, called vicariance biogeography, which emphasizes that the phylogenetic relationships of species combined with their geographic distributions can provide information both about the history of that group of species and about the geological history of the geographic areas they occupy.

Next S. J. Gould argues forcefully for the significance of the differences between historical sciences, such as evolutionary biology and geology, and experimental science, such as molecular biology and physics. We often cannot understand living organisms without knowing their evolutionary histories, and the attempt to apply the rules of experimental sciences to evolutionary problems can lead to foolish conclusions or even to dangerous misunderstanding of the subject.

The next two chapters describe two of the most important evolutionary events in the history of life. Neither of them can be understood from the fossil record; we must learn what we can from extant species. Fenchel and Finlay discuss the special problems faced by anaerobic organisms (those that cannot live in the presence of oxygen). In their efforts to avoid atmospheric oxygen, anaerobic species can become parasites, commensals, or mutualists, dependent on other species. It is quite likely that the first eukaryotic cells were derived from such a symbiotic association. Then Graham describes how the complex life cycle of land plants may have evolved. How this life cycle evolved and how it permitted the radiation of land plants is one of the great mysteries of botany.

The remaining chapters in this section describe several studies of particular groups. These studies are of interest in their own right because of the unusual or familiar features of each group, but they also illustrate more general evolutionary principles. Darwin began *On the Origin of Species* by using domesticated pigeons (which are not as popular now as they were in Darwin's day) to illustrate the power of selection. Similarly, the domestication of dogs, discussed by Morey, has quickly led to much greater diversity than is found in the wild relatives of dogs. Kabnick and Peattie then describe a group that is unfortunately also familiar to many of us, *Giardia* being an important parasite of humans. *Giardia* is a simple eukaryote that can help us understand the early evolution of eukaryotic cells.

The chapters by Holsinger and by Gorr and Kleinschmidt describe unfamiliar organisms. Cave-dwelling species (troglobites) are fascinating because they illustrate how readily organisms can adapt to novel and quite extreme conditions. Troglobites play an interesting role in evolutionary discussions of how and why unused characters (such as the pigments that protect skin from sunlight) are lost. As Gorr and Kleinschmidt describe, the coelacanth is almost legendary as a species whose discovery in the late 1930s was close to what has been portrayed in countless science fiction movies: a "prehistoric" species found by accident and finally identified by astounded scientists. The coelocanth is, fortunately, not a rapacious monster from the deep but a shy, almost pathetic fish that is fascinating to scientists because it is closely related to some of the earliest terrestrial vertebrates.

Cladistic Analysis and Vicariance Biogeography

Joel Cracraft

Evolutionary biology gains a new dimension from the reconstruction of systematic and biogeographic patterns

Evolutionary biology is concerned with deciphering and explaining the history of life, and the foundation on which that endeavor is based is systematics. Although considered out of fashion by some contemporary biologists, the importance of systematics cannot be overestimated: simply put, systematic analysis defines the structure of evolutionary pattern, from the lowest level at which populations become differentiated to those levels defined by the interrelationships of the higher taxa.

Evolutionary pattern itself has three primary components: form, in which similarities (whether of the expressed phenotype or of the genotype) have a hierarchical pattern of congruence among species; a taxic component, in which the different species of organisms have hierarchical relationships with one another; and a spatial component, in which different taxonomic groups, each distributed in the same areas of endemism, have patterns of taxic interrelationships that describe a congruent hierarchical arrangement for those areas. Thus, systematic analysis reveals, and then attempts to explain, the two great interests of evolutionary biology, the history of structural diversity and of taxonomic diversity.

In recent years systematics has undergone significant changes in theory and methodology, which have caused considerable controversy not only within systematics itself but throughout the field of evolutionary biology. At the heart of the intellectual ferment are the ideas embodied in the discipline called phylogenetic systematics, or cladistics.

The tenets of cladistics were introduced in the early 1950s by the German entomologist Willi Hennig, but it was not until his work was translated (Hennig 1966) and the studies of a Swedish entomologist, Lars Brundin, were widely known (Brundin 1966) that cladistics became an intellectual force. Although the theory of cladistics has shifted in emphasis over the years, two basic principles have continued to characterize its research program: First, natural groups are recognized by uniquely derived characters, termed synapomorphies. Second, only natural groups, defined by synapomor-

Joel Cracraft is Associate Professor of Anatomy at the University of Illinois and Research Associate in the Department of Zoology, Field Museum of Natural History. Since he received his Ph.D. in biology from Columbia University in 1969, his research has focused on systematic theory and methodology, historical biogeography, and avian evolution. The work reported here is supported by the NSF. Address: Department of Anatomy, University of Illinois, P.O. Box 6998, Chicago, IL 60680.

phies to be monophyletic (that is, descended from a common ancestor), are to be admitted into Linnaean classification schemes.

That biologists can cluster derived similarity (and, therefore, taxa) hierarchically confirms an evolutionary history for life. Moreover, the existence of hierarchical structure may be one reason that most systematists, including even staunch critics of cladistics, have had little difficulty in accepting the premise that we must formulate hypotheses about character polarity (that is, whether postulated homologies are primitive or derived) if we are to identify monophyletic groups. This does not mean, of course, that no controversy exists over how these hypotheses are to be constructed. Substantial disagreement has emerged, however, over the principle that classifications should precisely express the composition of natural groups (Eldredge and Cracraft 1980; Wiley 1981; Patterson 1982b).

One of the most important contributions of cladistics has been to focus attention on the vital importance of pattern analysis, for it is only by having some aspect of pattern that science has something to explain. As Platnick (1979) has remarked: "What Hennig may well have done [by formulating cladistics] . . . is to demonstrate the inadequacy of the [neo-Darwinian] syntheticist paradigm, by showing us that we are hardly likely to achieve any understanding of the evolutionary process until we have achieved an understanding of the patterns produced by that process, and that even today we have hardly begun to understand the patterns."

Reconstructing systematic pattern

Cladistic analysis is a method of systematics that attempts to summarize knowledge about the similarities among organisms in terms of a branching diagram, called a cladogram. Many recent workers have commented at length on the technical aspects of cladistic analysis, and only the general principles can be outlined here. (For detailed treatments of cladistic analysis, see Eldredge 1979; Gaffney 1979; Nelson 1979; Eldredge and Cracraft 1980; Cracraft 1981a; Nelson and Platnick 1981; Wiley 1980, 1981; Patterson 1980, 1982a, b.) Cladistics is designed to answer a specific problem, one that is easily generalizable to more complex cases: given, say, three taxa, which cladistic hypothesis, or cladogram, most economically explains the distribution of their similarities?

Consider, for example, three taxa that include a lamprey, a snake, and a dog. Our problem is to evaluate the three hypotheses of Figure 1 using, for example, the character information in Table 1. It is easily seen that characters 1–3, because they are present in all three taxa, are uninformative. All the other characters, in contrast, reveal similarities between two taxa, and if we merely add them, we note that the snake and dog share two (4, 5), the lamprey and snake two (6, 7), and the lamprey and dog none. How might we resolve the conflict in character congruence shown by the two informative cladograms? It is always possible, of course, to search for more shared characters in the hope that they will favor one hypothesis or the other, and indeed this has often been the method of choice within traditional systematics. The literature abounds, for example, with arguments over which taxa share the most characters. But it was Hennig's special insight to see that such a problem could be resolved in yet another way: similarities could be apportioned on a branching diagram according to the hierarchical level at which they characterize groups—that is, the level at which they are postulated to be a synapomorphy.

Cladists now generally agree that there are two comparative methods for evaluating character polarity, the use of an ontogenetic criterion or an outgroup criterion. Both approaches seek to establish the direction of transformation from a character that is primitive to one that is more derived; or, in other terms, a primitive character is more general, because it defines a group that is more inclusive than one defined by a less general, more derived condition of that character.

In applying the *ontogenetic criterion* to our example, we observe that during early development each of the three groups possesses a very similar, dorsally located axial skeleton, in which a notochord is formed and then enclosed by a fibrous sheath. As development proceeds, the lamprey forms small, segmentally arranged cartilages lying lateral to the notochord, and this remains the condition in the adult. In the snake and the dog, however, the axial skeleton continues to transform, with cartilaginous models of vertebrae being laid down and eventually replaced by bone. From this developmental sequence we can postulate that an axial skeleton composed of vertebrae is derived, relative to the more simple condition seen in the lamprey and in the embryos of the snake and the dog. Thus, character 4 unites the snake and the dog as a subset within the three-taxon problem.

Although the ontogenetic criterion is a potentially powerful method of assessing the direction of character transformation, comparative embryological data are not often available. Therefore, systematists usually must

Table 1. Comparative analysis of seven morphological characters

Character	Lamprey	Snake	Dog
Dorsal nerve cord	+	+	+
Notochord	+	+	+
Axial skeleton	+	+	+
Vertebral column	−	+	+
Jaws	−	+	+
Paired limbs	−	−	+
Long, fusiform body	+	+	−

employ the *outgroup criterion*, which, like ontogenetic comparison, identifies the hierarchical level at which characters define groups (Watrous and Wheeler 1981). By this criterion, if a shared character within the group being studied is also found outside the group (preferably in taxa thought to be closely related), then the character is too general, or primitive, to define a subgroup.

Critics of cladistics have generally accepted the method of outgroup comparison but sometimes claim that its effectiveness depends on the procedure of choosing an outgroup, which in turn entails having prior knowledge of higher-level relationships. In one sense this is true, of course, but it still does not constitute a serious difficulty for the method. Knowledge in science is always conjectural, and the choice of an outgroup only signifies tentative acceptance of a higher-level hypothesis about relationships, a hypothesis itself open to critical evaluation (Wiley 1975). For example, given our three-taxon problem, we can establish outgroups by asking which taxa are thought to be closely related. In actuality, the "protochordate" groups—urochordates (tunicates) and cephalochordates (amphioxi)—are known to share many unique similarities with the vertebrates and for that reason have generally been accepted as being closely related to them. What does this higher-level hypothesis, shown diagrammatically in Figure 2, tell us about the characters within our ingroup? From Table 1 we know that jaws (character 5) are absent in the outgroups, and thus it can be inferred that jaws are derived within the three taxa. Thus, the cladogram based

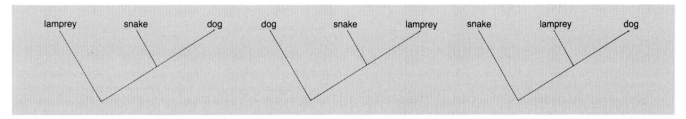

Figure 1. A cladogram, or branching diagram, shows the hierarchical relationships postulated to exist among groups. The cladistic hypotheses illustrated here for three taxa – a lamprey, a snake, and a dog – can be evaluated by reference to the seven morphological characters listed in Table 1. Three of the characters are shared by all the taxa and are therefore uninformative; of the

four remaining characters the snake and the dog share two, the lamprey and the snake two, and the lamprey and the dog none. According to these data, the left and middle cladograms appear equally tenable, and further information is required in order to resolve the conflict. The hypothesis depicted by the cladogram at the right conflicts with all the character information.

on the presence of jaws (Fig. 2, *bottom*) corroborates the first cladogram in Figure 1.

Ontogenetic and outgroup comparison also shed light on characters 6 and 7, which seem to be in conflict with the first cladogram of Figure 1. In the embryological sequences of the three forms, many similarities are observed during early development of the body wall; in contrast to the lamprey, however, the snake and the dog form two pairs of limb buds. These buds transform into definitive limbs in the dog, whereas the limb buds of snakes are extremely transitory and disappear soon after they arise. Ontogeny, therefore, shows that snakes are actually tetrapods, that our initial interpretation of the similarity (lack of paired appendages as a defining character of the lamprey and the snake) was incorrect, and that character 6 actually corroborates the first cladogram in Figure 1 instead of the second.

Given only the groups listed in Figure 2 (the dog, the snake, the lamprey, urochordates, and cephalochordates), outgroup comparison of adults alone would not enable us to resolve the exact nature of the character distribution of paired appendages. Because of the absence of paired appendages in the outgroups, their absence in the lamprey and the snake could be interpreted as a shared primitive character, or symplesiomorphy, which is uninformative with regard to delimiting relationships within a three-taxon statement, and which

yields the cladogram shown in the top half of Figure 3. The problem might be investigated in more detail, however, by the addition of other groups and characters, and when this is done it becomes evident that snakes are characterized not by the absence of paired appendages but by their loss (Fig. 3, *bottom*). Such a case also illustrates the principle that cladistic analysis seeks to maximize the congruence of characters when attempting to account for their distribution. For example, it is more economical to interpret character 6 as a loss in snakes than as a shared primitive character (absence of limbs), because the latter hypothesis would entail accepting numerous incongruities associated with assuming that the frog is more closely related to the dog than is the snake. Likewise, the long, fusiform body shared by the lamprey and the snake is easily resolved as a spurious resemblance by the examination of more taxa and characters.

It is not difficult to see that the methods of cladistics are generalizable to problems having more taxa and characters. This might seem a straightforward task, but although the relationships of some groups can be quickly resolved, others resist analysis because of the absence of easily detectable synapomorphies. The reasons for this seem to be twofold. Either the groups are exceedingly primitive, sharing very few characters that one might postulate to be derived, or else they are highly derivative, each possessing many derived characters not

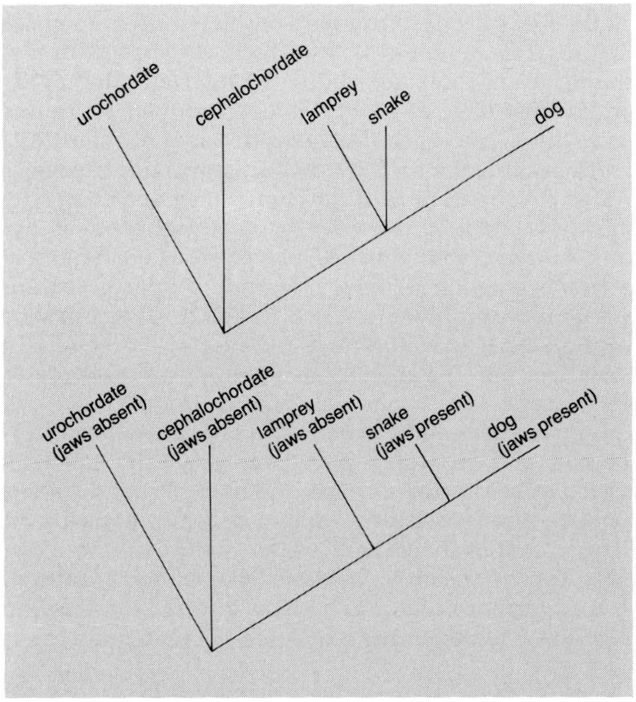

Figure 2. A cladogram can be based on "outgroup comparison." According to this method, if a character is present within the group under study and is also found outside the group, the character is considered too general, or primitive, to shed light on relationships within the group. With an "ingroup" comprising the three taxa of Figure 1 and an "outgroup" consisting of urochordates and cephalochordates, the character "presence of jaws" provides information about relationships within the ingroup. Before outgroup comparison, a cladogram (*top*) would show only a simple division between the outgroup and the group under study. Following comparison (*bottom*), the presence of jaws is inferred to be a less general, or derived, character, showing the snake and the dog to be more closely related than either is to the lamprey.

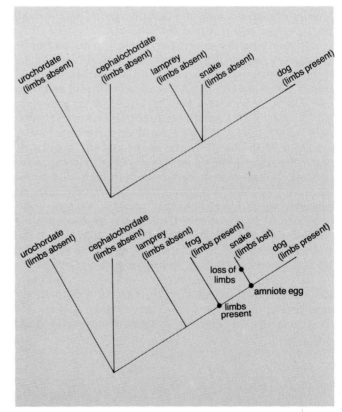

Figure 3. Using outgroup comparison to evaluate the character distribution of paired limbs fails to resolve the relationships of the ingroup (*top*). The absence of paired limbs is postulated to be primitive, and thus it cannot be used to unite the lamprey and the snake. However, if another taxon (for example, a frog) and another character (type of egg produced) are brought into consideration, then the interpretation changes: limbs in the snake are not primitively absent but are lost in an early stage of development. This cladistic hypothesis (*bottom*) is also confirmed by ontogenetic study.

shared with other groups (such characters are termed autapomorphies). Despite this difficulty, both situations can be resolved: the first by searching for other characters, some of which will be found to be derived and shared with other groups, and the second by analyzing the characters in more detail. An autapomorphy is itself the end point of a character transformation, and an understanding of such sequences—often through ontogenetic analysis—can allow us to identify shared characters.

Real-world data are seldom as accommodating as those presented in didactic exercises, and typically each possible cladogram for a group of taxa has one or more shared characters that conflict with its hierarchical structure. In such cases we need some method for evaluating the different hypotheses, and cladists have proposed that the principle of parsimony provides the necessary means (Farris 1983). Few aspects of cladistic analysis have been as misunderstood as the application of the principle of parsimony. Some critics have asserted that by applying parsimony cladists are claiming that evolution is parsimonious or that it is a method for determining truth. Actually, however, some form of parsimony seems to be a requirement of all science: it simply minimizes our acceptance of ad hoc assumptions when we are choosing among hypotheses.

In systematic analysis, the objective is to minimize the number of character conflicts, and we choose among alternative cladograms accordingly. This does not mean, of course, that the most parsimonious cladogram is true—for how could we evaluate the truth of that proposition objectively? Nor does it mean that we will necessarily prefer that cladogram as additional data become available. Indeed, there may be two cladistic hypotheses that are about equally good at explaining character distributions, and we may not want to choose between them. In such a case, the solution is simply to search for more characters that corroborate one hypothesis and conflict with the other. Nevertheless, there will be times when every competing hypothesis has some conflicting data, and in order to avoid the chaos of having all the hypotheses equally tenable, some criterion of choice must be introduced. Without question, systematic analysis has become more precise and objective as a result of the attention cladists have shown toward the problem of parsimony (Farris 1982, 1983).

Reconstructing spatial pattern

Just as cladistic analysis provides a method for revealing the degree of congruence among the characters of organisms, the method of vicariance biogeography assesses the degree of congruence in the distributional patterns of taxa. This use of the term "vicariance" dates from the late nineteenth century, when biologists recognized that closely related forms replaced each other geographically as ecological "vicariants" (or "vicars"). This implied that new species originated through a process of geographic isolation. By contrast with cladistics, the rationale for vicariance biogeography has been subject to considerable misunderstanding. Nevertheless, there is a far-reaching problem in this debate in that some traditionalists seem to deny the existence of congruent distributional patterns: "In complete opposition to the claims of the vicarianists, biotas are, therefore, highly

heterogeneous, *with each of the composing elements having a different history*" (Mayr 1982; italics mine). If this were entirely true, of course, there could not be a science of biogeography: we would not expect to detect nonrandom regularities in nature, nor would we propose hypotheses to explain them. In fact, biologists have been detecting common biogeographic patterns among very different kinds of organisms for over one hundred years (Nelson and Platnick 1981), and vicariance biogeography is a major advance over traditional methods simply because it provides a rigorous technique for revealing common elements in distributional pattern. As will be discussed below, knowledge of that pattern is essential if we are to understand evolutionary history and the processes postulated to have produced it.

Of the various types of biogeographic patterns that might be relevant to evolutionary analysis, that associated with geographic differentiation is particularly important. Present systematic data support the hypothesis that taxa arise in one area and, in the vast majority of cases, their close relatives or descendants arise in another. These areas may be very restricted in size, as in the case of some plants and small animals, or they may be very large, as with many species of birds and mammals. In any case, differentiation—the origin of a new species—is a spatial phenomenon, and in our quest to understand the general pattern of differentiation, we begin by asking whether taxa show congruence in their areas of distribution—in other words, whether there are any patterns of endemism. In fact, biologists have long recognized such patterns, which are easily discernible by inspection of distribution maps.

Two questions naturally arise from knowledge of this kind. First, why do these areas exist? Often this is not difficult to answer, because areas of endemism usually are defined by strongly marked geographic barriers or by noticeable ecological differences from adjacent areas. The second question—how have these areas arisen?—is more difficult, but a moment's reflection reveals one

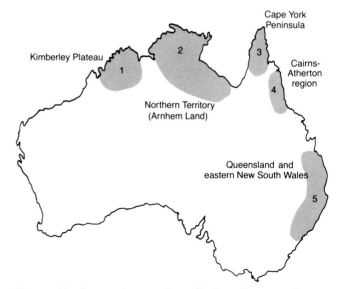

Figure 4. **Northern and eastern Australia show five areas of endemism, with various taxa having distributions defined by clearly marked geographic or ecological barriers. On the north are the savannas of the Kimberley Plateau and Northern Territory, or Arnhem Land; along the east coast, rain forests in Cape York Peninsula, the Cairns-Atherton region, and Queensland and eastern New South Wales are separated by drier woodland.**

intriguing possibility. If areas of endemism are where numerous taxa have differentiated, and if that differentiation has occurred in response to changes in the physical characteristics of those areas (that is, in geology or climate), then it might be conjectured that the areas of endemism will have an evolutionary history, and that the histories of the taxa and of the areas will exhibit congruence. Nearly all biologists would admit that some congruence must exist, but arguments over how much abound in the literature. Many, like Mayr, believe that nature is very complex ("heterogeneous"), with large amounts of random "noise"—that is, unique events—obscuring general historical patterns. Others, including vicariance biogeographers, maintain that we must at least search for the general pattern, because we can recognize unique historical events only in relation to a general pattern. A single painting by Jackson Pollock or Franz Kline may be viewed as chaotic, a random gesturing of paint on canvas, but when their work is examined as a whole, randomness disappears as common patterns of form and texture emerge. Furthermore, against the background of these common patterns, the unique characteristics of each work are also revealed.

When analyzing taxonomic differentiation it is appropriate, therefore, to begin with the problem of discovering congruence, or generality, in the histories of taxa and areas. A simple example will illustrate how this is done.

Northern and eastern Australia can be described biogeographically in terms of five areas of endemism, delineated in Figure 4. All five possess a more moist environment than do areas toward the center of the continent, and all have been viewed as "relict refuges" that survived widespread aridification during the Pleistocene (e.g., Keast 1961). The two northern areas, the Kimberley Plateau and the coastal Northern Territory, or Arnhem Land, are covered with savanna woodland (Ford 1978), whereas the three eastern areas, Cape York Peninsula, the Cairns-Atherton region, and coastal southeastern Queensland together with eastern New South Wales, include tracts of rain forest isolated by regions of drier woodland.

The first aspect of biogeographic pattern is easily established when the distribution maps of many different kinds of organisms are examined: clearly, the five areas are well-defined centers of endemism. To fulfill

Table 2. Character analysis for six species within the finch genus *Poephila* designates primitive characters with 0 and more derived characters with 1, 2, or 3. Each species is distinguishable by a unique combination of characters.

Character	Outgroups[a]	personata	leucotis	acuticauda	hecki	atropygialis	cincta
Color of back	0 dark gray or gray-brown; black barring	1 fawn-brown; no barring	1	1	1	1	1
Black band on flank	0 absent	1 present	1	1	1	1	1
Color of breast	0 white, red, or black, often with spots	1 buff; no spots	1	1	1	1	1
Color of bill	0 red or blue-gray	2 yellow	2	3 pink-red	2	1 black	1
Black color on face	0 at base of bill only	1 extensive, including chin	1	0	0	0	0
Color of throat	0 white, gray, or red	1 large black patch	1	0	0	0	0
Color of crown	0 dark gray or brown	0	0	1 light blue-gray	1	1	1
Shape of tail	0 rounded or slightly pointed	0	0	1 elongated to sharp point	1	1	1
Color of lower back or rump	0 black or gray	0	0	1 white; no black	1	0	0
Color of upper tail coverts	0 white or red	0	0	0	0	1 black	0
Color of face	0 white, gray, or red	1 fawn-brown	0	0	0	0	0

[a] These include *P. guttata*, *P. bichenovii*, and other genera of Australian estrildine finches.

the second component of biogeographic pattern, various taxonomic groups, each with differentiated taxa in three or more of these areas, should exhibit congruence in their phylogenetic patterns. In order to investigate this, it is necessary to examine the cladistic relationships of some of these groups, but at present only a small number of avian taxa have been studied in sufficient detail to resolve biogeographic patterns.

One group that has received attention is the finch genus *Poephila* (Cracraft 1982a), which has a well-defined subsection of six species distributed over the five areas. Table 2 presents a cladistic analysis for a suite of external morphological characters, and the distribution of these derived conditions leads to the phylogenetic hypothesis illustrated in Figure 5. The relationships shown can now be used to establish a preliminary cladistic hypothesis for the areas themselves, and three primary patterns can be hypothesized: areas 1 and 2 are more closely related to each other than either is to the three other areas; areas

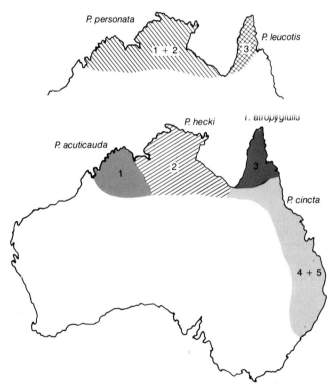

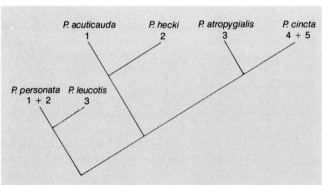

Figure 5. Six species of the finch genus *Poephila* are distributed in the areas of endemism of northern and eastern Australia, here numbered 1 through 5 to correspond with the map in Figure 4. The cladogram is based on the comparative analysis of 11 characters, listed in Table 2.

4 and 5 are more closely related than either is to area 3; and area 3 is more closely related to areas 4 and 5 than to areas 1 and 2.

To see whether in fact different lineages of birds show congruent patterns, it is necessary to undertake additional cladistic analyses. The results of four of these are shown in Figure 6. One problem with these cladograms is that each is only a three-taxon statement; much more could be learned if each lineage had representatives in four or five areas. Nevertheless, all are entirely congruent with the results for the *Poephila* finches, and taken together they provide the basis for postulating a general area-cladogram, which appears in Figure 7.

A general area-cladogram constitutes a hypothesis for the biogeographic history of the areas being examined. In this case, Figure 7 proposes that a vicariance event (a), possibly a climatic change, in the region of the Gulf of Carpentaria separated a widespread biota into western and eastern components. In the west a subsequent event (b) separated the biotas of the Kimberley Plateau and Arnhem Land. Ford (1978) has identified an arid region near the Joseph Bonaparte Gulf and the lowlands of the Victoria and Daly river valleys as the barrier between the Kimberley Plateau and Arnhem Land. In the east, another barrier developed (c), separating the Cape York Peninsula from eastern Australia. Judging from present-day geography, vicariance event c may have been associated with a change in elevation during uplift of the Great Dividing Range, in the Late Cenozoic. Finally, in eastern Australia, an arid barrier (d) developed, separating the Atherton Plateau rain forest area from that farther to the south.

What is the biogeographic significance of a general area-cladogram, particularly one based on such remarkable congruence as that shown by these five avian lineages? Clearly, it presents us with a hypothesis about the history of areas and their biotas. Moreover, the hypothesis proposes that, at least at one level of analysis, earth history is a major determinant of biotic history, and that area-cladograms based on geology (when and if they can be constructed) can be predicted to be congruent with those derived from the cladistic patterns of organisms. The general pattern of relationships among areas of endemism, furthermore, is best explained by the fragmentation or vicariance of once widespread biotas, rather than by many independent, random dispersal events, as has been the traditional explanation within historical biogeography.

If endemic taxa are found to have congruent patterns of cladistic relationships relative to their areas, then vicariance of the biotas is generally the most economical hypothesis, though not necessarily the only one, to explain the congruence. Yet, cladistic analysis can produce phylogenetic hypotheses that appear to be incongruent with the general pattern. The problem of identifying congruence and incongruence in biogeographic patterns has received considerable attention lately (Platnick and Nelson 1978; Nelson and Platnick 1978, 1980, 1981; Platnick 1981). Lineages that do not show differentiation each time an area becomes isolated—such as *Poephila*, illustrated in Figure 5—although entirely congruent with the history of the areas, can make comparisons among cladistic hypotheses exceedingly complex (see Platnick 1981 for an example). Actual incongruence can of course occur, but if we have a well-corroborated area-cladogram, based on the analysis of many clades, then at least we can offer some explanations for the incongruence.

Consider, for example, three parrots in the genus *Psephotus*, which have the relationship shown in the cladogram at the left in Figure 8. In this case, area 3 is more closely related to area 2 than to area 5, which conflicts with the general area-cladogram of Figure 7. Although the cladistic hypothesis of Figure 8 appears to be correct, considerations of parsimony would not make us abandon the general area-cladogram in the face of this single incongruity. Two hypotheses can be suggested to account for the pattern seen in *Psephotus*. First, as shown by the middle cladogram in Figure 8, we might assume that vicariance event c split areas 3 and 5, but that after differentiation in area 3 some members of *P. chrysopterygius* dispersed to area 2 and then differentiated into *P. dissimilis*. A scenario such as this would also imply that another taxon might be found in area 2 with relationships to all three species of *Psephotus*. Second, there may have been extinction, which would mean that our three-taxon analysis is actually embedded in a larger problem, illustrated in the cladogram at the right in Figure 8. Area 5 may be a composite of two areas of endemism, in which case the extinction of one species in area 5a has led us to perceive a conflict, when instead the problem is more complicated than had initially been conceived.

This example points to a significant problem within systematics and biogeography. In order to "explain" the conflict between the first cladogram in Figure 8 and the general area-cladogram, it was necessary to invoke either long-distance dispersal or extinction. Certainly each occurs in nature, but as first-order "explanations" both must be rejected, for, as we have seen, they can be invoked to explain any distribution pattern, and consequently they explain little or nothing.

Evolutionary analysis

Besides being methods of resolving historical pattern, cladistics and vicariance biogeography may also be able to tell us something about the evolutionary process. Whether they actually can do so depends on one's conception of that process. To most contemporary evolutionary biologists, "the process" probably means the causal factors bringing about change in gene content or allelic frequency within populations, and, thus (it is assumed axiomatically), phenotypic change. This transformational view of evolution can be interpreted as an extension of Darwinian adaptation and natural selection, which have always had difficulty in treating the question of species and their origins in any more than a superficial, narrative manner (Lewontin 1974). One can, however, look at the evolutionary process from a broader perspective, one that is delimited by five main questions: How do we explain the evolutionary imperative of life (what "drives" evolution as a whole)? How do populations become spatially isolated? How do evolutionary novelties, or derived characters, arise in individuals within isolated populations? How do these novelties spread through populations to characterize them as new taxonomic units? Lastly, how do we explain the common patterns of phenotypic and taxonomic diversity observed among clades?

Inasmuch as all these questions are concerned with patterns of form, taxonomic diversity, and distribution, the methods and data of cladistics and vicariance biogeography are obviously important. This is especially true in studies of taxonomic differentiation (Rosen 1978; Cracraft 1982a, in press a). By examining patterns of differentiation among different clades that show congruent cladistic-biogeographic histories, we have the means to compare the rates at which novelties are gained by populations, and to judge the concordance or dis-

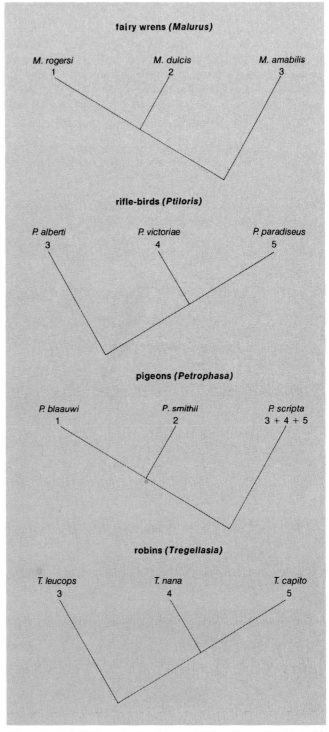

Figure 6. A cladistic analysis of four additional taxa distributed in the areas of endemism shown in Figure 4 reveals patterns that are congruent with those of the finch genus *Poephila*. The numbers 1 through 5 refer to the area of endemism of each species.

cordance between the amounts of phenotypic and genotypic change.

In the above examples, five clades of Australian birds were found to exhibit congruence in their history of differentiation in five areas of endemism. The probability that this degree of congruence could result by chance alone is vanishingly small, which strongly suggests that the evolution of each clade was influenced by the same sequence of geological or climatic changes. Yet, despite these similarities in cladistic pattern, each clade has its own unique aspects. For one thing, not every lineage responded to a given vicariance event by differentiating. For another, even if various lineages differentiate in the same area, it is obvious that they do so at very uneven rates. Some taxa are barely distinct from their close relatives and have been described as subspecies, whereas others are very different and are treated as species. What time emphasis, of course, in their taxonomic ranking—subspecies or species?—in the absence of a cladistic analysis is arbitrary and capable of obscuring interesting evolutionary questions about the pattern of differentiation and rates of change (Cracraft, in press a).

Because of the congruence in the cladistic and vicariance histories of the five taxa, it is possible to establish the relative age of origin of each branch point and lineage. If geological and climatic barriers can be dated, then an absolute time frame can be established to investigate the rate of change within and among lineages. Furthermore, if we can quantify phenotypic and genotypic change (for example, nucleotide or amino acid substitutions), then the two rates can be examined for the degree of their concordance or discordance.

It is at this level of differentiation within populations that changes in form and taxonomic diversity accumulate over time to become what has been called macroevolutionary change, defined as patterns of diversity among monophyletic groups. Cladistic analysis is essential for investigating macroevolutionary problems, for the simple reason that patterns of character change and systematic relationships are the major components of macroevolutionary pattern (Eldredge and Cracraft 1980; Cracraft 1981b, 1982b). A causal theory of macroevolution should be directed toward explaining the similarities in these patterns of morphological and taxonomic diversity from one clade to another. The

Darwinian, transformational view has long dominated macroevolutionary thinking: one need only be reminded of its emphasis on the "adaptive transformation" of one major group of organisms into another (the reptile-to-mammal transition, for example). This view is giving way to one in which changes in diversity within and among clades are interpreted as variation in rates of speciation and extinction that may have nothing to do

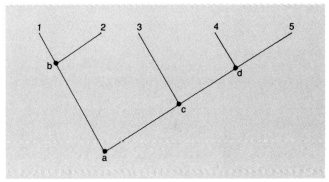

Figure 7. A general cladogram for the areas under study can be postulated, using the cladistic hypotheses for *Poephila*, *Petrophasa*, *Malurus*, *Tregellasia*, and *Ptiloris*. This cladogram postulates that four vicariance events split the biotas of northern and eastern Australia, thus leading to the systematic patterns shown in Figures 5 and 6.

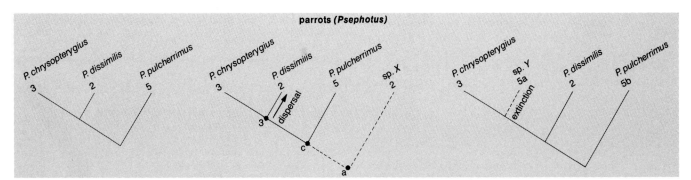

Figure 8. Parrots of the genus *Psephotus* show a phylogenetic pattern (*left*) that is incongruent with the general area-cladogram of Figure 7. Two explanations can account for the incongruity. The first possibility (*middle*) is that once vicariance event c split areas 3 and 5, the species *P. chrysopterygius* differentiated in area 3; some time thereafter, members of *P. chrysopterygius* dispersed

to area 2, where they differentiated into *P. dissimilis*. This hypothesis predicts that another closely related species should be found in area 2. A second possibility (*right*) is that an extinct species of *Psephotus*, as yet unknown, was actually present in area 5. If true, this would suggest that area 5 may actually be comprised of two distinct areas of endemism.

with the "adaptive" nature of the component species (Stanley 1979; Eldredge and Cracraft 1980; Vrba 1980; Cracraft 1982b). Tests of the theories that are emerging from this new view of macroevolution will rely heavily on the cladistic analysis of phylogenetic pattern.

A caveat on classification

Following the rise of the phylogenetic (cladistic) approach to classification in the 1960s, some contemporary systematists voiced strong objections (for example, Mayr 1974). At first glance this criticism may seem peculiar, because cladists propose only that classifications should express the hierarchical structure of natural groups— that is, those taxa postulated to have had a common phylogenetic history. As such, these classifications mirror precisely the cladistic hypotheses, or cladograms, on which they are based.

The Linnaean hierarchy is a system of classification in which taxa are assigned a categorical rank: species, genus, family, and so forth. Ranking is expressed in two ways, by subordination (a subfamily within a family, for example) and by the listing of taxa of equal rank. Because the logical structure of Linnaean hierarchies is one of groups within groups, the only information contained in these hierarchies is that of group membership (in particular, see Farris 1977; Eldredge and Cracraft 1980; Wiley 1981). It follows that cladistic relationships, because they too are hierarchical, can be unambiguously stored and retrieved from Linnaean classifications.

The outcome of the current controversies over classification is of critical importance to all areas of biology (Cracraft, in press b). At some point most biologists want to make comparisons among different kinds of organisms, and it is at such times that a classification becomes useful. Proponents of phylogenetic classification maintain that such comparisons will need to be based on our best knowledge of the composition of natural groups, because these groups have explicit ontological status as historical entities. On the other hand, advocates of alternative systems of classification contend that taxa do not have to be historical entities, that they can be defined by criteria (such as some aspect of similarity) that may be independent of the question of the group's ontological status. This is the crux of the current debate over methods of classification and why it is so important to all biology: it is literally an argument over the advisability of admitting fictitious taxa—those without independent ontological status—into our classifications. Cladists suggest that biological comparisons will prove more profitable when they are made within the context of natural groups, and hence that phylogenetic classifications should be a goal of systematic biology.

References

Brundin, L. 1966. Transantarctic relationships and their significance, as evidenced by chironomid midges. *Kungl. Svenska Vetenskap. Handl.* 11:1–472.

Cracraft, J. 1981a. The use of functional and adaptive criteria in phylogenetic systematics. *Am. Zool.* 21:21–36.

———. 1981b. Pattern and process in paleobiology: The role of cladistic analysis in systematic paleontology. *Paleobiology* 7:456–68.

———. 1982a. Geographic differentiation, cladistics, and vicariance biogeography: Reconstructing the tempo and mode of evolution. *Am. Zool.* 22:411–24.

———. 1982b. A nonequilibrium theory for the rate-control of speciation and extinction and the origin of macroevolutionary patterns. *Syst. Zool.* 31:348–65.

———. In press a. Species concepts and speciation analysis. In *Current Ornithology*, vol. 1, ed. R. F. Johnston. Plenum.

———. In press b. The significance of phylogenetic classifications for systematic and evolutionary biology. Proc. NATO Advanced Study Inst. on Numerical Taxonomy. Springer-Verlag.

Eldredge, N. 1979. Cladism and common sense. In *Phylogenetic Analysis and Paleontology*, ed. J. Cracraft and N. Eldredge, pp. 165–97. Columbia Univ. Press.

Eldredge, N., and J. Cracraft. 1980. *Phylogenetic Patterns and the Evolutionary Process*. Columbia Univ. Press.

Farris, J. S. 1977. On the phenetic approach to vertebrate classification. In *Major Patterns in Vertebrate Evolution*, ed. M. K. Hecht, P. C. Goody, and B. M. Hecht, pp. 823–50. Plenum.

———. 1982. Outgroups and parsimony. *Syst. Zool.* 31:328–34.

———. 1983. The logical basis of phylogenetic analysis. In *Advances in Cladistics*, vol. 2, ed. N. Platnick and V. A. Funk, pp. 7–36. Columbia Univ. Press.

Ford, J. 1978. Geographical isolation and morphological and habitat differentiation between birds of the Kimberley and the Northern Territory. *Emu* 78:25–35.

Gaffney, E. 1979. An introduction to the logic of phylogeny reconstruction. In *Phylogenetic Analysis and Paleontology*, ed. J. Cracraft and N. Eldredge, pp. 79–111. Columbia Univ. Press.

Hennig, W. 1966. *Phylogenetic Systematics*. Univ. of Illinois Press.

Keast, A. 1961. Bird speciation on the Australian continent. *Bull. Mus. Comp. Zool.* 123:303–495.

Lewontin, R. C. 1974. *The Genetic Basis of Evolutionary Change*. Columbia Univ. Press.

Mayr, E. 1974. Cladistic analysis or cladistic classification? *Z. Zool. Syst. Evolut.-forsch.* 12:94–128.

———. 1982. Review of *Vicariance Biogeography*, edited by G. Nelson and D. E. Rosen, p. 620. *Auk* 99:618–20.

Nelson, G. 1979. Cladistic analysis and synthesis: Principles and definitions, with a historical note on Adanson's *Familles des Plantes* (1763–1764). *Syst. Zool.* 28:1–21.

Nelson, G., and N. I. Platnick. 1978. The perils of plesiomorphy: Widespread taxa, dispersal, and phenetic biogeography. *Syst. Zool.* 27:474–77.

———. 1980. A vicariance approach to historical biogeography. *Bioscience* 30:339–43.

———. 1981. *Systematics and Biogeography*. Columbia Univ. Press.

Patterson, C. 1980. Cladistics. *Biologist* 27:234–40.

———. 1982a. Morphological characters and homology. In *Problems of Phylogenetic Reconstruction*, ed. K. A. Joysey and A. E. Friday, pp. 21–74. Syst. Assoc. Spec. Vol. no. 21. Academic Press.

———. 1982b. Cladistics and classification. *New Sci.* 94:303–06.

Platnick, N. I. 1979. Philosophy and the transformation of cladistics, p. 546. *Syst. Zool.* 28:537–46.

———. 1981. Widespread taxa and biogeographic congruence. In *Advances in Cladistics*, vol. 1, ed. V. A. Funk and D. R. Brooks, pp. 223–27. New York Botanical Garden.

Platnick, N. I., and G. Nelson. 1978. A method of analysis for historical biogeography. *Syst. Zool.* 27:1–16.

Rosen, D. E. 1978. Vicariant patterns and historical explanation in biogeography. *Syst. Zool.* 27:159–88.

Stanley, S. M. 1979. *Macroevolution*. W. H. Freeman.

Vrba, E. S. 1980. Evolution, species and fossils: How does life evolve? *S. Afr. J. Sci.* 76:61–84.

Watrous, L. E., and Q. D. Wheeler. 1981. The out-group comparison method of character analysis. *Syst. Zool.* 30:1–11.

Wiley, E. O. 1975. Karl R. Popper, systematics, and classification: A reply to Walter Bock and other evolutionary taxonomists. *Syst. Zool.* 24:233–43.

———. 1980. Phylogenetic systematics and vicariance biogeography. *Syst. Bot.* 5:194–220.

———. 1981. *Phylogenetics: The Theory and Practice of Phylogenetic Systematics*. Wiley.

Evolution and the Triumph of Homology, or Why History Matters

Stephen Jay Gould

In 1912, when the nation both needed and still had a good five cent cigar, Sigma Xi spent three dollars to rent a hall for its annual banquet. Receipts for 1912 totaled $${h}^{2}$$ ... against expenses of $4740.72 (including that three bucks), leaving a balance of $486.20, a fine improvement from the 1911 surplus of $295.67. Our society then included 8,200 members, 2,176 listed as active. In that year, Sigma Xi also decided, for the first time, to publish a journal, the *Sigma Xi Quarterly* (renamed *American Scientist* in 1942). In his "Salutatory" to the very first issue, president (and paleontologist) S. W. Williston wrote on page 1, volume 1, number 1: "Since its beginning Sigma Xi has stood for the encouragement of investigation, of research, rather than for the mere acquisition of knowledge."

In 1886 the founders of Sigma Xi had chosen for their motto "Companions in Zealous Research"—a phrase that we have happily retained despite its archaic ring. The original zealots were an uncompromising lot. Some roamed public places with hidden daggers to strike down supporters of Rome, others committed mass suicide at Masada. They were, above all, men of action—the *doers* of their generation. Our founders chose their words well. Science is doing, not just clever thinking. As Williston noted, our society stands for action expressed as research.

I have been assigned the impossible task of encapsulating the intellectual impact of evolution, both on other sciences and upon society in general, during the past 100 years. I have chosen this fundamental definition of Sigma Xi as prologue because I want to argue that Darwin's most enduring impact has generally been underestimated (or underesteemed). I will hold that his theory is, first and foremost, a guide to action in research—the first *workable* program ever presented for evolution. Darwin was, above all, a *historical methodologist*. His theory taught us the importance of history, expressed in doing as the triumph of homology over other causes of order. History is science of a different kind—pursued, when done well, with all the power and rigor ascribed to more traditional styles of science.

Stephen Jay Gould is Alexander Agassiz Professor of Zoology at Harvard University.

> How Darwin's "long argument" has changed the path of scientific thought during the past 100 years

Darwin taught us why history matters and established the methodology for an entire second style of science.

Darwin as a historical methodologist

Introducing the final chapter of the *Origin of Species* (1859), Darwin writes: "this whole volume is one long argument" (p. 459). Since Darwin was not a conscious or explicit philosopher, and since he crammed the *Origin* so full of particulars collected during twenty long years of preparation, readers often miss the unity of intellectual design. Indeed, Huxley commented that readers often misinterpret the *Origin* as a "sort of intellectual pemmican—a mass of facts crushed and pounded into shape, rather than held together by the ordinary medium of an obvious logical bond" (1893, p. 25).

What, then, is Darwin's "long argument," so deftly hidden amidst his particulars? It is not merely the specific defense of "natural selection," for most of the *Origin* is a basic argument for descent, not for any particular mechanism governing the process. But neither is it the most general marshaling of support for evolution—for transmutation was among the commonest of nineteenth-century heresies, and Darwin had something more special and personal to say.

The "long argument," as I read it, is the claim that *history* stands as the coordinating reason for relationships among organisms. Darwin's argument possesses a simple and beautiful elegance. Before the *Origin*, scientists had sought intrinsic purpose and meaning in taxonomic order. Darwin replied that the ordering reflects a historical pathway, pure and simple. (As just one example, numerological systems of taxonomy flourished in the decades before Darwin. These attempts to arrange all creatures in groups neatly ordered and numbered according to simple mathematical formulae—see Oken 1809–11 or Swainson 1835, for example—make sense if a rational intelligence created all organisms in an ordered scheme, but devolve to absurdity if taxonomy must classify the results of a complex and contingent history.) The eminent historian Edward H. Carr writes: "The real importance of the Darwinian revolution was that Darwin, completing what Lyell had already begun in geology, brought history into science" (1961, p. 71).

So much so good. But the simple statement that Darwin made history matter contains a dilemma, especially if we wish to defend the cardinal premise of Sigma Xi: that science is productive doing, not just clever thinking. History is the domain of narrative—unique, unrepeatable, unobservable, large-scale, singular events. One of the oldest saws of freshman philosophy classes asks: Can history be science? Many professors answer "no" because science seeks immanence by experiment and prediction, while the narrative quality of history seems to preclude just these defining features.

How then can we marry these two apparently contradictory statements—the claim that Darwin's "long argument" made history matter and the usual impression that Darwin was a great scientist? The problem vanishes when we locate Darwin's singular greatness in his extended campaign to establish a scientific methodology for history—to make history doable for the zealous researchers of science. Darwin was, more than anything else, a historical methodologist.

Michael Ghiselin's landmark book (1969) was the first to analyze all of Darwin's writing (not just the central trilogy of the *Origin*, the *Descent of Man*, and the *Expression of the Emotions*). He was also the first to suggest with proper documentation that Darwin's greatness as a scientist lay in the middle ground between his most basic elucidation of evolution as a fact, and his most general development of the radical implications (randomness, materialism, nonprogressionism) that so upset Western culture (but produced less immediate impact upon the day-to-day practice of science). This middle ground embodies Darwin's arguments for a methodology of research, for the actual *doing* itself. For Ghiselin, Darwin succeeded because he consistently used the hypothetico-deductive method so celebrated by recent philosophers of science—even though, as a loyal Victorian, he usually misportrayed himself (primarily in his *Autobiography*) as a patient and rigorous Baconian inductivist. (Ruse 1979 supports Ghiselin in the major work on Darwin's methodology written since.)

While I applaud Ghiselin's insight that Darwin must be viewed primarily as a methodologist—as someone who taught scientists how to proceed—I disagree that the central theme and sustaining power of Darwin's methodology lies in its hypothetico-deductive format. Philosopher of science Philip Kitcher has recently written that "if Darwin was a scientist practicing by the canons favored by Ghiselin and Ruse, then he was a poor practitioner"; in Kitcher's account, Darwin "answers to rather different methodological ideals" (1985, footnote 11). Kitcher views Darwin's theories as sets of "problem-solving patterns, aimed at answering families of questions about organisms, by describing the histories of these organisms" (p. 135)—the very aspect of life that had no relevance in the pre-Darwinian world of created permanence. But how can a naturalist do history in a scientific way, especially given the poor reputation of history as a ground for testable hypotheses? How can history be incorporated into science?

Darwin's long argument is not a simple brief for evolution; it is, above all, a claim for *knowability*—a set of methods that subjected evolution, for the first time, to zealous research. Previous briefs for evolution—and

many had appeared to much comment (Lamarck 1809; Chambers 1844)—had presented speculative systems suggesting little in the way of doable research. Lyell's strong distaste for Lamarck (an opinion shared by Darwin) centered upon the methodological vacuousness of his system: "There were no examples to be found. . . . When Lamarck talks of 'the efforts of internal sentiment,' 'the influence of subtle fluids,' and 'acts of organization,' as causes . . . he substitutes names for things; and, with a disregard to the strict rules of induction, resorts to fictions, as ideal as the 'plastic virtue,' and other phantoms, of the geologists of the middle ages" (1842, pp. 10–11).

Darwin's claim for knowability centers upon two themes: first, the uniformitarian argument that one should work by extrapolating from small-scale phenomena that can be seen and investigated; second, the establishment of a graded set of methods for inferring history when only large-scale results are available for study.

The uniformitarian argument

In a famous letter for once not overly immodest, Darwin stated that half his work came out of Lyell's brain. Lyell's insistent argument through three volumes of the *Principles of Geology*—that a historical scientist must work with observable, gradual, small-scale changes and extrapolate their effects through immense time to encompass the grand phenomena of history—won Darwin's allegiance, with a central commitment for its transfer, in toto, to biological realms. But, as a fateful event in the history of nineteenth-century science (Gould 1965; Rudwick 1972; Hooykaas 1963), Lyell advanced uniformity as more than a methodological postulate—work with small-scale events when you can, because they are all you have. It became a strong substantive claim as well—the world really works that way, all the time.

In Lamarck's system, small-scale adaptations (the giraffe's neck, the long legs and webbed feet of wading birds) are tangential—literally orthogonal—to a different, virtually unobservable, and more essential process that moves organisms up the ladder of life toward ever-greater complexity. Savor the paradox for a scientist committed by definition to doing: what you can know and manipulate is unimportant or irrelevant; what is essential cannot be directly observed.

Darwin broke through this disabling paradox by proclaiming that the tangible small-scale evidences of change—artificial selection as practiced by breeders and farmers, tiny differences in geographic variation among races of a species, for example— are, by smooth extrapolation, *the* stuff of all evolution. Darwin, for the first time, made evolution a workable research program, not just an absorbing subject for speculation. This methodological breakthrough was his finest achievement.

But Darwin, like Lyell, then ventured beyond the methodological issue, thereby setting the pathways of evolutionary debate ever since (including all the hubbub of the last decade). He argued that all change, at whatever apparent level, really did arise as the extrapolated result of accumulated selection within populations. The distinctive features of strict Darwinism—particularly its location of causality in struggles among organisms (denial of hierarchy), and its argument for continuity in rate, style, and effect from the smallest observable to the largest inferred events of change (see Gingerich 1983 for a modern defense; Gould 1984 for a rebuttal)—emerge from this substantive extension of the uniformitarian argument.

The questioning of this extension unifies the apparently diverse critiques prominently discussed during the past decade. Critics are denying the reductionistic causal premise (struggles among organisms) by outlining a hierarchical theory of selection, independent at several levels of genes, organisms, demes, and species, but with complex interactions across all levels (Gould 1982a; Vrba and Eldredge 1984; for a philosopher's defense of hierarchy as logically sound see Sober 1984). They are also denying causal continuity from competition in a crowded world (Darwin's "wedging") to delays and replacements of faunas in mass extinctions (Raup and Sepkoski 1984), thereby defending more randomness and discontinuity in *change* (rather than merely for raw material) than Darwin's vision allowed. (Punctuated equilibrium does not challenge the continuationist claim per se, since paleontological punctuations proceed tolerably slowly in ecological time, but rather the reductionistic argument about the primacy of selection on organisms, since trends mediated by differential speciation offer such scope for true species selection—see Eldredge and Gould 1972; Gould 1982b. Thus punctuated equilibrium leads to hierarchy, not saltationism.)

In short, Darwin made evolution doable for the first time, but by holding so strongly to the substantive side of uniformitarianism, ultimately offered a restrictive version that hierarchies of causal levels and tiers of time (Gould 1985a) must extend. This discussion has raged for ten years and continues unabated, but I shall pursue it no farther here because I want to concentrate on the character and meaning of Darwin's second great contribution to a science of history.

Inferring history from its results

The uniformitarian argument constructs history from an observable, small-scale present. But how can scientists proceed when they have only results before them? Past processes are, in principle, unobservable, yet science traffics in process. How, then, can we make history doable if our data feature only its results?

I have come to view Darwin's sequence of books as proceeding at two levels—an explicit and conscious treatment of diverse subjects (from coral reefs, to orchids, to insectivorous plants, to climbing plants, to worms, to evolution); and a covert, perhaps unconscious extended treatise on historical methodology, with each book featuring a different principle of historical reconstruction. We may arrange these principles—three in number—in terms of decreasing information for making inferences.

First, the large-scale results may lie before us, and we can also measure the rate and effect of the process that presumably produces them. In such cases of maximal information, we can use the uniformitarian method in its purest form: make rigorous measurements of the

modern process and extrapolate into available time to render the full result. *The Formation of Vegetable Mould, Through the Action of Worms* (1881) is Darwin's finest example of this method. This book, Darwin's last, may also be his most misunderstood. Often seen as a pleasant trifle of old age, Darwin's worm book is a consciously chosen exemplar of historical reasoning at its most complete. What better choice of object than the humble, insignificant worm, working unnoticed literally beneath our feet? Could something so small really be responsible both for England's characteristic topography and for the upper layer of its soil?

Punch's commentary on Darwin's last work on worms (*Punch* 22 October 1881, p. 190)

Darwin's argument is pure uniformitarianism, carefully extended in stages. He counts worms to see if the soil contains enough for the work needed. He collects castings to measure the rate of churning (about 1/10 inch per year). He then extends the time scale to decades, via natural experiments on layers, once at the surface, that now lie coherently below material brought up by worms (burned coals, rubble from demolition, flints on his own ploughed field)—and then even farther by measuring the rate of foundering for historical objects (the "Druidical" rocks of Stonehenge, for example).

Second, we may have insufficient data about modern rates and processes simply to extrapolate their effects, but we can document several kinds or categories of results and seek relationships among them. Here we face a problem of taxonomy. Darwin argues that we may still proceed in the absence of direct data for uniformitarian extrapolation. We must formulate a historical hypothesis and then arrange the observed results as stages of its operation. The historical process, in other words, becomes the thread that ties all results together causally. This method succeeds because the process works on so many sequences simultaneously, but beginning at different times and proceeding at different rates in its various manifestations; therefore, all stages exist somewhere in the world at any one time (just as we may infer the course of a star's life by finding different stars in various stages of a general process, even though we trace no actual history of any individual star).

Darwin's first theoretical book, *The Structure and Distribution of Coral Reefs* (1842), illustrates this powerful guide to history. Its argument rests upon a classification of reefs into three basic categories of fringing, barrier, and atoll. Darwin proposed a common theme—subsidence of islands—to portray all three as sequential stages of a single historical process. Since corals build up and out from the edges of oceanic platforms, reefs begin by fringing their islands, become barriers as their islands subside, and finally atolls when their platforms submerge completely. But the taxonomy itself guarantees no history. During the nineteenth century, Darwin's opponents developed a series of counterproposals that may be called, collectively, "antecedent platform" theories. They argued that since corals build at the edges of platforms, these fringing reefs, barriers, and atolls only record the extent of previous planation, not a historical sequence in coral growth—platforms eroded to a small notch develop fringing reefs; those planed flat by waves become substrates for atolls. (Lyell, before Darwin convinced him otherwise, had advanced an even simpler ahistorical theory: that atolls develop on the circular rims of volcanoes.) The two theories can be distinguished by a crucial test not available in Darwin's time: no correlation between vertical extent of the reef and its form for antecedent platforms, progressive thickening from fringing reef to atoll in Darwin's subsidence. Twentieth-century drilling into Pacific atolls has affirmed Darwin's view.

Third, we must sometimes infer history from single objects; we have neither data for extrapolation from modern processes, nor even a series of stages to arrange in historical sequence. But how can a scientist infer history from single objects? This most common of historical dilemmas has a somewhat paradoxical solution. Darwin answers that we must look for imperfections and oddities, because any perfection in organic design or ecology obliterates the paths of history and might have been created as we find it. This principle of imperfection became Darwin's most common guide (if only because the fragmentary evidence of history often fails to provide better data in the preceding categories). I like to call it the "panda principle" in honor of my favorite example—the highly inefficient, but serviceable, false thumb of the panda, fashioned from the wrist's radial sesamoid bone because the true anatomical first digit had irrevocably evolved, in carnivorous ancestors of the herbivorous panda, to limited motility in running and clawing. (The herbivorous panda uses its sesamoid "thumb" for stripping leaves off bamboo shoots.) I titled one of my books *The Panda's Thumb* (1980) to honor this principle of historical reasoning.

The panda principle is a basic method of all histori-

cal science, linguistics, and history itself, for example, not just a principle for evolutionary reasoning. In *The Various Contrivances by which Orchids Are Fertilized by Insects* (1862), the book that followed the *Origin of Species*, Darwin shows that the wondrously complex adaptations of orchids, so intricately fashioned to aid fertilization by insects, are all jury-rigged from the ordinary parts of flowers, not built to the optimum specifications of an engineer's blueprint. "The use of each trifling detail of structure," Darwin writes, "is far from a barren search to those who believe in natural selection" (1888 ed., p. 286).

Throughout all these arguments, Darwin also

We must look for imperfections and oddities, because any perfection in organic design or ecology obliterates the paths of history and might have been created as we find it

---

showed his keen appreciation for the other great principle of historical science—the importance of proper taxonomies. In a profession more observational and comparative than experimental, the ordering of diverse objects into sensible categories becomes a sine qua non of causal interpretation. A taxonomy is not a mindless allocation of objective entities into self-evident pigeonholes, but a theory of causal ordering. Proper taxonomies require two separate insights: the identification and segregation of the basic phenomenon itself, and the division of its diverse manifestations into subcategories that reflect process and cause. Consider, for example, Steno's *Prodromus* (1669). This founding document of geology is, fundamentally, a new taxonomy (see Gould 1983). Steno identifies solid objects enclosed in other solids as the basic phenomenon (a stunningly original and peculiar choice in the light of ordering principles generally accepted in his time); he then makes a fundamental division into objects hard before surrounded (fossils) and those introduced without initial solidity into a rigid matrix (crystals in geodes, for example). Using these divisions, Steno could identify the organic origins of fossils and the temporal nature of strata—the cornerstones of historical geology.

Darwin's *Different Forms of Flowers on Plants of the Same Species* (1877) is a fine illustration of how taxonomy informs history. The basic recognition of the phenomenon itself as a unitary puzzle poses a historical question. The work then becomes a long argument about subdivisions by function (heterostyly to assure cross-fertilization, cleistogamy to allow some advantageous selfing while retaining other forms of flowers for occasional crossing, for example), and about ancestral states and the paths of potential transformation.

The *Origin of Species* achieves its conceptual power by using all these forms of historical argument: uniformitarianism in extrapolating the observed results of artificial selection by breeders and farmers; inference of history from temporal ordering of coexisting phenomena (in constructing, for example, a sequence leading from variation within a population, to small-scale geographic differentiation of races, to separate species, to the origin of major groups and key innovations in morphology); and, most often and to such diverse effect, the panda principle of imperfection (vestigial organs, odd biogeographic distributions made sensible only as products of history, adaptations as contrivances jury-rigged from parts available).

I do not know whether Darwin operated by conscious design to construct his multivolumed treatise on historical method. Since great thinkers so often work by what our vernacular calls intuition (though the process involves no intrinsic mystery, as logical reconstruction by later intellectual biographers can attest), conscious intent is no criterion of outcome. Still, I like to think that the last paragraph of Darwin's last book records his own perception of connection—for he closes his last treatise on worms by remembering him first on corals, thereby linking both his humble subjects and his criteria of history:

It may be doubted whether there are many other animals which have played so important a part in the history of the world, as have these lowly organized creatures [worms]. Some other animals, however, still more lowly organized, namely corals, have done far more conspicuous work in having constructed innumerable reefs and islands in the great oceans.

Using the panda principle

Historical science is still widely misunderstood, underappreciated, or denigrated. Most children first meet science in their formal education by learning about a powerful mode of reasoning called "*the* scientific method." Beyond a few platitudes about objectivity and willingness to change one's mind, students learn a restricted stereotype about observation, simplification to tease apart controlling variables, crucial experiment, and prediction with repetition as a test. These classic "billiard ball" models of simple physical systems grant no uniqueness to time and object—indeed, they remove any special character as a confusing variable—lest repeatability under common conditions be compromised. Thus, when students later confront history, where complex events occur but once in detailed glory, they can only conclude that such a subject must be less than science. And when they approach taxonomic diversity, or phylogenetic history, or biogeography—where experiment and repetition have limited application to systems in toto—they can only conclude that something beneath science, something merely "descriptive," lies before them.

These historical subjects, placed into a curriculum of science, therefore become degraded by their failure to match a supposedly universal ideal. They become, in our metaphors, the "soft" (as opposed to "hard") sciences, the "merely descriptive" (as opposed to "rigorously experimental"). Every year Nobel prizes are announced to front-page fanfare, and no one who works with the complex, unrepeated phenomena of history can win—for the prizes only recognize science as designated by the stereotype. (I'm not bitching—since it makes for a much more pleasant profession—only making a social comment.) Plate tectonics revolutionized our view of the

earth, but its authors remain anonymous to the public eye; molecular phylogeny finally begins to unravel the complexities of genealogy, and its accomplishments rank as mere narrative. Harvard organizes its Core Curriculum and breaks conceptual ground by dividing sciences into the two major styles of experimental-predictive and historical, rather than, traditionally, by discipline. But guess which domain becomes "Science A" and which "Science B"?

In a perverse way, the best illustration of this failure to understand the special character of history can be found in writings by opponents of science, who use clever rhetoric to argue against evolution because it doesn't work like their simplistic view of physics. In his book *Algeny* (1983), for example (see Gould 1985b for a general critique), Jeremy Rifkin dismisses Darwin because evolution can't be turned into a controlled laboratory experiment: "To qualify as a science, Darwin's theory should be provable by means of the scientific method. In other words, its hypotheses should be capable of being tested experimentally" (p. 117). Rifkin then cites Dobzhansky's statement about history as though it represents a fatal confession: "Dobzhansky laments the fact that 'evolutionary happenings are unique, unrepeatable, and irreversible. It is as impossible to turn a vertebrate into a fish as it is to effect the reverse transformation.' Dobzhansky is chagrined" (p. 118). But Dobzhansky in this passage is neither chagrined nor troubled; he is simply commenting upon the nature of history. Rifkin concludes nonetheless: "Embarrassing, to say the least. Here is a body of thought, incapable of being scientifically tested. . . . If not based on scientific observation, then evolution must be a matter of personal faith" (pp. 118–19).

When creationist lawyer Wendell Bird took my deposition in pretrial hearings on the constitutionality of Louisiana's "creation-science" law (mercifully tossed out without trial by a federal judge), he spent an inordinate amount of time (and verbal trickery) trying to make me admit that a suspension of natural law—a miracle—might fall within the purview of science. At the close of this lamentable episode, I was astounded when he asked "Are you familiar with the term singularistic?" and then tried to argue that complex historical events (singularistic in that sense), as unrepeatable, are somehow akin to miracles (singularities) and therefore make such historical sciences as evolution either as good or as bad as the Genesis-literalism of so-called creation-science!

These arguments about history are red herrings and we would do well to suppress them by acknowledging the *different* strengths of historical science, lest the simplistic stereotype be turned, as in these cases, against all of science.

The "lesser" status of historical science may be rejected on two grounds. First, it is not true that standard techniques of controlled experimentation, prediction, and repeatability cannot be applied to complex histories. Uniqueness exists in toto, but "nomothetic undertones" (as I like to call them) can always be factored out. Each mass extinction has its endlessly fascinating particularities (trilobites died in one, dinosaurs in another), but a common theme of extraterrestrial impact (Alvarez et al. 1980) may trigger a set of such events, even perhaps on a regular cycle (Raup and Sepkoski 1984). Nature, moreover, presents us with experiments aplenty, imperfectly controlled compared with the best laboratory standards, but having other virtues (temporal extent, for example) not attainable with human designs.

Second, as argued earlier, Darwin labored for a lifetime to meet history head on, and to establish rigorous methods for inference about its singularities. History, by Darwin's methods, is knowable in principle (though not fully recoverable in every case, given the limits of evidence), testable, and different. We do not attempt to predict the future (I could already retire in comfort if someone paid me a dollar for each rendition of my "paleontologists don't predict the future" homily following the inevitable question from the floor at all presentations to nonscientists—"Well, where is human evolution going anyway?"). But we can postdict about the past—and do so all the time in historical science's most common use of repeatability (every new iridium anomaly at the Cretaceous-Tertiary boundary is a repeated postdicted affirmation of Alvarez's conjecture about impact, based upon just three sites in the original article).

Finally, history's richness drives us to different methods of testing, but testability (via postdiction) is our method as well. Huxley and Darwin maintained interestingly different attitudes toward testing in history. Huxley, beguiled by the stereotype, always sought a crucial observation or experiment (the destruction of theory by a "nasty, ugly, little fact" of his famous aphorism). Darwin, so keenly aware of both the strengths and limits of history, argued that iterated pattern, based on types of evidence so numerous and so diverse that no other coordinating interpretation could stand—even though any item, taken separately, could not provide conclusive proof—must be the criterion for evolutionary inference. (The great philosopher of science William Whewell had called this historical method "consilience of inductions.") Huxley sought the elusive crucial experiment; Darwin strove for attainable consilience. Di Gregorio's recent treatise on Huxley's scientific style contains an interesting discussion of this difference (1984). (Ironically, Whewell, a conservative churchman, later banned Darwin's *Origin* from the library of Trinity College, Cambridge, where he was master. What greater blow than the proper use of one's own arguments in an alien context.)

In an essay of 1860, for example, Huxley wrote: "but there is no positive evidence, at present, that any group of animals has, by variation and selective breeding, given rise to another group which was, even in the least degree, infertile with the first. Mr. Darwin is perfectly aware of this weak point, and brings forward a multitude of ingenious and important arguments to diminish the force of the objection" (quoted by di Gregorio, p. 61). Note particularly Huxley's subtle misunderstanding of Darwin's methodology. What Huxley views as a set of indirect arguments, presented faute de mieux in the absence of experimental proof, *is* Darwin's consilience, positively developed as the proper method of historical inference. Darwin complained of just this misunderstanding in a letter to Hooker in 1861: "change

of species cannot be directly proved . . . the doctrine must sink or swim according as it groups and explains phenomena. It is really curious how few judge it in this way, which is clearly the right way" (di Gregorio, p. 62). And, more specifically, in his *Variation of Animals and Plants Under Domestication* (1868):

Now this hypothesis [natural selection] may be tested—and this seems to me the only fair and legitimate manner of considering the whole question—by trying whether it explains several large and independent classes of facts; such as the geological succession of organic beings, their distribution in past and present times, and their mutual affinities and homologies. If the principle of natural selection does explain these and other large bodies of facts, it ought to be received. [I, 657]

Historical scientists try to import bodily an oversimplified caricature of "hard" science

Despite the ready availability of these powerful, yet different, modes of inference, historical scientists have often been beguiled by the stereotype of direct experimental proof, and have wallowed in a curious kind of self-hate in trying to ape, where not appropriate, supposedly universal procedures of *the* scientific method. Many of the persistent debates within evolutionary biology are best viewed as a series of attempts to divest evolution of history under the delusion that scientific rigor gains thereby—with responses by defenders that history cannot be factored away, and that good science can be done just splendidly with it.

In extreme versions, for example, the welcome and powerful movement of "equilibrium" biogeography and ecology, which developed in the 1960s and peaked in the 1970s, not only denied history, but viewed its singularities as impediments to real science. Equilibrium models avoid history by explaining current situations as active balances maintained between competing forces now operating. Such models apply a reverse panda principle by identifying nonequilibria as signs of history—situations not yet balanced and therefore in a relevant state of history. Equilibria, when reached, are timeless, changing only when the measurable inputs alter, and not by any historically bound "evolution" of the system.

Ironically, the founding document of this movement was written by two fine historical scientists who understood proper limits, and who used their models to identify nomothetic undertones of a valued history (MacArthur and Wilson 1967). They also explicitly discussed the interactions of history and equilibrium, and the long-term evolutionary adjustments that continue, albeit at slower rates, within systems at equilibrium: "The equilibrium model has the virtues of making testable predictions which were not immediately obvious and of making the individual vagaries of island history seem somewhat less important in understanding the diversity of the island's species. Of course the history of islands remains crucial to the understanding of the taxonomic composition of species" (1967, p. 64). But in the hands of singleminded and less thoughtful supporters, equilibrium ecology moved from suggestive simplification (or search for repeated undertones) to a hard substantive claim spearheading a crusade for bringing "real" science into an antiquated domain of descriptive natural history. The campaign quickly stalled, however; nature fights back effectively.

The most common denial of history made by self-styled Darwinian evolutionists resides in claims for optimality—conventionally for the mechanics of morphology, more recently for behavior and ecology. Again, optimality theory has its place and uses (primarily in designating ideals for assessing natural departures). Committed votaries think that they are celebrating evolution by showing how inexorably and fine the mills of natural selection can grind; in fact, they are attempting to abrogate Darwin's most important criterion of history—the panda principle of imperfection and oddity as signs of previous histories and affinities genealogically pre-

Evolution is a bush, not a ladder

served. Under certain conditions of minimal constraint, we may legitimately seek optimality (animal color patterns, often less subject than morphology to developmental covariance, represent one promising domain—see Cott 1940 for the classic statement). Usually, history and complexity must assert themselves prominently.

The sad tale goes on and on. Historical scientists, who should take legitimate pride in their different ways, try to import bodily an oversimplified caricature of "hard" science, or simply bow to pronouncements of professions with higher status. Some accepted Kelvin's last and most restrictive dates for a young earth, though fossils and strata spoke differently; many more foreswore their own data when physicists proclaimed that continents cannot move laterally. Charles Spearman misused factor analysis to identify intelligence as a measurable physical thing in the head, and then said of psychology that "this Cinderella among the sciences has made a bold bid for the level of triumphant physics itself" (see Gould 1981, chap. 6).

But the great historical scientists have always treasured both their rigorous, testable methods and their singular data. D'Arcy Thompson, whose own vision of optimal form, impressed directly upon organisms by physical forces, must rank among the most ahistorical of approaches to evolution (see Gould 1971), nonetheless knew that a retrievable history pervaded all objects—and that the panda principle can recover it. He wrote in his incomparable prose (1942):

Immediate use and old inheritance are blended in Nature's handiwork as in our own. In the marble columns and architraves of a Greek temple we still trace the timbers of its wooden prototype, and see beyond these the tree-trunks of a primeval sacred grove; roof and eaves of a pagoda recall the sagging mats which roofed an earlier edifice; Anglo-Saxon land-tenure influences the planning of our streets and the cliff-dwelling and cave-dwelling linger on in the construction of our homes! So we see enduring traces of the past in the living organism—landmarks which have lasted on through altered function and altered needs. [pp. 1020–21]

The triumph of homology

Louis Agassiz chose an enigmatic name for his institution—and for good cause. He called it the Museum of Comparative Zoology (I am sitting in its oldest section as I write this article) in order to emphasize that the sciences of organic diversity do not usually seek identity in repeated experiment, but work by comparing the similarities among objects of nature as given. Kind, extent, and amount of similarity provide the primary data of historical science.

As a problem, recognized since Aristotle, natural similarities come in two basic, largely contradictory styles. We cannot simply measure and tabulate; we must factor and divide. Similarities may be homologies, shared by simple reason of descent and history, or analogies, actively developed (independently but to similar form and effect) as evolutionary responses to common situations.

Systematics (the science of classifying organisms) is the analysis of similarity in order to exclude analogy and recognize homology. Such an epigram may sacrifice a bit of subtlety for crisp epitome, but it does capture the first goal of historical science. Homologous similarity is the product of history; analogy, as independent tuning to current circumstance, obscures the paths of history.

The major brouhaha about cladistics (see Hennig 1966; Eldredge and Cracraft 1980; any issue of *Systematic Zoology* for the past decade, or, for self-serving misuse by yet another opponent of science, Bethell 1985) has unfolded in needless acrimony because cladistics has not been properly recognized, even by some of its strongest champions, as a "pure" method for defining historical order and rigidly excluding all other causes of similarity. Cladistics allies objects in branching hierarchies defined only by relative times of genealogical connection. Closest, or "sister-group," pairs share a unique historical connection (a common ancestor yielding them as its only descendants). The system then connects sister-group pairs into ever-more inclusive groups sharing the same genealogical uniqueness (common ancestry that includes absolutely all descendant branches and absolutely no other groups). Cladistics is the science of ordering by genealogical connection, *and nothing else*. As such, it is the quintessential expression of history's primacy above any other cause or expression of similarity—and, on this basis alone, should be received with pleasure by evolutionists.

Nonetheless, several of the most forceful cladists never grasped this central point clearly; they buried their subject in frightful terminology and such exaggerated or extended claims that they antagonized many key systematists and never won the general approbation they deserved. In an almost perverse interpretation (literal, not ethical), some supporters, the self-styled "transformed" or "pattern" cladists, have actually negated the central strength of their method as a science of history by claiming—based on a curiously simplistic reading of Karl Popper—that science should eschew all talk of "process" (or cause) and work only with recoverable "pattern" (or the branching order of cladograms). Pattern cladists are not anti-evolution (as misportrayed by Bethell 1985); rather, as a result of narrow commitment to an extreme

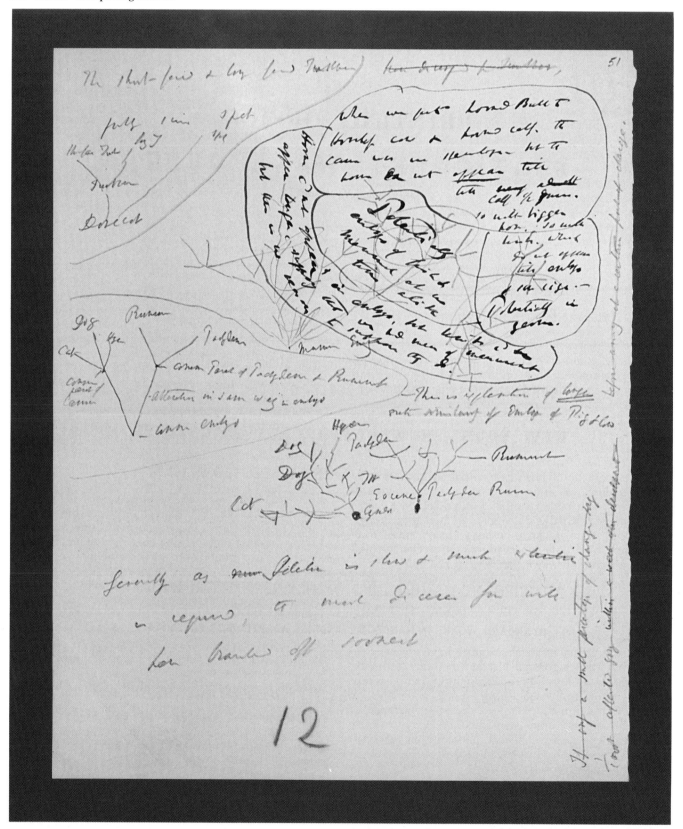

This unpublished page from Darwin's file "Embryology" shows Darwin constructing congruent trees of relationship, based in one case on developmental similarities, and in the other on time of divergence. The page, which dates from the mid-1850s, though by no means his first use of trees, is one of his most sophisticated. In the upper left, Darwin shows the descent of two breeds of tumbler pigeons from the common pigeon. Below, he arranges carnivores on one great branch and ungulates (divided into pachyderms and ruminants) on the other, which unite at a base labeled "common embryo." The central tree relates the same groups, but grows through geological time, rather than developmental space; here Darwin writes "Eocene Pachyderm Ruminant." On the right, he discusses the inheritance, expression, timing, and alteration of characters in development. (Summary by S. Rachootin; photograph of DAR 205.6:51 reproduced by permission of the Syndics of the Cambridge University Library.)

view of empiricism and falsification, they choose to ignore evolution as unprovable talk about process, and to concentrate on recovery of branching pattern alone. All well and good; it can be done with cladistic methods. But unless we wish to abandon a basic commitment to cause and natural law, branching order must arise for a reason (by a process, if you will). And that process is history, however history be made. In other words, the clearest method ever developed for discerning history has been twisted by some supporters to a caricatured empiricism that denies its subject. What an irony. We need to recover cladistics—a pure method for specifying those histories that develop by divergent and irreversible branching—from some of its own most vociferous champions.

Cladistics, as a methodology, is conceptually sound. In biological systematics, it has often proved inconclusive in practice (leading to a false suspicion that the method itself might be logically flawed) because taxonomists have worked, generally faute de mieux, or by simple weight of tradition, with the inappropriate data of morphology. Homology can often be recovered from morphology, but the forms of organisms often include an inextricable mixture of similarities retained by history (homology) and independently evolved in the light of common function (analogy). Morphology is not the best source of data for unraveling history. Thoughtful systematists have known this ever since Darwin, but have proceeded as best they could in the absence of anything better.

In principle, the recovery of homology only requires a source of information with two properties: sufficiently numerous and sufficiently independent items to preclude, on grounds of mathematical probability alone, any independent origin in two separate lineages. The "items" of morphology are too few and too bound in complex webs of developmental correlation to yield this required independence. Yet the discoveries and techniques of molecular biology have now provided an appropriate source for recovering homology—a lovely example of science at its unified best, as a profession firmly in the camp of repetition and experiment provides singular data for history. Molecular phylogenies work not because DNA is "better," more real, or more basic than morphology, but simply because the items of a DNA program are sufficiently numerous and independent to ensure that degrees of simple matching accurately measure homology. The most successful technique of molecular phylogeny has not relied upon sophisticated sequencing, but rather the "crudest" brute-force matching of all single-copy DNA—for such a method uses a maximum number of independent items (Sibley and Ahlquist 1981, 1984, and 1985).

Consider just one elegant example of the triumph of homology (as determined by molecular methods)—a case that should stand as sufficient illustration of the primacy of history as both a basic cause of order and a starting point for all further analyses. The songbirds of Australia have posed a classic dilemma for systematists because they seem to present a biogeographic and taxonomic pattern so different from the mammals. The marsupials of Australia form a coherent group bound by homology and well matched to the geographic isolation

of their home. But the songbirds include a large set of creatures apparently related to several Eurasian and American groups: warblers, thrushes, nuthatches, and flycatchers, for example. This classification has forced the improbable proposal that songbirds migrated to Australia in several distinct waves. Even though birds fly and mammals do not, the discordance of pattern between the two groups has been troubling, since most birds are not nearly so mobile as their metaphorical status suggests. But Sibley and Ahlquist (1985) have now completed the molecular phylogeny (true homology) of Australian songbirds—and they form a coherent group of homologues, just like the marsupials. The similarities to Eurasian and American taxa are all convergences—independently evolved analogies—not homologies. Marsupials, of course, have also evolved some astounding convergences upon placentals (our so-called "wolves," "mice," and "moles"), but systematists have not been confounded because all marsupials retain signatures of homology in their pouches and epipubic bones. We now realize that the apparent and deeply troubling discordance between Australian birds and mammals arose only because the birds did not retain such morphological signatures of homology, and systematists were therefore fooled by the striking analogies.

Once we map homologies properly, we can finally begin to ask interesting biological questions about function and development—that is, we can use morphology for its intrinsic sources of enlightenment, and not as an inherently flawed measure of genealogical relationships. The historical flow of protoplasm through branching systems of genealogy *is* the material reality that structures biology. But analogies have a different (and vital) meaning that the resolution of history finally permits us to appreciate. They are functional themes that stand, almost like a set of Platonic forms, in a domain for biomechanics, functional morphology, and an entire set of nonhistorical disciplines. "Wrenness," "mouseness," and "wormness" may not have the generality of forms so basic that they have rarely been confused with homologies (bilateral symmetry, for example), but they still represent iterated themes, standards of design external to history. The material reality of history—phylogeny—flows through them again and again, forming a set of contrasts that define the fascination of biology: homology and analogy, history and immanence, movement and stability.

If the primacy of history is evolution's lesson for other sciences, then we should explore the consequences of valuing history as a source of law and similarity, rather than dismissing it as narrative unworthy of the name science. I argued in the first section that Darwin cut through a tangle of unnecessary complexity by proposing "just history" as a disconcertingly simple answer in domains where science had sought a deeper, rational immanence (as for the ordering of taxonomy). I wonder how far we might extend this insight. Consider our relentless search for human universals and our excitement at the prospect that we may thereby unlock something at the core of our being. So Jung proposes archetypes of the human psyche in assessing the similarities of mythic systems across cultures, while others invoke brain structure and natural selection as a source of uncannily complex repetitions among human groups long separate. Yet evolution is a bush, not a ladder. *Homo sapiens* had a discrete and recent origin, presumably as an isolated local population, crowned with inordinate later success. Many of these similarities may therefore be simple homologies of a contingent history, not deep immanences of the soul. Such an offbeat idea might provide an astonishingly simple solution to some of the oldest dilemmas born of the Socratic injunction—know thyself.

Finally, history seems to be extending its influence to ever-widening domains. Soon we may no longer be able even to maintain the basic division of two scientific styles discussed in this paper (which only advocates equal treatment for the equally scientific, but different, historical sciences). The latest researches in cosmology are suggesting that the laws of nature themselves, those supposed exemplars of timeless immanence, may also be contingent results of history! Had the universe passed through a different (and possible) history during its first few moments after the big bang, nature's laws might have developed differently. Thus everything, ultimately, may be a product of history—and we will need to understand, appreciate, and use the principles of historical science throughout our entire domain of zealous research.

This has been an unconventional discharge of an appointed duty—to write a centennial essay on the impact of evolution. I have not written a traditional review. I have not chronicled the major advances and discoveries of evolution. I have tried, instead, to suggest that evolution's essential impact upon the practice of science has been methodological—validating the historical style as equally worthy and developing for it a rigorous methodology, outlined by Darwin himself in his most distinctive (but largely untouted) contribution, and continually refined to the kind of ultimate triumph for homology that molecular phylogeny can provide.

I have presented nothing really new, only a plea for appreciating something so basic that we often fail to sense its value. With a bow to that overquoted line from T. S. Eliot, I only ask you to return to a place well known and see it for the first time.

References

Alvarez, L. W., W. Alvarez, F. Asaro, and H. V. Michel. 1980. Extraterrestrial cause for the Cretaceous-Tertiary extinction. *Science* 208:1095–1108.

Bethell, T. 1985. Agnostic evolutionists: The taxonomic case against Darwin. *Harper's*. Feb., pp. 49–61.

Carr, E. H. 1961. *What Is History?* Vintage Books.

Chambers, R. 1844. *Vestiges of the Natural History of Creation.* London: John Churchill. (Published anonymously.)

Cott, H. B. 1940. *Adaptive Coloration in Animals.* Methuen.

Darwin, C. 1842. *The Structure and Distribution of Coral Reefs.* London: Smith, Elder.

———. 1859. *On the Origin of Species.* London: John Murray.

———. 1862. *The Various Contrivances by which Orchids Are Fertilized by Insects.* London: John Murray.

———. 1868. *Variation of Animals and Plants Under Domestication.* London: John Murray.

———. 1877. *Different Forms of Flowers on Plants of the Same Species.* London: John Murray.

———. 1881. *The Formation of Vegetable Mould, Through the Action of Worms.* London: John Murray.

di Gregorio, M. A. 1984. *T. H. Huxley's Place in Natural Science.* Yale Univ. Press.

Eldredge, N., and J. Cracraft. 1980. *Phylogenetic Patterns and the Evolutionary Process.* Columbia Univ. Press.

Eldredge, N., and S. J. Gould. 1972. Punctuated equilibria: An alternative to phyletic gradualism. In *Models in Paleobiology*, ed. T. J. M. Schopf, pp. 82–115. Freeman, Cooper, and Co.

Ghiselin, M. 1969. *The Triumph of the Darwinian Method.* Univ. of California Press.

Gingerich, P. D. 1983. Rates of evolution: Effects of time and temporal scaling. *Science* 222:159.

Gould, S. J. 1965. Is uniformitarianism necessary. *Am. J. Sci.* 263:223–28.

———. 1971. D'Arcy Thompson and the science of form. *New Lit. Hist.* 2 (2):229–58.

———. 1980. *The Panda's Thumb.* W. W. Norton.

———. 1981. *The Mismeasure of Man.* W. W. Norton.

———. 1982a. Darwinism and the expansion of evolutionary theory. *Science* 216:380–87.

———. 1982b. The meaning of punctuated equilibrium and its role in validating a hierarchical approach to macroevolution. In *Perspectives on Evolution*, ed. R. Milkman, pp. 83–104. Sunderland, Mass.: Sinauer Assoc.

———. 1983. *Hen's Teeth and Horse's Toes.* W. W. Norton.

———. 1984. Smooth curve of evolutionary rate: A psychological and mathematical artifact. *Science* 226:994–95.

———. 1985a. On the origin of specious critics. *Discover.* Jan., pp. 34–42.

———. 1985b. The paradox of the first tier: An agenda for paleobiology. *Paleobiology* 11:2–12.

Hennig, W. 1966. *Phylogenetic Systematics.* Univ. of Illinois Press.

Hooykaas, R. 1963. *The Principle of Uniformity in Geology, Biology, and Theology.* Leiden: E. J. Brill.

Huxley, T. H. 1893. The origin of species [1860]. In *Collected Essays*, vol. 2: *Darwiniana*, pp. 22–79. Appleton.

Kitcher, P. 1985. Darwin's achievement. In *Reason and Rationality in Science*, ed. N. Rescher, pp. 123–85. Pittsburgh: Stud. Phil. Sci.

Lamarck, J. B. 1809. *Philosophie zoologique.* Trans. 1984 by H. Elliot as *Zoological Philosophy.* Univ. of Chicago Press.

Lyell, C. 1842. *Principles of Geology.* 6th ed., 3 vols. Boston: Hilliard, Gray, and Co.

MacArthur, R. H., and E. O. Wilson. 1967. *The Theory of Island Biogeography.* Princeton Univ. Press.

Oken, L. 1805–11. *Lehrbuch der Naturphilosophie.* Jena: F. Frommand.

Raup, D. M., and J. J. Sepkoski, Jr. 1984. Periodicity of extinctions in the geologic past. *PNAS* 81:801–05.

Rifkin, J. 1983. *Algeny.* Viking Press.

Rudwick, M. J. S. 1972. *The Meaning of Fossils.* London: MacDonald.

Ruse, M. 1979. *The Darwinian Revolution: Science Red in Tooth and Claw.* Univ. of Chicago Press.

Sibley, C. G., and J. E. Ahlquist. 1981. The phylogeny and relationships of the ratite birds as indicated by DNA-DNA hybridization. In *Evolution Today*, ed. G. G. E. Scudder and J. L. Reveal, pp. 301–35. Proc. Second Intl. Cong. Syst. Evol. Biol.

———. 1984. The phylogeny of the hominoid primates, as indicated by DNA-DNA hybridization. *J. Mol. Evol.* 20:2–15.

———. 1985. The phylogeny and classification of the Australo-Papuan passerine birds. *The Emu* 85:1–14.

Sober, E. 1984. *The Nature of Selection.* MIT Press.

Steno, N. 1669. *De solido intra solidum naturaliter contento dissertationis prodromus.* Trans. 1916 by J. G. Winter as *The Prodromus of Nicolaus Steno's Dissertation.* Macmillan.

Swainson, W. 1835. *Classification of Quadrupeds.* London: Dr. Lardner's Cabinet Cyclopedia.

Thompson, D. W. 1942. *Growth and Form.* Macmillan.

Vrba, E. S., and N. Eldredge. 1984. Individuals, hierarchies and processes: Towards a more complete evolutionary theory. *Paleobiology* 10:146–71.

The Evolution of Life without Oxygen

Organisms in oxygen-free habitats engage in unique symbiotic relationships that provide clues to the evolution of the first eukaryotic cells

Tom Fenchel and Bland J. Finlay

In various nooks and crannies on the earth, whole communities of microscopic organisms go about their daily lives in the absence of oxygen. It is a form of existence utterly different from the aerobic lives we know. Yet these minute, anaerobic organisms do offer some valuable insights into the existence of oxygen breathers. Indeed, the first living cells—ancestors of all life on the planet—were themselves anaerobic organisms.

The story of the link between those who would and those who would not use oxygen in their lives begins with the ancestral anaerobes some three to four billion years ago. These ancient relatives were prokaryotes: single-celled organisms that lacked the ensemble of intracellular organelles (most notably a nucleus) found in their descendants, the eukaryotes (including human beings). The ancestral prokaryotes and the first eukaryotes were anaerobes by necessity; the atmosphere of the early earth bore only the smallest traces of oxygen.

Anaerobic organisms flourished on the surface of the planet for more than

Tom Fenchel is professor of marine biology at the University of Copenhagen and director of the Marine Biological Laboratory at Helsingør, Denmark. Bland J. Finlay is principal scientific officer at the Institute of Freshwater Ecology at Ambleside in England. They have worked together, on many aspects of the physiological ecology of protozoa, for more than 10 years. Their most significant joint achievements include the discovery of gravity perception in protozoa and the unraveling of the relevant bioenergetics that are fundamental to free-living protozoa in the presence and absence of oxygen. Fenchel received the Ecology Institute Prize in 1986 and Finlay received the Scientific Medal of the Zoological Society (London) in 1991. Fenchel's Address: Marine Biological Laboratory, DK-3000 Helsingør, Denmark.

500 million years before oxygen began to play a role in the evolution of life. Somewhere along the way, a group of prokaryotes, the cyanobacteria, developed the means to use the sun's energy in the process of photosynthesis. This event had the consequence of loading the atmosphere with oxygen, since cyanobacteria released the gas as waste. (Some of the oxygen molecules we breathe today were undoubtedly excreted by a cyanobacterium about two billion years ago.)

The advent of an oxygen-filled atmosphere opened the way for the evolution of organisms (prokaryotes and eukaryotes) that could use the gaseous molecule in their energy metabolism. It was an extremely successful event in evolution. For one thing, it permitted a tremendous increase in the efficiency of the organism's energy metabolism. Although many prokaryotic organisms do use oxygen in their metabolism, it is largely the eukaryotes that have evolved and diversified as oxygen-dependent organisms.

Nonetheless, many eukaryotes, such as human beings, still show signs of their anaerobic ancestry. This is evident in the biochemical significance of free oxygen. It is largely restricted to only two roles: energy metabolism and toxicity. All aerobic organisms must produce enzymes that detoxify oxygen radicals. Although aerobic organisms depend on oxygen for energy metabolism, with only a few exceptions, they do not use elemental oxygen in synthetic pathways. It is as if free oxygen began to have an impact on the history of life only after most biochemistry had been "invented."

Anaerobic organisms, on the other hand, go about their lives studiously avoiding oxygen because they lack protective enzymes. Although most species of anaerobes are prokaryotes, modern anaerobic eukaryotes do exist. These organisms include direct descendants of the earliest eukaryotes as well as forms that have secondarily adapted to life without oxygen. Most of them are protozoans, the smallest of all animals (less than one tenth of a millimeter in length), and all are unicellular.

During the last five years we have studied the biology and ecology of protozoa living in oxygen-free habitats. We have been particularly engaged by their strange and specialized symbiotic relationships with bacteria. These relationships are intriguing because they provide a contemporary analogy for the symbiotic origin of mitochondria, the organelles responsible for energy metabolism. They also shed light on the behavior of biological communities as they might have functioned three billion years ago, before the widespread distribution of oxygen. Our story ultimately suggests why oxygen was necessary for the diversification of eukaryotes and the evolution of multicellular animals.

Anoxic Habitats
Although oxygen has been generated by photosynthetic organisms for the last three-and-one-half billion years, anaerobic habitats have existed continuously throughout the earth's history. Such habitats can arise whenever dead organic material accumulates from the surrounding aerobic regions. In the process of converting organic carbon to form carbon dioxide (mineralization), anaerobic organisms consume (and deplete) the local oxygen. The worldwide distribution of black shales, a conse-

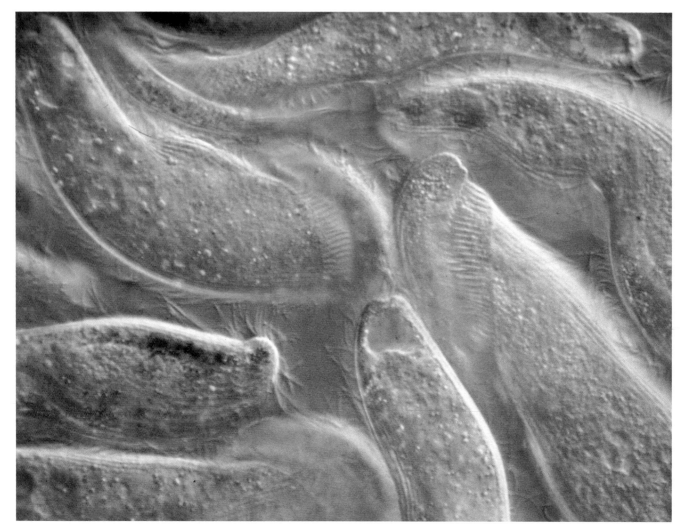

Figure 1. Ciliated protozoa of the species *Metopus contortus* live in an intimate metabolic union with at least two different species of symbiotic bacteria. The ciliate host provides organic molecules for the bacterial symbionts, and the bacteria improve the energy metabolism of the ciliate by removing certain metabolites. The symbiotic relationship offers an analogy for the types of interactions present in the earliest oxygen-free habitats about two billion years ago. (All photographs courtesy of the authors.)

quence of anoxic conditions, suggests that during some periods in earth's history, vast shallow seas were anoxic at certain depths. To this day there are a number of places where anoxic conditions persist.

The extent and distribution of anoxic habitats are often surprising to those who do not normally consider these niches. Marine sediments, for example, are often anoxic a few millimeters below the surface. Remarkably, they constitute an enormous, globally continuous anoxic environment. The ecological significance of such a habitat has yet to be fully explored or understood.

Sediments and detrital deposits of lakes also provide an oxygen-free environment. Here organic particles—dead algal cells, fecal pellets of planktonic animals and other debris—sink to the lake bottom. In the sediment, oxygen is supplied only by molecular diffu-

sion. This process is so slow over distances exceeding a few millimeters that it cannot meet the demand of aerobic organisms living beneath the sediment surface.

Even in shallow-water sediments where there is sufficient light to allow the growth of oxygen-producing microalgae, oxygen diffuses only as far as the upper five to eight millimeters. Digging in the sediment reveals the oxygen-free zone, distinguished by the contrast between its grey-black color (and its smell of hydrogen sulfide) and the yellowish oxidized zone. The black color comes from iron sulfides, compounds that are not stable in the presence of oxygen.

In biologically productive shallow waters, the anoxic zone may reach almost to the surface. When this happens a white veil of sulfur bacteria is often seen. These organisms make their liv-

ing by oxidizing hydrogen sulfide, which diffuses up from the anaerobic sediment. The presence of purple sulfur bacteria (which use hydrogen sulfide in a form of photosynthesis that does not produce oxygen) reveals that anaerobic conditions exist right up to the surface of the sediments.

Lakes are often thermally stratified so that the upper warm layer does not mix with deeper, colder water. As a result the deeper water is effectively isolated from contact with the atmosphere, and becomes anoxic. A similar phenomenon is often seen in marine fjords that have a sill at the entrance, and in bays with deeper basins. The Black Sea is the largest anoxic body of water in the world; oxygen is undetectable below a depth of about 150 meters. The deep waters of certain basins in the Baltic Sea and the Cariaco Trench in the Caribbean Sea also represent large anoxic marine basins.

Figure 2. Communities of purple sulfur bacteria cover a shallow inlet in Nivå Bay, north of Copenhagen. Purple sulfur bacteria use hydrogen sulfide (H_2S) in a form of photosynthesis that does not release oxygen. The presence of these anaerobic bacteria indicates that the sediments in the inlet are essentially free of molecular oxygen right up to the surface. The sediments consist of decaying seagrass leaves that form a layer about half a meter deep. Such habitats are a rich source of the anaerobic organisms described by the authors.

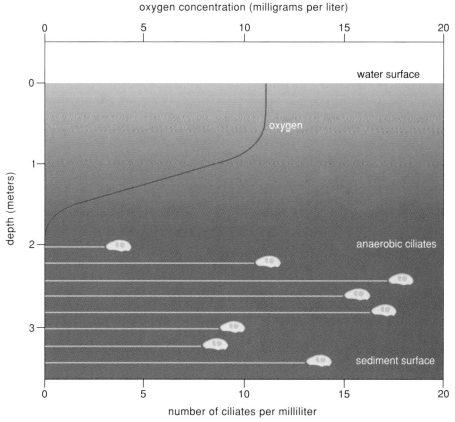

Figure 3. Concentration of dissolved oxygen *(red)* must fall to zero before anaerobic organisms can survive in the depths of a freshwater pond in summer. In this instance the anaerobic organisms first appear at a depth of about two meters below the surface of the pond.

There are other, less romantic, anoxic habitats. These range from anaerobic sewage treatment plants, to fermenters that produce useful methane gas from organic refuse, to landfills packed with domestic waste. The intestinal tracts of herbivorous animals also constitute an important class of anoxic (or nearly anoxic) habitats. Many herbivores depend for food on the metabolites of fermenting microorganisms that degrade plant structures such as straw and wood. The rumens of cows and sheep and the hindguts of termites have been extensively studied, but similar systems have evolved independently in other herbivores, including a varied groups of mammals, green turtles and sea-urchins.

It should be clear that anaerobic habitats are diverse and widely distributed. Even so, the microorganisms that live within them share a number of common features, including their interactions with each other.

Anaerobic Community Structure

Most anaerobic ecological systems are fueled almost entirely by dead organic material, typically plant debris, imported from the aerobic surroundings. Under anaerobic conditions, the material is decomposed primarily by fermenting bacteria, which break down large organic molecules into smaller sugars and amino acids. The dissolved compounds are then transported into the cells where they are fermented, providing energy for the bacteria.

The bacteria's fermentative pathways produce, among other things, acetate (which is made up of carbon, hydrogen and oxygen) and molecular hydrogen. Oxidizing a substrate by hydrogen production yields about twice as much energy as does glycolysis alone (leading to lactic acid or to ethanol and carbon dioxide). This is nevertheless a relatively modest yield of energy compared to aerobic respiration. Only about 10 percent of the substrate is incorporated into new cell matter (in microorganisms most of the energy is used for the synthesis of new macromolecules required for cell growth and renewal). The remaining material is released, primarily as acetate and hydrogen.

The excreted metabolites of fermenting bacteria are used by other types of bacteria. In environments where oxygen-supplying sulfate ions are in low concentrations (lakes and sewage di-

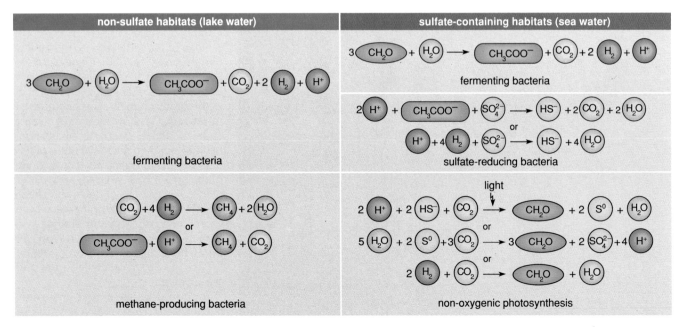

Figure 4. Metabolic processes in bacteria differ when sulfate is present or absent in oxygen-free environments. In either type of habitat, organic molecules (here represented by CH_2O) are fermented into acetate (CH_3COO^-), carbon dioxide and hydrogen *(top)*. In non-sulfate habitats these molecules are then transformed into methane (CH_4), water and carbon dioxide by methanogenic bacteria *(bottom left)*. In sulfate-containing habitats, sulfate-reducing bacteria oxidize the products of fermentation with sulfate (SO_4^{2-}) *(middle right)*. Photosynthetic bacteria in anoxic environments use the reduced sulfide (HS^-) as an electron donor to produce organic compounds and elemental sulfur or sulfate *(bottom right)*. These products can be recycled again by the sulfate-reducing bacteria. Because sulfate-reducing metabolism is energetically more efficient than the methanogenic system, it predominates in anaerobic communities where sulfate is present. These processes are quantitatively the most important. There are, however, other forms of fermentation, and some bacteria use electron acceptors other than sulfate.

gesters), methane-producing bacteria are responsible for the terminal mineralization process. The methanogens are capable of obtaining energy for growth by converting carbon dioxide (CO_2) and molecular hydrogen (H_2) into methane (CH_4) and water. Some methanogenic bacteria are also capable of transforming acetate into methane and carbon dioxide. When lake sediments are stirred, the bubbles of methane that rise to the surface are evidence of the activity of these bacteria.

Other types of bacteria predominate in seawater, which contains large amounts of sulfate (SO_4^{2-}) compounds. These anaerobes—the "sulfate reducers"—oxidize volatile fatty acids and hydrogen using sulfate rather than oxygen. In turn they produce hydrogen sulfide (H_2S) rather than water (H_2O) as their principal metabolite. Since sulfate respiration provides more energy than does methanogenesis, sulfate reducers are competitively superior to methanogens in regions where sulfate is available. Even so, a low level of methanogenesis is usually detectable in marine anaerobic environments. The presence of sulfate reducers or methanogens in the habitat means that organic material can be completely mineralized without oxygen. In anaer-

obic conditions this is accomplished by diverse types of bacteria, whereas in an aerobic habitat it can be accomplished by a single organism.

Hydrogen plays a key role as a substrate and a metabolite in anaerobic communities. Hydrogen produced by fermenting bacteria is rapidly metabolized by the methanogens and the sulfate reducers. This results in low hydrogen pressure, which is essential for the function of the whole ecological system. This is because fermentation that involves the release of hydrogen is thermodynamically feasible only if the ambient hydrogen pressure is very low. In a sense, fermenting bacteria and hydrogen-scavenging bacteria are engaged in a mutualistic relationship. Fermenting bacteria produce the substrates for methanogens and sulfate reducers, and the consumers maintain a favorable habitat for the producers by removing hydrogen. This interspecies hydrogen transfer is an example of a syntrophic interaction. It is crucial to the interaction of anaerobic microbial communities.

Where light is present, photosynthetic bacteria will re-oxidize the end products of mineralization. Purple and green sulfur bacteria use light to chemically reduce carbon dioxide to make

organic material. In this instance, hydrogen sulfide (H_2S) is used as an electron donor instead of water (H_2O) as in green plants. Consequently, sulfur-bacteria produce elemental sulfur or sulfate rather than molecular oxygen. Other photosynthetic bacteria use molecular hydrogen or organic compounds as electron donors. Photosynthetic systems that do not rely on oxygen are mechanistically simpler than those that do. It seems likely that oxygenic photosynthesis appeared later in evolutionary history.

In principle anoxygenic photosynthesis allows an anaerobic community to operate as a closed system fueled by light alone. The system has a complete cycle in which sulfur atoms function as electron acceptors in respiration and as electron donors in photosynthesis. In turn, the cycle produces substrates for fermentors and sulfate reducers. Such anaerobic communities may have dominated the early history of life.

Anaerobic Eukaryotes
Prokaryotes (bacteria) do not eat each other. They make a living from dissolved substances only. Eukaryotes, on the other hand, routinely ingest other organisms. Such predation, a type of interspecies interaction, is immensely important in aer-

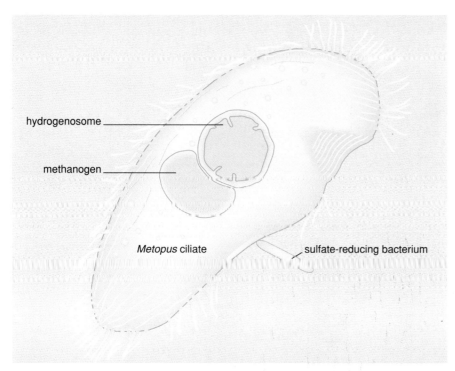

Figure 5. A single-celled anaerobic eukaryote, *Metopus*, harbors at least two types of symbiotic bacteria. Each *Metopus* cell contains about 7,000 methane-producing bacteria (methanogens) that live endosymbiotically within the cell, and 4,000 sulfate-reducing bacteria that live ectosymbioti-cally on the surface of the cell. Hydrogenosomes are intracellular organelles, closely related to mitochondria, which are thought to be highly modified endosymbiotic bacteria.

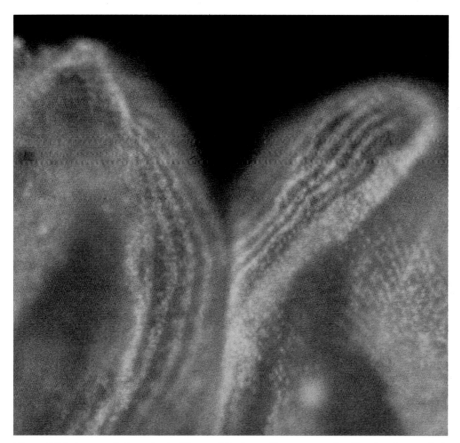

Figure 6. Methanogenic bacteria, inside two *Metopus* cells, are recognized by the characteristic emission of a bright blue fluorescence when illuminated by violet light. It has recently been discovered that nearly all anaerobic ciliates living in fresh water, and about half of those living in marine habitats, contain methanogens.

obic ecosystems, but it also occurs in anaerobic habitats. In this case, the predators are unicellular eukaryotes that engulf other cells. These predatory eukaryotes are the protozoa.

Anaerobic protozoa belong to two distinct groups. One group probably evolved directly from the ancient ancestral anaerobes; they are devoid of any mitochondria-like structures. The second group of protozoa consists of organisms that have secondarily adapted to anaerobic habitats.

Diplomonad flagellates (single-celled organisms with two nuclei) belong to the first group. They are best known as occasional inhabitants of animal intestines. *Giardia intestinalis*, for example, has been studied very closely because it can cause diarrhea in human beings. Other free-living species of diplomonads that feed on bacteria are also known. Because these organisms lack mitochondria, their energy metabolism is based on fermentation that does not involve hydrogen production.

Mitchell Sogin and his colleagues at the Marine Biological Laboratory at Woods Hole, Massachusetts, have recently studied the nucleotide sequence of the diplomonad's ribosomal RNA molecule. A comparison with the ribosomal RNA of other single-celled organisms suggests that the diplomonads branched off as an independent group during a very early stage in the evolution of eukaryotes. Some speculate that these organisms are the direct descendants of an anaerobic eukaryote that had not yet acquired mitochondria. It is possible, however, that the diplomonads lost their mitochondria during a later stage in evolution.

Other groups of anaerobic protozoa—certain flagellated amoeboid organisms—also lack mitochondria. In particular, species of the genera *Mastigella* and *Pelomyxa* (the giant freshwater "amoeba") may also be living fossils from the dawn of eukaryotic life. These organisms lack certain other organelles that are characteristic of most eukaryotic cells, including the Golgi apparatus, the endoplasmic reticulum and the microbodies.

Most anaerobic protozoa, however, belong to the second group, organisms that have secondarily adapted to life without oxygen. The ciliated protozoa, or infusoria, are the most common. Although there are probably more than 100 species of anaerobic infusoria, they all belong to taxonomic groups that include aerobic species. Anaerobic ciliates evolved independently within six different lineages. These organisms, which have secondarily adapted to anaerobic conditions, have been the focus of our own studies. In particular, we have studied the biology of five species, which we keep in controlled laboratory cultures.

The five species share a special sensitivity to oxygen. One species is killed within an hour of exposure to only about two percent of the atmospheric oxygen pressure. Other species seem capable of growth under the same conditions and may even recover from temporary exposure to atmospheric pressures of oxygen if they are returned to anoxic conditions. These organisms are sensitive to oxygen partly because they lack (or have low levels of) the enzymes that detoxify oxygen. They also lack respiratory enzymes (cytochromes), so they are unable to use oxygen in their energy metabolism.

Although they do not have respiratory enzymes, anaerobic ciliates have organelles that are almost identical to the mitochondria of aerobic ciliates. These organelles, known as hydrogenosomes, were originally discovered in 1973 by Donald G. Lindmark and Miklós Müller of Rockefeller University. Hydrogenosomes contain two enzymes that were previously found only in anaerobic bacteria. One of these enzymes, hydrogenase, catalyzes the oxidation of molecular hydrogen, yielding two protons and two electrons ($H_2 \longrightarrow 2H^+ + 2e^-$). Because of their structural similarities, it seems likely that the hydrogenosomes of anaerobic ciliates are modified mitochondria. Ultimately, the nucleotide sequence of the DNA in this organelle may provide a conclusive answer.

About 15 years ago one of us (Fenchel) observed that anaerobic ciliates often harbor symbiotic bacteria. In some instances, the bacteria were living as endosymbionts within the cytoplasm of the ciliate. In other cases, the bacteria formed a dense, fur-like cover on the surface of the ciliate. Some ciliate species (such as *Metopus contortus*) harbor both types of bacteria.

A few years later, Claudius Stumm and his colleagues at the University of Nijmegen, in the Netherlands, discovered that the endosymbionts are methane-producing bacteria. Methanogens can be recognized in the light

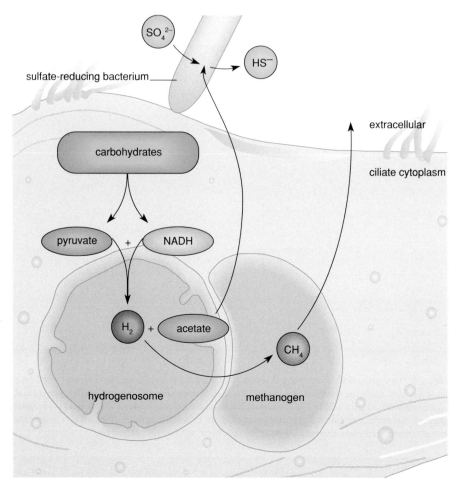

Figure 7. A chain of molecular events characterizes the symbiotic interactions between the *Metopus* ciliate and its attendant bacteria. The symbiotic community's energy metabolism begins with the ingestion of bacteria, which are hydrolyzed into smaller molecules, such as carbohydrates. These small molecules are converted by fermentation into pyruvate and the reduced form of nicotinamide-adenine dinucleotide (NADH). Hydrogenosomes oxidize pyruvate and the reduction equivalent of NADH (malate) to produce molecular hydrogen (H_2) and acetate. Methanogens oxidize the hydrogen with carbon dioxide (CO_2) and produce methane (CH_4) and water, which are released from the cell. Sulfate-reducing bacteria on the cell's surface oxidize metabolites such as acetate that diffuse out of the ciliate. Ultimately the symbiotic bacteria act to remove hydrogen from the ciliate, which increases the metabolic efficiency of the host cell.

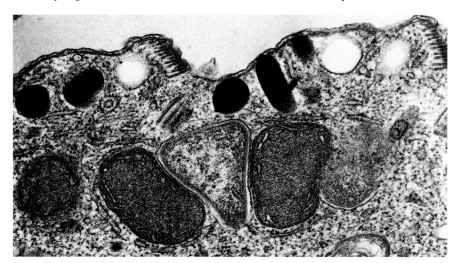

Figure 8. Hydrogenosomes *(large, dense structures)* and methanogens *(large, light structures)* are found relatively close to each other within the cytoplasm of a *Metopus* cell. The proximity of the structures facilitates the transfer of hydrogen from the hydrogenosome to the methanogen. Each of these structures measures about one micrometer in diameter.

microscope because they contain a coenzyme that emits a beautiful blue fluorescence when illuminated by violet light. It is now apparent that nearly all anaerobic ciliates living in fresh water, and about half of those living in

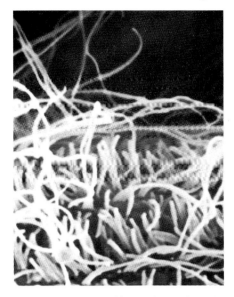

Figure 9. Putative sulfate-reducing bacteria (*short bristles*) are densely packed among the much longer cilia on the surface of the anaerobic ciliate *Parablepharisma pellitum*. The bacteria are about 2 to 3 micrometers long.

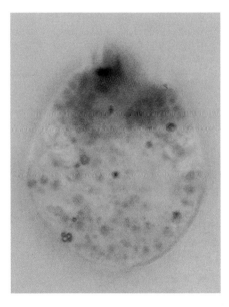

Figure 10. The ciliate *Strombidium purpureum* harbors 200 to 700 endosymbiotic purple bacteria that offer an analogy to the origin of mitochondria in eukaryotic cells from photosynthetic bacteria. The host ciliate is an anaerobic eukaryote that can tolerate low levels of oxygen in the dark because the photosynthetic endosymbionts remove the molecule through respiration. The symbiotic relationship shows how an anaerobic host can be gradually converted to an aerobic life-style.

marine habitats, contain methanogens.

Recently Niels Birger Ramsing, of the Max Planck Institute of Marine Microbiology in Bremen, and Fenchel found that the organisms living on the surface of at least two species of anaerobic marine ciliates are sulfate-reducing bacteria. The observation might explain the absence of such ectosymbionts where sulfate is nearly absent.

A Community of One

A symbiotic consortium consisting of a ciliate and one or two types of bacteria represents an anaerobic community that can completely mineralize ingested food. A *Metopus* cell, for example, harbors about 9,000 methanogenic endosymbionts and about 4,000 sulfate-reducing ectosymbionts. A brief overview of the process reveals the economic elegance of the community. The ciliate's food (mainly bacteria) is first hydrolyzed into small molecules. These are fermented into pyruvate and the reduced form of nicotinamide-adenine dinucleotide (NADH). These molecules are then oxidized in hydro-genosomes to produce acetate and hydrogen. Methanogenic endosymbionts then oxidize the hydrogen with CO_2 to produce methane and water. The ectosymbiotic sulfate-reducers oxidize the acetate (and any other metabolites such as lactate or ethanol) that diffuse out of the ciliate.

The symbiotic bacteria obviously gain from the association by receiving substrates from the ciliate host. But is there any advantage for the host? It is possible to test this possibility with some relatively simple experiments. Although ciliates always harbor methanogens in nature, they can be freed of the endosymbiotic bacteria by the addition of a compound (bromoethanesulfonic acid) that specifically inhibits the growth of methanogenic bacteria. In this way the ciliates can be maintained free of methanogens in laboratory cultures. Indeed, we have not been able to re-infect the ciliates with methanogens.

In two relatively large species of ciliates, the growth rate and metabolic efficiency of the eukaryotes decreased by about 25 percent when the methanogens were inactivated. (One smaller species appeared to be almost unaffected.) We considered the possibility that the methanogens excrete substances that are used by the ciliate host, but simple calculations show that this can-

not account for the large advantage of hosting the symbionts. A clue to the methanogens' significance came when we found that the symbiont-free ciliate host does not produce enough hydrogen to account for the production of methane in the normal symbiotic union. The observation suggests that the methanogens maintain low levels of hydrogen within the ciliate, making hydrogen production thermodynamically more favorable for the host.

At first it seemed unlikely that a ciliate could maintain high levels of hydrogen given the short diffusion path to the cell's surface and the very low levels of hydrogen outside of the cell. A simple theoretical model (assuming a spherical ciliate and a realistic rate of hydrogen production) suggests that hydrogen concentration would increase by 1,000-fold at the cell's surface in the absence of the methanogens. This would make hydrogen production considerably less favorable, especially for the re-oxidation of NADH. This effect may explain the adaptive significance of harboring methanogenic bacteria.

T. Martin Embley of the British Natural History Museum in London and Finlay have compared the ribosomal RNA sequences of some of the methanogen symbionts with the sequences of free-living methanogens maintained in laboratory cultures. The sequences of the symbionts are host-specific; they resemble (but are not identical to) sequences from free living species. Distantly related anaerobic ciliates can have symbionts that are closely related to each other. Conversely, some ciliates that are closely related to each other (different species within the same genus) have very different types of methanogens as their symbionts. These latter symbiotic interactions must have been established after the speciation of the hosts.

The associations may have started when ingested methanogens avoided digestion and survived by using the host's metabolites in their own digestion. Perhaps such a primitive stage in the evolution of symbiosis may still be discovered. In the cases we have studied the methanogens are no longer symbionts, but organelles. They are found only in their specific hosts, they are transmitted by cytoplasmic inheritance and, most importantly, the association between the host and the symbionts has become a unit of natural selection. It has little meaning to ask about the adaptive significance for one or the other component. Their mutual interaction is no longer symbiosis but rather the physiology of a single, complex cell.

In some ways the symbiotic relationship between methanogens and anaerobic ciliates presents an analogy to the endosymbiont theory for the origin of mitochondria, which holds that mitochondria originated as endosymbiotic bacteria about one to two billion years ago. An anaerobic ciliate such as *Metopus* is really a composite organism representing all three kingdoms of organisms. Eukaryotes are represented by the ciliate host, the prokaryotic eubacteria are represented by the hydrogenosomes (related to mitochondria) and the prokaryotic archaebacteria are represented by the methanogens. The sulfate-reducing ectosymbionts are also members of this complex. Remarkably, a *Metopus* cell and its symbiotic bacteria fulfill nearly all the roles of an entire anoxic microbial community.

Recently, Catherine Bernard and Fenchel discovered a new type of endosymbiosis in anaerobic protozoa. It consists of a phototrophic non-sulfur bacterium living inside the ciliate *Strombidium purpureum*. In many respects this symbiotic relationship is a closer analogy and a more useful model of the origin of mitochondria. The bacterium belongs to the alpha group of purple bacteria, which includes the ancestors of mitochondria. The particular type of purple bacteria to which the endosymbionts belong uses molecular hydrogen or low-molecular-weight organic compounds as electron donors in photosynthesis. In the absence of light, however, these bacteria become microaerobes capable of oxygen respiration.

The ciliates, on the other hand, avoid even minute traces of oxygen when they are in the light. The ciliates also tend to gravitate toward light, especially to wavelengths corresponding to the absorption spectrum of the photosynthetic pigments of the symbionts. In the dark, the ciliates prefer conditions that correspond to the oxygen requirements of the symbionts. Access to some oxygen improves their survival in the dark. In this instance the symbiont not only uses the metabolites of its anaerobic host, but it also transforms the ciliate into an oxygen-consuming organism in the dark.

Aerobes *vs.* Anaerobes

It remains to be explained why so few eukaryotes inhabit anaerobic environments and why those that do are so small. Consider for a moment the classic description of a "who-eats-who" food chain in an aerobic community. Pelagic algae are eaten by copepods, which are eaten by small fish, which are eaten by larger fish and so on. Ultimately the great white shark at the top of the chain has enough to eat because aerobic organisms are extremely efficient at converting food into energy.

Aerobic organisms are efficient because oxygen respiration is efficient. Although growth efficiencies vary somewhat, a realistic figure is 40 percent. So, if a copepod eats 100 units of algae, 40 units of copepods are produced. The 40 copepods translate into about 16 units of small fishes, which translate into 6.4 units of large fishes, which support the production of 2.5 units of sharks.

This scenario cannot take place in an anaerobic habitat. The low energy yield of anaerobic processes translates into a low growth efficiency, about 10 percent on average. This means that 100 units of organic matter will produce 10 units of fermenting bacteria, which support only one unit of anaerobic ciliates. Such a low yield is insufficient for any hypothetical anaerobic predator of the ciliates. In anaerobic communities the biomass production is simply too low to sustain more than a two-level food chain—there are no niches for larger animals.

In this light, it seems reasonable to propose that eukaryotes evolved into a diverse group of large and complex organisms mainly to swallow other organisms or to avoid being swallowed themselves. The evolution of such predatory interactions and complex food chains is dependent on a high level of bioenergetic efficiency. In earth's history this followed the evolution of oxygenic photosynthesis and aerobic respiration. Had this not taken place, the diversity of life would still resemble the foul-smelling sites where we collect our samples.

Bibliography

Bryant, C. (ed.). 1991. *Metazoan Life without Oxygen.* London: Chapman and Hall.

Embley, T. M., and B. J. Finlay. 1994. The use of small subunit rRNA sequences to unravel the relationships between anaerobic ciliates and their methanogen endosymbionts. *Microbiology* (in press).

Fenchel, T., and C. Bernard. 1993. A purple protist. *Nature* 362:300.

Fenchel, T., and B. J. Finlay. 1990. Anaerobic free-living protozoa: growth efficiencies and the structure of anaerobic communities. *FEMS Microbiology Ecology* 74:269–276.

Fenchel, T., and B. J. Finlay. 1990. Oxygen toxicity, respiration and behavioural responses to oxygen in free-living anaerobic ciliates. *Journal of General Microbiology* 136:1953–1959.

Fenchel, T., and B. J. Finlay. 1991. The biology of free-living anaerobic ciliates. *European Journal of Protistology* 26:201–215.

Fenchel, T., and B. J. Finlay. 1991. Endosymbiotic methanogenic bacteria in anaerobic ciliates: Significance for the growth efficiency of the host. *Journal of Protozoology* 38:18–22.

Fenchel, T., and B. J. Finlay. 1991. Synchronous division of an endosymbiotic methanogenic bacterium in the anaerobic ciliate *Plagiopyla frontata* Kahl. *Journal of Protozoology* 38:22–28.

Fenchel, T., and B. J. Finlay. 1992. Production of methane and hydrogen by anaerobic ciliates containing symbiotic methanogens. *Archives of Microbiology* 157:475–480.

Fenchel, T., T. Perry and A. Thane. 1977. Anaerobiosis and symbiosis with bacteria in free-living ciliates. *Journal of Protozoology* 24:154–163.

Fenchel, T., and N. B. Ramsing. 1992. Identification of sulphate-reducing ectosymbiotic bacteria from anaerobic ciliates using 16S rRNA oligonucleotid probes. *Archives of Microbiology* 158:394–397.

Finlay, B. J., and T. Fenchel. 1989. Hydrogenosomes in some anaerobic protozoa resemble mitochondria. *FEMS Microbiology Letters* 65:311–314.

Finlay, B. J., and T. Fenchel. 1991. Polymorphic bacterial symbionts in the anaerobic ciliated protozoon *Metopus*. *FEMS Microbiology Letters* 79:187–190.

Finlay, B. J., and T. Fenchel. 1992. An anaerobic ciliate as a natural chemostat for the growth of endosymbiotic methanogens. *European Journal of Protistology* 28:127–137.

Finlay, B. J., and T. Fenchel. 1993. Methanogens and other bacteria as symbionts of free-living anaerobic ciliates. *Symbiosis* 14:375–390.

Kabnick, K. S., and D. A. Peattie. 1991. *Giardia*: a missing link between prokaryotes and eukaryotes. *American Scientist* 79:34–43.

Margulis, L. 1981. *Symbiosis in Cell Evolution.* New York: W. H. Freeman and Company.

Müller, M. 1988. Energy metabolism of protozoa without mitochondria. *Annual Review of Microbiology* 42:465–488.

van Bruggen, J. J., K. B. Zwart, P. M. van Assema, C. K. Stumm, and G. D. Vogels. 1984. *Methanobacterium formicicum*, an endosymbiont of the anaerobic ciliate *Metopus striatus* McMurrich. *Archives of Microbiology* 139:1–7.

Wolin, M. J. 1982. Hydrogen transfer in microbial communities. In Microbial Interactions and Communities, ed. A. T. Bull and J. H. Slater, pp. 323–356. New York: Academic Press.

Zehnder, A. J. B. 1988. *Biology of Anaerobic Microorganisms.* New York: John Wiley & Sons.

The Origin of the Life Cycle of Land Plants

Linda E. Graham

A simple modification in the life cycle of an extinct green alga is the likely origin of the first land plants

The invasion of the land by aquatic plants about 400 million years ago was one of the most significant events in the history of life on earth. Botanists have long been concerned with various aspects of the evolution of land plants, but a particularly difficult problem has been the origin of the plant life cycle. Recently a significant body of evidence has emerged that may help solve this botanical mystery. This article will review the new evidence, which suggests a model of how the life cycle of land plants originated in ancestors among the green algae.

The life cycle of all land plants, both the bryophytes (such as mosses) and the more numerous and dominant vascular plants, involves the alternation of two distinct multicellular generations, the gametophyte and the sporophyte (see Fig. 1). The gametophyte, or gamete-producing generation, is haploid, meaning that it has a single set of chromosomes in its cells. The sporophyte is diploid, possessing twice the haploid number of chromosomes, and it produces spores by meiosis, a process that divides the diploid number of chromosomes in two; the haploid spores germinate asexually into gametophytes, which produce male gametes (spermatozoids) or female gametes (eggs) that combine sexually and then grow into new sporophytes, completing the cycle.

In vascular plants the sporophyte is the larger, more dominant generation; an oak tree, for instance, is primarily sporophyte, with its gametophytic generations located in the pollen grains and within the microscopic ovaries of the oak flowers. The new sporophyte, or embryo, is located in the acorn of oaks and, more generally, inside the seed of seed plants. In contrast, the sporophyte of bryophytes is often inconspicuous, while the green plant that one observes is the gametophyte. Because the chromosome number of cells in sporophytes is generally diploid, or twice that of haploid gametophytic cells, sporophytes are considered to have an increased potential for genetic variability and evolutionary flexibility as compared to the gametophytic part of the plant life cycle. This may explain the size dominance of the sporophyte over the gametophyte in most land plants.

Linda E. Graham is Associate Professor of Botany at the University of Wisconsin-Madison. A graduate of Washington University and of the University of Texas, she received her Ph.D. from the University of Michigan. Her scientific interests center on the ultrastructure, development, and evolution of green algae and lower plants. The work described here was supported by the NSF. Address: Department of Botany, University of Wisconsin, 430 Lincoln Drive, Madison, WI 53706.

Probably the most distinctive feature of the land-plant reproductive cycle is that eggs are retained on the parental gametophyte and fertilized there. The resulting young sporophyte, or embryo, then remains associated with the parental gametophyte, and derives nutrition from it for a time during early embryo development. It is for this reason that vascular plants and bryophytes are often referred to as embryophytes, or embryo-producing plants.

This close association between the two alternating generations in embryophytes has great evolutionary significance, as was recognized by Bold (1), who suggested that the retention and nurturing of the zygote within the tissue of the gametophyte was probably the stimulus that led to the profound modifications of the sporophyte generation in so many land plants. Recent studies have shown that the young embryo and parental gametophyte actually are involved in a reciprocal developmental relationship that in some ways parallels the relationship between mother and embryo in placental mammals. The plant embryo may induce the development of special placental transfer cells or cause other growth changes in the pregnant gametophyte (2). The gametophyte, in turn, may secrete ions, sugars, and other photosynthates such as amino acids that are absorbed and metabolized by the embryo as it begins to grow (2–5).

Thus, one of the major issues on which resolution of the mystery of land-plant evolution depends is how this close developmental and nutritional relationship between generations originated. Because green algae and land plants share many important features, most authorities agree that the ancestors of land plants most likely would be classified today among the green algae. Evolutionary theory predicts that phylogenetic pathways are constrained by prior genetic history and that natural selection generally fashions new features from preexistent ones. There is evidence that many biological, physiological, reproductive, and developmental features of higher plant cells were built on genetic foundations inherited from green-algal ancestors.

The problem, however, is that among modern green algae having alternation of generations, eggs and zygotes are not generally retained on parental plants. Rather, green-algal eggs or zygotes are usually released into the water, so that fertilization and zygote development are physically independent of the parent plant. The haploid and diploid components of green-algal life cycles can have no nutritional or developmental interrelationships. Green algae thus lack embryos, a fundamental difference from embryophytes that also provides a major distinction between the two kingdoms Plantae, which includes the embryophytes, and Protista (or Protoctista), which includes green algae (6). Therefore, the first appearance of the plant embryo was a major step in the evolution of land plants, and is of great concern to paleobotanists and other plant scientists interested in the origins of early plants.

Bower's hypothesis

The nature of the immediate algal ancestors of plants and their role in the origin of the land-plant life cycle has been the substance of much debate for over a century. The continuing controversy centers on two opposing theories, one first proposed in 1874 by Celakovsky (7) and the other developed in 1908 by Bower (8). Bower was the first to amass evidence in support of the idea that the sporophyte originated as a new component of the life cycle from algae that lacked a sporophyte (see Fig. 2); specifically, embryophytes arose from haploid, haplobiontic algae—algae having a single multicellular generation—resembling the present-day genus *Coleochaete*,

which is unusual among green algae in having diploid zygotes that are retained on the haploid parental form (Fig. 3). Bower proposed that a delay in zygotic meiosis could have produced the first multicellular diploid sporophytes that would be, like the embryos of land plants, associated with parental haploid gametophytes.

According to the alternative hypothesis, first suggested as a possibility by Celakovsky and seized upon by later workers who opposed Bower's theories, land plants arose from green algae that were diplobiontic—that already had alternation of two generations. This hypothesis has had considerable support for the past several decades (9) despite the major problem of being unable to explain how the sporophytes and gametophytes, which in present-day diplobiontic green algae are completely independent, or free-living, could have developed the intimate nutritional and developmental relationships that are characteristic of embryophytes. In other words, how could a free-living sporophyte become attached to—and parasitic upon—the gametophytic generation?

Resolution of this problem of the origin of the plant

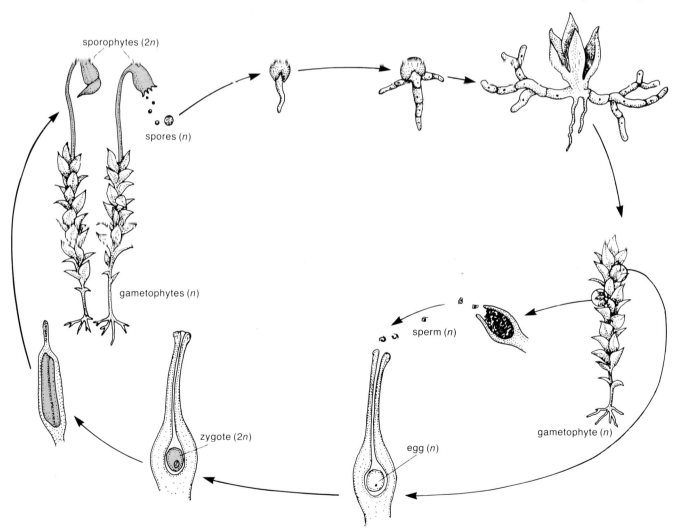

Figure 1. The life cycle of all land plants (shown here for a typical moss) involves the alternation of two multicellular generations. The gametophyte, the generation producing male and female gametes, is haploid; that is, its cells have a single set of chromosomes, *n*. The sporophyte generation is diploid, 2*n* (*shown as gray*), combining the chromosomes of the male and female gametes. Land plants are thought to have evolved from green algae, many of which also have alternation of generations, but land plants are distinguished by the retention of the zygote—the sporophyte embryo—within the nourishing tissue of the parental gametophyte. The understanding of how this relationship first evolved has been considerably advanced recently.

life cycle is now not merely of theoretical significance but will have practical importance in future work on plant biology. For example, understanding as much as possible about the genetic history of plants and the origin of their reproductive processes may be usefully applied to the genetic modification of economically important higher plants by haploid selection and by genetic-engineering techniques. There is special interest in understanding the plant-embryo relationship, for this may lead to development of techniques for the fertilization of isolated plant eggs in vitro, which in turn will facilitate genetic engineering (10).

Once identified, modern algae that are most closely related to plants are likely to be useful as simple systems for experimental study of several other poorly understood plant processes believed to be of ancient origin. These include photorespiration, which can decrease crop productivity, and phytochrome-mediated photomorphogenesis, which includes control of flowering and other processes of plant development. Thus, it is important to determine which hypothesis best explains the origin of the embryophytic life cycle and, as a corollary, which extant green algae are most closely related to land plants.

Until recently, however, little new evidence has been available with which to evaluate the two conflicting ideas. The fossil record has shed little light on the origin of the land-plant life cycle (11), probably because the earliest embryophytes were inconspicuous. However, the fossil record does provide some evidence that certain advanced green algae of the present day, such as *Chara* and *Coleochaete*, are quite ancient and may serve as models of the ancestors of land plants. The record indicates that the outward appearance or morphology of these forms has not changed greatly since the time land plants first appeared and diversified. Furthermore, the fossil record for the order Charales, which includes modern *Chara*, extends back about 400 million years to the Silurian (12), and the Upper Silurian–Lower Devonian genera *Parka* and *Pachytheca* strongly resemble extant *Coleochaete* in habitat and structure (11, 13). Such fossils indicate that study of present-day green algae may be of value in deducing the evolutionary origins of plants and of their life cycle.

The new evidence that does contribute significantly toward resolution of the problem of land-plant origins comes from recent studies of green-algal ultrastructure, systematics, and evolution, and from evolutionary theory. The weight of this evidence gives strong support to Bower's hypothesis.

Systematics and evolution

Recent, revolutionary changes in concepts of green-algal systematics and evolution have resulted from studies of features of reproduction and cell biology that are evolutionarily conservative and thus may be less susceptible to parallel and convergent evolution than are characters of external morphology. The conservative characters of greatest significance include certain biochemical features, the organization of the cell-division process, and the fine structure of reproductive cells, especially the flagellar apparatus and cytoskeleton (i.e., the protein-fiber structural framework) in motile reproductive cells (gametes and zoospores). Such data, accumulated by a

number of laboratories for numerous forms of green algae, collectively suggest that the evolutionary line which ultimately led to land plants diverged early from other mainstreams of green-algal diversification (14–18).

According to these data, the class Charophyceae (19), which includes the Charales and *Coleochaete*, is linked to the ancestry of embryophytes and separated from other algal lineages because, like land plants, advanced charophytes possess a phragmoplast, a distinctive array of microtubules and vesicles that appears during the final stages of cell division in plants. Phragmoplast microtubules are characteristically oriented at right angles to the direction of new cross-wall formation and are thought to be involved somehow in development of new cell walls. Most other green algae accomplish cytoplasmic division rather differently and lack a phragmoplast.

Charophytes are further distinguished by their flagellated reproductive cells, which contain a multilayered structure and microtubular cytoskeleton similar to those of all the land plants that produce flagellated spermatozoids, including bryophytes, fern allies, ferns, and certain gymnosperms. The multilayered structure is a distinctive layered part of the cell associated with the flagella of certain flagellates and with motile reproductive cells such as zoospores or spermatozoids. Its function has not yet been determined, but some workers think it might be involved in the synthesis and organization of microtubules, particularly those in flagella, or those of the cytoskeleton. Also, photorespiration in charophycean green algae is more similar to photorespiration in land plants than to this process in other green algae (20, 21). Finally, the only substantial evidence for the occurrence of phytochrome—a light-activated protein plant pigment involved in development—in green algae comes from members of the charophycean line (22).

For these reasons, it is becoming widely accepted that members of the Charophyceae represent the closest extant green-algal relatives of embryophytes. Given this information, new observations can be made concerning the two theories of the origin of the land-plant life cycle. First, all present-day members of the Charophyceae that are sexually reproductive lack alternation of generations; that is, they have haploid, haplobiontic life cycles. Meiosis occurs upon germination of the zygote, and thus

Figure 2. Most species of green algae display one of two types of life cycles. In haplobiontic, haploid species, such as of the unicellular genus *Chlamydomonas* represented here, there is only one generation, a gamete-producing plant whose cells are haploid, with a single set of chromosomes, *n*; pairs of gametes from different individual plants of each sex (designated + and −) combine to form a one-celled zygote, which has 2*n* chromosomes (*shown as gray*), and which then divides by meiosis to produce haploid spores. In contrast, the zygote of diplobiontic species, such as of the multicellular genus *Ulva*, does not undergo immediate meiosis, but grows to form a multicellular plant that itself produces spores by meiosis. This sporophyte, whose cells have the same diploid number of chromosomes as the zygote (2*n*), can produce a far greater number of spores than the meiotically dividing zygote of the haplobiontic life cycle, which is limited by the size of the zygote. The diplobiontic life cycle of algae – and of the land plants – is thought to have evolved from the haplobiontic by a delay in meiosis.

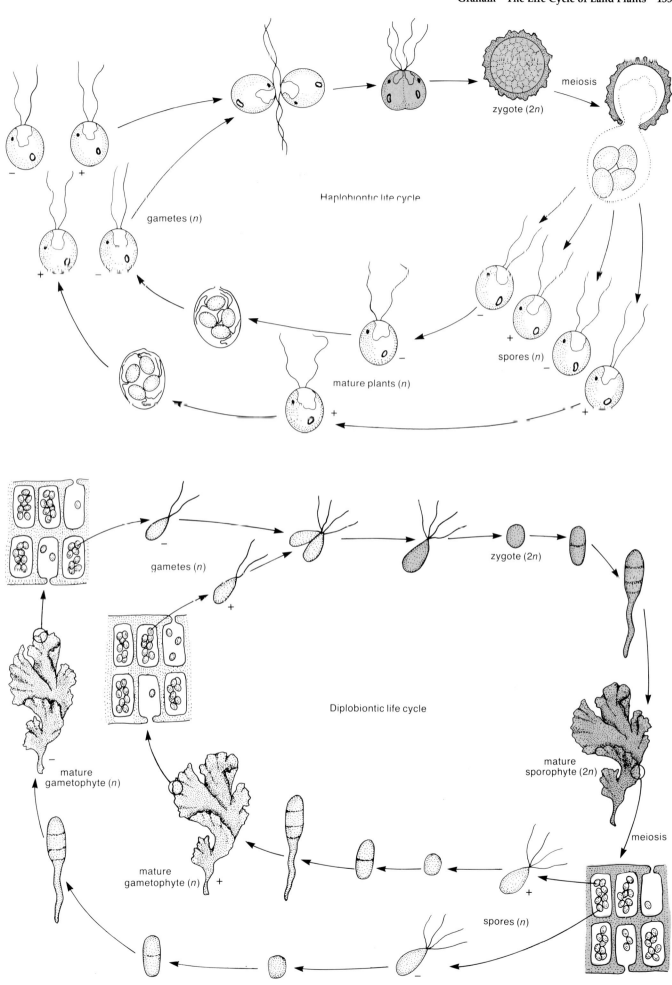

Haplobiontic life cycle

gametes (n)

zygote (2n)

meiosis

spores (n)

mature plants (n)

Diplobiontic life cycle

gametes (n)

zygote (2n)

mature
sporophyte (2n)

meiosis

spores (n)

mature
gametophyte (n)

mature
gametophyte (n) +

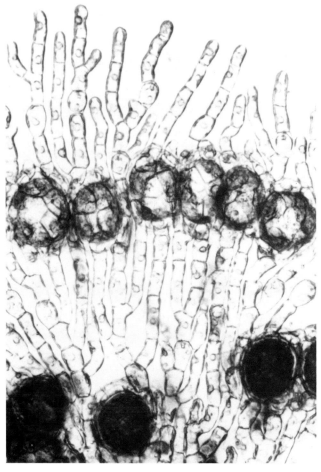

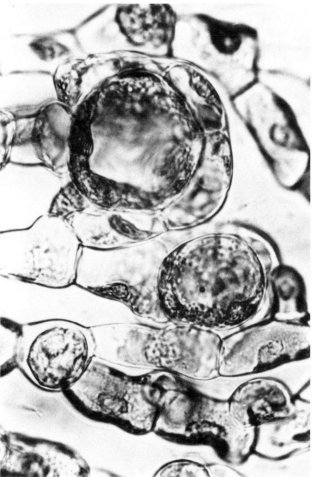

there is no multicellular diploid generation. Second, none of the extant green algae that do have alternation of multicellular generations have the combination of advanced, plantlike characteristics, such as phragmoplasts, multilayered structures, plantlike photorespiration, and phytochrome that are exhibited by charophycean algae. It seems unlikely that this constellation of conservative biochemical and ultrastructural characters arose convergently in some other lineage that gave rise to land plants and then became extinct.

Thus, on the whole, recent work in green-algal systematics strongly supports the hypothesis that embryophytes originated from haplobiontic, haploid charophycean algae as described by Bower (8), and that alternation of generations in other green-algal lineages arose in parallel. However, while the charophycean algae are now widely accepted as close relatives of embryophytes, there are workers who suggest that embryophytes arose from hypothetical extinct charophytes that were diplobiontic (23). But there are compelling theoretical reasons for rejecting this possibility.

Some theoretical considerations

Regardless of whether the land-plant sporophyte and its nutritional and developmental association with the gametophyte evolved from a diploid zygote or from a free-living sporophyte, the sequence of evolutionary steps must have been the same. The first step would have been development of oogamous sexual reproduction—that is, reproduction in which specialized, immobile eggs fuse with smaller, motile sperm, as opposed to isogamous reproduction, which involves unspecialized, indistinguishable male and female gametes, as in more primitive forms. The next step would have been retention of the egg on the parental gametophyte at the time of fertilization. This would be followed by retention of the zygote and its subsequent development on the gametophyte, and finally by establishment of a nutritional and developmental relationship between sporophyte and gametophyte. Because each of these four steps is dependent on the previous one, an alternative sequence of events is unlikely.

Bearing this sequence in mind, there are several major reasons for rejecting the hypothesis that the plant life cycle evolved from a diplobiontic one. First, there are no extant examples of green algae with alternation of generations that are also oogamous. Also, in present-day diplobiontic green algae, gametes are re-

Figure 3. In the highly branched species *Coleochaete pulvinata*, shown in the upper photograph magnified 280 times, eggs and sperm are produced at the growing edge (*top*). Following fertilization, the resulting zygotes enlarge greatly and acquire a cellular covering (*center*); older zygotes (*bottom*) appear darker because of the accumulation of food reserves. As can be seen at the greater magnification of the lower photograph (× 1,100), very young zygotes seem to attract neighboring filaments; as they enlarge, developing zygotes may actually stimulate unidirectional growth of neighboring cells, which then proliferate into a close covering around the zygotes. This retention of the diploid zygotes within the haploid tissue of the parental gametophyte, a characteristic of all land plants, occurs in no other genus of green algae and is the primary reason why *Coleochaete* may be considered as a model of an ancestor of land plants. (Lower photograph after ref. 41.)

leased from gametophytes, so that fertilization and subsequent zygote and sporophyte development are independent of the parental gametophyte.

In contrast, Bower's hypothesis that the land plants evolved from haplobiontic green algae similar to present-day *Coleochaete* has the great advantage that most of the evolutionary steps—oogamy, retention of the egg on the parental gametophyte, and retention of the zygote—would already have been accomplished in the green-algal ancestor. Of course, it is possible that diplobiontic, oogamous forms that retained eggs and zygotes became extinct after giving rise to land plants. However, the following theoretical consideration suggests that this is unlikely.

Haploid, haplobiontic life cycles are widespread among protists—one of the five kingdoms of organisms that includes algae, slime molds, and protozoa (6)—and therefore are probably primitive life cycles. A major disadvantage of such a life cycle is that relatively few products, generally only four, result from each zygotic meiosis. A number of different types of protists have solved this problem by a delay in meiosis long enough for the zygote to develop into a multicellular diploid structure that is capable of producing more than four meiotic products; in other words, these protists have developed a diplobiontic life cycle. The new diploid generation, or sporophyte, serves to protect the genome from the effects of deleterious mutations, as well as to increase the number and diversity of recombinant progeny (24).

If, in a diplobiontic green alga, the free-living, photosynthetic sporophyte were to abandon independent existence and assume an embryophyte-like association with the gametophyte, the size of the attached sporophyte, and consequently the number of meiotic products that could be produced, is likely to be reduced. In comparison to diplobiontic forms, such an alga is likely to be at a competitive disadvantage in environments that favor production of more spores for each fertilization event, or production of separate generations that can exploit seasonal or habitat variations. Indeed, it is difficult to conceive of any selective advantage for the multistep evolutionary pathway required to generate a land-plant life cycle from a diplobiontic one.

Interestingly, the origin of the life cycle of advanced red algae seems to offer a parallel to the origin of the sporophyte generation in plants. Advanced red algae have an alternation of three generations; two of these are usually free-living, and the third, called the carposporophyte, is attached to the female gametophyte and is probably partially parasitic on it (25). This carposporophyte may also stimulate development of a protective layer of gametophytic filaments called a pericarp. Thus, the red algae may exhibit an intimate developmental and nutritive interaction between generations that parallels that of embryophytes. Since male gametes of red algae lack flagella that would make them motile, fertilization rates may be low. The carposporophyte is thought to compensate by producing many copies of the products of any successful fertilization (26). Searles (26) has suggested that the evolutionary development of the land-plant sporophyte is related to reduced fertilization rates in drier terrestrial habitats, favoring production of greater numbers of spores for each fertilization. Thus, the selective pressures and evolutionary responses

leading to the origin of the red-algal carposporophyte and to the land-plant sporophyte may have been analogous.

It is also interesting to note that in developing the carposporophyte phase, red algae have not given up their original diploid generation (the tetrasporophyte), which is generally free-living. If diplobiontic green algae had acquired an attached sporophyte, one might expect to find some forms having three alternating generations such as occur among advanced red algae, but these do not exist. Collectively, such observations support the hypothesis that land plants arose from advanced charophycean algae by a single evolutionary step, a delay in meiosis.

Advanced charophycean algae

The evidence suggests that the present-day genus most closely resembling the now-extinct immediate ancestors of embryophytic land plants is *Coleochaete*. It is likely that some other present-day charophytes are more specialized than these ancestors (24). *Chara* and *Nitella*, for instance, have the most complex specialized plant bodies, gametangia (structures in which gametes are produced), and male gametes known among green algae. In spermatozoids, the thin plates of the multilayered structure are either highly modified, as in *Nitella* (27), or missing altogether, as in *Chara* (28, 29). These facts suggest that Charales (*Chara*, *Nitella*, and close relatives) have diverged substantially from the main evolutionary line leading directly to embryophytes.

The less-specialized bodies, gametangia, gametes, and multilayered structures of *Coleochaete* suggest a closer relationship to the direct ancestry of plants. *Coleochaete* has certain features—the photorespiratory enzyme glycolate oxidase (20), photorespiratory organelles or peroxisomes, a phragmoplast at cytokinesis (21), and multilayered structures in male gametes (30)—in common with other charophytes (19) and land plants. Since embryophytes lack zoospores (motile, flagellated spores), the widespread occurrence of zoospores in *Coleochaete* and in some other charophycean genera demonstrates the aquatic affinities of these green algae, and argues against a suggestion that charophycean algae originated and diversified on land and then became secondarily aquatic (23).

Certain advanced characters are shared by *Coleochaete* species and were probably also features of charophytes ancestral to the genus. These include ovoid spermatozoids resembling those of *Lycopodium* (30–31), which are thought to be the primitive type among lower land plants (32), production of a layer of cells covering zygotes (33), and production of more than four meiospores (i.e., spores resulting from meiosis) per zygote. In at least one species, this last feature is based on the occurrence of more than one round of DNA replication prior to meiosis (34). Some or all of these attributes probably characterized the ancestors of the Charales and land plants as well.

A number of embryophyte-like features occur in some, but not all, the species of *Coleochaete*: localized growth (a peripheral meristem) (35), parenchyma (36), putative placental transfer cells with localized wall ingrowths (37), and multicellular, internal antheridia (30, 38). Most likely, *Coleochaete* evolved these features in parallel with the charophytes that gave rise directly to plants in response to selective pressures operating in similar habitats.

A model for the origin of land plants

In regard to the origin of the embryophyte life cycle, the most significant feature of *Coleochaete*—retention and subsequent development of the zygote on the haploid parental body (Fig. 3)—makes it a model for the green-algal ancestor of embryophytic land plants. The parent-embryo relationship is likely to have first evolved as a result of particular selective pressures of the aquatic environment.

Most species of *Coleochaete* are littoral epiphytes—that is, they grow in waters near the shore, firmly attached to larger plants (macrophytes) or to inorganic substrates such as rocks or discarded bottles and cans. The adaptive advantage of zygote retention may be that zygotes are more likely to remain in the shallow water near the shore through winter and into spring, when they germinate and produce meiospores that swim a

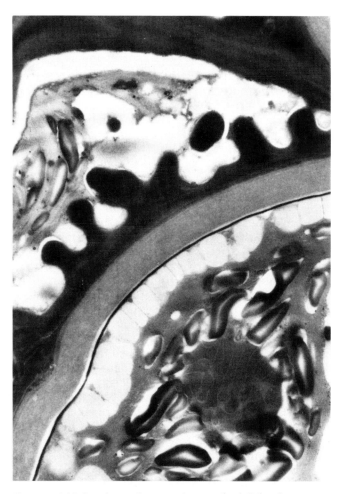

Figure 4. A high-voltage electron micrograph of *Coleochaete orbicularis* (× 6,700) shows the boundary between a zygote (*lower right*) and its neighboring cover cell (*upper left*), which has localized ingrowths from its outer wall into the cell. These ingrowths, similar to those of placental transfer cells in embryophytic land plants, are believed to function as do intestinal villi in humans; that is, they increase the surface area of membranes across which nutrients are transported. The structures within the zygote are starch grains and lipid droplets.

short distance before settling. Thus, upon their release, spores are close to suitable substrates for attachment and growth in a well-lighted environment. This may confer an advantage for spring colonization over other littoral epiphytes whose zygotes are released from the parental bodies and are thus more likely to overwinter in deeper water or in the sediments.

In *Coleochaete*, the attachment of the zygote occurs because a layer of vegetative cells belonging to the parental generation covers exposed surfaces of mature zygotes. Observations of the growth of this cellular cover suggest that zygotes probably induce its development. This phenomenon is best observed in the filamentous species *C. pulvinata* shown in Figure 3, where filaments in the vicinity of young zygotes grow toward the zygotes, eventually covering them (*39*). Such interaction during growth between cells of differing chromosome levels occurs in no other green-algal genus; it is comparable to developmental changes observed in gametophytic cells adjacent to zygotes in embryophytes, and to the growth of filaments around gametangia of Charales.

As Figure 3 shows, zygotes in *Coleochaete* are much larger than the parental vegetative cells. *Coleochaete* is unusual among haplobiontic, haploid green algae in that 8 to 32 spores are produced per zygote, rather than 4 or fewer as is usual. The large number of meiotic products in this genus may well be an adaptation allowing rapid colonization of substrate space at the beginning of the growing season (*34*).

Parka, *Coleochaete*'s presumed fossil relative, indicates that selective pressures in shoreline habitats during the Silurian (or earlier, when the first land plants are believed to have appeared) favored production of large zygotes and, consequently, of greater numbers of spores (*13*). *Parka*, probably also a littoral epiphyte associated with the macrophyte *Zosterophyllum*, produced very large sporangia (spore-producing structures), covered by a cellular layer, which contained numerous spores (*13*). Thus, production of large numbers of spores as an adaptation for rapid colonization (*40*) may have been common among charophycean epiphytes in the Silurian. In *Coleochaete* an additional cycle of premeiotic DNA replication apparently occurs, so that zygote nuclei may have DNA levels two (and perhaps even more) times higher than expected (*34*), an increase that probably represents extra copies of chromatids (the paired strands resulting from recent replication of chromosomes), which may then undergo genetic exchange and assort in various ways. This may confer the potential for an increased number of recombinant progeny, thus yielding greater genetic diversity as compared to organisms producing four or fewer meiotic products per zygote.

Production of more than four, and of more diverse, meiospores as an adaptation to littoral life may have served as a preadaptation (*41*) that led to the evolution of increasingly larger diploid phases of the life cycle by increasingly longer delays in meiosis. Indeed, the extra premeiotic DNA replication that occurs in *Coleochaete* might be viewed as a first step toward delay in meiosis. After shoreline habitats became accessible for colonization—perhaps because of reductions in ultraviolet levels resulting from increased levels of atmospheric oxygen and ozone (*42*)—an alga or early plant that could produce greater numbers of more diverse spores for every zygote (i.e., for every instance of successful fertilization) would presumably have an evolutionary advantage over similar organisms producing fewer, genetically less diverse meiotic products (43). In fact, green algae from lines of descent other than the Charophyceae have colonized the land. Examples include numerous genera of unicellular and colonial soil algae (44) and *Fritschiella*, a morphologically complex form once thought to be a land-plant progenitor. The highly specialized Trentepohliales may have originated on land from unicellular soil algae (18). But there is no evidence that any of these forms gave rise to any embryophyte group.

The close association between zygote and cover cells in *Coleochaete* also provides an opportunity for the haploid and diploid phases of the life cycle to develop a nutritional relationship similar to that occurring in embryophytes. Zygotes of *Coleochaete* contain chloroplasts (37), and thus can presumably photosynthesize. However, the zygotes become much larger than vegetative cells and accumulate large amounts of starch and lipid storage materials as they mature. There is circumstantial evidence that zygote photosynthesis may be supplemented by photosynthates secreted from covering cells during the time that reserves are stored. In at least one species, *C. orbicularis*, conspicuous, localized wall ingrowths occur in covering cells, as shown in Figure 4. These cover cells resemble gametophytic placental transfer cells of embryophytes in structure, location, and time of development. Among embryophytes, placental transfer cells facilitate movement of photosynthate across cell membranes and cell walls at the junction between sporophyte and gametophyte, where connecting strands of cytoplasm are lacking (2–4). Wall ingrowths of transfer cells function to increase the surface area of the wall-membrane complex (2–4), where transport enzymes are located (45).

In the aquatic environment, extensive transfer of solutes between zygotes and adjacent cells of most algae is unlikely, because cytoplasmic connections are disrupted by thickening of the zygote wall, and because photosynthates moving through cell walls and intercellular spaces can readily dissolve into the surrounding medium. Only in a tightly associated complex of zygote and parental cells, such as in *Coleochaete*, can short-distance transport across membranes and walls of adjacent cells occur to any great extent (41). The advantage of photosynthate importation by zygotes is that more resources are available for the production of spores at zygote germination.

Probably a major factor in the success of charophytes on land was the ability to maximize the result of sexual reproduction by virtue of a nutritional and developmental relationship between life-cycle phases. Phragmoplasts, multilayered structures, and other features of charophycean algae may have contributed to their ability to colonize the land. However, some of these characters may simply have been inherited by plants as components of a genome successful for other reasons. *Coleochaete* provides a model for the way in which similar charophycean algae could have acquired a variety of adaptations to littoral life, which later proved useful in the conquest of land.

Coleochaete also illustrates how charophycean algae could—and probably did—give rise to the first embryophytes by a simple, one-step process, delay in meiosis. Such a step is apparently an easy one, as it must have occurred each time alternation of generations arose in protists. The *Coleochaete* model also explains the origin of the nutritional and developmental relationship between generations that was apparently so influential in subsequent plant evolution. The evidence currently available suggests that continued study of *Coleochaete* is likely to result in further progress toward understanding the origins of plants and may also influence the direction of evolutionary studies in various groups of plants (9).

References

1. H. C. Bold. 1973. *Morphology of Plants*. Harper and Row.

2. A. J. Browning and B. E. S. Gunning. 1979. Structure and function of transfer cells in the sporophyte haustorium of *Funaria hygrometrica* Hedw. I. The development and ultrastructure of the haustorium. *J. Exp. Bot.* 30:1233–46.

3. A. J. Browning and B. E. S. Gunning. 1979. Structure and function of transfer cells in the sporophyte haustorium of *Funaria hygrometrica* Hedw. II. Kinetics of uptake of labelled sugars and localization of absorbed products by freeze-substitution and autoradiography. *J. Exp. Bot.* 30:1247–64.

4. A. J. Browning and B. E. S. Gunning. 1979. Structure and function of transfer cells in the sporophyte haustorium of *Funaria hygrometrica* Hedw. III. Translocation of assimilate into the attached sporophyte and along the seta of attached and excised sporophytes. *J. Exp. Bot.* 30:1265–73.

5. C. Caussin. 1983. Absorption of some amino acids by sporophytes isolated from *Polytrichum formosum* and ultrastructural characteristics of the haustorium transfer cells. *Ann. Bot.* 51:167–73.

6. L. Margulis and K. V. Schwartz. 1982. *Five Kingdoms*. Freeman.

7. L. Celakovsky. 1874. Bedeutung des Generationswechsels der Pflanzen. Prague.

8. F. O. Bower. 1908. *The Origin of a Land Flora*. MacMillan.

9. D. J. Paolillo, Jr. 1981. The swimming sperms of land plants. *BioScience* 31:367–73.

10. V. R. Tilton and S. H. Russell. 1984. Applications of in vitro pollination/fertilization technology. *BioScience* 34:239–42.

11. T. N. Taylor. 1982. The origin of land plants. A paleobotanical perspective. *Taxon* 31:155–77.

12. J. W. Schopf. 1970. Pre-cambrian micro-organisms and evolutionary events prior to the origin of vascular plants. *Biol. Rev.* 45:319–52.

13. K. J. Niklas. 1976. Morphological and ontogenetic reconstruction of *Parka decipiens* Fleming and *Pachytheca* Hooker from the Lower Old Red Sandstone, Scotland. *Trans. Roy. Soc. Edinburgh* 69:483–99.

14. J. D. Pickett-Heaps and H. J. Marchant. 1972. The phylogeny of the green algae: A new proposal. *Cytobios* 6:255–64.

15. O. Moestrup. 1974. Ultrastructure of the scale-covered zoospores of the green alga *Chaetosphaeridium*, a possible ancestor of the higher plants and bryophytes. *Biol. J. Linn. Soc.* 6:111–25.

16. K. D. Stewart and K. R. Mattox. 1978. Structural evolution in the flagellated cells of green algae and land plants. *BioSystems* 10:145–52.

17. H. J. Hoops, G. L. Floyd, and J. A. Swanson. 1982. Ultrastructure of the biflagellate motile cells of *Ulvaria oxysperma* (Kütz.). Bliding and phylogenetic relationships among ulvaphycean algae. *Am. J. Bot.* 69:150–59.

18. M. Melkonian. 1982. Structural and evolutionary aspects of the flagellar apparatus in green algae and land plants. *Taxon* 31:255–65.

19. K. D. Stewart and K. R. Mattox. 1975. Comparative cytology, evolution and classification of the green algae with some consideration of the origin of other organisms with chlorophylls a and b. *Bot. Rev.* 41:104–35.

20. S. E. Frederick, P. J. Gruber, and N. E. Tolbert. 1973. The occurrence of glycolate dehydrogenase and glycolate oxidase in green plants. An evolutionary survey. *Plant Physiol.* 52:318–23.

The Early Evolution of the Domestic Dog

Animal domestication, commonly considered a human innovation,
can also be described as an evolutionary process

Darcy F. Morey

Sometime within the past 12,000 or so years, most of humankind began to experience a profound shift in lifestyle. Stone Age hunters and gatherers of wild foodstuffs started to cultivate plants and raise animals for their own use. A landscape full of wild grasses, woolly mammoths and sabertooth cats gave way to giant-eared corn, fat cattle, toy poodles and many other new species. For reasons that remain obscure, the shift happened rapidly, by evolutionary standards, and in the mere space of a few thousand years, different domestic animals and plants appeared independently in several parts of the world.

The archaeological record indicates that humankind's best friend—the domestic dog, *Canis familiaris*—was likely also its first. Consequently, I think of dogs as the pioneers of an evolutionary radiation that had radical effects on the composition of the earth's biota and on the way people live. As such, dogs are an appropriate focal point for an ongoing debate about the origins and nature of animal domestication. Central to this discussion is the issue of intentionality—whether domestication must be understood as a human

Darcy F. Morey received his Ph.D. in anthropology in 1990 from the University of Tennessee at Knoxville. His primary training is as an archaeologist, with a specialization in zooarchaeology. His research on early domestication, the core of his doctoral project, grew out of a desire to integrate technical training in zooarchaeology with a long-standing interest in evolutionary theory and its application to sociocultural phenomena. He currently holds an adjunct affiliation with the University of Tennessee, where he teaches occasionally and does research. Address: Department of Anthropology, 252 South Stadium Hall, University of Tennessee, Knoxville, TN 37996-0720.

decision, as is commonly thought, or, rather, is best modeled strictly as an evolutionary process.

Those who explain domestication as a rational decision suggest that people recognized the potential benefits of bringing animals and plants under control. The assumption is that people intentionally sought to raise, cultivate and manipulate organisms in ways that enhanced their economically useful properties. In contrast, in the evolutionary view, the behavior, diets and, later, the physiology and morphology of certain animals changed from that of their wild counterparts in response to the selection pressures of a new ecological niche—a domestic association with human beings. This view holds, first, that knowing the intentions of prehistoric people is beyond the abilities of modern science. Second, and of greater importance, knowledge of people's rational intentions would not provide a scientific explanation for the process of domestication.

Domestication as Human Design
Given the pivotal role of domestication in shaping our present life-style, it is no surprise to find that prehistorians have argued vigorously about what domestication really is, how it originated, and why. Many classic definitions of the concept focus on human subjugation of other organisms. In a commonly drawn scenario, people isolated individuals of a particular species from their wild counterparts and then selectively bred them to exaggerate desirable traits and eliminate undesirable ones in a process known as artificial selection.

Such a scenario grows out of a combination of common-sense reflection on the conditions under which many modern domesticates live, with the

presumption that those ends were sought, at least in rudimentary form, by people of the past. According to this view, people turned to the domestication of plants and animals when increases in human population or environmental changes reduced the availability of wild foods. Given these pressures, people invented or otherwise made a decision to experiment with domestication, though not necessarily as a well-organized plan.

Theories that assume intentionality, however, may be rooted more in the biases of modern culture than in any objective measure. Life in the 20th century without domesticates is virtually unimaginable to us, so it is tempting to presume that people who lived without domesticates during the late Pleistocene and early Holocene surely wished to improve their lives.

Figure 1. Relationships between Stone Age people and wolves set the stage for dog domestication. People and members of the dog family have had a long association, as these 11,000–to–12,000-year-old remains attest. A puppy skeleton from either a dog or a wolf can be seen under the human skeleton's left hand. These burials were discovered at Ein Mallaha in northern Israel and were originally reported by zooarchaeologists Simon Davis and François Valla. Early dog remains have been found at sites in other parts of the world, suggesting that dog domestication may have taken place independently in different regions. Prehistorians have disagreed about whether different animals were intentionally domesticated by ancient people, or whether domestication is another example of evolution driven by natural selection. The author argues the latter, and proposes that dog evolution is best viewed as the product of selection pressures in a new ecological niche, in this case a domestic association with human beings. (Photograph by Alain Dagand.)

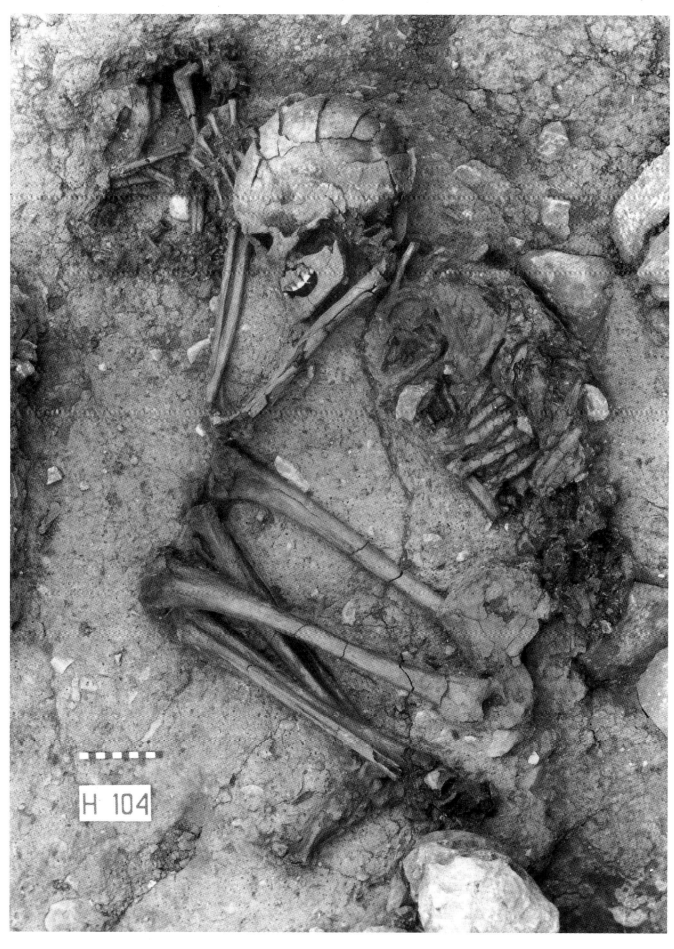

H 104

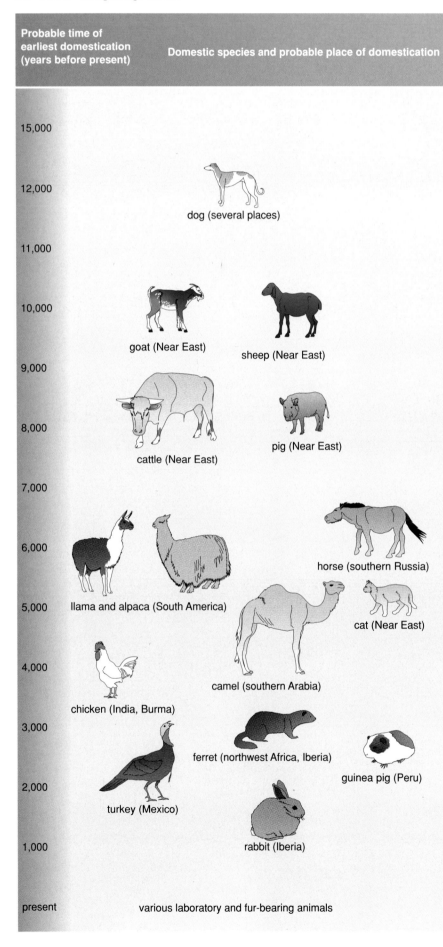

Probable time of earliest domestication (years before present)	Domestic species and probable place of domestication

15,000

12,000
dog (several places)

11,000

10,000
goat (Near East)   sheep (Near East)

9,000

8,000
cattle (Near East)   pig (Near East)

7,000

6,000
horse (southern Russia)

5,000
llama and alpaca (South America)   cat (Near East)

4,000
camel (southern Arabia)

chicken (India, Burma)

3,000
ferret (northwest Africa, Iberia)

guinea pig (Peru)

2,000
turkey (Mexico)

rabbit (Iberia)

1,000

present   various laboratory and fur-bearing animals

A second theme, this one anthropocentric, also underlies theories that assume intentionality—that people exercise rational control of their collective destiny. This perspective is appealing, for it places people at the evolutionary helm, charting the course from the start. To borrow anthropologist David Rindos's apt term, a "paradigm of consciousness" is our conceptual anchor, and from it stems the discussion of domestication as invention, decision, idea and so on.

Maybe the shift to economic reliance on domestic species was in some sense necessary, given human population growth and environmental changes in the Holocene. Maybe domestication was indeed a strategy that prehistoric people intentionally implemented. Both propositions are debatable, but my immediate objection stems from a problem more fundamental than the need for better data.

The human beings who participated in the earliest domestic relationships thousands of years ago are all dead. They cannot tell us what was in their minds or what they sought to accomplish. For early domestication, the data required to evaluate scenarios based on human intention are, by definition, unattainable. In other words, models that explain domestication this way cannot be empirically challenged, and on this basis alone, they are not scientific models.

The real issue is whether it is necessary to presume the intentions of prehistoric people to make sense of early domestication. Over the years, some scholars have attempted to describe domestication in more mechanistic terms, focusing on the implications of organisms sharing space and resources in symbiotic relationships. This approach, however, has not led to a uniform perspective. In 1959, for example, zoologist Charles Reed characterized domestication as "beneficial mutualism." At about the same time, in 1963, archaeologist F. E. Zeuner was using the term "slavery" as a virtual synonym for some cases of domestication. Nevertheless, such efforts can be viewed as the foundation for more recent attempts to model domestication as evolution.

Evolutionary perspectives differ from anthropocentric approaches in several

Figure 2. Humankind's best friend was likely also its first. This time line shows the estimated times and probable places of origin for several other important domesticates.

ways. First, they do not restrict domestic relationships to people. The complex symbiosis between ants and aphids is a handy example, and is even used in my dictionary to illustrate use of the term "domestication." Certain ants herd aphids, providing protection in exchange for the sugary, honey-like liquid they "milk" from the aphids. Second, domestic relationships involve two species. Focusing solely on the human role in domestication ignores the evolutionary stakes for participating animals and plants. The ubiquity of dogs, for example, suggests they have profited well from the domestic arrangement. Their wolf ancestors, on the other hand, have been extirpated from most of their formerly vast range, and many subspecies are now extinct. From a Darwinian perspective, wolves who took up residence with people a few thousand years ago made a smart move—at least from today's vantage point.

Finally, an evolutionary perspective discourages an assumption that changes in an animal's size or shape during domestication must be products of human selection.

Ancient Associations

If one is to eliminate rational intention as a scientific explanation for early animal domestication, one must conclude that the process originated with a natural association between people and the wild ancestors of dogs. Skeletal remains of early dogs from various archaeological sites around the world place the beginnings of their domestication in the late Pleistocene era, possibly as far back as 14,000 years ago. The data therefore indicate that canid domestication took place among people who still pursued a hunting-and-gathering way of life.

The ancestor of these early dogs can be identified with confidence as the wolf *Canis lupus*. This assertion rests on a growing body of molecular data and is buttressed by the striking physiological and behavioral similarities between the species. It is not currently possible to identify which subspecies of wolves gave rise to domestic dogs (although new advances in comparative DNA analyses to establish relatedness between species may soon change that). For now, scholars simply recognize the wolf as the dog's ancestral progenitor, and many people suspect that canid domestication involved several wolf subspecies in different parts of the world.

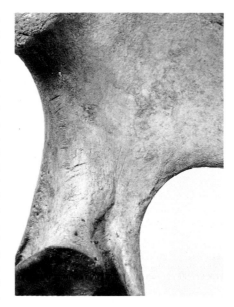

Figure 3. Dogs served a number of economic purposes in past human societies, the variety of which makes it difficult to glean a primary benefit that people derived from the animals during early domestication. This dog bone from Qeqertasussuk, a small island off of the west coast of Greenland, for example, was discarded by people along with large quantities of food debris almost 4,000 years ago. A series of cut marks on the bone indicate that the animal from which it came was skinned or butchered. Another dog bone from the site had been fashioned into what Danish archaeologist Bjarne Grønnow describes as a needle case. Later arctic peoples used dogs to pull sleds, and some skulls from later sites in Greenland and elsewhere in the Arctic bear marks that indicated blows to the head. (Photograph by Geert Brovad.)

Figure 4. Dog effigy vessel was made by a Colima artist. The Colima, who inhabited western Mexico about 2,000 years ago, and some other Precolumbian groups in Mesoamerica apparently used dogs as dietary fare, as did later groups, such as the Aztec. According to a Spanish observer at one Aztec market, 400 dogs were sold on a slow day. (Photograph used with permission from the Appleton Art Museum, Ocala, Florida.)

Wolves and late-Pleistocene hunters and gatherers undoubtedly came into contact regularly, since both were social species who hunted many of the same prey items. Wolves are also opportunistic scavengers; they were likely to have been familiar with human hunting practices and to have hung around human settlements regularly. Let us then assume that the road toward domestication began when some wolf pups became incorporated into a human social and residential setting. One could speculate endlessly about the conscious motivation people had for taking on wolf pups. It seems sufficient, however, to note that different people often kept wild animals for a variety of reasons without attempting to achieve long-term domestication.

Somewhere, at some time, one or more adopted pups managed to survive to adulthood in the new setting. To have a chance in human society, the animals minimally had to adjust to new social rules and to an altered diet.

Socialization, according to studies conducted by J. P. Scott during the 1950s and 1960s, is best achieved early in a dog's life. Scott and his colleagues at the Jackson Laboratory in Bar Harbor, Maine, conducted long-term studies of behavior and socialization in dogs and found that the first few weeks of a puppy's life are crucial for forming primary social bonds with both people and other dogs. Not surprisingly, wolves are similar. Several other studies have shown that young wolf pups also form lasting bonds with people, a process that becomes more difficult for the animals as they mature.

Bonding between people and wolves is facilitated by similarities in social structure and in nonverbal modes of communication. Wolves are organized hierarchically and they communicate status through vocal, facial and postural displays of dominance or submission. These displays involve many cues that are recognizable to people. Dogs use much the same repertoire of cues. Wolves and dogs can also respond appropriately to many human signals.

It is clear that animals living within human settlements had to learn that subordinate status to dominant humans was an inviolable rule. Some wolves were undoubtedly more adaptable than others to human dominance, and those that did not follow the rules were likely either killed or driven away. Some of those that adjusted be-

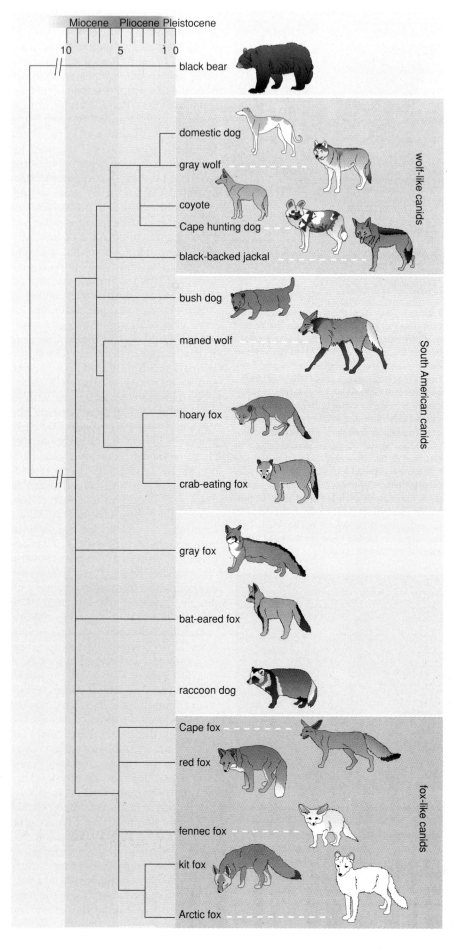

came tolerated in human society—a phenomenon that must have occurred within many human settlements. Selection for behavioral compatibility in a setting with new social boundaries was a strong force among founding domestic populations.

From the beginning of their domestic life, wolf pups would also have had to adjust to a different diet. Wild wolves take almost all their nutrition from meat. Adults often hunt cooperatively for large prey items, which for modern wolves includes deer, caribou or moose. Young wolves often accompany the adults and learn hunting skills, but that opportunity would be lost to wolf pups living in the domestic setting. Instead, they would have needed to rely more on people to share scraps of their own meals, a mixture of meat and plants. Adeptness at soliciting food from people was surely a valuable skill. To supplement this diet, wolf pups would have had to learn to scavenge competitively and to hunt small animals.

To maintain their toehold in the domestic niche, the domesticated wolves had to succeed in reproducing. One could assume that a male might leave the human setting and mate with wild animals. If he were successful, the progeny would be wild and would therefore not help perpetuate domestic populations.

Alternatively, the domestic setting might have included a male and female whose progeny remained in the human settlement. Although this scenario successfully creates more domestic animals, it also creates a genetically inbred population, which, in the long run, weakens the gene pool of the domestic population.

But a female surely had other options. A wild male that was unsuccessful in breeding within a wild pack might have found a domestic female an easier target. The female would most likely raise her offspring within the do-

Figure 5. DNA sequence comparisons and other lines of evidence allow scientists to establish the evolutionary relationships between members of the dog family. This analysis suggests that the gray wolf was the immediate ancestor of the domestic dog. The two species share so much genetic material in common that some scientists have described dogs as gray wolves with a few genetic alterations. The images do not depict true size relations between the species. Time is shown in millions of years ago. (Adapted from Wayne, 1993.)

mestic setting, although a few might attempt to return to the wild with their pups. The continuation of the domestic line requires that only some females raise offspring in a domestic setting.

An irony here is that canid domestication might have foundered if not for the role of wild males finding alternative reproductive opportunities. Still, their strategy ensured that the domestic population was not isolated genetically from wild populations. Genetic input from wild wolves was probably strong for many generations. Even today dogs and wolves are capable of mating and producing fertile offspring.

Evolution in a Domestic Setting

The new population of domestic wolves undoubtedly continued to expand. But at some point the animals began to change physically and behaviorally, evolving toward the form we recognize today as the dog. Early dogs conveniently exhibit consistent morphological changes when compared with wolves. Briefly (and not exhaustively), dogs became smaller overall, and the length of the snout became proportionally reduced. The result was a smaller animal with a shorter face, a steeply rising forehead and proportionally wider cranial dimensions. This general pattern suggests that adult animals retained juvenile characteristics, a phenomenon known as paedomorphosis. Paedomorphic dogs have a somewhat puppylike cranial morphology when compared with adult wolves.

In seeking to explain this pattern, many discussions presume that domestic animals must change in ways that serve people. For example, some discussions suggest that people involved in early canid domestication may have found paedomorphic features endearing and favored animals that retained them. Similarly, it has been suggested that people found smaller animals more manageable and favored them as well. Such suggestions appear reasonable, especially because they reflect common biases in people's present-day choices for good household pets. But these changes were taking place ubiquitously some 10,000 years ago, despite tremendous variability in cultural and geographic settings. It seems unlikely that all these human groups would have selected for exactly the same traits in dogs. Surely, the consistent appearance of these traits in animals living within so many different cultures raises

Figure 6. Gray wolf was almost certainly the ancestor of the domestic dog.

the possibility that some selection pressure other than human preference brought about the changes.

Specialists in life-history studies have developed some tools for probing this issue. The life-history analyst focuses on the entire life cycle of an animal, especially how changes in timing of developmental processes and important life events can have consequences that impact reproductive success. Life-history analysts might consider when and how often an animal should reproduce, or how big and how fast it should grow, depending on its situa-

tion. Different ecological circumstances pose different selection pressures, and the answers to these kinds of questions depend on the specific conditions faced by the animals.

In addition to selection for social compatibility, I propose that the conditions faced by early domestic canids led to strong selection on reproductive timing and body size. These selection pressures ultimately produced the smaller, paedomorphic animal known as the dog.

J. P. Scott, whose experimental work with dogs has already been noted, point-

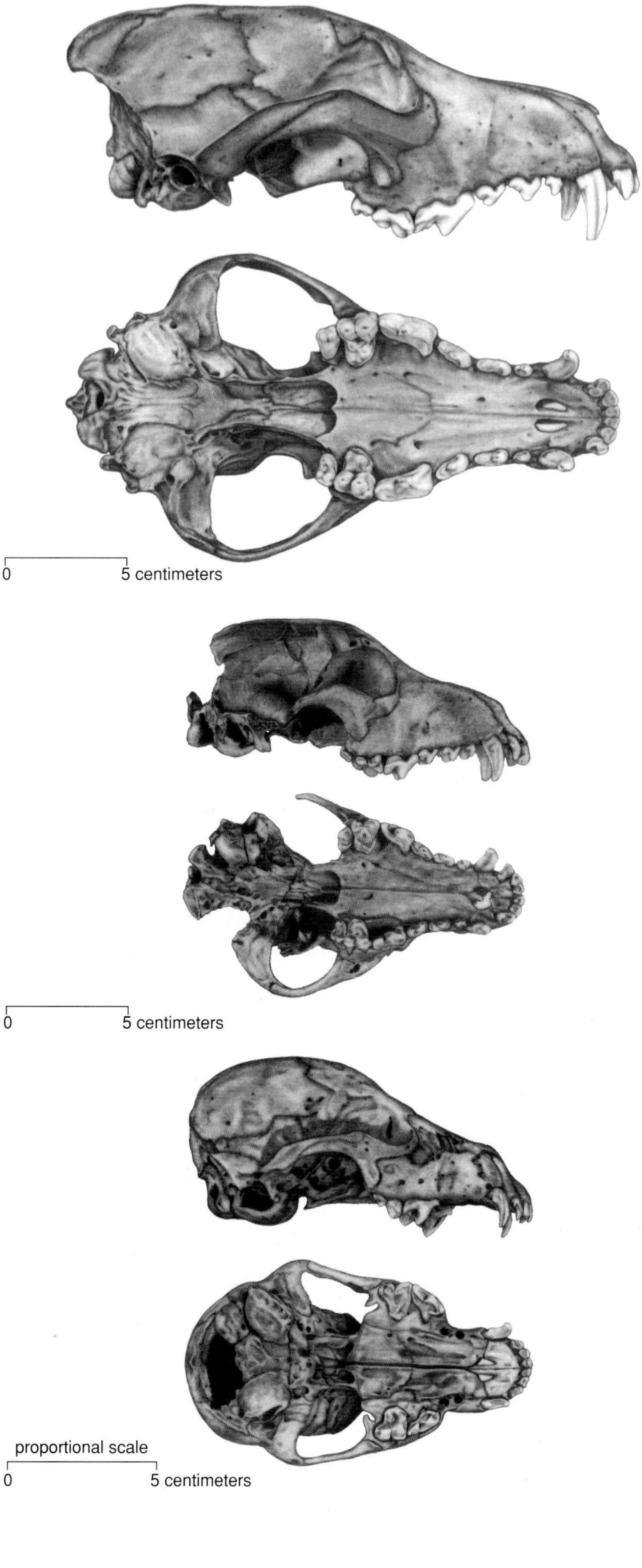

0 _____ 5 centimeters

0 _____ 5 centimeters

proportional scale

0   5 centimeters

ed out that canid domestication may be regarded as ecological colonization of a new niche. Population models view the hallmark of colonization as rapid population growth. One reason for this is that mortality becomes less dependent on population density compared with more stable conditions. Under these circumstances, a classical prediction of life-history models is that selection should favor lowered age at first reproduction. Increased fertility is at a premium then, and precocious maturation is a remarkably efficient way to achieve this. Evolutionary theory predicts that this change should result in size reduction and paedomorphosis in a descendant species, owing to a truncation of the growth period. In such a case, both consequences are only by-products of selection on reproductive timing. It is tantalizing to note that wild wolves reach sexual maturity at about the age of 2 years, whereas most modern dog breeds achieve maturity between 6 and 12 months. Unfortunately, it is difficult to know when in their history dogs started to reach sexual maturity earlier, and the current observed ages might just be an artifact of modern selective breeding programs.

A consideration of life-history studies also suggests that body size itself was a likely target of selection. An animal's body size plays a crucial role in defining its niche, and studies have shown that adult size is correlated with most life-history traits. Unfortunately, causes can be difficult to disentangle from effects. With early dogs, dietary change had to be pronounced, and I believe this placed smaller animals at a distinct advantage, because of their lower nutritional requirement. Admittedly this idea is difficult to test, and

Figure 7. Natural selection may have brought about many changes in the physiology and overall body size of domesticated wolves and led them eventually to form a separate species—the domestic dog. Skeletal remains show that early dogs were smaller and that adult dogs appeared juvenile in relation to their wolf ancestors. Here a prehistoric adult dog skull (*center*) is compared with an adult wolf skull (*top*) and a juvenile wolf skull. The dog skull bears a striking similarity to the juvenile wolf skull and is much less similar to the skull of the adult wolf. These changes suggest that the developmental program of the dog was altered in such a way that it would reach sexual maturity earlier than its wolf ancestors, while other aspects of its physical development were slowed down. (The juvenile wolf skull is enlarged here for the sake of comparison.)

other factors were probably involved.

Different lines of evidence at least suggest that dogs took a very direct route, genetically speaking, to get to smaller sizes. Zoologist Robert K. Wayne of the Zoological Society of London studied DNA sequences in modern canids and concluded that dogs basically are wolves, altered only by simple changes in developmental timing and growth rates. In related studies, Wayne also suggested that reduced fetal growth rates may be an important determinant of adult size in small dogs. Simple changes led to rapid size reduction in early dogs, probably at the cost of problems in the integration of different developmental processes during growth. For example, it is frequently observed that earliest dogs often have crowded teeth, sometimes even overlapping each other in jaws that are not really big enough to accommodate them efficiently. Overall, rapid size reduction with minimal genetic change suggests strong selection for smaller size among early dogs.

Consistent size reduction clearly took place in the early evolution of the dog, although causes are difficult to pinpoint. But evolutionary theory also predicts that the proposed developmental alterations should produce paedomorphic animals, and this requires a close look.

Evolutionary Paedomorphs
It is one thing to note that the cranial morphology of early dogs appears paedomorphic. It is quite another to argue that this pattern sets them apart from other canids or reveals something important about evolution under domestication. Other wild canids might also appear paedomorphic when compared with wolves. Dogs are frequently described as paedomorphic because modern small breeds resemble juvenile forms of larger breeds. But to have evolutionary significance, it is important to determine whether prehistoric dogs were paedomorphic relative to their ancestral species, the wolves.

To tackle these problems, I armed myself with calipers and a notebook and visited several American and European museums to measure canid crania. First, I took measurements from 65 adult prehistoric dog specimens from archaeological sites, the vast majority dated from between 3,000 and 7,000 years ago. Three-quarters of the specimens are from the United States, and the rest come from northern Europe. My choice of samples emphasized sites

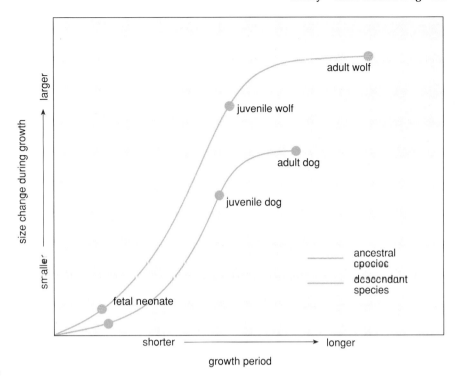

Figure 8. Size change is often a consequence of changes in growth rates and timing. This schematic illustrates a hypothetical model to account for differences in size and morphology between the wolf and the dog. This model postulates that the descendant species grows more slowly very early in life and finishes growing sooner than the ancestral species. In this way the dog comes to resemble the juvenile form of its wolf ancestor when it reaches its full size.

where people were still making their living primarily through hunting and gathering at the time corresponding to the age of the sample, and therefore where I had little reason to suspect systematic selective breeding.

Next, I measured crania from 222 modern wild canids representing four species. These are, in descending order of average size, the gray wolf, the red wolf, the coyote and the golden jackal. The wolves and coyotes are all North American, from the continental United States or southern Canada. Based on cranial measurements, I determined that most of the prehistoric dogs in my sample were roughly the size of golden jackals or the smaller coyotes. I did not have prehistoric samples of wild canids and must assume that modern samples provide a generally valid approximation of morphological variations in these species.

I was particularly interested in learning how several snout-length and cranial-width dimensions change in relation to the overall length of the skull as one moves from large to small animals. Size changes in animals are almost inevitably accompanied by patterned changes in proportions, a phenomenon known as allometry. Some allometric

patterns stem from basic laws of biomechanics. For example, an elephant's mass could not be supported on geometrically scaled-up mouse bones. To begin with, an elephant has to have proportionally thicker leg bones. Shape changes shown by dogs could reflect only this kind of allometry.

My analysis revealed some interesting results. First, it turns out that most dogs share snout-length proportions with comparably sized wild canids. What sets dogs apart is not changes in the length of their snouts, but the width of their palates and cranial vaults. The cranial morphology of dogs is unique and does not conform to allometric patterns among wild canids.

The issue then is whether this cranial morphology reflects evolutionary paedomorphosis. To determine this, I compared dog morphology with the morphology of its ancestral species, the wolf, as it grows. If the dog is in fact a paedomorphic wolf, I would expect to see the greatest similarities between dogs and juvenile wolves and less similarity between prehistoric dogs and adult wolves. Ideally, data for answering this question would include cranial measurements from juveniles of both species. Unfortunately, the archaeological record is not that cooperative, and skulls of juveniles are usually nothing more than a pile of fragile, fingernail-sized pieces. Without data from juvenile dogs, it becomes imperative to have data from juvenile wolves, and this cause is not as hopeless. I measured skulls of 64 modern juvenile wolves ranging in age from a few weeks to several months, a sample that includes several North American subspecies.

Using the allometric approach again, I compared juvenile wolf proportions with those of the adult wild canids and prehistoric dogs. By plotting snout-length measures against total skull length, I found that as a wolf grows, its snout gets longer at a rate that mirrors increasing snout length in the adult wild canids. These plots showed that all adult canid species, including adult dogs, look something like scaled-down adult wolves, if one considers only the ratio of snout length to total skull length.

When I plotted width-to-total-skull-length proportions, I saw some interesting differences. Adult dogs are distinct in these dimensions from all the adult wild canids. But adult dogs do resemble one wild canid group: juvenile wolves. Of all wild canid species, including adult wolves, the shape of adult dog crania most closely resembles that of juvenile wolves. The issue is not closed, but these data do support the hypothesis that dogs represent a paedomorphic form of their wolf ancestors. If that is true, it is possible that the dogs evolved as the evolutionary model would predict. Developmental changes in these animals might have come about as a response to selection pressures in a new niche, and these changes ultimately gave rise to a paedomorphic form of the ancestral species.

Behavioral Paedomorphosis
Many adult dogs not only appear juvenile, they also act juvenile. They display a sort of behavioral paedomorphosis. Dogs routinely solicit attention, play, grovel, whine, bark profusely and otherwise exhibit behavior that wolves more or less outgrow as they mature. Biologist Raymond Coppinger and linguist Mark Feinstein describe dogs as "stuck in adolescence." They also make the important point that the essence of tameness is the submissive, solicitous behavior style of juveniles. This leads to the question of whether physiological and behavioral paedomorphosis are interrelated.

Experiments directed by Russian geneticist D. K. Belyaev cause one to suspect that the answer is yes. Belyaev's group implemented a strict selective breeding program with silver foxes from a commercial fur farm. Their work sprung from the observation that although a majority of captive foxes were aggressive or fearful around people, a small number, about 10 percent, were less so. More than 30 years ago Belyaev began selectively breeding these calmer individuals only with other such individuals, through successive generations. Selection was for what Belyaev described as domesticated behavior.

The results after only about 20 generations were fascinating. Many foxes in the selected population now actively sought contact with people. The foxes would lick people's hands and faces, whine and wag their tails. Whereas

Figure 9. Behavioral alterations seem to accompany physical changes, so that dogs not only look more juvenile than wolves; they also act more juvenile. Behavior and physiology were shown to be linked by breeding experiments conducted by Russian geneticist D. K. Belyaev. Belyaev and his colleagues interbred foxes that responded well to people. After about 20 generations, foxes from this lineage actively sought contact with people, whined and wagged their tails. Like many dogs, some tame foxes had drooping ears and erect tails, features that were decidedly absent from the control fox population in this study. (Adapted from Belyaev 1979.)

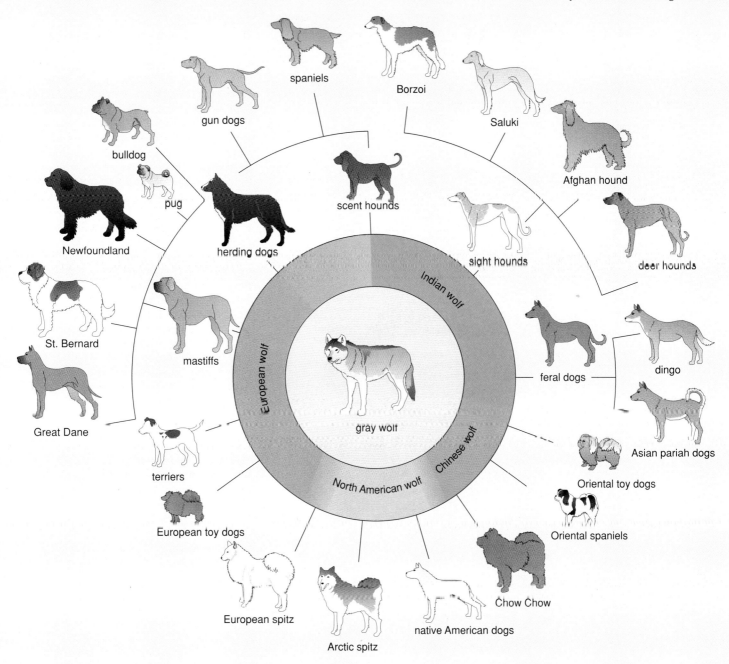

Figure 10. Different geographic subspecies of wolves may have given rise to different dog-breed groups. This model shows one interpretation of the ancestry of modern dog breeds. Modern dog breeds are the result of at least 2,000 years of breeding under human control, and no breed is derived solely from one geographic origin. Ultimately, DNA studies may help assess the accuracy of models like this one. The images do not depict the true size relations between breeds. (Adapted from Clutton-Brock and Jewell 1993.)

wild foxes, like wild wolves, breed only once each year, females in the selected population began a shift towards more frequent receptivity, with some later-generation females capable of breeding twice each year. Domestic dogs regularly breed more than once each year. Other changes in the selected population included a much longer moulting time, drooping ears and erect tails. These remarkably dog-like changes were absent in the unselected

fox population and are absent in wild wolves as well.

The experiments do not replicate, even roughly, the conditions of early domestication, but they show how strongly behavior is linked to physiology. Strict selection for certain behavioral traits can disrupt previously stable patterns of physiological development. Oddities of domestication, such as erect tails and drooping ears, make more sense in light of this work.

Scientists are still far from understanding precisely how different factors combined to produce the changed animal whose bones begin to turn up in late Pleistocene archaeological sites. Several important factors, however, at least seem to point in the same direction. Whether focusing on social behavior, diet or reproductive tactics, one should find that the evolution of a smaller, paedomorphic canid during domestication presents no surprise.

Figure 11. Canid domestication was undoubtedly helped along by the ability of the animals to form strong social attachments to people. For many modern dogs, social bonding is vital to their individual well-being. This scene, familiar to dog enthusiasts, emphasizes that bonding is a two-way street.

Beyond Dogs

A couple of years ago, a colleague commented that I was fortunate to have chosen dogs as my subject, because my perspective would not hold up for other cases of domestication. Naturally, I asked why not. He answered that dogs were first, but after that, the idea of domestication was in place. People then had a model, one they could apply to animals of considerably greater economic importance, for example goats or cattle. The domestication of such animals, my colleague argued, would best be understood as the product of people's purposeful efforts to achieve that goal.

Applying the same logic to Belyaev's experiments, we might just as well explain the evolution of modified, tame foxes as a consequence of Belyaev setting out to accomplish that. Such an explanation is not scientifically meaningful. The mechanistic explanation begins with the observation that foxes with certain heritable traits mated only with foxes bearing similar traits through successive generations.

The issue is not whether prehistoric people engaged in behavior that led to the domestication of goats or cattle. They certainly must have. The issue lies with the presumption that the eventual result—highly modified animals under conscious human subjugation—explains the process that started those animals toward that end. Figuring out what prehistoric people actually did that contributed to the evolution of domestic organisms is hard enough. To presume their purposes, and then proffer that as part of an explanation for evolutionary change, is to flirt with mysticism.

To be fair, my colleague's argument reflects a broader tendency for scholars to treat dogs as a special case because they are not perceived as economically important and therefore provided no compelling reason for people to have sought to domesticate them. Many societies, however, have made regular use of dogs as dietary fare. In addition, dog skins have served as clothing, and bones as raw material for tools, and the living animals have often been used as beasts of burden or as hunting aids.

Ultimately, the present exercise is only a minor part of the much larger issue of how to fit human cultural evolution into a scientific framework. Human culture, not being genetically determined, is widely assumed to su-

For a long time, early domestic dogs were consistently smaller compared with wolves. In contrast, modern dogs include breeds, such as the Great Dane, that are as large as or even larger than wolves. Given the context of domestication, only one set of circumstances is likely to account for large dogs or can account for the size range of modern breeds. That set of circumstances is selective breeding under human control.

It is important to stress that a domestic relationship does not mean that natural selection has become something other than natural. It is not a process that distinguishes human factors from others in the environment. Natural selection is simply the statistical summation of the reproductive fates of organisms that use their physical and behavioral equipment to compete for genetic representation in the next generation. Dogs are no exception. Tameness and other traits were the currency of competition from the onset of the domestic relationship, regardless of whether people had goals for the animals or were even aware of what changes were unfolding.

persede the Darwinian processes that explain how other organisms evolve. By extension, domestication is also frequently exempted from Darwinian models of evolution for the simple reason that it arises in a human sociocultural context. In a field hungry for genuine theory, however, anthropologists and archaeologists are currently debating the applicability of Darwinian theory to sociocultural evolution. Biologists should be keenly interested in this debate, for in the exclusion of cultural evolution from the Darwinian model makes it irrelevant to a good portion of life on this planet.

More than a decade ago, archeologist R. C. Dunnell suggested that if archaeology should achieve its widely professed goal of becoming scientific, few people would be pleased with the result. For one thing, there theories about cultural evolution would not be grounded in human intention. Even if we could document people's goals and intentions, they are phenomena to be explained, not explanations in themselves. Consider how difficult it is to take even the seemingly small step of bringing domestic organisms under the Darwinian umbrella. We are a long way from knowing whether Dunnell is right.

Acknowledgments

This research has been supported by the Jacob K. Javits Program of the U. S. Department of Education, the Smithsonian Institution, the American-Scandinavian Foundation and the Wenner-Gren Foundation for Anthropological Research. I thank Michael Logan for offering suggestions and helping locate sources for several illustrations in used in this article.

Bibliography

Belyaev, D. K. 1979. Destabilizing selection as a factor in domestication. *The Journal of Heredity* 70:301–308.

Clutton-Brock, J. 1981. *Domesticated Animals from Early Times*. Austin: University of Texas Press.

Clutton-Brock, J., and P. Jewell. 1993. Origin and domestication of the dog. In *Miller's Anatomy of the Dog*, 3rd edition, ed. H. E. Evans. Philadelphia: W. B. Saunders, pp. 21–31.

Davis, S. J. M. 1987. *The Archaeology of Animals*. New Haven:Yale University Press.

Dunnell, R. C. 1982. Science, social science and common sense: The agonizing dilemma of modern archaeology. *Journal of Anthropological Research* 38:1–25.

Hemmer, H. 1990. *Domestication—The Decline of Environmental Appreciation*. Cambridge, England: Cambridge University Press.

McKinney, M. L. and K. J. McNamara 1991. *Heterochrony—The Evolution of Ontogeny*. New York: Plenum Press.

Morey, D. F. 1992. Size, shape, and development in the evolution of the domestic dog. *Journal of Archaeological Science* 19:181–204.

Morey, D. F. and M. D. Wiant. 1992. Early Holocene domestic dog burials from the North American Midwest. *Current Anthropology* 33:224–229.

Olsen, S. I. 1985. *Origins of the Domestic Dog*. Tucson: University of Arizona Press.

Rindos, D. 1984. *The Origins of Agriculture—An Evolutionary Perspective*. New York: Academic Press.

Roff, D. A. 1992. *The Evolution of Life Histories*. New York: Chapman and Hall.

Scott, J. P. and J. L Fuller. 1965. *Genetics and the Social Behavior of the Dog*. Chicago: University of Chicago Press.

Wayne, R. K. 1993. Molecular evolution of the dog family. *Trends in Genetics* 9:218–224.

Giardia: A Missing Link between Prokaryotes and Eukaryotes

The emergence of eukaryotic cells was important in the evolution of complex multicellular life. But how did eukaryotes evolve?

Karen S. Kabnick and Debra A. Peattie

Like most inventions, life started out simple and grew more complex with time. For their first three billion years on earth, living creatures were no larger than a single cell. Gradually, the forces of natural selection worked on these simple organisms until eventually they became bigger, more sophisticated and more intricate. Organisms increased in size not only because the individual cells grew but also because multiple cells—in some cases many millions—came together to form a cohesive whole. The crucial event in this transition was the emergence of a new cell type—the eukaryote. The eukaryote had structural features that allowed it to communicate better than did existing cells with the environment and with other cells, features that paved the way for cellular aggregation and multicellular life. In contrast, the more primitive prokaryotes were less well equipped for intercellular communica-

Karen Kabnick received her Ph.D. in biology from MIT. She currently works with Debra Peattie as a postdoctoral fellow at the Harvard School of Public Health. In addition, she teaches cell biology in the Division of Continuing Education at Harvard University.

Debra Peattie is Adjunct Assistant Professor in the Department of Tropical Public Health at the Harvard School of Public Health and Staff Scientist at Vertex Pharmaceuticals Incorporated in Cambridge, Massachusetts. She obtained a B.A. in chemistry at Hollins College, Virginia, and a Ph.D. in biochemistry and molecular Biology at Harvard University. She is delighted that Giardia lamblia *occupies a significant niche in biological evolution and is very pleased never to have suffered the pangs of giardiasis. Address: Department of Tropical Public Health, Harvard School of Public Health, 665 Huntington Avenue, Boston, MA 02115.*

tion and could not readily organize into multicellular organisms.

Today both eukaryotes and prokaryotes still exist. Eukaryotes can be found variously as single-celled organisms called protists, and as organized systems in multicellular organisms. The cells of all plants, animals and fungi are eukaryotes. The prokaryotes live on in the two major divisions of bacteria—the eubacteria and the archebacteria. As in earlier times, prokaryotes are less likely than eukaryotes to form organisms larger than a single cell.

Not only do eukaryotic cells allow larger and more complex organisms to be made, but they are themselves larger and more complex than prokaryotic cells. Whether eukaryotic cells live singly or as part of a multicellular organism, their activities can be much more complex and diversified than those of their prokaryotic counterparts. In prokaryotes, all internal cellular events take place within a single compartment, the cytoplasm. Eukaryotes contain many subcellular compartments called organelles. Even single-celled eukaryotes can display remarkable complexity of function; some have features as specialized and diverse as sensory bristles, mouth parts, muscle-like contractile bundles, or stinging darts.

Much evidence from the fossil record and from molecular biology indicates that eukaryotes evolved from prokaryotes. But the details of this important transition are difficult to trace, having happened so long ago that most evidence of it has disappeared. One way we can devise plausible scenarios for the evolution of eukaryotes is to explore the vestiges of older sys-

tems that remain in existing cells and reconstruct how things might have happened. Especially useful for this purpose are many of the single-celled eukaryotes whose life-styles in some ways resemble those of their prokaryotic forebears, and which are thought to be among the earliest eukaryotes that are still in existence. Studies of such organisms have led to two main theories, which are not mutually exclusive, that seek to explain how eukaryotes evolved. Recent evidence suggests that one single-celled organism, the intestinal parasite *Giardia lamblia,* represents the first line of descent from the ancestral cells that took on eukaryotic features. As such, a study of the cell biology of this "missing link" organism can help to answer many questions about the way things might have been early in the history of life.

Prokaryotes and Eukaryotes

On a very fundamental level, eukaryotes and prokaryotes are similar. They share many aspects of their basic chemistry, physiology and metabolism. Both cell types are constructed of and use similar kinds of molecules and macromolecules to accomplish their cellular work. In both, for example, membranes are constructed mainly of fatty substances called lipids, and molecules that perform the cell's biological and mechanical work are called proteins.

Eukaryotes and prokaryotes both use the same chemical relay system to make protein. A permanent record of the code for all of the proteins the cell will require is stored in the form of DNA. Because DNA is the master copy of the cell's (or organism's) genetic make-up, the information it contains is absolutely

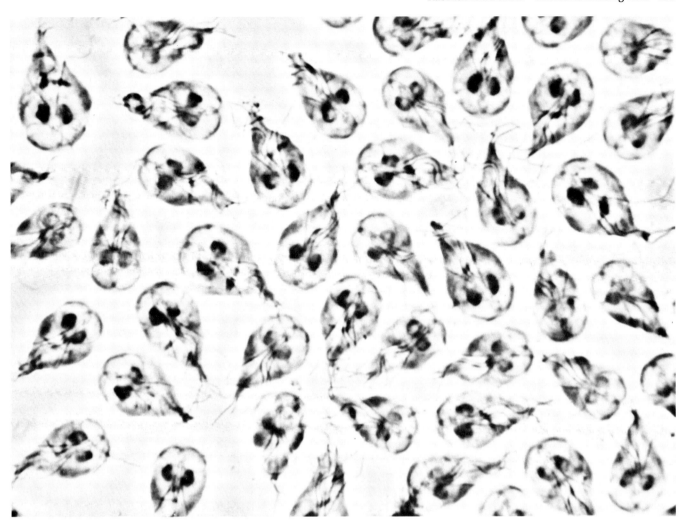

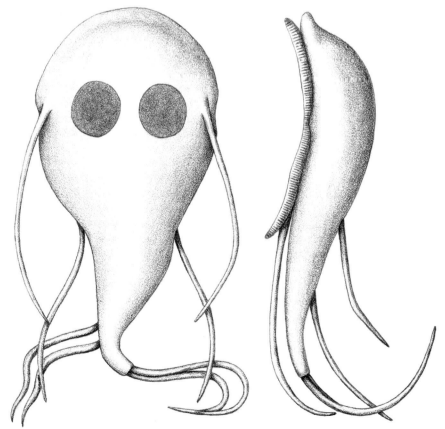

Figure 1. *Giardia lamblia*, a single-celled intestinal parasite, occupies a pivotal place in the progression from primitive cells to the more complex cells found in higher, multicellular organisms. *Giardia* belongs to the category of cells called eukaryotes, but in many respects it is not distant from more primitive prokaryotes. Thus *Giardia* may represent a missing link in the transition from prokaryote to eukaryote. Prokaryotes are single-celled organisms, and it is the emergence of eukaryotes that ultimately led to the evolution of complex multicellular life forms. Shown in a phase-contrast micrograph and in two drawings are trophozoites, the form *Giardia* takes in the upper intestine of infected animals and the form on which many studies have been conducted. The structures that resemble large eyes are nuclei, membrane-bounded compartments, that house the genetic material DNA. The presence of nuclei distinguished the eukaryotes from more primitive, prokaryotic, cells. Yet *Giardia* trophozoites are unusual, even for eukaryotes, in that they have two equal-sized nuclei. The side view (*lower right*) reveals the disk used by the parasite to attach to cells in the upper intestine. The tail-like structures are flagella, which *Giardia* uses to propel itself through its watery environment. Micrograph from Kabnick and Peattie 1990. Reproduced with permission from The Company of Biologists, Ltd.

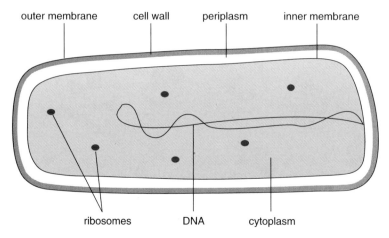

outer membrane   cell wall   periplasm   inner membrane

ribosomes   DNA   cytoplasm

Figure 2. Prokaryotes are a primitive cell type from which more complex cells, the eukaryotes, probably evolved. Today prokaryotes live on in the two major divisions of bacteria—eubacteria and archebacteria. A prokaryotic cell, schematized here, can be compared to a studio apartment in which all activities take place in a single chamber. The DNA of the prokaryote is attached to the inner cell membrane but is otherwise free-floating in the internal compartment. Ribosomes, the structures on which proteins are synthesized, are also in this compartment. When the organism breaks down nutrients, it releases digestive enzymes into the same space. The prokaryote gains structural support from an external cell wall, but the wall also limits the prokaryote's movement and its ability to communicate with other cells. These limitations restrict the size of most prokaryotic organisms to a single cell. According to one theory, the pivotal event in the evolution of complex cells and multicellular organisms was the loss of the cell wall.

crucial to the maintenance and perpetuation of the cell. As if to safeguard this archive, the cell does not use the DNA directly in protein synthesis but instead copies the information onto a temporary template of RNA, a chemical relative of DNA. Both the DNA and the RNA constitute a "recipe" for the cell's proteins. The recipe specifies the order in which amino acids, the chemical subunits of proteins, should be strung together to make the functional protein. Protein synthesis both in eukaryotes and prokaryotes takes place on structures called ribosomes, which are composed of RNA and protein. This illustrates one way in which prokaryotes and eukaryotes are similar and highlights the idea that differences between these organisms are often architectural. In other words, both cell types use the same bricks and mortar, but the structures they build with these materials vary dramatically.

The prokaryotic cell can be compared to a studio apartment: a one-room living space that has a kitchen area abutting the living room, which converts into a bedroom at night. All necessary items fit into their own locations in the one room. There is an everyday, washable rug. Room temperature is comfortable—not too hot, not too cold. Conditions are adequate for everything that must occur in the apartment, but not optimal for any specific activity.

In a similar way, all of the prokaryote's functions fit into a single compartment. The DNA is attached to the cell's membrane. Ribosomes float freely in the single compartment. Cellular respiration—the process by which nutrients are metabolized to release energy—is carried out at the cell membrane; there is no dedicated compartment for respiration.

A eukaryotic cell can be compared to a mansion, where specific rooms are designed for particular activities. The mansion is more diverse in the activities it supports than the studio apartment. It can accommodate overnight guests comfortably and support social activities for adults in the living room or dining room, for children in the playroom. The baby's room is warm and furnished with bright colors and a soft, thick carpet. The kitchen has a stove, a refrigerator and a tile floor. Items are kept in the room that is most appropriate for them, under conditions ideal for the activities in that specific room.

A eukaryotic cell resembles a mansion in that it is subdivided into many compartments. Each compartment is furnished with items and conditions suitable for a specific function, yet the compartments work together to allow the cell to maintain itself, to replicate and to perform more specialized activities.

Taking a closer look, we find three

main structural aspects that differentiate prokaryotes from eukaryotes. The definitive difference is the presence of a true (eu) nucleus (karyon) in the eukaryotic cell. The nucleus, a double-membrane casing, sequesters the DNA in its own compartment and keeps it separate from the rest of the cell. In contrast, no such housing is provided for the DNA of a prokaryote. Instead the genetic material is tethered to the cell membrane and is otherwise allowed to float freely in the cell's interior. It is interesting to note that the DNA of eukaryotes is attached to the nuclear membrane, in a manner reminiscent of the attachment of prokaryotic DNA to the cell's outer membrane.

Although DNA performs the same critical function in both cell types, the presence or absence of a nucleus has some profound implications for the form that the molecule takes and the way that the DNA template ultimately becomes translated into protein. In prokaryotes almost all of the organism's genetic information is carried on a single circular piece of DNA. The genetic material of the eukaryotic cell, on the other hand, consists of several linear pieces of DNA. The exact number of linear DNA segments varies from species to species. Generally, the DNA in a eukaryotic cell looks like a loose tangle of yarn, except during cell division, when the DNA becomes tightly wrapped into the structures called chromosomes. The membrane surrounding the eukaryotic cell's nucleus breaks apart during cell division and reappears intact in the daughter cells, one nucleus in each daughter.

Not only is the physical configuration of the DNA different in the two cell types, but they also differ in the number of sets of genetic instructions they contain. A prokaryotic cell contains only a single representation of the genetic information the organism requires; in this condition the cell is said to be haploid. In contrast, most eukaryotes have two sets of genetic information during some stage of their lives. Cells containing two sets of genetic information are referred to as diploid. Some simple eukaryotes pass through only a fleeting diploid stage, but higher eukaryotes spend most of their lives as diploid cells. Multicellular organisms can include both diploid and haploid eukaryotic cells. Most of the cells of the organism's body are diploid. The gametes—eggs and sperm—are haploid eukaryotes. During fertilization two haploid gametes fuse, thus restoring the diploid condition to the resulting embryo. Having two sets of genetic information offers the eukaryote certain advantages over prokaryotes, and the emergence of the diploid state was an important milestone in evolution.

The nucleus is one of several specialized compartments in the eukaryotic cell. Other compartments, called organelles, accommodate several other cellular activities. Prokaryotes do not have subcellular compartments, and this constitutes the second major distinction between the two cell types.

The organelles of eukaryotes include membrane-bounded compartments such as the lysosome, a highly acidic compartment in which digestive enzymes break down food. The endoplasmic reticulum is an interconnected system of membranes in which lipids are synthesized and some proteins are chemically modified. The endoplasmic reticulum communicates with another membrane system called the Golgi apparatus, where proteins are further processed and marked for transport to various sites inside or outside the cell. Eukaryotic cells contain special energy centers. In animal cells these are the mitochondria; plant cells have chloroplasts as well as mitochondria. Within mitochondria, organic compounds are broken down to generate the energy-rich molecule adenosine triphosphate (ATP). ATP is a sort of molecular fuel, which when degraded provides energy for many of the cell's biochemical reactions. ATP is also generated in the chloroplasts of plant cells, but the energy for its synthesis is derived from sunlight, in a process that also builds up carbohydrates and liberates oxygen.

The third distinguishing feature between the two cell types is the way in which the cell maintains its shape. Cells, like most animals, have skeletons. And, as in many animals, the cellular skeleton can be either internal or external. Prokaryotes have an external skeleton; a strong wall of cross-linked sugar and protein molecules surrounds the cell membrane and is made rigid by the turgor pressure of the cell. The wall lends structural support. It is also impermeable to many macromolecules and thus helps to maintain a barrier between substances inside and outside the cell. Such an external skeleton limits the ability of the prokaryotic cell to move. It also limits communication between cells, a condition that probably accounts for the vastly de-

creased ability of prokaryotes to form multicellular organisms.

The skeleton of the eukaryotic cell is internal; it is formed by a complex of protein tubules called the cytoskeleton. The internal placement of the cytoskeleton means the surface exposed to the environment is a pliable membrane rather than a rigid cell wall. The combination of an internal framework and a nonrigid outer membrane expands the repertory of motion and activity of the eukaryotic cell. For example, the cell can contract, as does a muscle cell. (The cells of most higher plants have a wall even more rigid than the prokaryotic wall.

Plant cell walls are chemically and structurally very different from prokaryotic walls; presumably they are a later, independent adaptation.)

The Way It Was

Two billion years ago, before the emergence of the first eukaryotes, life on earth was very different from what it is today. The organisms populating the earth were prokaryotes, similar to modern bacteria. But unlike the vast majority of modern organisms, even modern prokaryotes, these primordial organisms did not use oxygen. Free oxygen was scarce on the primordial earth, and

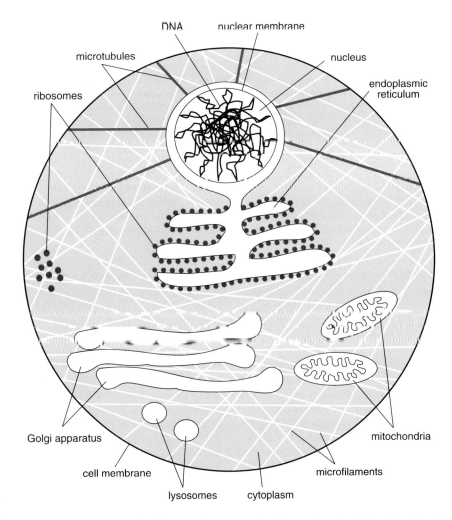

Figure 3. Eukaryotes are often larger and more complex than prokaryotes. The eukaryotic cell can be up to 100 times the size of a prokaryote. It is also more highly compartmentalized. The cells of all fungi, plants and animals are eukaryotes. The definitive difference between prokaryote and eukaryote is the presence of a membrane-delimited nucleus in the eukaryote. The organism's DNA is inside the nucleus, attached to the nuclear membrane. Ribosomes are outside the nucleus in the cytoplasm, and so that is where protein synthesis occurs. Digestive enzymes are kept apart from other cellular components in membrane-defined lysosomes. In animal cells, like the one schematized here, cellular respiration takes place in special compartments called mitochondria. Eukaryotes have no cell wall. Instead, their structural integrity is maintained by a system of protein tubules, called the cytoskeleton. Thin microfilaments form a meshwork underlying the cell membrane, while thicker microtubules radiate from the nucleus toward the periphery of the cell. Because the cell structure is internally supported, the outer membrane can remain somewhat fluid.

Comparison of Prokaryotes and Eukaryotes

	Prokaryotes	Eukaryotes
Organisms	Bacteria	Protists, fungi, plants and animals
Cell size	Generally 1 to 10 μm measured lengthwise	Generally 10 to 100 μm, lengthwise
Metabolism	Anaerobic or aerobic	Anaerobic or aerobic
Organelles	None	Nucleus, mitochondria, chloroplasts, endoplasmic reticulum, Golgi apparatus, lysosomes, etc.
Cell support	External cell wall	Internal cytoskeleton
DNA	Circular DNA in single cellular compartment	Very long linear DNA contained within a membrane-bounded nucleus
RNA and protein	RNA and protein synthesized in the single compartment	RNA synthesized and processed in nucleus; proteins synthesized in cytoplasm
Transmembrane movement	No endocytosis or exocytosis	Endocytosis and exocytosis
Cell division	Chromosomes pulled apart by attachments to inner membrane	Chromosomes pulled apart by attachments to cytoskeletal components
Cellular organization	Mainly unicellular	Unicellular or multicellular, with many differentiated cell types

Figure 4. Prokaryotes and eukaryotes share many metabolic and biochemical features, even though the architecture of the cells differs dramatically. Outlined here are some of the differences between the two cell types.

the earliest organisms evolved a metabolism based on sulfur and hydrogen sulfide (H_2S) rather than oxygen and water (H_2O). Many of these organisms were *obligate* anaerobes: Not only did they fail to make use of oxygen, but they could not survive in its presence.

How did eukaryotic cells, as well as modern aerobic prokaryotes, evolve from these anaerobic forerunners? Because of the importance of the eukaryotic cell in the evolution of complex living organisms, the question is of intense interest. Two theories offer competing explanations. Although the theories differ dramatically, they are not mutually exclusive. We can envisage a scenario in which both mechanisms contribute to the evolution of the eukaryotes.

You Are What You Eat
The first theory, proposed by Lynn Margulis of the University of Massachusetts at Amherst and others, suggests that a dramatic increase in atmospheric oxygen and the transition from anaerobe to aerobe were of primary importance in driving the evolution of eukaryotes. Ac-

cording to this theory, a population of primitive bacteria acquired the ability to photosynthesize. Photosynthetic organisms can use the energy of light to convert carbon dioxide into sugar. The sugar is then used as fuel to make ATP, which in turn provides energy for many other biochemical processes. A byproduct of photosynthesis is oxygen, and so a consequence of the evolution of photosynthetic bacteria was an overwhelming increase in atmospheric oxygen. The increasing abundance of oxygen posed a problem for those creatures that could not make metabolic use of it. Oxygen was toxic to these obligate anaerobes, and their continued survival depended on their developing the ability to use it, or at least to tolerate it.

Organisms that adapted to oxygen did so relatively quickly, according to Margulis's theory. Margulis proposes that an anaerobic organism engulfed a smaller aerobic organism believed to be the ancestor of mitochondria. The ingested aerobes were not digested, but lived on inside their new host. Hence was born a mutually beneficial arrangement, where the small aerobe

would convert oxygen into ATP for the energetic benefit of both cells. The host thus became tolerant to oxygen. In turn, the host organism eventually performed other functions, such as protein synthesis, for the aerobe.

The vestiges of that early union appear to live on today in modern eukaryotes. The mitochondria of both plant and animal cells and the chloroplasts of plants have many features that suggest they may have descended from free-living bacteria-like organisms. Both organelles have their own DNA, and both organelles replicate independently of cell division.

The theory advanced by Margulis postulates that other eukaryotic organelles were similarly derived from free-living organisms that became symbiotic with larger organisms. For example, the flagellum that helps to propel some eukaryotes by its whipping motion may have evolved from a primitive, unicellular, spiral-shaped organism, like a spirochete, which became associated with a larger host. The term "serial endosymbiosis" is used to describe the successive incorporation of smaller cells into a larger host to the benefit of both organisms.

Two major conclusions follow from the hypothesis of endosymbiotic evolution. One consequence is that the transition from prokaryote to eukaryote would have been relatively quick on the evolutionary time scale. Furthermore, if eukaryotic evolution occurred by endosymbiosis, then the first eukaryotes must have been aerobic. Anaerobic eukaryotes do exist, even today, but the endosymbiotic theory would hold that aerobic eukaryotes evolved first; some of these lost their mitochondria as a result of further selection pressures, giving rise later to anaerobic eukaryotes. Both of these points have generated some controversy, and we shall return to them later.

One important aspect of eukaryotic cells that is not addressed by an endosymbiotic mechanism is the origin of the cell nucleus and other membrane-defined systems such as the endoplasmic reticulum and the Golgi apparatus. Thomas Cavalier-Smith of the University of British Columbia in Vancouver has proposed a second theory that seeks to address the origins of membrane-delimited organelles as well as anaerobic and aerobic eukaryotes.

Cavalier-Smith suggests that early prokaryotes were set en route to becoming eukaryotes when they lost the

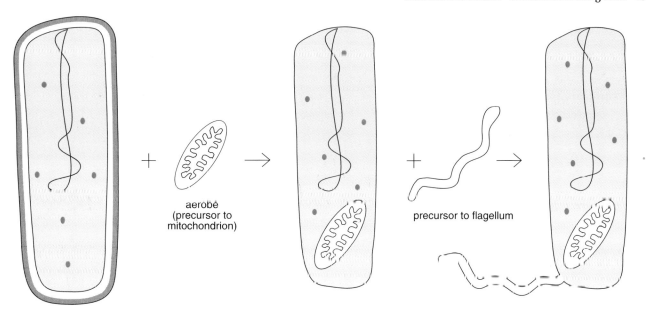

primordial bacteria-like cell

aerobe
(precursor to
mitochondrion)

precursor to flagellum

Figure 5. Subcellular compartments of eukaryotes may have evolved from previously free-living organisms, according to the theory of serial endosymbiosis. The first step toward the evolution of eukaryotes occurred when a primitive prokaryote-like cell, which could not use oxygen, ingested, but did not digest, a free-living oxygen-using organism. This mutually beneficial arrangement allowed the host to cope with the dramatic rise in concentrations of oxygen on the earth. The oxygen-using organism that resulted from the union went on to ingest another free-living creature and formed a symbiotic relationship with it. Here the oxygen user is shown ingesting a spiral-shaped organism that functions in the symbiote as a flagellum. Serial endosymbiosis would predict that many of the eukaryote's compartments were derived from the mutually beneficial union of a host and a smaller, free-living organism.

ability to manufacture muramic acid, an essential component of the cell wall in most bacteria. The loss of this sugar causes the rigid cell wall to break down, leaving the cell without support. Cells in this situation are vulnerable to external assaults and risk spilling their contents into the extracellular space. The organisms evolved two strategies for coping with the loss of muramic acid and thus diverged into two subsequent lines of descent. A new group of prokaryotes, now called archebacteria, developed a new type of rigid cell wall built without muramic acid. Cells that did not develop a new type of wall evolved an internal proteinaceous skeleton; that is, a cytoskeleton. It is at this point, according to Cavalier-Smith, that the modern eukaryote got its start.

In Cavalier-Smith's scheme, the key step in the evolution of eukaryotes is the development of the cytoskeleton. Since the cell's structural integrity is maintained by the cytoskeleton, the cell can afford to have a fluid outer membrane. The increased fluidity of the outer membrane allowed the development of two mechanisms, called endocytosis and exocytosis, which prepared the way for all subsequent steps of eukaryotic evolution.

Endocytosis and exocytosis are complementary processes whereby substances can enter (endocytosis) or exit (exocytosis) the cell through membrane-bounded vesicles. In endocytosis, incoming material enters the cell in a vesicle formed by the invagination of a small segment of the outer membrane; the invagination pinches off and seals itself up to form a vesicle, which carries its contents into the cell's interior. In the reverse process of exocytosis,

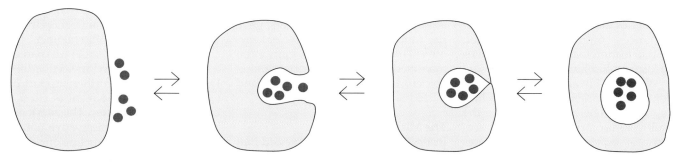

Figure 6. Transport of materials into and out of the cell is accomplished using membrane-bounded vesicles in the processes of endocytosis and exocytosis, respectively. In endocytosis, materials dissolved in the external aqueous environment gain entry to the cell when a small portion of the cell membrane surrounds them. The membrane invaginates and forms a pocket that completely surrounds the material. Eventually, the pocket seals itself up, breaks away from the membrane, and floats freely within the cytoplasm. Exocytosis works in the opposite direction to expel the same or different membrane-bounded materials from the cytoplasm into the external medium. Material is exocytosed when its membranous casing first fuses with the cell's outer membrane; this causes the vesicle to open and empty its contents into the extracellular medium. The flexibility of the membrane and its ability to pinch off, fold and seal may underlie the evolution of membrane-defined compartments in eukaryotes.

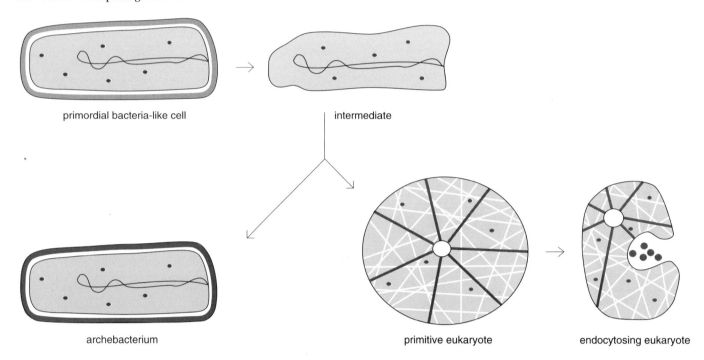

primordial bacteria-like cell   intermediate

archebacterium   primitive eukaryote   endocytosing eukaryote

Figure 7. Loss of the cell wall and the resulting fluidity of the outer cell membrane is a key event in the evolution of eukaryotes, according to one theory of eukaryotic evolution. Without a wall, the resulting cell lacks structural support, risks losing its contents and is vulnerable to external assaults. As shown in the diagram, cells that survived this situation adopted one of two solutions. Some acquired a new type of cell wall; these cells are now known as archebacteria to distinguish them from the older type of bacteria, the eubacteria. Other cells developed an internal skeleton, called the cytoskeleton, made from a network of proteinaceous fibers. The thicker microtubules are diagrammed here radiating from the cell's nucleus, which may have formed at about the same time as the cytoskeleton; thinner microfilaments form a flexible meshwork underlying the cell membrane. This protein skeleton provides support, so that the outer membrane can remain relatively fluid without jeopardizing the cell's structural integrity. With the cytoskeleton in place, the cell can develop the processes of endocytosis and exocytosis. The infoldings of the membrane led to the formation of the various subcellular compartments and membrane systems of the modern eukaryote. This theory predicts that the first eukaryotes were anaerobic, that is, they were unable to use oxygen. Later, possibly by endosymbiosis, anaerobic eukaryotes ingested a forerunner of the mitochondrion and gained the ability to use oxygen in generating energy. Recent evidence suggests that *Giardia lamblia* may represent the anaerobic eukaryote before it gained mitochondria.

particles leave the cell when the membrane of the vesicle enclosing them fuses with the outer cell membrane. In this case, the vesicle's contents are emptied into the extracellular space. The invaginations of the outer membrane could have given rise to the internal membranous structures of the eukaryotes, such as the cell nucleus, the endoplasmic reticulum and lysosomes. A second consequence of the increased fluidity of the cell membrane is that it enhances communication between cells, a feature that enables eukaryotes to form multicellular organisms.

Within the Cavalier-Smith paradigm, some of the various organelles, including the nucleus, evolved before the ability to use oxygen did. If this scenario is correct, the first eukaryotes would have been anaerobic. Later, these primitive anaerobes could have ingested a free-living, oxygen-using organism, via endosymbiosis, to give rise to aerobic eukaryotes.

Scientists often consult the fossil record when considering issues of evolution. In this matter, the record would appear to support some of the ideas of Cavalier-Smith. Prokaryotic cells were present on the earth 3.5 to 4 billion years ago, and eukaryotic cells did not appear until 1.4 to 1.5 billion years ago. Eukaryotic cells that contained mitochondria and were oxygen users, however, were not in evidence until as recently as 850 million years ago. Data from the fossil record reinforce the idea that primitive anaerobic eukaryotes arose from prokaryotes and then gave rise to more complex aerobic eukaryotes. This theory would gain even more credence if an appropriate anaerobic eukaryote could be identified, and indeed one has.

The Missing Link
In 1987 Cavalier-Smith suggested that the single-celled, anaerobic eukaryote *Giardia lamblia* might in fact be the missing link. *Giardia*, he suggested, might be the anaerobic eukaryote that ingested an oxygen-using bacterium; this union could have yielded the first aerobic eukaryote, from which all others may have descended. He based his prediction on an analysis of the types and structures of the organelles in *Giardia*. One important observation is that *Giardia* lacks mitochondria and is an obligate anaerobe. In further support of this notion, experiments in which *Giardia* ingested a marker molecule visible in electron micrographs show that the organism is capable of endocytosing particles from the extracellular space. It is conceivable that *Giardia* could have taken up a mitochondrion-like organism in a similar manner.

In 1989 one of us (Peattie) was part of a team that uncovered molecular-biological evidence in further support of Cavalier-Smith's placement of *Giardia* on the evolutionary tree. This work exploited the highly conservative nature of the ribosome, the structure on which proteins are synthesized. Ribosomes are found in all known cells—prokaryotic and eukaryotic alike. Their component RNA and protein molecules are assembled and folded to create a characteristic shape. There has been relatively little change over time in the molecules making up the ribosome. As a result, prokaryotic and eukaryotic ribosomes are fairly similar. The conserved nature of these molecules and their ubiquity makes them extremely useful for inferring evolutionary distances between organisms. Comparing the sequence of nucleotides in a ribosomal RNA shows how much the molecule has changed in the course of evolution from one organism to another.

Change is thought to be a function of time. If a great deal of time elapses between the emergence of organisms, there is more opportunity for the sequences of their nucleic acids and proteins to change. If two organisms evolve in a shorter space of time, there are fewer opportunities for the sequences to change. By analyzing the nucleotide sequences of ribosomal RNAs from different organisms and determining the degree of similarity or difference between these RNAs, we can reach some conclusions about how closely or distantly the organisms are related. With the aid of a computer, the sequences can be organized into a phylogenetic tree whose branching order indicates the likely order in which the organisms diverged from some common ancestor. Such phylogenetic trees can help clarify the order of branching among prokaryotes and eukaryotes and assess which organism represents the earliest line of descent among the eukaryotes.

The team in which one of us was a member constructed an evolutionary tree by comparing analogous segments of one type of ribosomal RNA from 54 organisms representing all levels of evolution. By this method we discovered that *Giardia lamblia* has a ribosomal-RNA sequence that is very close to that of prokaryotic cells. This *Giardia* ribosomal RNA shares more of its sequence with prokaryotes than does the corresponding RNA of any other eukaryote. Thus *Giardia* is evolutionarily closer to the prokaryotes than other eukaryotes are, and we can take this to mean that *Giardia* is a member of the earliest emerging eukaryotic lineage.

Given that *Giardia* lacks mitochondria and is necessarily anaerobic, its phylogenetic position provides compelling evidence for Cavalier-Smith's hypothesis that the anaerobic eukaryotes preceded the aerobes. At the same time, this evidence conflicts with Margulis's position that eukaryotes evolved in response to the build-up of oxygen on the primitive earth. The ability to use oxygen would appear to have arisen later, rather than

earlier, in the progression from prokaryote to eukaryote.

Valuable Lessons

Having established that *Giardia* occupies an important position in the transition from prokaryotes to eukaryotes, we have been interested in exploring aspects of its life history to see what we can learn about the early eukaryotes. But interest in this organism predates the discovery of its place on the evolutionary tree. *Giardia*, a unicellular organism, is a major intestinal parasite capable of infecting a variety of species, including human beings. The parasite can be found in both developed and underdeveloped countries, and causes diarrhea, abdominal cramps, malaise and weight loss. Because of its widespread distribution and the potential severity of infections, *Giardia* has been of interest to parasitologists and epidemiologists for some time.

There are two phases in the *Giardia* life cycle: trophozoites and cysts. Each cyst contains two trophozoites. Cysts are found in the feces of infected animals. Infected fecal matter can contaminate water supplies, where other animals can ingest the cysts. Inside the stomach, cysts are exposed to digestive acids, which cause the release of the trophozoites. Once released, a trophozoite attaches to cells of the upper intestine by means of a disc on the parasite's ventral surface. The parasites are thought to remain for a time in the up-

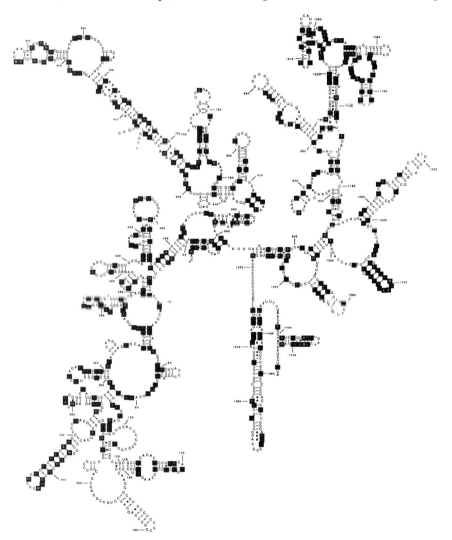

Figure 8. Comparisons of the sequences of macromolecules are useful in inferring evolutionary distances between organisms. Shown here is the sequence and proposed secondary structure of one of the RNAs making up the *Giardia* ribosome. This sequence has been compared with analogous eubacterial and archebacterial RNAs, and the positions where *Giardia* shares its sequence with such RNAs are shown in reverse type. This analysis has led investigators to believe that *Giardia* may represent the earliest lineage of cells to diverge from prokaryotes. Diagram courtesy of Mitchell Sogin, Marine Biological Laboratory at Woods Hole.

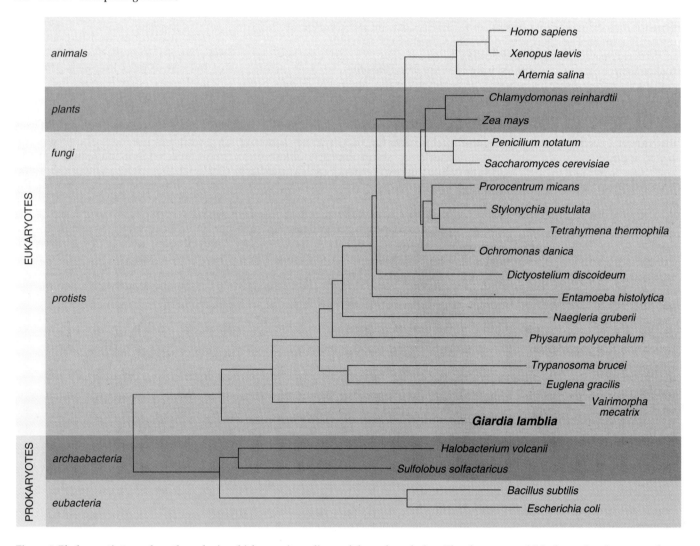

Figure 9. Phylogenetic trees show the order in which organisms diverged through evolution. The above tree, which shows the placement of *Giardia lamblia*, was constructed by comparing analogous ribosomal RNA sequences from each organism. The horizontal component of separation represents evolutionary distance between organisms. The diagram is based on data supplied by Mitchell Sogin, Marine Biological Laboratory at Woods Hole.

per intestine, where they feed and replicate. When they are forced further down the intestinal tract into the small bowel or colon, the trophozoites form cysts. These cysts are then excreted and the cycle is repeated. Because *Giardia* has the potential to infect a number of species, the possibilities for transmission are considerable.

The *Giardia* trophozoite lacks many of the subcellular organelles characteristic of higher aerobic eukaryotes. As mentioned before, it has no mitochondria. It also has no apparent Golgi apparatus. Some investigators report seeing a primitive endoplasmic reticulum, but this claim has yet to receive biochemical support. *Giardia* has an internal cytoskeleton as well as lysosomes that contain digestive enzymes. Its genetic material is encased in membrane-enclosed compartments. In our laboratory, studies are carried out using these trophozoites, graceful, tear-shaped

cells with four pairs of flagella.

Of all the cellular features within the trophozoite, the most puzzling and intriguing is that *Giardia* has not one nucleus, but two nuclei. Furthermore, these nuclei are equal in size. We have undertaken a study of the dual nuclei in the hope of contributing to a fuller understanding of the evolution of higher eukaryotic cells.

The Two Nuclei of *Giardia*

The presence of multiple nuclei is not unique to *Giardia*. Several other single-celled eukaryotes also have more than one nucleus, but only *Giardia* and a few closely related organisms making up the group called diplomonads have exactly two nuclei of equal size. In light of the evolutionarily significant position *Giardia* holds, we have been most eager to understand the importance of this unusual nuclear configuration. We have been trying to elucidate the struc-

tural and functional contributions made by the two nuclei.

Recently, we have shown that the two nuclei are not only equal in size, but also that they contain the same amount of DNA. In addition, using techniques that enable us to see the nucleic acids DNA and RNA under the microscope, we have demonstrated that each nucleus contains four major chromosomes.

We were then curious to learn whether the DNA in each nucleus encodes the same information. Since we know the sequence of one ribosomal RNA within the cell, and we know that the template for this RNA is archived in the DNA, we probed the DNA in each nucleus to see whether each contained this ribosomal sequence. We found that each nucleus did indeed contain sequences specifying this ribosomal RNA.

The mere presence of the sequence

in each nucleus, however, does not necessarily mean that each one is used as a template for ribosomal RNA. Thus we sought to establish whether the ribosomal RNA in the cell could have been derived from the DNA in either nucleus. We tagged all nascent RNAs with a radioactive label, and found radioactive RNA emerging from both nuclei. Since ribosomal RNA is by far the most abundant RNA species, we can infer that it was being copied from DNA templates in both nuclei. This suggests that the DNA in both nuclei is functionally equivalent and equally likely to serve as the template for the ribosomal RNA that makes its way out of the nucleus and into the cytoplasm.

Additional studies conducted on other multinucleated cells suggest that the DNA in these is not functionally equivalent. For example, in two well-studied single-celled organisms, *Tetrahymena* and *Paramecium*, there are unequal-size nuclei. *Tetrahymena* has one large nucleus and one small nucleus. The smaller nucleus contains two copies of the genome and is therefore diploid. The DNA in this micronucleus is not used as a template, but is passed on to progeny cells. The small nucleus then develops into a large nucleus, and only then does its DNA assume a template role. *Paramecium* has a large nucleus and two small diploid nuclei, which are likewise only passed on to future generations.

Since the arrangement of nuclei in *Giardia* is anomalous, even among multinucleated cells, the question arises: What is the possible evolutionary significance of the two equal-size nuclei of *Giardia* and their contents? We have already noted that we detect four major chromosomes in each nucleus, and others have reported that there are between four and five major chromosomes in the organism. The amount of DNA in each cell, and its complexity, have been determined. Taken together, these data and other experiments suggest that each nucleus of *Giardia* is haploid; that is, each contains a single representation of the organism's genetic information. The entire trophozoite, which contains two nuclei, would therefore be diploid.

The diploid state can be greatly advantageous, and most highly evolved, complex organisms have adopted this arrangement. If a cell has only a single copy of genetic information, any alteration or mutation of that information could result in nonfunctional proteins, with dire and possibly lethal consequences for the cell. But if the cell has two sets of instructions and one of them becomes nonfunctional, the second set can serve as a backup, and may compensate for the loss of the first. Furthermore, if a segment of the first set undergoes a mutation that provides a new beneficial function, the other copy can still perform the original function. With only one set of instructions, the organism risks losing an existing function to gain a new one. Again, this could ultimately lead to the cell's demise. A diploid organism has the advantage of retaining the old while developing new, advantageous functions.

The putative haploidy of each of the *Giardia* nuclei is intriguing with respect to the organism's evolutionary importance. It is possible that a single haploid nucleus gave rise to a second identical nucleus, thus giving the entire organism the various advantages of the diploid state. Later in evolution, the two haploid nuclei could have fused to produce the sole diploid nucleus characteristic of most higher eukaryotes. This hypothetical scenario explains the transition of a haploid prokaryote to a diploid eukaryote. It also predicts that the higher eukaryotes that contain a single diploid nucleus are the evolutionary descendants of a binucleated eukaryote.

Bibliography

Alberts, B., D. Bray, J. Lewis, M. Raff, K. Roberts and J. D. Watson. 1989. *Molecular Biology of the Cell.* Second Edition. Garland Publishing, Inc. New York.

Bockman, D. E., and W. B. Winborn. 1968. Electron microscopic localization of exogenous ferritin within vacuoles of *Giardia muris. Journal of Protozoology* 15:26-30.

Boothroyd, J. C., A. Wang, D. A. Campbell and C. C. Wang. 1987. An unusually compact ribosomal DNA repeat in the protozoan *Giardia lamblia. Nucleic Acids Research* 15:4065-4084.

Cavalier-Smith, T. 1975. The origin of nuclei and of eukaryotic cells. *Nature* 256:463-468.

Cavalier-Smith, T. 1981. The origin and early evolution of the eukaryote cell. *Symposia of the Society of General Microbiology* 32:33-84.

Cavalier-Smith, T. 1987a. Eukaryotes with no mitochondria. *Nature* 326:332-333.

Cavalier-Smith, T. 1987b. The origin of eukaryote and archaebacterial cells. *Annals of the New York Academy of Sciences* 503:17-54.

Cavalier-Smith, T. 1988. Origin of the cell nucleus. *BioEssays* 9:72-78.

Cavalier-Smith, T. 1989. Archaebacteria and Archezoa. *Nature* 339:100-101.

Doolittle, W. F. 1988. Bacterial evolution. *Canadian Journal of Microbiolog.* 34:547-551.

Dyer, B. D., and R. Obar, eds. 1985. *The Origin of Eukaryotic Cells.* Van Nostrand Reinhold Co. New York.

Feely, D. E. 1985 Histochemical localization of acid phosphatase in *Giardia. Anatomical Records* 202:54A

Friend, D. S. 1966. The fine structure of *Giardia muris. The Journal of Cell Biology* 29:317-332.

Halvorson, H. O., and A. Monroy, eds. 1984. *The Origin and Evolution of Sex.* MBL Lectures in Biology. Volume 7. Alan R. Liss, Inc. New York.

Kabnick, K. S., and D. A. Peattie. 1990. *In situ* analyses reveal that the two nuclei of *Giardia lamblia* are equivalent. *Journal of Cell Science* 95:353-360.

Lindmark, D. G. 1988. *Giardia lamblia:* Localization of hydrolase activities in lysosome-like organelles of trophozoites. *Experimental Parasitology* 65:141-147.

Margulis, L., 1981. *Symbiosis in Cell Evolution. Life and its environment on the early earth.* W. H. Freeman and Co. New York.

Margulis, L. and D. Sagan. 1986. *Microcosmos* Summit Books, New York.

Nemanic, P. C., R. L. Owen, D. P. Stevens, and J. C. Mueller. 1979. Ultrastructural observations on giardiasis in a mouse model. II Endosymbiosis and organelle distribution in *Giardia muris* and *Giardia lamblia. Journal of Infectious Diseases* 140:222-228.

Preer, J. R., Jr. 1989. Update on the molecular genetics of *Paramecium. Journal of Protozoology* 36:182-184.

Prescott, D. M., and G. E. Stone. 1967. Replication and function in the protozoan nucleus. In *Research in Protozoology,* vol. 2. (T.-T. Chen, ed.), pp. 117-146. Pergamon Press, New York.

Roberts-Thompson, I. C. 1984. Giardiasis In *Tropical and Geographical Medicine,* K. S. Warren and A. A. F. Mahmoud, eds., McGraw-Hill, New York. pp. 319-325.

Sagan, L. 1967. On the origin of mitosing cells. *Journal of Theoretical Biology* 14:225-274.

Shih, M.-C., P. Heinrich, and H. M. Goodman. 1988. Intron existence predated the divergence of eukaryotes and prokaryotes. *Science* 242:1164-1166.

Sogin, M. L., J. H. Gunderson, H. J. Elwood, R. A. Alonso and D. A. Peattie. 1989. Phylogenetic meaning of the kingdom concept: An unusual ribosomal RNA from *Giardia lamblia. Science* 243:75-77.

Sonneborn, T. M. 1974a. *Tetrahymena pyriformis.* In *Handbook of Genetics,* vol. 2: *Plants, Plant Viruses, and Protists* (R. C. King, ed.), pp. 433-467. Plenum Press, New York.

Sonneborn, T. M. 1974b. *Paramecium aurelia.* In *Handbook of Genetics,* vol. 2: *Plants, Plant Viruses, and Protists* (R. C. King, ed.), pp. 469-594. Plenum Press, New York.

Weisehahn, G. P., E. J. Jarroll, D. G. Lindmark, E. A. Meyer, and L. M. Hallick. 1984. *Giardia lamblia:* autoradiographic analysis of nuclear replication. *Experimental Parasitology* 58:94-100.

Woese, C. R. 1987. Bacterial evolution. *Microbiological Reviews* 51:221-271.

Woodard, J., E. Kaneshiro, and M. A. Gorovsky. 1972. Cytochemical studies on the problem of micronuclei in *Tetrahymena. Genetics* 70:251-260.

Yao, M.-C., and M. A. Gorovsky. 1974. Comparison of the sequences of macro- and micronuclear DNA of *Tetrahymena pyriformis. Chromosoma* 48:1-18.

Spelaeorchestia koloana

Speocirolana pelaezi

Palaemonias ganteri

Antriadesmus fragilis

Amblyopsis spelaea

Caconemobius varius

Cicurina buwata

Typhlomolge rathbuni

Troglobites: The Evolution of Cave-Dwelling Organisms

John R. Holsinger

Throughout the world, living in caves and other subterranean habitats, there are species of animals whose evolution has been driven by a life without sunlight and green plants, whose life cycles are completed in relatively simple, stable underground environments. These species, which include flatworms, segmented worms, snails, arachnids, crustaceans, millipedes, insects, fishes, and salamanders, are collectively referred to as troglobites. Because the majority of troglobites are relatively small and difficult to observe in nature without great effort, they are generally thought to be rare. However, they are more common and widespread than one might suspect. In North America alone, I estimate the number of species currently recognized as troglobites to be about 1,200, although the actual figure is probably much greater than this.

Troglobites are not mere curiosities. Naturalists and zoologists have long been challenged to explain the origins and geographic distributions of these creatures, and the explanations have important general implications for evolutionary biology.

It is widely accepted that troglobites evolved from ancestors living on the surface that were already partly adapted for life in a cave environment (Culver 1982, Sbordoni 1982, Barr and Holsinger 1985). The ancestors of troglobites presumably gained access to and colonized caves from freshwater, marine, and terrestrial environments (Vandel 1964; Barr 1968). These assumptions are strong-

---

Many species have survived in caves, long after their surface-dwelling ancestors became extinct

---

ly supported by the fact that nearly all troglobites belong to animal groups which are also well represented by species living in secluded surface habitats and having reduced eyes and pigment. These surface animals are commonly found in the cool, moist soil and ground litter of forest floors, in swamps, bogs, springs, and substrates of small streams; and in marine littoral (i.e., coastal) zones. Under the right circumstances, the invasion of caves from any of these habitats would be relatively easy for populations of a species already partly adapted to subterranean life. Subsequent genet-

ic isolation of the colonizers, followed by changes initiated through adaptation to life in caves, could lead to the evolution of troglobitic species.

One of the most interesting aspects of troglobite evolution is the strong possibility that many cave faunas are very old, isolated relicts that survived in cave refugia long after their ancestors either became extinct or migrated elsewhere because of changing conditions on the surface. Subterranean environments are ideal refugia: because they are protected against many of the perturbations that commonly affect surface environments, they can remain relatively stable over long periods of time.

The cave environment

Caves include both aquatic and terrestrial habitats (Fig. 2). Beyond entrance zones, where climatic conditions and food supplies tend to fluctuate rather widely, the environment is characteristically stable. Total darkness eliminates photosynthetic activity and all primary producers (except chemosynthetic autotrophs, whose contribution to cave energetics is probably negligible). The deep, insulated cave also has a relatively constant temperature that approximates the annual surface mean. Terrestrial underground habitats have a high relative humidity combined with a very low rate of evaporation.

The basic food resource in most cave ecosystems is organic matter from external sources. It may be transported underground by streams that enter caves through sinkholes and other openings, especially during floods, or by percolating groundwater that passes into caves through crevices and fissures. Probably most of this transported organic material is decomposed by microorganisms before it is consumed by detritus-feed-

Figure 1. Troglobites, typically blind and unpigmented organisms whose entire life cycles are spent underground, represent a wide diversity of animal groups and live in a variety of underground habitats. Examples of terrestrial troglobites are the amphipod *Spelaeorchestia koloana* (10 mm) and the small-eyed rock cricket *Caconemobius varius* (15 mm), which inhabit lava-tube caves in the Hawaiian islands, and the millipede *Antriadesmus fragilis* (7 mm) and the spider *Cicurina buwata* (6 mm) from limestone caves in the southern United States. Aquatic species include the isopod *Speocirolana pelaezi* (20 mm), the cave shrimp *Palaemonias ganteri* (25 mm), the cave fish *Amblyopsis spelaea* (80 mm), and the salamander *Typhlomolge rathbuni* (100 mm). Most troglobites are related to organisms living on the surface, although many are distributional relicts that have survived in a region in cave refugia long after their surface ancestors were forced out by climatic changes. In addition, some troglobites are phylogenetic relicts: for example, the genus *Palaemonias* includes only two species, both of which are troglobites. (Photographs of *A. fragilis*, *P. ganteri*, and *A. spelaea* by C. Clark, of *S. koloana* by W. Mull, and of *C. varius* by F. Howarth; the others by R. Mitchell.)

ing troglobites (Barr 1968; Culver 1982). These same microorganisms, especially fungi, also constitute an important item in the diet of many troglobites (Dickson and Kirk 1976). Other sources of nutrients are the eggs, feces, and dead bodies of cave inhabitants that periodically live on the surface, such as certain crickets and bats, and those of surface animals that enter caves by accident. In the systems of shallow lava caves in Hawaii, the major source of energy is tree roots (Howarth 1983).

Most caves form either in limestone or in basaltic lava. Solution caves, found primarily in limestone terranes termed karst areas, usually result from the dissolution of bedrock by carbonic acid. The abrasive action of debris transported in streams that enter caves from the surface may further enlarge some passages (Warwick 1976). Because limestone bedrock is common, solution caves have formed in many parts of the world and are more numerous than any other kind of cave. Lava caves or tubes develop from drained, riverlike channels of volcanic rock that are roofed over after the eruption, as the lava flow cools (Wood 1976). Compared to lava caves, limestone caves develop more slowly, most are much older, and they are more gradually destroyed by erosion, weathering, and collapse.

Approximately 40,000 caves are known at present in the United States, but this number is expected to increase considerably with new discoveries. Only caves with openings to the surface and with passages large enough for human exploration have thus far been extensively studied by biologists. Explorable caves vary greatly in size, ranging in length from a few meters to more than 500 km and in depth from several meters to over 1,250 m. However, since statistical estimates indicate that only about 10% of limestone caves have entrances that open to the surface, the total number of potentially explorable caves must be vastly greater than those now accessible to people (Curl 1958). More important, the cave environment is not limited to subterranean passages large enough to accommodate man but includes countless smaller tubes, cracks, and fissures.

The existence of diverse troglobite faunas in cracks and interstitial spaces filled with groundwater has been known for many years, a result of sampling wells, pumping groundwater, and collecting in and around the resurgence of small springs, seeps, and drain tiles (Vandel 1964; Husmann 1967). Only in recent years, however, have terrestrial troglobites been described from small, underground spaces outside larger caves (Uéno 1977). These studies have revealed extensive complexes of interconnected spaces of various sizes (ca. 0.1–20.0 cm) that in many areas form a continuum between larger caves (Howarth 1983). These spaces, which often contain habitats and organisms similar to those seen in cave passages, not only occur in limestone and volcanic rocks but are sometimes found in other types of rocks with open fissures (Juberthie 1983). In several parts of Europe, both within and outside karst areas, Juberthie and his colleagues discovered communities of troglobitic arthropods, such as collembolans (or springtails, tiny wingless insects), beetles, and millipedes, living in cracks and fissures in mantle rock just beneath the last layer of soil.

The ages of caves vary considerably. Some caves may be quite old—recent estimates suggest that certain limestone cave passages in North America could have formed 10 million years ago (Palmer 1981). Other caves could have formed as little as 350,000 to 700,000 years ago (Hess and Harmon 1981; Gascoyne et al. 1983). One might expect that the approximate age of caves would provide a reasonable time frame to help in estimating the age of troglobite faunas, but there is rarely if ever a direct correlation between the geological age of a cave and the age of its inhabitants. Not only were many caves likely colonized long after they formed, but it is also highly probable that the troglobitic faunas of some karst areas and lava flows are considerably older than the caves in which they live.

The development of solution caves is a continuous, dynamic process in karst areas with thick sequences of limestone. New passages form beneath older ones as the regional baselevel lowers in response to the incision of surface streams, and as the upper-level passages are destroyed by erosion. This makes it possible for younger passages to be colonized by the vertical migration of troglobites already present in the older parts of the cave system.

The reverse of this process probably occurred on islands such as the Bahamas. There the youngest limestone caves formed during low-sea stands in the Pleistocene (the time of the most recent glacial advances), but these caves are now partially or completely submerged. Under these conditions, new cave passages developed above old ones and could have been colonized by aquatic troglobites that moved upward with the water column, filling newly available habitats. Similarly, where limestone was deposited on volcanic rocks, such as in Bermuda, younger limestone caves could have been colonized by troglobites from older caves in the underlying basalt (Iliffe et al. 1983). In Hawaii, Howarth (1983) suggests, even newly formed lava tube systems, less than 100 years old, have been colonized by troglobites living in cracks and older lava caves in the same area. These observations have significant evolutionary implications, because, among other things, they strongly support the hypothesis that some troglobites may be much older than indicated by the ages of their present cave habitats. Moreover, they suggest that the developmental processes of caves, especially limestone caves, confer a kind of environmental continuity that allows troglobites to remain relatively unchanged in stable habitats for long periods of time.

Terrestrial troglobites

Considering the high probability that many troglobitic species are very old, it is not surprising that a substantial number of them are relicts. Relict species have been well documented in terrestrial troglobite faunas of many parts of the northern temperate latitudes. Caves in this region appear to have played an important role as refugia, probably in the Pleistocene but possibly even earlier for some species (Vandel 1964; Barr 1968; Peck 1981; Barr and Holsinger 1985). Although the evidence for bona fide relicts in terrestrial troglobite faunas of most tropical regions is still unclear, careful research in Hawaii has revealed few terrestrial relicts from lava caves (Howarth 1981). This is probably because Hawaiian troglo-

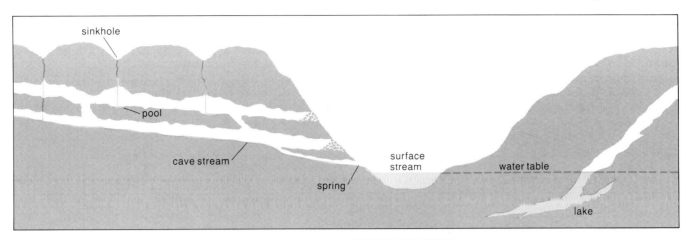

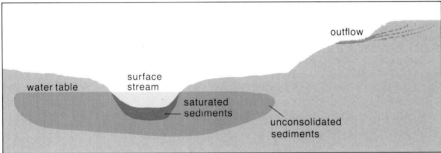

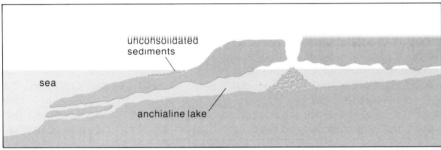

Figure 2. Cave habitats vary with the geomorphology of an area. Freshwater habitats in open caves (*top*), usually in karst, include pools fed by drips and seeps, streams in a zone above the water table, and bodies of groundwater below the water table. Interstitial habitats (*middle*) include the outflow of small springs or seeps through fine sediments or leaf litter, saturated sediments within several meters below the stream bed, and unconsolidated sediments beneath the water table that may extend over 70 m laterally. Habitats in coastal areas (*bottom*) include anchialine waters, which are brackish or marine waters that fill caves or fissures, and unconsolidated sediments saturated with brackish or marine water.

Ultimately, in concert with continued geographic and genetic isolation, many of these cave populations became troglobites. This model has been proposed by Barr (1985) to explain the evolution of troglobitic beetles, *Pseudanophthalmus*, of which approximately 240 species are recognized from ten states in the eastern United States. Barr suggests that surface ancestors of these species spread out from forest-floor habitats on the Allegheny Plateau during glacial maxima. Subsequently, during warmer interglacial periods, they colonized caves in karst areas on opposite sides of the plateau, in the Appalachians to the east, and the Interior Low Plateaus to the west.

The second theory to explain the evolution of terrestrial troglobites, the adaptive-shift theory, was originally advanced by Howarth (1973, 1981) to account for the evolution of troglobites in the Hawaiian Islands, but it may be applicable to other cave regions. This theory does not invoke isolation during climatic changes but instead proposes that the partly adapted ancestors shifted into newly developing food niches. Troglobites are therefore derived from the speciating native fauna of a region, and their evolution has been continual, rather than episodic as implied in the Pleistocene-effect model. The adaptive-shift model is based on data from Hawaiian lava caves, which are geologically young and contain a different food supply (tree roots) from most limestone caves. Moreover, many of the troglobitic species studied by Howarth (especially plant hoppers, crickets, and threadlegged bugs) are closely related to species living on the surface near the caves. Howarth suggests that the model is

bites have evolved not as a result of climatic changes but through adaptive shifts, and most are much younger than those of limestone caves in the temperate latitudes.

Two theories have been proposed to explain cave colonization and troglobite evolution in terrestrial species. The first, called the Pleistocene-effect theory, is the most widely accepted model for the evolution of terrestrial troglobites in the temperate latitudes, specifically in unglaciated regions of North America, Europe, and Japan, and it is based on fluctuating Pleistocene climates (Vandel 1964; Barr 1968; Peck 1981). During glacial maxima in areas just south

of the ice (and probably also on mountains in more southern latitudes), climates favored wide distribution of invertebrates inhabiting soil and humus at low temperatures. In the climate just south of the glacial margin, both caves and moist forest floors were inhabited by similar species. When the glaciers retreated, these species became progressively restricted to the cool, damp interiors of caves, sinkholes, deep wooded ravines, and cool forest floors at greater altitudes. With further warming and the probable changes in the surface vegetation during interglacial periods, most of the populations that survived were those living in caves.

applicable to tropical limestone areas outside Hawaii and probably to temperate karst regions as well. He agrees that glacial epochs had a significant impact on the evolution of troglobites in temperate regions but proposes that periodic changes in Pleistocene climates probably obscured the early history of troglobite evolution and distribution.

Whereas the Pleistocene-effect theory provides a mechanism for isolating populations geographically and genetically prior to their evolution into troglobitic species, the adaptive-shift theory implies that troglobites evolved without such geographic isolation. However, in view of differences in geological structure and climate among the major cave regions of the world, a single model for the evolution of terrestrial troglobites may not apply universally.

Still largely unexplained by either model is the origin of terrestrial troglobites in most tropical regions except Hawaii. Until a few years ago, terrestrial troglobites were thought to be rare in the tropics, where the climate was believed to have remained stable for millions of years. In the absence of climatic change, it was therefore further assumed that few terrestrial troglobites had evolved in tropical regions (Barr 1968; Mitchell 1969; Sbordoni 1982). However, a large number of terrestrial troglobites have recently been catalogued, and evidence of significant climatic changes in the tropics during the Pleistocene has been found (see, for example, Chapman 1980; Reddell 1981). Thus, while climatic changes might have played an important role in the evolution of terrestrial troglobites in tropical regions, neither their taxonomic relationships nor the Pleistocene climate are yet well enough understood to allow us to reach any firm conclusions. Finding a plausible explanation for the origin of terrestrial troglobites in tropical caves is an interesting challenge.

Aquatic troglobites

Unlike the terrestrial faunas, the aquatic troglobite faunas of both temperate and tropical regions contain many relict species, representing a number of important animal groups, such as flatworms, segmented worms, snails, crustaceans, fishes, and salamanders. Most are crustaceans, a remarkably diverse and widespread subphylum in subterranean groundwaters. It includes a considerable number of higher taxa (especially genera and families, but even orders) composed almost exclusively of troglobites, some of which are phylogenetic relicts, with no close living relatives, some of which are distributional relicts, having survived within a geographic region in cave refugia, and some of which are probably both.

Many troglobitic crustaceans of inland freshwater are only distantly related taxonomically to surface forms. Presumably they represent old, pre-Pleistocene colonizations of caves by freshwater ancestors. The freshwater amphipod genus *Stygobromus*, which is made up exclusively of troglobitic species, is a classic example of a relict group that might have lived in a cave environment for millions of years (See Figs. 3 and 4). The widespread distribution of *Stygobromus*, as shown in Figure 4, and its large number of species (98 from North America and 2 from Eurasia) suggest that this group of troglobites evolved and became widely distributed prior to the separation of North America and Eurasia by continental drift more than 70 million years ago (Holsinger 1986). Of more immediate interest, however, is the surprising discovery of several species of this genus in caves far north of the southern limits of Pleistocene glaciation, where troglobites were previously thought to be absent. These caves were covered but not destroyed by glaciers, and the species are not closely related taxonomically to the *Stygobromus* found south of glaciation. This indicates that certain species of troglobitic crustaceans could have survived one or more periods of glaciation in deep groundwater habitats beneath the ice (Holsinger et al. 1983).

In a review of the troglobitic decapod crustaceans of the Americas, Hobbs and his colleagues (1977) concluded that most of the shrimps and crayfishes recorded from freshwater caves in the southeastern United States are relatively old relicts. For example, two closely related species of the shrimp *Palaemonias* (shown in Fig. 1) inhabit cave systems approximately 280 km apart in northern Alabama and south-central Kentucky. They are the only members of this genus, as well as the only troglobitic members of the family Atyidae, in North America north of southern Mexico and the West Indies. Because most atyid shrimps now inhabit warmer waters farther south, these two species are likely relicts of a more widespread fauna that occurred in the southeastern United States sever-

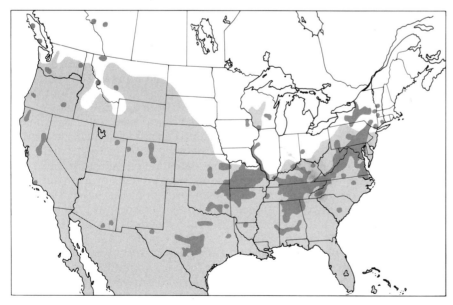

Figure 3. The distribution of the amphipod genus *Stygobromus* (*dark areas*) covers all the major cave regions in the United States (except the Florida karst region), an indication that the surface ancestors of this exclusively troglobitic genus were widespread and have long been extinct. Surprisingly, locally endemic species of *Stygobromus* are found in pockets far north of the maximum extent of the Pleistocene glaciers (*land areas in white*); apparently, these caves provided viable groundwater refugia beneath the ice.

al million years ago, when the climate of this region was much milder. According to Hobbs and his colleagues (1977), troglobitic species of crayfishes appear to have been derived from surface ancestors that colonized caves more than a million years ago in the late Tertiary. Major changes in aquatic surface habitats at this time eliminated surface ancestors or forced them to migrate elsewhere, leaving their troglobitic derivatives to survive in cave refugia.

Freshwater animals probably first became established in caves through stream capture—the diversion of surface waters into subterranean channels—and through the retreat of populations into cave streams from surface springs during episodic droughts. Isolation of these founder populations in underground streams probably followed when the springs were eliminated by erosional processes or when stream gradients and flow patterns were altered by regional uplifting and lowering of groundwater tables (Barr and Holsinger 1985). Evidence of both of these routes of invasion has been provided by recent studies. For example, there is good evidence that the ancestors both of troglobitic crayfishes of north-central Florida and of cave-adapted populations of the fish *Astyanax mexicanus* in east-central Mexico gained access to subterranean waters when surface streams were captured by sinkholes in these karst regions (Mitchell et al 1977, Franz and Lee 1982). Sweet (1982) presents data to suggest that spring-dwelling ancestors of troglobitic salamanders of central Texas migrated into cave streams to survive failure of their surface habitats during severe droughts.

In addition to these freshwater faunas, there are many troglobites of marine origin that now live in freshwater or brackish-water caves. The colonization of caves from marine sources is believed to have occurred primarily in karst areas that were formerly exposed to or covered by shallow marine embayments, or on islands that were slowly emerging from the sea (Stock 1980; Holsinger and Longley 1980; Holsinger 1986). These troglobites became adapted to the decreasing salinities that resulted from the regression of the sea or from tectonic uplifting.

A large number of troglobitic crustaceans that inhabit cave waters in Texas, Mexico, Central America, and the West Indies have strong taxonomic affinities with marine species and are apparently relics of old marine embayments (Stock 1977; Holsinger 1986). For example, one study sampling the outlet of deep artesian wells drilled into an aquifer in south-central Texas has revealed a remarkably diverse troglobite fauna that lives in an extensive network of submerged cave passages and fissures. To date, 21 species, 17 of which are crustaceans, have been recorded from a single well in the town of San Marcos (Holsinger and Longley 1980). They also include one species of planarian worm, one snail, one beetle, and one salamander. Significantly, more than half of the crustaceans are amphipods, representing 5 families, 8 genera, and 10 species—an amazing taxonomic diversity. Furthermore, approximately 8 of the amphipod species, plus 2 other crustaceans, are apparently old relics of marine embayments that covered the region in late Cretaceous and early Tertiary times (about 65 to 70 million years ago). Similarly, the present distributions of troglobitic crustaceans throughout this region from southern North America to the West Indies suggest that these species or their close relatives evolved in the areas where they now live, because these areas were last exposed to a marine environment millions of years ago in the late Cretaceous or early Tertiary.

Troglobitic species that apparently are closely related to these relics also occur in the Mediterranean region of southern Europe and North Africa. Some are found from eastern Africa to the western Pacific region as well. In the Mediterranean region, the present distributions of many troglobitic crustaceans correspond closely to shorelines of middle or late Tertiary embayments (Vandel 1964; Hutchinson 1967). Partly adapted marine ancestors were probably stranded in freshwater and brackish-water caves during the Mediterranean salinity crisis of the late Miocene (about 7 million years ago), when much of the Mediterranean Sea dried up, leading to the extinction of littoral marine organisms that did not find coastal cave refugia (Stock 1980; Por 1986). Additional support for this theory comes from genetic studies indicating that troglobitic isopods of the genus *Monolistra* in southern Europe diverged from a marine ancestor approximately 7 million years ago, at a time corresponding to the Miocene salinity crisis (Sbordoni 1982).

Discoveries of troglobites evolving from marine sources have recently been made by divers investigating anchialine habitats—landlocked pools or cave lakes that developed in limestone, coral, or basalt, with subterranean connections to the sea—in the Hawaiian, Galapagos, and Canary Islands, Bermuda, the West In

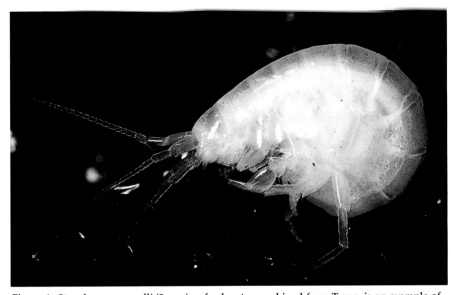

Figure 4. *Stygobromus russelli* (9 mm), a freshwater amphipod from Texas, is an example of an old troglobitic relict. This can be inferred from the fact that although all species of *Stygobromus* are troglobites, the genus is widespread in North America and also occurs in Eurasia, implying that the genus evolved before North America separated from Eurasia over 70 million years ago. (Photograph by R. Mitchell.)

dies, the Yucatan Peninsula, and elsewhere. These discoveries are beginning to reveal the potential richness of species in submerged caves and fissures near the ocean, habitats that had long gone unsampled.

Of particular interest is the origin of troglobitic crustaceans living in the brackish waters of anchialine caves on tropical islands that were built up from the sea floor by the deposition of limestone or lava or both. A few of these species are quite primitive and lack close taxonomic affinities with any other marine forms. Whereas some of them show relatively strong taxonomic relationships to deep-sea forms, and others are apparently related to shallow marine forms, most are taxonomically and ecologically distinct from species now living in an open marine environment, which suggests long periods of isolation and adaptation to anchialine caves (see Hart et al. 1985).

Among the most unusual and evolutionarily important of these crustaceans are the Remipedia, a new class recently discovered in explorations of anchialine caves in the Bahamas. Remipedes are believed to be very old relicts and perhaps the most primitive of living crustaceans (Schram et al. 1986). *Speleonectes*, one of four genera of living remipedes described so far, is composed of four species—two from limestone caves in the Bahamas, one from caves on the Yucatan Peninsula of Mexico, and one, shown in Figure 5, from a single, partially submerged lava tube on Lanzarote in the eastern Canary Islands (Yager 1987). Nothing is yet known about the dispersal potential of these organisms, but given their apparent restriction to anchialine caves, it would be surprising to find them in open marine waters outside caves. The presence of closely related species in caves on opposite sides of the Atlantic Ocean has exciting biogeographic implications. It can be interpreted to mean that these species evolved from a common ancestor, possibly before Africa and South America were fully separated by continental drift. At that time Lanzarote was still attached to the African continent and therefore situated much closer to the Bahama carbonate banks than it is at present (see also Iliffe et al. 1984).

Because crustaceans living in an-

Figure 5. This crustacean, *Speleonectes ondinae* (22 mm), found in the brackish waters of a lava-tube cave on Lanzarote in the eastern Canary Islands, belongs to a recently discovered class, the Remipedia. Remipedes consist entirely of troglobites, one indication that they are probably very old relicts. Another indication is that their morphology—the numerous, similar trunk segments bearing double-branched, paddle-like appendages—is perhaps the most primitive among living crustaceans. (Photograph by D. Williams.)

chialine caves exhibit a broad range of taxonomic affinities, it is likely that their preadapted ancestors colonized caves from several different sources at different times. Although it remains unclear what events might have led to isolation of colonizers in caves, some of them have almost certainly involved past changes in sea level.

Effects of isolation and dispersal

With some exceptions, the geographic ranges of troglobitic species are generally small and sometimes island-like. They tend to be correlated with isolated or separate exposures of cavernous rocks. In many limestone cave regions, closely related species are found in adjacent karst areas or in cave systems separated from each other by some kind of physical barrier. These patterns of distribution provide evidence that limits to underground dispersal resulted in significant geographic isola-

tion of troglobitic species. Then, when previously established populations of troglobites became restricted to different karst areas or cave systems, additional species evolved in the same general area.

A number of factors affect the dispersal of troglobites, but physical or extrinsic barriers that directly limit underground movement seem to have the most profound effect on geographic isolation. Although barriers can develop locally when segments of cave passages are destroyed by erosion, siltation, or collapse, on a much larger scale the most important physical barriers are those imposed by stratigraphy. In limestone cave regions, these barriers consist of clastic (i.e., fragmental) sedimentary rocks that do not form caverns, typically shales and sandstones, interposed between layers of cavernous limestone (Barr and Holsinger 1985). Stratigraphic barriers therefore tend to divide large cave regions into smaller, separate units that are composed of continuous limestone layers and that are referred to as areas of contiguous karst (Barr and Holsinger 1985).

The isolating effect conferred on species by barriers between areas of contiguous karst is seen in biogeographic studies of cave faunas in the Appalachians and the Interior Low Plateaus of the eastern United States (Barr 1968; Barr and Holsinger 1985; Holsinger and Culver, in press). They show that the ranges of many troglobites are significantly more delimited where areas of contiguous karst are narrowly delineated or island-like than where such areas are broad or corridor-like. Greatly restricted ranges are especially common to troglobitic species of terrestrial isopods, pseudoscorpions, millipedes, and beetles. As might be expected, these same studies also show that cave regions with the largest areas of contiguous karst have the greatest diversity of troglobitic species, a phenomenon partly attributable to greater dispersal potential for troglobites in a region with fewer barriers.

Not all troglobitic species are restricted to single areas of contiguous karst, however. On the average, aquatic troglobites have wider ranges than their terrestrial counterparts. For example, with small amphipod and isopod crustaceans, and even with the larger southern cavefish (*Typhlichtys subterraneus*), it is not uncommon to find the same species in several adjacent areas. Similarly, some terrestrial troglobites, especially spiders and collembolans, have wide ranges that exceed the boundaries of contiguous karst. In light of a strong case for dispersal barriers and geographic isolation, how can these exceptional distribution patterns be explained?

Many small aquatic troglobites occur outside karst areas and inhabit a diversity of minute spaces and interstices saturated with groundwater. Given the nature of groundwaters, which are generally more continuous than dry cave passages and open fissures above water tables, opportunities for dispersal by aquatic troglobites are usually much greater than for terrestrial troglobites (Culver 1982; Barr and Holsinger 1985). In addition, dispersal ability undoubtedly varies among terrestrial troglobites, inasmuch as some species can more readily exploit the tiny cracks, crevices, and shallow underground compartments that exist in certain noncavernous terranes between karst areas. Also, some troglobites, both aquatic and terrestrial, presumably have evolved from widespread surface ancestors that simultaneously invaded caves in separate karst areas (Barr and Holsinger 1985; Holsinger and Culver, in press). Many populations of these species may now be geographically and genetically isolated in different caves or karst areas, but lack of clear morphological differences among them has so far precluded taxonomists from recognizing the separated populations as separate species.

References

Barr, T. C., Jr. 1968. Cave ecology and the evolution of troglobites. *Evol. Biol.* 2:35–102.

———. 1985. Pattern and process in speciation of trechine beetles in eastern North America (Coleoptera: Carabidae: Trechinae). In *Taxonomy, Phylogeny, and Zoogeography of Beetles and Ants (Series Entomologia 33)*, ed. G. E. Ball, pp. 350–407. W. Junk.

Barr, T. C., Jr., and J. R. Holsinger. 1985. Speciation in cave faunas. *Ann. Rev. Ecol. Syst.* 16:313–37.

Chapman, P. 1980. On the invertebrate fauna of caves of the Serrania de San Luis, Edo. Falcon, Venezuela. *Trans. Brit. Cave Res. Assoc.* 7:179–99.

Culver, D. C. 1982. *Cave Life: Evolution and Ecology.* Harvard Univ. Press.

Curl, R. L. 1958. A statistical theory of cave entrance evolution. *Bull. Natl. Speleol. Soc.* 20:9–22.

Dickson, G. W., and P. W. Kirk, Jr. 1976. Distribution of heterotrophic microorganisms in relation to detritivores in Virginia caves (with supplemental bibliography on cave mycology and microbiology). In *The Distributional History of the Biota of the Southern Appalachians. Part IV. Algae and Fungi*, ed. B. C. Parker and M. K. Roane, pp. 205–26. Univ. Press of Virginia.

Franz, L. R., and D. S. Lee. 1982. Distribution and evolution of Florida's troglobitic crayfishes. *Bull. Fl. St. Mus. Biol. Sci.* 28:53–78.

Gascoyne, M. A., A. G. Latham, R. S. Harmon, and D. C. Ford. 1983. The antiquity of Castleguard Cave, Columbia Icefields, Alberta, Canada. *Arctic Alpine Res.* 15:463–70.

Hart, C. W., Jr., R. B. Manning, and T. M. Iliffe. 1985. The fauna of Atlantic marine caves: Evidence of dispersal by sea floor spreading while maintaining ties to deep waters. *Proc. Biol. Soc. Wash.* 98:288–92.

Hess, J. W., and R. S. Harmon. 1981. Geochronology of speleothems from the Flint Ridge–Mammoth Cave system, Kentucky. *Proceedings of the 8th International Congress of Speleology*, vol. 2, pp. 433–36.

Hobbs, H. H., Jr., H. H. Hobbs III, and M. A. Daniel. 1977. A review of troglobitic decapod crustaceans of the Americas. *Smithson. Contr. Zool.* 244:1–177.

Holsinger, J. R. 1986. Zoogeographic patterns of North American subterranean amphipod crustaceans. In *Crustacean Biogeography (Crustacean Issues 4)*, ed. R. H. Gore and K. L. Heck, pp. 85–106. A. A. Balkema.

Holsinger, J. R., and D. C. Culver. In press. The invertebrate cave fauna of Virginia and a part of eastern Tennessee: Zoogeography and ecology. *Brimleyana*, vol. 14.

Holsinger, J. R., and G. Longley. 1980. The subterranean amphipod crustacean fauna of an artesian well in Texas. *Smithson. Contr. Zool.* 308:1–59.

Holsinger, J. R., J. S. Mort, and A. D. Recklies. 1983. The subterranean crustacean fauna of Castleguard Cave, Columbia Icefields, Alberta, Canada, and its zoogeographic significance. *Arctic Alpine Res.* 15:543–49.

Howarth, F. C. 1973. The cavernicolous fauna of Hawaiian lava tubes. I. Introduction. *Pac. Insects* 15:139–51.

———. 1981. Non-relictual terrestrial troglobites in the tropic Hawaiian caves. *Proceedings of the 8th International Congress of Speleology*, vol. 2, pp. 539–41.

———. 1983. Ecology of cave arthropods. *Ann. Rev. Entomol.* 28:365–89.

Husmann, S. 1967. Die ökologische Stellung der Höhlen- und Spaltengewässer innerhalb der subterranaquatilen Lebensbereiche. *Intl. J. Speleol.* 2:409–36.

Hutchinson, G. E. 1967. *A Treatise on Limnology*, vol. 2. Wiley.

Iliffe, T. M., C. W. Hart, Jr., and R. B. Manning. 1983. Biogeography and the caves of Bermuda. *Nature* 302:141–42.

Iliffe, T. M., H. Wilkins, J. Parzefall, and D. Williams. 1984. Marine lava cave fauna: Composition, biogeography, and origins. *Science* 225:309–11.

Juberthie, C. 1983. Le milieu souterrain: Étendue et composition. *Mem. biospéol.* 10:17–65.

Mitchell, R. W. 1969. A comparison of temperate and tropical cave communities. *Southwestern Nat.* 14:73–88.

Mitchell, R. W., W. H. Russell, and W. R. Elliott. 1977. Mexican eyeless characin fishes, genus *Astyanax*: Environment, distribution, and evolution. *Spec. Publ. Mus. Texas Tech Univ.* 12:1–89.

Palmer, A. N. 1981. *A Geological Guide to Mammoth Cave National Park*. Zephyrus.

Peck, S. B. 1981. The geological, geographical, and environmental setting of cave faunal evolution. In *Proceedings of the 8th International Congress of Speleology*, vol. 2, pp. 501–02.

Por, E. D. 1986. Crustacean biogeography of the Late Middle Miocene Eastern land bridge. In *Crustacean Biogeography (Crustacean Issues 4)*, ed. R. H. Gore and K. L. Heck, pp. 69–84. A. A. Balkema.

Reddell, J. R. 1981. A review of the cavernicole fauna of Mexico, Guatemala, and Belize. *Bull. Texas Mem. Mus.* 27:1–327.

Sbordoni, V. 1982. Advances in speciation of cave animals. In *Mechanisms of Speciation*, ed. C. Barigozzi, pp. 219–40. Alan R. Liss.

Schram, F. D., J. Yager, and M. J. Emerson. 1986. Remipedia. I. Systematics. *San Diego Soc. Nat. Hist. Mem.* 15:1–60.

Stock, J. H. 1977. The taxonomy and zoogeography of the hadziid Amphipoda with emphasis on the West Indian taxa. *Stud. Fauna Curaçao* 55:1–130.

———. 1980. Regression model evolution as exemplified by the genus *Pseudoniphargus* (Amphipoda). *Bijdr. Dierk* 50:105–44.

Sweet, S. S. 1982. A distribution analysis of epigean populations of *Eurycea neotenes* in central Texas, with comments on the origin of troglobitic populations. *Herpetologica* 38:430–44.

Uéno, S. I. 1977. The biospeleological importance of noncalcareous caves. In *Proceedings of the 7th International Congress of Speleology*, pp. 407–08.

Vandel, A. 1964. *Biospéologie: La biologie des animaux cavernicoles*. Guthier-Villars.

Warwick, G. T. 1976. Geomorphology and caves. In *The Science of Speleology*, ed. T. D. Ford and C. H. D. Cullingford, pp. 61–125. Academic.

Wood, C. 1976. Caves in rocks of volcanic origin. In *The Science of Speleology*, ed. T. D. Ford and C. H. D. Cullingford, pp. 127–50. Academic.

Yager, J. 1987. *Speleonectes tulumensis* n. sp. (Crustacea: Remipedia) from two anchialine cenotes of the Yucatan Peninsula, Mexico. *Stygologia* 3:160–66.

John R. Holsinger is a professor of biological sciences at Old Dominion University, where he has taught since 1968. He received his Ph.D. from the University of Kentucky in 1966. His research has focused on the systematics and biogeography of subterranean crustaceans and on the distribution and ecology of cave animals in eastern North America. His field work has involved exploration of more than 1,000 different caves since 1960. Some of the work presented here was supported by the NSF. Address: Department of Biological Sciences, Old Dominion University, Norfolk, VA 23529–0266.

Evolutionary Relationships of the Coelacanth

Is the coelacanth a close cousin of land vertebrates? The bloodlines suggested by the hemoglobin molecule add fuel to a passionate scientific controversy

Thomas Gorr and Traute Kleinschmidt

In deep waters of the Indian Ocean, off the Comoro Islands, swims a creature once thought to have been extinct for 80 million years. The animal, a coelacanth, has evoked public fascination and attracted scientific attention ever since it was discovered more than 50 years ago. Part of the creature's allure is its appearance. Having changed little in the intervening millennia, the coelacanth can be aptly described as a "living fossil." More intriguing, however, is the coelacanth's pedigree: It may be the only living member of the crossopterygians—a group of fishes believed to include the direct ancestors of the first vertebrates that crawled onto land.

The crossopterygians had a long history before a living representative was discovered in the early part of this century. In the fossil record, crossopterygians span a period of time from about 400 million years ago—just before vertebrates took their first steps onto land—to their apparent extinction 320 million years later, just before the last dinosaur saw the light of day in the Cretaceous period. It is not surprising, then, that a living coelacanth (scientifically christened *Latimeria chalumnae*)

received a warm reception from the scientific community; the creature was a long-lost relative, perhaps even a window on the past.

For many years coelacanths were best known from the nearly 200 specimens that were caught and brought to shore. Typically these animals were entombed in a tank filled with a chemical preservative, and displayed in a museum. On occasion a specimen would be probed and dissected in order to gain some insight into the creature's anatomy and physiology, and perhaps its evolutionary provenance. Recently, however, submarine explorations by Hans Fricke of the Max Planck Institute for Behavioral Physiology in Germany have provided a means to study the coelacanth in its natural habitat. These ventures have not only provided insights into the coelacanth's behavior; they have also allowed investigators to estimate that only a few hundred coelacanths live in the Grande Comore region. The last point is critical: Because of the high price a coelacanth draws on the market, and an annual catch rate of about three specimens per year, the species appears to be threatened by real extinction. Ironically, the discovery of the coelacanth has placed the unique animal at its greatest peril in its 400 million-year history.

The recent investigations of the coelacanth have spawned renewed interest in its evolutionary status. With tissue samples from living animals, investigations of the coelacanth are no longer limited to examinations of gross anatomical structures. Laboratory techniques developed over the last three decades allow biologists to ascertain and compare the structure of key molecules from many species, including the coelacanth, for similarities that suggest

ancestral ties. The results have given rise to a passionate debate about the coelacanth's status as an evolutionary cousin to present-day land vertebrates, the tetrapods. It is a scientific controversy that we have entered with our own studies of the vertebrate hemoglobin molecule. We found not only that the coelacanth is the closest living relative of the tetrapods, but that the tetrapod with a hemoglobin molecule most similar to the coelacanth's is a frog tadpole.

A Fish in the Family

The significance of the coelacanth is best understood by considering what we know about its evolutionary history and about the origin of land vertebrates. The popular image of a fish crawling onto land and evolving into the first land-dwelling vertebrate has its real-world counterpart in a much more gradual (and complex) process, as evidenced in the fossil record. It is generally believed that the first tetrapods, evolved from a group of bony fishes called sarcopterygians (from the Greek *sarco*, meaning flesh, and *pteris*, meaning wing). The unifying characteristic of the group was the presence of paired, lobed (fleshy) fins—the likely precursors of legs in the ancestral tetrapod.

A little more than 400 million years ago, before the advent of land vertebrates, there were two major groups of sarcopterygians swimming in the waters in and around the ancient continents. One group, the crossopterygians, bore very sharp and pointed teeth and appear to have preyed on other fishes. Another group, the lungfishes, had a strikingly different form of dentition, consisting of tooth plates, which apparently were suited for crushing the shells of mollusks and other invertebrates.

Thomas Gorr received his B.A. in biology at the Philipps University in Marburg, Germany. His research on the structure of the hemoglobin molecule in the coelacanth is part of his doctoral research at the Max Planck Institute for Biochemistry. Traute Kleinschmidt is head of the research unit for Structure-Function Relationships of Hemoglobins at the Max Planck Institute for Biochemistry in Martinsried, Germany. She received her Ph.D. in chemistry at the Rheinische Friedrich-Wilhelms University in Bonn, Germany. Her research interests are concerned with the functional and evolutionary basis for the primary structure of the hemoglobin molecule. Address: Max Planck Institute for Biochemistry, Am Klopferspitz 18a, 8033 Martinsried bei München, Germany.

Figure 1. A coelacanth—the only living representative of the fishes considered to be ancestral to land vertebrates—swims idly in the depths of the Indian Ocean. The existence of a living coelacanth offers evolutionary biologists the opportunity to assess the fish's phylogenetic relationships based on the structure of its molecules. Comparisons of the coelacanth's hemoglobin molecule with those of other vertebrates suggest that it is the closest living relative of the land vertebrates. (Photograph courtesy of Hans Fricke, Max Planck Institute for Behavioral Physiology, Seewiesen, Germany.)

Crossopterygians and lungfishes are also distinguished from each other by the structure of their skulls. In particular, crossopterygians have a division between the front and the back half of their skulls, whereas lungfishes do not. The coelacanths, including *Latimeria,* are considered to be crossopterygians precisely because they bear such a division in their braincase (Andrews 1973, Schultze 1986).

Intriguingly, the earliest known tetrapods, the ichthyostegids, are characterized by features strikingly similar to those of the typical fossil crossopterygians, an extinct group called the rhipidistians. Most notably, the best-known representative, *Icthyostega,* had a rem-nant of a division in its skull very similar to the division in a rhipidistian skull. Because of these similarities, the traditional view of the evolution of tetrapods holds that the ichthyostegids evolved from a group of rhipidistians. It has been suggested that the adaptive advantages of these early amphibians drove the rhipidistians to extinction (about 290 million years ago) because they were competing for resources in their freshwater habitat. The only surviving crossopterygians, the coelacanths, may have persisted because their ancestors had adapted to a marine environment.

Because of its classification as a crossopterygian, the traditional view would accept the coelacanth as the clos-est living relative of the tetrapods. In the last decade or so, this view has been challenged on several fronts. Some anatomists have suggested that the lungfishes, of which six species survive, are more closely related to the tetrapods (Forey 1986, Robineau 1987, Forey 1990). This view was apparently substantiated by similarities between the mitochondrial DNA of lungfishes and tetrapods (Meyer and Wilson 1990). Some paleontologists still accept some rhipidistians as the closest extinct relatives of tetrapods, but deny the coelacanth's identity as a crossopterygian, preferring the lungfishes as the closest living relative (Miles 1977, Panchen and Smithson 1987, Benton 1990). Others

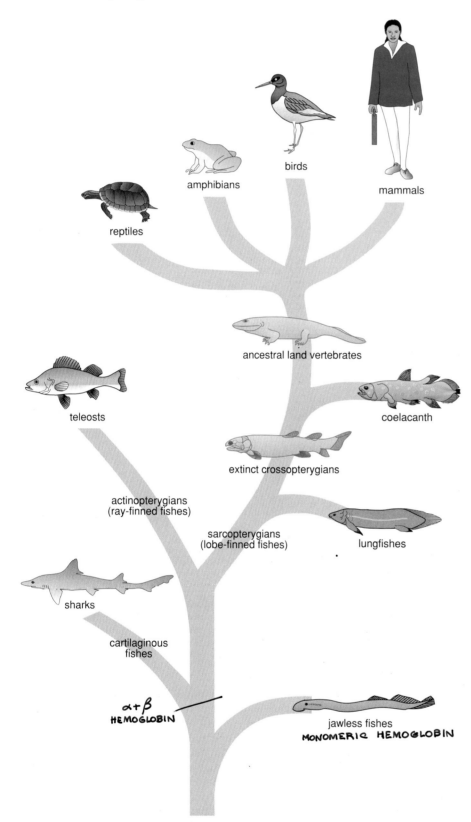

Figure 2. Traditional view of the vertebrate family tree identifies the lobe-finned fishes (sarcopterygians) as the ancestors of land vertebrates. The fossil evidence suggests that a subgroup of the lobe-finned fishes, the extinct crossopterygians, were the direct ancestors of land vertebrates, or tetrapods. In this view, the only living crossopterygian—the coelacanth (*Latimeria*)—is considered to be the closest living relative of the tetrapods. The other living lobe-finned fishes, the lungfishes, are considered to be evolutionary cousins of the crossopterygians, and therefore more distantly related to tetrapods. The ray-finned fishes (including the highly evolved teleosts), the cartilaginous fishes (such as sharks) and the jawless fishes (lampreys and hagfishes) are considered to be more distantly related to tetrapods.

deny any close relationship between crossopterygians and tetrapods, preferring both the fossil and living lungfishes as the closest relatives (Gardiner 1980; Rosen, Forey, Gardiner and Patterson 1981). Finally, another school of scientists would deny the close relationships of all sarcopterygians (crossopterygians and lungfishes) to the tetrapods. These scientists suggest that one or more groups of ray-finned fishes, such as the teleosts (tuna, carp, herring), are the most closely related to tetrapods (von Wahlert 1968, Baba et al. 1984, Maeda et al. 1984, Goodman et al. 1987, Bishop and Friday 1988).

Aside from these theories concerning the relationships between the bony fishes and the tetrapods, there are some anatomists who suggest other unconventional relationships for the coelacanth. Some believe that the coelacanth is most closely related to the cartilaginous fishes, the sharks and rays (Løvtrup 1977, Lagios 1982). Others hold that the coelacanth is a living representative of the stock that gave rise to all other bony fishes (Wiley 1979). Still others believe that the coelacanth is only distantly related to all other groups of living fishes (Bjerring 1973). In spite of the traditional view of the coelacanth's evolutionary status, when we began our study the phylogenetic relationships of this animal were mired in controversy.

Bloodlines

The existence of a living crossopterygian means that a biologist need not look solely at fossils to determine the possible relationships of these fishes to other vertebrates. Living tissues, examined on a molecular scale, provide another basis for comparison. The past three decades have seen the development of laboratory techniques that allow us to determine a molecule's structure and chemical composition. Computer programs can run algorithms that permit the comparison of thousands of molecules. These techniques provide a powerful complement to the classical methods of comparing gross anatomical structures.

The donation of blood samples from a living coelacanth by Hans Fricke provided our laboratory the opportunity to compare the molecules of this animal to those of other vertebrates. In our view the oxygen-binding molecule in blood, hemoglobin, seemed to be a natural choice because its structure and evolutionary history are relatively well known.

In the earliest vertebrates, the hemoglobin molecule consisted of a single (monomeric) chain; this is evident in the most primitive living fishes, the jawless hagfishes and lampreys, which have monomeric hemoglobins. In the ancestor of all other vertebrates, the single globin gene that coded for the monomeric chain duplicated, resulting in the production of two proteins: an alpha-hemoglobin chain and a beta-hemoglobin chain. The hemoglobin molecule of all living vertebrates other than hagfishes and lampreys consists of two alpha chains and two beta chains, forming a tetrameric molecule.

Reconstructions of the hemoglobin molecule's evolution place the duplication of the single globin gene about 450 million years ago in the common ancestor of all jawed vertebrates. About 400 million years ago another duplication of the alpha and beta chains took place. In this instance, however, the duplication resulted in the production of juvenile and adult forms of the alpha- and beta-hemoglobin chains (Goodman et al. 1982, Czelusniak et al. 1982). Most land vertebrates, including humans, have juvenile and adult versions of hemoglobin.

To find the chains with greatest similarity to those of *Latimeria*, we conducted a computer-aided search, comparing its alpha and beta chains to a pool of 522 hemoglobin molecules. Strikingly, the program selected two beta chains of the bullfrog tadpole as the closest matching sequences. As a consequence the tadpoles had to be included in all further studies. For our comparisons, we examined hemoglobin molecules from a coelacanth, a lungfish (*Lepidosiren paradoxus*), one species of shark (*Heterodontus portusjacksoni*) and five species of teleosts, as well as adult amphibians from five species and juvenile amphibians from three species. In all, our data set consisted of 522 hemoglobin chains, including all known amino-acid sequences from fishes and amphibians.

One of the first observations we made was that the alpha and beta chains of the hemoglobin molecule in fishes are most similar to the juvenile forms of hemoglobin expressed in tadpoles (Gorr et al. 1991a). Why is this so? We propose that the hemoglobin genes of the fishes and the tadpole evolved from a common ancestral gene. This means that the genes for the juvenile form of hemoglobin in amphibians and the hemoglobin genes that are expressed in adult fishes are both descended from the "juvenile" gene lineage that was formed *after* the adult-juvenile gene duplication in their com-

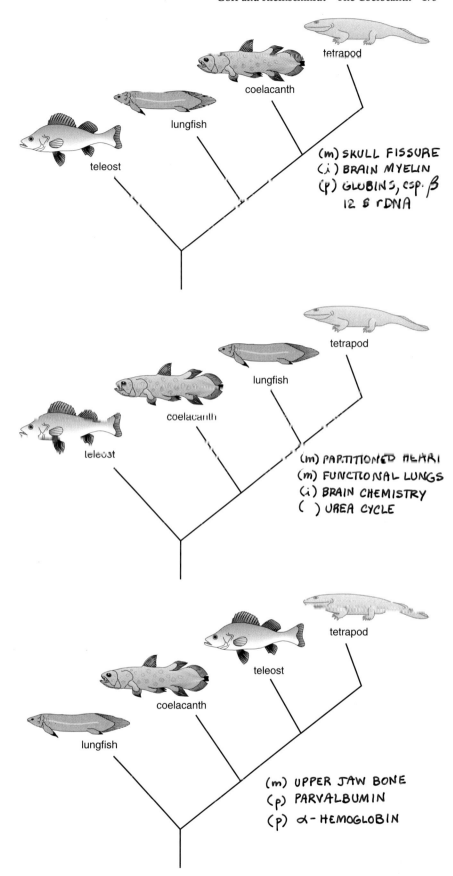

Figure 3. Three phylogenetic trees offer alternative hypotheses about the relatedness of tetrapods and fishes. The traditional view *(top)* holds that the coelacanth is the closest living piscine relative of the tetrapods. Recent proposals, based on both anatomical and molecular evidence, favor the lungfishes *(middle)* or the teleosts *(bottom)* as the evolutionary cousins of tetrapods.

mon ancestor. Genes related in this manner are said to be orthologous. In contrast, the hemoglobin genes expressed in adult frogs are paralogously related to the expressed forms of the fish hemoglobin genes because their similarities date back to the period *before* this gene duplication.

Other investigators have also found that the hemoglobin molecules of fishes are more closely related to the juvenile form of hemoglobin in tetrapods. Computer programs that reconstruct the most parsimonious phylogenetic trees based on the sequence of amino acids in the alpha and beta chains of the hemoglobin molecule place teleosts next to tadpoles (Goodman et al. 1987). Although this is one of the findings that led to the suggestion that teleosts are the tetrapods' closest relatives, it supports the notion of an evolutionary link between the juvenile hemoglobin in tetrapods and the fish hemoglobin molecule. Even where the amino-acid sequences do not match, the functional properties—volume, electrical polarity, hydrophobicity and tendency to dissociate—of the aligned amino acids are most closely matched in the hemoglobin molecules of fishes and juvenile tetrapods (Horimoto et al. 1990). Since amino acids that have similar functional properties usually have codons (triplets of nucleotides) that differ by only a single base, these similarities further support the hypothesis that these genes are orthologous.

Our next step was to determine which of the fish hemoglobins was closest to the tetrapod hemoglobin molecules. As we mentioned earlier, when we compared the amino-acid sequence of the coelacanth's hemoglobin to the data set, the matching algorithm selected two beta-hemoglobin molecules from the tadpole of a bullfrog (*Rana catesbeiana*) as the closest match. About 58 percent of the amino acids in the beta chain of the coelacanth's hemoglobin are identical to those in the beta chains of the tadpole's hemoglobin. (Only 40 percent of the amino acids in the beta chain of the adult bullfrog's hemoglobin match those of the coelacanth; this is consistent with the view that the hemoglobin genes of fishes and adult tetrapods are paralogous.) Other groups of fishes had significantly fewer matches to the beta chain of the tadpole's hemoglobin. Five teleost species weighed in with an average matching of about 48 percent, the lungfish had about 47 percent, and the shark matched about 45 percent of its

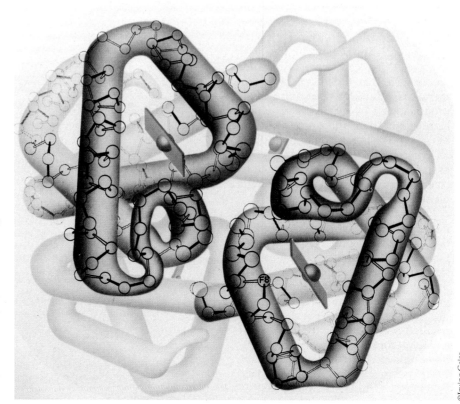

©Irving Geiss

Figure 4. Hemoglobin molecule of tetrapods and most fishes consists of two alpha chains *(bottom of molecule)* and two beta chains *(top of molecule)*. Because the amino-acid sequence in each chain has been determined in many different vertebrate species, the hemoglobin molecule is an ideal candidate for comparative investigations of evolutionary relationships. Here the position of the four oxygen-binding heme groups *(orange)* is shown nested within the four polypeptide chains *(blue)*.

amino acids with those of the tadpole.

The close link between the coelacanth and the tadpole was also evident when we attempted to reconstruct the phylogenetic relationships based on the beta-hemoglobin chains of the different species. The program produced a phylogenetic tree showing the coelacanth and the tadpole paired on one branch, followed by teleosts, the lungfish, adult frogs and sharks on successively distant branches. (Recall that the hemoglobin molecule of the adult frog is distantly related to the hemoglobin molecule of the tadpole because of the ancient duplication of the genes.)

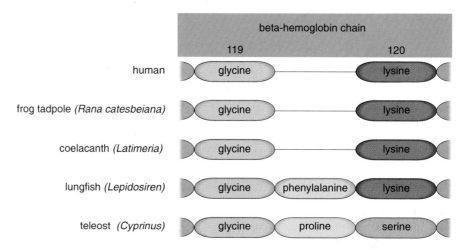

Figure 5. Additions and deletions of amino acids in the hemoglobin molecule offer evidence of evolutionary distances between species. With respect to length, the hemoglobin molecule of the coelacanth differs from that of the human only in having one insertion (threonine) between positions 46 and 47 in the alpha chain. In contrast, the alpha chain of

A distinctly different phylogenetic tree was produced when the alpha-hemoglobin chains were analyzed. In this instance the closest branches were between the teleosts and the amphibians. Increasingly distant branches held the coelacanth, the lungfish and the shark. Although these results contradict the outcome of the beta-hemoglobin comparisons, there is good reason to believe that they do not reflect the true phylogenetic relationships. In particular, it appears that the alpha-hemoglobin genes of the fishes have had variable and unusually high rates of mutation throughout their evolution, especially during the earliest phase (Goodman et al. 1975).

Our own analyses support the notion that the alpha-hemoglobin chain has evolved at widely varying rates in different species. One of us (Gorr) used a method called cladistic analysis, developed by the German entomologist Willi Hennig, to assess the evolutionary rates of the alpha-hemoglobin chain. One of the critical contributions of Hennig's methods was the distinction between different types of homologous characters (features inherited from a common ancestor) that are shared by two or more species. Homologous characters are said to be *primitive* if they are shared by a group of species that can trace the inheritance of the character back to an ancient ancestor. On the other hand, *derived* homologous characters are those shared exclusively by a more circumscribed group of species that can trace the inheritance of the character to their most recent ancestor. The shared derived characters are useful for inferring the relationships between species, whereas the conservation of primitive characters offers evidence for the rate of evolutionary change.

The primitive characters in the hemoglobin chains of bony fishes and tetrapods are those that were present before the adult and juvenile duplication of the hemoglobin genes. These can be identified by looking at the amino-acid residues that are shared between the hemoglobin chains of the tadpole and the adult frog. Thus we assume that these identities have been retained from a period before the adult-juvenile duplication rather than becoming identical independently afterward. When we looked at the alpha-hemoglobin chains of the bony fishes, we found a greater range of variability (from 31 to 46 primitive characters) compared to the beta-hemoglobin chains (from 31 to 40 primitive characters). Moreover, the highest number of preduplicational identities was found in the evolutionarily young teleost alpha chains (31 to 46), whereas the ancient *Latimeria* (39) and *Lepidosiren* (31) alpha chains showed lower values. In contrast, the situation in the beta chains was as expected: Most primitive matches (39 and 40) were found in the phylogenetic oldest chains of the coelacanth and the lungfish and fewer in teleosts (31 to 37). These differences suggest that the rate of evolutionary change of the alpha-hemoglobin genes has been highly variable in the bony fishes. The more variation there is in the rates of evolutionary change for a molecule, the less reliable is the molecule for inferring phylogenetic relationships.

The rates of change for the alpha-hemoglobin chains have not only been variable, they have also been relatively high. Only one primitive character was conserved in the alpha-hemoglobin chains of *all* the bony fishes, whereas 13 primitive characters were conserved in the beta-hemoglobin chains of all the bony fishes. The smaller number of primitive characters common to the alpha-hemoglobin chains of all the bony fishes suggests that the alpha-hemoglobin genes have undergone higher rates of evolutionary change. This means that the alpha-hemoglobin chains are not as reliable for inferring evolutionary relationships among these organisms as are the beta hemoglobin chains.

When only orthologously derived characters are considered, the results are consistent with those of the pairwise matching and the computer-generated phylogenetic tree. The beta-hemoglobin chains of the coelacanth and the tadpole had the greatest number of shared derived characters (18), followed by the lungfish (9) and a teleost, the carp (7). In contrast, analysis of the alpha-hemoglobin chains suggested that the closest affinities were between the tadpole and the teleosts, which had 17 shared derived characters. The alpha chain of the coelacanth shared 12 derived characters with the tadpole, whereas the alpha chain of the lungfish had 7 matches.

Critical Parts

Relationships between species can be deduced not only from comparisons of entire hemoglobin chains but also from certain parts of the molecule that are critical to its structure or function. In some respects, this approach is to be favored over attempts to form comparisons between large sequences of

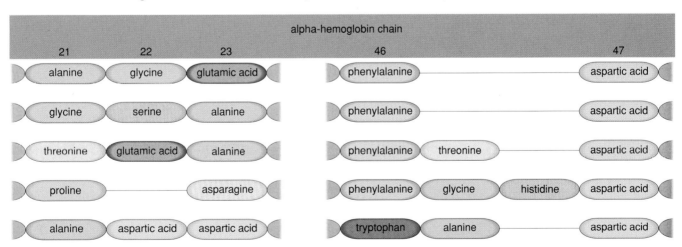

the lungfish has a deletion at position 22, two insertions (glycine and histidine) between positions 46 and 47 and an addition (not shown) at one end. There is also an insertion (phenylalanine) between positions 119 and 120 in the beta chain of the lungfish. The teleost (a carp) also has more additions and insertions than the coelacanth. Only those regions that alter the length of the chains relative to the human hemoglobin molecule are shown.

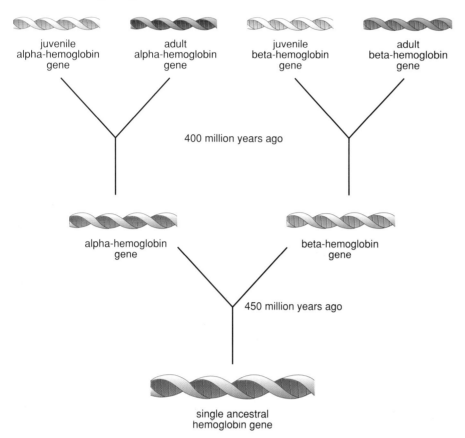

Figure 6. Evolution of the vertebrate hemoglobin genes has involved two duplications. About 450 million years ago a gene duplication produced the alpha- and beta-hemoglobin genes. A second duplication about 400 million years ago resulted in the formation of adult and juvenile forms of the alpha and beta genes. Comparisons between the hemoglobin molecules of fishes and tetrapods must consider both the juvenile and adult forms of the molecule.

amino acids or complementary pairs of chemical bases in DNA without regard to the relative significance of one part of the molecule over another. This follows because parts of the molecule that perform critical functions should be conserved in evolution because of their adaptive value. As a result, mutational changes in critical parts should be relatively rare in comparison to regions that have less critical roles. Consequently, the evolutionarily conserved regions should provide more reliable information about the phylogenetic relationships between species.

One of these critical regions is found in the alpha- and beta-hemoglobin genes. In all known instances the hemoglobin genes of vertebrates consist of three exons (DNA segments that code for the protein) and two introns (segments that are spliced out before protein synthesis). As it happens, the excision of the introns requires the presence of a precise sequence of DNA base pairs at the border between the adjacent exons and introns. Because of this requirement these border sites correspond to some of the most

highly conserved parts of a protein molecule (Hewett-Emmett, Venta and Tashian 1982). It turns out that the corresponding amino-acid sequences (adjacent to the first intron) in the alpha-hemoglobin chain of the coelacanth match those of the bullfrog and *Xenopus* tadpoles precisely, all having the sequence *arginine-leucine-phenylalanine*. In contrast, 144 out of 170 alpha chains from other animals (including the lungfish, shark and adult amphibians) replace the leucine with a methionine residue, and all teleosts have the sequence *arginine-methionine-leucine*.

The corresponding residues of the beta chain are also identical in the coelacanth and the bullfrog tadpole (both having the sequence *arginine-leucine-phenylalanine*). In contrast, 156 out of 166 beta chains (including some teleosts, adult amphibians, all birds and most mammals) have the sequence *arginine-leucine-leucine*. The distribution of these sequences suggests that the identities shared by the hemoglobin molecules of the coelacanth and the tadpoles are evolutionarily derived.

Two other qualities critical to the structure of hemoglobin are the binding between the chains in the tetrameric molecule and the binding of the heme group to the protein chains. In general, the stability of the molecule relies on the character of the amino acids at these binding sites. Although the sites have not been as stringently conserved as some of the others, they appear to be evolutionarily more conservative than most parts of the molecule. When we compared the amino acids at these positions in the different groups, we found that the highest degree of concordance occurred between the coelacanth and the tetrapods. At these sites, the coelacanth shared 33 percent of its amino acids with the bullfrog tadpole in the alpha chain and 44 percent in the beta chain. All other groups of animals shared no more than 28 percent of their amino acids in the alpha chain, and 33 percent in the beta chain (Gorr et al. 1991b). Again, these similarities further support the notion that the coelacanth is closely related to the tadpole.

Fishing for Relatives

How do we reconcile the different views of the relationships between fishes and tetrapods in the light of our own results? The issue does not appear to turn on whether the arguments are adduced on the basis of gross anatomy or molecular biology, since both types of evidence fall alternately on either side of the fence. Instead, each result must be considered on its own relative merits.

What evidence is there that the ray-finned fishes are the closest living relatives of the tetrapods? Anatomical arguments are based primarily on the similarities of the upper jaw of teleosts to those of the tetrapods and the rhipidistians (von Wahlert 1968). The coelacanths seems to lie outside these three groups because they lack a maxillary bone. The significance of this difference is difficult to ascertain since the coelacanth may have secondarily lost its maxilla during evolution.

Molecular evidence for the evolutionary affinities of the teleosts relies on the hemoglobin molecule and the muscle protein parvalbumin. Other investigators who have studied the hemoglobin molecule favor the teleosts over the lungfishes as most closely related to tetrapods (Goodman et al. 1987, Bishop and Friday 1988). These studies are not inconsistent with our results because the authors could not include the hemoglobin molecule of the coelacanth in their database. Rather, *Latimeria* was provisionally considered to be remotely related to the tetrapods based on earlier studies of the parvalbumin molecule. Phylogenetic trees based on this protein propose close genealogical ties between teleosts and tetrapods (Baba et al. 1984, Maeda et al. 1984). Although the coelacanth was included in these efforts, the lungfish was not. Unfortunately, their results seem to vary depending on which subunit of the molecule was considered. These authors did not provide a rationale for favoring some parts of the molecule over others. Moreover, the authors concluded that parvalbumin may not be suited for the study of higher-level phylogenetic relationships because the molecule evolved at very different rates in different lineages (Maeda et al. 1984).

Those who favor the lungfishes as the closest living relatives of the tetrapods also base their arguments on anatomical and molecular evidence. In particular, the lungfish's heart is like the typical tetrapod heart in having at least some separation of the oxygenated and deoxygenated bloodstreams (Rosen et al. 1981, Panchen and Smithson 1987). Such a similarity is difficult to draw with the coelacanth because of its adaptation to a marine environment. Because the coelacanth's lungs are no more than fat-filled sacs, its heart could not possibly have the same structure as that of a lung-bearing animal. The lungfish's lungs and the presence of a partition in its heart may have developed similarities to the tetrapod's heart and lungs through recent evolutionary convergences. In fact, paleontological evidence suggests that lungfishes evolved in the ancient oceans, and that the transition to freshwater was a recent evolutionary development. Moreover, some of the extinct species depended on gills rather than lungs (Panchen and Smithson 1987, Campbell and Barwick 1986, 1988).

Molecular evidence for close links between the tetrapods and the lungfishes is based on the genes for two mitochondrial molecules. Small regions (about 240 DNA base pairs) of the genes for 12S ribosomal RNA suggest that the lungfishes are more closely related to a species of frog (*Xenopus laevis*) than either the coelacanth or the teleosts (Meyer and Wilson 1990). One of the major problems with this study, however, is that the authors compared only 33 DNA base pairs in their phylogenetic analysis. However, given the evolutionary dynamics and

the algorithms they used, statistical considerations require at least 3,100 base pairs for such an analysis (Saitou and Nei 1986). Others have noted inconsistencies in the sequences of the frog's mitochondrial DNA used by Meyer and Wilson (Dunon-Bluteau et al. 1985, Cairns and Bogenhagen 1986, Johansen et al. 1990). Finally, because of its high rate of mutation relative to nuclear DNA, it is questionable whether mitochondrial DNA is suitable for the reconstruction of relationships between species that have not shared a common ancestor for at least 360 million years. As a result, certain genes of mitochondrial DNA may be best suited for phylogenetic questions where the species diverged about 150 million years ago, and no more than 300 million years ago (Mindell and Honeycutt 1990).

What evidence favors the coelacanth as the closest living relative of the tetrapods? Aside from similarities in the structure of its skull (notably the intracranial joint), the coelacanth has a hearing organ, the basilar papilla, apparently homologous to that found in the tetrapods (Fritzsch 1987). The

structure of the inner ear region of the fossil crossopterygians suggests that they also had a basilar papilla. In contrast, living lungfishes do not have a basilar papilla; instead they seem to rely on hearing organs with similarities to those found in cartilaginous and ray-finned fishes.

Molecular investigations of certain proteins in the nervous system also show that the coelacanth is most closely related to the tetrapods (Waehneldt and Malotka 1989, Waehneldt et al. 1991). In particular, certain proteolipid proteins of the myelin sheath that surrounds neuronal axons are found only in the lobe-finned fishes and the tetrapods, suggesting that they are a novel evolutionary acquisition of these animals. However, the proteolipid proteins of *Latimeria* and tetrapods share certain chemical features that distinguish them from the lungfishes. That is, they can pair to form dimers, and neither bears sugar residues. In contrast, the proteolipid proteins of lungfishes do not form dimers, and they do carry sugar molecules. Furthermore, studies of the immunoreactive properties of these

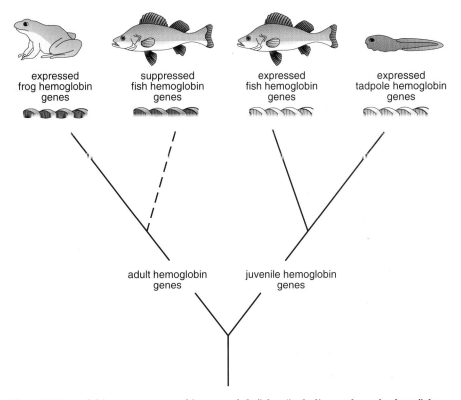

Figure 7. Hemoglobin genes expressed in most adult fishes (including coelacanths, lungfishes and teleosts) are more closely related to the genes of juvenile (tadpole) frogs than to those of adult frogs. It may be that the genes expressed in adult fishes and tadpoles are both derived from the "juvenile" hemoglobin genes (*right*) formed after the adult-juvenile gene duplication. In contrast, the genes that correspond to the expressed hemoglobin genes in the adult frog may be suppressed in adult fishes. Consequently, the evolutionary relationships between fishes and tetrapods is determined best by comparing the genes of adult fishes to those of juvenile tetrapods, such as the tadpole.

molecules also suggest that the coelacanth and the tetrapods have the closest affinities (Waehneidt and Malotka 1989, Waehneldt et al. 1991). Other investigators who have sequenced about 2000 base bairs of a type of ribosomal DNA (28S rDNA) from the nuclei of these animals have also concluded that the coelacanth is phylogenetically closest to tetrapods (Hillis and Dixon 1989, Hillis et al 1991). Unfortunately these investigators did not include any lungfishes in their study.

Our studies of the hemoglobin molecule support the view that the coelacanth is more closely related to the tetrapods than are the lungfishes or the teleosts. Our results also cast doubt on the view that coelacanths are most closely related to the cartilaginous fishes or that they belong to a group separate from the other bony fishes. These results are supported by comparisons indicating similarities in the length of the beta-hemoglobin chain, pairwise comparisons of the amino-acid sequences, computer-aided phylogenetic reconstructions of the molecule's evolution, a cladistic analysis of the molecule's evolution and similarities in the identity of the amino-acid residues at key locations in the molecule.

Why should the evidence based on the structure of the hemoglobin molecule be favored over the anatomical and molecular investigations that would deny a close relationship between the coelacanth and the tetrapods? Unfortunately, the arguments based on the anatomical similarities do not help to resolve the issue, since it is still difficult to choose among them. On the molecular side of the equation, however, the question rests primarily on the suitability of the molecule for inferring evolutionary relationships. The ideal molecule would have a rate of mutational change that was about average compared to other molecules. Its rate of evolutionary change should be fairly homogeneous throughout the course of its history. Homologous sequences from a relatively large number of representative species should be available. And finally, some forms of analysis also require the comparison of relatively large strings of sequences from a molecule. In our view the molecular investigations that favor the lungfishes or the teleosts as the closest living relatives of the tetrapods fail to achieve one or more of these criteria. In contrast, the beta-hemoglobin chain fulfills each of these requirements. The bloodlines, it seem, favor the coelacanth.

Postscript

Our study of the coelacanth's evolutionary relationships engendered a considerable amount of controversy after its initial publication (Gorr, Kleinschmidt and Fricke 1991, Stock and Swofford 1991, Sharp et al. 1991, Meyer and Wilson 1991). There was some question about our assumption that the beta-hemoglobin chains of the bony fishes evolved at the same rate in all species. In the view of our critics, the beta chains of coelacanths and tadpoles are similar because they evolved at similar (low) rates, whereas the beta chains of the lungfishes and the teleosts evolved at higher rates. The computer program we used (UPGMA, or the unweighted pair-group method with arithmetic mean) was also criticized because of the possibility that it could generate incorrect phylogenetic trees if the rates of molecular evolution varied widely among the species considered. In the light of these possibilities we took another look at our data.

In our original cladistic analysis we merely counted the amino acids that were shared derived characters. In reanalyzing the data we also made note of non-matching residues between the beta chains of individual fishes and tadpoles. That is, we distinguished between primitively retained (type I) characters and characters modified by further replacement (type II). In comparing the beta chain of the fishes with that of the tadpoles, a great number of type I amino acids would suggest a slow evolutionary rate, whereas a great number of type II amino acids would suggest a high evolutionary rate. In the new analysis we found that the lungfish did have about 1.4 times more type II amino acids than

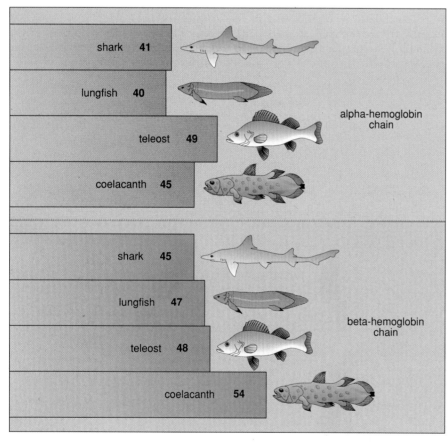

average amino-acid matches between fishes and tadpoles (percent)

Figure 8. Comparison of amino acids in the alpha- and beta-hemoglobin chains of fishes to the tadpole offers evidence of evolutionary relatedness. The coelacanth has the greatest percentage of amino-acid matches in the beta chain, whereas the teleosts have the greatest percentage in the alpha chain. Comparisons between the alpha-hemoglobin chains of different species, however, are not reliable for assessing evolutionary relationships because the alpha chain has experienced relatively high and variable rates of mutation. In contrast, the beta-hemoglobin chains of fishes and tetrapods have experienced lower and relatively homogeneous rates of mutation, thus offering a more accurate assessment of evolutionary relationships.

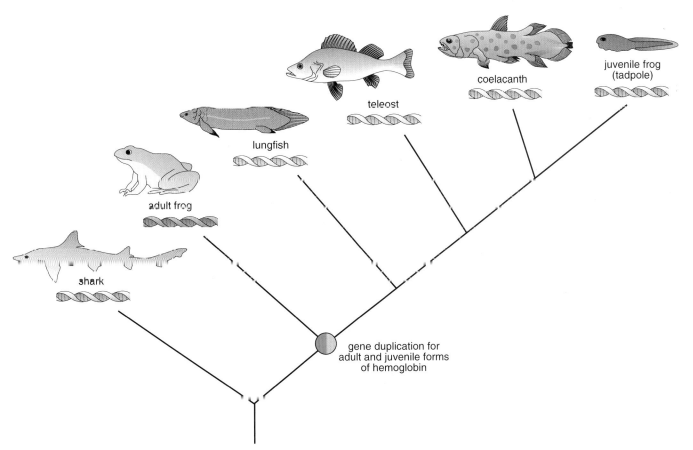

Figure 9. Phylogenetic tree based on the beta-hemoglobin chains of fishes and frogs places the coelacanth next to the tadpole. The tree was calculated with an algorithm that compared the beta chains of 17 species of fishes and frogs. The UPGMA method (or the unweighted pair-group method with arithmetic mean) that was used clusters the two amino-acid sequences that are most similar to each other and then treats the pairing as a single taxonomic unit. Subsequent comparisons repeat the process until only a single pairing of taxonomic units remains. For clarity, only the main branches of the tree are shown.

the coelacanth, but it also had 1.8 times the number of type I characters of the coelacanth. In conjunction with the shared derived characters, the most parsimonious grouping of the species still supports the coelacanth as the closest living piscine relative of the tetrapods.

There is also some justification for using the UPGMA algorithm. The evolution of the juvenile beta-hemoglobin chains (including those of the tadpoles) does appear to have progressed at a steady, clock-like, rate (Shapiro 1991). Moreover, the algorithm provides *rooted* trees, thus avoiding assumptions about which taxonomic group should be used as an outgroup. In other words, all groups are treated equally at the outset of the analysis.

There are several other arguments against the notion that the beta-hemoglobin chain of the lungfish has undergone a high rate of evolutionary change. First, the beta chains of the lungfish and the coelacanth retained the same number of shared primitive characters, suggesting similar rates of mutation. Second, with respect to the tadpole beta chain, the coelacanth and the lungfish

beta chains have the same number of conservative amino-acid substitutions (those that do not change the functional properties of the residue site). Furthermore, the number of identical amino acid residues shared by the lungfish and the teleost (43 to 49 percent) is about the same as the identities shared by the coelacanth with these fishes (45 to 50 percent). If the beta chains of the teleosts and lungfish had fast rates of mutation, then the number of matches should be fewer. As a result, even though the computer program we used to calculate the evolutionary trees does assume that the genes had equal rates of mutation, there is no evidence (such as large discrepancies in the number of shared primitive characters) to suggest that this was not the case. Finally, the critics imply that an analysis of the beta-hemoglobin chains suggests that the lungfishes and teleosts are more closely related to the adult frog than is the coelacanth. Such a statement, however, completely ignores the even greater number of matches between these fishes and the tadpoles (Gorr et al. 1991a). Even when all of the critics' ar-

guments are taken into consideration, there is no reason to doubt that the coelacanth is the closest living relative of the tetrapods.

Bibliography

Ahlberg, P. E. 1991. Tetrapod or near-tetrapod fossils from the Upper Devonian of Scotland. *Nature* 354:298–301.

Andrews, S. M. 1973. Interrelationships of crossopterygians. In *Interrelationships of Fishes*, ed. P. H. Greenwood, R. S. Miles and C. Patterson, pp. 137–177. London: Linnean Society.

Baba, M. L., M. Goodman, J. Berger-Cohn, J. G. Demaille and G. Matsuda. 1984. The early adaptive evolution of calmodulin. *Molecular Biology and Evolution* 1:442–455.

Benton, M. J. 1990. Phylogeny of the major tetrapod groups: Morphological data and divergence dates. *Journal of Molecular Evolution* 30:409–424.

Bishop, M. J., and A. E. Friday. 1988. Estimating the interrelationships of tetrapod groups on the basis of molecular sequence data. In *The Phylogeny and Classification of the Tetrapods, Vol. 1: Amphibians, Reptiles, Birds*, ed. (M. J. Benton, Ed.), Systematics Association Special Volume No. 35A, pp. 33–58. Oxford, U.K.: Clarendon Press.

Bjerring, H. C. 1973. Relationships of coelacanthiforms. In *Interrelationships of Fishes*, ed.. Greenwood, R. S. Miles and C. Patterson, pp. 179–205. London: Linnean Society.

Campbell, K. S. W., and Barwick, R. E. 1986. Paleozoic lungfishes. A review. *Journal of Morphology Supplement* 1:93–131.

Campbell, K. S. W., and Barwick, R. E. 1988. Geological and palaeontological information and phylogenetic hypotheses. *Geological Magazine* 1:93–131.

Cairns, S. S., and D. F. Bogenhagen. 1986. Mapping of the displacement loop within the nucleotide sequence of *Xenopus laevis* mitochondrial DNA. *The Journal of Biological Chemistry* 261:8481–8487.

Czelusniak, J., M. Goodman, D. Hewett-Emmett, M. L. Weiss, P. J. Venta and E. Tashian. 1982. Phylogenetic origins and adaptive evolution of avian and mammalian haemoglobin genes. *Nature* 298:297–300.

Dunon-Bluteau, D., M. Volovitch and G. Brun. 1985. Nucleotide sequence of a *Xenopus laevis* mitochondrial DNA fragment containing the D-loop, flanking tRNA genes and the apocytochrome b gene. *Gene* 36:65–78.

Forey, P. 1986. Relationships of lungfishes. *Journal of Morphology Supplement* 1:75–91.

Forey, P. 1990. The coelacanth fish: Progress and prospects. *Science Progress* 74:53–67.

Fritzsch, B. 1987. Inner ear of the coelacanth fish *Latimeria* has tetrapod affinities. *Nature* 327:153–154.

Gardiner, B. 1980. Tetrapod ancestry: A reappraisal. In *The Terrestrial Environment and the Origin of Land Vertebrates*, ed. A. L. Panchen, Systematics Association Special Volume No. 15, pp. 177–185. London: Academic Press.

Goodman, M., W. Moore and G. Matsuda. 1975. Darwinian evolution in the genealogy of haemoglobin. *Nature* 253:603–608.

Goodman, M., M. L. Weiss and J. Czelusniak. 1982a. Molecular evolution above the species level: Branching pattern, rates, and mechanisms. *Systematic Zoology* 31:376–399.

Goodman, M., M. M. Miyamoto and J. Czelusniak. 1987. Pattern and process in vertebrate phylogeny revealed by coevolution of molecules and morphologies. In *Molecules and Morphology in Evolution: Conflict or Compromise?* ed. C. Patterson, pp. 141–176. Cambridge, U.K.: Cambridge University Press.

Gorr, T., T. Kleinschmidt and H. Fricke. 1991a. Close tetrapod relationships of the coelacanth *Latimeria* indicated by haemoglobin sequences. *Nature* 351:394–397.

Gorr, T., T. Kleinschmidt, J. Sgouros and L. Kasang. 1991b. A "living fossil" sequence: Primary structure of the coelacanth *(Latimeria chalumnae)* hemoglobin—evolutionary and functional aspects. *Biological Chemistry Hoppe-Seyler* 372:599–612.

Hewett-Emmett, D., P. J. Vent and R. E. Tashian. 1982. Features of gene structure, organization, and expression that are providing unique insights into molecular evolution and systematics. In *Macromolecular Sequences in Systematic and Evolutionary Biology,* ed. M. Goodman, pp. 357–405. New York: Plenum Press.

Hillis, D. M., and M. R. Dixon. 1989. Vertebrate phylogeny: Evidence from 28S ribosomal DNA sequences. In *The Hierarchy of Life–Molecules and Morphology in Phylogenetic Analysis* (Proceedings from Nobel Symposium 70 held at Alfred Nobel's Björkborn, Karlskoga, Sweden, August 29–September 2, 1988), pp. 355–367. Amsterdam: Exerpta Medica.

Hillis, D. M., M. T. Dixon and L. K. Ammerman. 1991. The relationships of the coelacanth *Latimeria chalumnae*: Evidence from sequences of vertebrate 28S ribosomal RNA genes. *Environmental Biology of Fishes* 32:119–130.

Horimoto, K., H. Suzuki and J. Otsuka. 1990. Discrimination between adaptive and neutral amino acid substitutions in vertebrate hemoglobins. *Journal of Molecular Evolution* 31:302–324.

Johansen, S., P. H. Guddal and T. Johansen. 1990. Organization of the mitochondrial genome of Atlantic cod *Gadus morhua*. *Nucleic Acids Research* 18:411–419.

Lagios, M. D. 1982. *Latimeria* and the chondrichthyes as sister taxa: A rebuttal to recent attempts at refutation. *Copeia* 1982(4): 942–948.

Løvtrup, S. 1977. *The Phylogeny of Vertebrata.* London: Wiley & Sons.

Maeda, N., D. Zhu and W. M. Fitch. 1984. Amino acid sequences of lower vertebrate parvalbumins and their evolution: Parvalbumins of Boa, Turtle, and Salamander. *Molecular Biology and Evolution* 1:473–488.

Meyer, A., and A. C. Wilson. 1990. Origin of tetrapods inferred from their mitochondrial DNA affiliation to lungfish. *Journal of Molecular Evolution* 31:359–364.

Meyer, A., and A. C. Wilson. 1991. Coelacanth's relationships. *Nature* 353:219.

Miles, R. S. 1977. Dipnoan (lungfish) skulls and the relationships of the group: A study based on new species from the Devonian of Australia. *Zoological Journal of the Linnean Society* 61:1–328.

Mindell, D. P., and R. L. Honeycutt. 1990. Ribosomal RNA in vertebrates: Evolution and phylogenetic applications. *Annual Review of Ecology and Systematics* 21: 541–566.

Panchen, A. L., and T. R. Smithson. 1987. Character diagnosis, fossils and the origin of tetrapods. *Biological Reviews of the Cambridge Philosophical Society* 62:341–438.

Robineau, D. 1987. Sur la signification phylogénétique de quelques caractères anatomiques remarquables du Coelacanthe *Latimeria chalumnae* Smith, 1939. *Annales des Sciences Naturelles, Zoologie,* Paris 8:43–60.

Rosen, D. E., P. L. Forey, B. G. Gardiner, and C. Patterson. 1981. Lungfishes, tetrapods paleontology, and plesiomorphy. *Bulletin of the American Museum of Natural History* 167: 159–276.

Saitou, N., and M. Nei. 1986. The number of nucleotides required to determine the branching order or three species, with special reference to the human-chimpanzee-gorilla divergence. *Journal of Molecular Evolution* 24:189–204.

Schultze, H.-P. 1986. Dipnoans as sarcopterygians. *Journal of Morphology Supplement* 1:39–74.

Shapiro, S. 1991. Uniformity in the nonsynonymous substitution rates of embryonic beta-globin genes of several vertebrate species. *Journal of Molecular Evolution* 32:122–127.

Stock, D. W., D. L. Swofford, P. M. Sharp, A. T. Lloyd and D. G. Higgins. 1991. Coelacanth's relationships. *Nature* 353:217–219.

von Wahlert, G. 1968. *Latimeria und die Geschichte der Wirbeltiere: Eine Evolutionsbiologische Untersuchung.* Fischer Verlag: Stuttgart.

Waehneldt, T. V., and J. Malotka. 1989. Presence of proteolipid protein in coelacanth brain myelin demonstrates tetrapod affinities and questions a chondrichthyan association. *Journal of Neurochemistry* 52:1941–1943.

Waehneldt, T. V., J. Malotka, G. Jeserich, and J.-M Matthieu. 1991. Central nervous system myelin proteins of the coelacanth *Latimeria chalumnae*: Phylogenetic implications. *Environmental Biology of Fishes* 32:131–143.

Wiley, E. O. 1979. Ventral gill arch muscles and the interrelationships of gnathostomes, with a new classification of the Vertebrata. *Zoological Journal of the Linnean Society* 67:149–179.

Part III
Genetics and Evolution

It was not until 1900 that Mendel's laws of inheritance were rediscovered, but since that time genetics and evolution have been intimately associated. One of the fundamental questions about Darwin's theory is whether natural selection is sufficient to account for all evolution, or whether additional forces are needed to explain major evolutionary transitions. New discoveries in genetics, from macromutations to transposons, have been suggested as important forces that would permit transitions prohibited by natural selection alone. Modern studies in this area, including the one discussed by Koehn and Hilbish, look in detail at the genetic basis of adaptation by considering simultaneously genetics, physiology, and ecology. F. Gould has a similar theme but a more practical message—namely, that there is abundant genetic variation in species that are potential crop pests and that those species can respond quickly to shifts in cultivation methods. Thomson's essay calls attention to the more general problem faced by evolutionary biologists trying to make sense of genetics: Abundant genetic variation seems to permit a continuous series of changes, as envisioned by Darwin and Fisher, yet we do not find a smooth series of intermediate forms in nature.

Mutation has always been an important part of evolutionary genetics and one that has been difficult to characterize. Mutations are infrequent and unpredictable, yet they provide the only source for novel genetic variants. Part of the foundation of modern evolutionary theory is that mutations are random, meaning that they do not arise to fill a particular environmental need. This is the view supported by the classic experiments of Luria and Delbrück and of Lederberg in the 1940s and 1950s; but this view has been challenged recently by some experiments with bacteria that suggest the possibility of directed mutation. McPhee reviews this controversial topic, and Drake, Glickman, and Ripley describe what is known about the mechanistic basis of mutation.

The chapter by Hankin is somewhat different from the others in this section because it focuses on how morphological changes, particularly those associated with miniaturization, are achieved by changes in the development of an organism from an embryo to an adult. The subjects of developmental and evolutionary biology have grown close in recent years because specialists in both areas realize it is not possible to understand evolutionary transitions without also understanding the changes in developmental processes that underlie them.

The Adaptive Importance of Genetic Variation

Richard K. Koehn
Thomas J. Hilbish

Differences in appearance among individuals abound in nature. Walking down the streets of any major city like New York or Hong Kong would dramatically illustrate this point in the case of our own species, but this diversity of phenotypes—of genetically determined traits as they are manifested in the environment—is not restricted to humans. For biologists, it is impossible to compare individuals of any species without appreciating that nearly all sexually reproducing organisms are reservoirs of genetic and phenotypic variations.

For more than a century, evolutionists have sought to explain the origin, genetic basis, adaptive importance, and evolutionary role of the variations among the individuals of a species—in short, to understand genetic and phenotypic variations within the Darwinian paradigm of natural selection and adaptive evolution. The forces which create, maintain, or obliterate genetic variations within and among natural populations, as well as the importance of these variations in speciation, have always been subjects of active debate among evolutionary biologists.

The genetic basis for specific features that are polymorphic—that vary among individuals of a population—is usually impossible to determine with precision. Some features, such as eye color or blood type, are exceptions to this, each having a reasonably simple genetic basis. Nevertheless, the ecological circumstances that might favor or disfavor different genotypes for these single-gene polymorphisms are not obvious, and when we consider genetically more complex features, such as growth rate or metabolic rate, we are virtually ignorant of their genetic bases and of how each characteristic has come to be shaped by evolution.

There are some exceptions to this situation. Where individuals phenotypically differ in discrete ways, we

A multidisciplinary research effort provides one of the few mechanistic demonstrations of the importance of genetic variation

often have a reasonably complete understanding of the genetic basis of the polymorphism, and sometimes of how certain ecological circumstances lead to an evolutionary replacement of one genotype by another or, alternatively, to the maintenance of the variation as a stable, balanced polymorphism. It is, for example, impossible to imagine a course in introductory biology that does not include a description of industrial melanism in the moth *Biston betularia*—that is, a description of how the industrial revolution in Britain produced ecological circumstances that favored the increase by natural selection of a melanic (darker-colored) mutant. Although the melanic genotype had existed in *Biston* at low frequency for many years, collections spanning more than fifty years recorded its rise in frequency. This resulted from the enhanced protection enjoyed by the darker-colored moths against bird predation as pollution darkened the surfaces on which the moths rested during the day. In other words, when the environment changed, natural selection began to favor the more melanic genotype over the nonmelanic genotypes, which were preyed upon at a greater relative intensity. This has become a classic case study of the evolutionary process, particularly the action of natural selection, so much so that the preceding account was taken with only minor changes from a seventh-grade text on general science.

Unfortunately, of all the phenotypic variation in nature, the case of industrial melanism in *Biston* is not only a classic example, but one of the few examples where we understand the adaptive significance of a genetic polymorphism. When one considers the many polymorphisms that have been studied, the extent of our knowledge is very small compared to the vast array of phenotypic variation that we see in nature. There are many reasons for this, not the least of which is that relatively few examples of discrete and conspicuous variations in natural populations are known for which the genetic basis can be established with certainty. Yet, even when this is possible, it has been frustratingly difficult to identify the specific aspects of the environment that may be acting as a source of natural selection and that lead to the establishment of a balanced polymorphism.

A promising development occurred during the 1960s and 1970s when electrophoresis came into widespread use for the separation and detection of molecules

Richard Koehn is Dean of Biological Sciences and Director of the Center for Biotechnology at the State University of New York, Stony Brook, where he has been Professor of Ecology and Evolution since 1970. He attended Arizona State University (Ph.D. 1967) and has held appointments at the University of Kansas and the Institute of Genetics and Ecology, Aarhus University, Denmark. Thomas J. Hilbish is Assistant Professor of Biology at the University of South Carolina, Columbia. He received his Ph.D. from the State University of New York, Stony Brook, in 1984. The work reported here, representing more than 15 years of research, was supported by both the NSF and the USPHS. Address for Professor Koehn: Department of Ecology and Evolution, State University of New York, Stony Brook, NY 11794.

of differing physical characteristics. Electrophoretic surveys of animal and plant populations demonstrated a large number of molecular polymorphisms, primarily of enzymes. This discovery has created much interest among evolutionary biologists and excited optimism that we might gain from it a general understanding of the adaptive importance of genetic variation in natural populations. First, molecular polymorphisms occur as discrete phenotypes and the genetic basis for such variation can be easily established. Second, enzymes have known metabolic functions and measurable catalytic properties, and this makes it possible to erect specific hypotheses to test the phenotypic consequences, such as the metabolic or physiological effects, of catalytic variations. Such hypotheses might refer to the effect of specific environmental variables on the differential performance of enzyme variants, or to the different physiological or metabolic phenotypes that might result from enzymes with different catalytic properties, or ultimately to how these differences translate into genetic differences in such measures of evolutionary fitness as reproduction, survivorship, or longevity.

Despite the many advantages that molecular polymorphisms lend to the study of adaptation, there is no general agreement about their importance to adaptation and evolution (Lewontin 1974; Kimura 1982, 1983). On the one hand, mathematical studies of molecular polymorphisms lead to the conclusion that many of them have no evolutionary importance. That is, the number of molecular forms, and their relative frequencies in populations, correspond closely to mathematical expectations of neutral models, which do not incorporate forms of natural selection that produce polymorphism (reviewed by Kimura 1982). On the other hand, the catalytic properties of genetically varied forms of an enzyme are often different and produce different effects on metabolic performance that often seem to adapt individuals to varying ecological conditions (reviewed by Koehn et al 1983). These diametrically opposed explanations for molecular polymorphism—one that excludes a role for natural selection, the other that argues for its importance—have formed the basis for the neutralist-selectionist debate that dominated evolutionary biology during the 1970s and that has by no means been satisfactorily resolved.

The development of neutral models has proceeded at a much more rapid pace than the collection of experimental data on the biochemical and physiological consequences of enzyme polymorphism. The lag between theory and data is neither surprising nor unique to biology. More important, the experimental techniques that have been brought to bear on this problem are alien to most evolutionary biologists; yet biochemical and physiological information is critical to a resolution of this issue, a point that can be illustrated by considering a protein polymorphism that we do understand now as a result of multidisciplinary research.

The polymorphism that causes sickle-cell anemia in humans is the counterpart of industrial melanism in moths in that it is one of the few examples of molecular polymorphism that has a known evolutionary consequence. The sickle-hemoglobin polymorphism, which has stood as a paradigm for the belief that protein polymorphisms in general can have great adaptive import, has a simple genetic basis: one gene having two important alleles, the normal allele and the alternative

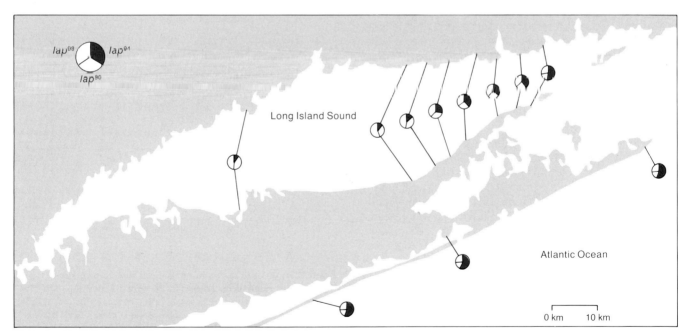

Figure 1. The frequency of the *lap*[94] allele among populations of the common mussel *Mytilus edulis* is much higher in open ocean than in estuaries, such as Long Island Sound. These differences in frequency are related to the higher levels of salinity in open ocean, a relationship borne out by the fact that the product of the *lap* locus, aminopeptidase-I, is directly involved in acclimating mussels to changes in environmental salinity (as illustrated in Fig. 2). The sharp decline from a *lap*[94] frequency of 0.55 in the ocean to 0.12 in the sound over a distance of just 30 km indicates that selection against this allele must be very strong in estuarine waters. Indeed, biochemical and physiological studies show that although mussels carrying the *lap*[94] allele become acclimated to changes in salinity much more efficiently than mussels without the allele, this comes at the cost of drawing energy away from other metabolic functions that are critical during periods of physiological stress in the sound. (After Hilbish and Koehn 1985a.)

allele with a protein product that can produce the sickle phenotype. The sickle allele differs by the substitution of a single amino acid in the product of the gene's β-hemoglobin locus. When homozygous (i.e., when identical alleles are paired at a gene locus), the sickle allele leads to early death. When heterozygous with the normal allele, this genotype can have either significantly beneficial or significantly negative effects on its carrier, depending on the presence or absence respectively of the malarial parasite *Plasmodium falciparum* (reviewed by Dickerson and Geis 1983). The sickling of red blood cells interferes with the delivery of oxygen to body tissues

---

It has been frustratingly difficult to identify the specific aspects of the environment that may be acting as a source of natural selection

---

and is therefore typically deleterious to a carrier of the sickle allele in circumstances of low oxygen availability, such as at high altitudes or in strenuous exercise. However, if the red blood cell is infected by *P. falciparum*, sickling tends to kill the parasite, thus ridding the carrier of the debilitating effects of malaria. This balance of effects leads to the selective maintenance of a balanced hemoglobin polymorphism where the parasite is present in the environment.

Why is human sickle hemoglobin essentially the only polymorphism whose adaptive importance is known? The obvious answer is that the sickle trait is a significant public health problem and as such has been the subject of a major research effort aimed at ameliorating its debilitating effects. The less obvious answer is that our understanding of this polymorphism has derived from a multidisciplinary research effort, one that has drawn on many traditional scientific fields, including protein chemistry, x-ray crystallography, cell and respiratory physiology, parasitology, population genetics, and human ecology.

We have taken this lesson from human hemoglobin and applied it over the past 15 years to another and quite different protein polymorphism. Our studies of aminopeptidase-I, an enzyme that is involved in regulating amino acid levels in the marine bivalve mollusk *Mytilus edulis*, demonstrate how a multidisciplinary research strategy—involving enzyme biochemistry, cell biology, physiological ecology, and population genetics—can provide a comprehensive understanding of the adaptive importance of a molecular polymorphism at a gene locus.

The *lap* polymorphism

M. edulis, the common mussel familiar to connoisseurs of Italian food as the principal ingredient in mussels marinara, has been a model species for biochemical, physiological, ecological, and genetic studies of marine invertebrates (Bayne 1976). The species has a circumpolar distribution in the cooler waters of the Northern Hemi-

sphere and is present in abundance in both intertidal and subtidal habitats. Adults are sedentary, affixing themselves to the substrate with proteinaceous threads. Females may each liberate up to 25 million eggs per season and as many as 12 million in a single spawn. Gametes are liberated into the surrounding water, where fertilization takes place and a larval life of 3 to 7 weeks begins. Larvae are passively transported by ocean currents, and this, in combination with the long larval period, endows the species with a strong ability for dispersal.

Studies by Slatkin (1981) confirm that gene flow is extensive among populations of *Mytilus*, which leads us to expect a high degree of genetic similarity among natural populations over vast geographic distances. However, populations of *Mytilus* are often genetically differentiated over relatively small distances, ranging from a few meters to several kilometers, which implies a high degree of differential mortality among genotypes in a species with enormous fecundity (Koehn et al. 1976). Genetically diverse individuals are dispersed over an environmental gradient, and natural selection in combination with gene flow acts to adjust the frequency of specific genotypes to local conditions; thus, we are able to investigate the mechanisms by which specific environmental agents bring about genetic changes in populations.

Aminopeptidase-I is genetically variable in all popu-

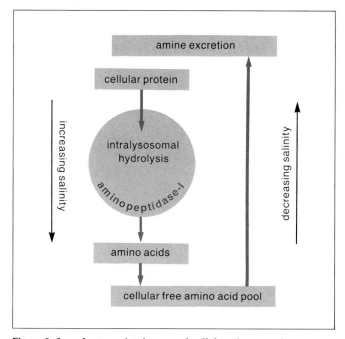

Figure 2. In order to maintain normal cell functions, marine invertebrates respond to changes in the level of environmental salinity with compensating changes in the concentrations of cellular amino acids, which osmotically balance the concentrations of salts in seawater. Aminopeptidase-I plays a critical role in the formation of this pool of amino acids within the cell; cellular proteins are broken down by lysosomes in the cell into polypeptides, which are further degraded by aminopeptidase-I to amino acids at the lysosomal membrane. The rate at which amino acids are formed in the cell—and at which amines are excreted when environmental salinity decreases—is higher in genotypes carrying the *lap*94 allele than in those without it.

lations of *Mytilus* worldwide (Levinton and Koehn 1976). It is the product of the *lap* locus (an acronym derived from an earlier assumption that the enzyme is a "leucine aminopeptidase"). Although a total of five different alleles segregate through electrophoresis at the *lap* locus, two of these are extremely rare in all populations studied so far. The three common alleles have been designated by numbers—*lap*[94], *lap*[96], and *lap*[98]—which reflect their relative electrophoretic mobility. The frequencies with which these three alleles occur vary among major geographic regions throughout the Northern Hemisphere, differing in, say, the Pacific coast of North America and the Baltic Sea (Koehn et al. 1976; Koehn and Gaffney 1984).

Allele frequencies at the *lap* locus also differ considerably between oceanic and estuarine populations in eastern North America. These differences are often greater than those observed between major geographic regions. It is generally observed that the *lap*[94] allele has a lower frequency in estuarine populations than in oceanic populations. For example, as illustrated in Figure 1, the frequency of the *lap*[94] allele progressively declines on both the northern and southern shores of Long Island Sound from 55% in oceanic populations to 12% in the sound (Koehn et al. 1976; Hilbish and Koehn 1985a). In view of the strong dispersal ability of pelagic larvae, this observation strongly violates our expectation of genetic homogeneity among contiguous populations. The fact that this pattern is observed repeatedly in many estuaries suggests that strong forces of natural selection, possibly related to environmental salinity, must be selecting against the *lap*[94] allele in waters of low salinity.

As a problem in adaptation, then, the question is sharply focused: How does aminopeptidase-I function metabolically in the response of *Mytilus* to salinity variations, and how do differences among allelic enzymes lead to selection against *lap*[94] in environments with low salinity? The answers to these questions arise not from population genetics, but from biochemical, metabolic, and physiological investigations.

The function of aminopeptidase-I

Because the salinity of seawater varies as a result of tides, rainfall, freshwater input from rivers, and so forth, marine organisms must possess some mechanism that allows cells to remain isosmotic when the salinity of the environment changes. In *Mytilus*, as in many marine invertebrates, the concentration of salts in seawater is osmotically balanced by an intracellular solute pool of amino acids, and changes in environmental salinity are met with compensating changes in the concentration of intracellular amino acids in order to maintain cell volume (Bishop 1976). As Figure 2 illustrates, when environmental salinity increases, cellular protein enters lysosomes, which are cellular organelles that degrade molecules by lysosomal enzymes; small polypeptides are then fully broken down into free amino acids by aminopeptidase-I and other exopeptidases.

The role of aminopeptidase-I is critical in the production of free amino acids during acclimation to increased salinity. The enzyme is present in all tissues and

intracellular compartments where there is active protein catabolism, such as in the microvillus border of the intestine (Moore et al. 1980); in mussels about 15% of the total aminopeptidase-I activity is associated with the lysosomal membrane.

The biochemical characterization of aminopeptidase-I demonstrates the manner in which it is responsible for the production of free amino acids. The enzyme hydrolyzes the terminal peptide bond of small polypeptides to cleave off a free amino acid (Young et al. 1979). The amino-acid products of this reaction are enzymatically converted by other enzymes to the specific residues

---

The polymorphism that causes sickle-cell anemia in humans is one of the few examples that has a known evolutionary consequence

---

that are important in the regulation of cell volume; in mollusks, these are primarily alanine and glycine. When environmental salinity increases, the increase in cellular concentrations of alanine and glycine in *Mytilus* is rapid, reaching new steady state concentrations in a matter of several hours (Deaton et al. 1984). Conversely, a decrease in environmental salinity leads to a rapid decrease in the volume of the pool of free amino acids, which are ultimately excreted directly or as metabolic waste products such as ammonia. Both the production and excretion of these free amino acids during cell-volume regulation are metabolically complex, but the overall rate at which they occur can be monitored by changes in the pool concentration when salinity is increased or by changes in the rate of amine and ammonia excretion when salinity is decreased.

Environmental salinity has a direct effect on lysosome function in general and on aminopeptidase-I activity in particular. First, in cell-free lysosomes prepared from mussels exposed to different salinities, many lysosomal enzymes differ in their activities. For example, the activity of the enzyme N-acetyl-β-hexosaminidase is greater in cell-free lysosomes isolated from mussels acclimated to high salinity than in those from low salinity (Koehn et al. 1980a). Second, these changes in enzyme activity also produce changes in the concentration of amino acids in lysosomes during the early stages of acclimation to an increase in salinity. The effect of environmental salinity on general lysosome function is paralleled by its specific effect on the total activity of the aminopeptidase-I enzyme (Moore et al. 1980). When mussels are moved from low to high salinity, there is a rapid increase in the activity of aminopeptidase-I that is correlated with blood osmolarity. When mussels are exposed to low salinity, there is a decrease in total enzyme activity to a lower steady state level after approximately nine days.

Field studies are entirely consistent with data from laboratory experiments. Natural populations of *Mytilus* exhibit differences in aminopeptidase-I activity in a way that correlates positively with environmental salinity, and enzyme concentration does not differ (Koehn 1978; Koehn et al. 1980a). Oceanic populations exhibit approximately 50% greater levels of specific enzyme activity (activity per amount of total cellular protein) than estuarine populations.

Biochemistry and physiology of adaptation

We have seen that the genetic composition of the *lap* locus in natural populations is a function of environmental salinity, with the *lap*[94] allele observed to predominate in high-salinity populations. We have also seen that the expression of this gene (that is, total level of aminopeptidase-I activity) is directly affected by environmental salinity and is intimately associated with the metabolic mechanism of cell-volume regulation. Given these obser-

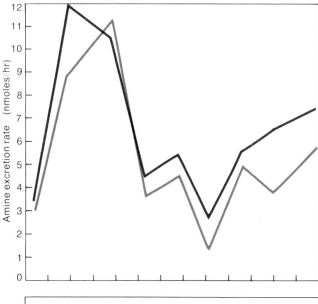

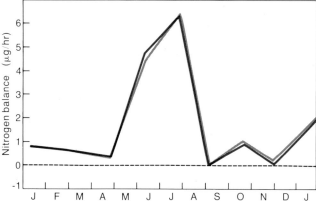

Figure 3. Nitrogen metabolism in *Mytilus* varies throughout the year, as is indicated by these amine excretion rates measured in a population in Long Island Sound during 1982 (*top panel*). The rate is significantly higher for *lap*[94] genotypes (*color*) than for mussels without this allele (*gray*), particularly during the fall months. This is a time of general physiological stress on all mussels and is therefore a time when the nitrogen balance (*lower panel*), especially for the *lap*[94] genotypes, approaches zero—when nearly all available nitrogen is exhausted in maintaining metabolic functioning. The *lap*[94] genotypes suffer higher rates of mortality during these months. (After Hilbish and Koehn 1985a.)

vations, we can now ask the question of principal interest to evolutionary genetics: How do the different aminopeptidase-I alleles function in the regulation of cell volume, and how are these differences important in the adaptation of individual mussels to varying environmental salinities? If allelic enzymes differ in enzyme activity, we would expect the more active allele to be most frequent in high-salinity environments.

In order to answer this question—to establish unequivocally the adaptive importance of allozymes (allelic enzymes of a single gene) in an enzyme polymorphism—it is necessary to demonstrate, first, that differences exist among the allelic enzymes of individual genotypes in some measure of catalytic function; second, that the catalytic differences among allozymes have physiological effects; third, that some characteristic of the natural environment has a direct effect on some measure of gene expression (e.g., the effect of salinity on aminopeptidase-I activity); and last, that biochemical and physiological differences among genotypes have an evolutionary consequence, ultimately manifested as differences in some measure of fitness, such as viability or fertility (Koehn 1978).

In addressing the first of these points, the biochemical basis of adaptation, we have investigated the dependence of aminopeptidase-I activity on genotype at the *lap* locus in natural populations. There are differences in the total levels of aminopeptidase-I activity not only among natural populations, but among *lap* genotypes themselves. In samples from natural populations, genotypes with the *lap*[94] allele exhibit significantly higher specific activities than do other genotypes (Koehn and Immermann 1981). This is true irrespective of total enzyme activity.

Differences in enzyme activity could be due to the kinetic properties (the rates of chemical reactions) of the different allozymes or to differences in enzyme concentrations. Since the concentrations of aminopeptidase-I were found not to differ among genotypes assayed by immunological methods, a detailed study of the enzyme kinetics of the separate allozymes was undertaken. The six genotypes (the six possible pairings of the three common *lap* alleles) do not differ in a number of catalytic properties but do differ in catalytic efficiency, which is the activity per enzyme molecule (Koehn and Siebenaller 1981); the catalytic efficiency of genotypes with *lap*[94] is about 20% greater than of genotypes that lack this allele. This is true irrespective of environmental salinity and the total amount of enzyme activity. These results, then, demonstrate significant differences in the rate at which different aminopeptidase-I genotypes might contribute to the increase in the concentration of cellular free amino acids during acclimation to higher salinity levels.

The next step is to determine the physiological basis of the adaptation of mussels to changes in salinity. The direct involvement of aminopeptidase-I in the production of free amino acids during acclimation to high salinity was tested by monitoring the change in the concentration of free amino acids in mussels following their transfer from low to high salinity (Hilbish et al. 1982; Deaton et al. 1984). The total concentration of amino acids in digestive gland tissue increases rapidly during acclimation to high salinity, and the rate of increase is greatest in those individuals with the lap^{94} allele, as predicted from the greater catalytic efficiency of this allele. After 48 hours at high salinity, the difference in the concentration of amino acids approaches statistical significance, and after 70 hours those genotypes with lap^{94} have a 24% net increase in amino-acid concentration.

The higher rate of increase in the concentration of free amino acids by lap^{94} allelozymes can also be demonstrated by a different experimental approach. Following 70 hours of acclimation to high salinity, the mussels were returned to low salinity. As indicated in Figure 2, differences in the concentrations of free amino acids between lap^{94} and other genotypes should be evident as different rates of amine excretion. This was indeed observed; upon return to low salinity the excretion rate of primary amines by lap^{94} genotypes significantly exceeds that of other genotypes (Hilbish et al. 1982; Deaton et al. 1984). Rates of ammonia excretion follow the same pattern. Both experimental designs unequivocally demonstrate that the different catalytic properties of the lap allelic enzymes, established in vitro, have predictable and measurable physiological consequences under laboratory conditions.

The differences in excretion rate detected in the laboratory were also observed in natural populations by monitoring changes in the energy status of individual mussels. The energy status of mussels can be characterized by determining the calories available from natural feeding rates relative to the calories necessary for metabolic maintenance, such as when growth is neither negative nor positive. When available food energy exceeds the maintenance requirement, individuals have a positive energy balance, with energy then available for growth or other activities that require energy. When the energy balance is negative, the maintenance requirement must be met from stored reserves, such as glycogen and protein; if a negative energy balance persists, the mussel will die eventually. Energy status can also be determined for specific elements, such as carbon and nitrogen, by determining their relative availability in comparison to metabolic need; thus, it is possible for a mussel to have a positive carbon balance, for example, and at the same time have a negative nitrogen balance, in which case death will occur when nitrogen reserves are exhausted.

We studied the energy status in a population at the midpoint of the allele-frequency cline at the entrance to Long Island Sound, where selection against the lap^{94} allele is very intense (Hilbish and Koehn 1985a). Although the overall rates of nitrogen excretion vary greatly throughout the year, individual mussels carrying the lap^{94} allele generally exhibit higher levels of amine excretion than other genotypes, a difference that is most pronounced between September and December (Fig. 3). The fall months represent a period of energetic and nutrient stress to all individual mussels in these natural populations, but particularly so for those mussels carrying the lap^{94} allele, which suffer the greatest net loss of nitrogen nutrients. As in the laboratory, rates of ammonia excretion depend on genotype. Other aspects of nitrogen metabolism, such as the rates of nitrogen acquisition, do not differ among genotypes. This period

of energetic stress corresponds to the time during which natural selection is most intense in Long Island Sound. Indeed, energetic stress and natural selection are one and the same in this case.

The structure of natural selection

The graded frequency of lap^{94} among populations of *Mytilus* in Long Island Sound, which is correlated with environmental salinity, is not stable, but is spatially and temporally dynamic. On an annual basis, mussel larvae emigrate into the sound from oceanic populations, as is indicated by the observation that juvenile mussels typically have the high frequencies of lap^{94} characteristic of oceanic populations (Koehn et al. 1980b; Hilbish 1985). However, the fact that resident populations of adults exhibit significantly lower allele frequencies than these immigrants indicates that frequencies among adults are determined by genotype-dependent mortality—that is, by selection against the lap^{94} allele (Koehn et al. 1980a).

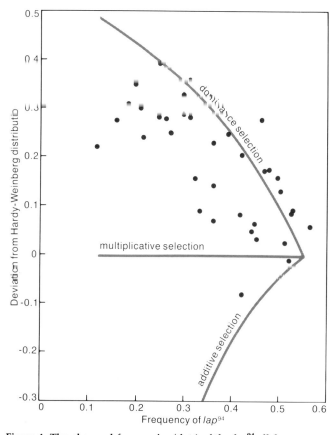

Figure 4. The observed frequencies (*dots*) of the lap^{94} allele among winter populations of *Mytilus* in Long Island Sound are compared to various mathematical models of selection against this allele (*lines*). Selection against lap^{94} is intense during the fall months, reducing its frequency from 0.55 among ocean populations to as low as 0.12 in the sound (see Fig. 1), and is expressed here in terms of deviations from a Hardy-Weinberg distribution of genotypes (which is the distribution expected in the absence of selection). The deviations are expressed as $(e - o)/e$, where e and o are, respectively, expected and observed frequencies of lap^{94} heterozygotes. The dominance selection model, which assumes that the lap^{94} allele is always genetically dominant, most closely predicts the observed pattern of lap^{94} frequencies. (After Hilbish and Koehn 1985b.)

Following settlement, immigrant mussels grow rapidly. Food is abundant during this period, and there are no significant differences among genotypes in their physiological condition, as measured by an index that compares dry tissue weight to shell length (Koehn et al. 1980a). However, during the period of physiological stress in October, all individuals decline in physiological condition, but the decline is greatest for animals with the lap^{94} allele—this is true if the lap^{94} allele is either heterozygous or homozygous. Furthermore, the rates of mortality are higher for individuals with the lap^{94} allele, indicating that selection against this allele results from a relatively lower net energy or nutrient balance of these individuals (Koehn et al. 1980b; Hilbish 1985).

It is impossible to imagine a course in introductory biology that does not include a description of industrial melanism in the moth Biston betularia

Natural selection can occur according to any of several specific models, and it is important to examine these models in order to deduce which, if any, can adequately explain the pattern of selective decrease in the frequency of lap^{94} observed in the annual cycle of immigration and selection in nature. In one model, for example, heterozygotes might exhibit higher mean fitness, leading to a stable genetic polymorphism, such as in human sickle hemoglobin; but this is not the case for selection at the lap locus in *Mytilus*. Other fitness models are possible: an additive model of selection against lap^{94}, in which the fitness of genotypes without lap^{94} is taken as unity, and the relative fitness of lap^{94} heterozygotes might be lower by a factor of s and that of the $lap^{94/94}$ homozygote by $2s$; multiplicative differences, whereby, for example, the $lap^{94/94}$ fitness is reduced by $(1-s)^2$; or dominance, whereby all genotypes heterozygous and homozygous for the lap^{94} allele are equally reduced in fitness (by s) relative to genotypes without this allele (because the lap^{94} allele would always be genetically dominant).

Phenotypically, the dominance model seems to prevail. The lap^{94} allele exhibits dominance over the lap^{96} and lap^{98} alleles in all biochemical and physiological phenotypes, ranging from in vitro measures of catalysis to nitrogen budgets in natural populations. That is, genotypes heterozygous of lap^{94} exhibit nearly identical phenotypes as the lap^{94} homozygote. Since natural selection operates on phenotypes rather than the genotype, natural selection should consist of an array of selection coefficients (values of s) for the various genotypes that reflect a high degree of dominance by lap^{94}.

We simulated the effects of various selection models on immigrant mussel populations, employing a range of selection coefficients within each of the additive, multiplicative, and dominance fitness models (Hilbish and Koehn 1985b). These simulations compared the frequency of lap^{94} after selection to deviations from a Hardy-Weinberg distribution—the distribution expected if no selection operated to shape it. As Figure 4 shows, the additive and multiplicative fitness models each yielded deviations from Hardy-Weinberg distributions that were clearly inconsistent with values observed in natural populations, whereas the dominance model produced the expected relationship. Thus, selection seems to act with equal stringency against both lap^{94} homozygotes and heterozygotes. This is the only form of selection that could be consistent with the biochemical and physiological phenotype of the genotypes at this locus.

The aminopeptidase-I polymorphism in *Mytilus* is now one of only a few cases of molecular polymorphism whose importance in adaptation can be mechanistically described. Genetic variation in the product of this single gene is demonstrably a factor in adaptation, but how much of a factor is a function of the specific environmental conditions. This last point is particularly important. In human sickle hemoglobin, the heterozygote enjoys enhanced relative fitness only in the presence of the malarial parasite; in the absence of this selective agent, the heterozygote is maladaptive. Because of its higher activity, lap^{94} is favored in habitats of high salinity, but in low salinity the lap^{94} allele is strongly selected against, because of the higher rate with which the lap^{94} genotypes expend nitrogen reserves, thereby reducing the energy available to carriers of this allele for other vital functions.

It is easy to imagine environmental situations under which the lap polymorphism might be neutral. For example, any environmental change that sufficiently ameliorated energy stress from September to December, such as an increase in the availability of food, would eliminate the differences in fitness between lap^{94} and other genotypes. Similarly, a decrease in environmental temperature would decrease temperature-dependent metabolic demands and would thereby increase the net energy status of all individuals.

Although still incomplete, results similar to those reported here for aminopeptidase-I in *Mytilus* are beginning to emerge for a variety of enzyme polymorphisms in *Drosophila melanogaster* (Zera et al. 1985), for lactate dehydrogenase in the teleost fish *Fundulus heteroclitus* (Powers et al. 1983), and for glutamate pyruvate transaminase in the copepod *Tigriopus* (Burton and Feldman 1983). As more molecular polymorphisms are investigated with regard to their effects on biochemistry, physiology, and fitness, we are gaining a better understanding of the evolutionary effects of quantitatively small biochemical variations that result from genetic polymorphism.

References

Bayne, B. L. 1976. The biology of mussel larvae. In *Marine Mussels: Their Ecology and Physiology*, ed. B. L. Bayne, pp. 81–120. Cambridge Univ. Press.

Bishop, S. H. 1976. Nitrogen metabolism and excretion: Regulation of intracellular amino acid concentration. In *Estuarine Processes*, ed. M. Wiley, vol. 5, pp. 414–31. Academic.

Burton, R. S., and M. W. Feldman. 1983. Physiological effects of an allozyme polymorphism: Glutamate-pyruvate transaminase and response to hyperosmotic stress in the copepod *Tigriopus californicus*. *Biochem. Genet.* 21:239–51.

Deaton, L. E., T. J. Hilbish, and R. K. Koehn. 1984. Protein as a source of amino nitrogen during hyperosmotic volume regulation in the mussel *Mytilus edulis*. *Physiol. Zool.* 57:609–19.

Dickerson, R. E., and I. Geis. 1983. *Hemoglobin: Structure, Function, Evolution, and Pathology*. Benjamin-Cummings.

Hilbish, T. J. 1985. Demographic and temporal structure of an allele frequency cline in the mussel *Mytilus edulis*. *Mar. Biol.* 86:163–71.

Hilbish, T. J., L. E. Deaton, and R. K. Koehn. 1982. Effect of an allozyme polymorphism on regulation of cell volume. *Nature* 298:688–89.

Hilbish, T. J., and R. K. Koehn. 1985a. The physiological basis of natural selection at the *Lap* locus. *Evolution* 39:1302–17.

———. 1985b. Dominance in physiological phenotypes and fitness at an enzyme locus. *Science* 229:52–54.

Kimura, M., ed. 1982. *Molecular Evolution, Protein Polymorphism, and the Neutral Theory*. Springer-Verlag.

———. 1983. The neutral theory of molecular evolution. In *Evolution of Genes and Proteins*, ed. M. Nei and R. K. Koehn, pp. 208–33. Sinauer.

Koehn, R. K. 1978. Physiology and biochemistry of enzyme variation: The interface of ecology and population genetics. In *Ecological Genetics: The Interface*, ed. P. F. Brussard, pp. 51–72. Springer-Verlag.

Koehn, R. K., B. L. Bayne, M. N. Moore, and J. F. Siebenaller. 1980a. Salinity related physiological and genetic differences between populations of *Mytilus edulis*. *Biol J. Linn. Soc.* 14:319–34.

Koehn, R. K., and P. M. Gaffney. 1984. Genetic heterozygosity and growth rate in *Mytilus edulis*. *Mar. Biol.* 82:1–7.

Koehn, R. K., and F. W. Immermann. 1981. Biochemical studies of aminopeptidase polymorphism in *Mytilus edulis*. I. Dependence of enzyme activity on season, tissue, and genotype. *Biochem. Genet.* 19:1115–42.

Koehn, R. K., R. Milkman, and J. B. Mitton. 1976. Population genetics of marine pelecypods. IV. Selection, migration, and genetic differentiation in the Blue Mussel *mytilus edulis*. *Evolution* 30:2–32.

Koehn, R. K., R. I. E. Newell, and F. W. Immermann. 1980b. Maintenance of an aminopeptidase allele frequency cline by natural selection. *PNAS* 77:5385–89.

Koehn, R. K., and J. F. Siebenaller. 1981. Biochemical studies of aminopeptidase polymorphism in *Mytilus edulis*. II. Dependence of reaction rate on physical factors and enzyme concentration. *Biochem. Genet.* 19:1143–62.

Koehn, R. K., A. J. Zera, and J. G. Hall. 1983. Enzyme polymorphism and natural selection. In *Evolution of Genes and Proteins*, ed. M. Nei and R. K. Koehn, pp. 115–36. Sinauer.

Levinton, J. S., and R. K. Koehn. 1976. Population genetics of mussels. In *Marine Mussels: Their Ecology and Physiology*, ed. B. L. Bayne, pp. 357–84. Cambridge Univ. Press.

Lewontin, R. C. 1974. *The Genetic Basis of Evolutionary Change*. Columbia Univ. Press.

Moore, M. N., R. K. Koehn, and B. L. Bayne. 1980. Leucine aminopeptidase (aminopeptidase-I), N-acetyl-β-hexosamidase and lysosomes in the mussel, *Mytilus edulis* L., in salinity changes. *J. Exp. Zool.* 214:239–49.

Powers, D. A., L. DiMichele, and A. R. Place. 1983. The use of enzyme kinetics to predict differences in cellular metabolism, developmental rate, and swimming performance between LDH-B genotypes of the fish *Fundulus heteroclitus*. In *Isozymes, Current Topics in Biological and Medical Research*, ed. M. C. Rattazzi et al., vol. 10, pp. 147–70. Alan R. Liss.

Slatkin, M. 1981. Estimating levels of gene flow in natural populations. *Genetics* 99:323–35.

Young, J. P. W., R. K. Koehn, and N. Arnheim. 1979. Biochemical characterization of "Lap," a polymorphic aminopeptidase from the blue mussel *Mytilus edulis*. *Biochem. Genet.* 17:305–25.

Zera, A. J., R. K. Koehn, and J. G. Hall. 1985. Allozymes and biochemical adaptation. In *Comprehensive Insect Physiology, Biochemistry, and Pharmacology*, ed. G. A. Kerkut and L. I. Gilbert, pp. 633–74. Pergamon.

The Evolutionary Potential of Crop Pests

Weeds, plant pathogens and insects are masters at surviving the farmer's assaults. New control strategies must anticipate pests' evolutionary responses

Fred Gould

One would be hard pressed to find a biology graduate who has not heard the story of the peppered moth, *Biston betularia*. In pre-industrial Britain the moths' light, peppered wings blended with the color of the lichen-covered tree bark on which they rested during the day. When industrial pollution killed the lichens and darkened the tree bark, the moths became more conspicuous targets for preying birds. Under intense selection pressure from these predators, moth populations in some polluted areas evolved dark wings and regained their cryptic status within a few decades (Kettlewell 1973).

This story of rapid adaptation is deserving of fame. Yet many equally or more spectacular cases exist in the scientific literature on crop pests and have considerable social relevance. Over the history of agriculture, farmers and plant breeders have applied selection pressure to plants to domesticate them. In doing so, and in attempting to protect their crops, they have forced the simultaneous adaptation of competing plants and of the fungi, bacteria, viruses and insects that feed on crops.

The pattern for the evolutionary battle between farmers and pests was set during the early days of agriculture, when farmers first separated weed seeds from desirable grain and when they selected the healthiest plants from one season as the source of seed for the next, thereby assuring that each generation would produce more of the repel-

lents and toxins needed to fend off pests. In response, weeds evolved seeds that mimicked the crop seeds the farmer saved for the next year's planting; pathogens and insects often developed resistance to toxins or modified their habits to avoid them.

This conflict has escalated sharply since World War II. As modern agriculture attempts to share less and less of the crop yield with pests, the intensity of the selection pressure for pest adaptation increases. New lessons about adaptive response seem to emerge every time a new agricultural technology is applied. The lessons have often been unpleasant ones: Many of the short-term triumphs of pest control have carried within them the seeds of longer-term failure.

During the past 10 to 15 years, evolutionary biologists and agricultural scientists have joined forces in examining patterns in the evolutionary history of crop pests. The question that brings them together is an essential one for the future of agriculture: Are there strategies for protecting the world's food supply from pests that can anticipate and slow down the pests' evolutionary responses?

Although collaboration between the two fields is in its infancy, it has already yielded several promising ideas and much new understanding. For instance, we have begun to understand how resistance develops, or fails to, when insects are challenged by multiple toxins or by a combination of a toxin and other plant defenses. We are investigating how insects adapt to toxins when they are expressed only in certain plant tissues, or only in some plants, or at different times in the season. The genetic basis for the adaptation of some fungi to plant toxins is being explained and may help us develop strategies for coexisting with these genetically flexible pests.

Even if teams of academic scientists

find solutions to the problems of pest adaptation, implementation of these solutions may be difficult. In the economically competitive environment of agriculture, the general orientation is toward short-term profits, whereas the concept of resistance management emphasizes long-term paybacks. In some cases, according to this approach, less is more: The lower the overall selective pressure challenging a pest, the longer the time for the pest to adapt. As a result of this approach, some pests may be left in the field. Even though these low densities of pests do not generally cause significant yield reduction, farmers may not be willing to take even small short-term risks for the promise of long-term stability of yield.

Over the next few decades, agriculture will continue its struggle with the problems of pests and resistance—a struggle that is likely to take some surprising turns as we experiment with the new strategies that genetic engineering offers the farmer. The connections between evolution and agricultural pest management are important both to agriculture's future and to science. Each crop-pest system has a unique mix of ecology and genetics, and experiments that elucidate the evolutionary pathways available in these systems might expand the range of potential solutions to the problems of pest management at a time when new directions are sorely needed. And agricultural systems may turn out to be the perfect testing ground for new evolutionary theories.

Later in this article I shall describe some of the ways in which evolutionary biology is being used to delay pest adaptation to control tactics. But it is important to set these developments against the backdrop of our past experience with pest evolution. The history of the war between farmer and pest teaches us not to underestimate the capacity of any pest species to resist attempts to

Fred Gould received his Ph.D. in ecology and evolutionary biology from the State University of New York at Stony Brook in 1977. He now teaches insect ecology at North Carolina State University and conducts research on the coevolution of plants and their herbivores, pest resistance and ecological aspects of pest management. Address: Department of Entomology, Box 7634, North Carolina State University, Raleigh, NC 27695-7634.

destroy it, whether it be a weed, a pathogen or an insect.

Weeds: Masters of Mimicry

Of all the crop pests, weeds boast the longest recorded history of adapting to agricultural practices. It is a history dotted with examples of one of nature's most interesting adaptive strategies: mimicry.

Within traditional agricultural systems there were two basic ways for weed seeds to survive the interval between cropping seasons. They could remain in the field, where they had to withstand the effects of weather, pathogens, seed feeders, burning and plowing, or they could hide among the crop seed that the farmer carefully stored for the next season's planting.

Success at the latter method requires that the weeds possess a number of important characteristics. They must ripen by harvest time. They must be held tight to their stems so that they do not fall to the ground on the way to threshing. And, finally, they must have a shape and density similar to that of the crop seed, so that they are not discarded during the winnowing operation, which separates crop seeds from anything that the wind blows less or more than the crop seeds. A surprising number of weeds have evolved all the characteristics required to become crop-seed mimics and lead a life of luxury between cropping seasons.

A great deal of morphological change lies within the evolutionary reach of a weed. One striking example comes from the mimicry of lentil seeds, *Lens culinaris*, by the common vetch, *Vicia sativa*. The lentil seed has a gently convex shape and, in fact, was the source of the word *lens*. Normal seeds of the common vetch are much more rounded than lentil seeds (*Figure 2*).

Early in this century botanists began speculating about a variant of the vetch seed that was causing trouble in the fields of central Europe. The variant had seeds that so closely resembled the lentil and looked so little like vetch that its origin was a puzzle. The change in seed shape was of tremendous practical importance: By mimicking the lentil seed the vetch could dominate a field planted for a lentil crop.

The prevailing hypotheses about the origin of the vetch variant ranged from hybridization of the taxonomically distinct vetch and lentil species to the view of V. S. Dmitriev (1952), who felt that the case offered evidence supporting

Figure 1. Winnowing, in which a farmer uses the wind to sift desirable seeds from weed seeds and debris, is one of the oldest of agricultural practices. But farmers' efforts to keep their fields from being overrun by weeds have often been defeated by the ability of some weeds to mimic the seed characteristics of crop plants. Seed mimicry is one of many evolutionary responses that have enabled crop pests—weed, plant pathogens and insects—to resist attempts to destroy them. The pest-control tactics used by modern farmers have increased the pressure on pests, and the pests' often-surprising adaptive responses suggest that agricultural scientists still have much to learn about the evolutionary biology of crop pests. (Reproduced from *The Grain Harvesters* with permission of the American Society of Agricultural Engineers.)

Trofim D. Lysenko's theory of species conversion. Breeding experiments in Wales in the late 1950s finally ended the speculation. By crossing normal vetch and the lentil-like variant, D. G. Rowlands (1959) demonstrated that the major change in seed shape could be attributed to a single recessive mutation. Farmers still occasionally struggle with vetch invasions of their lentil fields, especially in areas where traditional winnowing practices have not been supplanted by mechanized farming.

The Russian literature on species of the weed *Camelina* documents the most thoroughly studied case of mimicry in a weed (Sinskaia and Beztuzheva 1930). A number of *Camelina* subspecies are

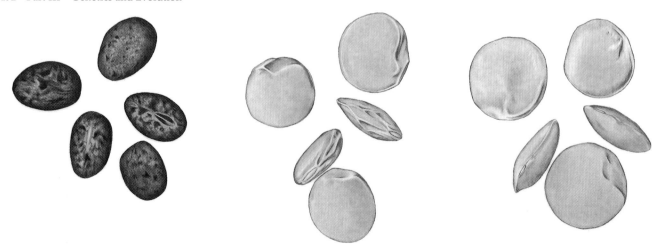

Figure 2. Success at seed mimicry has given the common vetch the ability to contaminate commercial lentil fields. At left is shown the typical seed shape of the common vetch, *Vicia sativa*. In a lentil field near Albion, Washington, a U.S. Department of Agriculture plant pathologist recently found vetch seeds that had a distinctly different shape *(center)* that was quite similar to the flatter shape of the lentil, *Lens culinaris (right)*. Breeding experiments conducted in the 1950s after a long debate over the origin of a vetch variant that had been infesting European lentil fields established that a single recessive mutation could cause the vetch to vary its seed shape to mimic the lentil, allowing it to make it through the winnowing process to the farmer's next planting. The seeds illustrated above were supplied by Richard M. Hannan of the USDA's Regional Plant Introduction Station in Pullman, Washington.

found in flax crops; they appear to have diverged from their nonweedy relatives by developing traits that resemble those of flax *(Figure 3)*. One variety has become so dependent on flax culture that it is found only in flax fields.

In the 1920s two Soviet botanists, E. N. Sinskaia and A. A. Beztuzheva, gathered *Camelina* seeds from a large area of central and eastern Europe and sowed them near Leningrad. They found a great deal of variation in characteristics such as height, branching pattern, seed size and the seeds' propensity for shattering, or dropping from the plant when ripe. Similarly, many varieties of flax were found in the region surveyed.

Sinskaia and Beztuzheva concluded not only that *Camelina* had evolved traits that mimicked flax in general, but also that some characteristics of local weed populations had evolved specifically either to fit into the flax culture of an area or to adapt to local climate, or a compromise between the two. Interestingly, the weedy subspecies had almost uniformly developed a nonshattering trait, matching the general habit of flax, but in certain small areas a shattering subspecies was found. In these areas farmers had planted a rare, primitive oil-flax cultivar that lacked the nonshattering trait.

Vetch and *Camelina* have been adept at getting their seed into the farmer's furrow. But surviving from one season to the next is only half the battle for a weed; the other half is avoiding the woman or man who wields the hoe. The distinction between a crop plant

and a weed is often but not always clear-cut in the field. For example, one of rice's most serious rivals, barnyard grass, is a skillful mimic. Spencer C. H. Barrett, now of the University of Toronto, and his colleagues discovered in weedy forms of barnyard grass so many ricelike traits—such as stem color, midrib size and leaf angle—that they found it harder to tell barnyard grass from rice than to distinguish two variants of barnyard grass from each other *(Figure 4)*. Barrett found only one telltale visual distinction: The rice plants have ligules (projections at the base of the leaf blade), but the weeds do not. This phenotypic trait is apparently not available within the taxonomic lineage of barnyard grass—but then, farmers are unlikely to notice the absence of a ligule in the field (Barrett 1983).

Vetch, *Camelina* and barnyard grass are not closely related to the crops they mimic, and they appear to have acquired their useful traits by mutation. Some weeds, however, are so closely related to crops that hybridization between them is often noted. Wild rices are major weeds of rice in India and Africa, where they have sometimes reduced yields by 50 percent. Their normal resemblance to rice makes hand weeding a difficult chore. Their ability to respond to changes in rice culture, furthermore, has allowed them to resist eradication efforts.

Some Indian plant breeders decided that they could make weeding easier by breeding rice plants with reddish-pur-

ple coloration(Dave 1943). This approach worked well until the wild rice plants also developed reddish-purple color, presumably by exchanging the color-coding gene with cultivated rice through hybridization. According to Keith Moody of the International Rice Research Institute, farmers in Orissa, India, have taken a further step: alternating over time the planting of red and green rice seedlings. Some of the weeds will always make it through this temporally changing selection regime, but theoretically and practically the alternation with intensive weeding limits the population size of the weed. On a recent trip to India, Moody found a farmer planting rice that had a red leaf-collar and a generally green stem. The farmer told Moody that now he could eliminate both the red and green weeds. Moody wonders how much time will pass before red-collared wild rice appears.

In the mechanized farming dominant in the U.S., hand weeding (along with traditional methods of winnowing seed for the next season) may be a thing of the past, but the battle between farmers and weeds goes on. Currently, there is no premium on looking like rice if you are a weed in a California rice field; the chemical herbicides used to control weeds do not discriminate on the basis of appearance. The nature of the game has switched to biochemical mimicry. Agricultural industries spend millions of dollars each year inventing chemical agents that kill weeds without harming crops. They have succeeded marvelously. But this success has put enormous selection pressure on weeds to biochemically mimic crops, so that any agent that kills them will also kill the crop. The first cases of herbicide resistance were reported in the 1960s, and today many weeds appear to be starting on their way toward such a mimetic state. At his last count, Homer LeBaron estimated that there were 84 cases of weeds with resistance to at least one chemical herbicide, and some weeds of wheat in Australia have become resistant to a broad array of herbicides (Green, LeBaron and Moberg 1990).

Genetic engineers have recently succeeded in putting new genes into cotton plants that make them resistant to a previously deadly herbicide (Stalker, McBride and Malyj 1988). If genes for herbicide resistance are engineered into Indian rice, agronomists will not be surprised to find wild rices "borrowing" these engineered genes in the same way they borrowed genes for red plant color.

Pathogens: Moving Targets

Plant-pathogenic fungi and bacteria are old hands at dealing with toxic chemicals. Long before the arrival of human beings, these pathogens and naturally reproducing plants entered a protracted battle for survival that prominently featured chemical weapons. The mortality caused by pathogens in ancient times is thought to have selected for our modern flora, which produce hundreds of microbial toxins and other physiological defenses that thwart the attack of pathogens. Those who enjoy spicy food can be grateful that plants have experimented with a flavorful array of biochemical defenses against pathogens. If the taste of ginger was a gift of Dionysus, it was also a useful tool for the plant's early survival.

Consciously or unconsciously, farmers and plant breeders have entered this biochemical war. Just as the first farmers are thought to have collected seed for the next season from their best-yielding, healthiest plants, modern plant breeders collect superior seed, but in a more organized and precise manner. Sometimes unknowingly, ancient and modern breeders have often selected for plants that produce toxins that defend against specific pathogens, which in turn have adapted to defend themselves against the toxins.

Today, plant breeders know that pathogens are moving targets. When they breed a plant for cold tolerance, they expect that trait to be maintained

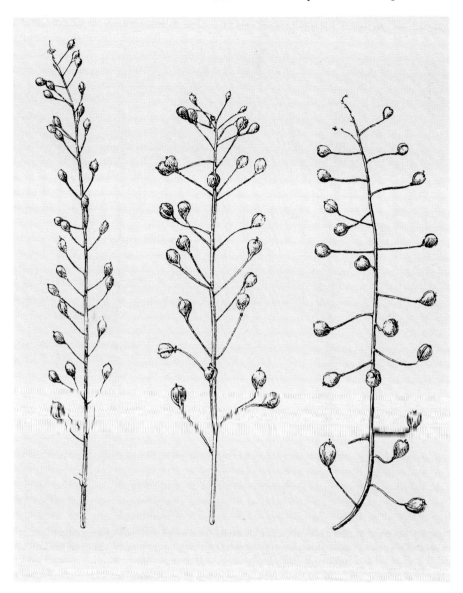

Figure 3. *Camelina*, a weed that is a skillful crop mimic, has adapted to many variations in agricultural practices. Soviet botanists found that *Camelina* had evolved different forms in order to survive in the flax fields of eastern Europe. The plant mimics many characteristics of flax and has been known to adapt to local farming practices, to local flax varieties and to variations in climate. Above are drawings of three forms of *Camelina*. On the left is the wild form of *Camelina sylvestris* subspecies microcarpa, which has small fruits that "shatter"—that is, they drop their seeds when ripe. In the center is a weedy form of this subspecies with larger fruits that hold their seeds when ripe, as do most flax varieties. At right is a rare weedy *Camelina* that has large fruits but has a shattering characteristic similar to that of an old local variety of oil-flax. The botanists found that the characteristics of various *Camelina* forms often matched the characteristics of flax growing in the same area. (From Sinskaia and Beztuzheva 1930.)

in the plant's progeny and assume that their job is done. When, on the other hand, they breed a plant that is resistant to a pathogen, they know that the plant's offspring will be genetically similar, but they can never be sure that the pathogen's response to the resistance trait will not change. Indeed, it would be an enormous job to catalogue all the cases in which a pathogen evolved a means of undoing the work of a plant breeder. It is quite common

for such adaptation to occur in less than three years.

Like weed resistance to herbicides, the resistance of plant-pathogenic fungi to synthetic fungicides is a recent phenomenon, but a significant one. It was first observed in the early 1960s after topically applied fungicides that did not penetrate the plant were replaced with systemic fungicides. Although the resistance to the new compounds was a surprise to plant pathologists at the time,

Figure 4. Survival in a hand-weeded field is easier for a weed that looks like a crop plant. A barnyard-grass seedling is easily mistaken for a cultivated-rice seedling, making barnyard grass (*Echinochloa crus-galli*) a serious nuisance in rice fields. In these renderings of a young rice plant (*Oryza sativa*) and two barnyard-grass seedlings, one can see how a rice-mimicking barnyard-grass plant can look more like a rice plant than like another variety of its own species. Left to right, the plants shown are cultivated rice, the *oryzicola* variety of barnyard grass and another barnyard-grass seedling, *Echinochloa crus-galli* var. *crus-galli*. In his research Spencer C. H. Barrett has found only one major visual distinction between rice and its mimic: the presence of a ligule on the rice.

some retrospective studies show that there was sufficient genetic variation in the original fungal populations to have allowed the rapid adaptation to have been predicted. By 1984 more than 100 species of fungi were known to be resistant to at least one fungicide (Green, LeBaron and Moberg 1990).

Plant pathologists and breeders have been working to devise evolutionary hurdles that will be more difficult for pathogens to jump. The conventional wisdom is that pathogens have more difficulty overcoming pathogen resistance that is based on many genes and, presumably, many diverse resistance factors. Other approaches are also being considered and will be discussed in the last section of this article.

Molecular biologists have begun to throw their expertise into the battle. They have found that by inserting into a plant's genome a gene that causes the plant to produce an excess of a pathogenic virus's coat protein, they can make the plant resistant to the virus (Beachy 1990). The mechanism of this resistance is the subject of continuing investigation, and there is currently no way to predict whether the pathogenic virus will evolve to circumvent the effect of this gene.

Molecular biology has made a very different but important contribution to this war by elucidating details of the biochemical battle between plants and pathogens. Willi Schäfer and his colleagues reported recently in *Science* that they had moved from one species of pathogenic fungus to another a gene that coded for a special detoxifying enzyme (Schäfer et al. 1989). The recipient fungus, which previously could attack corn plants but not peas, became capa-

ble of surviving within pea plants because it could now metabolize a toxin produced by the pea plants. This work proved that the limits of host range in some pathogens may involve as little as a single gene, coding for the right detoxification enzyme. If such a small change could extend a pathogen's range across the great taxonomic divide of the plant world from monocotyledons to dicotyledons, it is no wonder that a fungus's adaptation to a new variant of a crop species is often so rapid.

Insects: Winners in Chemical Warfare
Fungi have adapted to synthetic pesticides with impressive speed, but the real experts at chewing up the synthetic chemical agents of postwar pest control are the insects. Resistance to DDT, detected shortly after its introduction as one of the first so-called modern insecti-

cides, is frequently cited as a textbook case of rapid adaptation. Since the DDT case the insects have, as a group, never met a chemical they couldn't take to the mat. George P. Georghiou has carefully documented more than 500 instances of insect adaptation to insecticides. In some situations insects have adapted to insecticides within a single season, even when the insecticide featured a new chemical twist. And there are now a few severe pests that have adapted to all or almost all pesticides that can legally be used to kill them.

Today most pesticide chemists are modest when predicting the life expectancy of a new type of insecticide. In the late 1960s, however, a different attitude prevailed in some scientific circles. In a 1967 *Scientific American* article, the reknowned insect physiologist Carroll Williams proclaimed that investigators were on the verge of developing "resistance proof" insecticides. His optimism seemed warranted at the time, for the new insecticides he described were mimics of insect juvenile hormones. How could an insect possibly become immune to the effects of its own hormones without wreaking havoc on its developmental and reproductive systems?

Five years after Williams's pronouncement, bits and pieces of information started coming in that demonstrated that insects can indeed adapt to the new hormone mimics, which interrupt the normal pattern of development in susceptible insect strains. The most precise work in this area is the research of Thomas Wilson and his colleagues in Vermont, who worked with natural and induced genetic variation for tolerance of juvenile hormone and its synthetic equivalents in the fruit fly, *Drosophila* (Shemshedini and Wilson 1990). Wilson's group found that a strain exposed to the mutagen EMS (ethyl methane sulfonate) developed 100-fold resistance to juvenile hormone. The resistant strain showed little decrease in fitness when reared on food with or without juvenile hormone. Recent molecular work by Wilson's group has demonstrated that the resistance in *Drosophila* can be traced to a single genetic change, induced by the mutagen, that affects the binding characteristics of one cytosolic juvenile-hormone binding protein.

If a single gene change can neutralize a hormone mimic, can we expect any control tactics to hold their own in the face of evolutionarily flexible pests? Biological control has often been held out

as the solution when new problems arise with pesticide resistance. We would not have these problems, the argument goes, if we used naturally occurring insect pathogens, parasites and predators to control pests. This may be true in some cases, but there is now ample evidence that insect pests can adapt to some of their natural control agents if these agents exert sufficient selection pressure on the pest population.

For example, a colony of cabbage moths maintained at Cambridge, England, for five years contracted a viral disease. Over 90 percent of the population was wiped out, but the colony finally recovered from the disease outbreak. Later studies showed that the colony had become significantly more resistant to the virus than were other moth colonies sampled in that general area of England (David and Gardiner 1960). Additional support comes from experiments in which specific selection regimes have been imposed on insect populations by bringing them into contact with natural control agents in the laboratory, these experiments have generally given rise to insects with elevated resistance to pathogens. There are, however, exceptions where the resistance

level has not changed, even following repeated generations of selection.

A noteworthy case of virus resistance was documented by L. L. J. Ossowski in 1980. Ossowski demonstrated that the wattle bagworm, a caterpillar pest in South Africa, was more tolerant of local strains of a virus than it was of foreign strains of the virus. Ossowski concluded that the caterpillars had developed a defense against only the specific virus strains it had encountered over time. He suggested that the best biological control agents may be those collected far from the area where the pest problem exists.

Today, as genetic engineers attempt to use biological systems to control pest populations, there are still lessons to be learned about the nature of genetic variability. Ten years ago there was a belief among genetic engineers that a stable way to combat caterpillar pests would be to incorporate into crop plants insect-toxin genes derived from the bacterium *Bacillus thuringiensis*, or *B.t.* Since the bacteria and the caterpillars had been in contact for millions of years, it seemed logical that the caterpillars would have already adapted to the toxins if they had the genetic po-

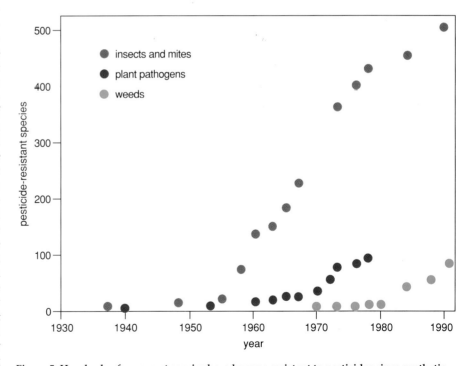

Figure 5. Hundreds of crop-pest species have become resistant to pesticides since synthetic chemicals were first used on a large scale for controlling agricultural pests in the 1940s. Insecticide resistance became a problem first, and today more than 500 insect species are known to be resistant to one or more insecticides. Resistance to pesticides has also developed in plant pathogens, primarily in fungi exposed to systemic fungicides. Genetic resistance to herbicides began to appear among weeds in the 1960s and has been reported in at least 84 species to date. The data are from George P. Georghiou and Homer LeBaron and from Green, LeBaron and Moberg 1990.

tential to do so. What was apparently forgotten in this argument was the fact that in natural environments outbreaks of these bacteria are extremely rare, and so the selection pressure for pest adaptation is low in nature. The caterpillars' genetic "potential" may never have had the occasion to prominently manifest itself. Proving this point are findings that some insect populations have recently developed over 100-fold resistance to these bacterial toxins as a result of unusually heavy reliance on *B.t.* for their control (Shelton and Wyman 1991). The stability of natural biological-control agents may reside not in their being immune to pest adaptation but in their reaching an evolutionary equilibrium with the pest, since both the pest and the biological-control agent can evolve.

If one were to dream of control measures to which insect pests truly could not adapt, food deprivation might be an obvious candidate. Indeed, the age-old practice of crop rotation is based on this approach: The farmer alternates planting of an insect's normal host plant with a plant that it cannot feed on, and the pest dies of starvation. This strategy has proved highly effective over hundreds of years, but insects are never completely static components in such a situation.

J. L. Krysan and his colleagues at Brookings, South Dakota, received calls during the early 1980s that indicated that some farmers who were rotating corn and soybean crops were still expe-riencing problems with the northern corn rootworm. Krysan's team determined that in some areas where corn and soybeans were rotated, the corn rootworm had a genetically altered diapause, or resting stage (Krysan et al. 1986). In large areas of the Midwest where corn is grown every year, almost all of the northern corn rootworms produce eggs that remain in the soil for one winter and then hatch and feed on the young corn roots in spring. In certain areas where farmers rotate corn and other crops that rootworms cannot feed on, about 40 percent of the eggs remain in diapause for a second winter. In this way they are synchronized to feed on the rotated corn crop. Krysan's colleagues in Illinois have recently reported a significant correlation ($p < 0.04$) between the percentage of rotated corn crops within a county and the percentage of rootworms that have an prolongeddiapause (*Figure 6*) (Levine, Oloumi-Sadeghi and Fisher, in press). Fortunately, this adaptation to crop rotation has not caused widespread problems, at least partially because eggs remaining in the soil for a long period of time are subject to mortality from both biotic and abiotic forces.

Evolutionary Biology on the Farm
Looked at from the farmer's viewpoint, the history of pest control is the saga of a long struggle to stay a step ahead of pest adaptation. Some of the techniques used to combat pests have proved rela-tively resistance-proof, but the successes have been limited. The results of society's recent experiment with synthetic chemical pesticides have been particularly disappointing.

Agricultural scientists now recognize that they need to maintain an arsenal of pest-control tools in anticipation of pests' evolutionary responses. That arsenal contains some potentially powerful weapons, among them the novel approaches offered by biotechnology and the promise of new developments in pesticide chemistry. But with or without the new weapons (whose use may be limited by economic, technological or social considerations and the high regulatory costs associated with their development), advances in managing pest resistance depend on improving our ability to predict the evolutionary future of pests.

Much of the discussion of resistance management over the past 10 to 15 years has centered on ways to reduce the rate at which pests adapt to conventional pesticides—a theme that dominated a major 1984 meeting on the management of pesticide resistance sponsored by the National Academy of Sciences (National Research Council 1984). Yet pests adapt not only to pesticides but also to other agricultural pressures, and they interact with other parts of their environment in important ways. The most interesting solutions may lie not only in more careful pesticide use but also in alternative strategies, such as manipulating plant-

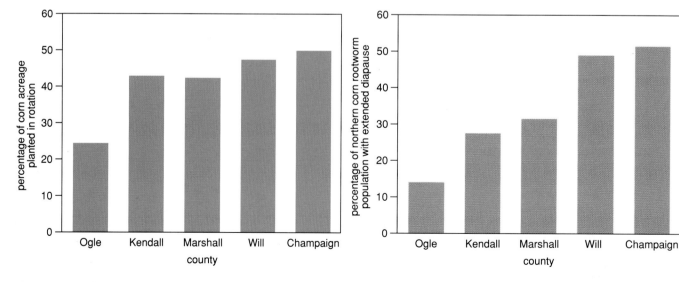

Figure 6. Eggs of the northern corn rootworm, a major pest in cornfields, typically remain in diapause, a resting stage, for one winter. The insect has recently evolved a longer diapause in areas where corn is rotated with soybeans. This genetic adaptation allows the insect egg to survive in the soil between the every-other-year planting cycles of its host plant instead of hatching too early among soybean roots, where it would starve. The bars show the relationship in five Illinois counties between the predominance of crop rotation as a practice and the proportion of the corn rootworm population with prolonged egg diapause. Crop rotation often succeeds in reducing pest populations by depriving the pests of their food, but some pests may adapt to the practice. Data are from Levine, Oloumi-Sadeghi and Fisher, in press.

pest interactions or combining the limited use of toxins with biological controls.

One idea, the multiple-toxin approach, provides a lesson in the complexity and importance of the population-genetic factors at work in pest adaptation. It has been suggested that one way to slow down a pest's adaptation to pesticides and to pest-resistant host plants is to challenge the pest with two or more different pesticides or plant-defense mechanisms. This notion is based on an intuitively appealing idea: The more hurdles placed in the path of a pest, the harder it is for the pest to adapt. When this view was explored mathematically through the use of population genetics–based models, it was found that in some cases the conventional wisdom was reasonable; in other cases, it could be very misleading (Gould 1986).

The success of the multiple-toxin approach depends on a number of specific attributes of the pests and of the toxins being used to kill them. If the inheritance of pest resistance to each of the toxins is recessive, and if high enough doses of persistent toxins are used so that most pests will die even if they are resistant to one of the toxins—and if, furthermore, there are some untreated pest habitats offering refuge in or near the crop—then a multiple-toxin approach is likely to work extremely well. On the other hand, if resistance to the toxins is inherited as an additive or dominant trait, and if the toxins degrade over time or are used at low doses, large populations of sexually reproducing pests can adapt to two toxins used in combination as fast as or faster than they would adapt to the two when used separately. And if, instead of reproducing sexually every generation, the pest goes through a number of parthenogenic generations between bouts of sexuality (as is the case with many aphids), recessive inheritance does not hinder adaptation as much. A further caveat is that the toxins must be distinct enough biochemically that the insect is unlikely to adapt to multiple toxins with a single genetic change.

These results have obvious utility. Even though most pesticides are too dangerous or expensive to apply as mixtures at high doses, plant breeders and genetic engineers can apply multiple-toxin approaches to their work. The same dynamics of pest resistance that would be at work in a field sprayed with pesticides will apply if a crop plant is given pest resistance by

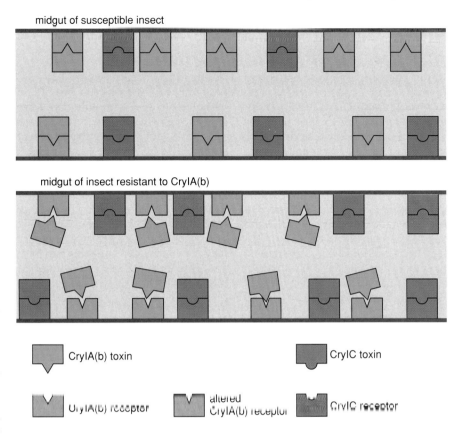

midgut of susceptible insect

midgut of insect resistant to CryIA(b)

CryIA(b) toxin   CryIC toxin

CryIA(b) receptor   altered CryIA(b) receptor   CryIC receptor

Figure 7. Insect resistance to toxins produced by the bacterium *Bacillus thuringiensis*, or *B.t.*, seems to be mediated by heritable changes in receptor proteins on the inner surface of the insect's midgut. Two of the *B.t.* toxins are insecticidal crystal proteins designated *CryIA(b)* and *CryIC*. In *B.t*-susceptible strains of the Indian meal moth, receptor proteins in the lining of the midgut bind to both toxins. Insects resistant to *CryIA(b)* have been found to have an altered *CryIA(b)* receptor in the midgut; the alteration greatly reduces the receptor's affinity for the toxin. However, the resistant insects have a slightly greater than normal abundance of *CryIC* receptors, and so they remain susceptible to this second toxin. In principle the Indian meal moth might evolve resistance to both *B.t.* toxins, but no such doubly resistant strain has been observed. Work aimed at creating transgenic crop plants that express *B.t.* toxins is now under way; it may be possible to control some insects for long periods of time by engineering such plants to express multiple *B.t.* toxins. (Adapted from Van Rie 1991.)

the insertion of two or more genes that express toxins at high levels.

The multiple-toxin approach is currently receiving detailed attention as such crops as cotton, corn and tomatoes are engineered to produce the *Bacillus thuringiensis* toxins discussed earlier. Different strains of the bacteria produce distinct toxins injurious to insects, and in many strains each bacterium produces a number of toxins. Some of the toxins are quite similar in their amino acid sequences; a single genetic change in an insect may produce resistance to both. On the other hand, studies with resistant colonies of the diamondback moth and the Indian meal moth have shown that adaptation to one type of toxin can be independent of adaptation to other distinct toxin types. And cross-breeding of resistant and susceptible insects has shown that *B.t.* toxin resistance

is often inherited as a recessive or semi-recessive trait.

Working with the meal moth and the diamondback moth, molecular biologists have developed a reasonably good understanding of why resistance to one type of *B.t.* toxin has not led to cross-resistance to other *B.t.* toxins (Van Rie 1991). Their experiments have demonstrated that the *B.t.* toxins they worked with are effective only if the toxin binds to a receptor protein in an insect's midgut. Distinct types of toxins turn out to bind to different receptors. Insects with resistance to one type of toxin were found to have a single altered receptor protein, the one responsible for binding the specific toxin to which they were resistant (*Figure 7*).

The alteration that led to resistance generally involved a decrease in the affinity of the receptor for that toxin, so that it took a lot more toxin to cause a fatal lesion in the gut. Because the other receptors in the gut were specified by different genes, a change in one receptor did not alter the receptors that bound other *B.t.* toxins, and so there was no cross-resistance. The critical experiments of simultaneously selecting these insect species with two toxins to be more certain that they will not come up with a single genetic change that makes them immune to both toxins have not been done, but they are in the planning stage. If such experiments indicate that cross-resistance is truly unlikely, and confirm the recessive nature of the resistance traits, we will be in a position to recommend testing the multiple-toxin strategy at a small-scale field level. Such tests could be conducted on an isolated island, just in case of some unexpected evolutionary event.

My laboratory has recently collaborated with scientists in Alabama, Belgium and Spain to investigate the question of whether the multiple-toxin approach is as likely to be effective with other insect species. We are aiming our efforts at one species in the *Heliothis* complex, a four-species group of caterpillars that attack cotton, corn, tomatoes and several other crops. *Heliothis* is one of the world's most severe insect pests and is a major target for control with genetically engineered plants. We selected *Heliothis virescens* for resistance to combinations of toxins and to single toxins, and exposed the insects to the toxins at different doses and for different portions of their larval stage.

With the *Heliothis* complex, or at least with *Heliothis virescens*, we are not sure that multiple *B.t.* toxins will be useful because preliminary results indicate that strains resistant to one toxin may be developing resistance to other toxins. If these preliminary findings hold true, it means that if we are to use multiple toxins for *Heliothis* control, we need to find and combine classes of toxins that are biochemically more distinct from each other than are pairs of *B.t.* toxins. Some possible candidates are insect-specific toxins produced by mites and scorpions, which sound horrendous but may be safer for human beings than the chemicals that give basil leaves their delightful flavor. Although genetic engineers are currently limited to working with protein-based toxins, it is hoped that in the future they will be able to manipulate the levels of expression of safe, natural plant-defense compounds

that are generally more difficult to manipulate than single proteins.

When Is Less More?
Another idea for delaying pest adaptation is that of partial resistance. Plant pathologists and entomologists have long thought that if you could choose between a crop variety that had very strong resistance to a pest and one that had partial resistance to a pest, the partially resistant variety would probably last longer in the field than the variety that initially conferred strong resistance (Lamberti, Walker and van der Graaff 1981). Plant pathologists have some historical evidence that supports this view, and there are a number of potential explanations. One is that the selection pressure on the pest population is less in the case of partial resistance than it is when there is strong resistance.

Although partial resistance of crops to insect pests may not provide sufficient control in some cases, entomologists have found that combining partial resistance with the action of natural biological-control agents could offer useful protection. It was once generally assumed that the action of pest-resistance factors in plants differed so greatly from the action of biological-control agents that these natural enemies would not influence the rate at which pests adapted to partial plant resistance. It was therefore somewhat surprising when ecologically based population-genetic models showed that natural enemies of pests could significantly increase or decrease the rate of pest adaptation to the plant, depending on the characteristics of the natural enemy, including its hunting behavior (Gould et al. 1991).

Behavioral interactions between a pest and a crop with resistance to it can also be important, and an understanding of these interactions offers another intriguing prospect for managing adaptation: the expression of toxins in specific parts of crop plants. In a number of natural insect-plant associations, it has been shown that the plant does not produce an equal amount of toxin all season long or in all of its parts. In many cases it seems as if evolution has selected for plants that produce more of the protective toxins in their most vulnerable tissues at times of the year when insects can do the most harm. Some insects appear to respond to this heterogeneous defense strategy by avoiding the heavily defended tissues.

Biotechnology may offer a way to ex-

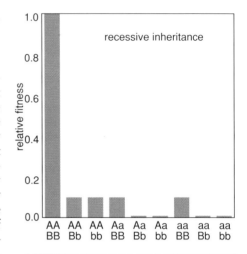

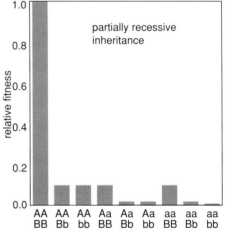

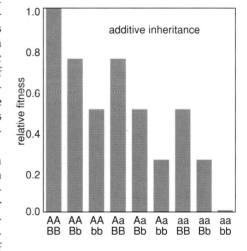

Figure 8. Onset of resistance to plant-produced toxins in a pest population was studied in a series of computer simulations, which showed that the useful lifetime of a plant's defensive strategy depends strongly on the intensity of the selection pressure applied to the pest and on how the resistance traits are inherited. The simulations examined a pest species with two genetic loci for resistance to plant-produced toxins; the *A* and *B* alleles confer resistance, whereas the *a* and *b* alleles do not. The effect of selection pressure is most

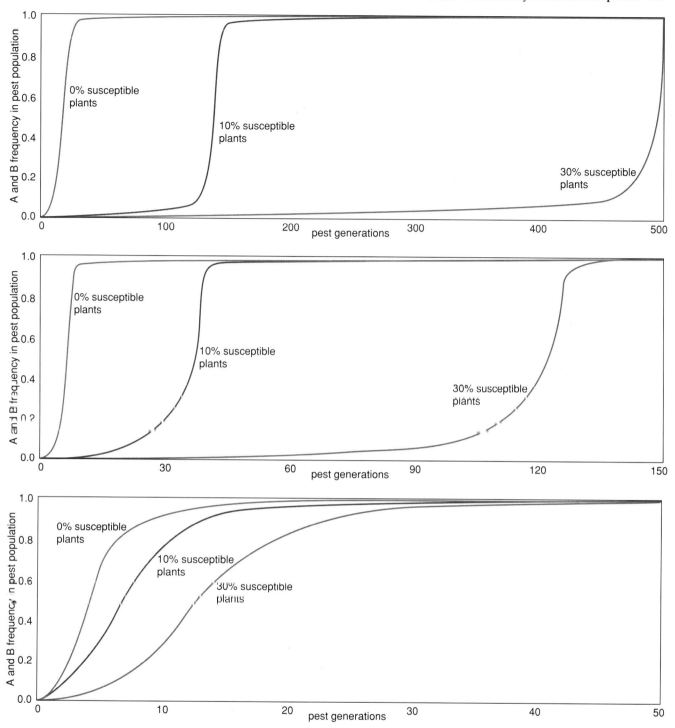

dramatic when resistance is inherited as a recessive trait *(top)*. In this case only the *AABB* genotype has high fitness when the pest must live on a host plant that produces both toxins. (All the genotypes are equally fit when the host plant has no defensive toxins.) If the simulated pests are exposed exclusively to toxin-producing plants, resistance emerges quickly; within about 30 pest generations the frequency of the *A* and *B* alleles goes from near 0 to near 1. Adding just 10 percent susceptible plants delays the development of resistance for almost 150 generations, and with 30 percent susceptible plants the resistant pests do not dominate the population until after 500 generations. The benefits of reduced selection pressure are smaller but still significant when resistance in the pest is inherited as a partially recessive trait *(middle)*. In this case, when individuals with a single *A* or a single *B* allele feed on plants expressing both toxins, their fitness is slightly higher than the fitness of *aabb* individuals (0.02 versus 0.01). If the pests feed exclusively on toxin-producing plants, the population becomes resistant in fewer than 10 generations. A 30-percent admixture of susceptible plants delays the onset of resistance until about generation 120. If resistance to the toxins is an additive trait, so that each *A* or *B* allele contributes incrementally to fitness on toxin-producing plants, the advantage of adding susceptible plants decreases further but is not completely lost *(bottom)*. Note that the three graphs have different horizontal scales. In all cases the initial frequencies of alleles *A* and *B* are set at 0.01. The effects would be more dramatic at lower initial frequencies, but the true initial frequencies are as yet unknown.

Figure 9. Tissue-specific expression of toxins by host plants, a concept being explored in experiments involving the caterpillar *Heliothis virescens (above),* **may be one way to delay the development of resistance in crop pests. (Photograph by Karl Suiter.)**

ploit this interaction to protect important parts of plants while delaying the evolutionary response of insects to controls. It may become possible to restrict pests to nibbling on less-important, nontoxic parts of a plant, thus relieving the pressure on the pest for physiological adaptation while preserving tissues essential to a good harvest. Laboratory experiments with *Heliothis virescens* have shown that larvae, when given a choice of synthetic food with or without *B.t.* toxin in it, eat much more of the unadulterated food. Experimental results on growth and survival of *H. virescens* strains in situations where there is either choice or no choice indicate that having a choice of foods could slow adaptation to less than one-fifth the rate found in the situation in which *B.t.* toxin is present in all of the food (Gould and Anderson 1991).

My colleagues and I are currently conducting experiments that are similar to these, with the exception that we are using genetically engineered plants that produce *B.t.* toxin. We have chosen tobacco as our model plant because it is a major host of *H. virescens* and has become the "white rat" of plant genetic engineering. We have developed a technique with tobacco that enables us to mimic a crop plant that produces *B.t.* toxin solely in the apical bud area, usually the favorite part of the plant for *Heliothis virescens* larvae. From an agricultural perspective this is useful because

when *H. virescens* feeds on the bud, it eliminates apical dominance (the controlling effect of the terminal bud on development of lateral buds), and the plant becomes deformed. If the larvae abandon the toxin-laden bud tissue to feed on older, larger leaves that lack the toxin, just as they abandon the toxin-laden synthetic food, their activity will cause much less reduction in yield. Such a system could have real advantages in many crops if the insect survived but there was little yield lost. In our experiments we have to perform an operation akin to grafting the top of a *B.t.*-toxin-producing plant to the lower part of a normal tobacco plant because plants expressing *B.t.* toxin only in specific tissues are not available. Although the technology for tissue-specific expression exists, it will take a number of convincing ecological and behavioral experiments to get genetic engineers to construct such plants. Our next step with this system will be to determine how natural enemies fit into such tissue-specific defense systems.

The utility of tissue-specific expression of toxins or other resistance factors is not limited to insects. Mike Bonman and his co-workers at the International Rice Research Institute have found that the most severe losses from rice blast disease occur when the blast-disease organism (*Pyricularia grisea*) attacks the panicle, or flower cluster, of the plant (Bonman et al. 1991). The growth of the

blast organism on leaf tissue is less detrimental to yield. Bonman has found some rice genotypes that are more resistant to panicle infection than to leaf infection, and he has suggested that molecular genetics could be used to develop even more specific panicle resistance. This type of tissue-specific resistance would protect the rice against major losses while limiting selection pressure to the brief part of the season during which the panicle is exposed to infection.

Up to this point, I have been assuming that insecticides or resistant crops will start out being very effective and will sooner or later lose their effectiveness. But evolutionary theory holds out the tantalizing possibility that resistance-management approaches might be applied in ways that allow evolution to enhance rather than undo the effects of control tactics. I used a genetic model to explore a system in which an insect can feed on a crop or on other vegetation, but prefers the crop (Gould 1984). I plugged into the model, at low frequency, a single mutation that made the insect resistant to a new pesticide being sprayed on the crop. I also introduced at low frequency a mutation that programmed the insect to lay more of its eggs on the alternative vegetation. In many cases the insect population became resistant to the pesticide. However, at certain initial frequencies of the two novel traits the insect population evolved to a state in which it abandoned the crop in favor of the alternative food, thereby indirectly increasing the effectiveness of the pesticide over time.

These theoretical results suggest that there should be cases in which insects adapt to pesticides by avoiding them or by avoiding the types of plants that are often coated with them. Empirical work is being conducted in this area, and although some cases of such behavioral avoidance of pesticides can be found, they are rare compared with cases of physiological resistance. It may be that, contrary to the conventional biological wisdom that suggests that behavior evolves faster than physiology, it is easier for these pests to adapt physiologically than behaviorally when confronted with toxic substances.

Most of the work on developing evolutionarily sustainable pest-control strategies has focused on the manipulation of natural and synthetic toxins. As noted earlier, toxins are only one component of an agricultural system to which pests adapt. In the future, the evolutionary approach may help us to design better cultural and biological control strategies. For example, we have information indicating that some weed species can be divided into specific strains that are best adapted to distinct crops; however, we have yet to examine whether the rotation of certain types of crops makes it difficult for a weed population to adapt to all of the crops in the rotation. Similarly, it is likely that a weed population that is adapted to survive in fields where the soil is turned over with a moldboard plow may not be as adapted to survive in fields farmed with new no-tillage techniques. Temporal rotation of these farming practices could keep weed populations from reaching an optimal genetic solution to either practice. Recent thesis research by Heather Henter has shown that within a single 10-acre field, some lineages of pea aphids are far more resistant to their parasite, *Aphidius ervi*, than are others. (Parasite eggs laid within the bodies of resistant aphids usually degenerate before hatching.) Will studies of the genetic interaction between other parasites and pests reveal such striking variation at this fine scale? If so, understanding how such variation is maintained may help us to develop more efficient and sustainable biological-control programs. And if it is more difficult for insect pests to adapt behaviorally than physiologically, then instead of engineering plants to kill insects, it may be desirable to engineer plants that do not attract insects in the first place.

The need to understand more about pest adaptation to all components of agricultural systems may become more acute as replacing evolutionarily outmoded pesticides with new ones becomes more difficult for technological and social reasons. We are just starting to explore some of the ways in which we could hold pest evolution in check for at least a few more years. It will be a great challenge to agricultural scientists and evolutionary biologists to see just how far they can push the limits of their research fields to predict and direct the evolutionary future of pests.

It is sometimes said that necessity is the mother of invention. The needs of agriculture require more accuracy and precision from evolutionary theory than has previously been demanded. Perhaps

this need will lead to a reexamination of old techniques of prediction and the development of new ones. As young evolutionary biologists sit and ponder what organism should be the subject of their thesis research, I hope they will consider the benefits that could accrue should they choose one of the hundreds of intriguing pests that plague the world's harvest.

Acknowledgments

This article had its origins in a previous paper (Gould 1990) and in a Sigma Xi lecture delivered at Kansas State University in April 1991. I would like to thank C. R. Carroll, D. J. Futuyma, R. Prokopy and R. L. Rabb for inspiring and fostering my early work in this area. M. T. Johnson and C. Nalepa offered helpful comments on the manuscript.

Bibliography

Barrett, Spencer C. H. 1983. Crop mimicry in weeds. *Economic Botany* 37:255–282.

Beachy, R. N., P. P. Abel, R. S. Nelson, J. Register, N. Tumer and R. T. Fraley. 1990. Genetic engineering of plants for protection against virus diseases. In *Plant Resistance to Viruses*, ed. D. Evered and S. Harnett, pp. 151–158. Ciba Foundation Symposium 133. New York: Wiley & Sons.

Bonman, J. M., B. A. Estrada and J. M. Bandong. 1989. Leaf and neck blast resistance in tropical lowland rice cultivars. *Plant Disease* 73:388–390.

Dave, B. B. 1943. The wild rice problem in the central provinces and its solution. *Indian Journal of Agriculture* 13:46–53.

David, W. A. L., and B. O. C. Gardiner. 1960. A *Pieris brassicae* (Linnaeus) culture resistant to a granulosis. *Journal of Insect Pathology* 2:106–114.

Dmitriev, V. S. 1952. Questions of the development of species and the control of weeds. *Soviet Agronomy* 4:17–27.

Georghiou, George P. 1986. The magnitude of the resistance problem. In *Pesticide Resistance: Strategies and Tactics for Management*, National Research Council. Washington: National Academy Press.

Gould, F. 1984. Role of behavior in the evolution of insect adaptation to insecticides and resistant host plants. *Bulletin of the Entomological Society of America* 30:33–41.

Gould, F. 1986. Simulation models for predicting the durability of insect-resistant germ plasm: a deterministic, two locus model. *Environmental Entomology* 15:1–10.

Gould, F. 1990. Ecological genetics and integrated pest management. In *Agroecology*, ed. C. R. Carroll, J. H. Vandermeer and P. M. Rosset, pp. 441–458. New York: McGraw-Hill.

Gould, F., and A. Anderson. 1991. Effects of *Bacillus thuringiensis* and HD-73 delta-endo-

toxin on growth, behavior, and fitness of susceptible and toxin-adapted *Heliothis virescens* (Lepidoptera: Noctuidae) strains. *Environmental Entomology* 20:30–38.

Gould, F., G. G. Kennedy and M. T. Johnson. 1991. Effects of natural enemies on the rate of herbivore adaptation to resistant host plants. *Entomologia Experimentalis et Applicata* 58:1–14.

Green, N. G., H. M. LeBaron and W. K. Moberg. 1990. *Managing Resistance to Agrochemicals: From Fundamental Research to Practical Strategies*. Washington: American Chemical Society.

Kettlewell, B. 1973. *The Evolution of Melanism.* Oxford: Clarendon Press.

Krysan, J. L., D. E. Foster, T. F. Branson, K. R. Ostlie and W. S. Cranshaw. 1986. Two years before the hatch: Rootworms adapt to crop rotation. *Bulletin of the Entomological Society of America* 32:250–253.

Lamberti, F., J. M. Walker and N. A. van der Graaff. 1981. *Durable Resistance in Crops*. New York: Plenum.

Levine, E., H. Oloumi-Sadeghi and J. R. Fisher. In press. Discovery of multiyear diapause in Illinois and South Dakota Northern Corn Rootworm (Coleoptera: Chysomelidae) eggs and incidence of the prolonged diapause trait in Illinois. *Journal of Economic Entomology*.

National Research Council. 1986. *Pesticide Resistance: Strategies and Tactics for Management.* Committee on Strategies for the Management of Pesticide Resistant Pest Populations. Washington: National Academy Press.

Ossowski, L. L. J. 1960. Variation in virulence of a wattle bagworm virus. *Journal of Insect Pathology* 2:35–43.

Rowlands, D. G. 1959. A case of mimicry in plants—*Vicia sativa* L. in lentil crops. *Genetica* 30:435–446.

Schäfer, W., D. Straney, L. Ciuffetti, H. D. Van Etten and O. C. Yoder. 1989. One enzyme makes a fungal pathogen, but not a saprophyte, virulent on a new host plant. *Science* 246:247–249.

Shelton, A. M., and J. A. Wyman. 1991. Insecticide resistance of diamondback moth (Lepidoptera: Plutellidae) in North America. *Proceedings of the Second International Diamondback Moth Workshop.* Taiwan.

Shemshedini, L., and T. G. Wilson. 1990. Resistance to juvenile hormone and an insect growth regulator in *Drosophila* is associated with an altered cytosolic juvenile hormone-binding protein. *Proceedings of the National Academy of Sciences* 87: 2072–2076.

Sinskaia, E. N., and A. A. Beztuzheva. 1930. The forms of *Camelina sativa* in connection with climate, flax and man. *Trudy Po Prikladnoi Botanike (Genetike I Selektsii)* 25:98–200.

Stalker, D. M., K. E. McBride and L. D. Malyj. 1988. Herbicide resistance in transgenic plants expressing a bacterial detoxification gene. *Science* 242:419–423.

Van Rie, Jeroen. 1991. Insect control with transgenic plants: resistance proof? *Trends in Biotechnology* 9:177–179.

Williams, C. M. 1967. Third-generation pesticides. *Scientific American* 217:13–17.

Marginalia

Fisher's microscope, or the gradualist's dilemma

Keith Stewart Thomson

In an earlier life, I occasionally led seminars for graduate students on the subject of "how to teach" (admittedly, I sometimes felt like the baseball player who, although he was a poor fielder, couldn't hit either). One of the exercises I gave students was to describe, using no visual aids and with hands behind the back, how to set up a deck chair. The smart students used to ask me "would you describe which sort of chair you mean—without using your hands of course." Normal conversation turns out to be very difficult without waving of hands, facial gestures, and so on. Similarly, written exposition of scientific ideas, particularly counterintuitive ones (the best sort), is usually difficult without resort to simile, analogy, or metaphor; familiar examples are Maxwell's demon, the blind watchmaker, the selfish gene, Einstein's twins paradox, and so on.

If a picture is worth a thousand words, what price a well-chosen analogy? Nothing could be more useful, although the trouble is that sometimes the analogy is so good that it lives on long after the principle it was intended to illustrate ought to have faded into oblivion. A perennial favorite in evolutionary theory used to be R. A. Fisher's microscope analogy for the role of selection. It dates from 1929, but lo and behold, it has recently been resurrected (1).

Evolutionary theory, in whatever its neo-Darwinian, postclassical Darwinian, or post-New Synthetic guise, is quintessentially a theory of gradual change. It is a theory of continuity, and evolutionary change must therefore, by definition, be the result of mechanisms that only work through very small changes. This produces a dilemma, however, one that Darwin himself puzzled over (see especially chapters 4 and 6 of *Origin of Species*), although most later evolutionists gloss over it. The gradualist's dilemma is this: is a mechanism of slow accumulation of insignificant changes sufficient to account for the magnificent diversity of adaptation seen in the living and fossil record—the running of the cheetah, the eye of the hawk, and the ponderous enormity of some dinosaurs? If evolution is a process of very gradual adaptation, must there not have been countless millions of intermediate forms, all of equal adaptive value? Where are (were) they? These are questions that give anti-evolutionists great comfort, and a few authors (Dawkins, for example, ref. 1) have recently been trying to tackle the problem head on.

The traditional alternatives to gradualism—evolutionary saltationism or macromutationism—have long ago been defeated, and quite rightly, although it sometimes appears that they have been abolished by the simple device of defining them away. In a rational theory of continuity, saltation (a discontinuous variation) is merely that which is irrational and inexplicable—in short, either an error or a dream. The hypothesis of punctuated equilibrium appears saltatory but is merely a version of gradualism dealing with the question of how small changes are patterned in time.

How did evolutionary theory come to have at its foundation a view of mechanism that makes change sure but so infinitely graded, one that explains the origin of the magnificently improbable from the ineffably trivial? The source is Darwin, to be sure, but Darwin was not dogmatic on the question of scale. Another dominating influence is R. A. Fisher and his 1930 book *The Genetical Theory of Natural Selection* (2). There is no ambivalence about Fisher's gradualism. He sought to show mathematically that nothing except the most insignificant variation in phenotype was compatible with the operation of natural selection:

[with respect to] either the organism or its environment, we should conclude that any change on either side has, when this change is extremely minute, an almost equal chance of effecting improvement or the reverse; while for greater changes the chance of improvement diminishes progressively, becoming zero, or at least negligible, for changes of sufficiently pronounced character.

After 1930, and particularly under the influence of the book's second chapter, "The Fundamental Theorem of Natural Selection," evolution became a play in which the theme was Darwin's but the language was increasingly Fisher's and then also Sewall Wright's. A sharp debate between Fisher and Wright further shaped the field in fundamental ways, but its essential gradualism was unshaken (3, 4).

Naturally enough, in proposing so extreme a view of gradualism, Fisher was also opposing something, namely the "mutationism" of the 1920s, led among others by R. C. Punnett (5). In a mutationist scheme the direction, tempo, and mode of evolutionary change are dictated by the mechanisms that produce variation, not by selection. In the genetics of 1929 mutationism was wrongheadedness, but the approach had good popular support. Fisher sought to place natural selection back in center stage as the force that shaped evolutionary change. In his preface he notes how neglected natural selection had become. Ironically, under his influence a new imbalance was formed, in which the sources and role of variation, the internal factors of evolution, would now be neglected in favor of the external mechanisms of selection.

Fisher captured the essence of his gradualism in the following analogy with a microscope:

The conformity of these statistical requirements with common experience will be perceived by comparison with the mechanical adaptation of an instrument, such as a microscope, when adjusted for distinct vision. . . . It is sufficiently obvious that any large derangement [of the instrument] will have a very small probability of improving the adjustment, while in the case of small alterations much less than the smallest of those intentionally effected by the maker or the operator, the chance of improvement should be almost exactly one half.

Mr. Thomson is president of the Academy of Natural Sciences, 19th and the Parkway, Logan Square, Philadelphia, PA 19103.

Is this really sufficiently obvious and common experience? What the analogy mostly shows is that while Fisher was a good statistician, he was not much of a microscopist. In Fisher's analogy of a light microscope, "deranging" the system appears to mean focusing (usually there is a fine and a coarse adjustment). Actually, while one focuses a camera or telescope by changing the arrangement of the lenses, the focus of a microscope is fixed, and one "focuses on" the object by moving the whole system nearer to or farther from the object. What he calls the "adjustment" is the bringing of an object into clear view. In any case, changing the adjustment is the analogue of the introduction of phenotypic variation, and the field of view containing the object must be the selective environment. The sharpness achieved is fitness.

It is a powerful analogy, but it is flawed. It works only in a simple world that can be reduced to one infinitesimally confined plane—the world of idealized models. But it is amusing to follow up the analogy and discover that it also demonstrates exactly the opposite of what Fisher intended.

First, as with a microscope, the pattern of evolutionary change is a function of scale. If the object is sufficiently large relative to the potential range of adjustments, continued smaller adjustments and even large ones may still not cause loss of an image. This is the equivalent of a generalized and stable adaptation, the vertebrate eye for example. By contrast, a single very small object (i.e., a specialized adaptation) would be lost from view (become extinct) by the slightest adjustment of the instrument.

In most cases, once a microscope has been set up and an object brought into clear focus, any change in adjustment greater than an infinitesimally small one will cause the sharpness of that image (fitness) to be reduced. Only if the image were not clear to start with is there any chance that a change would improve its clarity. If the system were to undergo a series of minute random changes, they might average out to no change at all. But this is stasis, not evolution.

Fisher must have forgotten that when one is using a microscope on any sort of complex object—a slice of tissue, for example—a shift in the adjustment simply takes one plane out of focus and brings another one in. Potentially, at every point *something* is sharply focused, and the focus is never any better for one variation in the system than for another.

Now consider the case when the object field consists of a number of discrete items—say, a suspension of diatoms in a sample of pond water. A slight change in adjustment will indeed spoil the sharpness of the image of an organism, but a more pronounced shift has a finite chance of bringing in another one (3). In an evolutionary sense, a significantly different variant is not automatically at a disadvantage but may have a chance of survival in a new context if the environment, as in this example, is not smoothly continuous but is much more like Wright's "adaptive landscape," with its sharp peaks and deep valleys. If organisms were to vary only minutely from one another, in this analogy, they would all become extinct. Survival of the lineage may depend on greater variations. This is not at all what Fisher intended (or Wright, for that matter).

A major fallacy of Fisher's microscope analogy is

therefore that it models an unrealistic evolutionary world. It fails to recognize that every variant phenotype potentially functions in, and is tested against, a different version of what G. Evelyn Hutchinson called the n-dimensional hyperspace of the environment. Each calls forth its own niche and can only be judged on its own new terms, not the terms of its sister or parent. Even if the original state of adaptation were "perfect" (in its own context), a variant from that would not *automatically* be less fit.

A microscope analogy turns out to show (unsurprisingly) that long-term success of the observer (survival of the lineage) can depend both on the nature of the object field and on different strategies. One could elect to remain fixed on a single cell by dint of making only extremely small changes that average out (with any luck) to no change at all. If the object field is dense and continuous like a slice of tissue, then one could move (for example from cell to cell) via relatively small changes, any of which would result in a clear image,

---

Sometimes an analogy is so good that it lives on long after the principle it was intended to illustrate ought to have faded into oblivion

---

with little chance of missing altogether and becoming extinct. In this case, large phenotypic variants would also have a significant chance of finding a context for survival. However, if the object field is complex but discrete, with gaps between the elements, a third strategy is needed. Very small changes would allow one to hold the status quo for a while, a certain range of medium-sized changes would inevitably cause loss of the image (extinction), and larger changes would have a better chance of finding a new target than the smaller or medium-sized ones. The difficulty then becomes that, if one continues to make large changes in the system, the target will just as soon be lost. This is, I suppose, something one could call the saltationists' dilemma.

Fisher's version of the microscope analogy also fails to give a satisfactory account of evolutionary change, because it postulates only changes in the adjustment of the microscope (variation). To get closer to common experience, let us therefore imagine that Fisher was taking a course in introductory biology and trying to focus on a moving *Paramecium* in the pond-water sample. This is a better analogy, because in life both environments *and* phenotypes vary. This also turns out to get closer to Fisher's goals, because it is patently disastrous for the adjustment of the microscope (i.e., variation) to move faster or slower than the moving object (environmental change), and vice versa.

Fisher postulated (in an early formulation of the "arms race" and the "Red Queen hypothesis") that the inorganic and organic environment of organisms is always deteriorating relative to the state of adaptation. In other words, that wretched *Paramecium* will not stay still. What would Fisher do? He would first follow one *Paramecium* through slow, careful, and continuous (i.e., gradual) changes until it is eventually lost; then he would scan the field with relatively large adjustments until another target is found and then minutely followed again, and so on. Furthermore, the environment is not always deteriorating; occasionally, a *Paramecium* will swim right into view—or, without warning, a rotifer or a *Didinium* instead. Success of the observer (survival of the lineage) therefore depends on a mixed strategy of small and large adjustments (variants), a diverse changing environment, and chance.

One should really extend the analogy further; we need a whole population of microscopists. We can imagine Fisher, Wright, Punnett, Bateson, Waddington, Schmalhausen, and a host of others sitting in the class (perhaps even Goldschmidt is over in the far corner—retaking the course!), and we will then find every strategy being employed, ensuring that somewhere in the room at any point at least one organism is in view.

Similarly, modern evolutionary enquiry encompasses a wide range of possible mechanisms. At last, we have come out from under Fisher's shadow and are beginning to pay more attention to the wonderfully complex internal factors in genetics and development that shape the nature and scale of variation. Evolution is still a theory of continuity, but we need no longer insist that every evolutionary change requires the same vast number of intermediate steps graded with equal minuteness and represented by large populations of organisms.

This is not to say that we are reopening the Pandora's box of saltationism and macromutationism. The search for pattern and process in the generation of variation depends on a wealth of new information about genetic and morphogenetic mechanisms and is anchored by the study of "developmental constraints" (6). And, of course, unless we do this, we will never be completely comfortable about "saltations." In fact, one could never be positive from the empirical evidence of phylogeny and systematics whether they did or did not exist; the only evidence would be negative evidence—a gap within a lineage. And one can never be sure that a gap is an artifact due to an imperfect record or an imperfect analysis. All the more reason to study the mechanisms by which variation is caused and the patterns in which they occur, independently of how natural selection works on them. Pass me a new analogy, this one is worn out.

References

1. R. Dawkins. 1986. *The Blind Watchmaker*. Norton.

2. R. A. Fisher. 1958. *The Genetical Theory of Natural Selection*, 2nd ed. Dover.

3. J. R. G. Turner. 1985. Fisher's evolutionary faith and the challenge of mimicry. *Oxford Surv. Evol. Biol.* 2:159–96.

4. W. B. Provine. 1985. The R. A. Fisher-Sewall Wright controversy and its influence upon modern evolutionary biology. *Oxford Surv. Evol. Biol.* 2:197–219.

5. R. C. Punnett. 1915. *Mimicry in Butterflies*. Cambridge Univ. Press.

6. J. M. Smith et al. 1985. Developmental constraints and evolution. *Quar. Rev. Biol.* 60:265–87.

Directed Evolution Reconsidered

What appeared to be a serious challenge to Darwinism may be as easily explained by facets of bacterial metabolic regulation

Donald MacPhee

We who teach biology tend to think that the basis of modern evolutionary theory is well established. As an article of faith, we accept the idea that organisms evolve by a combination of random genetic change and natural selection, the tenets laid out by Darwin. Fundamental to Darwinian theory is the orthodox view that spontaneous genetic changes, or mutations, and the environment act as two fully independent forces in evolution. That is, mutations arise frequently and randomly, and sometimes the changes they bring about make an organism more able to cope with its environment than are its kin that lack the mutation. As a result, the individual with the mutation is more likely to leave offspring than others. Eventually organisms with the mutation overtake the general population and come to represent the standard type.

Any notion that the right kinds of mutations arise in response to particular environmental stresses is antithetical to Darwinian dogma and is tantamount to arguing that the environment

Donald G. MacPhee is a Reader in Microbiology at La Trobe University in Melbourne, Australia, where his research is primarily concerned with fundamental aspects of spontaneous and induced mutagenesis. After graduating from Edinburgh University in 1964 with a degree in bacteriology, he went on to obtain a Ph.D. in microbial genetics in 1967, and later had postdoctoral fellowships at Stanford University and at the University of East Anglia in England. MacPhee is a reviewing editor for the journals Environmental and Molecular Mutagenesis, Mutagenesis, Mutation Research *and the* Thai Journal of Toxicology. *He is currently president of the International Association of Environmental Mutagen Societies. His work has been supported by the Australian Research Council. Address: Department of Microbiology, La Trobe University, Bundoora, Victoria 3083, Australia.*

directs the evolution of new species. Moreover, the notion of purpose in evolution is also discounted by Darwinian theory; the idea that camels evolved humps that store water as a response to desert conditions is usually seen as a totally inappropriate model for the acquisition of new characteristics and their subsequent transmission to future generations. In fact, this notion harks back not to Darwin, but to an earlier theorist, Jean Baptiste de Lamarck, who suggested that organisms evolve by acquiring characteristics in response to environmental stresses. Although Lamarckism has attracted a following from time to time over the years, modern biologists on the whole are very uncomfortable with the notion that the environment might restrict genetic change to beneficial mutations.

With this background, then, it came as a major surprise to many people when John Cairns, a prominent biologist and cancer researcher, and his colleagues at the Harvard School of Public Health, Julie Overbaugh and Stephan Miller, wrote in a widely publicized article in *Nature* in 1988 that "cells may have mechanisms for choosing which mutations will occur." The Cairns paper raised the possibility that mutation could arise nonrandomly, yielding a product that enhanced the individual's chances of survival. The contention that environmental pressures actually cause an appropriate genetic change contrasts sharply with the view of the scientific community in general; for some, it may even border on heresy. Furthermore, although they make no explicit claim of support for Lamarckism, Cairns and his colleagues do suggest in their 1988 *Nature* article that organisms can somehow sense their

needs in a particular environment and mutate accordingly. However unpalatable this claim may be (even, apparently, to the authors themselves), it carries with it a Lamarckian implication that organisms can adapt their genes to suit a new environment.

In spite of the strong Darwinian bias in the scientific community, the *Nature* article, and the concept it spawned, directed evolution, have been taken very seriously by many prominent geneticists and other biologists. This is in part because of the distinguished reputation of the journal itself and partly because the views expressed in the article received support from a significant group of geneticists, including, for example, Franklin Stahl, who is world-renowned for his discovery, with Matthew Meselson, of the mechanism of DNA replication. In addition, the article's credibility results in no small part from the reputation of its authors. John Cairns has had a long and distinguished career in biology. First he made some key observations about the structure of the bacterial chromosome, and later he helped to discover the major enzyme responsible for its replication (after another enzyme had been thought to be the only one capable of performing that function). After delving into cancer research, Cairns became the director of the Cold Spring Harbor Laboratory on Long Island, New York, and most recently he has been outspoken in his advocacy of public-health measures in the fight against cancer. So, although the findings in the 1988 *Nature* paper run contrary to evolutionary dogma, it is not possible to dismiss them out of hand. Moreover, the experiments themselves are well conducted, and the results seem perfectly sound and reproducible.

Figure 1. Students of evolution, like the ones depicted in this early 19th-century British cartoon, have long debated how organisms become adapted to their environments. The Darwinian tenets of random mutation and natural selection have become orthodoxy for most scientists. Nevertheless, some periodically explore the possibility that mutations arise in response to environmental pressures. Nineteenth-century philosopher Jean Baptiste de Lamarck is the most famous proponent of such a theory. More recently, a well-known biologist resurrected this philosophy and provided some compelling evidence. Still, many in the scientific community wonder whether it is necessary to abandon Darwin, or whether the recent findings can be explained within conventional evolutionary dogma.

Nevertheless, publication of the paper led to a vigorous and ongoing exchange of correspondence and a flurry of follow-up articles about evolutionary processes. Although most of the papers are clearly favorable to the ideas expressed by Cairns and his colleagues, a number of commentators have included alternative explanations and interpretations.

Because of the very radical nature of the hypothesis of directed evolution, some interpretations have likewise been quite radical. One in particular, in seeking to explain a hypothesis that is counter to Darwinian tenets, proposes a mechanism that runs counter to standard molecular biological theory as well. Still, not everyone who has studied Cairns' experiment and accepts the notion of directed evolution agrees that such radical solutions are necessary. And others, myself included, believe that what may appear to be evidence for directed evolution may just as easily be explained by well-documented facets of bacterial metabolic regulation. Research performed in my laboratory has recently pointed to just such an explanation, one that requires a revision neither of Darwinian theory nor of molecular biological theory.

Mutations Made to Order

Experiments testing the Darwinian notion of random mutation date back to 1943, when Salvador Luria, then at Indiana University, and Max Delbrück, working at Vanderbilt University, devised a statistical way, called the fluctuation test, to distinguish bacterial mutations that arise independently from the environment (random mutations) from those that arise in response to an environmental pressure (nonrandom mutation). As their test case, Luria and Delbrück chose to count the number of bacteria that developed a resistance to a bacterial virus, also known as a phage.

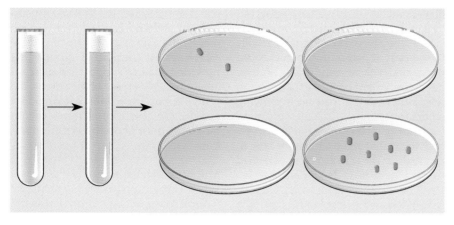

Figure 2. Randomness of mutation is tested in experiments similar to the one devised by Salvador Luria and Max Delbrück in 1943. Bacteria are first grown without any selection pressure in a test tube in a medium containing all of the necessary nutrients. Then the bacteria are transferred to culture plates in which a selection pressure is applied. In the Luria-Delbrück experiment, the culture plates contained a virus that was potentially lethal to the bacteria. Even though all of the bacteria initially placed in the test tube (*green*) were vulnerable to viral killing, some of the bacteria on the culture plates nevertheless survived the viral assault. These bacteria (*red*) had obviously mutated and acquired the ability to resist the bacteria. By analyzing the distribution of surviving bacteria, Luria and Delbrück determined that the resistant bacteria had mutated randomly, before they were exposed to the virus.

Bacteria were grown in test tubes, in the absence of the virus, for several generations and then transferred to culture plates on which the virus was present. Luria and Delbrück then observed the number and the distribution of the colonies that were able to resist viral infection. Bacteria that could not resist the virus were killed.

The scientists expected that one of two things would happen. In the first scenario, mutations converting virus-sensitive to virus-resistant bacteria could arise before the bacteria ever encountered a virus. In that case, all of the bacteria that could resist the virus on the culture plates would be the progeny of a resistant parent that arose before the bacteria were plated. Luria and Delbrück suggested that if this first scenario were correct, they should be able to detect it in the distribution of resistant bacteria on the various culture plates. They would expect to see a wide variation in the number of resistant bacteria from one culture plate to the next, reflecting the probability that a particular plate received a resistant progenitor bacterium.

In the second scenario, mutants would arise only after the bacteria encountered the virus, which they would do after being spread onto culture plates. If this were the case, reasoned Luria and Delbrück, then each plate should have the same probability of generating resistant bacteria, and therefore they would expect to see approxi-

mately the same number of mutants on each plate. When Luria and Delbrück conducted this experiment, they observed a broad variation in the number of resistant bacteria from plate to plate, indicating that the mutations had arisen before the bacteria ever encountered the virus. In other words, their data supported a model in which mutations are random. Almost 10 years later, the Luria and Delbrück results gained further support from work done by Joshua and Esther Lederberg, then at the University of Wisconsin, who came to the same conclusion using a different experimental design. Those conclusions remained essentially unchallenged until the 1988 Cairns paper.

Why, then, would Cairns and his colleagues question what generations of scientists have come to accept as the almost axiomatic truth of random mutation? The Cairns group does not dispute that most changes are brought about by random mutation. Clearly, random mutation accounts for the Luria and Delbrück results, as well as the Lederberg data. But the Cairns group wanted to know whether mutations are always completely random, and they questioned whether the Luria and Delbrück experiments disprove nonrandom mutations. They pointed out in their 1988 *Nature* paper that the test used by Luria and Delbrück was a rather harsh one. If bacteria had a mutation that made them resistant to the virus, they would live; bacteria with-

out the mutation to viral resistance would be killed by the virus. What if nonrandom mutations require that the bacteria be exposed to the environment for a period of time before the mutations can be made or become evident, they asked. Under the harsh conditions used by Luria and Delbrück, the bacteria would die before they could mutate and adapt to the new environment. So Cairns and his colleagues decided to apply the fluctuation test to bacteria that were not facing lethal conditions. To do that, they took advantage of bacterial metabolic needs.

Bacteria can use for food a number of different sugars, including sucrose, glucose and lactose. They can use these sugars because they possess proteins, encoded in their genes, that degrade the sugars to simpler compounds. The breakdown of each sugar requires a different set of enzymes—proteins that facilitate sugar breakdown to provide the cell with energy—encoded by different genes. The ability of the bacterium *Escherichia coli* to make use of lactose, for instance, requires a set of enzymes encoded by a series of genes referred to collectively as the Lac operon. *E. coli* bacteria that possess a functioning Lac operon are said to be Lac^+, and those in which the Lac operon does not code for a functional protein are said to be Lac^-. Often, the difference between a Lac^+ and a Lac^- bacterium boils down to very small changes at the level of the DNA encoding the Lac proteins. Cairns and his colleagues performed the fluctuation test with *E. coli* in which the Lac operon was present but contained an alteration that precluded the manufacture of Lac proteins. For all practical purposes, then, these bacteria were unable to metabolize the sugar lactose.

The scientists allowed the Lac^- *E. coli* to grow for several generations in test tubes that contained medium with a number of different nutrients and then transferred the bacteria to culture plates that contained lactose as the sole nutrient. The rationale was that all the bacteria had started out as Lac^- and could not use lactose. Some of the bacteria would have mutated spontaneously, in the absence of the selection pressure, and these would be expected to make use of the lactose on the culture plates right away. Those that could not use the lactose right away would not die, and the Cairns group wanted to know whether, given enough time, any of the *Lac⁻* bacteria plated on culture plates could mutate and acquire the ability to use lactose. When they looked at the resulting numbers of mutants, they found a mixed distribution. In other words, they saw that some of the mutants had arisen randomly before the bacteria were put on culture plates. But many others arose several days following plating, indicating that they had formed after being forced to use lactose as the only nutrient. These, the Cairns group surmised, had mutated nonrandomly in order to make use of the only nutrient available to them in their new environment.

When Cairns and his colleagues analyzed their data according to the predictions of the fluctuation test, they saw two distribution patterns: one indicative of the random mutation that happened prior to plating, and a second suggesting that nonrandom mutations had taken place following plating. Furthermore, they confirmed that the second, later wave of mutations did, indeed, occur many days after the bacteria were exposed to the lactose-only medium, whereas the first wave of mutants were evident almost immediately after plating.

Cairns and his colleagues recognized the possibility that any number of muta-

tions could have arisen after plating, but by supplying a medium containing only lactose, they were skewing their results to see only those mutants that could thrive under those conditions. So they did an important control experiment in which bacteria that had been growing on the lactose-only medium were overlaid with agar containing glucose, a second sugar that the bacteria are able to metabolize. The scientists then screened the bacteria to see whether any had become resistant to the normally toxic effects of the amino acid valine. By doing so, the Cairns group was able to see whether another mutation had arisen in the same bacteria but in genes totally unrelated to lactose metabolism. In other words, they wanted to see whether these bacteria were just susceptible to mutation in general or whether the mutations were localized in the genes of the Lac operon in specific response to the environmental conditions on the lactose-containing plates.

The crucial result here was the inability of the investigators to demonstrate a significantly increased yield of valine-resistant mutants. The result was used to argue that mutants did not arise randomly on the lactose-containing plates. Rather, the mutation arising with the greatest frequency was the

one that conferred the greatest advantage. In addition to their own experiments, the Cairns group reviewed research results from other groups that provided further support for directed evolution. From these observations, the Cairns group drew their often-quoted conclusion that "cells may have a mechanism for choosing which mutations will occur."

Mutation Mechanisms

When Darwin proposed his theory of natural selection, he did not know the biochemical basis of heredity or mutation. Over the past 40 years, the biochemistry involved has become better understood. Scientists now know that the instructions for all of the proteins that provide structure for a cell or an organism and the instructions for all of the enzymes are contained within that cell or organism's genes. For most organisms, the genes are made of DNA. Permanent, stable and heritable changes in an organism involve alterations in its DNA, whether the changes are random or nonrandom. Still, the two kinds of change may well happen at different stages of a cell's life and may involve different mechanisms.

Random changes are believed to come about as the cell prepares to di-

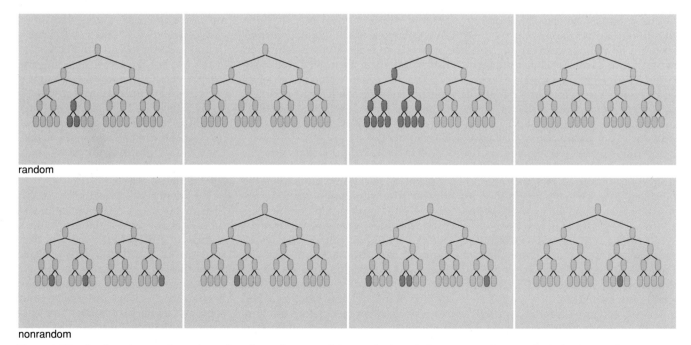

random

nonrandom

Figure 3. Distribution of mutant bacteria on the culture plates containing a selection medium is an indication of whether bacterial mutation is random. If mutation occurs randomly in the test tube before the selection pressure has been applied, as illustrated in the upper panel, the number of mutants found on a culture plate is a reflection of the probability that the plate will receive a bacterial mutant. In this case, there is a wide variation in the numbers of mutants on each plate. In their experiment, Luria and Delbrück observed a variable distribution of mutants from which they concluded that mutation is random. If however, mutation occurs nonrandomly, as in the lower panel, then the bacteria must have mutated after being exposed to the selection pressure. In this case, each culture plate has an equal chance of containing bacteria capable of mutation. One would therefore expect to see nearly equal numbers of mutants on each culture plate after selection pressure has been applied.

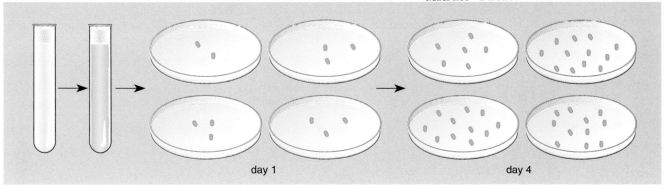

Figure 4. Attempted refinement of the Luria-Delbrück experiment took place in 1988, when John Cairns and his associates reached a different conclusion regarding the nature of mutants. Reasoning that the selection pressure in the 1943 experiments was lethal to the bacteria and would not allow them enough time to adapt, Cairns and colleagues applied a nonlethal selection pressure. Bacteria were transferred from a test tube to culture plates containing lactose *(yellow)* as the only source of carbon. Initially, the bacteria lacked the ability to metabolize lactose . Some of the bacteria *(orange)* acquired the lactose-metabolizing ability in the test tube and were able to use the sugar immediately after encountering it on the culture plates. These had mutated randomly, and their distribution on the culture plates was as expected for random mutations. After a few days on the culture plates, additional lactose-metabolizing mutants were apparent. These, concluded Cairns and his colleagues, may have arisen specifically in response to the pressure to use lactose. Their distribution on the culture plates conformed to that of nonrandom mutation. The Cairns group suggested that the environment had specifically directed the mutation to allow the bacteria to use lactose.

vide. At that time, the cell's DNA is copied so that each daughter cell will have a full set of genetic instructions. But, in spite of proofreading enzymes that compare the copy with the original and correct copying errors, the copy is not always completely faithful to the original. The differences in the copied DNA may result in a mutation that alters a function or the appearance of the daughter cell.

The mechanism that might be operating to form nonrandom mutations is more difficult to imagine. The Cairns experiments were structured in such a way

that cells were not dividing, and therefore were not duplicating DNA when they were placed on culture plates.

Among those who agree with the premise of directed evolution, there is still considerable debate about how such changes could arise. How can a cell possibly "know" that changing a particular gene would be advantageous? And if a cell does have a way of anticipating how genetic changes will enhance its ability to deal with an environmental pressure, how are the alterations to the DNA actually made?

Of all of the proposed mechanisms,

the most radical by far was offered by the Cairns group itself. The notion of directed evolution threatened Darwinism, and the proposed mechanism of such genetic change challenged a theory of information transfer within the cell so entrenched in scientific thinking that it is actually referred to by biologists as the "central dogma."

The theory of information transfer holds that although DNA is the archive of all of the cell's genetic information, it does not serve as the direct template for making protein. Rather, a go-between molecule of RNA, which is chemically

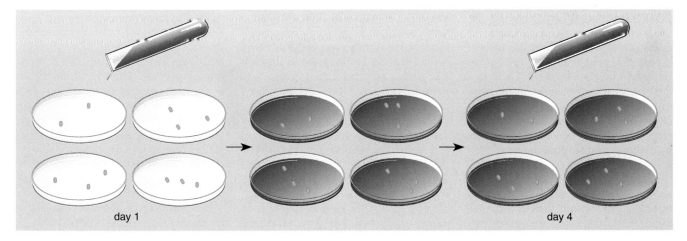

Figure 5. General mutation in the face of starvation was a possibility. The Cairns group tested the notion that many genes had mutated under the harsh metabolic conditions of the lactose-only medium. As a control experiment, bacteria that had been grown on lactose were overlaid with fresh agar *(violet)* and exposed to a new selection pressure. The top layer of agar contained the amino acid valine, which is generally toxic to bacteria. Some bacteria can mutate and resist valine toxicity, and the Cairns group reasoned that if widespread and general mutation were taking place, valine-resistant mutants would be apparent in increased numbers. In addition to valine, the top agar contained glucose as a nutrient sugar rather than lactose. The Cairns group observed no increase in the number of valine-resistant mutants under these conditions. From this they surmised that the bacteria on the original lactose-only medium had specifically mutated in order to use lactose, but had not mutated in the chromosomal region conferring valine resistance. Mutation was not general, but specifically affected the genes that conferred an adaptive advantage. Thus, in some cases, mutation and hence evolution, could be directed.

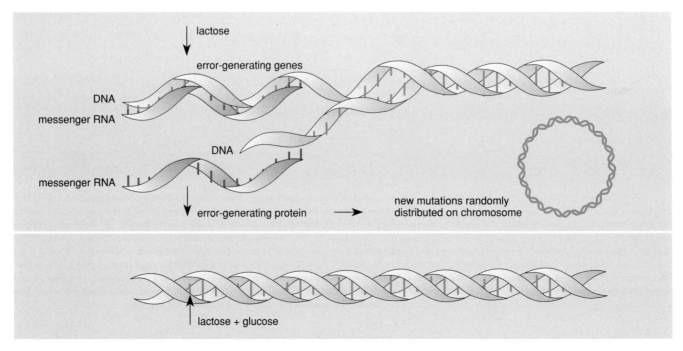

Figure 6. Mechanisms for directed evolution are difficult to envision, and some of the most radical proposed solutions require a reworking of well-established molecular biological theory. Catabolite repression—a well-known metabolic regulatory mechanism in bacteria—can account for all of the observations made by the Cairns group and others without challenging the existing molecular biological and evolutionary framework. The bacterial cell prefers glucose over all other metabolic energy sources. If glucose is not present, the cell is able to switch on the genetic and enzymatic machinery necessary to process more exotic sugars, such as lactose. When lactose alone is present, several genetic programs are initiated that would normally be quiescent, or repressed, in the presence of glucose. Among the genes activated when lactose is present are genes that code for proteins that generate errors, or mutations, in other genes. Activation means that the DNA for the error-coding genes is copied into the form of messenger RNA and then translated into proteins, some of which may alter the composition of other genes on the bacterial chromosome (*top*) and lead to new and sometimes adaptive mutations. In the presence of lactose or other exotic sugars, one would expect to see a large number of new mutations in the bacterial genes. These mutations are, however, random, occurring in genes whether or not the changes are adaptive. When glucose is present (*bottom*) the situation is reversed. There is a general repression of the expression of genes that allow the use of exotic energy sources. In addition, expression of the error-generating genes is also repressed. When glucose is present in the medium, one would expect to see a general decrease in the number of mutations. These observations suggest a new interpretation of the control experiment depicted in Figure 5. (Note: genes and chromosomes not drawn to scale.)

very similar to DNA, acts as the template. So, although DNA may contain the instructions for many thousands of genes, an RNA copy is made of only the specific gene that is required at the time. At a later stage, the RNA copy is destroyed. Thus, in most organisms, only the DNA from which RNA is copied is permanent. The dogma of molecular biology concerns the way information is transmitted in this system. It says that alterations in the information molecules DNA and RNA will show up in the proteins they encode, but if the protein somehow becomes altered, it will not bring about a change in RNA or DNA. That is, information flows in only one direction, from the information molecules to proteins. The mechanism for directed evolution initially proposed by the Cairns group (they have since backed away from this suggestion) would require a revision of this dogma.

Mutations first arise in the RNA molecule, suggested Cairns and his colleagues in the 1988 *Nature* paper. These mutations yield altered proteins, some of which may confer an advantage over nonmutated organisms in coping with an environmental stress. If this is the case, the Cairns group suggested that some as yet undiscovered process exists for the novel and advantageous protein to exert feedback of some sort onto the information content of a cell. This feedback would cause the mutant RNA template to be copied into the permanent DNA record. Although it is conceivable that RNA can be copied into DNA—indeed some organisms proceed this way routinely, and some strains of *E. coli* have recently been discovered to have the correct molecular machinery to carry out this process—the idea of a protein directing the informational content of a cell's DNA still stretches plausibility for most scientists.

Nevertheless, many biologists, although they reject Cairns' proposal, still support the theory of directed evo-

lution and have suggested more theoretically conservative mechanisms. Franklin Stahl, for example, proposed that mutations might arise through faulty repair of existing DNA. Even during periods when DNA is not actively replicated, portions of the chromosome are routinely scanned for nicks and changes that may come about in the normal course of cellular events. If mistakes are detected, the erroneous portion of DNA is usually excised and replaced by a segment true to the original code.

Normally, error correction is crucial for maintaining genetic integrity. But genetic integrity may be the last thing a cell needs during stressful periods, when, for example, cells are starving, as they are under the conditions of the Cairns experiment. Under those conditions, argues Stahl, the cell may somehow slow down its DNA error-repair systems in order to generate as many new versions of encoded proteins as possible. If one of these proteins is in

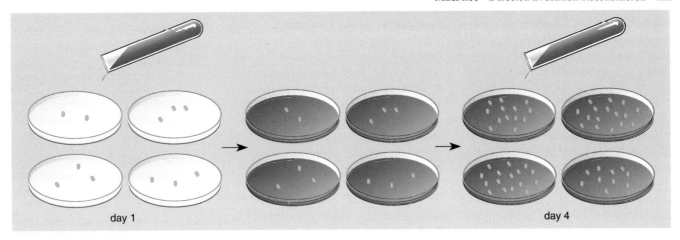

Figure 7. Catabolite-repression hypothesis can be tested by a variation on the experiment shown in Figure 5. Instead of using glucose as a source of energy, glycerol (*purple*) is used. Catabolite repression would predict that the use of glucose should lead to a general repression of genetic mutation. Glycerol-rich medium, on the other hand, should lead to a high mutation rate. Cells growing on culture plates containing lactose were overlaid with agar containing valine plus either glucose or glycerol. The number of valine-resistant mutants was assessed. In contrast to the findings of the Cairns experiment, many valine-resistant mutants were evident when glycerol was provided instead of glucose in the top agar. These findings are consistent with the catabolite-repression theory. They also suggest that the original lactose-metabolizing bacteria arose as a result of random, nondirected mutation.

fact advantageous, Stahl suggests, some mechanism might exist to make sure that the mutation is not corrected but instead remains as part of the permanent DNA record. Stahl asks the question of how the environment might direct a change in the efficiency of error-repair mechanisms. The answer to that question may be very close at hand. Work in my laboratory supports the idea that the mechanism may well be a variation on a well-studied process already in place in the bacterial cell.

Darwin Redux

The model I prefer assumes that mutations arise continuously and spontaneously, in the best tradition of Darwin. The rates at which mutations appear are regulated but not directed in any way. Not only does this approach leave Darwinian tenets intact, but the genetic mechanisms for regulating mutation rates are also well within the framework of known metabolic activities for bacterial cells. In short, this model also spares the central dogma.

The foundation for this model is the observation that, given a choice of food sources, a bacterium will prefer a simple sugar like glucose to a more complicated sugar like lactose. There are two stages involved in the preferential system for sugar usage. First, glucose inhibits the formation of the specific enzymes required for the breakdown of other sugars—lactose, for example—in a process known as catabolite repression. Second, when and only when

the entire glucose supply is exhausted will enzymes for the metabolism of other sugars be produced.

In other words, given an abundant food supply, the genes encoding the enzymes for the metabolism of the more unusual sugars are kept in a switched-off state, or are repressed; they are switched on only when they are actually required to provide enzymatic activity of the appropriate sort. Similar regulatory models were first proposed about 30 years ago by Francois Jacob and Jacques Monod, and their operation at the level of gene expression is now a standard theme in texts on molecular biology. Since Jacob and Monod developed this model, a number of variations on this theme have been uncovered.

The Jacob–Monod model of gene expression has normally been applied to the type of biochemical or metabolic pathway for which it was first proposed—that is, for sugar metabolism and biosynthetic pathways. I now contend that it may also apply to a pathway concerned with generating spontaneous mutations.

If this is true, we would expect to see a generally lower rate of mutation in the presence of glucose, where catabolite repression would be most active. Mutation rates should be higher when bacteria must rely on more exotic sugars, such as lactose, for their nutrition. Put another way, when glucose is present and acting generally to produce catabolite repression, it will prevent expression of all sorts of genes, including the genes

whose products are actually involved in making mistakes, or mutations, in DNA molecules. In contrast, when another sugar is the only one available, catabolite repression would not be operating, and the spontaneous mutation rate would be high. It should be noted that during periods when mutation rates are high, genes at all positions in the bacterial chromosome, not just specific genes, are mutated randomly.

If the normal cellular mechanisms for regulating gene expression that I have just outlined do apply to the pathway for generating spontaneous mutations, the results reported by Cairns and his colleagues in the 1988 *Nature* paper can be explained without difficulty and without the need to invest bacteria with the ability to make choices.

Assuming that such a system was operating during the Cairns experiment, it might be possible to reinterpret some of their conclusions. The first finding—that high levels of spontaneous mutations are observed under starvation conditions—is consistent with a model where catabolite repression has been lifted in the absence of glucose and in the presence of lactose.

In fact, it is the absence of catabolite repression and the corresponding expression of the mutation-generating system that accounts for the appearance of the late lactose-using colonies recorded by Cairns and associates. Their claim that specifically *Lac*⁺ mutants appeared in response to the culture conditions provided the basis for their argument that only beneficial mutations were being "directed" to appear. In support of these claims, they then performed the experiment showing that valine-resistant mutants did not appear at the same levels.

However, when they performed the experiment measuring the number of valine-resistant mutants, they provided glucose in the medium as a source of nutrition. Yet the choice of glucose also ensured that catabolite repression would take place. The genes for using lactose and other exotic sugars would be switched off again and so too would the genes whose products give rise to spontaneous mutations. The upshot is that when growth conditions are unfavorable, bacteria have an increased tendency to mutate at a great many sites, whereas when conditions are more favorable, the tendency to mutate is much reduced.

My colleagues Sue Thomas, Louise Hafner and George Kopsidas and I have repeatedly found that the ability of glucose to shut down spontaneous mutation is characteristic of a wide range of mutation test systems. We have also found that when a carbon source other than glucose is present in the medium used to detect valine-resistant mutants, the number of new is at least 10 times greater than the number found on medium containing glucose, When glucose is added back to the medium, the number of mutants again drops. This is precisely what one would expect if the mutational pathway was, indeed, subject to catabolite repression. In our experiments, catabolite repression, rather than "directed evolution," best explains the differential yields of lactose-positive and valine-resistant mutants.

At the moment it is a matter of pure speculation as to which mutation-generating genes are responsible for causing the alterations seen when catabolite repression is lifted. It is nevertheless possible to suggest a few ways in which increased mutation rates might come about in bacterial cells. For example, DNA polymerase III, the enzyme that duplicates *E. coli* Dna prior to cell division is composed of several subunits, the cooperation of which is essential in order to faithfully replicate the parental DNA. One subunit of this enzyme complex is known to be responsible for the enzymes's overall proofreading and editing capacities. Any significant derepression of a gene or genes coding for the polymerizing subunits should engender a relative decrease in the amount and, possibly, the quality of proofreading associated with the editing subunit. As a result of such a change DNA replication will be less accurate overall and more mutations will be produced.

In addition, relief from catabolite repression may cause an increase in levels of another enzyme important for filling in nicks and gaps in existing DNA. Increased levels of this enzyme could yield more promiscuous and less accurate gap-filling activity. Other possibilities also exist, and indeed, evidence has recently been obtained in my laboratory that indicates several processes may be involved in generating the errors that lead to spontaneous mutations.

Organisms always seem so remarkably suited to their environments that it becomes a temptation to think that there must be some sort of intent to their adaptations and a direction to their evolution. Certainly it was a temptation to Lamarck, and apparently it continues to tempt modern-day molecular biologists. But Darwin, working long before the era of bacterial genetics, resisted that notion. And now that scientists can look at the stuff of heredity directly, we can see that molecular genetics does, after all, proceed according to Darwin's theories of random mutation.

Dedicated to the memory of a great friend and scholar, Professor Frederik H. Sobels.

Bibliography

Brenner, S. 1992. Dicing with Darwin. *Current Biology* 2:167—168.

Cairns, J., and P. L. Foster. Adaptive reversion of a frameshift mutation in *Escherichia coli*. *Genetics* 128:695—701.

Cairns, J., J. Overbaugh and S. Miller. 1988. The origin of mutants. *Nature* 335:142—145.

Charlesworth, D., B. Charlesworth, J. J. Bull, A. Grafen, R. Holliday, R. F. Rosenberg, L. M. Van Valen, A. Danchin, I. Tessman and J. Cairns. 1988. Origin of mutants disputed (Correspondence). *Nature* 336:525—528.

Foster, P. 1992. Directed mutation: between unicorns and goats. *Journal of Bacteriology* 147:1711—1716.

Goodman, B. 1992. Heredity made to order. *Mosaic* 23:24—31.

Hall, B. G. 1990. Spontaneous point mutations that occur more often when advantageous than when neutral. *Genetics* 126:5—16.

Keller, E.F .1991. Between language and science: The question of directed mutation in molecular genetics. *Perspectives in Biology and Medicine* 35:292—306.

Lenski, R. E., and J. E. Mittler. 1993. The directed mutation controversy and Neo-Darwinism. *Science* 259:188—194.

Luria, S. E., and M. Delbrück. 1943. Mutations of bacteria from virus sensitivity to virus resistance. *Genetics* 28:491—511.

MacPhee, D. G. 1985. Indications that mutagenesis in Salmonella may be subject to catabolite repression. *Mutation Research* 151:35—41.

MacPhee, D. G. 1993. Is there evidence for directed mutation in bacteria? *Mutagenesis* 8:3—5.

MacPhee, D. G. 1993. Directed mutation: paradigm postponed *Mutation Research* 285:109—116.

Stahl, F. 1988. A unicorn in the garden. *Nature* 335:112—113.

Erratum

In this article, the term "Darwinian," as in "Darwinian theory" or "Darwinian tenets," should be replaced by the phrase "Darwinian and neo-Darwinian" at the first mention and by the term "neo-Darwinian" thereafter.

John W. Drake
Barry W. Glickman
Lynn S. Ripley

Updating the Theory of Mutation

De mutatis mutationum mutandis: recently discovered dynamic aspects of DNA structure and metabolism have fostered a fundamental reshaping of the theory of mutation

In recent years an extraordinary increase has occurred in the attention, both popular and scientific, paid to mutation and its consequences. The sources of this interest are the recognition that components of our environment pose a largely unevaluated threat to the conservation of genetic material and the realization that mutations frequently have serious consequences for human health that encompass, at the least, birth defects and cancer. The resulting renewed effort has improved our understanding of the fundamental genetic substance, DNA, and of the intricacies of its metabolism and organization into genes.

Modern investigations into the mutation process closely intertwine the structure of DNA and all the processes that impinge upon it. Inherent in the now-classical description of DNA structure by Watson and Crick in 1953, and immediately recognized by them, was the notion that variations in the electronic structures of the DNA bases could cause incorrect base pairings, and hence mutations. In the early models, however, DNA was viewed as structurally static when not undergoing replication. More recently, the identification of numerous families of alternative structures has led to an expanded view of DNA as far more variable in form. Some of these structures provide explanations for mutational events that were previously mysterious, and others offer intriguing hints for future exploration.

Mutagenesis reflects not only the structure of DNA, but the plasm in

The authors are members of the Laboratory of Genetics at the National Institute of Environmental Health Sciences, and have carried out studies of fundamental mechanisms of mutagenesis for a number of years. Address: Laboratory of Genetics, NIEHS, Research Triangle Park, NC 27709.

which it resides, the proteins that adhere to it and induce its higher-order structures, and, above all, the many enzymes that mediate its replication, recombination, and repair. These enzymes achieve levels of accuracy during the repair and replication of DNA that far exceed simple expectations. In this discussion we will consider most closely the properties of the DNA polymerases, which are the ultimate catalysts of replication and are remarkable in frequently operating their own enzymatic editorial offices. In addition, other enzymes act subsequent to replication to improve accuracy still further.

We will also consider the characteristics of mutational events themselves. Mutations have classically been attributed to DNA damage or to misprocessing. However, a new candidate has recently emerged: mobile genetic elements, discovered in many organisms and often present in large numbers in each cell. The movement of these elements to new locations often generates mutations at the sites of insertion.

Mutations are most precisely described as changes in the sequence of the four bases that provide the informational content of DNA. These bases are the purines adenine (A) and guanine (G) and the pyrimidines thymine (T) and cytosine (C). In double-stranded DNA they are arranged in the four base pairs A·T, T·A, G·C, and C·G (see the top of Figs. 1 and 2), and base pairs, in turn, are arranged in linear sequences. Each strand of DNA has a chemical polarity defined by the asymmetry of the sugar-phosphate backbone. One end of the sugar is called the 5′ end and the other the 3′ end, and DNA strands are conventionally written in the 5′→3′ direction. The two complementary strands of a double helix have opposite polarities and are

written in a form such as

$$...5' A G G C T A 3'...$$
$$...3' T C C G A T 5'...$$

Any discussion of the mutation process ultimately draws on the roster of elementary changes in the sequence of the base pairs.

When one base (or base pair) is replaced by another, the change is called a base or base pair substitution. Base pair substitutions are further classified into two classes known as transitions and transversions. In a transition, a purine is replaced by a purine, and at the same time a pyrimidine is replaced by a pyrimidine: for instance, A·T → G·C or G·C → A·T. In a transversion, a purine is replaced by a pyrimidine and a pyrimidine by a purine: for instance, A·T → T·A or A·T → C·G.

Mutations can also result from the addition or deletion of one or more base pairs. An important example of this type occurs in the DNA sequences that encode polypeptides. Such changes, called frameshift mutations, are important for their ability to disrupt gene function. Because the genetic code relates codons of three contiguous bases to each amino acid, the addition or deletion of any nonthreefold number of bases throws thr eadingf rameo uto fo rder.

There also exist mutations of even greater extent, affecting from tens to many thousands of base pairs. The largest of these, called chromosome mutations, may involve the rearrangement of portions of chromosomes, or the addition or deletion of DNA sequences.

Bent and battered bases

In classical theory, the hydrogen-bonding potential between the coding faces of bases determines both

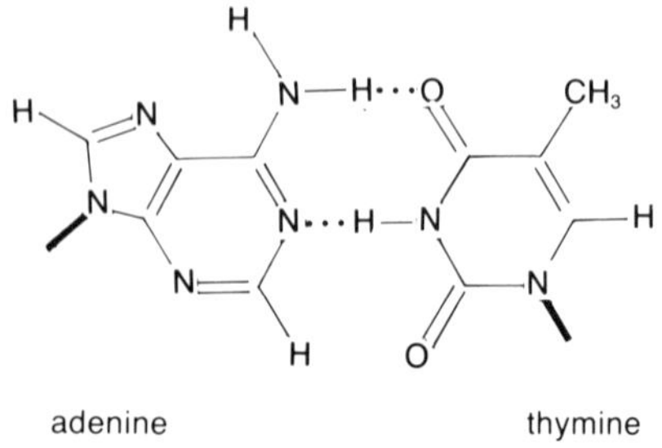

the adenine · thymine base pair

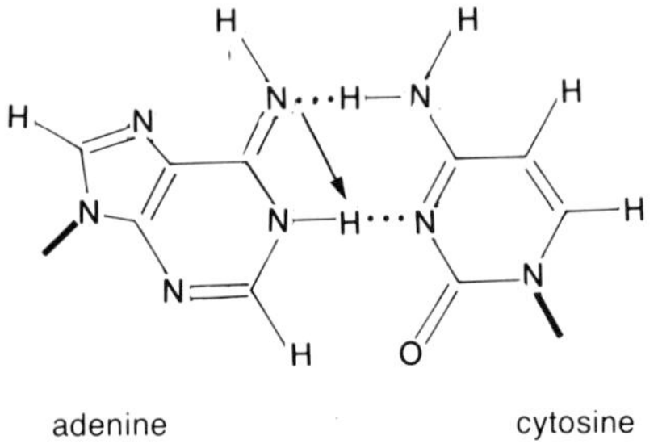

an adenine · cytosine mispair

A · T → A* · C → G · C

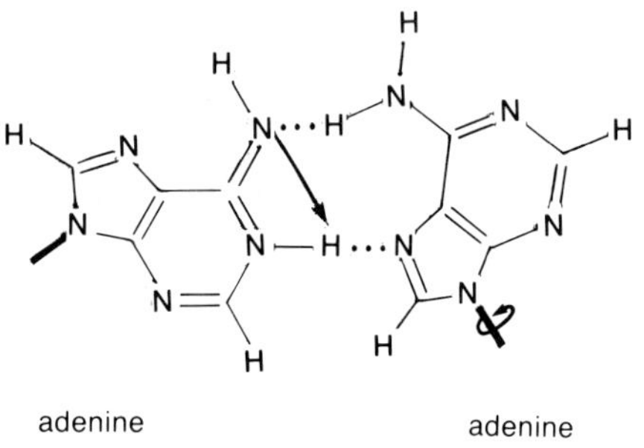

an adenine · adenine mispair

A · T → A* · A' → T · A

Figure 1. Proton migration within base pairs can set off a chain of modifications that ends in DNA mutation. At the top, the normal A·T base pair has two hydrogen bonds (*dotted lines*), and each base is connected to the helical DNA backbone (not shown) by the glycosidic bonds between the indicated nitrogen atom of the base and the first carbon atom of the deoxyribose portion of the backbone. In the middle structure, the adenine·cytosine mispair acts as an intermediate step in the mutation A·T → G·C (see the top of Fig. 2 for the structure of the G·C base pair). A proton has migrated (*arrow*), and the resulting rearrangement of electronic structure permits two hydrogen bonds to form with the incorrect base, cytosine. The possibility of such a mechanism for mutation was perceived as early as 1953 by Watson and Crick. In the structure at the bottom, an adenine·adenine mispair acts as an intermediate in the mutation A·T → T·A (where the T·A base pair is the same as the A·T shown at the top, but viewed from its underside). Again, proton migration has occurred (*arrow*), and the adenine on the right has rotated 180° around its glycosidic bond into the *syn* configuration. In this mispair, both adenines are abnormal.

the structure of DNA and the specificity with which it is replicated. However, hydrogen-bonding potential, and hence base-pairing specificity, can vary, either by brief, spontaneous changes in the electronic structure of a base or by permanent covalent modifications. Many spontaneous errors of DNA synthesis are believed to result from the former type of change, and many induced mutations from the latter.

Transitions may arise from any of several proton migrations within bases. Although such base tautomers may be rare and short-lived, they may produce mutations when they occur at the moment of base addition to the growing chain. Figure 1 gives an example of such a mechanism, postulated by Watson and Crick (1953) immediately after the announcement of their model of double-helical DNA.

Transversions have been more difficult to explain, since neither of the two possible aberrantly paired intermediates, the purine·purine or pyrimidine·pyrimidine base pairs, fits well into the conventionally conceived double helix. Indeed, more than two decades passed before a satisfactory scheme was offered (Topal and Fresco 1976). It was proposed that transversions arise by the apposition of two errors, one a proton migration such as those mediating transitions, and the other a 180° rotation of a base around its bond to the DNA backbone (from the common *anti* to the infrequent *syn* configuration). Such a mechanism for an A·T → T·A transversion is shown in Figure 1.

This class of models may have been overlooked for many years for a simple reason: whereas a double-error model suggests that transversions should be rare as compared with transitions, the fact is that they are usually not rare. However, the ratio of *syn* to *anti* configurations is not very small either: it is approximately 1:10, whereas the frequency of proton migration is usually estimated at around 1:10,000. Thus the model predicts that transversions would originate at most only about tenfold less frequently than transitions—a small difference when compared to the large natural variation in mutation rates at different sites.

The picture thus far shows spontaneous mutations arising by

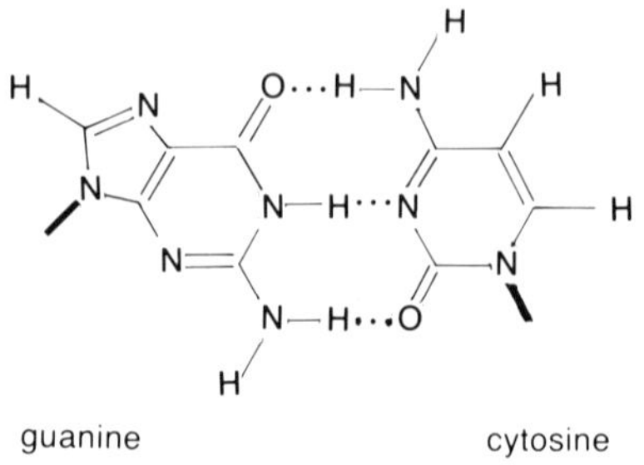

the guanine · cytosine base pair

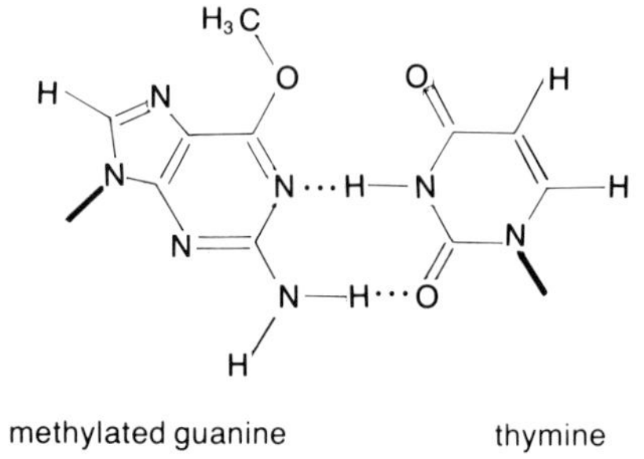

a methylguanine · thymine mispair

G·C → G'·C → G'·T → A·T

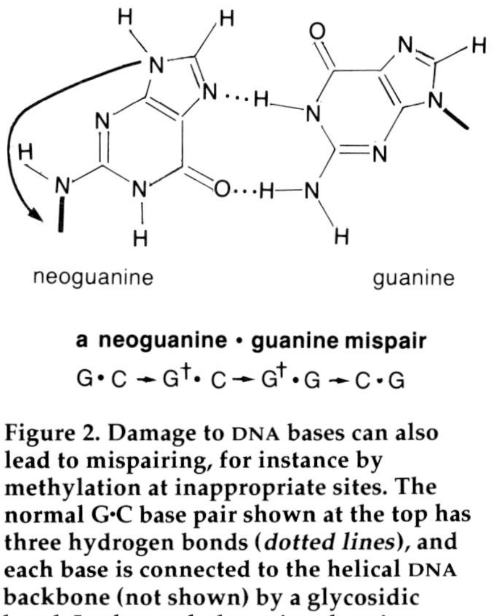

a neoguanine · guanine mispair

G·C → G†·C → G†·G → C·G

Figure 2. Damage to DNA bases can also lead to mispairing, for instance by methylation at inappropriate sites. The normal G·C base pair shown at the top has three hydrogen bonds (*dotted lines*), and each base is connected to the helical DNA backbone (not shown) by a glycosidic bond. In the methylguanine·thymine mispair, the oxygen at the top of the guanine has been methylated, also causing the loss of one proton from a nearby nitrogen and producing a base able to form two hydrogen bonds with thymine, and thus ultimately substituting an A·T base pair (the structure of which is shown at the top of Fig. 1). In the neoguanine·guanine mispair, the bond from a guanine to the DNA backbone has shifted from its usual position to an extracyclic nitrogen (*arrow*), reorienting the modified guanine and permitting it to form two hydrogen bonds with an ordinary guanine. The final result, a C·G base pair, is the same as the G·C base pair shown at the top, but viewed from its underside.

means of the mispairing properties of transitory tautomers of bases. However, DNA and its precursors are subject to constant physical and chemical attack from both environmental and endogenous sources, which can damage bases permanently. It is useful to assign damaged bases to one of two categories: those in which base-pairing specificity has been altered, and those in which it has been obliterated.

Figure 2 gives two examples of bases driven to mispair by damage, one generating transitions and the other transversions. The methylguanine·thymine mispair (Loveless 1969) results from the alkylation—specifically, the methylation—of guanine. This adduct promotes an electronic rearrangement similar to that shown in the middle of Figure 1, and thus allows aberrant hydrogen bonding. DNA methylation can result from exposure to exogenous chemicals, but even normal cellular methyl donors occasionally attack DNA. The proposed neoguanine·guanine mispair (Bingham et al. 1976) begins with heat-induced rupture of the glycosidic bond that attaches a guanine to the DNA backbone, followed by rotation of the guanine within its plane and the subsequent formation of a novel bond (a process called repurination). Heat-induced DNA lesions occur at a significant rate even at ordinary mammalian body temperatures. Indeed, so many take place per day in each cell that, as will be explained below, it has been necessary to postulate the existence of an efficient repair process for reversing the damage.

Certain types of base damage altogether preclude hydrogen bonding. These include depurination (the complete loss of a purine), gross base distortion (such as the dimerization of adjacent bases, twisting one coding face out of reach), and the formation of bulky adducts (akin to the simple methylation shown in Fig. 2, but adding a group so large as to interfere with base·base interactions). Such kinds of damage are quite common. Depurination, for instance, occurs in humans about 10,000 times per cell per day at body temperature; base dimerization is induced by the ultraviolet component of sunlight; and bulky adductors are common among such environmental carcinogens as aflatoxin and benzpyrene. Base damages like these terminate

the 2-aminopurine · thymine base pair

a 2-aminopurine · cytosine base pair

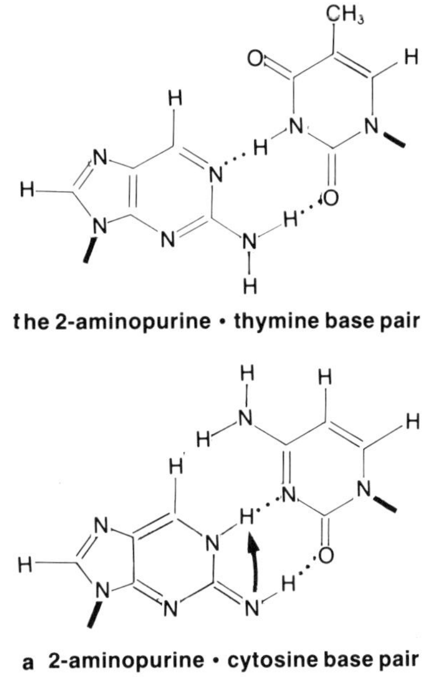

Figure 3. Artificial bases resembling the natural bases of DNA can be helpful in studying mechanisms of mutations. The synthetic analog to adenine, 2-aminopurine, can form two hydrogen bonds with thymine (top), but a proton migration (arrow) produces an electronically modified base that can form two hydrogen bonds with cytosine (bottom). This intermediate participates in both A·T → G·C and G·C → A·T transitions. It thus promotes transitions in both directions (A·T ↔ 2AP·T ↔ 2AP·C ↔ G·C).

DNA synthesis, and are thus apt to kill the cell. However, as we shall see, in certain circumstances they may have surprising alternative consequences.

Perspicacious polymerases

Since few mutations appear to confer an advantage to the organism that harbors them, and many are harmful, it is not surprising that cells have evolved mechanisms to reduce rates of mutation. We have noted that errors might be expected to occur as frequently as 10^{-4}, owing to mispairing caused by base tautomers. However, studies with DNA polymerases in vitro often reveal error frequencies of only about 10^{-7} (Loeb and Kunkel 1982).

Analyses of the enzymatic determinants of mutation rates suggest that the DNA polymerase plays a central role. Some mechanisms by which polymerases reduce error rates have been rewardingly probed by examining the properties of mutant polymerases. For example, certain mutationally modified DNA polymerases often increase mutation

rates, and are therefore called mutator polymerases. Conversely, other mutant polymerases reduce mutation rates below the normal level; these polymerases are called antimutators.

DNA polymerases are large and complex proteins, containing approximately 1,000 amino acids and interacting physically and functionally with numerous other proteins involved in DNA metabolism. Many DNA polymerases express two distinct enzymatic functions: a $5' \rightarrow 3'$ polymerizing (or DNA-synthesizing) activity and a $3' \rightarrow 5'$ exonuclease (DNA-degrading) one. The discovery of the exonuclease activity led to the suggestion that it might serve as a "proofreader" of newly synthesized DNA, and subsequent experiments have supported this notion. For example, the 3'-exonuclease removes mismatched bases at the ends of polynucleotides in preference to correctly paired bases (Brutlag and Kornberg 1972). Moreover, a striking relationship has been observed between polymerase fidelity, as measured in bacteriophage T4 in vivo, and the ratio of T4 exonuclease to polymerase, as measured in vitro: the mutator polymerases often have relatively less exonuclease, and the antimutator polymerases more exonuclease, than the normal enzyme (Muzyczka et al. 1972). This is precisely what is predicted by the model that assigns a proofreading function to the exonuclease.

Subsequent theoretical considerations led to the view that DNA polymerases improve their accuracy through a series of coupled steps in which transiently incorporated bases are tested for the goodness of their fit, mainly in terms of hydrogen bonding to the templating base; poorly paired bases are then removed by the exonuclease. Base-pairing is thus examined twice: first during base incorporation and then, during proofreading, by the exonuclease. These two steps forge an accuracy that approaches the product of the two individual error rates. In this example, the mispairing rate may thus be decreased from about 10^{-4} to about 10^{-8}.

But just how does the enzyme catalyze the accurate incorporation and removal of bases? The simplest view is that the polymerase is passive with respect to the binding of incoming bases; only the ability of the base to form hydrogen bonds with the templating base determines the length of its stay in the polymerization site, and hence its chance of incorporation. Similarly, only the probability that an incorporated base will fail to remain hydrogen-bonded with its complement determines its susceptibility to the exonuclease. A more complex view is that the polymerase somehow senses additional properties of the templating and incorporated bases and makes use of this information to improve fidelity.

A number of the properties of DNA polymerases strongly suggest that the simple passive-polymerase model is inadequate, and that more subtle modes of discrimination are available. For instance, proofreading models based exclusively on hydrogen bonding predict that antimutator polymerases with increased exonuclease activities should reduce all base-pair substitutions. In the case of the T4 antimutator polymerases, however, the rate of A·T → G·C transitions is strongly reduced, whereas there is almost no effect on the rate of spontaneous G·C → A·T transitions, and the rate of transversions at A·T base pairs is actually increased (Ripley 1982a). Does this mean that only A·T → G·C transitions arise via mispaired intermediates? Or, as seems more likely, do DNA

polymerases discriminate on the basis of determinants other than hydrogen bonding?

An important hint that properties of a base other than its hydrogen-bonding potential may determine its specificity in replication comes from studies of chemically induced mispairing. These studies employed a synthetic base analog, 2-aminopurine (2AP), not found in normal DNA but similar to the natural base adenine. Figure 3 shows how 2AP can pair normally with thymine but can mispair with cytosine as the result of an electronic rearrangement; because this rearrangement occurs more frequently in 2AP than in adenine, 2AP is a strong mutagen. It promotes transitions in both directions (A·T ↔ 2AP·T ↔ 2AP·C ↔ G·C). The mispaired intermediate has two orientations: an incoming C mispairing with a template 2AP, or an incoming 2AP mispairing with a template C. As compared with a normal polymerase, an antimutator polymerase reduces the frequency of 2AP-induced mutations far more when the 2AP resides in the template than when it is the incoming base. This result argues against the notion that accuracy depends only upon the length and strength of hydrogen bonding—in this case, in 2AP·C (Ripley 1981).

There are many ways in which

a polymerase might sense the steric properties of a base at the incorporation as well as at the proofreading step of DNA synthesis. Although the precise molecular details remain to be defined, it is likely that mutagenic and antimutagenic activities can be expressed during the incorporation of a base, as well as during the proofreading step (Hershfield 1973; Gillin and Nossal 1976). In addition, other factors, such as the surrounding DNA bases, influence accuracy. For example, a base change such as A·T → G·C occurs at widely differing rates at different sites; but the molecular basis of the influences of neighboring bases remains obscure. Indeed, within the critical region of the DNA replication fork (wherein one double helix becomes two), the structure of DNA is completely unknown. Thus, while it is clear enough that parental bases form the templates for progeny bases, it remains unknown whether they do so mainly by direct base·base interactions or through an indirect mechanism mediated by DNA polymerases.

It should be stressed that polymerases do not act solo parts but are accompanied by numerous enzymes of DNA metabolism that are already known to contribute substantially to accuracy. Many of these proteins function cooperatively within a replication complex. This aggregate of enzymes unwinds the double helix prior to synthesis, maintains the parental strands in an extended configuration suitable for a template, and solves the topological problems of local unwinding and rewinding of double helixes (Kornberg 1980; Hibner and Alberts 1980). It may even serve to link the synthesis of progeny bases directly to the sites of their incorporation.

Repair and misrepair

We have seen that the polymerase gains fidelity by coupling proofreading to polymerization. In theory, a chain of subsequent proofreading steps might pursue the moving replication fork, adding numerous factors of improvement, and indeed such a step has been identified (Glickman and Radman 1980). Mismatch repair, as this step is known, was initially identified because its elimination caused mutation rates to rise sharply. Thus it appears to be an

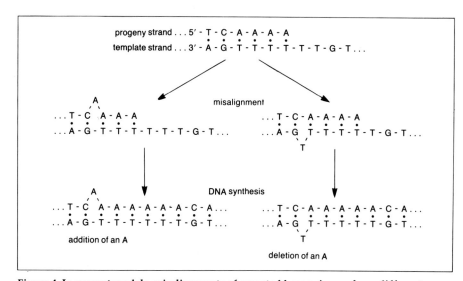

Figure 4. In current models, misalignments of repeated base pairs can have different mutagenic consequences, depending on whether the misalignment occurs by swinging a base out from a newly synthesized progeny strand (*left*), or from a parental template strand (*right*). Whereas the normal progeny strand of this sequence would contain a string of 6 adenines, misalignment mutations give results of either 7 adenines or 5 adenines. (Here and throughout, base-pairing is indicated by dots.) Subsequent DNA synthesis traps the misalignment. The next round of DNA replication (not shown) will segregate these structures into purely mutant and purely normal base-pair sequences. Simple variations on such schemes can also produce additions or deletions of two or more base pairs. (After Streisinger et al. 1966.)

important mechanism for the control of mutation rates.

Although the system detects base mismatches resulting from replication errors, it follows some distance behind the replication fork, and thus encounters an inherent challenge: which base of the mispair is erroneous? Which base should be kept, which discarded and replaced? In *Escherichia coli*, for instance, mismatch repair appears to mark occasional bases of the DNA in such a way that the parental DNA strand can be distinguished from the daughter strand. In *E. coli*, mismatch repair requires a gene called *dam*. The enzyme encoded by *dam* methylates adenine residues in the sequence

$$...5'\ G\ A\ T\ C\ 3'...$$
$$...3'\ C\ T\ A\ G\ 5'...$$

which occurs frequently in DNA. Because of the time lag between DNA replication and methylation, the GATC sequences in the parental strands are methylated while those in the progeny strands are transiently unmethylated. This difference between parental and progeny strands permits the cell to discern the "wrong" base of any mismatch. There are indications that mismatch repair occurs in a wide variety of organisms, including higher eukaryotes, but the particular signals used to discriminate between correct and incorrect bases of the mismatch may not always be the same.

A number of other DNA repair systems operate not only at or near the replication fork but throughout the genome, recognizing and repairing damaged bases. These systems are as diverse as are the kinds of damage they repair (Lindahl 1982). They fall into two broad classes: those that directly reverse the damage (for instance, by stripping off the offending methyl group, as in Fig. 2, or by breaking the linkages between dimerized bases), and those that excise damaged bases and resynthesize double-stranded DNA, using the complementary strand as a template. This second process, called excision repair, is capable of recognizing and removing a broad range of DNA damages.

Although they are highly effective, these repair systems cannot remove every instance of damage before it enters a replication fork. Should such unrepaired damage cause mispairing, mutations are likely to result. However, if the damage actually precludes pairing, a quite different chain of events may ensue, as outlined in the following popular hypothesis.

The first consequence of nonpairing would be chain termination: the polymerase simply cannot proceed past the damaged base, possibly because whatever base happens to be incorporated cannot bond properly with its parental-strand complement, and is therefore promptly removed by the proofreading exonuclease. Under these conditions, reinitiation of DNA synthesis can occur farther along, leaving an embarrassing gap in the daughter strand.

Such a gap triggers a remarkable response in many organisms; in *E. coli* it is known as the SOS response (Radman 1974; Witkin 1976). A number of DNA repair genes are activated in coordination, some causing the gaps in the daughter strand to be filled accurately by a recombinational mechanism. However, in the present context the most interesting mechanism is one that permits DNA synthesis past the point of damage. Because such "bypass synthesis" would be poorly templated, at best, by damaged bases, it is decidedly mutagenic. (For this reason it has been called error-prone repair, misrepair, or mutagenic repair.) Mutagenesis by agents that generate noncoding or synthesis-blocking lesions depend uniformly on the induction of bypass synthesis for their mutagenic consequences.

Misalignment mutagenesis

We have focused thus far on base-pair substitutions produced by mispairing. However, another important component of mutagenesis proceeds through transient intermediates in which the bases are correctly paired, in the sense that A pairs with T and G with C, but in which the pairing occurs out of register. The products of such anomalous alignments may be not only base-pair substitutions, but also additions and deletions

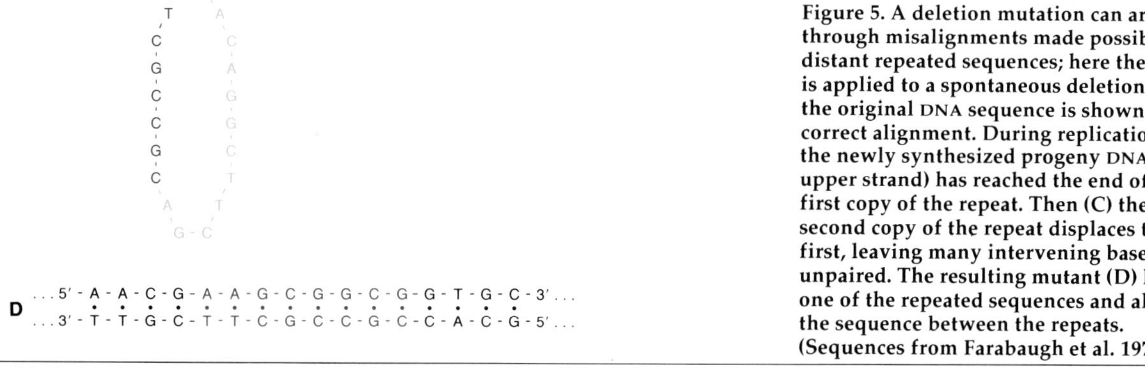

Figure 5. A deletion mutation can arise through misalignments made possible by distant repeated sequences; here the model is applied to a spontaneous deletion. In A, the original DNA sequence is shown in its correct alignment. During replication (B), the newly synthesized progeny DNA (the upper strand) has reached the end of the first copy of the repeat. Then (C) the second copy of the repeat displaces the first, leaving many intervening bases unpaired. The resulting mutant (D) has lost one of the repeated sequences and all of the sequence between the repeats. (Sequences from Farabaugh et al. 1978.)

...5'-A-T-T-A-C-T-C-G-A-T-G-C-C-T-T-A-A-G-G-C-A-T-C-G-A-G-T-G-C-G-3'...
...3'-T-A-A-T-G-A-G-C-T-A-C-G-G-A-A-T-T-C-C-G-T-A-G-C-T-C-A-C-G-C-5'...

Figure 6. An important source of mutation in double-stranded DNA appears to be the palindrome, wherein the two strands bear the identical base sequence when read from their 5' ends to their 3' ends. When the usual base-pairing complementarity between strands is combined with the symmetry of DNA palindromes, the result is complementarity within a single strand. This permits the DNA to form hydrogen bonds by base-pairing within a strand (*right*), as well as by pairing between strands (*above*).

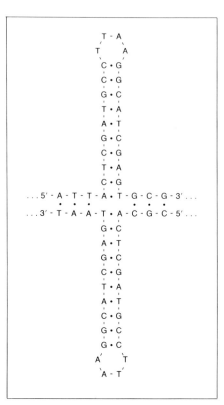

The first model of misalignment mutagenesis was offered to explain frameshift mutations and arose from the observation that additions or deletions of one or a few base pairs often occurred within short, redundant sequences (Streisinger et al. 1966). The model outlined in Figure 4 shows such events as they may take place during DNA synthesis, particularly at a strand discontinuity near a region of local redundancy that may promote misalignments. This model successfully explains the existence of sites in many genetic systems at which mutations are unusually frequent (mutational "hot spots"). In bacteriophage T4 such a hot spot consists of a repeated base pair, for example

...A A A A A A...
...T T T T T T...

at which a frameshift mutation may add or delete an A·T base pair (Okada et al. 1972; Pribnow et al. 1981). Frameshift mutations arise in the same manner within a more complex sequence at an *E. coli* mutational hot spot, the wild-type sequence being

...C T G G C T G G C T G G...
...G A C C G A C C G A C C...

with the mutation either adding or deleting one CTGG tetramer. The general model is convincingly confirmed here, since the frequent occurrence of four-base-pair duplications of an existing sequence is highly unlikely to occur by any mechanism short of templated DNA synthesis.

Additions and deletions of much larger extent are explicable by a minor variation on this theme. The termini, or ends, of such large mutations often bridge short, repeated sequences separated by tens to hundreds of nonrepetitious base pairs. A deletion of this type is shown in Figure 5. The crucial aspect of the misalignment schemes shown in Figures 4 and 5 is their reliance on correct base-pairing in an incorrect context.

Unfortunately, however, such misalignments cannot explain many frameshift and deletion mutations that clearly do *not* arise within or between repetitious sequences. Recently, a second class of models for misalignment mutagenesis has been proposed to explain at least some of these puzzles (Ripley 1982b; Ripley and Glickman 1983). The new models describe misalignments generated by DNA palindromes—sequences in which one strand read in the usual 5'→3' direction is identical to that of the complementary strand, also read

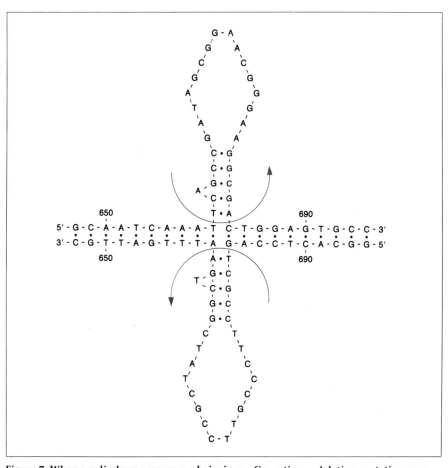

Figure 7. When a palindrome assumes a hairpin configuration, a deletion mutation may result. In the *E. coli lacI* gene, a palindrome could lead to the misalignment shown here, with hairpin structures projecting out from both DNA strands. Thus the terminal bases of a deletion would be juxtaposed instead of remaining separated by 27 base pairs. The sequence between base pairs 657 and 685 may then be deleted either by the enzymatic removal of the hairpin at its base (*arrows*) or by aberrant DNA synthesis across the base of the stem; in the latter case, the daughter double helix would look as if one of the hairpins above had been precisely excised. (Deletion sequence from Farabaugh et al. 1978.)

in its 5'→3' direction. Because of the symmetry of such sequences, palindromes are complementary not only between opposite strands, but also within a single strand. The example in Figure 6 demonstrates this complementarity in both the conventional, linear, double-stranded configuration of DNA and an alternative, hairpin configuration.

The significance of the hairpin structure for deletion mutagenesis is illustrated in Figure 7. In this example, deletion termini fall not within repeated sequences, but at palindromes. When the termini are juxtaposed by a palindrome-directed misalignment, the deletion can be effected simply by the enzymatic removal of the hairpin, or else by DNA synthesis across the stem of the hairpin.

As a slightly more complicated example, consider the deletion generated by the DNA structure shown in Figure 8. Here the DNA misalignment is a hybrid between those illustrated in Figures 5 and 7, and again it brings the termini of the deletion into exact apposition. Repeated sequences mediate a misalignment topologically like that shown in Figure 5, but the palindrome also provides pairing within the displaced (and later deleted) sequence, as in Figure 7. The structure is thus stabilized by two elements of misalignment, one within the strand and the other between strands. The coincidence of repeated and palindromic elements at the ends of deleted sequences has been frequently observed, and it suggests that the additional hydrogen bonding available in such composite structures greatly increases the opportunities for deletion mutagenesis.

In addition to large deletions, many frameshift mutations and base-pair substitutions can be uniquely explained by the metabolism of palindromes or, more exactly, imperfect or quasipalindromes. The salient characteristic of these models is the nonrandom nature of the mutations produced, a result of the use of a nearby DNA sequence as the template.

Consider, for example, a class of complicated mutations originally observed in yeast (Stewart and Sherman 1974) and inexplicable by classical models. The mutation

$$\begin{array}{ccc} C\,G\,G & & A\,C\,C\,T \\ {\scriptstyle \cdot\ \cdot\ \cdot} & \rightarrow & {\scriptstyle \cdot\ \cdot\ \cdot\ \cdot} \\ G\,C\,C & & T\,G\,G\,A \end{array}$$

is composed, in a formal sense, of one base addition plus at least two base substitutions, but the whole mutation appears to arise in a single step, and it occurs repeatedly. As shown in Figure 9, the origin of this complex mutation can be readily understood as a quasipalindrome that is rendered more perfect by DNA metabolism. For instance, it can be imagined to arise by removal of the three nonpaired bases on the left side of the hairpin stem and the subsequent closure of the gap by DNA synthesis, using the opposite side of the stem as a template. Thus, instead of random sequence changes, the mutation is templated by the misaligned sequence.

An even more complicated mutation, which arises in bacteriophage T4 (de Boer and Ripley, unpubl.), is shown in Figure 10. In this example, some of the changes are separated by unchanged bases, and the mutation spans a total of ten base pairs. As with the yeast mutations, all the changes can be predicted by a misalignment, rather than by random base changes or deletions.

The quasipalindrome model provides extraordinarily attractive explanations for complex mutations. Although the model can often also explain simple frameshift or base-pair substitution mutations, the frequency with which it is actually responsible for these simpler mutations remains unknown. It is also difficult to assess just how frequently mutagenic secondary structures may form in vivo. The important point for the moment, however, is that secondary structures need form only occasionally and briefly in order to serve as significant intermediates in a process that is itself both rare and anomalous.

The mutagenic propensities of palindromes may also provide new glimpses into evolutionary processes. One can speculate, for instance, that palindromes are subject to a novel kind of nonrandom mutation pres-

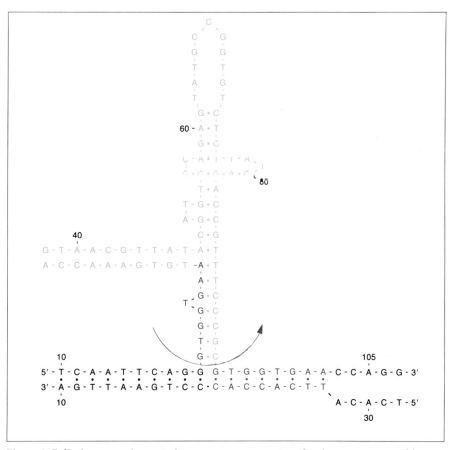

Figure 8. Palindromes and repeated sequences can occur together in a sequence, making possible a combination of palindromic misalignment, as shown in Figure 7, and repeated-sequence misalignment, as shown in Figure 5. Such two-component misalignments are frequently observed in deletion mutations, as in this spontaneous deletion in the *E. coli lacI* gene. Here the palindrome consists of the bases shown in blue, plus the vertical sequence shown in red. The repeated sequence, composed of the bases in red, partly overlaps the palindrome. The enzymatic removal of the misaligned structure at its base (*arrow*) generates the deletion. (Deletion sequence from Farabaugh et al. 1978.)

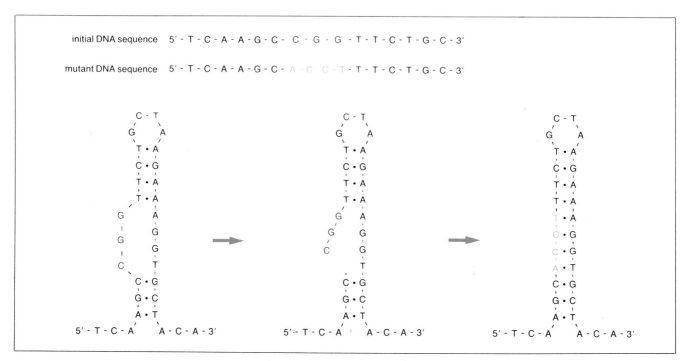

Figure 9. An imperfect palindrome, or quasipalindrome, can form a misaligned DNA structure that provides a template for frameshift mutation, as in the iso-1-cytochrome c gene of yeast. Removal of the imperfect part of the palindrome, CGG (*red*), may occur by mismatch or excision repair. The mutant sequence is then produced (*blue*), with the opposite side of the hairpin stem used as a template for repair DNA synthesis. Thus the initial DNA sequence CGG is changed to ACCT. (Deletion sequence from Stewart and Sherman 1974.)

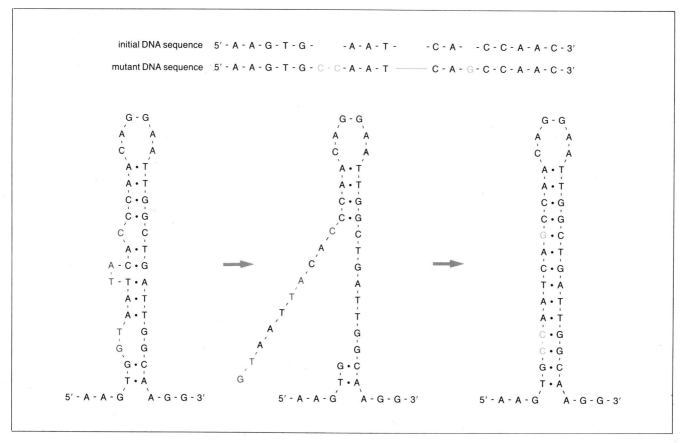

Figure 10. Although this complex mutation in the bacteriophage T4 *rIIB* gene contains three separate base substitutions and a two-base deletion, it can be explained as a single event. In the initial DNA sequence listed at the top, all the bases to be substituted or deleted are given in red. In the original hairpin structure these bases are unpaired, their opposites being either of the wrong type or missing altogether. The removal of a portion of the hairpin bounded by the unpaired bases—with, as the next step, DNA synthesis with the opposite side of the hairpin stem used as a template—can account for the generation of the mutant sequence. (After de Boer and Ripley, unpubl.)

sure. Specifically, imperfect palindromes will occur by chance much more frequently than good palindromes. Because of the tendencies illustrated in Figures 9 and 10, poor palindromes may be driven relatively rapidly toward perfection, at least in their stems. Once perfected, however, they may become particularly prone to deletion.

In another context, it is common practice to estimate evolutionary divergence by measuring the divergence of DNA sequences among homologous genes. The number of differences in the sequences is then taken to be directly proportional to the time elapsed since divergence, with only uncomplicated and usually minor corrections for overlapping mutations. If, however, a significant fraction of mutations arise as multiple changes within a single event, then a number of evolutionary distances may have to be systematically reevaluated.

Self-propelled genetic vehicles

Two lines of investigation, initiated many years ago in organisms as diverse as *E. coli* and maize, have recently converged in the discovery that a major fraction of spontaneous mutations are caused by special DNA sequences able to move among chromosomes (Shapiro 1983). Because the sequences move frequently, the sites they occupy are often recognized as genetic instabilities—that is, sites having high mutation rates. The nature of the DNA sequences responsible for these instabilities has been most fully explored in bacteria, which harbor many different elements, each ranging from a few hundred to a few thousand base pairs long. The general scheme that has emerged is that most such sequences contain genes whose products can steer the sequence to virtually all sites within chromosomes. A number of colorful names are currently used for these elements: jumping genes, insertion elements, transposons, nomadic species, mobile elements, and so on.

The special significance of mobile elements for mutagenesis is the discovery that they are a major component of spontaneous mutation. This first became apparent in *E. coli*, in which a large fraction of spontaneous mutations are the result of the

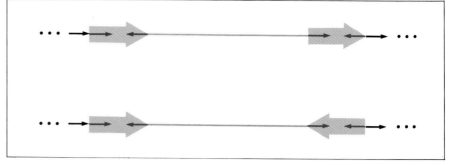

Figure 11. Two general structures for mobile genetic elements can now be postulated on the basis of a number of known DNA sequences. These general structures are shown schematically. At each end, in black, is the original chromosomal DNA sequence, a small part of which has been repeated during the insertion of the mobile element (*black arrows*). At each end of the element are long DNA repeats (*large red arrows*); in the bottom structure these take the form of inverted repeats—which are the same as palindromes! Within each of these long terminal repeats, or palindromes, are short terminal palindromes (*small red arrows*). The DNA sequence in the center of each element (*gray*) is not repetitious and can sometimes code for proteins that appear to be involved in motility.

inactivation of genes by insertions. A similarly large frequency of insertions was soon reported in yeasts, and an even greater frequency has recently been reported in *Drosophila*. There are indications that even mammals may be riddled with such molecular parasites (see, for instance, Jaenisch et al. 1983).

The DNA sequences of a number of mobile elements have now been determined, and a consensus structure is shown in Figure 11. The repeated sequences, if inverted, can become palindromes, and the sequence in the center can often code for proteins, some of which may be involved in mobility. The large repeats often contain small internal repeats at their ends, and the entire element is flanked by short repeated sequences not belonging to the mobile element, which are generated during the insertion of the element into a new site. This structural complexity provides a number of potential secondary structures that may play important roles in the behavior of mobile elements. These elements usually seem to be spun off the chromosome by DNA replication, leaving behind one copy and generating another that can insert elsewhere. Sometimes, however, the elements leave their original sites altogether. Such departures are not always precise: sometimes a portion of the element is left behind, and at other times additional DNA, beyond the mobile element, is deleted.

Although insertion mutagenesis may be a ubiquitous component of spontaneous mutation, there is as yet

a striking lack of evidence that mobility, and hence mutagenesis, can be enhanced by chemical or physical mutagens. DNA damage, therefore, seems unlikely to engender mobility. On the other hand, mobility is likely to involve DNA replication, and thus to be controlled by a variety of proteins. Perhaps there exist mutagens that activate mobile elements by attacking proteins rather than DNA, but what such mutagens may be remains an open question.

Future directions

The analysis of mutagenesis has often been frustrated by the rarity of mutations and the multiplicity of mechanisms by which they arise. The chemical analysis of DNA lesions is difficult, and by itself rarely provides a satisfactory account of the cause of a mutation, mainly because the actions of enzymes on DNA that can lead to mutations are numerous and complex. As a result, the bridges of inference that must be built between mutational and chemical measurements are often long, and they frequently fall.

The list of mutagenic mechanisms is long, and it is far more difficult to write the encyclopedia of all possible errors than the few chapters of correct procedures. Important mechanisms of mutation are probably still lurking unseen, just as did the ways of secondary structures and mobile elements until very recently. The critical questions of the moment, however, are strongly implied by our story. Do mobile elements contribute only to spontaneous mutation, or can they also be activated by environmental influences? How do DNA polymerases sense the shapes of bases and use that information in their pursuit of perfection? What are the mechanics of mismatch repair, and how does mutagenic bypass work around nonpairing DNA lesions? There remain also the larger issues of how far the analysis of alternative DNA structures can take us in understanding mutagenesis, and whether there are yet higher orders of DNA structure that are important in mutagenesis. In many cases, the technology already exists to attack these questions, and answers can be expected soon.

References

Bingham, P. M., R. H. Baltz, L. S. Ripley, and J. W. Drake. 1976. Heat mutagenesis in bacteriophage T4: The transversion pathway. *PNAS* 73:4159–63.

Brutlag, D., and A. Kornberg. 1972. Enzymatic synthesis of deoxyribonucleic acid. XXXVI. A proofreading function for the 3′→5′ exonuclease activity in deoxyribonucleic acid polymerases. *J. Biol. Chem.* 247:241–48.

de Boer, J. G., and L. S. Ripley. Unpubl. DNA secondary structures generate frameshift mutations.

Farabaugh, P. J., U. Schmeissner, M. Hofer, and J. H. Miller. 1978. Genetic studies of the *lac* repressor. VII. On the molecular nature of spontaneous hotspots in the *lacI* gene of *Escherichia coli*. *J. Mol. Biol.* 126:847–63.

Gillin, F. D., and N. G. Nossal. 1976. Control of mutation frequency by bacteriophage T4 DNA polymerase. II. Accuracy of nucleotide selection by the L88 mutator, CB120 antimutator, and wild type phage T4 DNA polymerases. *J. Biol. Chem.* 251:5225–32.

Glickman, B. W., and M. Radman. 1980. *Escherichia coli* mutator mutants deficient in methylation-instructed DNA mismatch correction. *PNAS* 77:1063–67.

Hershfield, M. S. 1973. On the role of deoxyribonucleic acid polymerase in determining mutation rates. Characterization of the defect in the T4 deoxyribonucleic acid polymerase caused by the *ts* L88 mutation. *J. Biol. Chem.* 248:1417–23.

Hibner, U., and B. M. Alberts. 1980. Fidelity of DNA replication catalysed *in vitro* on a natural DNA template by the T4 bacteriophage multi-enzyme complex. *Nature* 285:300–05.

Jaenisch, R., et al. 1983. Germline integration of Moloney murine leukemia virus at the *Mov13* locus leads to recessive lethal mutation and early embryonic death. *Cell* 32:209–16.

Kornberg, A. 1980. *DNA Replication.* W. H. Freeman.

Lindahl, T. 1982. DNA repair enzymes. *Ann. Rev. Biochem.* 51:61–87.

Loeb, L. A., and T. A. Kunkel. 1982. Fidelity of DNA synthesis. *Ann. Rev. Biochem.* 51:429–57.

Loveless, A. 1969. Possible relevance of O–6 alkylation of deoxyguanosine to the mutagenicity and carcinogenicity of nitrosamines and nitrosamides. *Nature* 223:206–07.

Muzyczka, N., R. L. Poland, and M. J. Bessman. 1972. Studies on the biochemical basis of spontaneous mutation. I. A comparison of the deoxyribonucleic acid polymerases of mutator, antimutator, and wild type strains of bacteriophage T4. *J. Biol. Chem.* 247:7116–22.

Okada, Y., G. Streisinger, J. E. Owen, J. Newton, A. Tsugita, and M. Inouye. 1972. Molecular basis of a mutational hot spot in the lysozyme gene of bacteriophage T4. *Nature* 236:338–41.

Pribnow, D., et al. 1981. rII cistrons of bacteriophage T4. DNA sequence around the intercistronic divide and positions of genetic landmarks. *J. Mol. Biol.* 149:337–76.

Radman, M. 1974. Phenomenology of an inducible mutagenic DNA repair pathway in *E. coli*: SOS repair hypothesis. In *Molecular and Environmental Aspects of Mutagenesis*, ed. L. Prakash, F. Sherman, M. W. Miller, C. W. Lawrence, and H. W. Taber, pp. 129–40. Springfield, IL: C. C Thomas.

Ripley, L. S. 1981. Influence of diverse gene 43 DNA polymerases on the incorporation and replication *in vivo* of 2-aminopurine at A·T base pairs in bacteriophage T4. *J. Mol. Biol.* 150:197–216.

———. 1982a. The infidelity of DNA polymerase. In *Induced Mutagenesis: Molecular Mechanisms and Their Implications for Environmental Protection*, ed. C. W. Lawrence, L. Prakash, and F. Sherman, pp. 85–116. Plenum.

———. 1982b. Model for the participation of quasipalindromic DNA sequences in frameshift mutation. *PNAS* 79:4128–32.

Ripley, L. S., and B. W. Glickman. 1983. The unique self-complementarity of palindromic sequences provides DNA structural intermediates for mutation. *Cold Spring Harbor Symp. Quant. Biol.* 47:851–61.

Shapiro, J. A., ed. 1983. *Mobile Genetic Elements.* Academic Press.

Stewart, J. W., and F. Sherman. 1974. Yeast frameshift mutations identified by sequence changes in iso-1-cytochrome *c*. In *Molecular and Environmental Aspects of Mutagenesis*, ed. L. Prakash, F. Sherman, M. W. Miller, C. W. Lawrence, and H. W. Taber, pp. 102–25. Springfield, IL: C. C Thomas.

Streisinger, G., et al. 1966. Frameshift mutations and the genetic code. *Cold Spring Harbor Symp. Quant. Biol.* 31:77–84.

Topal, M. D., and J. R. Fresco. 1976. Complementary base pairing and the origin of substitution mutations. *Nature* 263:285–89.

Watson, J. D., and F. H. C. Crick. 1953. The structure of DNA. *Cold Spring Harbor Symp. Quant. Biol.* 18:123–31.

Witkin, E. M. 1976. Ultraviolet mutagenesis and inducible DNA repair in *Escherichia coli*. *Bacteriol. Rev.* 40:869–907.

Development and Evolution in Amphibians

James Hanken

In Paris in 1865, an event occurred that rocked the intellectual centers of Europe and North America. Two years earlier, the first live specimens of the axolotl—a large, aquatic, gilled salamander endemic to the lakes and river drainages of the Valley of Mexico had arrived in Paris courtesy of General Forey of the French Expeditionary Forces (Smith 1989). Of the 34 larval specimens that survived the trans-Atlantic voyage, six (five males and one female) were given to Auguste Duméril at the menagerie of the Musée d'Histoire Naturelle. Within the first year of Duméril's care, in January 1865, the axolotls, which until that time had been known only from preserved specimens, attained sexual maturity and bred. This apparently confirmed the status of the axolotl as a distinct species (and genus, *Siredon*) of "perennibranchiate" (permanently gilled) amphibians (Duméril 1865). Such species differ from other salamanders in which the gills are lost following a metamorphosis to a terrestrial stage. What happened later that year, however, was astonishing. Four of the laboratory-reared offspring, followed by several more the following year, did metamorphose into gill-less salamanders of a seemingly different genus, *Ambystoma*, which also had been formally described several years earlier (Duméril 1865, 1866).

Announcement of this apparent developmental transformation between what for decades had been considered distinct species in different genera met with great skepticism from the scientific community, who felt that either the reported transformation was fabricated, or the taxonomy of these salamanders was incorrect. More significant, however, was the impact on the prevailing recapitulationist doctrine, which held that morphological evolution proceeds by the addition of novel features to an ancestral ontogeny, or developmental sequence, which is recapitu-

> *The evolution of morphological diversity in amphibians has been achieved by modifications in development*

lated in descendants (Gould 1977). Under the recapitulationist doctrine, perennibranchiate salamanders, such as the axolotl, were considered ancestral forms from which advanced species had evolved by adding a metamorphosis and a resulting nonbranchiate form. If, however, metamorphosing forms could also mature as larvae (thus eliminating later stages of their ontogeny), then the recapitulationist interpretation was clearly wrong.

Duméril's discoveries triggered, over the next several decades, a flurry of studies of both the developmental transformation known as metamorphosis and the validity of the recapitulationist doctrine as a model of organic evolution. (In the light of subsequent observations, Duméril's discoveries are no longer astonishing. All the salamanders he worked with are now known to belong to a single species, *Ambystoma mexicanum*. Moreover, larval reproduction has proved to be an extremely common mode in the life history of *Ambystoma*, which includes several species found in North America [Shaffer 1984].) Although intense interest in fundamental processes of development—both in amphibians and in other organisms—has continued unabated, by the early part of the twentieth century, evolutionary biologists were devoting less attention to development as an important influence in evolutionary change.

The last few years, however, have witnessed a resurgence of interest in the relation between development and evolution. A large number of studies conducted in this period have contributed enormously to our basic understanding of how developmental processes are modified in the evolution of structural diversity (e.g., Raff and Raff 1987). These studies have also revealed more clearly than ever before the dual role that developmental processes play as both a source of and constraint on morphological change (Alberch 1982; Roth 1982). This renewed interest in the role of internal or "structural" factors in mediating evolutionary change has restored a more balanced view of evolution and its causes, away from the strictly functionalist view—with its emphasis on adaptation in response to external processes such as natural selection—which has dominated much of evolutionary thought for the last 40 to 50 years (Lauder 1982). And again, as when Duméril made his dramatic discoveries more than a century ago, amphibians occupy center stage. This can be attributed to the great structural and phylogenetic diversity of amphibians,

James Hanken is assistant professor of environmental, population, and organismic biology at the University of Colorado, Boulder. He received a Ph.D. in zoology from the University of California, Berkeley, and a Killam postdoctoral fellowship in developmental biology at Dalhousie University in Nova Scotia. He is interested in evolutionary vertebrate morphology, and his current research centers on the development of the skull in amphibians. He has won numerous awards for his photographs, which have appeared in a variety of textbooks, field guides, and magazines. Address: Department of EPO Biology, University of Colorado, Boulder, CO 80309-0334.

Hyla rufitella

Ensatina eschscholtzi

Ichthyophis kohtaoensis

Figure 1. The morphologies of the three living orders of amphibians have changed drastically since they last shared a common tetrapod ancestor. The three orders—Anura, Caudata, and Gymnophionaare illustrated here by a frog, a salamander, and a caecilian. These modern amphibians provide clues to the relation between developmental processes and the evolution of morphology. (All photos are by the author except the caecilian, which is courtesy of David M. Dennis.)

their complex yet evolutionarily plastic life cycle, and their suitability for laboratory investigation, which is unmatched by other vertebrates. In this article I review the relation between development and evolution in amphibians, highlighting some of the more conspicuous and important features of this relation.

Amphibians were the first vertebrate class to colonize the terrestrial environment successfully and extensively, beginning some 400 million years ago in the Devonian period. From these archaic forms evolved the reptiles (and through the reptiles other amniotes—birds and mammals) as well as the amphibians alive today. Living amphibians, however, are a far cry from their Devonian prototype. They constitute three orders which have diverged substantially since they last shared a common tetrapod ancestor (Fig. 1). Indeed, it is easier to identify ways in which they differ from each other than to name the uniquely "amphibian" characteristics that they share (Hanken 1986). The frogs (Order Anura) and salamanders (O. Caudata) are probably more familiar to people than is the third order, the caecilians (O. Gymnophiona)—secretive, limbless burrowers found in many tropical regions. Collectively, these three orders display an impressive diversity in morphology, physiology, ecology, and behavior which has allowed them to occupy a wide range of environments worldwide, from wet Amazonian rainforests to dry Saharan deserts. In terms of the total number of described living species, which is 3,438 for frogs, 352 for salamanders, and 162 for caecilians (Duellman and Trueb 1986), they fall far short of extant amniotes, but they arguably match or even exceed these groups in their evolutionary diversity.

In analyzing the relation between development and evolution in extant amphibians, three features emerge as particularly important: phyletic size change; spatial and temporal repatterning; and paedomorphosis—the retention of juvenile characteristics of an ancestor in later stages of a descendant. These features, either singly or in combination, illustrate how development has been modified in the evolution of much of the morphological diversity in the group. They also help to pinpoint the specific developmental processes involved in each instance of morphological change. In the following sections each of these features is treated separately, although as will be apparent, they are often closely linked.

Phyletic size change

Living amphibians vary tremendously in size, from the tiny Brazilian rainforest frog *Psyllophryne didactyla*, which measures less than 1 cm from snout to rump, to Colombian caecilians, genus *Caecilia*, and the Asian salamander, *Andrias davidianus*, both of which measure over 1.5 m in length (Duellman and Trueb 1986; Taylor 1968). Some extinct species were even larger. Naively, we tend to consider large size or increase in size as being evolutionarily advantageous. Indeed, the evolutionary tendency for lineages to evolve to larger and larger body sizes is sufficiently widespread to be embodied in what is called Cope's rule, named after Edward Cope, the sensational and outspoken nineteenth-century vertebrate paleontologist who drew attention to the trend. Ironically, phyletic size decrease—and especially extreme decrease in size, or

Figure 2. The salamander *Thorius* is an example of evolutionary miniaturization; adults can be as small as 1.3 cm in length, snout to vent. The specimen shown is sitting on a blade of grass. At the time of hatching, these salamanders are less than half the size of the specimen shown.

miniaturization—seems to be more important in the evolution of truly novel morphological features.

An excellent example of the role of miniaturization in the evolution of morphological novelty is the Mexican salamander genus *Thorius,* shown in Figure 2. The 15 species of *Thorius* (only nine are formally named) represent the smallest salamanders known. Sexually mature adults are as small as 1.3 cm, snout to vent (Hanken 1983a); they are clearly pushing the lower limit for body size in terrestrial vertebrates. They are found under logs or in leaf litter on the montane forest floor. Only after examining their internal anatomy by specialized staining procedures can one appreciate how unusual they are (Fig. 4). In the head, for example, the brain and the three paired, primary sense organs—the eyes, the (inner) ears, and the nose (olfactory organ)—predominate at the expense of the bony skull, which is reduced in many places to little more than thin scaffolding. Some bones are absent entirely (Hanken 1983b, 1984). Other cranial fea-

tures, ranging from the branching pattern of nerve dendrites within the brain to musculoskeletal structures involved in feeding, are very different from those in closely related genera (Lombard 1977; Lombard and Wake 1977; Roth et al. 1988).

In the limbs, things are even more complicated. Most tetrapod species have a single, characteristic configuration of the wrist or ankle skeleton. *Thorius,* however, displays a total of 18 different skeletal patterns containing from as few as four to as many as nine separate cartilages (Fig. 3; Hanken 1982, 1985). A species typically will have several patterns, and as many as four different patterns in the forelimb alone are found in single populations of several species. Even individual salamanders commonly have different patterns on right and left sides. Many of these configurations are as different from one another as those that routinely distinguish other salamander genera.

Thus, in *Thorius* there is an obvious association between size change and the evolution of morphological novelty. But what links these two phenomena? The answer is development. Predominance of the brain and sense organs, for example, is largely an expression of the way that these structures scale to body size during ontogeny. In the development of virtually all vertebrates, absolute size of the brain and sense organs (especially the eye and inner ear) scales to body size with negative allometry; that is, the relative size of each structure is inversely proportional to body size. This relation holds for most comparisons among adults of different species as well. We typically think of negative allometry in terms of its consequences for size increase; for example, as an explanation for the relatively small eye in an elephant compared to a mouse, or for the relatively tiny brain in enormous dinosaurs compared to smaller, living reptiles. In *Thorius,* the mathematical relation is turned around so that a miniscule head (a skull length approximating 3 mm in adults of some species) contains a relatively enormous brain and sense organs.

Secondary changes also result. For example, another feature that distinguishes *Thorius* from larger salamanders is the orientation of the jaw suspension—that is, the bones, principally the quadrate, that connect the lower jaw to the skull in nonmammalian vertebrates. In larger salamanders, the jaw suspension descends ventrolaterally from the otic capsule (a bony chamber at the back end of the skull which houses the inner ear) to its articulation with the

Figure 3. In the case of *Thorius,* miniaturization has been accompanied by morphological novelty. Seen here are nine different forelimb skeletal patterns found in modern species. The patterns differ in the number and arrangement of the carpal, or wrist elements that lie at the base of the fingers.

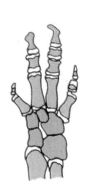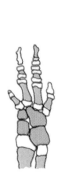

1 mm

mandible at the jaw joint. In *Thorius,* the jaw suspension descends vertically from the otic capsule toward the mandible, a rearrangement that may have important functional consequences for the way the jaw is used in feeding. Reorientation of the jaw suspension during the evolution of *Thorius* may have been brought about by a relative increase in the size of the inner ear (Hanken 1983b); the articulation between quadrate and otic capsule—one of the most evolutionarily "conservative" joints in vertebrates—apparently moved laterally as the otic

There is an obvious association between size change and the evolution of morphological novelty

capsule increased in relative size to accommodate the expanding inner ear. The quadrate-mandible articulation, on the other hand, was not directed laterally. Unlike the otic capsule, the lower jaw does not enclose one of the primary sense organs and thus does not exhibit strong negative allometry. The lower jaw acted as a fulcrum about which the quadrate gradually pivoted during the evolution of small size.

The proliferation of novel skeletal patterns in the limbs might also be a scaling effect of miniaturization on development. Many theoretical models of limb development emphasize the size-dependance of pattern formation in the limbs (e.g., Oster et al. 1985; Solursh 1984). The point is that the configuration and number of skeletal elements initially produced in the hand or foot are a consequence of the absolute size of the undeveloped limb, either directly or indirectly in response to other developmental parameters. These models predict that reducing the size of the developing limb would lead to a decrease in the number of rudimentary cartilages, which are among the first visible signs of limb skeletal pattern. This is exactly what is observed in *Thorius,* where the evolutionary trend is toward a smaller number of cartilages in the wrist and ankle (Hanken 1985). The relation between the size of the developing limb and the skeletal pattern has been demonstrated by comparisons among other amphibian lineages and by experimentation (Alberch and Gale 1983, 1985).

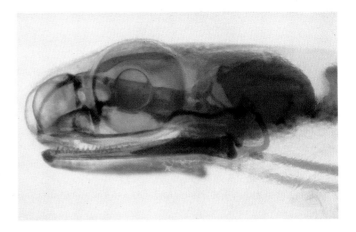

Figure 4. This stained lateral view of the head of an adult *Thorius* reveals a startling case of negative allometry: the brain and sense organs are disproportionately large compared to the tiny skull. Skeletal tissues are stained red (bone) or blue (cartilage). The cartilaginous nasal capsule encloses the olfactory organ; the transparent eye with inner lens appears yellow; the bony otic capsule, which encloses the inner ear, is on the right.

Spatial and temporal repatterning

At a basic level, every change of form is a change in pattern. Thus, morphological evolution can be thought of as phyletic alteration of the developmental mechanisms of pattern formation. Size change in *Thorius,* for instance, includes several examples of altered spatial patterning that are either a direct consequence of or at least closely correlated with miniaturization. Pattern change, however, need not always be tied to changes in absolute size. Repatterning also may involve change in the timing of development, or heterochrony (coined by the influential and highly controversial nineteenth century German biologist Ernst Haeckel in the context of the recapitulationist doctrine, and later redefined by de Beer [1958]). Heterochrony is evolutionary change in the timing of developmental events. It may affect a wide range of developmental phenomena, from the sequence in which bones form in the skull, to the timing of earlier inductive events in the embryo (Gould 1977). Most important in the context of this article, repatterning may also affect evolutionary success. Some of the best examples of spatial and temporal repatterning and its evolutionary consequences are centered on amphibian metamorphosis, and especially an advanced life-history mode derived from it: direct development.

Metamorphosis is a critical event in the biphasic life history followed by many amphibians. Aquatic larval and terrestrial adult stages are well adapted for life in their respective environments, and this is reflected in the specialized features of their anatomy, physiology, and behavior. Metamorphosis effects an abrupt yet orderly transition between these two stages. Many amphibians, however, do not undergo this primitive transition. Earlier I described the Mexican axolotl, which routinely abandons metamorphosis and its resulting terrestrial stage, and consequently lives its life as a larva, albeit a sexually mature one. A far more common alternative, however, is direct development, in which the free-living, aquatic lar-

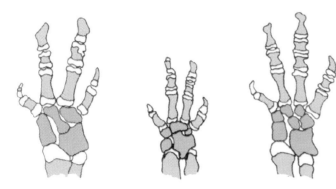

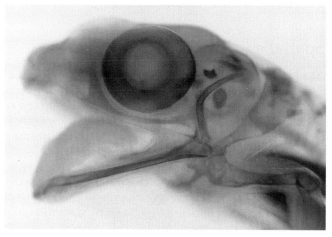

Figure 5. Direct-developing species such as the Puerto Rican frog coqui (*Eleutherodactylus coqui*) have eliminated the free-living, aquatic larval stage (the tadpole) and hatch from the egg as fully terrestrial frogs. In the developing fetus (*above*), note the well-developed forelimb, which never forms during embryogenesis in metamorphosing species. The cleared and stained head of a newly hatched coqui (*below*) reveals the lack of a distinctive larval skull characteristic of metamorphosing species.

val stage is "abandoned." In this case, eggs are laid on land (instead of in ponds or streams), and at the end of embryonic development a fully developed juvenile frog, salamander, or caecilian hatches, grows, and matures. Other reproductive modes are sometimes considered direct development, such as viviparity, or the retention of the developing embryo within the maternal oviduct until and beyond hatching.

Direct development is found in hundreds of amphibian species and has probably evolved repeatedly in each extant order (Duellman and Trueb 1986). It is also tightly linked with the evolutionary success of many groups. One obvious benefit that it confers is emancipation from aquatic breeding sites, thereby allowing the species to disperse across or even permanently occupy areas that do not con-

tain such habitats. Not surprisingly, direct development has received a great deal of attention by biologists, but most of this has concerned the ecological factors that promote its evolution and the sequence in which it evolves (e.g., McDiarmid 1978). In contrast, the developmental basis of direct development has received little attention. For example, it is commonly assumed, and stated in many textbooks, that direct developers undergo a metamorphosis in the egg; that is, that direct developers recapitulate the ontogeny of ancestral metamorphosing species. Yet there are few studies that document this phenomenon, at least with respect to important internal features such as the skeleton, and there are other well-documented cases in which this phenomenon has been shown not to be the case. In fact, what one sees in groups such as frogs is a gra-

In recent years the role of internal, or structural, influences on evolution has moved to the fore

dient of developmental patterns, from species that do at least superficially recapitulate the ancestral ontogeny (including forming a tadpole within the egg), to others that essentially bypass many ancestral stages and add new ones—a phenomenon called ontogenetic repatterning (Roth and Wake 1985).

One of the potentially most important examples of spatial and temporal repatterning is found in a group of tropical New World frogs, genus *Eleutherodactylus*. "Potentially," because these frogs have been studied very little compared to other groups. These frogs are a conspicuous component of the vertebrate fauna in most parts of their range, and would have to be considered an evolutionary success story by almost any criterion. Anyone who has found himself in the rain forests of Puerto Rico at night can attest to the deafening chorus of the coqui, *Eleutherodactylus coqui*. With more than 400 named species, Eleutherodactylus is the largest genus of vertebrates alive today (other, unnamed species await formal description). And from what is known, all species exhibit direct development, including *E. jasperi* from Puerto Rico, which is viviparous (see Fig. 5).

Cranial development in *Eleutherodactylus* illustrates well the extensive repatterning that has occurred in the evolution of direct development in the genus. If cranial development recapitulates the ontogenetic sequence typical of metamorphosing ancestors, then the skull of *Eleutherodactylus* should first form the distinctive tadpole skull, with its specialized, cartilaginous jaws and gill arches. This skull, while still in the embryo, should then abruptly "metamorphose" into an adult skull by a combination of resorption and remodeling of existing larval cartilages, and by the formation of new cartilages and bone. Instead, however, embryos of *Eleutherodactylus* never form the distinctive larval skull. Rather, from its earliest recognizable stage, the skull closely resembles that of the adult (Fig. 5; Hanken and Summers 1988; Lynn 1942).

Even the sequence in which the bones ossify is altered. In *Eleutherodactylus,* the first bones to form are the squamosal and angulosplenial, which together form the jaw joint. Precocious ossification of jaw elements, however, is not seen in any metamorphosing frogs (Trueb 1985). In fact, the only other amphibian that displays precocious ossification of these elements is the viviparous caecilian *Dermophis mexicanus,* which also has lost the free-living, aquatic larval stage (Wake and Hanken 1982; Fig. 6). In *Dermophis,* this feature is part of a suite of adaptations for nutrition of both the developing embryo and the fetus, which is retained in the mother's oviduct long after yolk reserves are exhausted. The developing fetus uses its developing jaws and teeth to scrape and ingest a milky secretion from the lining of the oviduct. In *Eleutherodactylus,* early ossification of the jaws probably assures their proper function in capturing prey soon after hatching, by providing both a well-developed joint and solid points of attachment for the jaw and tongue musculature.

Does spatial and temporal repatterning promote evolutionary success? In *Eleutherodactylus,* the association between extreme repatterning and proliferation of species is, pending additional study, no more than a correlation, albeit a striking one. Data from other amphibians, however, suggest that there may be a causal link. Perhaps the most compelling evidence comes from the lungless salamanders, family Plethodontidae. Plethodontids are by far the predominant group of salamanders alive today, comprising more than 220 species divided among 27 genera. The remaining eight living families of salamanders comprise 133 species (Duellman and Trueb 1986). A few plethodontids retain the ancestral biphasic life history with aquatic larvae that metamorphose into terrestrial adults. Most genera, however, have direct development. The bolitoglossines are such a subgroup; they are spread widely throughout the New World tropics (Wake and Lynch 1976). The tiny salamander *Thorius* is a bolitoglossine of Central America.

David Wake of the University of California has studied plethodontids extensively. With students and other collaborators, Wake has discovered a remarkable diversity in the structure and function of the feeding apparatus in many forms with direct development as compared to metamorphosing taxa (Lombard and Wake 1977; Wake 1982). The diversity includes novel arrangements of the skeleton, musculature, and nerves in the mouth and throat—the hyolingual apparatus—which allow the tongue to be extended to a distance of up to one-half the length of the body to capture prey. Among plethodontids, the greatest diversity, complexity, and functional versatility of the hyolingual apparatus are seen in the bolitoglossines, who also exhibit the most derived ontogeny compared to less specialized taxa.

Wake and colleagues argue that two sequential events permitted the observed repatterning (Roth and Wake 1985; Wake 1982). The first event was the loss of lungs, which occurred early in the history of the family (all living forms are lungless). Presumably this occurred as an adaptation to life in cool, aerated mountain streams, in which cutaneous respiration can accommodate modest

Figure 6. The Guatemalan caecilian, *Dennophis mexicanus,* is viviparous, that is, the developing young are retained in the maternal oviduct until and beyond hatching. Precocious ossification of the fetal jaws and early-formed teeth (*stained red*) allow the young to scrape a nutritive secretion from the lining of the oviduct.

respiratory needs and the buoyancy of lungs might be a hindrance. Because the two main functions of the hyolingual apparatus in adult lunged salamanders are lung ventilation and feeding, loss of lungs in plethodontids left feeding as the sole function. Moreover, this removed an important constraint on the morphology of the hyolingual apparatus, which in lunged salamanders represents a structural compromise between the conflicting demands for feeding and respiration.

The second key event was the evolution of direct development. With the loss of the larval stage, the need to form the larval hyobranchial apparatus (precursor of the adult hyolingual apparatus), which is anatomically specialized for aquatic feeding and respiration, was also removed (Fig. 7). Wake and his colleagues argue that the need to form a specialized, larval hyobranchial apparatus constrains the morphology of the adult hyolingual apparatus that forms from it in metamorphosing species; in other words, there is a limit to the extent of metamorphic

Figure 7. This stained skull of a larval long-toed salamander, *Ambystoma macrodactylum,* reveals the complex hyobranchial apparatus that will eventually be remodeled in metamorphosis—giving way to the adult hyolingual apparatus. The absence of a larval hyobranchial apparatus in some direct-developing species may eliminate constraints on the development of the hyolingual apparatus.

transformation. When the larval constraint is removed, however, the adult structure is free to evolve, and this is what happened in bolitoglossines.

Thus two events seemingly far removed from feeding—lung loss and direct development—eliminated two constraints on the structure of the feeding apparatus. Bolitoglossines responded with spatial and temporal repatterning: in the embryo, the hyolingual apparatus initially assumes the derived, adult configuration, never

---

At a basic level, every change of form is a change in pattern

---

recapitulating the ancestral larval structure (Alberch 1987). It should be noted that repatterning and consequent specialization of feeding structures did not follow these two events in all groups. For example, in another group of lungless, direct-developing plethodontids, the plethodontines (which include the common red-backed salamander of eastern North America), the adult hyolingual apparatus is not nearly as specialized, and development recapitulates, at least in part, the larval precursors (Dent 1942).

Paedomorphosis

The third principal feature characterizing amphibian development and evolution is a specific kind of heterochrony called paedomorphosis. In certain respects, paedomorphosis is far easier to understand than other kinds of temporal repatterning. Paedomorphosis is often not so much a change in ancestral developmental timing, as it is a failure to complete the ancestral sequence. In other words, the adult descendant retains "juvenile" characteristics of the ancestor.

Two instances of paedomorphosis have already been described: the axolotl becomes sexually mature while retaining an otherwise larval morphology; *Thorius* retains a flimsy skull which lacks many late-forming bones typically present in salamanders (Hanken 1984). Paedomorphosis in the axolotl, in which the rate of development of somatic tissues is slowed relative to that of reproductive structures, is commonly called neoteny, whereas that in *Thorius*, which probably involves precocious sexual maturation, is called progenesis (Gould 1977).

The significance of paedomorphosis for amphibians, and the reason I distinguish it from other instances of temporal repatterning, can be appreciated by considering two facts. First, paedomorphosis is an extremely common mode of evolutionary change. The extensive literature of amphibian morphology is replete with species, genera, and higher taxa—even the entire subclass Lissamphibia, to which living amphibians belong—that are paedomorphic compared to their ancestors or living relatives (e.g., Bolt 1977; D. B. Wake 1966; M. H. Wake 1986). Thus evolutionary change often represents variations on an ancestral theme. This, however, is not to say that novel changes, involving extensions beyond or drastic alterations to the ancestral ontogeny, never occur. Clearly, such events have

occurred and some have been very significant. Nor should paedomorphosis be perceived as confining or limiting change. Rampant morphological novelty in *Thorius*, which is the product of paedomorphosis combined with extreme decrease in body size, proves the opposite. Rather, predominance of paedomorphosis illustrates the bold stamp that phylogenetic legacy leaves on morphological evolution in these vertebrates.

Second, paedomorphosis provides an alternative, or at least a complement, to strictly adaptationist explanations of trends such as convergent or parallel evolution. For example, several lineages of frogs have independently lost one or more bones in the skull, which apparently were present in their common ancestor. Among these is the columella, a small but important bone that conducts sound from the surface of the head to sensory cells in the inner ear. One might be tempted to interpret the repeated loss of the columella primarily as the result of natural selection for a particular kind of acoustical acuity. Indeed, such an explanation probably accounts for the loss of the columella in certain groups. A fuller understanding is achieved, however, when one considers that the columella is among the last bones to form in an anuran skull. If paedomorphosis occurred in a given lineage, for whatever reason, then there is a good chance that the columella would be lost as a consequence.

Thus paedomorphosis allows one to make specific, testable hypotheses of morphological change. In the case of the missing columella, for example, one might predict that additional late-forming bones would be absent as well, regardless of their role in hearing. This is indeed the case (Trueb 1985; Trueb and Alberch 1985). Loss of such bones in combination with the columella would be difficult to explain by purely selectionist explanations.

Evolution and development

Evolution is the net result of a series of influences, some promoting change, others limiting it. During much of this century, evolutionary biologists have tended to perceive the predominant influences as residing largely in the external environment of the organism. This functional, adaptationist approach has not been without success. It has contributed greatly to our understanding of many important evolutionary processes, such as natural selection. In recent years, however, the role of internal, or structural, influences on evolution has moved to the fore, a position occupied in earlier times both before and after Darwin (Goodwin 1984; Lauder 1982; Russell 1916). Development is one internal influence that can foster greater understanding of evolution.

The consideration of development need not deny an important role for external factors. Clearly, internal and external influences may be intimately related. In *Thorius*, miniaturization interacting with developmental phenomena such as allometry and scale-dependent patterning resulted in profound changes in the morphology of the head and limbs. Yet this provides no explanation for the trend toward small body size, a trend which probably results from natural selection for some life history or other ecological parameter (Gould 1977; Hanken 1984). And whereas features of limb development may promote the appearance of novel variants, these variants must function adequately or they will be quickly eliminated from the population. The path to greatest understanding of evolution entails an approach that considers the role of both internal and external influences in evolutionary change.

It is important to remember that while phyletic size change, spatial and temporal repatterning, and paedomorphosis may effectively describe characteristic features of the relation between development and evolution in amphibians, they reveal little of the molecular, cellular and developmental processes that underlie the observed evolutionary changes. A major challenge for future research is to reveal the developmental and genetic bases of these features, and how they interact with evolutionary processes at the individual, population, species, and even community level.

References

Alberch, P. 1982. The generative and regulatory roles of development in evolution. In *Environmental Adaptation and Evolution*, ed. D. Mossakowski and G. Roth, pp. 19–36. Stuttgart: G. Fischer.

———. 1987. Evolution of a developmental process—irreversibility and redundancy in amphibian metamorphosis. In *Development as an Evolutionary Process* ed. R. A. Raff and E. C. Raff, pp. 23–46. Alan R. Liss, Inc.

Alberch, P., and E. A. Gale. 1983. Size dependence during the development of the amphibian foot. Colchicine-induced digital loss and reduction. *J. Embryol. Exp. Morphol.* 76:177–97.

———. 1985. A developmental analysis of an evolutionary trend: Digital reduction in amphibians. *Evolution* 39:8–23.

Bolt, J. R. 1977. Dissorophoid relationships and ontogeny, and the origin of the Lissamphibia. *J. Paleontol.* 51:235–49.

de Beer, G.R. 1958. *Embryos and Ancestors*. 3rd ed. Oxford Univ. Press.

Dent, J.N. 1942. The embryonic development of *Plethodon cinereus* as correlated with the differentiation and functioning of the thyroid gland. *J. Morphol.* 71:577–601.

Duellman, W. E., and L. Trueb. 1986. *Biology of the Amphibians*. McGraw-Hill.

Duméril, A. 1865. Reproduction, dans la Ménagerie des Reples au Musée d'Histoire Naturelle, des axolotls, batraciens urodèles à branches persistantes, du Mexique (*Siredon mexicanus vel Humboldtii*) qui n'avaient encore jamais été vus vivants en Europe. *C. R. Acad. Sci.* 60:765–67.

———. 1866. Observations sur la reproduction dans la Ménagerie des Reptiles du Musée d'Histoire Naturelle, des axolotls, batraciens urodèles à branches extérieures du Mexique sur leur développement et sur leurs métamorphoses. *Nouv. Archs. Mus. Hist. Nat.* Paris 2:265–92.

Goodwin, B. C. 1984. Changing from an evolutionary to a generative paradigm in biology. In *Evolutionary Theory: Paths Into the Future*, ed. J. W. Pollard, pp. 99–119. Wiley.

Gould, S. J. 1977. *Ontogeny and Phylogeny*. Harvard Univ. Press.

Hanken, J. 1982. Appendicular skeletal morphology in minute salamanders, genus *Thorius* (Amphibia: Plethodontidae): Growth regulation, adult size determination, and natural variation. J. Morphol. 174:57–77.

———. 1983a. Genetic variation in a dwarfed lineage, the Mexican salamander genus *Thorius* (Amphibia: Plethodontidae): Taxonomic, ecologic, and evolutionary implications. *Copeia* 1983:1051–73.

———. 1983b. Miniaturization and its effects on cranial morphology in plethodontid salamanders, genus *Thorius* (Amphibia, Plethodontidae): II. The fate of the brain and sense organs and their role in skull morphogenesis and evolution. *J. Morphol.* 177:255–68.

———. 1984. Miniaturization and its effects on cranial morphology in plethodontid salamanders, genus *Thorius* (Amphibia: Plethodontidae). I. Osteological variation. *Biol. J. Linn. Soc.* 23:55–75.

———. 1985. Morphological novelty in the limb skeleton accompanies miniaturization in salamanders. *Science* 229:871–74.

———. 1986. Developmental evidence for amphibian origins. *Evol. Biol.* 20:389–417.

Hanken, J., and C. H. Summers. 1988. Developmental basis of evolutionary success: Cranial ontogeny in a direct-developing anuran. *Am. Zool.* 28:12A.

Lauder, G. V. 1982. Introduction to *Form and Function* by E. S. Russell, pp. xi–xlv. Univ. of Chicago Press.

Lombard, R. E. 1977. Comparative morphology of the inner ear in salamanders (Caudata: Amphibia). *Contrib. Vert. Evol.* 2:1–140.

Lombard, R. E., and D. B. Wake. 1977. Tongue evolution in the lungless salamanders, family Plethodontidae. II. Function and evolutionary diversity. *J. Morphol.* 153:39–80.

Lynn, W. G. 1942. The embryology of *Eleutherodactylus nubicola* an anuran which has no tadpole stage. *Contrib. Embryol.* no. 190 541:27–62.

McDiarmid, R. W. 1978. Evolution of parental care in frogs. In *The Development of Behavior: Comparative and Evolutionary Aspects*, ed. G. M. Burghardt and M. Bekoff, pp. 127–47. Garland STPM Press.

Oster, G. F., J. D. Murray, and P. K. Maini. 1985. A model for chondrogenic condensations in the developing limb: The role of extracellular matrix and cell tractions. *J. Embryol. Exp. Morphol.* 89:93–112.

Raff, R. A., and E. C. Raff, eds. 1987. *Development as an Evolutionary Process*. Alan R. Liss, Inc.

Roth, G. 1982. Conditions of evolution and adaptation in organisms as autopoietc systems. In *Environmental Adaptation and Evolution*, ed. D. Mossakowski and G. Roth, pp. 37–48. Stuttgart: Gustav Fischer.

Roth, G., B. Rottluff, and R. Linke. 1988. Miniaturization, genome size and the origin of functional constraints in the visual system of salamanders. *Naturwissenschaften* 75:297–301.

Roth, G., and D. B. Wake. 1985. Trends in the functional morphology and sensorimotor control of feeding behavior in salamanders: An example of the role of internal dynamics in evolution. *Acta Biotheor.* 34:175–92.

Russell, E. S. 1916. *Form and Function: A Contribution to the History of Animal Morphology*. London: John Murray. (Paperback reprint: Univ. of Chicago Press, 1982.)

Shaffer, H. B. 1984. Evolution of a paedomorphic lineage. I. An electrophoretic analysis of the Mexican ambystomatid salamanders. *Evolution* 38:1194–1206.

Smith, H. M. 1989. Discovery of the axolotl and its early history in biological research. In *Developmental Biology of the Axolotl*, ed. J. B. Armstrong and G. M. Malacinski, pp. 4–12. Oxford Univ. Press.

Solursh, M. 1984. Ectoderm as a determinant of early tissue pattern in the limb bud. *Cell Diff.* 15:17–24.

Taylor, E. H. 1968. *The Caecilians of the World. A Taxonomic Review*. Univ. of Kansas Press.

Trueb, L. 1985. A summary of osteocranial development in anurans with notes on the sequence of cranial ossification in *Rhinophrynus dorsalis* (Anura: Pipoidea: Rhinophrynidae). *S. Afr. J. Sci.* 81:181–85.

Trueb, L., and P. Alberch. 1985. Miniaturization and the anuran skull: A case study of heterochrony. In *Functional Morphology of Vertebrates*, ed. H. R. Duncker and G. Fleischer, pp. 113–21. Stuttgart: Gustav Fisher.

Wake, D. B. 1966. Comparative osteology and evolution of the lungless salamanders, family Plethodontidae. *Mem. South. Calif Acad. Sci.* 4:1–111.

———. 1982. Functional and developmental constraints and opportunities in the evolution of feeding systems in urodeles. In *Environmental Adaptation and Evolution*, ed. D. Mossakowski and G. Roth, pp. 51–66. Stuttgart: Gustav Fischer.

Wake, D. B. and J. F. Lynch. 1976. The distribution, ecology, and evolutionary history of plethodontid salamanders in tropical America. *Bull. Los Angeles Co. Mus.* 25:1–65.

Wake, M. H. 1986. The morphology of Idiocranium russeli (Amphibia: Gymnophiona), with comments on miniaturization through heterochrony. *J. Morphol.* 189:1–16.

Wake, M. H. and J. Hanken. 1982. The development of the skull of *Dermophis mexicanus* (Amphibia: Gymnophiona), with comments on skull kinesis and amphibian relationships. *J. Morphol.* 173:203–23.

Part IV
Sex and Behavior

Much of evolution depends on compromises and tradeoffs. A species may increase performance in some ways only at the expense of decreasing it in others. This problem becomes especially important when considering interactions among individuals of the same species. The gain by some individuals usually results in a loss to others, and in such cases what is favored by natural selection is by no means obvious. For example, in species with separate sexes, males and females must find each other in order to produce offspring, but the greatly different costs of producing sperm and eggs (a female spends a great deal more energy to produce eggs than a male spends to produce sperm) impose different constraints on their choices. How these choices are made determines the outcome of sexual selection, a topic introduced by Darwin but not subject to detailed analysis until quite recently. Furthermore, characteristics that are advantageous in finding a mate may be detrimental to survival.

The first three chapters in this section deal with the problem of sexual selection. Thornhill and Gwynne describe how exquisitely choosy insects can be in picking a mate. Females appear to make subtle calculations of how much a male can help provision her and her young. The overriding importance of such calculations is clear, because each extra gram of nutrients is directly converted into additional eggs. The chapter by Small addresses the seeming paradox of female choice. In some cases, including several of the insect species discussed in the previous chapter, the benefits of choosing one male over another are clear. In many other species, however, the basis for choosing is far less clear and seems (to the human observer, at least) to be arbitrary and even counterproductive. Females seem to choose males with characteristics that *reduce* male survivorship, implying that females choose mates that will produce male offspring with reduced survivorship. An alternative to this view is that females are choosing males with characteristics that advertise their overall vigor, and that females are actually choosing males with "good genes" to pass on to their offspring. The details of female choice are poorly understood in most species but are likely to differ widely among species.

The chapter by Ryan emphasizes another aspect of female choice and sexual selection, this time in frogs. Females of many frog species find their mates by the male's call; the female not only chooses among males within her species based on their calls, but also distinguishes males of her species from those of other species. This auditory-based female choice behavior gives the observer the opportunity to modify calls experimentally in order to find what different females prefer.

When individuals must fight one another for access to limited resources, the resource rarely justifies the risk of death or serious injury. How do animals resolve such conflicts without either giving up too easily or risking too much? Riechert shows that some spiders behave as if they understand the theory of games, as introduced to evolutionary biology by Maynard Smith and Price in the 1970s. The spiders seem to calculate their chances of winning contests and to "give up" when their long-term interests are not served by continuing. The evolutionary theory of games provides a way to formalize the notion of what constitutes "long term interests."

In the next chapter, Shear describes another aspect of spider behavior, the web. Our knowledge about the evolution of spider webs comes from a variety of sources, including the biochemistry of the silk, the morphology of the spider's silk-spinning organs, and the characteristics of the webs themselves. This chapter shows that a phylogenetic analysis can reveal many clues to the sequence of transitions that led to the current diversity of webs.

The subject of sociobiology, founded in the 1970s by E. O. Wilson, encompasses all aspects of the evolution of social behavior. In many ways, the pinnacle of social behavior among nonhuman species was reached by social insects: bees, ants, wasps, and termites. Many social insects exhibit such extreme cooperation that most females do not lay eggs, instead devoting their lives to the care of siblings and other close relatives. Naked mole rats, described by Honeycutt, are a mammalian group that approaches the social insects in their degree of cooperation, with only a few of the females being able to reproduce. Only recently have evolutionary biologists begun to examine the reasons for the evolution of this extraordinary social system.

Social behavior in primates is not developed to the extremes of that in social insects or naked mole rats, but it is of special interest to humans because the behavior of living primates gives us the best clues to the behavior of our immediate ancestors. Jolly describes some of what has been learned from field studies of primate behavior. Many primate behaviors are so similar to our own that it is impossible not to describe them in anthropocentric terms. One of the current controversies in the study of primate behavior is the extent to which primates have a "consciousness" in the sense that humans have. As difficult as this subject is to analyze objectively, it cannot help but better inform us about our own consciousness.

The last chapter, by Altmann, is an unusual and provocative "discussion" of primate behavior and society. It poses as many questions as it answers and conveys the spirit of pure curiosity that motivates evolutionary biologists, who are confronted with the rich diversity of the natural world and try to explain it to themselves and to others.

Randy Thornhill
Darryl T. Gwynne

The Evolution of Sexual Differences in Insects

The ultimate cause of sexual differences in behavior may be the relative contribution of the sexes to offspring

Evolutionary biologists strive to understand the diversity of life by the study of the evolutionary processes that produced it. Among the more fundamental of these processes is sexual selection, which has probably been a major form of selection in the evolutionary background of all organisms with two sexes. An important question for evolutionary biologists, as one theorist (Williams 1975) has put it, is "Why are males masculine and females feminine and, occasionally, vice versa?" This question focuses on evolutionary causation by natural or sexual selection rather than on the proximate causes of sexual differences, such as genetic influences, hormones, or development.

Sexual selection is distinguished from natural selection in terms of how the differential in the reproduction of individuals is brought about (Darwin 1874). Sexual selection is differential reproduction of individuals in the context of competition for mates. Natural selection is differential reproduction of individuals due to differences in survival. Since reproduction is necessary for selection

Randy Thornhill is Professor of Biology at the University of New Mexico. He received his B.S. and M.S. from Auburn University and his Ph.D. (1974) from the University of Michigan. His research interests include sexual selection, the evolution of sexual differences, insect mating systems, and human social behavior. Darryl Gwynne attended the University of Toronto and Colorado State University (Ph.D. 1979). He was a postdoctoral fellow at the University of New Mexico and is currently a Research Fellow at the University of Western Australia. His interests include sexual selection and communication in insects. The research reported here was supported by grants from the NSF, a Queen Elizabeth II Fellowship (Australia), and the Australian Research Grants Scheme. Address for Dr. Thornhill: Department of Biology, University of New Mexico, Albuquerque, NM 87131.

to act, natural selection also includes differential reproduction of individuals in the context of reproductive acts, such as obtaining a mate of the right species, proper fertilization, and so on. Although both forms of selection involve competition between individuals for genetic representation, competition for mates is a key factor for distinguishing sexual from natural selection. The competition among members of one sex (usually males) for the opposite sex may take the form of attempting to coax choosy individuals to mate, leading to intersexual selection, or may involve striving to obtain access to already receptive individuals who are willing to mate with any individual of the opposite sex, leading to intrasexual selection.

In his treatise on sexual selection, Darwin (1874) compiled an encyclopedic volume of comparative support for the crucial role of the process in the evolution of morphological and behavioral traits important in sexual competition. Current studies of sexual selection involve several approaches. Some researchers seek to describe the consequences and nature of sexual selection by the study of behavioral and morphological traits important in sexual competition as well as by observing the types of mating associations (monogamy and polygyny, for example) in animals and plants (e.g., Bradbury and Vehrencamp 1977; Emlen and Oring 1977; Thornhill and Alcock 1983). Another approach is to measure the intensity of sexual selection, focusing on variation in the reproductive success of individuals in nature (e.g., Payne 1979; Wade and Arnold 1980; Thornhill 1981, 1986; Gwynne 1984a). Other studies are attempting to elucidate how sexual selection works, and there are several compet-

ing hypotheses (reviewed in Thornhill and Alcock 1983). Subtle forms of female mate choice and male-male competition for females have been discovered and are under investigation (Parker 1970; Thornhill 1983; Smith 1984). The area of study we will address in this paper concerns factors that control the operation of sexual selection—factors that govern the extent to which one sex competes for the other.

The evidence of sexual selection in nature raises a number of questions about these factors. When reproducing, why are males usually more competitive and less discriminating of mates than females and thus subject to greater sexual selection? And why in a few exceptional species is the intensity of sexual selection on the sexes apparently reversed, with females competing for males and males discriminating among mates? Moreover, why does the extent of sexual selection vary in the same species?

We will address these questions using evidence from insects, which, as one of the most diverse groups of animals, exhibit a variety of different reproductive biologies and thus provide a wealth of comparative information with which to examine the theory of sexual selection. We will first discuss theory concerning the control of sexual selection and then examine the theory in light of what is known about insects.

Control of sexual selection

Bateman (1948) argued that males typically are more sexually competitive than females primarily because of the sexual asymmetry in gamete size. He noted that female fertility is limited by the production of large,

Figure 1. The female in this mating pair of hangingflies (*Hylobittacus apicalis*) is feeding on a blow fly captured and provided to her by the male. This nuptial feeding by the male enhances the female's fecundity, reduces the risks that must be taken by the female to obtain food, and therefore promotes the male's reproductive success. (From Thornhill 1980.)

costly gametes; for the same amount of reproductive effort, a male pro-duces vastly more gametes. There-fore the reproductive success of males is limited by their success at inseminating females and not, as in females, by their ability to produce gametes. Bateman's work with fruit flies, *Drosophila melanogaster,* also demonstrated empirically that the in-tensity of sexual selection is greater on males than on females, and the difference is due to greater variation in mating success among males.

Williams (1966) and Trivers (1972) built a more comprehensive theory than Bateman in noting that what controls the intensity of sexual selection and explains the evolution of sexual differences in reproductive strategy is not just prezygotic invest-ment by the sexes in gametes but all goods and services that contribute to the next generation—that determine the number and survival of offspring. The large disparity in gamete size itself predicts neither the reduced sexual differences seen in monoga-

mous species nor the competitive fe-males and choosy males seen in spe-cies with reversals in sex roles.

Material contributions by each sex to the next generation determine the reproductive rate of the popula-tion; therefore, sexual competition is ultimately for these contributions be-cause the greater the amount ob-tained, the higher the reproductive success of a competitor (Thornhill 1986). Simply put, when one sex (usually the females) contributes more to the production and survival of offspring, sexually active members of this sex are in short supply and thus become a limiting resource for the reproduction of the opposite sex; and the extent of sexual competition in the sex contributing least should correspond with the degree to which the opposite sex exceeds it in this contribution. Furthermore, the sex with the greater contribution is sub-ject to a greater loss of fitness if it makes an improper mate choice, be-cause its contribution represents a large fraction of its total reproductive

contribution. This asymmetry, cou-pled with the availability of the sex investing less, is expected to favor mate choice by the sex contributing more.

An important point to note is that not all forms of effort expended by the sexes in reproduction are ex-pected to control the extent of sexual selection. Energetic expenditures by males that are used in obtaining fer-tilizations but that do not allow great-er reproduction by females or do not promote the fitness of offspring are excluded (Trivers 1972; Thornhill and Alcock 1983; Gwynne 1984b).

Male efforts that are expected to control the extent of sexual selection encompass an array of resources that are of material benefit to females, offspring, or both. Such resources include nutrition, protection, and, under certain conditions, genes in spermatozoa. Bateman argued per-suasively that female reproductive success is rarely limited by sperm per se. However, a high variance in the genetic quality of males available as mates may result in female competition for the best mates if genetic variation among males affects offspring survival and if males of high genetic quality limit female reproductive success. Although there is little information with which to examine the influence of high-quality sires on the operation of sexual selection, there are a number of studies, which we will now discuss, that examine sexual selection in species in which males provide immediate, material services.

Contributions to offspring

Both males and females can provide for offspring in a variety of ways. Females invest directly in their offspring both through the material investment in eggs and zygotes as well as through maternal care. The better-known examples of male investment concern direct paternal care of offspring; this has been observed in a large number of species in a variety of animal groups (Ridley 1978). However, males can also contribute indirectly to offspring by providing benefits to their mates, both before and after mating. Examples include the nutritional benefits of "courtship feeding," which is observed in certain birds (Nisbet 1973) and insects, such as the hangingfly *Hylobittacus apicalis* shown in Figure 1 (Thornhill 1976). Protection of the mate is another example of such benefits (Gwynne 1984b; Thornhill 1984). The nature of selection leading to the evolution of benefit-providing males is still poorly understood (Alexander and Borgia 1979; Knowlton 1982). But regardless of the evolved function of the phenomenon, with the evolution of benefit-providing males there may be a change in the action of sexual selection on the sexes.

Contributions by one sex that affect the number and survival of offspring potentially limit the reproduction of the opposite sex. Thus the relative investment of the sexes in these sorts of reproductive efforts should determine the extent to which each sex competes for the opposite sex. This hypothesis can be tested by comparing species or populations with differing investment patterns or by directly manipulating resources that limit the reproduction of the population. Examples we will review use these methods.

There have been few attempts to estimate the extent of sexual selection on the sexes in nature. However, variance in the reproductive success of the sexes has been estimated for *Drosophila melanogaster* (Bateman 1948), a damselfly (Finke 1982), red-winged blackbirds (Payne 1979), and red deer (Clutton-Brock et al. 1982). In these species, the parental contribution by the male is smaller than that of the female; as predicted, all species show greater sexual selection on the males.

Observed sexual differences, the consequences of sexual selection, typically serve as evidence for the relative intensity of sexual selection on the sexes in the evolutionary past. In most species, females provide a large amount of parental contribution and males little, and it is primarily the males that show secondary sexual traits of morphology and behavior which function in competition for mates. It is also well known that sexual differences are greatly reduced under monogamy. This is as expected, because both sexes of monogamous species engage in similar levels of parental care. However, for this comparative test to succeed, a sex reversal in the courtship and competitive roles should be observed in species in which males provide a greater portion of the total contribution affecting offspring number and survival.

Parental care provided only by the male is found throughout the vertebrates, particularly in frogs and toads, fishes, and birds, and is likely to represent a limiting resource for female reproduction. In certain seahorses and pipefishes (Syngnathidae), males care for eggs in a specialized brood pouch (Breder and Rosen 1966). In these fishes, male parental care appears to limit female reproductive success, and females are larger and more brightly colored than males, as well as being more competitive in courtship (Williams 1966, 1975; Ridley 1978). In frogs of the genus *Colostethus*, it is the male in one species and the female in another that provide parental care by carrying tadpoles on their backs. In both species, as predicted by theory, it is the sex emancipated from parental duties that defends long-term mating territories and has a higher frequency of competitive encounters (Wells 1980). In species of birds in which males provide most of the parental care, the roles in courtship behavior are reversed; females compete for mates and sometimes are the larger or more brightly colored sex (reviewed by Ridley 1978).

Exclusive paternal care of eggs or larvae is restricted to about 100 species of insects, all of which are within the order Hemiptera, or true bugs (Smith 1980). In the giant water bugs (Hemiptera: Belostomatidae), females adhere eggs to the wing covers of their mates, and the males aerate the eggs near the water surface and protect them from predators. For *Abedus herberti,* Smith (1979) provides evidence that male back space is a limiting resource for females and that male parental care is essential for offspring survival; females actively approach males during courtship, and males reject certain females as mates.

Although direct investment in offspring through parental care is uncommon within the insects, indirect paternal contributions, with males supplying the females with nutrition or other services such as guarding, is widespread in a number of taxa.

The guarding of the female by the male after mating is usually thought of as functioning to prevent other males from inseminating the female (Parker 1970). However, an alternative hypothesis is that guarding evolved in the context of supplying protection for the female and that it thereby enhances male reproductive success (Gwynne 1984b; Thornhill 1984). Male guarding is known to benefit the female in several species: in damselflies (*Calopteryx maculata*), guarding by males after mating allows females to oviposit undisturbed by other males (Waage 1979); in waterstriders (*Gerris remigis*), harassment of guarded females by other males is similarly reduced, allowing females much longer periods during which to forage for food (Wilcox 1984). At present there is no information for these species concerning whether certain males protect females better than others, which would lead to female competition for more protective males. If female competition occurs, selection should favor mate choice by males.

Mate choice by males has been observed in species in which males provide protection or other services to females. In brentid weevils (*Brentus anchorago*) males prefer large females as mates and are known to assist their mates in competition for oviposition sites by driving away nearby ovipositing females (Johnson and Hubbell 1984). Male lovebugs (*Plecia nearctica*), so named for their two- to three-day-long periods of copulation, also prefer to mate with large females (Hieber and Cohen 1983). Lengthy copulation in this species may be beneficial for females in that copulating pairs actually fly faster than unattached lovebugs (Sharp et al. 1974). Similar benefits may be obtained by paired amphipod crustaceans (*Gammarus pulex*); pairs in which males are larger than females have a superior swimming performance that minimizes the risk of being washed downstream (Adams and Greenwood 1983). Perhaps these sorts of services supplied by male crustaceans explain the presence of male choice of mates seen in certain groups (e.g., Schuster 1981).

Males can supply nutrition in several ways. Our research has dealt with courtship feeding, where food items such as prey or nutritious sperm packages (spermatophores) are eaten by females, and we discuss this behavior in detail below for male katydids and scorpionflies. There are also more subtle forms of contribution; in several insect species spermatophores or other ejaculatory nutrients are passed into the female's genital tract at mating (Thornhill 1976; Gwynne 1983; Thornhill and Alcock 1983). A number of researchers have done some interesting work on a similar phenomenon in crustaceans. Electrophoretic studies of proteins in the ovaries and the male accessory gland of a stomatopod shrimp (*Squilla holoschista*) strongly suggest that a specialized protein from the male's accessory glands is transferred with the ejaculate into the female's gonopore and then is translocated intact into the developing eggs; females of this species usually initiate mating and will mate repeatedly (Deecaraman and Subramoniam 1983). In a detailed study of another

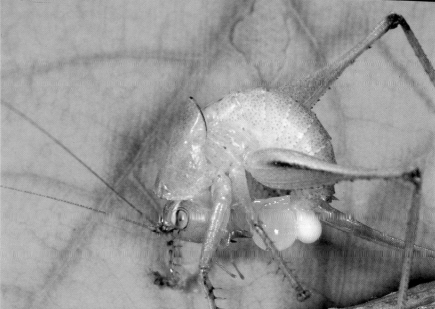

Figure 2. A female katydid (*Requena verticalis*) just after mating shows the large spermatophore that has been attached by the male to the base of her ovipositor (*top*). The female grasps the nutritious spermatophylax (*middle*) and eats it (*bottom*), leaving the sperm ampulla portion of the spermatophore in place. After insemination, the ampulla is also eaten. The nutrients in the spermatophore represent a considerable material contribution by the male in the reproductive success of the female. (Photos by Bert Wells.)

Figure 3. While this female Mormon cricket (*Anabrus simplex*) is atop the male, the male apparently weighs his potential mate and will reject her if she is too light. Males select mates among females that compete for access to them, preferring females that are larger and therefore more fecund. This represents a reversal of the sex roles much more commonly found in nature. (Photo by Darryl Gwynne.)

stomatopod, *Pseudosquilla ciliata,* Hatziolos and Caldwell (1983) report a reversal in sex roles, with females courting males that appear reluctant to mate; in the absence of obvious male parental contribution, these researchers cite work with insects in suggesting that male *Pseudosquilla* may provide valuable nutrients in the ejaculate.

Studies with several butterfly species have used radiolabeling to show that male-produced proteins are incorporated into developing eggs as well as into somatic tissues of females (e.g., Boggs and Gilbert 1979). Lepidopteran spermatophores potentially represent a large contribution by the male (up to 10% of body weight), and proteins ingested by females are likely to represent a limiting resource for egg production in these insects that feed on nectar as adults (Rutowski 1982). Preliminary experiments by Rutowski (pers. com.) with alfalfa butterflies (*Colias* spp.) indicate that females receiving larger spermatophores lay more eggs. Consistent with theory, there is evidence of males choosing females and of competition by females for males. For example, in the checkered white butterfly (*Pieris protodice*), males prefer young, large (and thus more fecund) females to older, small-er individuals (Rutowski 1982). And in *Colias,* certain females were observed to solicit courtship by pursuing males; these females may have had reduced protein supplies, as they were shown to have small, depleted spermatophores in their genital tracts (Rutowski et al. 1981). Although there is variation between species of butterflies in the size of the male spermatophore, this variation apparently does not result in large differences between species in the male contribution; a review of the reproductive behavior of several butterfly species did not show consistent differences in courtship when species with small spermatophores were compared to those with large spermatophores (Rutowski et al. 1983). However, as shown by Marshall (1982) and confirmed by our studies described below, spermatophore size is not always a useful measure of the importance of the male nutrient contribution.

Reversal of courtship roles in katydids

Katydids (Orthoptera: Tettigoniidae) are similar to butterflies in that males transfer spermatophores to their mates, and, as shown by radiolabeling, spermatophore nutrients are used in egg production (Bowen et al. 1984). In contrast to the mated female butterfly, the katydid female ingests the spermatophore by eating it (Fig. 2). The spermatophore consists of an ampulla which contains the ejaculate and a sperm-free mass termed the spermatophylax (Gwynne 1983). Immediately after mating, the female first eats the spermatophylax; while this is being consumed, insemination takes place, after which the empty sperm ampulla is also eaten (Gwynne et al. 1984). However, the katydid spermatophylax appears not to function as protection of the ejaculate from female feeding. The spermatophylax of the katydid *Requena verticalis* is more than twice the size necessary to allow the transfer both of the spermatozoa and of substances that induce a four-day nonreceptive period in females (Gwynne, unpubl.).

Spermatophore nutrients are important to the reproductive success of the female katydid. Laboratory experiments have shown that as consumption of spermatophylax increases, both the size and the number of eggs that females subsequently lay also increase (Gwynne 1984c). Furthermore, the increase in the size of eggs appears to be determined only by male-provided nutrient; an increase in protein in the general diet increases egg number but does not affect egg size (Gwynne, unpubl.).

The size of the spermatophore produced by male katydids varies from less than 3% of male body weight in some species to 40% in others (Gwynne 1983). Differences in the size of the male contribution conform with the predictions of sex-difference theory: in two species of katydids that make very large investment in each spermatophore (25% or more of male weight) and that have been examined in detail—the Mormon cricket (*Anabrus simplex*) and an undescribed species (*Metaballus* sp.) from Western Australia—there is a complete reversal in sex roles, with females competing aggressively for access to males that produce calling sounds, and males selecting mates, preferring large, fecund females (Gwynne 1981, 1984a, 1985). Figure 3 illustrates this reversal in the Mormon cricket. There is no evidence of such a reversal of courtship roles in species with smaller spermatophores; in these species males compete for mating territories and females select mates (Gwynne 1983).

It is evident, however, that a complete estimate of the contribution to offspring requires more than a simple measure of the relative contribution by the sexes to offspring such as the weight of the spermatophore relative to the weight of a clutch of eggs. Both species of katydids showing a role reversal in courtship behavior also had populations that showed no evidence of the reversed roles. For the Mormon cricket, the simple measure of relative contribution did not show a higher contribution by males at the sites of role reversal (Gwynne 1984a). However, these sites had very high population densities, with individuals of both sexes competing vigorously for food in the form of dead arthropods and certain plants. These observations suggest the hypothesis that the limited food supplies at these sites resulted in few spermatophores being produced and that spermatophore nutrients were thus a limiting resource for female reproduction. Food did not appear to be scarce at sites of low population density where the reversal in courtship roles was not observed. Support for the hypothesis that food is a limiting resource at high-density sites came from dissections of the reproductive accessory glands that produce the spermatophore in a sample of males from each of the sites. Only the few calling males at sites of high density had glands large enough to produce a spermatophore, whereas most males at the low-density site had enlarged glands. This difference between the males at the high- and low-density sites was not a result of a higher number of matings by males at the high-density site.

Differences between individuals from the two sites indicate that sexual selection on females at high-density sites was intense compared to the low-density site. (Sexual selection is measured by variance in mating success; see Wade and Arnold 1980.) Some females were very successful at obtaining spermatophores. These tended to be large females that were preferred by males as mates. The evolutionary consequences of the apparently greater sexual selection on high-density females was not only aggressive female behavior in competition for calling mates but also a

larger female body size at this site relative to males. This sexual dimorphism was not seen at sites of low density.

Variation in the expression of sexual differences within the same katydid species suggested that behavior might be flexible; that is, females become competitive and males choosy when they encounter certain environments. This hypothesis was examined using the undescribed *Metaballus* species of katydid from Western Australia, which is similar to the Mormon cricket in that only certain populations show female competition for mates and show males that reject smaller, less fecund females. In this species, discriminating males call females by producing a broken "zipping" song from deep in the vegetation. Sites where courtship roles are reversed consist of mainly the zipping male song, whereas at sites of male competition, males produce continuous songs that appear to be louder. An experiment was conducted which involved shifting a number of males and females from a site where role reversal was not observed to one in which it was noted. The behavior of the males that were moved to the role-reversed site changed to resemble that of the local males: their song changed from a continuous to a zipping song, the duration of courtship increased (possibly to assess the quality of their mates), and they even rejected fe males as mates. Thus, sexual differences in behavior are plastic; courtship roles of the sexes appear to be dependent on the environment encountered.

For the Mormon cricket, it is likely that the relative contributions of the sexes is the factor controlling sexual selection. A comparison of the weights of spermatophores and egg clutches is undoubtedly a poor estimate of relative contribution by the sexes; spermatophores seem to be important to the reproduction of females at both sites (Gwynne 1984a). However, if food supplies limit spermatophore production at sites where reversals in courtship roles are observed, and if females cannot obtain spermatophore nutrients from other food sources, then spermatophores are likely to have a greater influence on female fecundity and thereby are more valuable to female reproduction at these sites. Thus, the total

contribution from the males at these sites is probably larger than that of the females.

Nuptial feeding in scorpionflies

Most of the evidence supporting the hypothesis that the relative contribution of the sexes to offspring is an important factor controlling the extent of sexual selection has been derived from comparisons between or, in the katydid work, within species. In contrast, studies were conducted in which the relative contribution of males was manipulated to determine its effect on the extent of sexual selection (Thornhill 1981, 1986). This research has focused on scorpionflies of the genus *Panorpa* (Panorpidae), in which males use either dead arthropods or nutritious products of salivary glands to feed their mates.

Males must feed on arthropod carrion, for which they compete through aggression, before they can secrete a salivary mass. Males in possession of a nuptial gift release pheromone that attracts conspecific females from some distance. Females can obtain food without male assistance, but doing so is risky because of exposure to predation by web-building spiders. Movement in the habitat required to find dead arthropods exposes females and males to spider predation, and dead arthropods unattended by males are frequently found in active spider webs. The gift-giving behavior of males is an important contribution, because dead arthropods needed by females to produce eggs are limited both in the absolute sense and in terms of the risks in obtaining them.

In a series of experiments, individually marked male and female *Panorpa latipennis* were placed in field enclosures, and variances in mating success of the sexes were determined in order to estimate the relative intensity of sexual selection. Dead crickets taped to vegetation represented the resource that males defended from other males and to which females were attracted. In one experiment, three treatments were established in which equal numbers of males and females were added to each enclosure and the number of dead crickets varied—two, four, or six crickets per enclosure. As predicted, competition among males was greatest in the enclosures with two crickets; the intensity of sexual selection, calculated by variance in male mating success, was greatest in this treatment and was lowest in the treatment with six crickets.

Variance in female mating success was low and was not significant across cricket abundances over the seven days of the experiment. Sexual selection on females probably often arises from female-female competition for the best mates regardless of the number of mates. *Panorpa* females prefer males that provide large, fresh nuptial gifts of dead arthropods over males that provide salivary masses, and males only secrete saliva when they cannot compete successfully for dead arthropods (Thornhill 1981, 1984). This female mating preference is adaptive in that females mating with arthropod-providing males lay more eggs than females mating with saliva-providing males. Thus an accurate measure of sexual selection on female *Panorpa* would include the variation in egg output by females in relation to the resource provided by the mates of females. This information is not available at present.

However, the results on males from this experiment clearly support the hypothesis that sexual selection is determined by the relative contribution of the sexes. As food is a limiting resource for reproduction by female scorpionflies, the total contribution of food by males in enclosures with more crickets was greater than in enclosures with fewer crickets, and the intensity of sexual selection on males declined as males contributed relatively more.

Such studies of the factors controlling the operation of sexual selection are important for two major reasons. The first is simply that sexual selection has been such an important factor in the evolution of life. Sexual selection seems inevitable in species with two sexes, because, as Bateman (1948) first pointed out, the relatively few large female gametes will be the object of sexual competition among the males, whose upper limit to reproductive success is set by the number of ova fertilized rather than by production of the relatively small, energetically cheap sperm. The role of sexual selection in the history of life can best be explored when such controlling factors are fully under-

stood. The second reason is related to the first: the difference in the operation of sexual selection on the sexes may ultimately account for all sexual differences. Only sexual selection acts differently on the sexes per se (Trivers 1972). Natural selection may act on and may even magnify sexual differences in behavior and morphology, but probably only after these differences already exist as a result of the disparate action of sexual selection.

The insight of Williams (1966) and Trivers (1972) is that the relative contribution of materials and services by the sexes in providing for the next generation is the most important factor controlling the operation of sexual selection. In insects, contributions supplied by males to their mates include not only the paternal care of young, a well-studied phenomenon in vertebrates, but also other services such as courtship feeding, subtle forms of nutrient transfer via the reproductive tract, and "beneficial" guarding of mates.

References

Adams, J., and P. J. Greenwood. 1983. Why are males bigger than females in precopula pairs of *Gammarus pulex?* *Behav. Ecol. Sociobiol.* 13:239–41.

Alexander, R. D., and G. Borgia. 1979. On the origin and basis of the male-female phenomenon. In *Sexual Selection and Reproductive Competition in the Insects*, ed. M. S. Blum and N. A. Blum, pp. 417–40. Academic.

Bateman, A. J. 1948. Intrasexual selection in *Drosophila*. *Heredity* 2:349–68.

Boggs, C. L., and L. E. Gilbert. 1979. Male contribution to egg production in butterflies: Evidence for transfer of nutrients at mating. *Science* 206:83–84.

Bowen, B. J., C. G. Codd, and D. T. Gwynne. 1984. The katydid spermatophore (Orthoptera: Tettigoniidae): Male nutrient investment and its fate in the mated female. *Aust. J. Zool.* 32:23–31.

Bradbury, J. W., and S. L. Vehrencamp. 1977. Social organization and foraging in emballonurid bats. III. Mating systems. *Behav. Ecol. Sociobiol.* 2:1–17.

Breder, C. M., and D. E. Rosen. 1966. *Modes of Reproduction in Fishes*. Nat. Hist. Press.

Clutton-Brock, T. H., F. E. Guinness, and S. D. Albon. 1982. *Red Deer: Behavior and Ecology of Two Sexes*. Univ. of Chicago Press.

Darwin, C. 1874. *The Descent of Man and Selection in Relation to Sex*, 2nd ed. New York: A. L. Burt.

Deecaraman, M., and T. Subramoniam. 1983. Mating and its effect on female reproductive physiology with special reference to the fate of male accessory sex gland secretion in the stomatopod, *Squilla holoschista*. *Mar. Biol.* 77:161–70.

Emlen, S. T., and L. W. Oring. 1977. Ecology, sexual selection, and the evolution of mating systems. *Science* 197:215–22.

Finke, O. M. 1982. Lifetime mating success in a natural population of the damselfly *Enallagma hageni* (Walsh) (Odonata: Coenagrionidae). *Behav. Ecol. Sociobiol.* 10:293–302.

Gwynne, D. T. 1981. Sexual difference theory: Mormon crickets show role reversal in mate choice. *Science* 213:779–80.

———. 1983. Male nutritional investment and the evolution of sexual differences in the Tettigonidae and other Orthoptera. In *Orthopteran Mating Systems: Sexual Competition in a Diverse Group of Insects*, ed. D. T. Gwynne and G. K. Morris, pp. 337–66. Westview.

———. 1984a. Sexual selection and sexual differences in Mormon crickets (Orthoptera: Tettigoniidae, *Anabrus simplex*). *Evolution* 38:1011–22.

———. 1984b. Male mating effort, confidence of paternity, and insect sperm competition. In Smith 1984, pp. 117–49.

———. 1984c. Courtship feeding increases female reproductive success in bushcrickets. *Nature* 307:361–63.

———. 1985. Role-reversal in katydids: Habitat influences reproductive behavior (Orthoptera: Tettigoniidae, *Metaballus* sp.). *Behav. Ecol. Sociobiol.* 16:355–61.

Gwynne, D. T., B. J. Bowen, and C. G. Codd. 1984. The function of the katydid spermatophore and its role in fecundity and insemination (Orthoptera: Tettigoniidae). *Aust. J. Zool.* 32:15–22.

Hatziolos, M. E., and R. Caldwell. 1983. Role-reversal in the stomatopod *Pseudosquilla ciliata* (Crustacea). *Anim. Behav.* 31:1077–87.

Hieber, C. S., and J. A. Cohen. 1983. Sexual selection in the lovebug, *Plecia nearctica*: The role of male choice. *Evolution* 37:987–92.

Johnson, L. K., and S. P. Hubbell. 1984. Male choice: Experimental demonstration in a brentid weevil. *Behav. Ecol. Sociobiol.* 15:183–88.

Knowlton, N. 1982. Parental care and sex role reversal. In *Current Problems in Sociobiology*, ed. King's College Sociobiology Group, pp. 203–22. Cambridge Univ. Press.

Marshall, L. D. 1982. Male nutrient investment in the Lepidoptera: What nutrients should males invest? *Am. Nat.* 120:273–79.

Nisbet, I. C. T. 1973. Courtship-feeding, egg size, and breeding success in common terns. *Nature* 241:141–42.

Parker, G. A. 1970. Sperm competition and its evolutionary consequences in the insects. *Biol. Rev. Cambridge Philos. Soc.* 45:525–67.

Payne, R. B. 1979. Sexual selection and intersexual differences in variance of breeding success. *Am. Nat.* 114:447–66.

Ridley, M. 1978. Paternal care. *Anim. Behav.* 26:904–32.

Rutowski, R. L. 1982. Mate choice and lepidopteran mating behavior. *Fla. Ent.* 65:72–82.

Rutowski, R. L., C. E. Long, and R. S. Vetter. 1981. Courtship solicitation by *Colias* females. *Am. Midl. Nat.* 105:334–40.

Rutowski, R. L., M. Newton, and J. Schaefer. 1983. Interspecific variation in the size of the nutrient investment made by male butterflies during copulation. *Evolution* 37:708–13.

Schuster, S. M. 1981. Sexual selection in the Socorro Isopod *Thermosphaeroma thermophilum* (Cole) (Crustacea: Peracarida). *Anim. Behav.* 29:698–707.

Sharp, J. L., N. C. Leppala, D. R. Bennett, W. K. Turner, and E. W. Hamilton. 1974. Flight ability of *Plecia nearctica* in the laboratory. *Ann. Ent. Soc. Am.* 67:735–38.

Smith, R. L. 1979. Paternity assurance and altered roles in the mating behaviour of a giant water bug, *Abedus herberti* (Heteroptera: Belostomatidae). *Anim. Behav.* 27:716–25.

———. 1980. Evolution of exclusive postcopulatory paternal care in the insects. *Fla. Ent.* 63:65–78.

———, ed. 1984. *Sperm Competition and the Evolution of Animal Mating Systems.* Academic.

Thornhill, R. 1976. Sexual selection and paternal investment in insects. *Am. Nat.* 110:153–63.

———. 1980. Sexual selection in the black-tipped hangingfly. *Sci. Am.* 242:162–72.

———. 1981. *Panorpa* (Mecoptera: Panorpidae) scorpionflies: Systems for understanding resource-defense polygyny and alternative male reproductive effort. *Ann. Rev. Ecol. Syst.* 12:355–86.

———. 1983. Cryptic female choice in the scorpionfly *Harpobittacus nigriceps* and its implications. *Am. Nat.* 122:765–88.

———. 1984. Alternative hypotheses for traits believed to have evolved in the context of sperm competition. In Smith 1984, pp. 151–78.

———. 1986. Relative parental contribution of the sexes to offspring and the operation of sexual selection. In *The Evolution of Behavior,* ed. M. Nitecki and J. Kitchell, pp. 10–35. Oxford Univ. Press.

Thornhill, R., and J. Alcock. 1983. *The Evolution of Insect Mating Systems.* Harvard Univ. Press.

Trivers, R. L. 1972. Parental investment and sexual selection. In *Sexual Selection and the Descent of Man, 1871–1971,* ed. B. Campbell, pp. 136–79. Aldine.

Waage, J. K. 1979. Adaptive significance of postcopulatory guarding of mates and non-mates by *Calopteryx maculata* (Odonata). *Behav. Ecol. Sociobiol.* 6:147–54.

Wade, M. J., and S. J. Arnold. 1980. The intensity of sexual selection in relation to male sexual behaviour, female choice, and sperm precedence. *Anim. Behav.* 28:446–61.

Wells, K. D. 1980. Social behavior and communication of a dendrobatid frog (*Colostethus trinitatis*). *Herpetologica* 36:189–99.

Wilcox, R. S. 1984. Male copulatory guarding enhances female foraging in a water strider. *Behav. Ecol. Sociobiol.* 15:171–74.

Williams, G. C. 1966. *Adaptation and Natural Selection.* Princeton Univ. Press.

———. 1975. *Sex and Evolution.* Princeton Univ. Press.

Female Choice in Mating

The evolutionary significance of female choice depends on why the female chooses her reproductive partner

Meredith F. Small

The large, pink rear end of a female monkey bobbed though the juniper scrub. The skin on her rear end was swollen like a balloon as a result of the hormonal changes that trigger estrus. The swelling showed males, even those at a great distance, that she was ready to mate. She soon approached a young male and swung her hindquarters into his face; he mounted her. Both of them ignored the rattle of paper and scratchy pencil noises as I noted this copulation.

I came to this group of Barbary macaques, housed on 10 hectares of oak forest in southwestern France, to study the mating behavior of females. My job was to follow one of 14 females for half an hour, several times a week, and note her sexual partners. Barbary macaques breed seasonally, from September to January. As a female comes into estrus the swelling on her hindquarters indicates that she is sexually receptive and that ovulation is imminent. A female selects a male by turning her hind end into his face; if he is interested, they copulate. Some males wait for females to come calling. A more assertive male might approach a female and give her a slight nudge from behind; if she is willing, they

Meredith F. Small is associate professor of anthropology at Cornell University. She received an A.B. in 1973 from San Diego State University, an M.S. in 1975 from the University of Colorado at Boulder and a Ph.D. in 1980 from the University of California at Davis. She has studied female macaque reproductive strategies for the past 14 years, working with three species—rhesus, bonnets and Barbarys. She is currently writing a book on female choice, Nympho's Daughters: The Evolution of Sexual Assertiveness and Mate Choice in Female Primates, *to be published next year by Cornell University Press. Address: Department of Anthropology, McGraw Hall, Cornell University, Ithaca, NY 14853.*

copulate. The female typically emits a loud call during the copulation; afterwards, she spends a few minutes grooming her partner. The female always ends the interaction by moving on, usually making a beeline for the next male.

Initially, the data that I gathered on mating by Barbary macaques fit nicely into a relatively recent development in the theory of animal behavior. Over the years, evolutionary biologists have discarded the image of females as passive, coy creatures and have embraced the notion that females, just like males, have been selected to tend to their own reproductive interests during mating. But what are those interests?

For any organism, the fundamental evolutionary interest is passing genes to future generations. Nevertheless, males and females pursue this goal through different strategies because of physiological constraints. One conspicuous asymmetry between the sexes is that females invest more heavily in offspring than males do; females gestate and lactate while males are free to inseminate other females. This difference in investment suggests that a female should be careful about selecting a potential father for her offspring. Mate selection by females, however, might be a significant evolutionary force acting on males, affecting the passage of particular male genes into future generations. Current evolutionary theory strongly supports a female effect on the mating process.

My observations showed clearly that Barbary females decide which males get to mate and when. These female monkeys are a perfect example of the sexually assertive female primate. But by the end of the breeding season, having observed 506 copulations, I

Pat and Tom Leeson (Photo Researchers, Inc.)

Figure 1. Differences between the sexes hampered Darwin's theory of evolution by natural selection. If an animal's environment creates the same problems for males and females, why would the sexes be different?

Primary sexual characteristics, such as testes and ovaries, did not cause a problem. These differences are necessary for sexual reproduction, and therefore evolved by natural selection. Secondary sexual characteristics caused the fundamental difficulty. These traits and behaviors are those that either appear in only one sex, such as horns, or are exaggerated in one sex, such as large tearing teeth. To Darwin these characteristics did not appear essential for reproduction; but they are often different between the sexes. To solve this dilemma, Darwin proposed a second type of selection—sexual selection. Sexual selection could induce exaggerated traits in males—such as the impressive tail of the peacock shown here.

Figure 2. Male-male competition affects sexual selection. Darwin offered the possibility that competition between males, fighting for the chance to mate with females, could create secondary sexual characteristics, such as the horns of the male bighorn sheep shown here. This type of sexual selection is now called intra-sexual selection, selection within one sex. A characteristic such as horns could be enhanced through reproduction. For example, a male bighorn sheep is more likely to mate if he displaces all of the competing males. Likewise, he might do better in this competition if he has the biggest horns. So if the male with the biggest horns is the most likely to mate, his male offspring are also likely to have big horns.

Tom Branch (Photo Researchers, Inc.)

found myself questioning the current consensus about female choice. Yes, female Barbary macaques do make choices, but they seem to choose every male in the group, one after the other. As the breeding season progressed, I recorded a steady increase in the number of different male partners for each female. If Barbary females are supposed to be selective about which males will father the next batch of infants, why were these females moving from male to male with apparently indiscriminate abandon? The day that I watched a female copulate with three different males in the span of six minutes, I knew it was time to reevaluate the current concept of female choice.

Darwin's Feelings on Females

The theoretical investigation of female choice began, as did much evolutionary theory, with Charles Darwin. His theory of evolution by natural selection implies that all individuals are under similar selection pressures. But if this is so, why are there morphological and behavioral differences between males and females? Many of these differences, ones that Darwin called primary sexual characteristics, are required for reproduction. Ovaries, testes, eggs and sperm are all necessary for sexual reproduction, and thus their development can be explained through the conventional mechanisms of natural selection. But Darwin had a more difficult time explaining secondary sexual characteristics—traits and behaviors that appear at puberty and are either limited to one sex or exaggerated in one sex, such as horns, manes and facial hair. Darwin thought that these traits arose through competition for mates—a process that he called sexual selection.

In 1871 Darwin published a further analysis of sexual selection in *The De-scent of Man and Selection in Relation to Sex*. He was explicit about how sexual selection operates, and about which sex is affected more by the process. As far as evolution is concerned, it is not enough for animals simply to survive; they must also pass on genetic material to win in the game of reproductive success. Darwin wrote: "This depends, not on a struggle for existence, but on a struggle between males for the possession of females; the result is not death to the unsuccessful competitor, but few or no offspring."

Darwin described two ways in which sexual selection could operate. First, it could arise through competition between males, as they battle to gain access to females. This male-male competition is now referred to as intra-sexual

selection. Many male traits can be explained in this way by the need for weaponry and armor during male-male contests over females. For example, the massive horns of male bighorn sheep grow as males reach sexual maturity, and the horns help the males in battles for females. Male lions have huge manes to protect their necks during fights with other males. Male baboons sport giant canine teeth to intimidate opponents who want access to the same females.

In a second aspect of sexual selection, Darwin saw males winning the favor of females by first attracting attention and then waiting to be selected over other males. The peacock's tail is often cited to illustrate this point. The extravagant plumage of peacocks serves no survival

al selection was minor; even when a female chooses a certain male over others, the female's behavior only serves to explain male traits. Darwin's emphasis on males over females was based on what he considered the difference in passion between the sexes. Darwin felt that males were the more passionate sex, and therefore they would fight to gain females, whereas females were not interested in sex. Darwin wrote of this supposed difference in ardor: "The female..., with the rarest exceptions, is less eager than the male. As the illustrious [John] Hunter long ago observed, she generally 'requires to be courted'; she is coy, and may often be seen endeavouring for a long time to escape from the male." Males, with their zealous passion, would be competitive, whereas females, with their passive approach to sex, would be choosy. Darwin clearly thought that female choice, as a force of sexual selection, was secondary to male-male competition, and rather unimportant.

Ruth Hubbard, a historian of science at Harvard University, has suggested that Darwin's view of female sexuality was more influenced by his Victorian times than by the facts of animal behavior. In defense of Darwin, he had few reports of distinctively female animal behavior to guide his conclusions, and as for human models, he had only the behavior of the females around him—his social milieu—to form a picture of femaleness. Darwin's writings about women sound very quaint to modern ears. He saw men as more "courageous, pugnacious, and energetic than women," and thought that a woman differed from a man "in mental disposition, chiefly in her greater tenderness and less selfishness." And it seems he believed the sexual behavior of female animals generally would be like that of "proper" Victorian ladies —passionless and passive. It would take years of field and laboratory research to prove Darwin wrong on this point. Female animals are anything but sexually passive creatures.

Female Choice Affects Females
For almost a century, biologists virtually ignored female choice as a potential evolutionary force. R. A. Fisher, a leader in both statistics and genetics during the first half of the 20th century, wrote briefly about female choice in his volume *The Genetical Theory of Natural Selection*, a classic evolutionary text published in 1930. Fisher proposed that

purpose, and peacocks do not use their tails for fighting. But peahens are attracted by the large fans, and choose the most demonstrative males as mates. The lavish tail of the peacock has, therefore, evolved because females are attracted to it.

In 1982 Malte Andersson of the University of Göteborg in Sweden empirically demonstrated a direct relationship between female choice and the exaggeration of a male trait in African widowbirds. Male widowbirds have an extremely long tail, about 50 centimeters in length, whereas the females have a tail more in proportion with their body size. In an ingenious experimental design, Andersson lengthened the tails of some males by adding pieces of tail feathers and shortened the tails of oth-

ers; for controls he left some males as they were and in other cases clipped a segment of tail and then glued it back onto the same bird. Andersson found more new nests in territories owned by males with artificially lengthened tails. He also showed that males do not use their exaggerated tails in male-male competition. Andersson concluded that the only explanation for the evolution of tail-length exaggeration in widowbirds is female choice. Female widowbirds consistently choose males with the longest tails. Today we call this process inter-sexual selection or female choice.

In both intra-sexual and inter-sexual selection, Darwin emphasized that sexual selection explains how males evolve odd and exaggerated characteristics. Darwin felt that the female role in sexu-

Figure 3. Long tail of the male widowbird *(above)* attracts the female *(right)*. Malte Andersson found that the males with the longest tails have the most nests in their territories. In other words, a longer tail translates into more matings and more offspring. Darwin proposed that attracting females is another possible force that drives the evolution of secondary sexual characteristics in males. In this case, however, the trait does not confer any survival advantage; the trait simply attracts females. Because females are attracted to a certain trait, they tend to mate with males who have an exaggerated example of the trait, such as a longer tail. Then, the offspring are also likely to have an exaggerated version of the trait. In widowbirds, this type of sexual selection has produced males with extremely long tails, about half a meter in length. This type of sexual selection is now called inter-sexual selection, mate choice or female choice. (Photographs courtesy of Malte Andersson.)

mate choice can have an evolutionary effect only if a consistent choice by the female and the favored trait of the male are passed on together. Fisher held that females choose males because of a particular trait even though the trait probably has little effect on their offspring. The trait in the male and the choice by the female pass through generation after generation, co-evolving in a runaway manner. Natural selection stops the exaggeration only when the trait becomes a hindrance.

In the 1950s John Maynard Smith of the University of Sussex in England began working on the mating process in the fruit fly *Drosophila*. Although Maynard Smith was initially interested in male fertility and the mating process in general, his experiments produced some unexpected information about female mating behavior. In one experiment, Maynard Smith and his colleagues worked with a strain of flies in which

many of the males were infertile because of their inbred heritage. The investigators also noticed a ritualized courtship dance of male and female flies. At first, when females bobbed right and left in front of a courting male, Maynard Smith assumed that the females were trying to get away. But other experiments with wax models of female flies showed that female participation in the dance was necessary for mating to proceed smoothly. And in many cases the female started dancing just to see if the male could keep up. When inbred males, who were clumsy dancers with bad timing, tried to mount females, they were often too far forward or too far back, and the female would eventually kick them off altogether. As Maynard Smith put it for these poor males: "The spirit is willing but the flesh is weak."

Maynard Smith proposed that the dance evolved on the female's behalf. In other words, females judge males by

their dancing ability, and the dance is a true indicator of male fertility. Remember that the inbred, less-fertile males are the poor dancers. Maynard Smith predicted that selfish choices made by a female might, as a secondary consequence, affect the appearance of male characteristics and behaviors.

This was a new kind of female choice, one based on the reproductive interests of the females rather than on male-male competition or on females mindlessly choosing males with the most impressive displays. Unfortunately, no one listened. Maynard Smith recently wrote: "When, in 1956, I published a paper showing at least to my own satisfaction, how female fruit flies choose males, I do not remember receiving a single reprint request." Two decades passed before anyone seriously considered females as effective factors in sexual selection.

In 1972 Robert Trivers of the University of California at Santa Cruz wrote a paper on parental investment that forever changed the structure and meaning of female-choice theory. Trivers argued that Darwin's dichotomy between mate competition as a male domain and mate choice as a female domain is reasonable, but not because of a difference in passion between the sexes. The same conclusion can be reached because of a difference in reproductive strategies. Males, who produce effectively endless amounts of sperm, and typically spend no time caring for offspring, do best in evolutionary terms when they gain as many mates as possible. Females, on the other hand, produce fewer gametes, and they gestate and usually care for the infants. Females should be choosy, picking the best father for their offspring. This male-female difference is especially critical for mammals because females spend months nursing infants, and each batch of offspring represents a large investment. Trivers suggested that

Genevieve Renson (Jacana/Photo Researchers, Inc.)

Figure 4. Male mandrill's brightly colored face distinguishes him from the female. This difference in coloration could have arisen from a type of selection best called "Fisherian" female choice. Darwin and R. A. Fisher, a mathematician of the 20th century, raised the possibility that females might select males because of a specific trait. To qualify as an example of Fisherian female choice, a trait must be either exaggerated in one sex or found only in one sex, and it must not be the result of male-male competition. The mandrill offers one such example. The faces of the male and female are colored differently, and this cannot be explained by competition among males, as far as anyone knows. The face of the male mandrill is, probably, brightly colored because the females choose to mate with gaudy males. After many generations, the coloring of the male's face became progressively more elaborate.

George Holton (Photo Researchers, Inc.)

Figure 5. Black lemurs are sexually dichromatic: The males are black and the females are brown. This difference in color is likely another example of Fisherian female choice, because the male's coloration probably has no direct effect on fitness.

these biological differences produce males who battle for females, and females who should be very selective about their reproductive partners.

Female-choice theory is now somewhat different from what Darwin envisioned. Gone is the supposed difference in passion between males and females. The passive role for females is replaced by a new sexual assertiveness. And females gained a further dimension from Trivers: Females are selected to address their own reproductive requirements, choosing a mate who will pass on the best genes to the next generation. This change in perspective toward female behavior, initiated in the 1970s and still running strong, was socially timely, and it would be naive to ignore the influence of social trends on the acceptance of the theory. The feminist revolution in Western culture paved the way for open-minded thinking about female roles, and more women entered the field of animal behavior. Today animal-behavior journals abound with data on female behavior, especially information on female mating behavior. We have learned that females are active participants in mating, but oddly enough we remain unsure about the impact of female choices on inherited traits, behaviors and individual reproductive success.

Fishing for Fitness

Ryne Palombit, a colleague in animal behavior at the University of California at Davis, and I believe that part of the confusion over the effect of female choice on an animal's life is caused by a basic confusion in the theoretical framework. Between the days of Darwin and today, evolutionary theorists have really identified two types of female choice.

Following the traditional theory of Darwin and Fisher, females might choose specific males because the females are attracted to some male trait that appeared in the first place by natural selection. For example, the male widowbird first needed a tail for stability in flight, not for attracting females. The co-evolution of the male's trait and the female's choice results in the exaggeration of the male feature. This kind of "Fisherian" female choice explains the evolution of male traits and differences between males and females, just as Darwin predicted. To look for this type of female choice, we must ask the question: Are there traits that are exaggerated in or exclusive to one sex, and that cannot be explained by male-male competition?

For the primate order, the group of animals that I study, the search for traits that might have evolved by Fisherian female choice is difficult. Male primates are usually bigger than females, but this is due to intense pressure on males to compete with other males for matings. Male baboons have huge canines, but females have canines too, and the male exaggeration is probably due to fighting among males. There are only a few examples in primates of male traits that could, perhaps, be explained by Fisherian female choice. For example, several lemur species are sexually dichromatic: The males are one color and the females are another. This trait probably did not evolve to help males in fighting. Therefore, it may have evolved by female choice, even if coloration has nothing to do with male fitness. The only other clear example is the brightly painted red and blue face of the male mandrill.

The other kind of female choice is what I call "Triverian" female choice, where females are making choices based on what is best for them. In this type of female choice, the effect on males can be secondary. The only time that a male is affected is when the specific trait on which females base their choice also has a link to the fitness of the male. Torbjörn van Schantz and his colleagues at the University of Lund in Sweden showed a direct connection between a male trait (the spurs of pheasants), female choice and improved reproductive success for females. Van Schantz factored out male size, wing span, territory and age by changing the kinds of males available to females. Only spur length was consistently important to females. And females who mated with long-spurred males hatched the largest clutches. If spur length is a heritable trait, then the males from these clutches should also have long spurs. In other words, if a male trait is correlated with health and vigor and females are attracted to that trait, then the females' choices will affect the evolution of the male trait. Traits with this property represent "truth in advertising" on the part of males. But to females, how their choice affects male evolution is not important; the female is only interested, in an evolutionary sense, in how her choice affects her offspring. From this perspec-

Figure 6. Male pheasants with long spurs are more attractive to females. And females have larger clutches when they mate with long-spurred males, such as the male silver pheasant shown here. This is an example of what could be called "Triverian" female choice. Robert Trivers pointed out that males and females have different levels of investment in their offspring. In general, males produce effectively endless amounts of sperm. Conversely, females produce a limited number of eggs. Because of this asymmetry, Trivers suggested that males should battle for females, and females should be choosy in selecting a reproductive partner. Triverian female choice also implies that a female's choice is based on her reproductive interests, not on the male's. In the case of pheasants, the female's choice affects the length of spurs in her male offspring, but this is secondary. The primary effect is that the female who chooses a long-spurred male will produce more offspring.

Tom McHugh (Photo Researchers, Inc.)

tive, the male trait, and how it evolved, is secondary to the motivation of the female making the choice.

These two kinds of female choice, Fisherian and Triverian, are lumped together by most biologists, but there is an important distinction between them. Fisherian female choice is always sexual selection in the manner described by Darwin; it explains differences in male and female traits and the exaggerated appearance of those traits. Triverian female choice is really an expression of ordinary natural selection because it is inconsequential if the female's choice affects male traits. The female has been naturally selected to choose the best male as her fertilizing partner.

Most of the confusion about what females are really doing stems from misunderstanding the differences between these two types of female choice. There is no question that female animals do make choices. At question is the evolutionary effect of a female's choice. Does it simply affect male traits and maintain the difference between males and females, or does it improve the female's fitness? Fisherian female choice gives rise to differences between males and females, without necessarily directly affecting the female's fitness. Triverian female choice may also create differences between males and females, but its primary effect is to enhance the viability of the female's offspring.

Primate Picks

Primates are likely candidates for studies of female choice, because of their big brains, high intelligence and flexible behavior. Twenty years of primatology, including laboratory and long-term field studies, has shown that female primates are active participants in the mating game. They often initiate sexual activity, and they walk away from males as well. Female primates are highly sexual—mating not just for conception at the moment of ovulation but repeatedly during the estrus cycle. Although these females are clearly sexually assertive, we do not know what the evolutionary effect of this assertiveness might be or why it evolved. And we are not sure how a female primate's choice of a partner has shaped the evolution of primate mating systems.

Reproduction by a female primate should be constrained by one critical factor—she has a limited reproductive potential. Female primates tend to reach sexual maturity late (in comparison with other mammals), and they usually bear

Figure 7. Female Barbary macaques choose which males get to mate. When these female monkeys come into estrus, hormonal changes cause the pink tissue around the female's hind end to swell. The swelling serves as a signal to males that the female is ready to mate. However, the female selects the male. To show her interest, she approaches the male and swings her hind end into his face. If the male is also interested, which he generally is, the two monkeys mate. (Photograph by the author.)

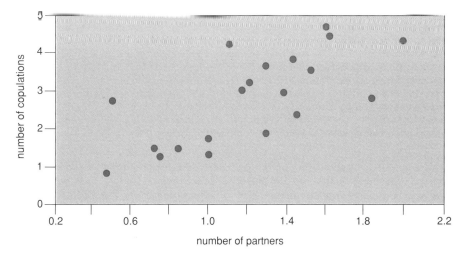

Figure 8. Female Barbary macaques mate with nearly every available male of reproductive age. In this graph each point represents the mating history of a single female. (The data are weighted for the length of observation, thereby creating fractional values for the number of partners on the x axis.) The data show that, as the females mated more and more during the breeding season, they continually mated with more new partners. Clearly, these females did not choose a preferred male and mate with him repeatedly. If the females had behaved monogamously, the points would create a roughly vertical line. Instead, the females mated with any male who would mate, giving the scatter of points a positive slope. This implies that these female primates are not following the evolutionary scenario of a female carefully selecting just the right reproductive partner. (From Small 1990.)

Figure 9. Female primates invest a disproportionate amount of energy in their offspring, as compared with males. The female produces a limited number of eggs, each being an important opportunity to perpetuate her genes in future generations. Moreover, the female carries the baby in her uterus during the months of pregnancy. Following birth, she nurses the baby monkey. Then she cares for her offspring, sometimes for years. In contrast, the male plays a role only during mating. This photograph of a female Barbary macaque with twin offspring conveys just how much energy the mother must provide. Given that the female primate has a finite amount of energy to expend on reproduction and that she can produce only a limited number of offspring, she should select the mate who is most likely to produce strong offspring—offspring who will survive to reproduce themselves. (Photograph by the author.)

only one offspring at a time, with long periods between births. Furthermore, the female invests considerable energy in her offspring. Infants are nursed for many months, and mothers usually carry them until the infants initiate independence. One has only to think of the human infant, with its years of dependency and need, to see the far end of the primate continuum. Considering that a female has a limited amount of energy to expend on the production of offspring, she should carefully select a mate who will enhance the survival of her offspring and, hence, the survival of her genes. Female choice, when it occurs,

should reflect the reproductive interests of the female.

But how can the female judge the fitness of a male? Primate females cannot count sperm, do health checks or predict male vigor. Nevertheless, the females do choose on the basis of proximate cues provided by males. These cues are both physiological and behavioral.

In many species of primates, female choice appears to depend at least in part on a male's rank, his place in the troop's hierarchy. Not all primate species have such hierarchies, but when they do, females seem to pay particular attention. In theory, females

should prefer males of high status because this is generally correlated with access to resources. In addition, high-status males are often older and more powerful than low-status males. The stronger males might provide some protection from predators, or aid females during interactions within the troop. In a survey of female responses to male rank, I found that females in nine primate species seem to prefer high-status males. For example, female rhesus monkeys, vervet monkeys and savannah baboons choose high-ranking males when given the chance. These males also tend to be the older males in the group, which guarantees mature sexual physiology. But the preference for high-status mates is not absolute or invariant; even in species that have a status hierarchy, some females do not pursue a high-status male.

In addition, female primates may consider the familiarity of the prospective mate. In a few species, females choose familiar males over unknown males. Barbara Smuts of the University of Michigan at Ann Arbor reports that female olive baboons often have two male friends who gain preferred access during estrus. Correspondingly, orangutan females actively resist nonresident males. But this penchant for the familiar in some species is balanced by a taste for the exotic in others. Many female primates are attracted to unknown males. This selection for novel males may have evolved to avoid inbreeding. Females in nine primate species have been reported to show a preference for "foreign" males. Some females—such as those of patas monkeys and rhesus monkeys—will actively seek males lurking on the periphery of the troop. Japanese macaques, conversely, seem equally willing to mate with either a familiar or an unfamiliar male.

And we must consider the factor of popularity. People base many of their mating decisions on "attractiveness." Perhaps nonhuman primates also have some concept of attractiveness, or beauty. In fact, many of the choices made by nonhuman-primate females that seem inexplicable to human observers might fall into this category. One male in my group of Barbary macaques was repeatedly the target of female attention. To my eyes, he seemed a brute—he bit females and never engaged in mutual grooming. But the Barbary females evidently saw in him "a certain something" that only a female macaque could explain. His rate of copulation was higher than that of any other male.

In essence, our knowledge of female choice in primates presents a confusing picture. Sometimes the females choose a high-status male; sometimes they don't. Sometimes the females choose a familiar male; sometimes they don't. Part of this confusion may arise from a lack of data. We do not have a single example of a female primate making a specific mating choice that can be confirmed to increase her reproductive success. Likewise, we lack any direct evidence of a female primate making a choice that affects a male characteristic. Maybe we lack such examples because we have yet to ask the right questions.

There is, however, another potential explanation: Female choice may not be a powerful evolutionary force in primates. For female choice to have any evolutionary impact, females must make consistent choices; yet some female primates do not seem to make any choice. Female chimpanzees seem to have no clear preferences at all; they mate with just about every male. As I have shown, the same is true for Barbary macaque females. However, these females are not passive or indifferent; they do have an agenda of their own, but that agenda is simply to mate with any male in reproductive condition. I believe that some primate females are less choosy because they are under pressure to conceive. Ovulation is an event with a short window of opportunity, and seasonal breeding means there are few chances to conceive before females fall into an anestrous state. Although all females might prefer the "best" male, best is probably a category that expands and contracts with the timing of ovulation. If there is no time to dawdle, there is no time to be choosy.

The behavior of female Barbary macaques and of other female primates suggests that our current notion of female choice is already antiquated. We have empowered the behavior of females by acknowledging their sexual assertiveness, but we often stop short of accepting that sexually assertive behavior might result in less than choosy behavior. A passionate female with reproduction in mind must do what she must do. It may, in fact, be impossible to be sexually assertive and choosy at the same time. It is not that the contribution of male genes is unimportant to a female; but she may be more interested in simply conceiving, rather than conceiving with a particular male. Lowering her standards, and taking anyone who is interested, must then be one of the strategies available to a female primate.

Bibliography

Andersson, Malte. 1982. Female choice selects for extreme tail length in a widowbird. *Nature* 299:183–186.

Darwin, Charles. 1859. *The Origin of Species*. London: John Murray and Sons.

Darwin, Charles. 1871. *The Descent of Man and Selection in Relation to Sex*. London: John Murray and Sons.

Fisher, R. A. 1930. *The Genetical Theory of Evolution*. New York: Dover.

Hubbard, Ruth. 1979. Have only men evolved? In *Women Look at Biology Looking at Women*, ed. Ruth Hubbard. Boston: G. K. Hall and Company.

Maynard Smith, John. 1955. Fertility, mating behavior and sexual selection in *Drosophila subobscura*. *Genetics* 54:261–279.

Small, Meredith F. 1989. Female choice in nonhuman primates. *Yearbook of Physical Anthropology* 32:103–127.

Small, Meredith F. 1990. Promiscuity in Barbary macaques (*Macaca sylvanus*). *American Journal of Primatology* 20:267–282.

Smuts, Barbara B. 1985. *Sex and Friendship in Baboons*. New York: Aldine.

Trivers, Robert L. 1972. Parental investment and sexual selection. In *Sexual Selection and the Descent of Man*, ed. B. Campbell. New York: Aldine.

Signals, Species, and Sexual Selection

Michael J. Ryan

Many species of animals, especially birds and frogs, are readily identifiable to human observers by their distinctive visual and acoustical displays. These displays often characterize males that are attracting and courting females. Females rely on such species-specific displays to identify males; in particular, their concern is whether the males are conspecific or heterospecific, that is, members of their own or another species. Because heterospecific matings rarely yield viable offspring, it is important for females to recognize males of their own species, lest they waste a considerable investment in producing eggs.

The process of speciation involves a decrease in reproductive interactions and therefore a decrease in genetic exchange among populations. Because evolutionary change is more likely to occur in small groups of individuals, speciation enhances the probability of evolution. The understanding of how reproductive isolation evolves has therefore been a cornerstone of evolutionary biology. Reproductive isolation can result from the geographical isolation of taxa, but geographic barriers do not persist indefinitely. Reproductive isolation can also be maintained by behavioral differences, especially by differences in mate-recognition systems, which involve both the male's display and the female's preference for the display. Studies of the role of mate-recognition systems in promoting the integrity of species represent perhaps the main contribution of the field of animal behavior to the modern synthesis of evolutionary biology (Mayr 1982).

Many studies have documented a species-recognition function for male courtship. For example, Blair (1964) and his colleagues showed that female frogs are more likely to be attracted to a conspecific advertisement call than to a heterospecific call. The sensory basis of this mate-recogni-

> *Studies of mate recognition in frogs and fish reveal preferences for individuals, populations, and even members of closely related species*

tion system has been identified. Capranica (1976) and his colleagues demonstrated that the frog's auditory system is biased or "tuned" so that a conspecific call is more likely to elicit a neural response than is a heterospecific call.

Because of the importance of species-specific courtship signals in species isolation, and the success with which the function of these signals has been identified, there has been a tendency to ignore variations of courtship signals within species. However, a renewed interest in sexual selection has led to the finding that variations in these signals among conspecific males influence the male's ability to acquire mates (Campbell 1972). It is now clear that mate-recognition systems not only result in conspecific mating preferences, but also influence preferences of mates within and between populations of the same species, and in some very unusual cases they even generate heterospecific mate preferences.

Mate preference in túngara frogs

The túngara frog, *Physalaemus pustulosus*, is unusual among frogs because of its complex advertisement call (Fig. 1). This call consists of a "whine" that is followed by up to six "chucks." The whine is fairly tonal, and decreases from a starting frequency of 900 Hz to a final frequency of 400 Hz in about 400 msec. The chuck is much briefer—only 30 msec—and has a much richer spectrum of frequencies. A typical chuck has a fundamental frequency of 220 Hz and 15 harmonics of that frequency. Especially when calling in isolation, a male tends to produce simple calls—a whine and no chuck. In a large chorus, however, the calls are complex and include both whines and chucks (Rand and Ryan 1981). This vocal system was first studied by A. Stanley Rand of the Smithsonian Tropical Research Institute in Panama. Rand and I have been collaborating on studies of these frogs for the past decade.

We have discovered that if a male hears calls broadcast from a tape recorder, he adds chucks to his own calls. He tends to add more chucks to his calls in response to chucks added to the broadcast calls (Rand and Ryan 1981). This response to vocal competition appears to be the reason that most males in large choruses produce complex calls.

Michael J. Ryan is an associate professor in the Department of Zoology at the University of Texas. He received his Ph.D. in 1982 from Cornell University. He was subsequently a Miller Fellow at the University of California, Berkeley, for two years, and arrived at the University of Texas in 1984. Professor Ryan is also a research associate at the Smithsonian Tropical Research Institute in Panama, where he has conducted research on communication in frogs. His general interests are in the evolution and mechanisms of animal behavior. Address: Department of Zoology, University of Texas at Austin, Austin, TX 78712-1064.

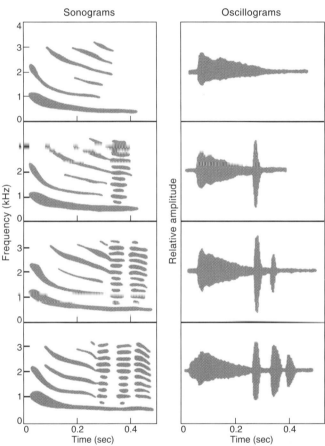

Figure 1. The mating call of the male túngara frog, *Physalaemus pustulosus,* **comprises combinations of a "whine" and a number of "chucks." The whine is necessary and sufficient to attract the female; however, when competitors are present, the male adds chucks to his call. Sonograms and oscillograms reveal the structures of a simple call containing only a whine (***top graphs***) and more complex calls containing chucks (***proceeding down***).**

Experiments in female phonotaxis suggest the advantages of complexity in male calls. A female is attracted to a speaker producing a simple whine. If the frequency structure of the whine is changed, however, the female is not attracted. Furthermore, if the whine is removed from a complex call, leaving only chucks, the female ceases to exhibit phonotaxis. The whine is therefore both necessary and sufficient for species recognition

by the female (Ryan 1983a). In addition, given a choice between calls with and without chucks, the female prefers the call with chucks. Therefore males enhance their attractiveness to females by increasing the complexity of calls. Females rely on the whine to discriminate among species and use the chuck to discriminate among individuals within the species.

In measuring the mating success of male túngara frogs during two breeding seasons, I found that females were more likely to mate with larger males—both on a nightly basis and throughout the season. As a frog increases in size, so do his vocal cords, and because more massive vocal cords vibrate more slowly, larger frogs tend to have lower-pitched calls. This is true both among and within species. I tested the hypothesis that the greater mating success of larger males results from the preference of females for lower-frequency calls by conducting phonotaxis experiments using synthetic calls in which the whines were identical but the chucks had different frequencies. The experiments demonstrated that females prefer calls with chucks of lower frequency, suggesting that at least some of the mating advantage of larger males accrues from this female preference (Ryan 1980, 1983b).

These results, however, suggested a paradox. If females prefer calls with chucks, why do males bother to produce simple calls? There must be a cost involved; perhaps males conserve energy by producing complex calls only in the face of vocal competition. Some colleagues and I measured the increase in the rate of oxygen consumption in calling frogs. We found that calling is indeed energetically expensive; during calling, the rate of oxygen consumption increased fourfold to fivefold (Bucher et al. 1982). A very small increase in lactic acid suggested that it is primarily aerobic metabolism that supports calling behavior (Ryan et al. 1983). However, no difference between the energy used to produce a complex call and the energy used to produce a simple call was observed.

There is another potential cost in calling: not only do calls attract females, they can also attract predators. In fact, Marler (1955) suggested that pressures of predation have led to the convergence of structure and function in bird calls. Tuttle and I conducted a series of studies on the frog-eating bat, *Trachops cirrhosus,* which locates prey by orienting to the frog's advertisement call (Tuttle and Ryan 1981) (Fig. 2). Like female túngara frogs, frog-eating bats are attracted to a simple call, and when given a choice between a simple and a complex call, they too prefer the call with chucks (Ryan et al. 1982). The ability of the male túngara frog to vary the number of chucks in his call allows him to balance this cost of predation with the benefit of mate attraction.

The two functions of courtship display in the túngara frog probably evolved in response to different selection forces. The whine, used for species recognition, evolved under selection forces associated with the advantages of conspecific relative to heterospecific matings. The female preference for calls with chucks, and especially chucks with lower frequencies, evolved under the influence of sexual selection generated by female choice and the countervailing selection force of predation.

Mate preference in cricket frogs

The mate recognition system consists of not only the signal but also the receiver. Variations in signals have been more extensively documented than variations in receivers because signals are more accessible to the researcher. It is much easier to compare the colors and calls of different species than to compare the properties of the visual and auditory systems that decode those stimuli.

Anurans have emerged as a model system in the study of communication for a number of reasons (Wilczynski and Ryan 1988). The male frog's call is relatively simple compared to bird song, and therefore it can be more easily quantified and synthesized. Also, female frogs readily exhibit phonotaxis in response to broadcasts of natural or synthetic calls, allowing experimental determination of the importance of various parameters. Another important advantage, perhaps unique to frogs among all vertebrates, is the detailed understanding of the properties of the auditory system responsible for decoding the conspecific advertisement call. This allows for the investigation of both aspects of the mate recognition system: the signal and receiver.

Unlike other vertebrates, amphibians have two organs in the inner ear that are stimulated by airborne sound: the amphibian papilla and the basilar papilla. Each papilla is enervated by fibers from the eighth cranial nerve. These two organs differ in several ways, one being their sensitivity to frequencies. The nerve fibers emanating from the amphibian papilla tend to be most sensitive to lower frequencies, usually below 1,500 Hz, whereas the fibers that enervate the basilar papilla are tuned to higher frequencies, usually above 1,500 Hz. The frequency to which each inner ear organ is most sensitive—called the best excitatory frequency (BEF)—is usually matched to the more energetic frequencies of the advertisement call. For example, the adver-

tisement calls of the bullfrog and the green treefrog have two concentrations of spectral energy; one of these is matched by the BEF of the amphibian papilla and the other by the BEF of the basilar papilla (Zakon and Wilczynski 1988). Not all calls stimulate both inner ear organs. For example, the whine of the túngara frog stimulates primarily the amphibian papilla (Ryan et al., in press.).

The call of the cricket frog (*Acris crepitans*) sounds like a loud click, and these clicks are organized into complex call groups. The call has a dominant frequency of 2,800 to 4,100 Hz, and stimulates primarily the basilar papilla. Nevo and Capranica (1985) documented considerable call variation in this species across its range in North America. They also showed that between two populations separated by 2,500 km, there were differences in the tuning of the auditory system that tended to match the dominant frequency of the local call (Capranica et al. 1973). Because a colleague and I are interested in the coevolution of signals and receivers of mate recognition systems, we decided to investigate correlated differences in the call and the auditory system in cricket frogs over relatively small geographic distances in which the potential for biological interactions was significant (Ryan and Wilczynski 1988).

Initially, we studied two populations of cricket frogs in central Texas; one in grasslands of Austin, and the other in pine forests of Bastrop, 65 km away. Calls differed in a number of ways, most obviously in the dominant frequency—frogs from Austin had lower-frequency calls (Fig. 3). There were also differences in the BEF of the basilar papilla. The BEFs of frogs from Austin were, on average, lower than the BEFs of the frogs from Bastrop. However, the BEF of each population was not significantly different from the dominant frequency of the local advertisement call.

Just as the dominant frequency of the call can vary with body size, so too can the BEF of the basilar papilla.

Figure 2. In addition to attracting a female frog, the call of the male túngara frog can attract the frog-eating bat, *Trachops cirrhosus*. The bat responds to complexities in the frog's call in much the same way that the female frog does. In the photograph above a bat feeds on a male túngara that had been calling. (Photo by M. Tuttle.)

Several authors have suggested that congruence between the signal and receiver of a mate recognition system can be maintained by incidental effects of body size (Passmore 1981; Paterson 1982). For example, selection might favor larger body size in a population living in a drier habitat because of its advantage in minimizing desiccation rates. If so, the mate recognition systems of this population and a population living in a wetter habitat would diverge while remaining congruent within each population. The larger frogs would have lower-frequency calls and lower BEFs as a result of correlated responses of the signal and receiver to selection on body size, despite any direct selection on the communication system. These differences might even result in frogs from the different populations that do not recognize each other as potential mates. Nevo and Capranica (1985) made such a suggestion in order to explain the correlated variation in calls and tuning of the two populations of cricket frogs they studied (Capranica et al. 1973).

The frogs from Austin and Bastrop that we studied differed in body size: the Austin frogs were bigger and, as expected, had calls with lower dominant frequencies and basilar papillae with lower BEFs. However, size did not explain differences in the signals and receivers. An analysis of covariance showed that even after adjusting for differences in body size, call frequencies and BEFs differed between populations but not within each population.

We considered whether these population differences in the mate recognition system are biologically meaningful. If frogs from these two populations were to come into contact, would females prefer local males over males from the other population? We created call groups representing the two populations that were identical in the number of calls and call repetition rate, and found that females from Austin preferred the local calls. We also constructed synthetic calls that were identical in all aspects except dominant frequency. Again, females from Austin exhibited a significant preference for the local call.

Although like most frogs, cricket frogs have an advertisement call that results in females preferring males of their species rather than heterospecific males (Nevo and Capranica 1985), there is variation in both the signal and the receiver between populations of different species. This variation, which is not attributable to differences in body size alone, could generate mate preferences among populations.

Our study in some ways parallels research on bird dialects. Those studies have shown that there are significant and abrupt differences in the songs of conspecific birds from neighboring populations. Researchers have suggested that this variation, coupled with female mate preference, could result in genetic structuring of populations; that is, matings would be more likely to occur within than between call variants (Baker and Cunningham 1985). This idea is controversial because of the difficulties of conducting female phonotaxis experiments with birds and characterizing the sensory basis of the female preference (Andrew 1985). Our studies of cricket frogs, however, suggest that variations in the conspecific advertisement call between geographically close populations could lead to local mate preferences and possibly to genetic differentiation among populations.

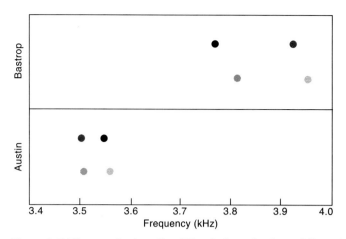

Figure 3. Differences in the calls of identical species from different geographical regions can be significant. Shown above are the average dominant frequencies of calls (*black dots*) and the best excitatory frequencies of the basilar papilla (*red dots*) for cricket frogs from two areas in Texas, Austin and Bastrop. The dots with lighter shading represent the data after being adjusted for differences in body size.

Heterospecific mate preference

The selection of mates is usually hierarchical. Among conspecific mates, choice, or sexual selection, usually proceeds only within the constraints of species recognition. This is exemplified by the mate-recognition systems discussed above. A female túngara frog relies on the whine of the male to select the correct species, and then proceeds to discriminate among conspecifics using the male's chuck. However, species-specific courtship signals do not always result in conspecific mate preferences. Two species of insects of the genus *Drosophila* exhibit mating asymmetries. The females of one species of this pair of sister species demonstrate conspecific mate preference, while the females of the other species mate randomly with males of either species (Kaneshiro 1980). Similar results have been reported for fish of the genera *Gasterosteus* (McPhail 1969; Moodie 1982) and *Trichogaster* (McKinnon and Liley 1987).

Our studies of fish of the genus *Xiphophorus*, which includes the platys and swordtails (Fig. 4), suggest that sexual selection for large body size can result in females of one species preferring to mate with males of another species. Larger males of many species have greater mating success, either because they are better able to compete for access to females or, as in the case of túngara frogs, because females prefer larger males. In most of these species, it is not clear whether differences in body size are the result of environmental effects or genetic differences. Because evolution proceeds only in the presence of genetic variation, this lack of knowledge is not trivial.

Swordtails and platys are unusual in that much of the variation in body size is attributable to allelic variation at a single Y-linked locus, the pituitary locus (Kallman 1984). This locus controls the timing of sexual maturity. Because males in this genus cease to grow upon reaching sexual maturity, this locus also influences body size. In the swordtail, *X. nigrensis,* from the Rio Choy in Mexico, males can have one of three alleles at the Y-linked pituitary locus. Males with the *s* allele mature early and have a small body size, those with the *L* allele mature later and have a large size, and males with the *I* allele are intermediate with respect to both body size and time to maturity. For this species, altering the availability of food affects the time required to attain sexual maturity but not the body size at that point. Because the pituitary locus on the X chromosome is fixed for *s*, females mature early and with a small body size, but unlike males, they continue to grow after maturing.

Because the variation at the pituitary allele occurs only on the Y chromosome, the body size of a son is determined by the body size of the father, which makes possible a paternity analysis. By collecting females and raising their offspring, the genotype (relative to the pituitary locus) is revealed. When these data are compared to the frequency distribution of the three genotypes in nature, the relative reproductive success of each pituitary allele can be determined. Because in our experiments the females were fertilized by males present at the time of sampling, much of the variance in reproductive success of the pituitary alleles was due to sexual selection—some combination of female choice and male competition.

Colleagues and I showed that small males were at a significant reproductive disadvantage; across generations there was a decrease in the *s* allele. Furthermore, some of this decreased reproductive success derived from female choice. Individual males of various sizes were placed at either end of a large aquarium, separated from a center section by glass partitions. A female was placed in the center, where she could consort with the male at either end. In most comparisons females spent significantly more time with the larger male (Ryan, et al., in press). Female preferences are therefore an important source of selection on male size, although the greater swimming endurance

of larger males suggests a role for male competition in male reproductive success (Ryan 1988).

A study of male mating behavior in swordtails revealed striking differences correlated to male size. Larger males performed a conspicuous display of courtship, whereas smaller males did not attempt to court females (Ryan and Causey 1989) (Fig. 5). Instead, the smaller males chased after females, trying to force copulation—a difficult task when faced with internal fertilization and quickly retreating females. Within the intermediate-size class, it was also found that smaller males chased while larger males courted. The transition between chasing and courting occurred at a length of about 29 mm. The results of female choice tests coincided with these results; females usually discriminated among males if one male was shorter and one longer than 29 mm. No discrimination was observed when both males were on one side of this transition.

Unlike other studies, our study reveals that this selection favoring larger males results in changes in allelic frequencies across generations; that is, our study documents genetic evolution by sexual selection. *X. nigrensis* males that are preferred less adopt alternative mating behaviors, and to some extent, there is a correlation between genotype and mating behavior.

The closest relative of *X. nigrensis* is *X. pygmaeus*, found in the nearby Rio Axtla. All *X. pygmaeus* males are small, encompassing the size range of the small-size class and the smaller males of the intermediate-size class of *X. nigrenis*. Wagner and I wondered if the pituitary alleles responsible for large body size in *X. nigrensis* would be favored by sexual selection if they were to appear in the *X. pygmaeus* population. Is the female preference present in the absence of the male trait? This might be true if the preference were present in the common ancestor of *X. pygmaeus* and *X. nigrensis* and were not lost in *X. pygmaeus* after the two taxa diverged.

We presented female *X. pygmaeus* with a choice between an *X. pygmaeus* male and a large *X. nigrensis* male. There was a strong preference for the larger, heterospecific male. Noting that the male *X. nigrensis* possesses a well-developed sword, which is lacking in *X. pygmaeus*, we decided to remove the sword of the *X. nigrensis* male and repeat the experiments. Female *X. pygmaeus* still preferred the larger *X. nigrensis*. Surprisingly, the female *X. pygmaeus* preferred the heterospecific male when both males were 26 mm long. The heterospecific preference was extinguished only when both males were small and of the same size. Under those circumstances, females did not exhibit any preference. In all cases, female *X. nigrensis* preferred her own conspecifics over *X. pygmaeus* males (Ryan and Wagner 1987).

Differences in body size alone cannot explain the asymmetric mating

Figure 4. In experiments, the swordtail, *Xiphophorus nigrensis*, demonstrates a startling behavior: the female prefers a male of a closely related but different species if the heterospecific fish is larger than males of her own species. Shown here are a male (*top*) and female of the species. (Photo by H. R. Axelrod.)

preferences observed. Behavior seems to be important as well. Franck (1964) reported that male *X. pygmaeus* lacks the display that characterizes the courtship behavior of its sister species and many other swordtails. Causey and I reconfirmed this, and showed that male *X. pygmaeus* behave toward females as do small male *X. nigrensis*—chasing the females in attempts to force copulation. In most of the *X. nigrensis–X. pygmaeus* pairs tested, heterospecific males were not only larger, they also possessed the characteristic courtship display. Only when both males were small, and both lacked the display, did the heterospecific preference cease to occur. The preference for the 26-mm heterospecific male is nevertheless confusing—*X. nigrensis* males of this size usually do not court.

It is not clear why the mating behavior of an entire species consists of what is considered alternative behavior. Courtship behavior is clearly favored by sexual selection through female choice in *X. nigrensis,* and it appears as if it might be favored if it were to evolve in *X. pygmaeus.* Obvious hypotheses, such as increased predation on courting males, have yet to be tested. Other possibilities such as phylogenetic influences and genetic constraints are being investigated. The preference for large, courting males in female *X. pygmaeus* and the lack of such a trait in their male counterparts has led to an interesting situation in which sexual selection can override considerations of species recognition. These species do not occur together in nature, but they do hybridize in the laboratory. If they were to come into contact, sexual selection could cause gene pools of the two species to merge. Furthermore, the study suggests that in some cases the female's preference, although not expressed, is "waiting" to be exploited by males with certain traits. Andersson (1982) has made a similar interpretation as a result of his study of female preference for long tails in widow birds; females preferred males with tails that were artificially lengthened beyond the maximum length exhibited by the species.

Evolution of mate recognition

There is little debate that mate-recognition systems effect mating between conspecifics. However, there is disagreement over the factors involved in the evolution of these systems. The disagreement highlights the important distinction between the evolved function of a trait and its incidental effects (Williams 1966; Gould and Vrba 1982). The function, in a strict sense, is that initial effect for which selection favored the trait. An extreme example of an effect not favored by selection is the attraction of bats to the chuck of male túngara frogs.

Dobzhansky (1937) suggested that mate-recognition systems evolved to serve the function of species isolation. This suggests the function is negative—one of avoidance. Paterson (1982) criticized this thesis because it viewed the species as an adaptive mechanism. He argued instead for the positive effects, suggesting that mate-recognition systems evolved to promote mating between individuals of similar genotypes (conspecifics).

Dobzhansky and Paterson both emphasized strong stabilizing selection on male courtship signals, and they tended to discount the significance of intraspecific variation. The studies reviewed here have suggested that both views are

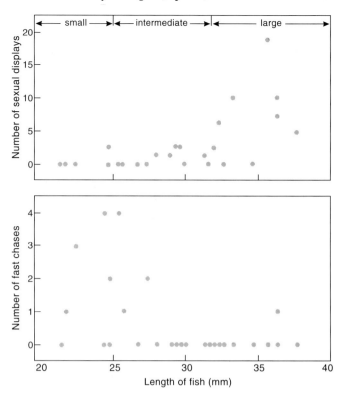

Figure 5. In the presence of females, large *X. nigrensis* males engage in courtship displays, whereas smaller *X. nigrensis* males simply chase the females. This may be related to the tendency of females to be attracted to larger males.

too typological, regardless of whether the evolved function of mate-recognition systems is one of repulsion or attraction. Courtship signals vary among males in the same population (e.g., túngara frogs and swordtail fish), and among populations of the same species (e.g., cricket frogs). And this variation is biologically meaningful, being the target of sexual selection by female choice. At least for the chuck component of the túngara frog's call, there is ample phylogenetic evidence that the vocal structures that allow males to produce the chuck evolved under the influence of sexual selection and not species recognition (Ryan 1985). Finally, there is the example of *X. pygmaeus,* in which female preference for courtship and larger size, a clear example of sexual selection and not species recognition, overrides the consideration of mating with conspecifics and results in females preferring heterospecific males.

Species recognition might be an evolved function, but it might also be an incidental effect of male courtship signals. A number of factors can be responsible for the divergence of signals that result in conspecific mate recognition. I have given examples of the importance of sexual selection—a possibility discussed extensively by West-Eberhard (1979, 1983, 1984; also Lande 1981).

Studies of mate-recognition systems are now moving away from notions of typology and embracing the idea of the rich and diverse variation within species as an important biological phenomenon. Some studies have revealed considerable variation in preferences among conspecific females (Majerus et al. 1982; Breden and Stoner 1987; Houde 1988). Others have investigated how the sensory basis of the preference enhances or constrains the divergence of courtship signals (Ryan 1986; Christy 1988; Ryan, et al., in press) or biases the direction of their evolution (Endler and McLellan 1988; Ryan 1990). Still needed are more studies of the receiver component of the recognition system. And finally, more attention should be given to studies involving rigorous phylogenetic comparisons. The common ancestor of sister taxa defines the common starting point from which two mate-recognition systems diverged. Perhaps knowledge of the system's history will provide further insight into the phylogenetic constraints under which these traits have evolved.

An understanding of how females recognize potential mates has been a cornerstone of modern evolutionary biology and an important pursuit of those interested in behavioral evolution. With the current interest in sexual selection and variability within species, this pursuit will remain an important, if more complexly defined, endeavor. Look for future studies to include approaches from the fields of sensory biology and phylogenetics.

References

Andersson, M. 1982. Female choice selects for extreme tail length in widow birds. *Nature* 299:818–20.

Andrew, R. J. 1985. Questions about the evolution of bird song. *Behav. Brain Sci.* 8:100.

Baker, M. C., and M. A. Cunningham. 1985. The biology of bird song dialects. *Behav. Brain Sci.* 8:85–100.

Blair, W. F. 1964. Isolating mechanisms and interspecies interactions in anuran amphibians. *Quart. Rev. Biol.* 39:334–44.

Breden, F., and G. Stoner. 1987. Male predation risk determines female preferences in the Trinidad guppy. *Nature* 329:831–33.

Bucher, T. L., M. J. Ryan, and G. A. Bartholomew. 1982. Oxygen consumption during resting, calling, and nest building in the frog *Physalaemus pustulosus*. *Physiol. Zool.* 55:10–22.

Campbell, B., ed. 1972. *Sexual Selection and the Descent of Man, 1871–1971.* Aldine.

Capranica, R. R. 1976. Morphology and physiology of the auditory system. In *Frog Neurobiology*, ed. R. Llinas and W. Precht, pp. 552–75. Springer-Verlag.

Capranica, R. R., L. S. Frischkopf, and E. Nevo. 1973. Encoding of geographic dialects in the auditory system of the cricket frog. *Science* 182:1272–75.

Christy, J. H. 1988. Pillar function in the fiddler crab *Uca beebei* (II: Competitive courtship signalling). *Ethology* 78:113–28.

Dobzhansky, T. 1937. *Genetics and the Origin of Species.* Columbia Univ. Press.

Endler, J., and T. McLellan. 1988. The processes of evolution: Towards a newer synthesis. *Ann. Rev. Ecol. Syst.* 19:394–421.

Franck, D. 1964. Vergleichende an lebendgebärenden Zahnkarpfen der Gattung *Xiphophorus*. *Zoologisches Jahrbuch* 71S:117–70.

Gould, S. J., and E. Vrba. 1982. Exaptation—a missing term in the science of form. *Paleobiol.* 8:4–15.

Houde, A. 1988. Genetic differences in female choice between two guppy populations. *Animal Beh.* 36:510–16.

Kallman, K. D. 1984. A new look at sex determination in poeciliid fishes. In *Evolutionary Genetics of Fishes*, ed. B. Turner, pp. 95–171. Plenum.

Kaneshiro, K. Y. 1980. Sexual isolation, speciation and the direction of evolution. *Evolution* 34:437–44.

Lande, R. 1981. Models of speciation by sexual selection on polygenic characters. *Proc. NAS* 78:3721–25.

Marler, P. 1955. Characteristics of some animal calls. *Nature* 176:6–8.

Majerus, M. E. N., P. O'Donald, and J. Weir. 1982. Female mating preference is genetic. *Nature* 300:521–23.

Mayr, E. 1982. *The Growth of Biological Thought.* Harvard Univ. Press.

McKinnon, J. S., and N. R. Liley. 1987. Asymmetric species specificity in response to female sexual pheromone by males of two species of *Trichogaster* (Pisces:Belodontidae). *Can. J. Zool.* 65:1129–34.

McPhail, J. D. 1969. Predation and the evolution of a stickleback (*Gasterosteus*). *Canadian Journal of the Fisheries Research Board* 26:3183–3208.

Moodie, G. E. E. 1982. Why asymmetric mating preferences may not show the direction of evolution. *Evolution* 36:1096–97.

Nevo, E., and R. R. Capranica. 1985. Evolutionary origin of ethological reproductive isolation in cricket frogs. *Acris. Evol. Biol.* 19:147–214.

Paterson, H. E. H. 1982. Perspectives on speciation by reinforcement. *So. Afr. J. Sci.* 78:53–7.

Passmore, N. 1981. The relevance of the specific mate recognition concept to anuran reproductive biology. *Monitore Zoologica Italiano* 6:93–108.

Rand, A. S., and M. J. Ryan. 1981. The adaptive significance of a complex vocal repertoire in a neotropical frog. *Zeitschrift für Tierpsysiologie* 57:209–14.

Ryan, M. J. 1980. Female mate choice in a neotropical frog. *Science* 209:523–25.

———. 1983a. Frequency modulated calls and species recognition in a neotropical frog, *Physalaemus pustulosus*. *J. Comp. Physiol.* 150:217–21.

———. 1983b. Sexual selection and communication in a neotropical frog, *Physalaemus pustulosus*. *Evolution* 37:261–72.

———. 1985. *The Túngara Frog. A Study in Sexual Selection and Communication.* Univ. Chicago Press.

———. 1986. Neuroanatomy influences speciation rates among anurans. *Proc. NAS* 83:1379–82.

———. 1988. Swimming endurance, genotype, and sexual selection in a swordtail *Xiphophorus nigrensis*. *Copeia* 1988:484–87.

———. In press. Sexual selection, sensory systems, and sensory exploitation. *Oxford Surv. Evol. Biol.*

Ryan, M. J., G. A. Bartholomew, and A. S. Rand. 1983. Energetics of reproduction in a neotropical frog, *Physalaemus pustulosus*. *Ecology* 64:1452–62.

Ryan, M. J., and B. J. Causey. 1989. "Alternative" mating behavior in the swordtails *Xiphophorus nigrensis* and *Xiphophorus pygmaeus* (Pisces: Poeciliidae). *Beh. Ecol. Sociobiol.* 24:341–348.

Ryan, M. J., J. Fox, W. Wilczynski, and A. S. Rand. In press. Sexual selection for sensory exploitation in the frog *Physalaemus pustulosus*. *Nature*.

Ryan, M. J., D. K. Hews, and W. E. Wagner, Jr. In press. Sexual selection on alleles that determine body size in the swordtail *Xiphophorus nigrensis*. *Beh. Ecol. Sociobiol.*

Ryan, M. J., M. D. Tuttle, and A. S. Rand. 1982. Bat predation and sexual advertisement in a neotropical frog. *Am. Naturalist* 119:136–39.

Ryan, M. J., and W. E. Wagner, Jr. 1987. Asymmetries in mating preferences between species: Female swordtails prefer heterospecific mates. *Science* 236:595–97.

Ryan, M. J., and W. Wilczynski. 1988. Coevolution of sender and receiver: Effect on local mate preference in cricket frogs. *Science* 240:1786–88.

Tuttle, M. D., and M. J. Ryan. 1981. Bat predation and the evolution of frog vocalizations in the neotropics. *Science* 214:677–78.

West-Eberhard, M. J. 1979. Sexual selection, social competition, and evolution. *Proc. Am. Phil. Soc.* 123:222–34.

———. 1983. Sexual selection, social competition, and speciation. *Quart. Rev. Biol.* 58:155–83.

———. 1984. Sexual selection, competitive communication and species-specific signals in insects. In *Insect Communication*, ed. T. Lewis, pp. 283–324. Academic Press.

Wilczynski, W., and M. J. Ryan. 1988. The amphibian auditory system as a model for neurobiology, behavior and evolution. In *The Evolution of the Amphibian Auditory System*, ed. B. Fritzsch et al., pp. 3–12. Wiley.

Williams, G. C. 1966. *Adaptation and Natural Selection. A Critique of Some Current Thought.* Princeton Univ. Press.

Zakon, H., and W. Wilczynski. 1988. The physiology of the anuran eighth nerve. In *The Evolution of the Amphibian Auditory System*, ed. B. Fritzsch et al., pp. 125–55. Wiley.

Spider Fights as a Test of Evolutionary Game Theory

Susan E. Riechert

The behavioral differences between two populations of the same species can be largely predicted and explained by game theory

The extent to which the behavior of a species changes from one local environment to another is an area of current ecological and evolutionary theory for which the spider has made an excellent test subject. Differences in traits between populations of the same species have been termed ecotypic variation (Turesson 1922). Although most studies of ecotypic variation deal with morphological and physiological characteristics, such as body color, the timing of reproduction, and temperature tolerances, it is well known that in animal evolution behavior tends to change before morphology (von Wahlert 1965; Krebs and Davies 1981). Mayr (1963) even states that for animals "a shift into a new niche or adaptive zone is almost without exception initiated by a change in behavior."

I have been working on a territorial system in spiders which lends itself to the use of game theory to analyze how behavior may adjust populations to local conditions. I share my findings here to demonstrate both the value of spiders as tools in ecological research and the importance of such studies in understanding evolutionary processes. Readers might wish to consult papers by Mitchell and his colleagues (1977) and Brockmann and Dawkins (1979), which also consider the variation in behavioral traits between populations.

The genus *Agelenopsis* belongs to the funnel-web spider family (Araneae, Agelenidae) and consists of the "grass spiders," so called because they frequent grassy areas throughout North America. They are, in fact, common inhabitants of lawns and hedgerows. I chose to work with the western species, *A. aperta* (Gertsch), because it has the widest geographic distribution and resides in the broadest range of habitats of any member of the genus: its populations are distributed from northern Wyoming to southern Mexico and from California to central Texas and are abundant in such divergent habitats as wet woodland and cactus scrub (Fig. 1).

Like all spiders, *A. aperta* is a predator that feeds on a diverse array of insects, other spiders, and their allies. Its web-traps are nonsticky sheets horizontal to the ground. Because the sheet is not sticky, it is used more for the detection of prey than for their actual capture, and it does not need to be replaced each day, being instead merely repaired and added to. The spider itself spends most of its time within the protection of a silk-lined funnel that is attached to the sheet and extends under a rock or into leaf litter, grasses, or shrub branches.

A. aperta overwinters in the juvenile stage and matures in the early summer just prior to the onset of seasonal rains (Riechert 1974). Spiderlings emerge from egg cases in August and September, generally weeks after the deaths of their mothers.

Levels of competition in different habitats

Food, water, shelter, and potential mates are often scarce in natural systems. For *A. aperta*, the availability of suitable locations for building webs is a major problem. Such sites must provide the structural support needed for attachment of the web. Their temperatures must be favorable; body temperature in spiders is determined by external factors that vary with local topography—factors such as solar and thermal radiation, air temperature, wind speed, and humidity—and *A. aperta* can capture prey only when its body temperature is between 21 and 35°C (Riechert and Tracy 1975). Finally, a web site must provide an abundance of prey, because the web-building spider does not actively search for prey but relies on prey coming to it.

I have studied populations of *A. aperta* at two habitats that differ markedly in the number of suitable web sites: a desert grassland in south-central New Mexico and a desert riparian habitat, a woodland bordering a stream, in the Chiricahua mountains of southeastern Arizona (Fig. 2). The grassland habitat is characterized by daily temperature extremes and strong winds. As a result, only 12% of the available space is capable of providing both shelter and the levels of prey necessary to support the growth and reproduction of *A. aperta* (Riechert and Tracy 1975). In this habitat, spiders settle in the limited number of sites that provide enough shade to decrease solar radiation, enough ground litter to decrease the amount of heat that would otherwise be radiated if the web were placed over dirt or rock substrates, and enough insect attractants, such as flowering herbs and shrubs and cow, deer, and rabbit feces (Riechert 1976).

Susan Riechert, professor in the Department of Zoology and in the Graduate Program in Ecology at the University of Tennessee, received her B.S., M.S., and Ph.D. (1973) from the University of Wisconsin. She is an evolutionary ecologist and, using the spider as her experimental tool, specializes in social structure, competition, and predator-prey relationships. The research reported here was supported by grants from the NSF and by a fellowship from the Fogarty Foundation. Address: Department of Zoology, University of Tennessee, Knoxville, TN 37996.

Figure 1. The funnel-web spider *Agelenopsis aperta* at the entrance to the funnel that extends from its web. (Photo by P. Riechert.)

The riparian habitat offers a much more favorable environment, with over 90% of the available space suitable for occupation by *A. aperta*. The tree canopy provides protection from wind and more constant temperatures. The permanent spring-fed stream both attracts insects from the surrounding woods and fields and offers a rich supply of aquatic insects on which spiders can feed; even in drought years, spiders anywhere in this habitat are assured an abundant supply of prey. And the structurally complex substrate of grass sod, fallen tree branches, and low shrubs is well suited for building webs.

A. aperta is capable of using visual, chemical, temperature, and vibratory senses to discriminate among habitats of different quality in selecting a suitable location for building a web (Riechert 1985). The spider seeks shade, and once in shade, it moves along a temperature gradient, seeking a location that offers a temperature of approximately 30°C. At the same time, the spider uses vibratory and olfactory cues from insects to locate patches where prey is abundant. In the case of the grassland population, this behavior leads to the construction of webs near animal feces, which attract flies, and near flowering plants, which are visited by a variety of insect pollinators.

The location of a web in the grassland habitat is strongly correlated with the number of healthy offspring a female spider produces (Riechert and Tracy 1975). Protected sites afford both more prey and more time for capturing them, and females that consume more prey

produce more and heavier eggs. Male spiders in the grassland also benefit from the increased consumption of prey at protected sites, because heavier males can wander farther in search of potential mates and, furthermore, have a much higher probability of being accepted by females than lighter males, who may even be eaten rather than mated with. In the riparian habitat, there is no correlation between the site of a web and reproductive success, because prey levels are generally high, and the entire habitat is protected from unfavorable winds, temperatures, and levels of humidity by a tree canopy.

By itself, a difference in the availability of web sites between grassland and riparian habitats does not prove that different levels of competition for these sites exist. The grassland spiders may merely cluster in the more favorable patches, and the riparian spiders may disperse more evenly throughout the habitat. However, *A. aperta* is a territorial species, and territorial behavior can limit the number of individuals a given area will support (Whitham 1979; Riechert 1981). With the exceptions of newly hatched juveniles and males searching for mates, all *A. aperta* defend an area around the web against intrusion by other members of their population (Riechert 1978a, 1981). Unlike a person defending his yard against tresspassers, however, no specific boundaries are patrolled. Rather, an intolerance is exhibited toward the construction of webs within distances that are genetically determined for the respective populations (Riechert 1978a, in press).

The territories defended by *A. aperta* are much larger

Figure 2. The desert grassland of south-central New Mexico (*top*) can support growth and reproduction among *A. aperta* on only 12% of its surface at best, whereas nearly all of the riparian habitat in southeastern Arizona (*bottom*) is inhabitable. Competition for suitable web sites is therefore expected to be much greater among grassland than among riparian spiders. (Photos by S. Riechert.)

in the grassland than in the riparian, with a mean size of 3.7 m^2 versus 0.6 m^2. This difference is determined by the accessibility of food. By having sole occupancy of high-quality grassland territory or of any riparian territory, a spider is assured of the food needed for survival and for reproduction, even during times of food shortage (Riechert 1981). Using artificial sticky webs to assess the difference in the amount of prey that would be available in shared versus unshared territories, I found that a spider would lose approximately 40% of its food supply if it did not defend a territory of the size specified for each of these habitats, a reduction that would place the spider under food stress and would ultimately limit its potential to produce offspring (Riechert 1978a).

The system of fixed territory sizes can limit population size, something that is realized in the grassland habitat. Since *A. aperta* produces approximately 125 eggs per clutch, it is obvious that there might be more individuals than can be supported by the grassland

habitat, where only 3% of the available space is adequate to ensure survival to reproduction in drought years, and only 12% in most years (Riechert 1981). Spiders in this habitat compete for precious few sites. In contrast, most riparian spiders obtain territories and survive to reproduction, regardless of the year's weather. Here, other factors, such as predation by birds, spider wasps, and other spiders, appear to maintain population size below the threshold of competition for available web sites.

Territorial disputes and game theory

Because the two populations of *A. aperta* exist under markedly different levels of competition for web sites, it is reasonable to expect differences in the fighting behavior they exhibit in settling territorial disputes. This hypothesis deviates from classical ethology's view of animal conflict as being highly ritualized and constant within a species. The species-specific model supported by classical ethology assumes that the repetitive use of the same visual and vocal displays and the lack of escalated fighting evolved to prevent injury to competing members of a species (e.g., Lorenz 1966). By convention, the contestant that exhibits the "best" display wins the contested resource. Male Galapagos tortoises, for instance, settle contests over mates on the basis of head height; the ritualized display exhibited by competing tortoises, then, consists of two animals facing one another and stretching their necks skyward, with the tortoise perceived as being "taller" by this means winning the mating opportunity (Fritts 1984).

In *Agelenopsis*, however, fights are not highly ritualized, and the sequence of events varies greatly from contest to contest. For example, the number of distinct behavior patterns might be as few as 2 (approach and retreat) and as many as 28, and contests may last anywhere from a few seconds to 21 hours (Riechert 1978b). Fighting among these spiders is not limited to displays. Biting, shoving, dragging, and tumbling are common in the disputes (Fig. 3).

A recently developed model, evolutionary game theory, provides a closer fit to *Agelenopsis* territorial disputes than does the species-specific model of classical ethology, because it allows for changes in conflict behavior with varying contexts, such as differences in size, experience, and age. Evolutionary game theory is based on the costs and benefits to individuals of particular strategies. By this theory, if a spider, say, fails to engage in biting and other physical forms of interaction during the course of a dispute, it is because such direct fighting is not in the spider's best interest in that instance. There may be a risk of retaliation, or perhaps the value of the disputed resource is so low that the energy expenditures and the risk of injury do not warrant escalated fighting. Consider, for example, a woman whose purse is grabbed while she is walking down a street; one would expect that she would put up far more resistance to the theft if she had her life savings in the purse than if it contained but a few coins.

Evolutionary game theory deviates from the simple calculation of the maximum ratio of benefit to cost by the addition of a factor called frequency dependence. For example, a student's performance on an exam that is graded on a curve is frequency dependent; his grade depends not only on his but also on his classmates' performances. Thus, evolutionary game theory fits those cases in which the success of an individual using a particular behavioral strategy is not independent of the performances of other members of its population. An example from biology is sex ratio allocation by parents: the optimum proportion of males to females a mother should produce depends on the proportion present in the population; if there are, say, more females than males, then an individual parent will achieve a higher reproductive success by producing a higher proportion of males to mate with the existing females. Other examples from biology to which this theory might be applied include animal contests, parent-offspring conflict, optimal growth patterns and other life-history traits, social structure (e.g., when to cooperate), and local patterns of distribution.

Evolutionary game theory was adapted from classical game theory developed by von Neumann and Morgenstern (1944) to explain human behavior in conflict situations. It is called game theory because the mathematics underlying it is similar in structure to that which forms the basis of such parlor games as chess and checkers. In both classical and evolutionary games, "decisions" are made as to what strategy or action is to be taken in a given context. Each strategy has associated with it a set of payoffs which specify what an individual's level of success will be against contestants exhibiting the same and other strategies. That set of actions which provides the best average payoff is expected to prevail in the system. Classical game theory has been widely applied in economics and business (e.g., McDonald 1975; Schotter and Schwodiauer 1980), the social sciences and politics (Brams 1975), the military (Aumann and Maschler 1966), and social psychology (Bartos 1967).

Evolutionary game theory is a relatively new introduction. John Maynard Smith is largely responsible for the application of classical game theory to evolutionary contexts (e.g., Maynard Smith and Price 1973; Maynard Smith 1983; reviewed in Riechert and Hammerstein 1983; Parker 1984). There are two major differences between the classical and evolutionary theories. First, whereas in classical game theory it is assumed that rational thought is used in determining which action to take, evolutionary game theory assumes that natural selection ultimately determines the strategies that are exhibited, individuals being merely the performers of inherited programs. The other difference is in the characterization of the payoffs: in classical game theory, payoffs are indicated by an individual's personal value judgment of what constitutes success; in evolutionary game theory, the payoffs are expressed in terms of individual fitness, which is defined as the reproductive success of one's offspring but is often estimated by individual weight gain or reproductive rate.

The solution to the evolutionary game is referred to as the evolutionarily stable strategy, or ESS, and thus the theory is frequently referred to as the ESS theory. The ESS specifies the set of strategies that will be exhibited in all roles and situations an individual may find itself in; if most members of a population utilize this set of strategies, which provides the best average payoff in fitness, then mutants exhibiting a different set of strategies will have little success in the population. Hence, we say the ESS is stable against invasion by a mutant strategy set.

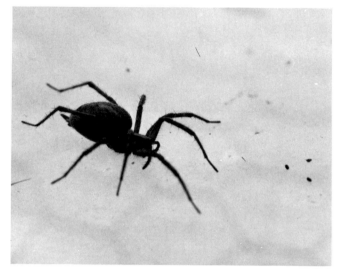

Figure 3. A large variety of characteristic behaviors are used in territorial disputes among *A. aperta*. A number of these fall under the category of assessment (*top*), which is indicated by subtle moves, such as an adjustment of the spider's position or a spreading of the front legs, made while the opponent is on the web but beyond visual contact. Display (*middle*) involves both vibratory and visual signals to the opponent, such as waving the front legs. Fighting (*bottom*) comprises all acts of physical contact, including shoving, biting, and tumbling. (Photos by S. Riechert.)

The number of biological systems to which game theory might be applied is enormous. However, because detailed data are required to determine the payoffs associated with different sets of strategies in natural contexts, few empirical tests of the theory have been completed. Behavioral applications include work on competition among dung flies for mates at cowpats; an ESS was obtained specifying how long a male should hover at a cowpat, given that the rates at which females visit a cowpat decrease with its age (Parker 1970). In another study involving behavioral strategies, an ESS model was developed to explain the choice exhibited by digger wasps between digging a new burrow and using an existing one (Brockmann et al. 1979). This particular study fits into the more general problem of whether animals should be producers or should steal the products of other individuals' labor, a line of investigation that has been pursued in the case of foraging house sparrows (Barnard and Sibly 1981). The ESS theory has also been applied to cooperative foraging systems, specifically to foraging bird flocks in which individual birds spend a proportion of their time watching for predators instead of feeding (Pulliam et al. 1982).

Evolutionarily stable strategies and ecotypic variation

Because the fighting behavior of *A. aperta* is frequency dependent and because my long-term studies of its population biology included estimates of the fitness of individuals from both the riparian and grassland populations occupying sites of different quality, I was interested in applying ESS theory to the ecotypic variation observed in the levels of competition for web sites. The aim was to determine whether each of the populations is at the expected ESS—whether the predicted strategy is the prevalent one in the population.

Although spider contests vary greatly and can involve dozens of different behaviors, they do show a definite structure, which consists of four basic categories of behaviors that range from assessment and display to threat and, finally, to actual fighting—from lower to higher levels of energy expenditure and risk of injury. The shorter contests rarely go beyond the display phase; most often, a retreat signifies a withdrawal from the territory, and a contest consists only of one bout. Many contests, however, consist of multiple bouts separated by retreats from the web.

John Maynard Smith, Peter Hammerstein, and I undertook game-theory analyses of territorial disputes among *A. aperta* (Maynard Smith 1983; Hammerstein 1981; Riechert 1978b, 1979, 1984). Based on my observations of the territorial system, our current analysis includes the following strategy sets: withdraw if the opponent is larger, otherwise display; display only; display only, if the site quality is low, if the probability of winning is low, or both, otherwise escalate; always escalate to fighting (Hammerstein and Riechert, unpubl.). A large number of parameters were required to describe the payoffs for these complex sets of strategies, including the probability that the territory owner will win a random contest, the encounter rate, the costs of biting and display, the time spent on the web exposed to predators during territorial disputes, the rate of preda-

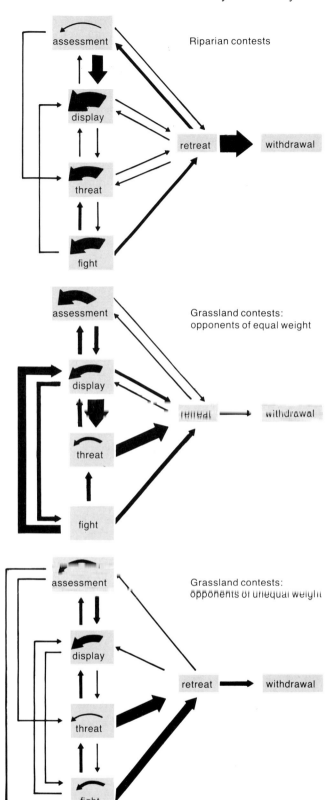

Figure 4. The sequence of events that occur during territorial disputes among *A. aperta* are summarized in these flow diagrams, in which the different widths of the arrows represent differences in the probabilities of transition between various levels of the disputes. For example, riparian contests often escalate from assessment to display, but are far less likely to escalate further, presumably because an abundance of suitable territories reduces the potential benefits of such risky behavior. In contrast, the scarcity of suitable grassland territories means that disputes over them (between equal opponents) are much more likely to escalate.

tion on *A. aperta* in the habitat, the daily increment to reproductive success associated with gaining or keeping the territory in dispute, and the probability of winning a subsequent site if this dispute is lost. It was possible to collect these data because *A. aperta* is locally abundant and can be readily observed and manipulated with no discernible disruption of its natural behavior.

The results of the analyses indicate that members of the grassland population should exhibit the following strategy: display only, if site quality is low, if the probability of winning is low, or both, otherwise escalate. For the riparian population, the optimum strategy is to withdraw if the opponent is larger, otherwise display.

It is apparent from Figure 4 that the contest behavior observed in riparian spiders deviates from the predicted ESS for that population. Contrary to what the model predicts, the majority of riparian spiders do not withdraw from occupied territories when the owner is encountered. Rather, both engage in disputes and escalate to potentially injurious behavior. Indeed, if escalation is reached in fights involving riparian spiders, the opponents tend to stay there rather than returning to less risky behavior as grassland spiders typically do.

Conflicts among grassland spiders apparently do exhibit the ESS predicted by evolutionary game theory. As Figure 4 and Table 1 show, the time and energy expended by these spiders in fights varies with their probabilities of winning them, which for these animals are functions of the opponents' relative weights. The intensity of the contests also corresponds to the potential reproductive value of the different sites under dispute, with far greater energy expended and risk of injury taken in disputes over high-quality sites.

Why is the behavior for settling territorial disputes at its predicted ESS within the grassland population but not within the riparian? To answer this question, it is helpful to compare some of the characteristic differences between the two populations outlined in Table 1. First, there is a much greater variability in the parameters associated with the contests in the grassland disputes than in the riparian (Riechert 1979). This variability is largely attributable to the greater disparity in quality among different locations in the grassland habitat. Furthermore, there is an owner bias in the grassland disputes: owners tend to win disputes with intruders of similar weight. This bias is not observed in the riparian disputes, where, even if there is a sizable weight difference between opponents, the outcomes of the disputes are not as predictable as in the grassland (Maynard Smith and Riechert 1984). There thus appears to be a relaxation of the rules of decision that govern fighting in the riparian population; that is, the riparian spider can sometimes get away with failing to implement the optimum strategy. I noted one other interesting but puzzling difference. Biting and other escalated behaviors in the riparian disputes are ritualized in that no injury has been observed to result from them. This is despite the fact that such fighting is more lengthy when it does occur than in the grassland disputes. In the grassland contests, 50% of these escalated contests result in some form of injury to one of the opponents.

These differences in behavior between populations, especially the level of aggression individual spiders exhibit in the contests, are to some extent under genetic control (Maynard Smith and Riechert 1984). The ritualization of the fighting behavior, however, is more flexible; when I pitted riparian spiders against grassland spiders at quality sites in the grassland habitat, the behavior of the riparian spiders changed and they bit and injured their grassland opponents in response to being bitten by them.

What, then, can be concluded from these observations? Historically, *A. aperta* is a desert species, and most populations exist under higher levels of competition for limited sites than observed for the riparian population. Therefore, the fighting behavior of the riparian spiders, in many respects similar to that of the grassland spiders but with some significant modifications, is probably derived from the type of contest observed in the grassland population. The derived riparian ecotype has resulted, in part, from a relaxation of the rules of decision governing the outcome of disputes and from the ritualization of potentially injurious behavior.

But why have riparian contests not reached the level of change predicted by our ESS analysis? If one assumes that the model is correct—that it has taken into account all the important parameters and includes all possible sets of strategies—then there must be some biological explanation for the observed deviation. A number of hypotheses have been proposed as to why some populations fail to reach a predicted ESS, and several of these are applicable to the riparian ecotype of *A. aperta*. One possibility is that the release from strong competition is a recent event and that there just has not been sufficient time for natural selection to operate on the behavioral traits to complete the expected change. Another possibil-

Table 1. Comparison of contests between opponents of differing weights and for sites of varying quality

Site quality (opponents equal in weight, within 10%)	Cost Estimated energy expended	Length Number of acts	Length Number of bouts	Outcome Probability that owner will win
Grassland				
Poor: surface	123.3	11.9	1.9	0.56
Average: holes	344.0	31.4	3.0	0.76
Excellent: holes +	556.7	51.6	3.7	0.92
Riparian				
Excellent: rocks	126.2	13.5	1.8	0.92
Excellent: grasses	146.2	14.5	2.1	0.60
Excellent: leaf litter	185.5	16.1	2.1	0.89
Weight of opponents (*site quality excellent*)				
Grassland				
Owner heavier	493.7	40.8	2.9	0.96
Opponents equal (within 10%)	556.7	51.6	3.7	0.92
Intruder heavier	1,012.5	75.9	4.0	0.28
Riparian				
Owner heavier	160.4	16.9	2.0	0.85
Opponents equal (within 10%)	215.4	19.9	2.1	0.70
Intruder heavier	145.5	15.6	2.1	0.17

NOTE: A minimum of 25 contests were used in each context; the values shown represent averages. Estimated energy expended is given as a rank-score based on intensity (after Riechert 1979). All contests took place in natural habitats.

ity is that the expected or "best" set of strategies has been vitiated by interbreeding with individuals from populations existing under stronger levels of competition for sites. In the case of the riparian habitat, there might be an influx of individuals from nearby cactus-scrub and mesquite habitats, where the levels of competition for limited web sites are similar to the grassland habitat. Finally, a major change in the wiring of *A. aperta*'s nervous system might be required to achieve the new ESS, and such a mutant may simply not have arisen yet, a delay referred to as phylogenetic inertia. It is not yet clear which if any of these possibilities is operating in the case of *A. aperta*. These are ongoing studies.

References

Aumann, R. J., and M. Maschler. 1966. Game theoretic aspects of gradual disarmament. In *Development of Utility Theory for Arms Control and Disarmament, Report to the US Arms Control and Disarmament Agency*. Contract 80:1–55.

Barnard, C. J., and R. M. Sibly. 1981. Producers and scroungers: A general model and its application to captive flocks of house sparrows. *Anim. Behav.* 29:543–50.

Bartos, O. J. 1967. *Simple Models of Group Behavior*. Columbia Univ. Press.

Brams, S. J. 1975. *Game Theory and Politics*. Macmillan.

Brockmann, H. J., and R. Dawkins. 1979. Joint nesting in a digger wasp as an evolutionarily stable preadaptation to social life. *Behaviour* 71:203–45.

Brockmann, H. J., A. Grafen, and R. Dawkins. 1979. Evolutionarily stable nesting strategy in a digger wasp. *J. Theor. Biol.* 77:473–96.

Fritts, T. H. 1984. Evolutionary divergence of giant tortoises in the Galapagos. *Biol. J. Linn. Soc.* 21:165–76.

Hammerstein, P. 1981. The role of asymmetries in animal contests. *Anim. Behav.* 29:193–205.

Hammerstein, P., and S. Riechert. Unpubl. Payoffs and strategies in spider territorial contests.

Krebs, J. R., and N. B. Davies. 1981. *An Introduction to Behavioral Ecology*. Sinauer.

Lorenz, K. 1966. *On Aggression*. Methuen.

Maynard Smith, J. 1983. *Evolution and the Theory of Games*. Cambridge Univ. Press.

Maynard Smith, J., and G. R. Price. 1973. The logic of animal conflict. *Nature* 246:15–18.

Maynard Smith, J., and S. E. Riechert. 1984. A conflicting-tendency model of spider agonistic behavior: Hybrid-pure population line comparisons. *Anim. Behav.* 32:564–78.

Mayr, E. 1963. *Animal Species and Evolution*. Harvard Univ. Press.

McDonald, J. D. 1975. *The Game of Business*. Doubleday.

Mitchell, D. E. T., E. T. Beatty, and P. K. Cox. 1977. Behavioral differences between two populations of wild rats: Implications for domestication research. *Behav. Biol.* 19:206–17.

Parker, G. A. 1970. The reproductive behavior and the nature of sexual selection in *Scatophaga stercoraria* (Diptera: Scatophagidae). II. The fertilization rate and the spatial and temporal relationships of each sex around the site of mating and oviposition. *J. Anim. Ecol.* 39: 205–23.

———. 1984. Evolutionarily stable strategies. In *Behavioral Ecology*, ed. J. R. Krebs and N. B. Davies, pp. 30–61. Sinauer.

Pulliam, H. R., G. H. Pyke, and T. Caraco. 1982. The scanning behavior of juncos: A game theoretical approach. *J. Theor. Biol.* 95:89–103.

Riechert, S. E. 1974. The pattern of local web distribution in a desert spider: Mechanisms and seasonal variation. *J. Anim. Ecol.* 43:733–46.

———. 1976. Web-site selection in a desert spider, *Agelenopsis aperta* (Gertsch). *Oikos* 27:311–15.

———. 1978a. Energy-based territoriality in populations of the desert spider *Agelenopsis aperta* (Gertsch). *Symp. Zool. Soc.* 42:211–22.

———. 1978b. Games spiders play: Behavioral variability in territorial disputes. *Behav. Ecol. Sociobiol.* 4:1–28.

———. 1979. Games spiders play. II. Resource assessment strategies. *Behav. Ecol. Sociobiol.* 6:121–28.

———. 1981. The consequences of being territorial: Spiders, a case study. *Am. Nat.* 117:871–92.

———. 1984. Games spiders play. III. Cues underlying context-associated changes in agonistic behavior. *Anim. Behav.* 32:1–5.

———. 1985. Decisions in multiple goal contexts: Habitat selection of the spider, *Agelenopsis aperta* (Gertsch). *Zeitschrift fur Tierpsychol.* 70:53–69.

———. In press. Between population variation in spider territorial behavior: Hybrid-pure population line comparisons. In *Colloquium on Behavioral Genetics*, ed. M. Huettel. Plenum.

Riechert, S. E., and P. Hammerstein. 1983. Game theory in an ecological context. *Ann. Rev. Ecol. Syst.* 14:317–409.

Riechert, S. E., and C. R. Tracy. 1975. Thermal balance and prey availability: Bases for a model relating web-site characteristics to spider reproductive success. *Ecology* 56:265–84.

Schotter, A., and G. Schwodiauer. 1980. Economics and the theory of games: A survey. *J. Econ. Lit.* 18:479–527.

Turesson, G. 1922. The genotypic response of the plant species to the habitat. *Hereditas* 3:211–350.

von Neumann, J., and O. Morgenstern. 1944. *Theory of Games and Economic Behavior*. Princeton Univ. Press.

Wahlert, G. von. 1965. The role of ecological factors in the origin of higher levels of organization. *Syst. Zool.* 14:288–300.

Whitham, T. G. 1979. Territorial defence in a gall aphid. *Nature* 279:324–25.

Untangling the Evolution of the Web

A spider's web leaves no trace in the fossil record. How, then, can the evolutionary history of webs be deciphered?

William A. Shear

Max Meier

Figure 1. *Linyphia triangularis*, a close relative of spiders that weave geometric orb webs, constructs not an orb but an aerial sheet with scaffolding. Linyphiid sheet webs pose an intriguing problem for evolutionary biologists. The orb web, once considered the pinnacle of spider-web evolution, may have evolved from a single origin, or it may have appeared during the evolution of at least two lines of spiders, only to be lost or replaced in some families. New research suggests that web architecture, and web-building behavior, may have evolved in a com-

The delicate tracery of a spider's web must be one of the most unlikely candidates for fossilization in all of nature. Only a few threads of ancient spider silk have been preserved, and these in relatively recent deposits of amber; we know of no complete fossil spider webs.

Arachnologists who would reconstruct the evolutionary history of the web must examine, then, the wonderful record found in the garden, grassland and forest: the webs built by living spiders. By comparing these webs and integrating the information with evolutionary trees based on spider anatomy, it should be possible to discern the course of web evolution. After all, ephemeral though the web may be, the spider is nearly unique among animals in leaving a detailed record of its behavior.

And what a varied record it is! The careful exploration of tropical rain forests brings to light new species and new webs every year. There are orbs: two-dimensional, point-symmetrical arrays, a strong silk frame enclosing a series of radiating lines. Then there are other aerial webs, so unlike the orb: suspended sheets and three-dimensional space-filling webs, or cobwebs, that lack any obvious organization.

On the ground, spiders living in burrows or under objects weave silken collars or sheets that extend outward from the mouth of a burrow. Still others have abandoned their burrows entirely and construct short silk tubes on tree bark, camouflaged by bits of bark and lichens, and sometimes closed by hinged doors at either end. Some construct webs that they use more as weapons than traps, throwing them at passing insects or holding them under tension to release them when prey blunders into a thread.

How does a scientist interpret the story written in the spider's web? The answer has changed substantially over the past century. A few years after Darwin proposed his theory of evolution by natural selection in 1859, biologists turned this powerful analytical tool on the Araneae, the order of spiders. In 1895, the British arachnologist and biogeographer Reginald Innes Pocock proposed a scheme describing the course of evolution in spider webs. His work was followed by other proposals, including, most notably, those of William Bristowe in l930, and B. J. Kaston in 1964.

These scenarios were essentially static, based on observations and descriptions of finished webs. Students of animal behavior, however, have added a new and dynamic dimension to the study of web evolution by carefully examining the actual process of web construction. It turns out that some spiders previously thought to be unrelated share patterns of web-building behavior, which is tightly controlled by a spider's genetic program, even though their webs may look radically different to us.

Meanwhile systematists have been rearranging spider classification itself as new tools (such as the scanning electron microscope) for observing anatomical features have become available. Detailed studies of tropical and Southern Hemisphere spiders have revealed undetected relationships among groups. The earlier hypotheses about web evolution no longer, in many cases, line up with the evidence about the evolution of the spiders themselves.

The web, though a wonderfully detailed record, is now known to tell only part of its own ancestral story. In the full account, as it continues to unravel, is seen all the richness of the new evolutionary biology that has grown from the natural-history studies of Darwin's century. Information from anatomy, systematics, ecology and ethology can be eclectically combined to produce and test new hypotheses. The result, in the case of the spider web, has been a picture far less simple and linear than the old taxonomy. The familiar garden spider's orb web, for example, may have been tried and then abandoned by some species; for all its magnificence, the orb may be not the pinnacle of web evolution but an intermediate form.

Spiders and Their Silk

Arachnologists now recognize three main groups of spiders, differentiated by anatomical and behavioral traits

plex, nonlinear fashion separately from spider anatomy, the traditional basis for classifying spiders and discerning their evolutionary history.

William A. Shear is Charles Patterson Distinguished Professor and chairman of the Biology Department at Hampden-Sydney College and a research associate in the Department of Entomology, American Museum of Natural History. He received his doctorate in 1971 from Harvard University. He has published more than 100 articles and chapters on the systematics and evolution of arachnids and myriapods. Recently his research has focused on the fossil evidence for early terrestrial ecosystems, and he wrote about this subject with Jane Gray for American Scientist in the September–October 1992 issue. Address: Department of Biology, Hampden-Sydney College, Hampden-Sydney, VA 23943. Internet: bills@tiger.hsc.edu.

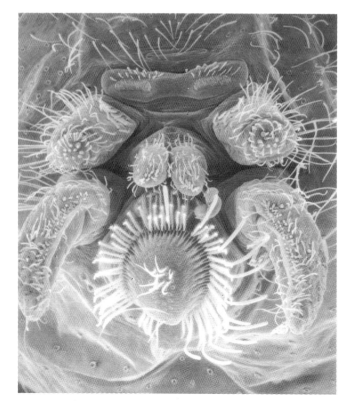
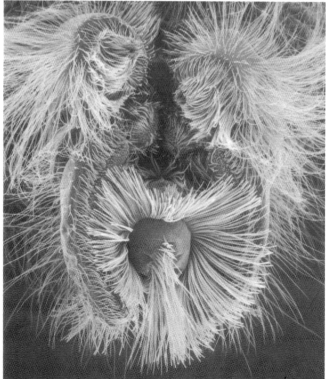

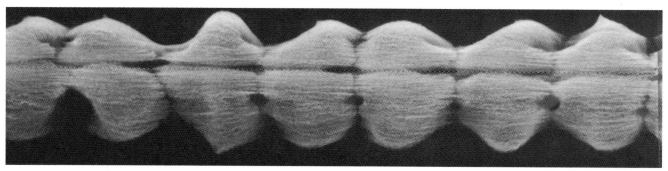

Figure 2. Presence or absence of a cribellum, a broad median plate that replaces one of four pairs of spinnerets (silk-spinning organs) in many spider families, was used by early taxonomists to divide araneomorph spiders into two ancestral groups. *Oecobius*'s cribellum is evident above its spinnerets and anal tubercle in the upper-left image, produced by a scanning electron microscope. The underside of another spider, *Uroctea (upper right)*, displays only the spinnerets and tubercle. Cribellate spiders produce a woolly, puffy silk *(bottom micrograph)* that functions as an effective insect trap. Surprisingly, many araneomorphs have lost the cribellum. It is no longer considered the basis for separating families of spiders; in fact, *Oecobius* and *Uroctea* are now known to be closely related. (Micrographs courtesy of Charles Griswold, California Academy of Sciences *(top)* and Brent Opell, Virginia Polytechnic Institute and State University.)

and some general differences in their webs. The most primitive of these, the Mesothelae, are known from living examples found from Japan south to Indonesia, and from fossils as old as 300 million years. They differ from all other spiders in having an obviously segmented abdomen, and in having their spinning organs, or spinnerets, located near the middle of the abdomen, rather than at the posterior end.

Tarantulas, now becoming popular as pets, belong to a second group, the Mygalomorphae. Although the mygalomophs resemble the mesotheles in some characteristics, their spinnerets are at the end of the abdomen, and there are nev-

er more than six. Mygalomorphs are common and diverse in the tropics; most species are sedentary, some almost never leaving their burrows.

The third group of spiders, the Araneomorphae, include most North American spiders and are the "true spiders" best known to most of us. Unlike the mesotheles and mygalomorphs, their fangs point toward each other at right angles to the long axis of the body, and most have only a single pair of lungs.

Their silk glands and use of silk unambiguously define all these groups as spiders. Not all living spiders spin webs, but since 1950 web-building species have been found in almost all

the families of spiders once thought of as wandering hunters. It now seems very likely that all spiders who actively hunt their prey, or who use little or no silk in prey capture, are descendants of web builders. We also know that modern-looking, functional spinnerets were characteristic of spiders that lived 375 million years ago. So a fundamental problem in the study of web and spider evolution is the origin of silk itself.

A little more than a century ago, Henry McCook, one of the earliest American observers of spider behavior, proposed a hypothesis for the origin of silk that today remains the best-supported idea. McCook suggested that primitive proto-

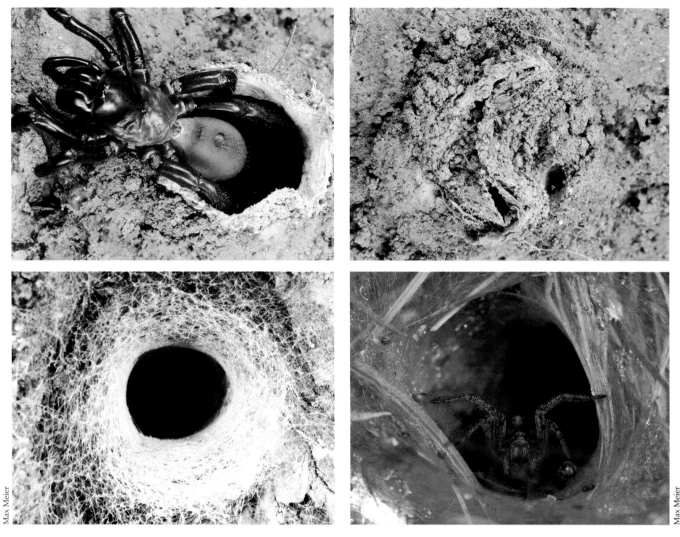

Max Meier

Max Meier

Figure 3. Early stages of web evolution are thought to be represented by silk-lined burrows, sometimes with triplines to extend the spider's sensory area. Next a silk collar is constructed as an extension of the lining, followed by the sheet webs developed by such spiders as the araneomorph family Agelenidae, which incorporate a retreat for the spider. Primitive web building is seen among mygalomorphs (*Atypoides unicolor*, upper two photographs) that build silk-lined burrows and cover them with trap doors. A transitional stage is evident in the silk collar extended by *Amaurobius ferox*, an araneomorph (lower left). Finally, an agelenid, *Agelena labyrinthica*, weaves a ground-level sheet with a retreat. (Upper photographs courtesy of Fred Coyle, Western Carolina University.)

spiders, like modern centipedes, trailed excretory matter from kidneylike glands at the bases of the legs as they walked about. The chemical trails so laid down would have been useful in finding mates and returning to burrows or hiding places under stones.

Eventually, McCook reasoned, the excretory function of these many coxal glands was taken over entirely by a few in the anterior (forward) part of the body, leaving those in the abdomen to function entirely in trail-making. The trail of excretory material was replaced by longer-lasting protein—silk—and some of the abdominal appendages became transformed into spinnerets.

Even today, most spiders continuously trail out a dragline of silk as they move about, and the silk lines of females

can be followed by males in search of mates. Studies of development have shown that the spinnerets do indeed originate from the rudiments of abdominal appendages.

There remain two alternative views, one of them originating with Pocock and Bristowe, who thought that the original function of silk was to protect eggs. In this hypothesis, silk was first produced from the mouth region and smeared over the egg bundles. Unfortunately, this scheme rests partly on the argument that the gum produced from the jaws of one spider, *Scytodes thoracica*, is a primitive "pre-silk," and it turns out that *Scytodes thoracica* is not a primitive spider. There is also the problem of transferring the production of silk from the mouth region to the abdomen.

The second alternative has been offered recently by Arthur Decae of the National Museum of Natural History in Leiden, Holland, who suggested in 1984 that spiders developed silk even before they became terrestrial. The function of the silk would have been to keep burrows in marine mud from collapsing or being filled with sediment, and the silk might have served as a sort of gill for later (and entirely hypothetical) amphibious spiders who would periodically be submerged by tides. Decae did not speculate on how silk might actually have originated.

Anatomy and Evolution

A functional explanation for the origins of silk and the spinning habit may be impossible to achieve, but the evolution of silk-spinning *organs* has been studied, and debated, extensively. Revealing evidence has come from the histology of silk glands—the details of their cellular construction—and from the embryological development of the spinnerets themselves. Histological evidence allows us to draw connections, or homologies, between silk glands in different spider groups, and embryology shows clearly that the spinnerets are paired abdominal appendages, with the silk issuing from modified setae, or hairs. So much information is available on the anatomy of the spinning apparatus, in fact, that the traditional view of web evolution rests heavily on a classification derived from the form and position of spinnerets.

As mentioned above, the spinnerets are located near the middle of the abdomen in the primitive spiders, the mesotheles, but at the end of the abdomen in the other two families. With the evolution of the araneomorphs there came a further development: The frontmost pair of spinnerets (presumably inherited from a mesothele-like ancestor) became a broad, median plate called a cribellum. The cribellum is covered with minute tubules, each capable of producing an extremely fine silk fiber, and the araneomorphs that have this plate are called cribellate spiders.

Using special bristles on the last pair of legs, the cribellate spiders tease these fibers into a woolly ribbon that is laid on core fibers produced by other, less modified, spinnerets. The result is an effective insect trap. The tiny cribellate fibers not only entangle bristles and hairs on insects, but also may adhere by means of electrostatic attraction to even the smoothest surface. At least two families of cribellate spiders make orb webs, in which the catching spiral consists of this kind of silk.

Surprisingly, many groups of araneomorphs have lost the cribellum. In their webs insects do not adhere to the silk but are simply impeded by it—long enough for the web's owner to capture them. Among the groups in which the cribellum has evidently been lost—called ecribellates—members of one superfamily, Araneoidea, have substituted a new kind of sticky silk. This silk is actually wet. Special adhesive glands add a liquid cement to ordinary silk fibers as they emerge from the spinnerets. The adhesive is extremely sticky, but it loses this property when it dries out, so that most spiders making webs including this kind of silk (called viscid silk) must periodically renew the sticky threads. Among the araneoids are many makers of intricate orbs, including the common garden spider.

The role of the cribellum in the evolution of spider webs has been the subject of considerable debate. Without the cribellum, the mesotheles and the mygalomorphs never achieved the orb web. Mesothele webs are generally silk linings for their burrows. Mygalomorphs make various webs, including aerial sheets, but they have not evolved orbs or space-filling cobwebs. Only araneomorphs make orbs and cobwebs, and only some araneomorphs have cribella. The cribellum poses one of evolutionary biology's most intriguing ques-

Max Meier

Figure 4. Orb web of an ecribellate araneoid, the garden spider *Araneus diadematus* (top), differs only in detail from the orb of a cribellate uloborid spider, the New Zealand species *Piha waitkerensis*. The leg movements used by both during web construction are very similar, making it likely that there is a close evolutionary relation between them, despite their anatomical differences. The orb web may, however, have arisen in both groups by convergent evolution—a common adaptation to similar environmental pressures. (Bottom photograph courtesy of Brent Opell.)

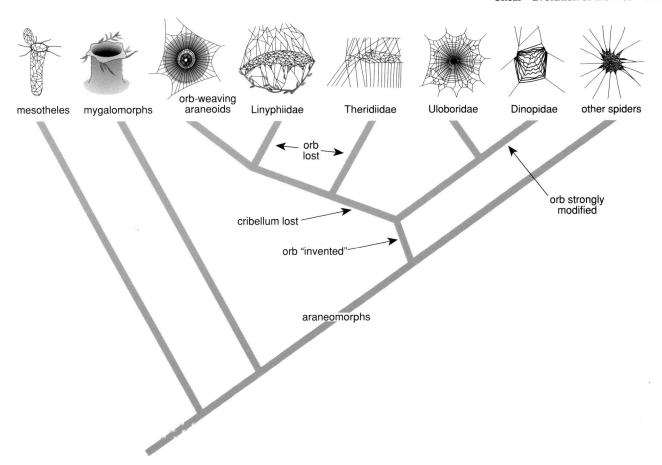

mesotheles mygalomorphs orb-weaving araneoids Linyphiidae Theridiidae Uloboridae Dinopidae other spiders

orb lost

orb strongly modified

cribellum lost

orb "invented"

araneomorphs

Figure 5. Phylogenetic tree shows how some families of spiders may have arrived at similar and different web designs. The Mesothelae are general-ly believed to have evolved first from the common ancestor of all spiders, followed by the Mygalomorphae and the "true spiders," the Araneomorphae. The monophyletic hypothesis of orb-web origin (which is incorporated into this diagram) holds that the orb web was invented by an araneomorph, the common ancestor of araneoid and uloborid spiders, that had a cribellum. The cribellum was acquired by a spider that was the common ancestor of all araneomorphs, including the araneoid superfamily and the uloborids. The araneoids lost the cribellum, and some araneoid families later lost the orb. Among the uloborids and their close relatives, the dinopids, are many species that have modified the orb.

tions: What is the relation between the evolution of anatomy and of behavior?

The spider taxonomy of the late 19th century, which relied heavily on ana-tomical distinctions, proposed an an-swer. Pocock considered the cribellum a stable anatomical trait, important enough to divide the araneomorphs into two major groups, the cribellates and the ecribellates. This distinction was maintained by Bristowe and Kaston, but a Finnish taxonomist, Pekka Lehti-nen, pointed out in 1967 that there are many pairs of spider taxa that are very similar, except that one has a cribellum and the other does not. In the new scheme of spider phylogeny a single family or genus sometimes includes both cribellate and ecribellate spiders.

A case in point involves the two spi-der genera *Uroctea* and *Oecobius*. Lehti-nen pointed out that these two genera of anatomically peculiar spiders, then seg-regated in their separate families, are vir-tually identical except that *Oecobius*

species have a cribellum and *Uroctea* species do not. The similarities extend to many fine details of their anatomy and behavior. In 1970, I studied *Oecobius* and found that upon sexual maturity males lose the calimistrum, or comb, used to process cribellate silk, and that in both sexes of many species, the cribellum ap-pears degenerate.

Today it is accepted that the two gen-era are each other's closest relatives and that they belong in the same family—*Uroctea* was derived from an *Oecobius*-like ancestor through the loss of the cribellum and calimistrum. The main outcome of this change in our view of anatomical evolution has been that we can no longer be certain that similar webs woven by cribellate and ecribellate spiders were in-dependent developments.

This is not to say that convergent and parallel evolution have no place in the scheme. It seems clear that when, for ex-ample, mygalomorph and araneo-morph spiders make similar advanced

webs, the design is unlikely to be attrib-utable to descent from a common an-cestor. Indeed, the division of spiders into the three main lines of evolution (mesothele, mygalomorph and araneo-morph) probably took place when the founders of all three lines were still bur-row-dwellers. Earlier schemes of web evolution erred, in my judgment, not only in assuming that there was exten-sive convergence between the "distinct" cribellate and ecribellate lines, but also in arranging web types in lockstep lin-ear sequences. A phylogenetic diagram of web evolution (*Figure 5*) shows in-stead a reticulate pattern in which dif-ferent lines of spiders (which would in-clude both cribellate and ecribellate species) may have followed different pathways to the same web design.

Interestingly, the orb web, the most ex-tensively studied of all webs, probably originated only once, though from what precursor is still not clear. I shall return to the evolutionary problem of the orb later.

Figure 6. Uloborid orb may have evolved along the lines that web-making follows during the lives of cribellate spiders of the New Guinean genus *Fecenia*. *Fecenia* species make near-orbs (shown is *Fecenia angustata*'s). *Fecenia ochracea* alters the form of the web from a sheet to a near-orb over its lifetime, incorporating a retreat. To achieve an orb from a *Fecenia* web it is only necessary to dispense with the retreat and complete the circle. (Photograph courtesy of H. W. Levi, Harvard University.)

Figure 7. *Synotaxus turbinatus*'s web resembles a fishnet, incorporating regularly arranged threads. As a close relative of the cobweb-weaving theridiid spiders, and thus part of the superfamily Araneoidea, which includes most of the orb-weaving groups, *Synotaxus* would be expected to arrange its threads in an orb. The fact that it does not supports the idea that the orb developed in separate families by convergent evolution, not from a single origin. (Photograph by Jonathan Coddington, courtesy of H. W. Levi.)

Tubes, Trap Doors and Triplines

My own consideration of web types and their distribution among spider taxa has led me to propose a nonlinear evolutionary scheme. It appears probable that several web types are the product of convergent evolution—that is, that the same web has evolved in unrelated species that have adapted to similar environmental circumstances. Convergence provides an explanation of the appearance of similar web types in different families: These webs may be as much a product of a spider family's ecology as of its phylogenetic relationships.

The simplest and probably the oldest spider's web is simply a silk lining for the retreat in which the animal spends much of its time. Many living spiders in all three major groups modify crevices or holes in their environment in this way. Others actively dig burrows in soft soil or sand and line them with silk. The retreat or burrow may be closed by an elaborately hinged door or by a collapsible collar that is an extension of the silk lining.

The design of such webs, and the behavior of the spiders that construct them, is an intriguing story in itself and has been the subject of extensive study by Fred Coyle of Western Carolina University. Coyle has shown that making a collapsible collar for a trap door to a burrow can improve predatory efficiency and still give a modicum of protection. He has also demonstrated that vibrations carried by the ground are the most important sensory cue used by these spiders to aim and time their lunges at prey.

These vibrations suggest the reason for a modification: the lines of silk that many spiders extend from their burrows. Coyle has hypothesized that these lines could be used by the myopic spider as triplines to extend its sensory area. The importance of an extended sensory area is shown by the fact that many burrowers that build trap doors and rarely exit their tunnels incorporate twigs and leaves, or even tabs of tough silk, in their entrances in a radiating pattern. Prey touching the twigs, leaves or tabs is attacked.

A burrow with silk lines extending from the entrance is found, for example, in *Liphistius batuensis*, a mesothele. The lines are not produced accidentally, but are deliberately laid out and later reinforced. Tweaking them with a stick induces the spider to strike. In addition to this primitive spider, such arrangements also turn up among a variety of mygalomorphs and araneomorphs.

The Sheet-Web Weavers

Most living spiders do not make their webs in burrows. Indeed, by far the most common web is the agelenid sheet web, which appears to represent the next stage in web evolution. These webs, made by members of the araneomorph family Agelenidae, include a tubular retreat reminiscent of the burrow. From this retreat extends a dense, horizontal sheet of silk. It seems likely that this sheet might have developed in at least two ways, perhaps by extension from an original turret, or by the addition of a complex of cross lines to the original triplines. In any case, the sheet not only signals the presence of prey over a wide area, it also impedes the movements of the prey and gives the spi-

der more time to reach a victim. Perhaps 90 percent of living spiders make sheet webs with a retreat.

Many agelenids also produce an extensive, irregular tangle of threads above the sheet. As B. J. Kaston pointed out in his reexamination of the evolution of web-building in 1964, the tangle confers multiple advantages. It can make the sheet structurally more rigid so that it better conducts vibrations made by crawling prey. It has also been observed to intercept and knock down low-flying insects so that they fall on the sheet and can be captured. A number of families related to the agelenids also construct these sheet-plus-retreat webs near the ground. Species in several mygalomorph families have adopted this way of life, and a few have achieved aerial sheet webs. But

relatively few of them have added the aerial tangle, and no known mygalomorph species have gone past the sheet-web stage of web design.

Agelenids and their relatives run over the top surface of the sheet, but other families of sheet-web weavers hang from beneath it. This may provide some additional protection from predators. In both groups of sheet-weavers, some have dispensed with the retreat entirely and have moved the sheet up into vegetation, where the abundant supply of flying insects may be exploited.

The distribution of sheet webs among spider families follows ecological constraints more closely than family relationships, making a strong case for convergence. The mygalomorph spiders of the genus *Euagrus* make retreat-plus-sheet webs difficult to dis-

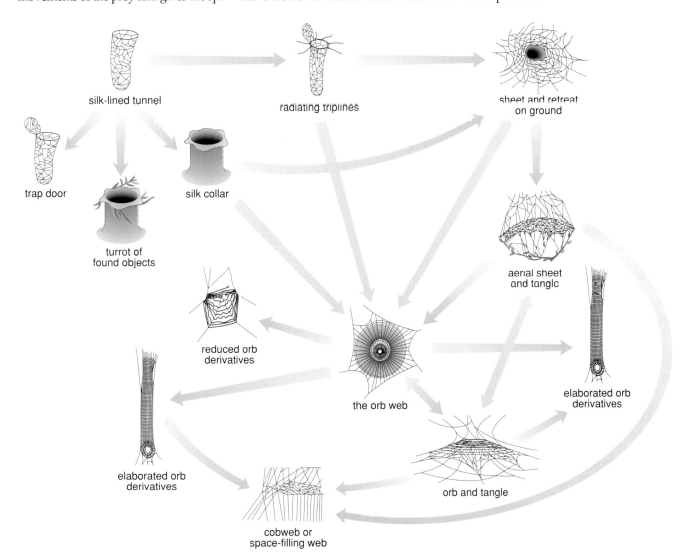

Figure 8. Hypothetical pathways of spider-web evolution form a tangled web of their own, with the question of the orb's origin, and its role as a possible precursor to other webs, at the center. In several cases it is not clear which web is ancestral; it is possible that some aerial sheet webs preceded the orb web, whereas others developed from the orb. Pathways that are less likely are indicated by light-orange arrows; for some of them there is no direct evidence.

tinguish from those of the araneo-morph agelenids; these spiders also replace the agelenids ecologically in the deserts of the southern United States and in Mexico. In New Zealand, Ray Forster of the Otago Museum has described a number of families of spiders that make aerial sheets, just as do other, unrelated families in the Northern Hemisphere. Such examples suggest that the common possession of an unspecialized type of web cannot be used to argue for relationships between spider groups, since the resemblance of the webs may be a result either of the retention of a primitive ancestral pattern common to many spiders, or of convergent evolution.

Enter the Orb

At the center of the phylogenetic Gordian knot of web evolution lies the orb. The geometry of the orb webs fashioned by cribellate and ecribellate araneomorphs is nearly identical, yet the spiders that make them seem quite different. Are the resemblances among the orb webs the results of common ancestry, or are they the product of convergent evolution? The evidence is mixed, and the controversy in this case may not soon be resolved.

The debate over the orb takes the shape of two proposed scenarios. One view, called the "monophyletic hypothesis," states that all orb webs have a common origin; that is, all orb-weaving spiders descend from a common ancestor. This proposal is the older of the two, having first been suggested by Teodor Thorell in 1886.

But the alternative, the convergence hypothesis, has been dominant in scenarios of web-building evolution for more than 50 years, because the dominant thinking has been that all ecribellate spiders were related to one another and formed a group not necessarily close to the cribellates. This distinction meant that any resemblances between the cribellates and ecribellates, including web form, had to result from convergent evolution.

When arachnologists realized that having a cribellum was the primitive condition for all araneomorphs, it became clear that the ecribellate spiders do not form a single group but originated many times by multiple losses of the cribellum. The monophyletic hypothesis again surfaced, and has been persuasively argued in recent years by Jonathan Coddington of the Smithson-

ian Institution. According to Coddington, the cribellate orb weavers and the ecribellate ones had a common ancestor, a cribellate that was probably also an orb weaver.

Much of the evidence marshaled by Coddington comes from careful observations of leg movements that take place in the process of web construction. These observations, reported by William Eberhard of the University of Costa Rica, have had a significant effect not only on the debate over web evolution but also on the views of how behavior ought to be considered in classifying spiders. Eberhard has established that most of the spiders that weave geometrical orbs follow a highly stereotyped sequence of leg movements, even if the orb web has become modified to the point that it no longer resembles a "typical" orb.

Orb weavers are found among five families of an ecribellate superfamily of spiders mentioned above, the Araneoidea, and a cribellate family, the Uloboridae. The studies of Eberhard and Yael Lubin of the Ben Gurion University of the Negev have found that the uloborids' leg movements are identical to

Figure 9. Reduced orb webs reflect ingenious predatory strategies in which activity appears to be substituted for silk. *Mastophora* plays out a single line of silk with a large glue blob at the end, luring male moths to the blob with a volatile substance that mimics the female pheromone of the desired species. Reduced orbs may be considered evolutionary outgrowths of the orb. (Photograph by Mark Stowe, University of Florida.)

those of all five araneoid families of ecribellate orb weavers. Of course, the silk in the webs is different; the uloborids use cribellate silk for the catching spiral, whereas the garden spider and other araneoids use viscid silk.

The origin of the uloborid orb web is not difficult to understand. In 1966, Raja Szlep of the Hebrew University of Jerusalem described the web of a cribellate sheet-weaver, *Titanoeca albomaculata*. She found that around the periphery of its small sheet, *Titanoeca* weaves regularly arranged arrays of threads surprisingly similar in appearance to partial orbs. The regular sectors had numbers of radiating lines, and across these were laid adhesive cribellate threads in a back-and-forth pattern which, if continued entirely around the web, could be visualized as a spiral. *Titanoeca*'s web suggested a route to the orb.

Later, similar behavior was observed by Michael Robinson of the Smithsonian Institution and Lubin. Working in New Guinea on the cribellate *Fecenia ochracea*, a member of a family possibly related to *Titanoeca*'s, Robinson and Lubin discovered that in the course of its lifetime, an individual of this species alters its web form from a typical sheet to what could only be described as a near-orb, the whole web consisting of a *Titanoeca*-like sector, with the radiating lines converging on a retreat. Since then, other examples of sheets with regularly arranged sectors have been found, but only among cribellate araneomorphs. To achieve the orb, it seems only necessary to dispense with the retreat of a *Fecenia*-like web and complete the circle of radial lines.

We are still left puzzling over the question of where the Araneoidea got the orb web. The monophyletic hypothesis urges that the orb developed among certain cribellates that are the common ancestors of araneoid and uloborid orb weavers. In this view the uloborids and the araneoids are each other's closest relatives, differing in that the araneoids have since lost the cribellum. The convergent hypothesis, on the other hand, maintains that the araneoids lost their cribella, and then independently invented the orb web. In this view, uloborids and araneoids are not each other's closest relatives.

The origin of the orb may, then, lie in a *Titanoeca-Fecenia* scenario carried to its geometric conclusion by a common ancestor, followed by the loss of the cribellum among the araneoids. Or a similar scenario may have been played out in similar environments by separate ancestors. The riddle can only be solved by independent evidence. If a close relationship between uloborids and araneoids can be demonstrated by means independent of web features, the monophyletic hypothesis is supported. If, on the other hand, it turns out that the uloborids' closest relatives are some other group of cribellates that do not make orbs, the convergent hypothesis is supported.

Coddington has indeed found independent evidence supporting the monophyletic hypothesis. He has found at least two anatomical characters, or stable traits, that occur only in uloborids and araneoids, and that therefore were also probably inherited from a common ancestor. Both groups have specialized silk glands connected to the posterior lateral spinnerets, and both have a special muscularized valve in the anterior lateral spinnerets. Admittedly, only a few spider families have been examined for these characters, but of those looked at so far, the specializations occur only in Uloboridae and Araneoidea. In addition, Coddington has listed nine detailed behavioral characters connected with orb web construction. An examination of the list suggests that if there was a common cribellate ancestor of uloborids and araneoids, it too wove an orb web and passed down several common behavioral traits to both its descendant groups.

The strongest argument so far advanced for the convergent-evolution hypothesis is the fact that two large families in the Araneoidea, the Linyphiidae and the Theridiidae, do not make orbs, and their behavior, as currently understood, includes no trace of the characteristic silk-handling movements discovered by Eberhard. If there is no evidence that these araneoids descended from an orb-making ancestor, then the common behavioral traits of cribellate and ecribellate orb weavers might be better explained as adaptation to common environments, rather than expressions of a shared inheritance.

The members of the Linyphiidae make aerial sheets. It could be argued that these webs are derived from horizontal orbs with added elements, but similarly persuasive is a scenario in which, following the traditional linear-phylogeny argument, the linyphiid sheets are ancestral to orbs.

Figure 10. *Cyrtophora* has elaborated rather than reduced the orb. Above and below the horizontal orb, the spider has added an extensive tangle of threads. The addition of a tangle, so common in aerial sheet webs, suggests a pathway from which aerial sheets might have evolved from orb webs. It is possible that the orb arose from a sheet web, but that some species have gone from weaving orbs to making a new form of sheet web.

The crucial evidence is missing; linyphiid web-building is not well enough understood. If the special silk-handling movements of orb weavers are indeed completely absent in the Linyphiidae, their ancestors were probably never orb weavers, and the convergent hypothesis is supported because of the close relationship of the linyphiids to the five orb-weaving families.

The second non-orb-weaving family in the Araneoidea, the cobweb weavers of the Theridiidae, is one of the largest spider families in numbers of species. The arguments just stated for linyphiids apply to theridiids as well, but there is an additional point. Eberhard has discovered a theridiid spider, *Synotaxus* (now considered not a theridiid at all but placed in its own family, Synotaxidae), that makes a web with regularly arranged threads. The problem this presents for the monophyletic hypothesis is that the web is not an orb, but a totally different design using rectangular modules that make the whole web resemble a fisherman's net. If the monophyletic hypothesis is correct, one might reasonably predict that such a web would resemble an orb; the fact that it does not supports the idea of convergence.

Beyond the Orb
Among all six of the orb-weaving families I have just mentioned, there are some members whose webs do not closely resemble orbs, nor are they sheets. A few make no webs at all. They can be recognized as family members by their anatomical features and, if webs are still present, by the characteristic movements they use to handle silk. The webs and behavior of these spiders suggest that the orb itself is ancestral to various ingenious modified webs, some of them more complex and others elegant for their simplicity and efficiency.

The most interesting may be the reduced webs. Web construction is of course only part of a spider's approach to predation and self-protection. Among some species activity has been substituted for silk. In the Uloboridae, Brent Opell of Virginia Tech has studied members of the genera *Hyptiotes* and *Miagrammopes*. These spiders hold their webs under tension, releasing them when they come in contact with prey. With the use of this stratagem an insect can be effectively entangled with a simpler web. In *Hyptiotes*, the triangle spider, the web consists of only a pie-shaped sector of the orb, and in *Miagrammopes* only one or a few single sticky threads make up the entire web.

Jonathan Coddington has recently found that *Dinopis*, a cribellate spider of the family Dinopidae (neither a uloborid nor an araneoid), exhibits the characteristic movements of an orb builder. *Dinopis*, however, makes a small, rectangular web best described as the outer half of a pie-shaped sector of an orb, and is famous for its habit of throwing itself and its web at pedestrian and flying prey. It is tempting to propose that muscular movement is cheaper than silk, and thus action has replaced the elaborate web. Recent work by Opell provides indirect support for this idea.

Mark Stowe of the University of Florida argues persuasively that another route to web reduction lies through prey specialization. His field studies have shown that certain araneoids catch mostly moths and have evolved an especially sticky glue for their webs for that purpose. The "super glue" is needed because moths can escape most spider webs by shedding the scales that cover their bodies, leaving the scales stuck to the web. The presence of this glue has allowed the New Guinean spider *Pasilobus* to reduce its web to only a few threads, which, however, remain extraordinarily effective in catching moths.

Stowe and Eberhard have also been able to document that some moth specialists have carried specialization to an extreme: They catch prey of only one or a few species, and only the males of those species. To do so they produce a volatile substance that mimics the female pheromones of the moth species they catch. In the case of the moth-attracting spiders of the genus *Mastophora*, the web is reduced to a single line, with a large glue blob at the end, which is manipulated by the spider. Only their anatomy connects these spiders to the orb weavers.

Robert Jackson of Canterbury University, New Zealand, and I have independently suggested that yet another route to web reduction involves the habit of kleptoparasitism, in which one spider species lives in the web of another and steals prey. Some species of the genus *Argyrodes* still make their own webs and catch insects for themselves, but others invade the webs of unrelated species and cut out part of the host web, replacing it with their own threads. From this base, they make forays into the host web to steal food. Still other species go beyond stealing prey; they kill and eat their host spiders, making web-building virtually superfluous. All known members of the large ecribellate family Mimetidae make no webs of their own. By imitating the struggles of prey in others' webs, they entice other spiders near enough to be killed and eaten.

Finally, there appear to be orb weavers that have added structures to their webs. Lubin has found that some uloborids construct a second orb beneath the first and pull it into a cone. *Cyrtophora*, an ecribellate orb weaver, adds an extensive tangle of threads above and below its horizontal orb. These strong lines probably provide *Cyrtophora*, which sits on its web during the day, a modicum of additional protection from parasites and predators, and may also increase predatory efficiency by knocking down flying insects, which then fall on the horizontal orb. Similar tangles are found above and below many linyphiid sheet webs, which have also recently been found to incorporate viscid silk. The tangle itself, without the horizontal orb, resembles a cobweb. Discovering the characteristic movements of orb weavers in the makers of such webs would reinforce the hypothesis that these spiders originated from orb-weaving ancestors.

Despite the almost complete lack of a fossil record for spiders' webs, and only a very sketchy one for spiders themselves, information from anatomy, systematics, ethology and ecology has been combined to produce hypotheses about the course that evolution has taken in forming this fascinating arachnid artifact. Predictions from these hypotheses can be checked by careful studies of web types old and new, and the results of these observations will lead to further refinements. There are still many closely woven threads to be untangled in the story of web evolution.

Bibliography

Coddington, J. A. 1990. Cladistics and spider classification: araneomorph phylogeny and the monophyly of orbweavers (Araneae: Araneomorphae; Orbiculariae). *Acta Zoologica Fennica* 190:75–87.

Coddington, J., and C. Sobrevila. 1987. Web manipulation and two stereotyped attack behaviors in the ogre-faced spider *Deinopis spinosus* Marx (Araneae, Deinopidae). *Journal of Arachnology* 15:213–225.

Coyle, F. A., and N. D. Ketner. 1990. Observations on the prey and prey capture behavior of the funnelweb mygalomorph spider genus *Ischnothele* (Araneae, Dipluridae). *Bulletin of the British Arachnological Society* 8:87–104.

Eberhard, W. G. 1975. The 'inverted ladder' orb web of *Scoloderus* sp. and the intermediate web of *Eustala* (?) sp. Araneae: Araneidae. *Journal of Natural History* 9:93–106.

Eberhard, W. G. 1980. The natural history and behavior of the bolas spider *Mastophora dizzydeani* sp. N. (Araneidae).

Eberhard, W. G. 1982. Behavioral characters for the higher classification of orb–weaving spiders. *Evolution* (36(5):1067–1095.

Eberhard, W. G. 1990. Function and phylogeny of spider webs. *Annual Review of Ecological Systems* 21:341–372.

Eberhard, W. G. 1990. Early stages of orb construction by *Philoponella vicinia, Leucauge mariana,* and *Nephila clavipes* (Araneae, Uloboridae and Tetragnathidea), and their phylogenetic implications. *Journal of Arachnology* 18:205–234.

Jackson, R. R., and M. E. A. Whitehouse. 1986. The biology of New Zealand and Queensland pirate spiders (Araneae, Mimetidae): Aggressive mimicry, araneophagy and prey specialization. *Journal of Zoology, London (A),* 210:279–303.

Kaston, B. J. 1964. The evolution of spider webs. *American Zoologist* 4:191–207.

Kullmann, E. J. 1972. The convergent development of orb-webs in cribellate and ecribellate spiders. *American Zoologist* 12:395–405.

Levi, H. W. 1978. Orb-webs and phylogeny of orb-weavers. *Symposium Zoological Society of London* 42:1–15.

Lubin, Y. D., B. D. Opell, W. G. Eberhard and H. W. Levi. 1982. Orb plus cone-webs in Uloboridae (Araneae), with a description of a new genus and four new species. *Psyche* 89(1-2):29–64.

Opell, B. D. 1990. Material investment and prey capture potential of reduced spider webs. *Behavioral Ecology and Sociobiology* 26:375–381.

Platnick, N. I., and W. J. Gertsch. 1976. The suborders of spiders: A cladistic analysis (Arachnida, Araneae). *American Museum Novitates* 2607:1–15.

Reed, C. F., P. N. Witt, M. B. Scarboro and D. B. Peakall. 1970. Experience and the orb web. *Developmental Psychobiology* 3(4):251–265.

Robinson, M. H., and B. Robinson. 1975. Evolution beyond the orb web: The web of the araneid spider *Pasilobus* sp., its structure, operation and construction. *Zoological Journal of the Linnean Society* 56(4):301–314.

Robinson, M. H., and Y. D. Lubin. 1979. Specialists and generalists: The ecology and behavior of some web-building spiders from Papua New Guinea. II. *Psechrus argentatus* and *Fecenia* sp. (Araneae: Psechridae). *Pacific Insects* 21(2-3):133–164.

Shear, W. A., ed. 1986. *Spiders: Webs, Behavior, and Evolution.* Stanford, Calif.: Stanford University Press.

Szlep, R. 1966. Evolution of the web spinning activities: The web spinning in *Titanoeca albomaculata* luc. (Araneae, Amaurobidae). *Israel Journal of Zoology* 15:83–88.

Vollrath, F. 1992. Spider webs and silks. *Scientific American* 266(3):70–76.

Witt, P. N., and C. F. Reed. 1965. Spider-web building. *Science* 149(3689):1190–1197.

Naked Mole-Rats

Like bees and termites, they cooperate in defense, food gathering and even breeding. How could altruistic behavior evolve in a mammalian species?

Rodney L. Honeycutt

Biological evolution is generally seen as a competition, a contest among individuals struggling to survive and reproduce. At first glance, it appears that natural selection strongly favors those who act in self-interest. But in human society, and among other animal species, there are many kinds of behavior that do not fit the competitive model. Individuals often cooperate, forming associations for their mutual benefit and protection; sometimes they even appear to sacrifice their own opportunities to survive and reproduce for the good of others. In fact, apparent acts of altruism are common in many animal species.

It is easy to admire altruism, charity and philanthropy, but it is hard to understand how self-sacrificing behavior could evolve. The evolutionary process is based on differences in individual fitness—that is, in reproductive success. If each organism strives to increase its own fitness, how could natural selection ever favor selfless devotion to the welfare of others? This question has perplexed evolutionary biologists ever since Charles Darwin put forth the concepts of natural selection and individual fitness. An altruistic act—one that benefits the recipient at the expense of

Rodney L. Honeycutt is an associate professor in the Department of Wildlife and Fisheries Sciences and a member of the Faculty of Genetics at Texas A&M University. He began his research on the genetics and systematics of African mole-rats in 1983 during his tenure as assistant professor of biology at Harvard University and assistant curator of mammals at Harvard's Museum of Comparative Zoology. He is interested in the evolution and systematics of mammals and has taught courses in mammalian biology for the past seven years. His research has taken him to regions of Africa, South America, Central America and Australia. Address: Department of Wildlife and Fisheries Sciences, Texas A&M University, 210 Nagle Hall, College Station, TX 77843.

the individual performing the act—represents one of the central paradoxes of the theory of evolution.

In seeking to explain this paradox, biologists have focused their attention on the social insects—ants, bees, wasps and termites. These species exhibit an extreme form of what has been called reproductive altruism, whereby individuals forgo reproduction entirely and actually help other individuals reproduce, forming entire castes of sterile workers. Since reproductive success is the ultimate goal of each player in the game of natural selection, reproductive altruism is a remarkable type of self-sacrifice.

Helping behavior is common in vertebrate societies as well, and some species cooperate in breeding. But until recently there did not appear to be a close vertebrate analogue to the extreme form of altruism observed in social insects. Such a society may now have been found in the arid Horn of Africa, where biologists have been studying underground colonies of a singularly unattractive but highly social rodent.

The naked mole-rat, *Heterocephalus glaber*, appears to be a eusocial, or truly social, mammal. It fits the classical definition of eusociality developed by Charles Michener (1969) and E. O. Wilson (1971), who extensively studied the social insects. In the burrow colonies of naked mole-rats there are overlapping adult generations, and as in insect societies brood care and other duties are performed cooperatively by workers or helpers that are more or less nonreproductive. A naked mole-rat colony is ruled, as is a beehive, by a queen who breeds with a few select males. Furthermore, the other tasks necessary to underground life—food gathering, transporting of nest material, tunnel expansion and cleaning and defense against predators—appear to

be divided among nonreproductive individuals based on size, much as labor in insect societies is performed by the sterile worker castes.

The naked mole-rat is not the only vertebrate that can be described as eusocial, but no other vertebrate society mimics the behavior of the eusocial insects so closely. The fact that highly social behavior could evolve in a rodent population suggests that it is time to reexamine some old theories about how eusocial behavior could come into being—theories that were based on the characteristics of certain insects and their societies. In the past decade, since Jennifer U. M. Jarvis first revealed the unusual social structure of a naked mole-rat colony, a number of biologists have been at work considering how a eusocial rodent could evolve. I shall discuss the state of that work briefly here, examining what is known about the naked mole-rat's ecology, behavior and evolution and about altruistic animal societies.

Introducing the Naked Mole-Rat

The naked mole-rat is a member of the family Bathyergidae, the African mole-rats—so named because they resemble rats but live like moles. Many rodents burrow and spend at least part of their life underground; all 12 species of Bathyergidae live exclusively underground, and they share a set of features that reflect their subterranean lifestyle and that demonstrate evolutionary convergence, the independent development of similar characteristics. Like the more familiar garden mole, a mole-rat has a stout, cylindrical body, a robust skull, eyes that are small or absent, reduced external ears, short limbs, powerful incisors and sometimes claws for digging, and a somewhat unusual physiology adapted to the difficulties of life underground, including a burrow

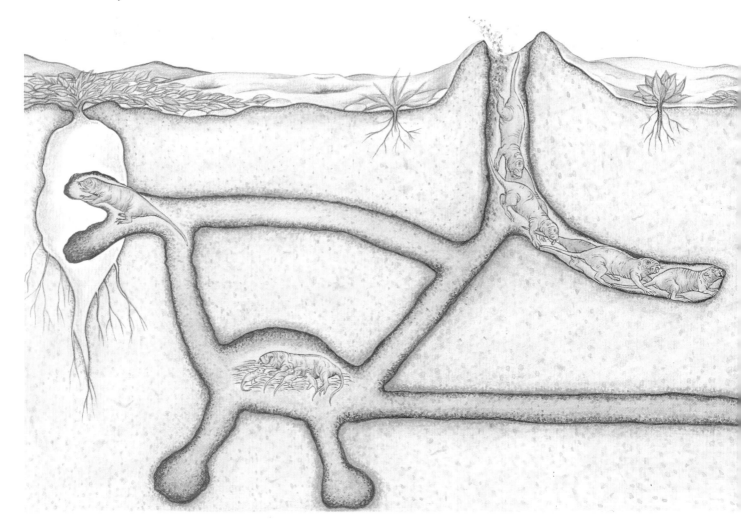

Figure 1. Burrow system built by naked mole-rats beneath the East African desert illustrates the complex social organization that makes the subterranean species unusual. Reproduction in a naked mole-rat colony, which usually has 70 to 80 members, is controlled by a queen, the only breeding female, shown here nursing newborns in a nest chamber. Digging tunnels to forage for food is one of the functions of

atmosphere high in carbon dioxide. All Bathyergidae species are herbivorous, and all but one sport fur coats.

Field biologists who encountered naked mole-rats in the 19th century thought that these small rodents—only three to six inches long at maturity, with weights averaging 20 to 30 grams— were the young of a haired adult. But subsequent expeditions showed that adult members of the species are hairless except for a sparse covering of tactile hairs. Oldfield Thomas, noting wide variations in the morphological characteristics of the naked mole-rats, identified what he thought were several species. *H. glaber* is currently considered a single species, within which there is great variation in adult body size.

Naked mole-rats inhabit the hot, dry regions of Ethiopia, Somalia and Kenya. Like most of the Bathyergidae species, they build elaborate tunnel systems. The tunnels form a sealed, compartmentalized system interconnecting nest sites, toilets, food stores, retreat routes and an elaborate tunnel system allowing underground foraging for tubers *(Figure 1)*. Like the morphology of the animals, the tunnel system is an example of convergent evolution, being similar to those of the other mole-rats in its compartmentalization, atmosphere and more or less constant temperature and humidity. Naked mole-rats subsist primarily on geophytic plants (perennials that overwinter in the form of bulbs or tubers), which are randomly and patchily distributed. The mole-rats forage broadly by expanding their burrows, but their distribution is limited by food supply and soil types. Like most rodents that live underground, they are not able to disperse over long distances.

The tunnel systems of naked mole-rats can be quite large, containing as many as two miles of burrows. The average colony is thought to have 70 to 80 members. In order to study the social organization of the naked mole-rats, biologists have had to devise ways to capture whole colonies and recreate their burrow systems in the laboratory. This is not an easy task, but it is possible because the rodents have a habit of investigating opened sections of their burrow systems and then blocking them. One can create an opening, then capture the naked mole-rats as they come to seal it. Cutting off their retreat requires quick work with a spade, hoe or knife, and the procedure must be repeated in various parts of the tunnel system in order to retrieve an entire colony. A carefully reconstructed colony can survive quite well in captivity, and naked mole-rats are beginning to become an attraction at zoos.

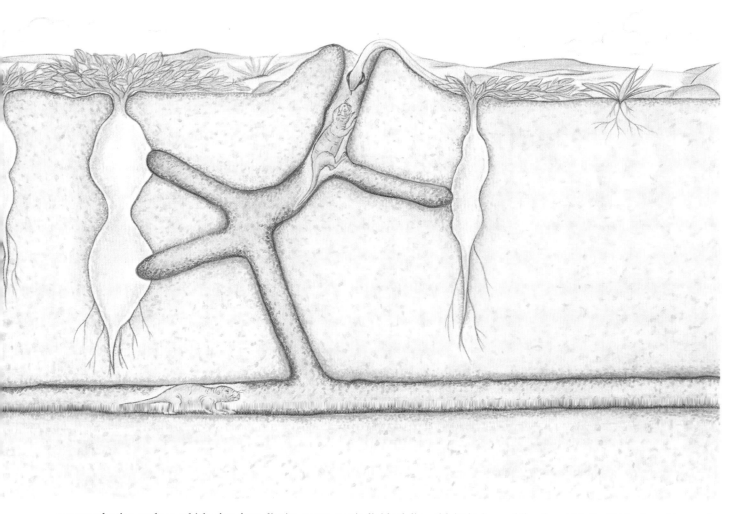

nonreproductive workers, which often form digging teams; one individual digs with its incisors while others kick the dirt backward to a mole-rat that kicks it out of the tunnel. The molehills or "volcanoes" formed in this way are plugged to create a closed environment and deter predators such as the rufous-beaked snake. Tubers and bulbs are the naked mole-rats' food source.

Most African mole-rats excavate by digging with their large incisors, removing the dirt from the burrow with their hind feet. The digging behavior of naked mole-rats, which are most active during periods when the soil in their arid habitat is moist, appears to be unlike that of the other mole-rats in two respects. First, instead of plugging the surface opening to a tunnel during excavation, the naked mole-rats "volcano," kicking soil through an open hole to form a tiny volcano-shaped mound. When excavation is complete, the tunnel is plugged to form a relatively airtight, watertight and predator-proof seal (Figure 4). Second, naked mole-rats have been observed digging cooperatively in a wonderfully efficient arrangement that resembles a bucket brigade. One animal digs while a chain of animals behind move the dirt backward to an

Figure 2. Wrinkled, squinty-eyed and nearly hairless, the first naked mole-rats found by biologists were thought to be the young of a haired adult. The rodents are just three to six inches long at maturity, although there is great variation in body size within each colony. Other morphological features reflect the fact that the naked mole-rats live entirely underground: small eyes, two pairs of large incisors for digging, and reduced external ears. (Except where noted, photographs courtesy of the author.)

Figure 3. Habitat of the naked mole-rats is hot, dry and dotted with patches of vegetation. Visible in the foreground of this photograph, taken in Kenya, are the molehills formed by the rodents.

Figure 4. "Volcanoes" formed when naked mole-rats kick sand out of a tunnel, then plug the opening, make the animals' burrows easy to find. Naked mole-rats are most vulnerable to predators while forming volcanoes; the activity often attracts the attention of snakes.

animal at the end, which kicks the dirt from the burrow. One 87-member colony was seen to remove about 500 kilograms of soil per month by this process. Another colony of similar size moved an estimated 13.5 kilograms in an hour—about 380 times the mean body weight of a naked mole-rat. A team kicking dirt through a surface opening is vulnerable to attack from snakes; the mounds also make *H. glaber*'s colonies easy for scientists to find.

Naked mole-rats are long-lived animals and prolific breeders. Several individuals caught in the wild are surviving after 16 years in captivity; two of these are females that still breed. In captive colonies females have produced litters as large as 27, and in wild populations litter sizes can be as high as 12. The naked mole-rat breeds year-round, giving birth about every 70 to 80 days. This fecundity is unusual among the Bathyergidae. The other highly social species of African mole-rat, *Cryptomys damarensis*, is also a year-round breeder but produces smaller litters, with an average size of five.

The major threat to the longevity of a naked mole-rat, and probably to all of the mole-rats, is predation. On at least two occasions I have encountered the rufous-beaked snake in a mole-rat burrow; one snake had three mole-rats in its stomach. Similar field observations have been made by other investigators. Encounters between mole-rats and snakes in the laboratory suggest that avoidance may not be the mole-rat's only strategy against predators; individuals have also been seen attacking the predator in their defense of the colony.

The naked mole-rat's closest relatives are the 11 other species in the Bathyergidae, which are all of exclusively African origin and distribution (*Figure 5*). It has been difficult to determine which of the 32 other rodent families shares a common ancestry with the Bathyergidae, but a consensus arising from recent studies places the family in the rodent suborder Hystricognathi, which includes caviomorph rodents from the New World—porcupines, guinea pigs and chinchillas—and porcupines and cane rats from the Old World. The naked mole-rat is the most divergent species within the Bathyergidae, its evolutionary branch splitting off at the base of the family's phylogenetic tree (*Figure 6*).

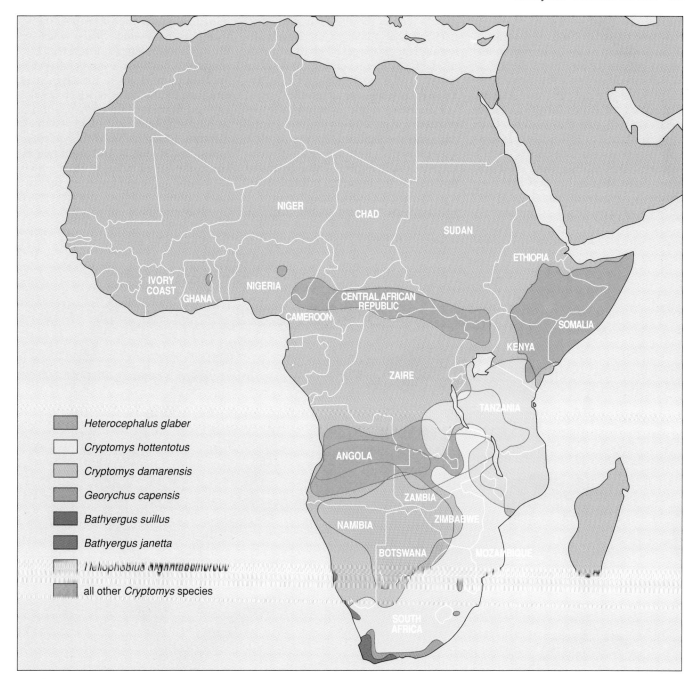

Figure 5. Geographic range of the naked mole-rat, *Heterocephalus glaber*, is limited to the hot, dry region called the Horn of Africa—parts of Ethiopia, Kenya and Somalia. On the map are shown the areas inhabited by other species of African mole-rats. All species in the family Bathyergidae live entirely underground. Most are solitary or colonial; the other species with a highly developed social structure, *Cryptomys damarensis*, is found in Southern Africa.

How Do Altruistic Societies Evolve?
Darwin called the development of sterile castes in insect societies a "special difficulty" that initially threatened to be fatal to his theory of natural selection. His solution to the problem was surprisingly close to current hypotheses based on genetic relatedness, even though he did not have a knowledge of genetics. Darwin suggested that traits, such as helping, that were observed in sterile form could survive if individuals that expressed the traits contributed to the reproductive success of those individuals that had the trait but did not express it.

Today the notion of *inclusive fitness* forms the foundation for theories about how reproductive altruism might evolve. The idea arose in 1964 from William Hamilton's remarkable genetic studies of the Hymenoptera, the insect order that includes the social ants, bees and wasps. Hamilton showed that if the genetic ties within a generation are closer than the ties between generations, each member of the generation might be motivated to invest in a parent's reproductive success rather than his or her own. Inclusive fitness is a combination of one's own reproductive success and that of close relatives.

In the Hymenoptera, Hamilton found an asymmetric genetic system that could contribute to the development of reproductive altruism by giving individuals chances to maximize their inclusive fitness without reproducing. Hymenopteran males arise from unfertilized eggs and thus have only one set of chromosomes (from the mother); females have one set from each parent. The males are called haploid, the females diploid, and this system of sex determination is referred to as *haplodiploidy (Figure 9)*. The daughters of a monogamous mother share identical genes from their father and half their mother's genes; they thus have three-quarters of their genes in common. A female who is more closely related to her sister than to her mother or her offspring can propagate her own genes most effectively by helping create more sisters. Sterile workers in hymenopteran insect colonies are all female.

Hamilton's work prompted a flurry of interest in genetic asymmetry, but he and others recognized that it was not a general explanation for how eusocial societies might evolve. There are many limitations; for instance, multiple matings by females reduce the closeness of relationships between sisters, and it is hard to explain the incentives for females to tend juvenile males, which are not as closely related as are sisters. Furthermore, although eusociality has evolved more times in the Hymenoptera than in any other order, it has also evolved in parts of the animal world in which both sexes are diploid— namely Isoptera, which includes the social termites, and Rodentia, the order that includes the naked mole-rat. Finally, there are many arthropod species that are haplodiploid and have not developed highly social behavior.

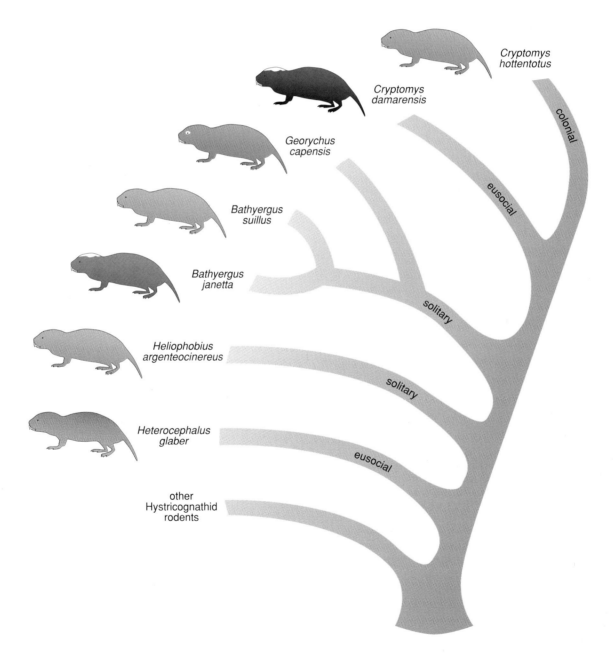

Figure 6. Phylogenetic tree for the family Bathyergidae, the African mole-rats, shows that the two eusocial, or truly social, species are quite divergent. Among other rodents, the suborder Hystricognathi, which includes porcupines, guinea pigs and chinchillas, appears to have the closest genetic link with the African mole-rats. Although there is much similarity among the Bathyergidae species in their physiological characteristics and their subterranean lifestyle, the phylogenetic distance between the eusocial species of mole-rats suggests that complex social behavior evolved separately in the two cases.

There is another way that close kinship might develop among the members of a generation, and it is considered a possible explanation for the evolution of the termite and naked mole-rat societies. Several generations of inbreeding could result in a higher degree of relatedness among siblings than between parents and offspring *(Figure 10)*. When male and female mates are unrelated, but each is the product of intense inbreeding, their offspring can be genetically identical and might be expected to stay and assist their parents for the same reasons set forth in the haplodiploid model. The inbreeding model was developed by Stephen Bartz in 1979 to explain the development of eusocial behavior in termites, which live in a contained and protected nest site conducive to multigenerational breeding.

Genetics alone cannot provide a comprehensive explanation for the evolution of eusociality. Other possible explanations, especially relevant to termites and vertebrate helpers, lie in combinations of ecological and behavioral factors. These factors perhaps provided preconditions or starting points for the eventual evolution of a eusocial lineage or species. The best way to understand the development of eusociality may be to consider the costs and benefits associated with remaining in the natal group and helping, as compared to the costs and benefits of dispersing and breeding.

Probably one of the most important preconditions for the development of eusociality is parental care in a protected nest, where offspring are defended against predators and provided with food. If there is a high cost associated with dispersal—in terms of restricted access to food, lack of breeding success or increased vulnerability to predators—then there may be an incentive for juveniles to remain in the protected nest and become helpers. Helpers that remain in the nest for multiple generations may forgo reproduction indefinitely as a consequence of maternal manipulation.

The short-term benefits of group living seem to accrue mainly to those individuals who are reproducing, since they benefit from the help others provide with defense and obtaining food. In fact, there is a correlation between the breeder's reproductive fitness and the number of helpers in cooperatively breeding vertebrate species. Thus the long-term effect of helping may be an

Figure 7. Catching naked mole-rats requires some understanding of their behavior. Mole-rat catchers create an opening from the surface to a burrow, which is normally kept sealed by the animals, and wait quietly for a mole-rat to investigate. A spade, hoe, pick or knife blade is driven quickly into the tunnel to block the mole-rat's escape. (Photograph courtesy of Stan Braude, University of Missouri at St. Louis.)

Figure 8. Captive naked mole-rats, carrying identifying tattoos, adapt well to being placed together in bins, apparently because the highly social animals tend to huddle together for warmth in their burrows in the wild. These rodents are part of Jennifer U. M. Jarvis's collection at the University of Cape Town.

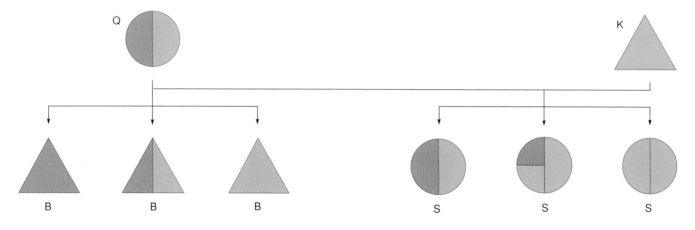

degrees of relatedness in haplodiploid species

	daughter	son	mother	father	sister	brother
female	$\frac{1}{2}$	$\frac{1}{2}$	$\frac{1}{2}$	$\frac{1}{2}$	$\frac{3}{4}$	$\frac{1}{4}$
male	1	0	1	0	$\frac{1}{2}$	$\frac{1}{2}$

Figure 9. Haplodiploidy, an asymmetric genetic system, is thought to contribute to the development of reproductive altruism in ants, bees and wasps—species with intricate social systems that include sterile castes of workers. In a haplodiploid species, males *(triangles)* arise from unfertilized eggs and have only one set of chromosomes, whereas females *(circles)* have one set of chromosomes from each parent. The relatedness between sisters—the fraction of their genes that are shared—is thus greater than the relatedness of mother and daughter *(bottom panel)*. William D. Hamilton hypothesized that females seeking to increase their inclusive fitness—a combination of their own reproductive success and that of close relatives—might in a haplodiploid species become helpers, advancing the continuation of their own genetic heritage by helping with the reproduction of sisters rather than their own offspring. Although haplodiploidy is not considered a full explanation of how eusocial behavior would evolve in ants, bees and wasps, it is notable that most species in which reproductive altruism has evolved are haplodiploid, and that the sterile workers among the haplodiploid insects are all female. In this illustration, the parents are labeled *Q* and *K* and the offspring *S* and *B*, following the scheme in Figure 10; for simplicity, the effects of any recombination of genes are not depicted.

increase in inclusive fitness for the helpers. This may prove to be a very important consideration in species where the probability of a dispersing individual procuring a nest site and eventually breeding is extremely low.

Naked Mole-Rat Society
In some ways the social organization observed in naked mole-rat colonies is more akin to the societies of the social insects than to the social organization of any other vertebrate species. In other respects, mole-rats are unique and may always remain a bit of a mystery.

Some similarities between naked mole-rat societies and the insect societies are striking. A naked mole-rat colony, like a beehive, wasp's nest or termite mound, is ruled by its queen or reproducing female. Other adult female mole-rats neither ovulate nor breed. The queen is the largest member of the colony, and she maintains her breeding status through a mixture of

behavioral and, presumably, chemical control. She is aggressive and domineering; queenly behavior in a naked mole-rat includes facing a subordinate and shoving it along a burrow for a distance. Queens have been long-lived in captivity, and when they die or are removed from a colony one sees violent fighting among the larger remaining females, leading to a takeover by a new queen.

Most adult males produce sperm, but only one to three of the larger males in a colony breed with the queen, who initiates courtship. There is little aggression between breeding males, even upon removal of the queen. The queen and breeding males do not participate in the defense or maintenance of the colony; instead, they concern themselves with the handling, grooming and care of newborns.

Eusocial insect societies have a rigid caste system, defined on the basis of distinctions in behavior, morphology

and physiology. Mole-rat societies, on the other hand, demonstrate behavioral asymmetries related primarily to reproductive status (reproduction being limited to the queen and a few males), body size and perhaps age. Smaller nonbreeding members, both male and female, seem to participate more in gathering food, transporting nest material and clearing tunnels. Larger nonbreeders are more active in defending the colony and perhaps in removing dirt from the tunnels. Jarvis has suggested that differences in growth rates may influence the length of time that an individual performs a task, regardless of its age.

Naked mole-rats, being diploid in both sexes, do not have an asymmetric genetic system such as haplodiploidy. As Bartz has proposed for termites, inbreeding in naked mole-rats may create a genetic asymmetry that mimics the result of haplodiploidy. There is genetic evidence suggesting that naked mole-rats are highly inbred within colonies and even between colonies in a local area. An important part of the question about breeding within and between colonial groups cannot be answered, however, since there is very little information on how mole-rat colonies are established. This makes it difficult to evaluate the naked mole-rats using Bartz's model of inbreeding and eusociality in termites.

Still, among the eusocial insects termites offer the closest comparison with the naked mole-rats. Termites are the only eusocial insects outside the Hymenoptera, and all termites are diploid, with two sets of chromosomes. Worker groups include nonreproductive males and females, and they perform primarily tasks associated with maintaining and defending the colony. The queen termite is more passive than a naked mole-rat queen and uses chemical control. Termite colonies are much larger, sometimes having more than 10,000 workers, and the definition of castes is more rigid.

The naked mole-rat cannot be considered the only eusocial vertebrate species, but it does represent the most advanced form of vertebrate eusociality and the one most analogous to eusociality in insects. Helping or cooperative breeding has evolved many times in vertebrates, and in many of those species the social system includes both a small number of reproducing individuals (usually a dominant breeding pair) and a or nonbreeding individuals (males and females), representing offspring from previous years, that serve as helpers or alloparents. As in naked mole-rats, these nonbreeders participate in foraging for food, care of young and defense against predators. Unlike naked mole-rats, most cooperatively breeding vertebrates (an exception being the wild dog, *Lycaon pictus*) are dominated by a pair of breeders rather than by a single breeding female. The division of labor within a social group is not as pronounced in other vertebrates, and the colony size is much smaller. In addition, mating by subordinate females in many social vertebrates is not totally suppressed, whereas in naked mole-rat colonies subordinates are not sexually active, and many may never breed.

Several ecological and behavior factors may have facilitated the evolution of eusociality in naked mole-rats. Richard Alexander, Katharine Noonan and Bernard Crespi (1991) have sug-

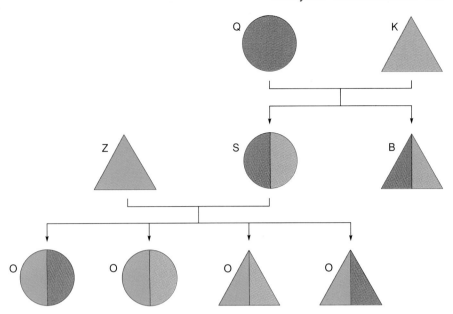

Figure 10. Genetic asymmetry can be produced by cycles of inbreeding and outbreeding in a way that may encourage the evolution of reproductive altruism. Stephen Bartz developed a genetic model to explain how complex social behavior could have evolved in termites living within the confines of a bark-covered chunk of rotting wood. Bartz's hypothesis begins with the mating of a male and a female who are unrelated but are each the product of intense inbreeding (the "queen" and "king," or Q and K, *above*), so that for each, both halves of the genotype are essentially identical. The products of this union (S and B) are essentially identical and therefore more related to one another than to their parents; this genetic asymmetry is thought to encourage helping behavior in both sexes because each sibling can increase its inclusive fitness by assisting in the creation of brothers and sisters. If one of the offspring mates with a similarly inbred but unrelated individual, as in the case of S and Z, the new parents and the new offspring (O) are less closely related than than are the original siblings, S and B. The result mimics the close ties between siblings that are produced by haplodiploidy (*Figure 9*), but the genetic asymmetry disappears in subsequent generations unless specific patterns of inbreeding and outbreeding are followed. (Adapted from Bartz 1979.)

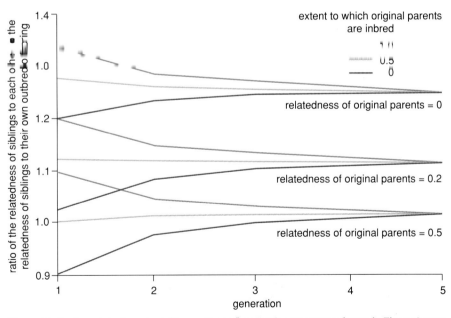

Figure 11. Brother-sister incest might perpetuate the genetic asymmetry shown in Figure 9 over several generations. On this graph, a ratio of relatedness greater than 1.0 means that siblings are more related to one another than to their offspring and are therefore encouraged to become helpers rather than breeders. It is evident that helping behavior is most encouraged when the original parents are highly inbred but unrelated; brother-sister mating makes the inbreeding of the parents unimportant after a few generations, but the importance of the relatedness of the original parents persists. A similar pattern might have contributed to the evolution of social behavior in the confined quarters in which naked mole-rats breed. (From Bartz 1979.)

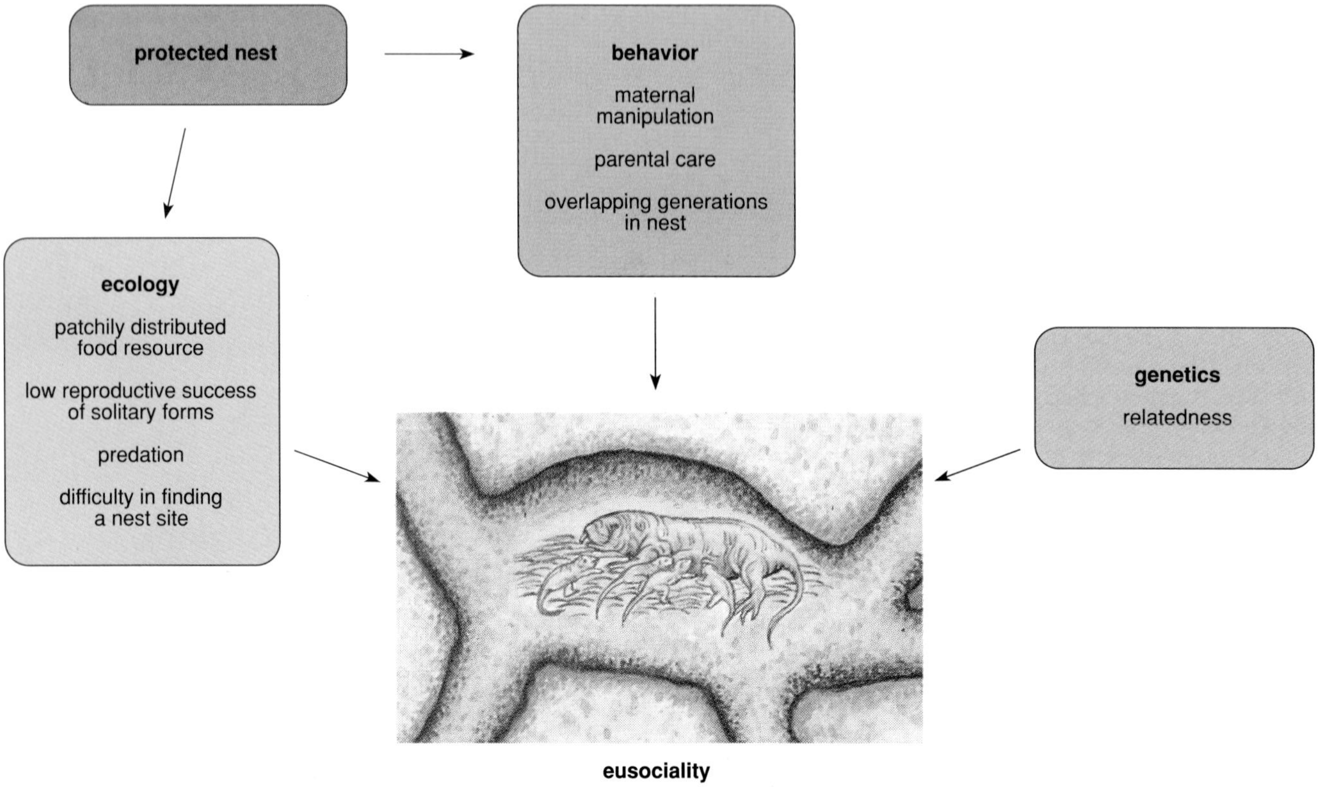

protected nest

behavior

maternal
manipulation

parental care

overlapping generations
in nest

ecology

patchily distributed
food resource

low reproductive success
of solitary forms

predation

difficulty in finding
a nest site

genetics

relatedness

eusociality

Figure 12. Genetic, ecological and behavioral factors probably combine to promote the development of eusociality in an animal species. All of the factors shown above may have been important in the evolution of the complex social organization of naked mole-rat colonies. Inbreeding in the rodents' underground burrows may have created a high degree of genetic inbreeding within generations, promoting helping behavior. In the ecosystem inhabited by the naked mole-rats, the costs associated with leaving the nest may be high compared to the benefits of group living. Behavioral patterns such as parental care may also have predisposed the species to large-scale group living. A closed burrow system that provides a protected nest environment might be crucial in tipping the ecological and behavioral balance toward organized group living and cooperative breeding.

Figure 13. Ruler of a famous group of naked mole-rats, the queen of Jennifer U. M. Jarvis's captive colony at the University of Cape Town in South Africa is distinguished from her subjects by her large size. She is still breeding after 16 years of captivity. Jarvis's colony served as the basis for the first description of eusocial behavior in a mammal.

gested that the subterranean niche shared by termites and naked mole-rats may be an important precursor for the evolution of eusociality. Life underground provides relative safety from predators and access to a readily available food source that does not require exit from the underground chamber. It also offers an expandable living place that can accommodate a large group.

Since the naked mole-rats share their subterranean niche with the other mole-rat species, it is interesting to speculate about why eusocial behavior has or has not evolved among the other Bathyergidae. Of the other 11 species, all are solitary but two—one of which, *Cryptomys damarensis*, may be termed eusocial. *C. damarensis* is not a particularly close relative of the naked mole-rat; whereas *H. glaber* diverged at the base of the family phylogenetic tree, *C. damarensis* is a distantly related and much more recent species, suggesting that complex social behavior in the two species evolved quite separately *(Figure 6)*. Another species in the *Cryptomys* genus, *C. hottentotus*, is the only other social member of the family; its small colonies (two to 14 members) have less well-developed social structures and vary in size and organization.

C. damarensis colonies are somewhat smaller than those of the naked mole-rat, having eight to 25 members. They also include a single reproductive female and one or more reproductive males and exhibit a division of labor among reproductive individuals based on size. One important difference between the two species has been suggested: *C. damarensis* colonies appear to be less stable over time, and the effects of multigenerational group living and inbreeding may be less pronounced. The significance of the presumed differences is a matter that will require further study because the dynamics associated with the duration of colonies and the founding of new colonies in wild naked mole-rats are not well understood. For instance, new colonies presumably are formed from existing colonies by budding, or fissioning, but the frequency of this event and its causes are not known.

The features of the subterranean niche may supply part of the explanation of social living in mole-rats, even though many solitary, non-social species of rodents in the Bathyergidae and other families occupy a similar niche. Restricted access to food and an unpredictable environment may also provide clues to the evolution of eusociality in both naked mole-rats and *C. damarensis* because as resources become more difficult to find, the energetic cost associated with finding them increases. Several authors have suggested that cooperation in food foraging and communal living might be promoted by the patchy distribution of the food source.

There is no simple explanation for the evolution of eusociality, and the hypotheses that fit the naked mole-rats and the other social species should not be considered mutually exclusive. Reproductive altruism is more likely to occur among genetically related individuals, but relatedness is not a sufficient explanation. Each eusocial species has a unique combination of life-histo-

Figure 14. *Cryptomys damarensis* is an African mole-rat distantly related to the naked mole-rats but sharing many kinds of eusocial behavior. Its somewhat larger colonies appear to be less stable over time. The species is found in Southern Africa.

ry characteristics associated with both its ecology and its behavior, and some or perhaps all of these characteristics may have predisposed a particular species for group living and cooperative breeding. The fact that various factors can work together in the development of eusociality may provide the ultimate explanation for the novelty, and therefore the mystery, of each example of eusocial behavior.

Bibliography

Alexander, R. D., K. M. Noonan and B. J. Crespi. 1991. The evolution of eusociality. In *The Biology of the Naked Mole Rat*, ed. P. W. Sherman, J. U. M. Jarvis and R. D. Alexander, 3–44. Princeton, N.J.: Princeton University Press.

Allard, M. W., and R. L. Honeycutt. 1992. Nucleotide sequence variation in the mitochondrial 12S rRNA gene and the phylogeny of African mole-rats (Rodentia: Bathyergidae). *Molecular Biology and Evolution* 9 (in press).

Andersson, M. 1984. The evolution of eusociality. *Annual Review of Ecology and Systematics.* 15:165–189.

Bartz, S. H. 1979. Evolution of eusociality in termites. *Proceedings of the National Academy of Sciences (U.S.A.)* 76:5764–5768.

Bennett, N. C., and J. U. M. Jarvis. 1988. The social substructure and reproductive biology of colonies of the mole-rat, *Cryptomys damarensis* (Rodentia, Bathyergidae). *Journal of Mammalogy.* 69:293–302.

Brown, J. L. 1987. *Helping and Communal Breeding in Birds.* Princeton, N. J.: Princeton University Press.

Emlen, S. T. 1991. Evolution of cooperative breeding in birds and mammals in *Behavioral Ecology: An Evolutionary Approach.* 3rd edition, ed. J. R. Krebs and N. B. Davies, 301–337. Palo Alto, Calif.: Blackwell Scientific Publications.

Genelly, R. E. 1965. Ecology of the common mole-rat (*Cryptomys hottentotus*) in Rhodesia. *Journal of Mammalogy* 46:647–665.

Hamilton, W. D. 1964. The genetical evolution of social behavior. *Journal of Theoretical Biology* 7:1–52.

Jarvis, J. U. M. 1981. Eusociality in a mammal: Cooperative breeding in naked mole rat colonies. *Science* 212:571–573.

Macdonald, D. W., and P. D. Moehlman. 1982. Cooperation, altruism, and restraint in the reproduction of carnivores. In *Perspective in Ethology*, Vol. 5, ed. P. P. G. Bateson and P. H. Klopfer, 433–467. New York: Plenum Press.

Michener, C. D. 1969. Comparative social behavior of bees. *Annual Review of Entomology* 14:277–342.

Reeve, H. K., D. F. Westneat, W. A. Noon, P. W. Sherman and C. F. Aquadro. 1990. DNA "fingerprinting" reveals high levels of inbreeding in colonies of the eusocial naked mole-rat. *Proceedings of the National Academy of Sciences (U.S.A.).* 87:2496–2500.

Trivers, R. 1985. *Social Evolution.* Menlo Park, Calif.: The Benjamin/Cummings Publishing Company, Inc.

Wilson, E. O. 1971. *The Insect Societies.* Cambridge, Mass.: Harvard University Press.

Alison Jolly

The Evolution of Primate Behavior

A survey of the primate order traces the progressive development of intelligence as a way of life

Primates stand at a turning point in the course of evolution. Primates are to the biologist what viruses are to the biochemist. They can be analyzed and partly understood according to the rules of a simpler discipline, but they also present another level of complexity: viruses are living chemicals, and primates are animals who love and hate and think.

The primates are an order of mammals that is difficult to characterize by any single feature. However, a number of anatomical trends are apparent within the order (Le Gros Clark 1960). Most are directly related to behavioral complexity. Free and precise movement of the hands and forelimbs culminates in our own cleverness with tools. A shift from reliance on smell to reliance on vision leads to the capability for detailed spatial patterning of a world full of objects. The cerebral cortex increases in size and complexity. Finally, the lengthening of prenatal and postnatal life demands prolonged care of our dependent young and allows time for them to learn the resources of their environment and the manners of their tribe. If there is an essence of being a primate, it is the progressive evolution of intelligence as a way of life. Such

Alison Jolly is a guest investigator at The Rockefeller University. She has done pioneering fieldwork on the ringtailed lemur and the sifaka, and has written and edited books on the dilemma of conservation in Madagascar: A World Like Our Own *(1980) and* Madagascar *(1984), as well as on the primates:* Lemur Behavior *(1966),* The Evolution of Primate Behavior *(1972), and* Play, *with J. Bruner and K. Sylva (1976). The present article is adapted by permission of the publisher from* The Evolution of Primate Behavior, *2d edition, published in January 1985 by Macmillan Company. Address for Dr. Jolly: The Rockefeller University, 1230 York Avenue, New York, NY 10021.*

trends long predate the emergence of humanity and, to a surprising degree, are represented at different levels of development among the species living today.

The modern primates fall into four groups: the strepsirhines (from the Greek for "turned nose"), the new-world monkeys, the old-world monkeys, and the hominoids, or apes together with humans. Twenty-eight of the 185 primate species live on Madagascar, and about 50 each live in South America, Africa, and Asia. Representatives of the four groups are shown in Figure 1.

At least 80% of all primate species live in rain forest. This was probably the original home of the group, and it is not surprising that the most diverse array still live there. A few are specialized to this habitat, but many are able to occupy both moist and dry forest. Half the species on each continent may at times range into dry woodland; only in Africa and Asia do some primates live on the open savannah. Humans, of course, are terrestrial rather than arboreal; but at what point our ancestors left the forests to take to the open plains is a matter of lively debate, with many interpretations possible because of the lack of analogous species surviving today and the fragmentary nature of the fossil record.

In the last ten years, four developments have challenged long-held assumptions in the study of primate behavior. First, far more data are now available on the ranging patterns, food choice, and population dynamics of wild primates. Ecological principles, as formulated by Hutchinson in *An Introduction to Population Ecology* (1978), have finally penetrated primate studies. This means we have a far clearer idea than before how environmental pressures

shaped primate society and intelligence.

Second, Wilson, in his book *Sociobiology* (1975), crystallized the possibility of calculating the evolutionary advantages of social behavior. He was certainly not the only one; he built on work by Hamilton, Trivers, and, chiefly, Darwin. Nonetheless his book provoked outcry at the thought that we might quantify the evolutionary advantages of love. Meanwhile, data on primate kinship and mutual aid began to do just that.

The third development is the recognition of consciousness in animals other than ourselves. Griffin points out, in *The Question of Animal Awareness* (1976) and *Animal Thinking* (1984a, b), that behaviorists cannot have it both ways. They cannot equate the workings of the mind to the workings of the nervous system and then deny conscious mind to creatures with nervous systems very much like our own. By this reasoning, consciousness is a real property of the complex organization of a brain, just as the capacity of a virus to reproduce itself is a property of its complex chemical architecture. Although the issue of whether apes use language as we do is still far from settled, on one point there is a clear consensus: it is no longer possible to doubt conscious awareness in the great apes. Figure 2 shows some of the complex interactions of a primate group, as a young chimpanzee reaches out to touch her newborn brother and is gently prevented by the mother.

These three currents of thought have clarified some of the links between primate environment, social emotions, and the emergence of mind. The fourth development is the realization that the urgent need in primate studies is conservation.

This realization has been painful. It began for me in Madagascar, where the tragedy of forest felling, erosion, and desertification is a tragedy without villains. Malagasy peasant farmers are only trying to change the wild environment in order to feed their own families, as mankind has done ever since the invention of agriculture.

Thus, the study of primates describes a circle that starts and ends with ecology. We can faintly trace the biological steps that led from the dangerous, lush, complicated environment of the early primates to the first grouping in loose societies for defense, reinforcement, and communication, and then to the fostering of wider-ranging, quicker mental abilities. The development of intelligence leads us back to ecology again, for the future of our environment and that of all other species is now within the scope of the human mind to foresee and, in large part, to determine.

Figure 1. The living primates are generally divided into four groups: the strepsirhines (lorises, bushbabies, and lemurs), the new-world monkeys, the old-world monkeys, and the hominoids (apes and humans). Representatives of each group are shown here: top left, the slender loris, *Loris tardigradus*, photographed in Sri Lanka; bottom left, the woolly spider monkey, *Brachyteles arachnoides*, the largest South American primate; top right, the savannah baboon, *Papio anubis*, shown here in Tanzania; bottom right, the Bornean orangutan, *Pongo pygmaeus*. (Photographs courtesy of C. M. Hladik; R. Mittermeier; T. W. Ransom; P. Coffey and the Jersey Wildlife Preservation Trust.)

Challenges in the primate diet

Primates, like other animals, need to eat protein for growth and replacement of tissues, carbohydrates and fat for energy, and various trace elements and vitamins for chemicals which they cannot produce themselves.

Proteins come from leaves, particularly young leaves, and from insect and vertebrate prey. To some extent, leaves and prey are alternates in the diet of a primate. Animals that can digest leaves have less need of protein from prey, particularly as they also harvest the leaf-fermenting microbes of their gut as an additional source of protein.

The energy provided by carbohydrates and fat is used for metabolism, primarily for basal metabolism. This means that body size is the most important single measure of the amount of energy needed. Secondary factors are the amount of activity and whether the animal maintains a constant temperature. Many prosimians, for example, save energy by letting their temperature drop several degrees at night, and basking in the sun to warm themselves as the day begins. Fruit containing sugar, starch, or oil is the most common

source of energy; meat and insects are more concentrated sources, but obtaining them requires more skill, more time, and more risk of wasted time and energy. Vitamins and trace elements come mainly from the normal diet of fruit, leaves, and prey.

Fruit is the staple for most species, often accounting for nearly half the total intake of food, at least among diurnal primates. Fruit-eating can be handled in more than one way. Most primates tolerate a high proportion of green or bitter fruits, which means medium-sized sources of food at medium distances. Some primates, such as the spider monkey and the chimpanzee, specialize in ripe fruit. These animals range widely, because there is usually little ripe fruit on a single tree. Their social groups join and split, with members often foraging singly or in small subgroups.

Among the fruits eaten by primates, one holds a special place. The fig tree may have played a distinctive role in primate evolution (MacKinnon 1979). There are some 900 species of *Ficus*, a genus extraordinary in many ways. The fruits are eaten by a large number of vertebrates, mostly seed dispersers rather than seed predators. Flowering and fruiting do not coincide from one fig

tree to another, but on any one tree most of the figs tend to ripen at the same time. Many species of fig coexist in a tropical forest, and yet they do not compete for pollinators, for each is fertilized by its own coevolved fig wasp which functions almost like the active gametes of an animal. There is frequently a fig tree in fruit somewhere, and each tree puts colossal energy into the bonanza of fruit that attracts seed dispersers (Janzen 1979). In return, primates may expend considerable energy to reach a ripe fig tree, as shown in Figure 3.

The vertebrates that eat figs have at least one qualification for social tolerance: a large clump of food to eat all at once. If early primates traveled together from one fig tree to another, they had already begun to fulfill a condition of longer-term social bonding. In such forests as the Krau game reserve in Malaysia, fig trees are still major plants that determine the movements of primate groups (MacKinnon and MacKinnon 1980).

Leaves are another important element in the primate diet. The amount of foliage eaten varies widely; in most cases it makes up between about 10% and 30% of the diet, but a few species may take half or three-quarters of their food in this form. Leaf-eating involves specializations of teeth, gut, and behavior, and, like fruit-eating, can be carried out in more than one fashion. There is a gradation from more active, wide-ranging animals that concentrate on new leaves with an admixture of fruit, to those that eat more mature leaves and rely on energy-saving and sedentary habits. The contrast appears consistently in pairs of closely related species: the wide-ranging hanuman langur and the purple-faced langur in Sri Lanka (Hladik 1975), the ringtailed lemur and the brown lemur in western Madagascar (Sussman 1974), and the red colobus and the guereza colobus monkey in East Africa (Clutton-Brock 1975). In Figure 4, a brown cebus monkey shows the heavy jaw muscles necessary for eating palm pith.

Insects, although significant in terms of foraging time and protein supply, make up a minimal proportion of the diet. The chimpanzee, famous for its "fishing" with a stripped twig for termites in a dead log, actually takes in as little as 4% of its diet in the form of insect prey. However,

Figure 2. The kin group of a mother and young offspring is basic to most primate social troops. Younger siblings may learn by imitating older ones, and are commonly defended and sometimes fed by them. The newborn, however, must be protected for a short time from the curiosity of siblings. Here a young chimpanzee (*Pan troglodytes*) of the Gombe Stream, Tanzania, reaches out to touch her infant brother but instead finds her hand gently held off by her mother. (Photograph courtesy of H. van Lawick.)

insect-eating is probably very ancient in the primate line, and it is practiced today not only by small-bodied, "primitive" primates but by members of every primate group, including humans.

There are three main techniques for catching insects: the slow stalk, the quick grab, and poking into things. Cartmill (1974) points out that our forward-facing eyes and grasping hands are characteristic of arboreal predators like the potto and the slender loris. Our earliest steps toward binocular vision and fine manipulation may have evolved for stalking cockroaches. Later, emphasis on extracting concealed prey by poking into things favored a longer attention span, manual skill, and the imagination to work for something that is out of sight (Parker and Gibson 1979). A Lowe's guenon, shown in Figure 5, regularly feeds on insects found within tightly rolled leaves.

The eating of meat among primates is a matter of considerable interest, because meat-eating, and hunting, are thought by many to have provided an impetus to the course of human evolution. Meat can of course also be obtained by scavenging—eating what is left of an abandoned carcass, or stealing from a less alert predator—but this is far rarer than true hunting in wild primates (Butynski 1982). Most primates are at least adept enough to bite the head and neck off their prey, although without the deadly precision of many carnivores (Steklis and King 1978).

Hunting seems not to be a fixed, innate tendency, but it is readily learned. Baboons at Gilgil Ranch, in Kenya, gradually developed the tradition. At first only the adult males hunted, but a few females also took to chasing prey, and both females and infants ate prey if they could get a piece; hunting as a whole increased in frequency. Infants and juveniles at first associated casually with others around a carcass, but once a young baboon had tasted meat, it actively tried to get a share the next time. Andrew (1962) and others have attributed the long-term increase in mammalian brain size to selection by predators for quicker-thinking prey and by prey for quicker-thinking, more strategically minded predators. The "hunting hypothesis" as one major selective trend in human evolution still stands, even though

Figure 3. A squirrel monkey (*Saimiri sciureus*) of Manu National Park, Peru, leaps between fig trees, while her baby clings tightly to her back. The fig is a favorite fruit of many primates, and squirrel monkey groups will travel a considerable distance to reach a single tree on which the figs are ripe. Once arrived, the animals may remain and feed for several days, because all the figs on one tree tend to ripen at the same time. (Photograph courtesy of C. Janson.)

Figure 4. A brown cebus monkey (*Cebus apella*) feeds on the pith of palm leaves in Manu National Park, Peru. The massive jaw muscles of this species are a specialized trait which lets it strip tough bark or crack hard-shelled nuts. (Photograph courtesy of C. Janson.)

modified by the recent realization that gathering insects and seeds, with the necessary tool use and multiple-step attention, has filled a parallel role.

Eating gum, the sticky sap exuded from the bark of various trees, is a speciality little considered ten years ago. It now appears that many prosimians and a few new-world monkeys are specialized gumnivores; their mark on a tree, once seen, is unmistakable, as in Figure 6. Feeding on flowers, another little-known specialization, may be important in helping an animal through a vulnerable stage of life.

The soft acacia flower, for example, is an ideal weaning food for young baboons lucky enough to mature in the proper season (Altmann 1980).

Just as some primates have been observed partaking of foods previously unknown, others have been found to draw fine distinctions between the edible and inedible parts of a familiar food, especially in plants. Leaves are not just young or old. Frequently only the petiole or the leaf tip is consumed. The "fruit" may be merely a particular seed coat, meticulously scraped from pulp and seed, while the monkey discards all the rest.

Adaptations for feeding

The challenge of maintaining a sufficient, varied, and digestible diet can be met by physical or behavioral adaptation, or both. For the red colobus monkey, to take an example, nearly half the diet comes from so-called toxic plants (Struhsaker 1978). The combination of physiological resistance and great selectivity in the part of leaf or the age of leaf eaten allows the red colobus to survive. The home of this species, the Kibale forest in Uganda, is one of the richest primate habitats in the world, but even there the monkeys must choose from among the available food.

With the realization that what looks like food can often be poisonous, our view of habitats has changed. No longer an abundant larder, the jungle is a treacherous place demanding great discrimination of taste (Freeland and Janzen 1974).

The primates offer some curious examples of physical adaptations for feeding. Most striking is the tooth-comb of lemurs and lorises, which probably evolved as a tool for scraping gum from bark, although it is too fragile actually to bore holes; instead, these prosimians depend on the holes of wood-boring insects for their source of gum (Szalay and Seligsohn 1977). The association between small body size, nocturnality, gum-eating, and the primitive six-tooth comb suggests that it was a feeding adaptation at the start, later modified in the larger and more gregarious animals as a tool for social grooming. In South America the marmosets also have specialized, procumbent lower incisors, permitting them to drill holes for sap (Moynihan 1976).

Many species are anatomically specialized, such as the colobine with its sacculated stomach for fermenting leaves, or the aye-aye, shown in Figure 7, with its long, skeletal third finger for extracting wood-boring grubs from the holes of trees. Like the toothcomb of the lemur, however, these physical structures are made more versatile by the animals' behavior. The aye-aye uses its insect-eating teeth and its specialized hand to chisel open coconuts and flick out the pulp. The colobine not only eats fruit as well as leaves but uses the same digestive apparatus to ferment mature leaves or a more

Figure 5. Campbell's guenon (*Cercopithecus cambelli*), an old-world monkey, unrolls a palm leaf to search for insects. The ability to uncover hidden prey is clearly of adaptive value to insect-eating primates such as the guenon, the mangabey, the macaque, and the chimpanzee. (Photograph courtesy of F. Bourlière.)

usual diet of new leaves, or even terrestrial herbs.

Perhaps most characteristic of primates are the adaptations that exist entirely in the behavior of the animal. In La Marcarena National Park, in Colombia, the blackcapped cebus monkey obtains food from the black palm nut, or cumare, by one of several approaches, depending on the ripeness of the nut (Izawa and Mizuno 1977). At its earliest stage of ripening, the monkey can bite open the base of the nut and sip the milk inside as from a cup. Later in the season, it finds the soft "eye" and punctures it with a canine tooth to drink the milk; then it taps the soft-shelled nut on a bamboo joint, licking the contents, which resemble yogurt, from the bamboo after every three strokes or so. Still later, when the nuts are hard-shelled, the monkey makes a fulcrum of its hind legs and tail, and bashes the nut on a bamboo joint with all its strength.

This set of alternatives is a local adaptation, absent in other populations of blackcapped cebus monkeys. It seems to have developed at La Marcarena because the cumare palm grows next to many clumps of the hard bamboo, and because the terrain is hilly, which means that there are trees and vines adjacent to the cumare palms at the right height to permit monkeys to jump past the lethal spines of the trunk and land at the fruit. At Manu National Park, in Peru, the cebus monkey uses a different strategy (Terborgh 1984). It investigates the fallen palm nuts, choosing those that have been bored by a beetle (which weakens the shell), but only those in which the beetle has left some of the meat. These nuts it cracks open on branches' or against one another. Even here, it is only the cebus that has developed nutcracking. Woolly and spider monkeys and bearded sakis in the same forest bite open the green fruit but are baffled thereafter, whereas cebus monkeys of many species, in many environments, hit food onto branches or cages (Izawa and Mizuno 1977). It seems that a propensity for bashing things pays off.

Like most mammals, primates in the wild have traditions about which foods to eat in each area and which predators to avoid. Primates also have local habits for the handling of food. Marais (1969) describes troops

of baboons that hammered the gourdlike baobab fruit with stones, and a troop that cooled the water from a hot spring by scooping drainage channels in the soft mud beside the spring.

Figure 6. The black-penciled marmoset (*Callithrix penecillata*), a new-world monkey, gouges slits into the tree bark using procumbent incisors. Then it licks and chisels the gum that is exuded. (Photograph courtesy of W. Kinzey.)

Chimpanzees in some West African populations use large sticks in fishing for insects; unlike their East African counterparts, they peel off the bark (McGrew et al. 1979). Adjacent populations, in East Africa, use

Figure 7. The Malagasy aye-aye (*Daubentonia madagascariensis*) is unusual for its extremely specialized hand, with one skeletal finger with which it probes for insects in tree branches. This animal also has enlarged, very sensitive ears, and can hear the sounds made by insects within the wood. (Photograph courtesy of J. J. Petter.)

different tools and techniques to deal with different species of termite (Nishida and Uehara 1980; Uehara 1982). Apparently only West African chimpanzees use hammerstones and anvils to crack palm nuts (Sugiyama and Koman 1979).

Although local differences may appear random or arbitrary in some cases (for example, why do East African chimpanzees *not* use stones to crack nuts as their western neighbors do?), they clearly have an adaptive value in others. One group of vervet guenons has invaded some artificial clearings in true rain forest, far from its normal habitat in the savannah or forest fringe. In these manmade clearings the vervets forage in unpredictable patterns and communicate with their softest calls. If dogs approach, the monkeys suppress all noise and hide, whereas in the savannah they would give loud alarms. These local habits keep them safe from humans, including the habit of treating dogs as a warning about the presence of humans (Kavanagh 1980). The two specialized strategies of the cebus monkey in La Marcarena, Colombia, and in Manu, Peru, are also evidently adaptive to their specific regions.

Local traditions in foods, in tool-using, and in defense against predators are dependent on the ability of a small, more or less cohesive group of primates to learn from one another. Occasionally tool-using

and the growth of knowledge combine in the social group, with dramatic results, as in the chimpanzee group of Boussou, Guinea (Sugiyama and Koman 1979). This group had in its range a huge fig tree whose trunk was too thick to climb. There were no adjacent trees allowing direct access but a thorny kapok tree that extended below. The fig is a favorite fruit of the chimpanzee, as well as of other primates, and this group persistently climbed the kapok and grappled with the problem, for some time without success. One day for fifty minutes the dominant and the third-ranking male alternated positions on the kapok branch. They broke kapok branches, peeled off the thorny bark, and flailed at the fig branch with a total of nine different stick tools. Whenever a stick caught momentarily, all the watching chimpanzees called and barked. All at once the third-ranking male began quickly to break branches from the limb he was standing on and drop them to the ground without any attempt to use them. This so lightened the limb that it rose slightly, until by bouncing and stretching upright the chimpanzee was able to seize a twig of the fig tree. He climbed up, and then the second-ranked male succeeded in hanging a stick on the dangling fig. Taking advantage of one another's weight to pull the fig branch lower, the whole group swarmed upward.

Learning in primate society

A species or a local population may modify its form or behavior by means of evolutionary change, which comes through the selection of advantageous genes, or by historical change, which can be passed along to the offspring directly. There is ample feedback between the two levels of change. A chance mutation may lead to quicker or more practical learning ability, and so be selected for. Learning ability may buffer the rigors of the environment, favoring genes for bodily vigor at later ages, or allowing formerly lethal genetic anomalies to live and make their own contribution to society.

There are many current attempts to quantify and explain these interactions (Lumsden and Wilson 1981; Bonner 1980; Pulliam and Dunford 1980). One of the major themes is that of polymorphism, or variability. Does mammalian social life allow or depend on a diversity of genotype and behavior and on diverse roles within the group? Or is there an "ideal type" toward which all the individuals of a species tend? Other major questions are how knowledge accumulates within the social group and how quickly such knowledge can change with changing circumstances.

One of the dangerous tendencies of humans is that we so often

Figure 8. The young primate develops behavioral and locomotor skills through the practice of familiar actions in play. At the left, a gorilla (*Gorilla gorilla*) plays at the species-specific gesture of beating its chest; at the right, a chimpanzee practices walking bipedally and carrying a stick. (Photographs courtesy of P. Coffey and the Jersey Wildlife Preservation Trust; H. van Lawick.)

picture ideal types: the Aryan superman, the Hollywood goddess, the high school senior who scores perfectly on a standardized test. The workings of biology, however, do not support this tendency; instead, the great advances seem to involve randomization. We go through all the confusion of sexual reproduction just to mix up our genes.

Hutchinson (1981) suggests that selection has favored some "noise," even in the creation of our proud brain. If the reading of the genetic instruction or the pattern used to record experience contains a random element, this allows polymorphism of intellect within a kin group, which may in turn be adaptive. Differing powers of intelligence from innovative genius to complaisant follower, and differing styles of intelligence from quick-witted hunter to tribal bard have allowed us to mix ideas, not merely genes.

Studies in both the field and the laboratory tend to show that what and how primates learn can vary with their age, their sex, and even their rank within the social group. On the whole, it is semi-independent infants and juveniles who approach and handle new objects most often and for the longest time. They thus perpetrate most of the useful innovations.

The Japanese macaque troop of Koshima Island is famous for its cultural innovations. One infant female called Imo began to wash sweet potatoes to remove the grit when she was eighteen months old. The innovation spread to her playmates and her mother, and from mother to baby sibling. Imo was likewise among the first to swim, and to "placer wash" wheat kernels by throwing a handful of wheat and sand in the water so that the sand would sink and the kernels would float. These discoveries also spread quickly through the troop.

Infants may be most playful, but adolescents are perhaps particularly quick to learn formal tasks. Tsumori (1966, 1967; Tsumori et al. 1965) tested the entire Koshima troop by burying peanuts in the beach sand, patiently arranging the situation so that each troop member in turn had a chance to dig without too much interference from others. Late adolescents, 6 to 7 years old, were quickest and most successful at unearthing the peanuts. This result agrees with laboratory tests that show learning speed to increase until near-adulthood.

Although older adults are slower to solve individual tasks, they have a greater store of knowledge in which to integrate new facts. When Menzel (1969) released a group of chimpanzees in a new enclosure, the adults glanced around and apparently accumulated a great deal of information, whereas the youngsters probably learned little from bouncing several times up and down each tree.

Social rank, as well, appears to affect learning ability. Within two captive troops of rhesus monkeys, the three most dominant males performed worse than other males on several types of learning and reasoning tasks (Bunnell and Perkins 1980; Bunnell et al. 1980). It is not clear what underlay this effect—perhaps a simple circumstance, such as that dominants are not as hungry and therefore not as highly motivated to perform well in experiments. Age may have been a factor as well, since the animals ranged from 4 to 16 years old. Their performance shifted as their rank shifted, however, which suggests that the effect is related to dominance, rather than to individual age or intelligence.

Such tests confirm the observation in the wild that dominant males are less likely than others to take up new habits. On Koshima Island the dominants continued to eat their sweet potatoes gritty, and would never dream of going swimming, whereas juveniles splashed into the water all around them. This conservatism may in turn be useful. One dominant Japanese macaque kept his troop away from a novel object, which was, in fact, a trap. In another case, an adult male chacma baboon frustrated seven successive attempts to trap his troop with drugged oranges. Each time he approached, tasted, and discarded an orange first, then chased away the infants and juveniles who tried to eat (Fletemeyer 1978).

In addition, differences between males and females in their feeding patterns may reflect two distinct casts of mind. It is possible that such differences underlay the evolution of food-sharing and division of labor in our own line. Among orangutans, for example, the huge males forage on the ground and are thus more likely than females to find termites nesting in dead logs. In one study lasting eight and a half years, males were seen on three occasions to carry termite-infested logs into the trees and

Figure 9. A young chimpanzee cautiously uncovers a hidden rubber snake that had previously been shown to her companion at the far right, in an experiment designed to test communication among chimpanzees. The chimpanzee at the right alone had been shown the snake earlier and has led the other chimpanzees to this site and conveyed to them that a frightening object is found here. If the hidden object had been food, the chimpanzees would have searched for it with their hands rather than probing with a stick. (Photograph courtesy of E. Menzel.)

share them with their consorts (Galdikas and Teleki 1981). Although very rare, these episodes seem similar to the more frequent sharing of vertebrate prey by hunting male chimpanzees, who commonly give pieces of the carcass to females and young.

If the foraging of our ancestors differed by sex, it may have become increasingly worthwhile for males and females to exchange food. Furthermore, it could have been adaptive to evolve slightly different mentalities, initially for the particular blend of stamina, patience, and attention to detail that would be appropriate either for hunting vertebrates or for gathering insects and fruit. Then, as sharing food became normal, it would have been advantageous to both sexes and to their jointly supported offspring if the *other* sex was good at its tasks. Perhaps we can see the foundation for this long history even today, in the patience of the female chimpanzee who squats for hours fishing at a termite mound, while her baby plays alongside (McGrew 1979, 1981).

Communicating new ideas

We know that human babies achieve the use of language in several stages: from acts that are involuntarily repeated, such as crying, to the apparently conscious imitation of acts such as babbling and clapping, to the effortful imitation of novel actions such as the forming of words. Great apes and some monkeys also imitate not only familiar acts, as in Figure 8, but novel actions as well. For instance, orangutans of the Tanjung Puting Reserve, in Indonesian Borneo, imitated using logs as bridges after observing a workman who was in such a hurry to escape (they had sunk his boat and charged him) that he dragged a log to the river and scrambled over. He pulled the log up after him, but the two most aggressive orangutans, among eight watching, dragged everything they could find toward the river and succeeded in crossing on a vine before the end of the day. In the years before this incident no orangutan had ever been known to make a bridge, but thereafter the scientists were obliged to collect and destroy every usable log, and even then the orangutans sometimes crossed the

river to the camp using vines they had pulled down from the forest canopy (Galdikas 1982).

Even a relatively simple act may be enough to transmit information, particularly if it is about biologically important, easily learned matters, such as predation (Hall 1963). Young vervets apparently learn which predators are worthy of eagle alarms, and baboons must learn whether to fear Landrovers (DeVore and Hall 1965). In wild troops, animals tend to learn from close kin or associates. Subordinates are more likely to copy dominants, possibly because they are keeping a wary eye on the dominants' moves in general (Miyadi 1967).

Although it is clear that animals that are observing are actively learning, it has long been supposed that there is no active teaching. However, it is sometimes difficult to distinguish the two. Many mammals place their young in situations conducive to learning (Ewer 1968).

The active passing of information, if not teaching as such, also occurs among peers and between social ranks in the primate group. Menzel (1971) kept a group of eight young chimpanzees in an observation house with access to a 4-hectare field. He took out one chimpanzee at a time and showed it a hidden pile of fruit, then returned it to the group and let them all into the field. The apes were too young to venture out alone; instead, the guiding ape would lead its companions to the trove. If dominant, it might stride off confidently, sure that the others would follow. If subordinate, it begged and tugged the others' hands and fur. Sometimes when they paid no attention the guide would fling itself on the ground in a tantrum.

Once the group knew what to expect, Menzel made his experiments more elaborate. The chimpanzees learned to distinguish which of two guides had seen a bigger reward. Now they would march past an apple on a stick, following a guide with more to offer. Next, Menzel hid frightening objects such as rubber snakes. Again the group followed the guide, but with bristling fur and tentative approach, unearthing the reptile with sticks and slapping the ground. Figure 9 shows the cautious method of uncovering a rubber snake. When Menzel removed his

rubber snake before the group arrived, they searched the area around its hiding place, slapping piles of leaves and poking along the boundary fence.

The form of this communication is not mysterious: it consists of bodily cues which are obvious to everyone, unambiguous and at the same time flexible enough to suit changing circumstances. However, as a means of passing messages about facts removed in space and time, this level of communication approaches social control of the environment, for which language was invented and through which the human intellect evolved. We should perhaps not be surprised that the chimpanzee Washoe, taught American Sign Language since her infancy, has shown her own adopted infant a chair and modeled the sign *chair* five times, while looking at him, or that she has signed *food* to him and then molded his hands in hers into the sign for *food* (Chevalier-Skolnikoff 1981). The use of sign language among trained primate subjects is a rich field for inquiry.

A human responsibility

What conclusions can be drawn from the study of primate behavior? The inferences shed a harsh light on our treatment of other primates. Too often we cage them without regard for their sociability and their manipulative curiosity. We breed them without regard for their own preferences, or their long-evolved incest taboos. We rear their infants in isolation, which was fascinating when we could not imagine the results, but which can now be seen as cruelty, based on a fallacy that primates other than ourselves are bodies without minds.

Far more dangerous is our treatment of primates in the wild. Many species are in danger of losing their habitat altogether. Meanwhile, there have been no bounds set on the human habitat—even in the United States, which pioneered the preservation of wilderness land. When we omit to guard a tropical rain forest or a mountain watershed, we are condemning not just individuals but entire species and ecosystems. For every endangered species that breeds in captivity and every park that is protected, far more species and wildlands are lost.

It would be hubris to claim that no organism other than *Homo sapiens* has so transformed the earth's environment. After all, the plants and their offspring created our oxygenated atmosphere. We are, however, approaching the same power. We have tilled land, felled forests, polluted at least the smaller oceans, and developed the potential for nuclear mutual assured destruction. We do not yet know whether our technological venture will succeed or fail, or even whether success would leave room for any species other than our crops, our parasites, and ourselves.

The evolutionary ventures of being alive, being cellular, and then being multicelled were all successful. Yet there are intermediate creatures still present in the world today that illustrate other viable modes of existence: viruses, oozing slime molds, and sponge cells, which when sieved and separated creep together to reconstruct their communal form.

The primates living today are such transitional forms, instructing us with their alien and yet familiar minds, their richly complex societies, their rudimentary tools. The primates stand at the hinge of evolution. Whether they will continue to do so depends on us.

References

Altmann, J. 1980. *Baboon Mothers and Infants.* Harvard Univ. Press.

Andrew, R. J. 1962. Evolution of intelligence and vocal mimicking. *Science* 137:585–89.

Bonner, J. T. 1980. *The Evolution of Culture in Animals.* Princeton Univ. Press.

Bunnell, B. N., and M. N. Perkins. 1980. Performance correlates of social behavior and organization: Social rank and complex problem solving in crab-eating macaques (*M. fascicularis*). *Primates* 21:515–23.

Bunnell, B. N., W. T. Gore, and M. N. Perkins. 1980. Performance correlates of social behavior and organization: Social rank and reversal learning in crab-eating macaques (*M. fascicularis*). *Primates* 21:376–88.

Butynski, T. M. 1982. Vertebrate predation by primates: A review of hunting patterns and prey. *J. Human Evol.* 11:421–30.

Cartmill, M. 1974. Rethinking primate origins. *Science* 184:436–43.

Chevalier-Skolnikoff, S. 1981. The Clever Hans phenomenon, cueing and ape signing: A Piagetian analysis of methods for instructing animals. In *The Clever Hans Phenomenon*, ed. T. A. Sebeok and R. Rosenthal, pp. 60–94. Annals of New York Acad. of Science, 364.

Clutton-Brock, T. H. 1975. Feeding behavior of red colobus and black-and-white colobus in East Africa. *Folia Primatol.* 23:165–207.

DeVore, I., and K. R. L. Hall. 1965. Baboon ecology. In *Primate Behavior*, ed. I. DeVore, pp. 20–52. Holt.

Ewer, R. F. 1968. *The Ethology of Mammals.* London: Logos.

Fletemeyer, J. R. 1978. Communication about potentially harmful foods in free-ranging chacma baboons, *Papio ursinus. Primates* 19:223–26.

Freeland, W. J., and D. H. Janzen. 1974. Strategies in herbivory by mammals: The role of plant secondary compounds. *Am. Nat.* 108:269–89.

Galdikas, B. M. F. 1982. Orangutan tool use at Tanjung Puting Reserve, Central Indonesian Borneo (Kalimantan Tengah). *J. Human Evol.* 11:19–33.

Galdikas, B. M. F., and G. Teleki. 1981. Variations in subsistence activities of female and male pongids: New perspectives on the origins of hominid labor division. *Current Anthropol.* 22:241–56.

Griffin, D. R. 1976 (2d ed. 1981). *The Question of Animal Awareness.* The Rockefeller Univ. Press.

———. 1984a. *Animal Thinking.* Harvard Univ. Press.

———. 1984b. Animal Thinking. *Am. Sci.* 72:456–64.

Hall, K. R. L. 1963. Tool using performances as indications of behavioral adaptability. *Current Anthropol.* 4:479–94.

Hladik, C. M. 1975. Ecology, diet, and social patterning in Old and New World primates. In *Socioecology and Psychology of Primates*, ed. R. H. Tuttle, pp. 3–35. The Hague: Mouton.

Hutchinson, G. E. 1978. *An Introduction to Population Ecology.* Yale Univ. Press.

———. 1981. Random adaptation and imitation in human development. *Am. Sci.* 69:161–65.

Izawa, K., and A. Mizuno. 1977. Palm-fruit cracking behavior of wild black-capped capuchin (*Cebus apella*). *Primates* 18:773–92.

Janzen, D. H. 1979. How to be a fig. *Ann. Rev. Ecol. Systemat.* 10:13–52.

Kavanagh, M. 1980. Invasion of the forest by an African savannah monkey: Behavioral adaptations. *Behaviour* 73:238–60.

Le Gros Clark, W. E. 1960. *The Antecedents of Man.* Quadrangle Books.

Lumsden, C. J., and E. O. Wilson. 1981. *Genes, Mind, and Culture.* Harvard Univ. Press.

McGrew, W. C. 1979. Evolutionary implications of sex differences in chimpanzee predation and tool use. In *The Great Apes*, ed. D. A. Hamburg and E. R. McCown, pp. 441–64. Benjamin/Cummings.

———. 1981. The female chimpanzee as a human evolutionary prototype. In *Woman the Gatherer*, ed. F. Dahlberg, pp. 35–72. Yale Univ. Press.

McGrew, W. C., E. G. Tutin, and P. J. Baldwin. 1979. New data on meat eating by wild chimpanzees. *Current Anthropol.* 20:238–39.

MacKinnon, J. R. 1979. Reproductive behavior in wild orangutan populations. In *The Great Apes*, ed. D. A. Hamburg and E. R. McCown, pp. 257–74. Benjamin/Cummings.

MacKinnon, J. R., and K. S. MacKinnon. 1980. Niche differentiation in a primate community. In *Malayan Forest Primates*, ed. D. J. Chivers, pp. 167–90. Plenum.

Marais, E. 1969. *The Soul of the Ape.* London: Anthony Blond.

Menzel, E. W. 1969. Responsiveness to food and signs of food in chimpanzee discrimination learning. *J. Comp. Physiol. Psychol.* 56:78–85.

———. 1971. Communication about the environment in a group of young chimpanzees. *Folia Primatol.* 15:220–32.

Miyadi, D. 1967. Differences in social behavior among Japanese macaque troops. In *Neue Ergebnisse der Primatologie*, ed. D. Stark, R. Schneider, and H. J. Kuhn. Stuttgart: Fischer.

Moynihan, M. 1976. *The New World Primates.* Princeton Univ. Press.

Nishida, T., and S. Uehara. 1980. Chimpanzees, tools, and termites: Another example from Tanzania. *Current Anthropol.* 21:671–72.

Parker, S. T., and K. R. Gibson. 1979. A developmental model of the evolution of language and intelligence in early hominids. *Brain Behav. Sci.* 2:367–408.

Pulliam, H. R., and C. Dunford. 1980. *Programmed to Learn: An Essay on the Evolution of Culture.* Columbia Univ. Press.

Steklis, H. D., and G. F. King. 1978. The craniocervical killing bite: Toward an ethology of primate predatory behavior. *J. Human Evol.* 7:567–81.

Struhsaker, T. T. 1978. Interrelations of red colobus monkeys and rain forest trees in the Kibale Forest, Uganda. In *Ecology of the Arboreal Folivores*, ed. G. G. Montgomery, pp. 397–492. Smithsonian Inst. Press.

Sugiyama, Y., and J. Koman. 1979. Tool-using and -making behavior in wild chimpanzees at Boussou, Guinea. *Primates* 20:513–24.

Sussman, R. W. 1974. Ecological distinctions in sympatric species of *Lemur*. In *Prosimian Biology*, ed. R. D. Martin, G. A. Doyle, and A. C. Walker, pp. 75–108. Duckworth.

Szalay, F. S., and D. Seligsohn. 1977. Why did the strepsirhine tooth comb evolve? *Folia Primatol.* 27:75–82.

Terborgh, J. 1984. *Five New World Primates: A Study in Comparative Ecology.* Princeton Univ. Press.

Tsumori, A. 1966. Delayed response of wild Japanese monkeys by the sand-digging method, II. Cases of the Takasakiyama troops and the Ohiragama troop. *Primates* 7:363–80.

———. 1967. Newly acquired behavior and social interactions of Japanese monkeys. In *Social Communication among Primates*, ed. S. A. Altmann, pp. 207–20. Chicago Univ. Press.

Tsumori, A., M. Kawai, and R. Motoyoshi. 1965. Delayed response of wild Japanese monkeys by the sand-digging method. *Primates* 6:195–212.

Uehara, S. 1982. Seasonal changes in the techniques employed by wild chimpanzees in the Mahale Mountains, Tanzania, to feed on termites (*Pseudacanthus spiniger*). *Folia Primatol.* 37:44–76.

Wilson, E. O. 1975. *Sociobiology, The New Synthesis.* Harvard Univ. Press.

The Monkey and the Fig

A Socratic Dialogue on Evolutionary Themes

Stuart A. Altmann

Socrates: Look, Eusebius, what's that?

Eusebius: Where, Socrates?

Soc.: In that tree.

Eus.: It's a monkey (1).

Soc.: What is it doing?

Eus.: Just eating figs, that's all.

Soc.: Are you sure, Eusebius? Watch carefully! How is it getting at the figs?

Eus.: Oh, is that what you meant! It's hanging by its tail.

Soc.: Can all monkeys do that?

Eus.: No, only some of the New World monkeys. You can't hang that way without a special gripping surface on the last part of the tail, something like the palm of your hand. A hairy tail would be just too slippery.

Soc.: What else does he need in order to hang that way?

Eus.: Strong tail muscles.

Soc.: And?

Eus.: What do you mean, Socrates?

Soc.: What controls those tail muscles?

Eus.: Why, the brain, of course! These monkeys have large specialized areas in the sensory and motor centers of their brain, devoted just to controlling that fancy tail of theirs. (2).

Soc.: See how well the prehensile tail keeps the monkey from falling out of the tree as it plucks fruit.

Eus.: It does far more than that! An ordinary mammal in the trees can feed only on the fruits it can reach from the tops of branches. But with the addition of a prehensile tail, it can also reach those underneath. It has a much larger "feeding sphere." Also, the monkey's

prehensile tail enables it to climb onto terminal branches that would otherwise be inaccessible, and that's where the fruit is. A prehensile tail, combined with unusually long arms and legs, means that there's hardly any fruit that these monkeys can't reach (3). Their prehensile tail also helps them when they are brachiating—swinging by their arms from one branch to another.

Soc.: But doesn't that kind of suspensory locomotion take a lot of energy?

Eus.: Yes, somewhat more than walking the same distance (4), but brachiating actually saves energy because a brachiator can take short-cuts through the forest: with prehensile tails, these monkeys can cross otherwise impassable gaps in the forest canopy. Brachiation also saves time. These monkeys routinely move through the forest at speeds that ordinary monkeys wouldn't dare. For an animal that exploits widely scattered food sources, like figs, rapid and efficient locomotion is essential. Otherwise, search time would take up the whole day!

Soc.: Such arboreal locomotion must require a lot of well-coordinated information from the monkeys' eyes.

Eus.: Indeed! Monkeys are like owls and like us: their eyes are on the front of their heads, so they have good binocular vision.

Soc.: It seems that a lot of this monkey's anatomy and physiology are specialized for fruit-eating.

Eus.: Well, they use the same equipment in other activities, too.

Soc.: Which came first, Eusebius?

Eus.: I don't know.

Soc.: How could you find out?

Eus.: I don't know that either.

Soc.: Then you didn't understand the first question! To understand a question is to know how it could be answered (5). What else is special about the monkey's eyes?

Eus.: They can see colors.

Soc.: So what? So can we.

Eus.: Yes, but most mammals can't, or do so only poorly.

Soc.: How does the monkey use its color vision?

Stuart Altmann is a professor of ecology and evolution at the University of Chicago. This dialogue is based on his Charles Michener Lecture on Social Biology given in 1988 at the University of Kansas. Eusebius is a creation of the composer Robert Schumann, one of several fictitious characters who provided lively discussions in Schumann's journal of music criticism, Neue Zeitschrift für Musik. *Socrates, by asking probing questions and making provocative generalizations as a way of clarifying ideas, is being Socratic. Address for Professor Altmann: Department of Ecology and Evolution, University of Chicago, Chicago IL 60637-1454.*

Eus.: Probably to detect when the fruit is ripe.

Soc.: I wonder why so many types of fruit change color when they ripen.

Eus.: Maybe so they can tell the fruit-eaters when they are ripe.

Soc.: Now, Eusebius, do you mean that plants have volitions and intentions, just like people?

Eus.: No, what I meant is, maybe plants benefit by such advertising, and so these color changes evolved, along with color vision (6).

Soc.: Benefit! What's so beneficial about being eaten?

Eus.: Most of the fig seeds go through the monkey's gut undigested, then get deposited somewhere else, neatly packaged with fertilizer (7). Besides, if the figs aren't eaten before they drop, many of the seeds will be destroyed by lygaeid bugs and other insects. So the fig tree benefits by advertising its ripeness. Ripe fruits are adapted to being eaten, whereas leaves are adapted to not being eaten. Fruits are usually nutritious; leaves are often toxic (8).

Soc.: So when we watch a monkey eat a fig, we are seeing the result of co-evolution of plants and animals?

Eus.: Well, sort of, though that's a bit of an exaggeration.

Soc.: And the monkeys are the slaves of the fig trees: in exchange for nothing more than a little food, the monkeys carry their load for them.

Eus.: I wouldn't call them "slaves." That's a loaded term borrowed from human behavior, with all sorts of connotations about social classes, control, subjugation, and so forth.

Soc.: Still, frugivorous monkeys and apes are doomed to a life of wandering through the forest in search of ripe fruit and other food. That's a tough way to make a living, but it may be one reason for their cleverness. Locating and selecting nutritious fruits, and remembering where all the good fruit trees are, may have selected for mental abilities. Foraging is the problem and intelligence is the solution (9).

Eus.: Is that so? What about howler monkeys? Don't they eat figs and have prehensile tails? Yet they are as phlegmatic as can be, and they don't impress me as being very clever.

Soc.: Howlers do eat figs, but they also eat large quantities of leaves, and they pay the penalty!

Eus.: What's the penalty of leaf-eating?

Soc.: The penalty is lethargy. Leaves are everywhere in a tropical forest, but they aren't very nutritious and they take a long time to digest, partly because of the toxins and the fiber in them. Leaf-eaters are obliga-

tory resters (10). By contrast, this sort of rambunctious suspensory locomotion requires rapidly mobilizable energy, which fruit-eaters get from sugars. Fruit-eating not only *requires* long-range locomotion, it also provides the fuel for it.

Eus.: Fruits and leaves typify the basic alternatives: you either eat a high-bulk diet that is readily available but not very nutritious, or a low-bulk, high-energy diet that requires a lot of searching (11). That's the basic division among Old World monkeys: the colobines are sluggish leaf-eaters, whereas the more active cercopithecines, such as the macaques and baboons, are very selective omnivores that manage to find the most nutritious foods available at each time of the year (12).

Soc.: So you might say that fruit-eaters live by their wits, whereas leaf-eaters live by their stomachs!

Eus.: Another of your exaggerations, dear Socrates, but with an element of truth in it.

Soc.: Much of the year, the most nutritious and least toxic parts of plants are in short supply. So small animals, like insects, birds, and little monkeys, can sustain themselves on high-energy foods such as fruits and seeds, but big animals can't—unless they are unusually clever, like some large monkeys and apes. But tell me, Eusebius, why don't all the fig trees in this forest ripen at the same time of year? Surely not just to provide monkeys with a year-round supply of food! There must be some time of the year that would be best for the figs.

Eus.: Oh, no! From the fig's standpoint, simultaneous ripening would be ruinous. You see, a fig isn't really a fruit, it's a flower, or rather, a cluster of flowers lining a cavity, with the tops of the flowers on the inside of the fig. The cavity contains both male flowers, with anthers full of pollen, and female flowers, with stigmas ready to receive pollen. Because the female flowers in a fig mature well before the male flowers, and because the figs on any one tree are synchronous with each other, fig trees never fertilize themselves. They are cross-pollinated by fig wasps coming from other trees. Every species of fig has its own species of fig wasps that carry the pollen from one fig plant to another.

The way it works is this. After a female fig wasp enters a fig, she lays her eggs in some of the female flowers and pollinates them too. Such flowers become sterile, however, because the fig wasp larva eats the seed. Several weeks later, when the wingless male fig wasps emerge, they run around in-

side the fig to other flowers, find females that are still inside, and inseminate them. After a female emerges into the cavity of the fig, she gathers pollen from the male flowers, which have now matured, and carries this pollen in a special pouch on her body. She leaves the fig through a hole cut by the males, then flies off to another fig tree. There, she probes for flowers in which to lay her eggs, and as she does so, she spreads the pollen that she carries

over the stigmas of female flowers. Without this pollination, the fruit would be aborted by the tree and her offspring would die: cheaters are automatically eliminated. Those seeds that are eaten by the larvae are, as it were, the "cost" that the fig pays for pollination (13).

Because the pollen is carried from one fig tree to another only by these wasps, the female flowers of each fig tree must mature at about the same time as the male flowers of a nearby donor fig tree. Similarly, the male flowers must not mature until the female fig wasps are ready to emerge. The timing is critical, at every stage.

Soc.: But how does the first fig of the year get pollinated? What's the source of its pollen?

Eus.: The first fig of the year is pollinated by pollen coming from the last fig of the previous year. It's a cycle: they keep ripening all year 'round.

Soc.: Now I understand! Because figs are pollinated by wasps, they fruit asynchronously throughout the year, and because of that, fig-eating primates are fast and smart. The evolution of human intelligence rests on the sex life of tropical plants and insects!

Eus.: Another of your wild exaggerations, Socrates!

Soc.: Perhaps. It sounds like the wasps and figs of a local population are a chronological Rassenkreis, or breeding cycle.

Eus.: Meaning what?

Soc.: Meaning that the fig wasps of January cannot mate with those of June but only with those whose birthdays are near theirs, and so on 'round the calendar. The same is true of figs. For this reason, the fig wasps of January could even be somewhat different genetically from those of June. Are they?

Eus.: Hmm! Nobody has bothered to look (14).

Soc.: Now, Eusebius, what does all this have to do with ripening, which is how we got into this fig business?

Eus.: From the wasps' standpoint, it would be disastrous if the figs ripened too early, before the larvae have emerged. So the wasp larvae secrete a substance that inhibits fig ripening. After the wasps emerge, the figs ripen and are eaten by fig-eaters, like our monkey friend here, and they in turn distribute the seeds.

Because the feces of monkeys and apes often land high up in trees, the figs often sprout there. The strangler figs have taken advantage of this. They use the tree for support and send roots from this upper world to the ground. The entwining roots prevent the trunk of the host tree from expanding and eventually kill it, leaving a fig tree in its place.

Soc.: How long has this fig and monkey business been going on?

Eus.: Well, the fig genus (Ficus) is one of the oldest genera of flowering plants. Figs have been around a long time.

Soc.: Longer than monkeys?

Eus.: Oh, yes! More than 40,000,000 years (15).

Soc.: Then how did figs get along before there were monkeys?

Eus.: Lots of animals eat figs—birds, coatis, insects, bats—probably more than eat any other tropical fruits.

Soc.: Do other fig-eating animals compete with monkeys?

Eus.: Well, they do reduce the number of figs that are available.

Soc.: Does that matter? Are monkey populations food-limited?

Eus.: This time, I do understand the question. You are asking whether the monkey's populations would increase if they got more food, and decrease if they got less. Well, yes, I think they would (*16*).

Soc.: So the whole future of the species might hinge on whether this monkey finds another fig?

Eus.: You are exaggerating as usual, but I suppose so. Something like the straw that broke the camel's back.

Soc.: Except that in that case, all the straws contributed equally (*17*).

Eus.: I don't follow you.

Soc.: Then follow the monkey. What's he doing now?

Eus.: Dropping half-eaten figs. Just a bite out of each.

Soc.: That seems very wasteful (*18*), and it seems to contradict your claim that monkeys are food-limited.

Eus.: Wrong on both counts! The figs are not identical. Some have higher concentrations of nutrients. Some may be only partly ripe and have more toxins, like ficin. The monkey is probably searching for the best figs. So long as figs are abundant, he can afford to be choosy. As for the population of monkeys, they aren't fig limited, they are nutrient limited. The monkey's problem isn't to maximize his fig intake but only his nutrient intake. By sorting through the fruit, he invests a little time and energy, but increases his nutrient intake.

Soc.: What nutrients does he get out of the figs?

Eus.: Lots, including vitamins A and C, phosphorus, calcium, and especially carbohydrates, which provide energy. Figs are among the most nutritious of tropical fruits (*19*).

Soc.: How does the monkey know which figs to reject and which to eat?

Eus.: By taste. That's what taste buds are for! Look it up in a physiology textbook (*20*).

Soc.: Do you mean to say that animals detect the presence of nutrients in their foods by taste, and can thereby select those foods that they need to obtain a balanced diet?

Eus.: Yes. Mammals have "specific hungers." Years ago, Curt Richter showed that if an animal is deficient in, say, sodium, it selects salty foods (*21*). Similarly, if it is thirsty, it searches for water. If it is low on oxygen it breathes more vigorously, and if it isn't getting enough energy, it prefers a high-calorie diet. For each of these food components, the body has elaborate and specific homeostatic mechanisms, both sensory and effector, including the liver, the kidneys, the lungs, and specialized detectors in the medulla.

Soc.: But the four items that you named, sodium, water, oxygen, and energy, are the only ones, perhaps with the addition of proteins, for which mammals have such genetically determined selection systems. What about all the other nutrients?

Eus.: Well, let's see. It's been suggested that diets that lead to deficiencies are like slow poisons: they become aversive, and the animal switches to other foods (*22*).

Soc.: But which new foods? If the animal is deficient in nutrient X, does it just try other foods at random until it eats something that contains X, starts to feel better, and gets reinforced for eating foods that taste of X?

Eus.: Sure. Some mammals that are deficient in thiamine learn to select thiamine-flavored foods.

Soc.: What about nutrients that do not have a distinctive taste? Vitamin C tastes pretty much like the other organic acids in fruits, malic acid, fructic acid, and so forth. What about pantothenate, which is tasteless? Mammals can't develop a specific hunger for it even by conditioned learning (*21*).

Eus.: No, not by itself, but if you combine pantothenate with a distinctive color or flavor, they can. Even in the absence of specialized physiological mechanisms, specific hungers can develop as a result of aversive learning whenever a deficiency occurs, and in this way the animal learns to select a well-balanced diet.

Soc.: Well, that's what experimental psychologists claim, and it might work on a long time scale, say several weeks or months, depending on the turnover rate of each nutrient, but it cannot over short periods. Phenological changes in a tropical forest occur too rapidly. Even if a monkey settles on an ideal food mix now, the same foods would not be available in a week or two. In a changing world, the animal would constantly be up against one deficiency or another. And surely, Eusebius, a monkey doesn't take a bite out of a fig, see if he develops a deficiency, and if so, drop the fig and try another! So on what basis, then, is he selecting among the figs?

Eus.: Maybe the fig combines sugars, for which the monkeys develop a specific hunger, with other nutrients, like vitamins, which the monkeys can't taste, but need anyway, because they are otherwise deficient in the monkey's diet. The fig might be using colors and odors to cue the monkeys, sugars to motivate them, and vitamins to sustain them.

Soc.: You mean, figs might provide nutrients that are otherwise missing in the monkeys' diet, even though the monkeys are unaware of what they are getting?

Eus.: That's right. For plants like figs that depend on animals for seed dispersal, that would be advantageous….

Soc.: As if fig trees know more about the monkeys' deficiencies than do the monkeys themselves! The biochemical evolution of figs depends on the biochemistry of the other food plants of the fig-eaters (*23*).

Eus.: I hadn't thought of it that way.

Soc.: Now, tell me, Eusebius, does every baby monkey go through this elaborate process of figuring out what to eat?

Eus.: Oh, no! They no doubt learn much on their own, but mostly they learn what to eat by watching their mother….

Soc.: . . . who in turn learned from her mother, and so on (*24*)?

Eus.: Yes.

Soc.: Why, that's culture!

Eus.: No, it isn't, and I do wish you would stop using terms borrowed from human behavior! You're being anthropocentric!

Soc.: Well, monkeys are anthropoids. Besides, do you want me to make up a new word for a phenomenon for every species that shows it? Should geneticists stop talking about inheritance because that term was borrowed from economics?

Eus.: Let's not get into a semantic argument. Besides, there may be an indirect way for infants to learn about foods from their mother that has nothing to do with culture. If a lactating female rat eats onion-flavored food, certain chemicals from the onions get into her milk. Drinking such milk makes her pups more likely to select onion-flavored foods (*25*). And so it may be with the young monkey: it may learn something about which foods to eat at its mother's breast.

Beyond that, I think mother's milk affects learning in a more important way. Milk provides the infant mammal with a long period during which it doesn't have to meet its own nutritional requirements. Milk is a concentrated food, easy to consume and digest, that gives young mammals the time and energy to explore, to try things, and to learn from other members of their group (*26*).

Soc.: Think of it, Eusebius! The evolution of the mammalian cerebral cortex was made possible by lactation. We're smart because we drink milk!

Eus.: You're exaggerating again, Socrates! Let's get back to figs. Ripe figs and fig seeds are unusual in apparently having no toxins, but many other seeds are protected by toxic secondary compounds. Spider monkeys eat *Strychnos* fruit, seeds and all, but because they don't chew the seeds, they are not affected by the strychnine in them (*27*).

Many legume seeds (pulses) contain another toxin, called trypsin inhibitor, yet pulses are favorite foods of many primates. Trypsin inhibitor blocks the gut's ability to digest proteins (*28*). It also makes you very sick, as I found out once when I ate partly cooked beans. Baboons in Africa eat so many green acacia pods that they get sick from the trypsin inhibitor. But they keep forcing their vomit back down. I think they must have some way to detoxify the trypsin inhibitor if they can keep it down long enough. From the baboons' standpoint, legume seeds are too nutritious to pass up: they are more than 20% protein (*29*).

The adult males eat the entire pod of acacias. They chew up the whole green pod and spit out just the fiber. The smaller baboons don't have such powerful jaw muscles, but they are able to be more selective.

It's a matter of size. First they hull the pods, and put the seeds in their cheek pouches. Later they remove the seed coat and swallow just the naked seed. The pod and seed coat, which are rejected, have much more trypsin inhibitor in them, and less in the way of nutrients (*30*). Food manipulation is a way to increase the concentration of nutrients in your food and decrease the concentration of useless or harmful materials.

Soc.: Apparently, the animal's basic problem in resource exploitation lies not so much in finding the essential resources as in solving the packaging problem: nutrients seem always to be packaged with hazards (*31*).

What's our monkey doing now, Eusebius?

Eus.: Still eating figs.

Soc.: Alone?

Eus.: That's the only way, Socrates.

Soc.: Why is that?

Eus.: Because figs of this species occur in widely scattered clusters in the forest and a cluster contains hardly enough ripe fruit for one monkey, let alone two or more.

Soc.: So if two monkeys started eating figs from the same cluster, they would soon be fighting over them. Yet once the fruits of a cluster have all been eaten, there's nothing left to fight about, right?

Eus.: I see what you're getting at. Maybe that's why these monkeys aren't territorial. You have to gain at least as much from being territorial as you lose from the cost of territorial defense. Costs can't exceed benefits.

Soc.: What do you mean by the "cost of defense"? Monkeys don't hire mercenaries to fight for them.

Eus.: That's just ecological jargon. In the short run, territorial defense requires time and energy. It also involves a certain element of risk: some of these territorial battles end in bloodshed. In the long run, however, costs are measured in terms of reproductive success, of "biological fitness."

Soc.: How do you equate them? How many calories or minutes spent on territorial defense are equivalent to one fitness unit?

Eus.: Why do you care?

Soc.: Because I wondered how you know that animals have territories only when the cost is less than the benefits. Besides, if we're going to develop a predictive theory of adaptations, we ought to be able to tell whether, for example, one monkey that expends 1,000 calories and 30 minutes in a territorial dispute is more (or less) fit than another monkey that spends 30 calories and 1,000 minutes.

Eus.: You look to see which has the most babies. That's what fitness is all about!

Soc.: But I thought that's what we wanted to predict. Besides, today's fight is just an isolated event in a whole life history of events. How do we measure the contribution to an organism's fitness of each event in its life history?

Eus.: Hmm. That would be easy if every time animals did something adaptive they popped out another baby, and every time they did something maladaptive they fell over dead.

Soc.: But that's not what happens. So what do we do?

Eus.: I don't know, Socrates.

Soc.: Are you sure?

Eus.: Yes.

Soc.: That's too bad, Eusebius. I was hoping you did, because the answer to that question should be worth a Nobel Prize (*32*). But let's get back to our monkey. Tell me, Eusebius, if these monkeys go off by themselves to feed on figs, how do they ever have a social life? How do they get a mate and raise a family?

Eus.: Oh, I can answer this one! During the rainy season, figs of another species ripen. These are on big trees, and for a while, enormous numbers of figs are all ripe at once. When that happens, all the monkeys in the area come to one or two favorite fig trees and stuff themselves. They stop fighting over figs. Why fight when there's more than enough for everyone? After a few weeks of this gorging, the mating season starts (*33*).

Soc.: Food and sex!

Eus.: It's all tied into aggression, too. The three F's: feeding, fighting, and . . .

Soc.: Watch your language, Eusebius!

Eus.: Anyway, the males start running and swinging wildly through the trees, displaying to the females. Then each female picks one or another of the males to copulate with.

Soc.: Why all the wild running through the trees?

Eus.: Oh, the males are just showing off.

Soc.: You've forgotten what Ronald Fisher said about female mate choice.

Eus.: You mean, that females select males on the basis of the male's ability to increase the *female's* fitness (*34*)? I guess I see what you are driving at. The males are displaying their locomotor ability, which is very useful for traveling through the forest, searching for figs, escaping predators, and so forth. And that ability just might get transmitted to their offspring.

Soc.: After the females select their mates, do they all go off in pairs and raise broods of baby monkeys?

Eus.: Oh, no! The females raise the infants alone. There's not much the male can do for them (*35*). After all, male mammals don't lactate (*36*).

Soc.: Why not?

Eus.: I don't know, Socrates. As I was saying, the female monkey nurses the infant until it can feed itself (*37*), which it can do at an early age: ripe figs are easy to eat.

Soc.: But not always easy to find.

Eus.: No, but the infant rides on the mother from one fig tree to another and learns about such things. Even after infants can walk and climb by themselves, they follow their mothers around until they are about two years old (*9*). And since the male would just compete with the mother and infant for food, they're better off without him. From his standpoint, that's just fine! He can devote more time to trying to mate with other females.

Soc.: Wouldn't the males be helpful at defending the mother and young from predators?

Eus.: Not really. These monkeys don't counterattack predators the way baboons do. They count on their agility in the trees. There isn't a predator in the forest that can keep up with them.

Soc.: Do all fruit-eaters live this way? Widely dispersed, with an open social system, no permanent pair bonds, and no paternal care?

Eus.: Not enough frugivores have been studied to know whether that's the universal system, but it's certainly common. Chimps live that way. So do fruit-eating bellbirds and some fruit-eating bats (*38*). Their social options are constrained by the nature of their food supply.

Soc.: You realize, I suppose, that you are talking like a Marxist.

Eus.: Marxist! Marxist! I never mentioned Marx. And I never mentioned politics. I'm a registered Republican.

Soc.: Karl Marx claimed that the means of making a living determines the structure of society (*39*).

Eus.: Just because Marx and I share an idea doesn't make me a Marxist!

Soc.: But that idea was central to Marx's whole political philosophy.

Eus.: Well, it isn't to mine!

Soc.: You were telling me earlier that the incredible loco-motor abilities of these monkeys—their prehensile tail and so forth—are an adaptation to feeding on widely dispersed food clumps.

Eus.: Yes, in part, but I am beginning to understand that the parts are all interconnected. Maybe we should talk about an "adaptive complex."

Soc.: Which would be what?

Eus.: The rapid-arboreal-locomotion, long-armed, prehensile-tailed, binocular-color-vision, terminal-branch-dispersed-feeding, seed-distributing, milk-drinking, nonterritorial, no-paternal-care, predator-fleeing complex.

Soc.: That is indeed complex! It seems that Darwin was right about baboons after all.

Eus.: When did Darwin get into this conversation?

Soc.: He's been in it all along, Eusebius!

Eus.: I mean, about baboons, what did he say?

Soc.: "He who understands baboon[s] would do more towards metaphysics than Locke" (*40*).

Eus.: Only a little exaggerated, Socrates, only a little!

Soc.: Look there, Eusebius! What do you see?

Eus.: Another monkey!

Soc.: What's he doing?

Eus.: He's . . . he's eating figs!

Soc.: Is he doing anything else?

Eus.: Indeed he is!

Soc.: What else, Eusebius?

Eus.: Why, everything, Socrates, just *everything*!

Notes and references

1. Both the monkeys and the figs described herein are composites of several species. The monkeys are essentially spider monkeys, *Ateles* (Robinson and Janson; van Roosmalen; van Roosmalen et al.), portrayed with some poetic license. The natural history of figs and fig wasps is based largely on traits common to many lowland neotropical species, superbly reviewed by Janzen.
   J. G. Robinson and C. H. Janson. 1987. Capuchins, squirrel monkeys, and atelines. . . . In *Primate Societies*, ed. B. B. Smuts, D. L. Cheney, R. M. Seyfarth, R. W. Wrangham, and T. T. Struhsaker, ch. 7. Univ. of Chicago Press.
   M. G. M. van Roosmalen. 1985. Habitat preferences, diet, feeding strategy and social organization of the black spider monkey (*Ateles paniscus paniscus* Linnaeus 1758) in Surinam. *Acta Amazonica* 15(3/4) (supplement).
   M. G. M. van Roosmalen, P. Loth, and L. L. Klein. In press. The spider monkeys, genus *Ateles*. In *Ecology and Behaviour of Neotropical Primates*, vol. 2, ed. A. F. Coimbra-Filho & R. A. Mittermeier. Brazilian Acad. Sci.
   D. H. Janzen. 1980. How to be a fig. *Ann. Rev. Ecol. Syst.* 10:13–51.

2. B. H. Pubols and L. M. Pubols. 1971. Somatic organization of spider monkey somatic sensory cortex. *J. Comp. Neurol.* 141:63–76. The corresponding motor cortex areas of prehensile primate tails have not yet been mapped.

3. T. I. Grand. 1972. A mechanical interpretation of terminal branch feeding. *J. Mammal.* 53:198–201.

4. P. E. Parsons and C. R. Taylor. 1977. Energetics of brachiation vs. walking: A comparison of a suspended and an inverted pendulum mechanism. *Physiol. Zool.* 50:182–88.
   Gibbons and siamangs are extraordinary brachiators, yet have no tails. The relative efficiency and riskiness of brachiating with or without a prehensile tail have not been investigated.

5. Socrates's comment reflects the empiricist perspective, that the meaning of a statement or question is its means of verification, or, put the other way around, if no conceivable observation would answer a question, it is empirically meaningless.
   H. Reichenbach. 1951. The verifiability theory of meaning. *Proc. Am. Acad. Arts and Sci.* 80:46–60.

6. G. H. Jacobs. 1981. *Comparative Color Vision*. Academic Press.
   Snodderly, D. M. 1979. Visual discriminations encountered in food foraging by a neotropical primate: Implications for the evolution of color vision. In *The Behavioral Significance of Color*, ed. E. H. Burt, Jr., pp. 237–79. Garland Press.

7. Many animal-dispersed seeds have characteristics that enable them to pass intact through the vertebrate gut (Janzen). Some species of tropical trees are reported to be completely dependent on primates for seed dispersal (van Roosmalen, ref. *1*).
   D. H. Janzen. 1983. Dispersal of seeds by vertebrate guts. In *Coevolution*, ed. D. J. Futuyma and M. Slatkin, ch. 11. Sinauer.

8. D. McKey. 1979. The distribution of secondary compounds within plants. In *Herbivores: Their Interaction with Secondary Plant Metabolites*, ed. G. A. Rosenthal and D. H. Janzen, ch. 2. Academic Press.

9. K. Milton. 1981. Distribution patterns of tropical plant foods as an evolutionary stimulus to primate mental development. *Am. Anthropol.* 83:534–48.

10. Leaf-eating primates, such as colobines and howlers, spend inordinate amounts of time stationary, compared with other primates. The extent of lethargy or obligatory resting time is reflected, albeit imperfectly, in basal metabolic rate. Among mammals, both arboreal leaf- and fruit-eaters tend to have depressed metabolic rates.
    B. K. McNab. 1986. The influence of food habits on the energetics of eutherian mammals. *Ecol. Monogr.* 56:1–19.

11. S. J. C. Gaulin. 1979. A Jarmen/Bell model of primate feeding niches. *Human Ecol.* 7:1–20.

12. S. Altmann and J. Altmann. 1970. *Baboon Ecology: African Field Research.* Univ. of Chicago Press.

13. D. H. Janzen. 1979. How many babies do figs pay for babies? *Biotropica* 11:48–50.

14. Eusebius failed to catch an error in reasoning by Socrates. Unless fig wasps enter diapause and then become sexually active a year after they are conceived, the fig wasps of, say, a given January cannot mate with those of the next January. Therefore, the fig wasps of a particular season do not constitute a gene pool.

15. The oldest fossils recognizable as *Ficus* date from the Lower Tertiary (Chandler), so figs are at least 40 million years old. The oldest known monkey fossil is that of *Prohylobates tandyi*, a Miocene fossil (Simon) and so about 25 million years old.

M. E. J. Chandler. 1961–64. *The Lower Tertiary Floras of Southern England. . . .* Brit. Mus. (Nat. Hist.).

Simons, E. 1972. *Primate Evolution.* Macmillan.

16. J. G. H. Cant. 1980. What limits primates? *Primates* 19:525–35.

Iwamoto, T. 1978. Food availability as a limiting factor on population density of the Japanese monkey and gelada baboon. In *Recent Advances in Primatology,* ed. D. J. Chivers and J. Herbert, pp. 287–303. Academic Press.

17. Contrary to implications of the expression "the straw that broke the camel's back," the masses of various straws contribute additively to a camel's burden. By contrast, organisms are integrated systems in which many traits are correlated with each other, and the effect of correlated traits on fitness are not necessarily additive. This phenomenon of coadaptation (or, at the genetic level, epistasis) is well known but has only recently been incorporated into formal models of well-adapted organisms (Altmann) or of contributions to fitness (Lande and Arnold).

S. A. Altmann. 1984. What is the dual of the energy-maximization problem? *Am. Nat.* 123:433–41.

Lande, R., and S. J. Arnold. 1983. The measurement of selection on correlated traits. *Evolution* 37:1210–26.

18. H. Howe. 1980. Monkey dispersal and waste of a neotropical fruit. *Ecology* 61:944–59.

19. J. A. Duke and A. A. Atchley. 1986. *CRC Handbook of Proximate Analysis Tables of Higher Plants.* CRC Press.

20. C.M. Lang. 1970. Organoleptic and other characteristics of diet which influence acceptance by nonhuman primates. In *Feeding and Human Nutrition,* ed. R. S. Harris, pp. 263–75. Academic Press.

21. C. P. Richter. 1943. Total self regulatory functions in animals and human beings. *Harvey Lecture Ser.* 38:63–103.

Rozin, P. 1976. The selection of foods by rats, humans, and other animals. *Adv. Study Behav.* 6:21–76.

22. L. M. Barker, M. R. Best, and M. Domjan, eds. 1977. *Learning Mechanisms in Food Selection.* Baylor Univ. Press.

23. Socrates is speculating that in some cases, plants with animal-dispersed seeds have been selected to produce fruits with nutrients that are otherwise in short supply in the diet of their major seed-dispersers. For example, fruits that are eaten by partially frugivorous birds tend to be high in water and carbohydrates but deficient in proteins and other nutrients, whereas those eaten by specialized frugivorous birds also supply lipids and proteins.

D. McKey. 1975. The ecology of coevolved seed dispersal systems. In *Coevolution of Animals and Plants,* ed. L. E. Gilbert and P. H. Raven, pp. 159–91. Univ. of Texas Press.

24. For tropical, omnivorous primates and many other group-living animals, social learning of what to eat and what not to eat may be a major factor selecting for group living and for prolonged immaturity. A recent study of young howler monkeys suggests that they use social cues from adults when learning which leaves to eat, whereas trial-and-error learning is used for fruits. Leaves are more likely to be toxic, whereas fruits containing animal-dispersed seeds are typically nutritious, colorful, flavorful, and scented.

J. Whitehead. 1988. The development of feeding selectivity in mantled howling monkeys. In *Proc. 10th Congr. Intl. Primatol. Soc.,* ed. J. Else and P. Lee. Cambridge Univ. Press.

25. B. G. Galef, Jr. 1976. Social transmission of acquired behavior. . . . *Adv. Study Behav.* 6:77–100.

26. C. M. Pond. 1977. The significance of lactation in the evolution of mammals. *Evolution* 31:177–99.

27. van Roosmalen, ref. *1.*

28. C. A. Ryan. 1979. Proteinase inhibitors. In *Herbivores: Their Interaction with Secondary Plant Metabolites,* ed. G. A. Rosenthal and D. H. Janzen, ch. 17. Academic Press.

29. S. A. Altmann, D. G. Post and D. F. Klein. 1987. Nutrients and toxins of plants in Amboseli, Kenya. *Afr. J. Ecol.* 25:279–93.

30. S. A. Altmann. Unpubl. *Foraging for Survival: Weanling Baboons In Africa.*

The primary nutritional consequence of discarding the pod and seed coat of *Acacia tortilis* is to increase the protein concentration of the diet and decrease its fiber content. Rejecting the seed coat reduces trypsin inhibitor intake by 62%; the trypsin inhibitor content of the pods is not yet known.

31. S. A. Altmann. 1985. More on hominid diet before fire. *Curr. Anthropol.* 26:661–62.

32. Repetitions of actions or events in a life history do not always contribute equally to an organism's fitness. The contribution of a given fig's protein to the monkey's fitness depends on whether the monkey's diet at the time is otherwise lacking in protein, the effect of a birth on the mother's fitness depends on her age, the contribution of an egg to a bird's fitness depends on how many other eggs are in the clutch, and so on. Thus, measuring the contribution of behavior to fitness is more difficult than it is for abiding traits, such as those of morphology or physiology.

33. The role of food in triggering primate breeding seasons is unknown. Smuts et al., ref. *1.*

34. This concept is implicit in Fisher's discussion of sexual selection. It is now widely accepted, although the empirical evidence is inadequate.

R. A. Fisher. 1958. *The Genetical Theory of Natural Selection,* 2nd ed. Dover Press.

35. Eusebius is wrong here. The male could do much to increase the fitness of his offspring, by teaching them, feeding them, guarding them, and so forth. However, extensive paternal care is unlikely in species in which males have a lower expected fitness if they care for their present brood than if they desert them and seek additional mating opportunities elsewhere.

R. L. Trivers. 1972. Parental investment and sexual selection. In *Sexual Selection and the Descent of Man, 1871–1971,* ed. B. Campbell. Aldine.

36. M. Daly. 1979. Why don't male mammals lactate? *J. Theoret. Biol.* 78:325–45.

37. For limits on a female primate's ability to provide parental care, see J. Altmann, 1980, *Baboon Mothers and Infants,* Harvard Univ. Press.

38. T. H. Kunz, ed. *Ecology of Bats.* Plenum.

Rodman, P. S. 1984. Foraging and social systems of orangs and chimpanzees. In *Adaptations for Foraging in Nonhuman Primates,* ed. P. S. Rodman and J. G. H. Cant, ch. 5. Columbia Univ. Press.

B. K. Snow. 1970. A field study of the bearded bellbird in Trinidad. *Ibis* 112:299–329.

39. Marx expressed this idea in various ways: for example, "The mode of production in material life determines the general character of the social, political, and spiritual processes of life." Similarly, a widespread assumption in behavioral ecology is that the diversity of social systems in the animal kingdom primarily reflects adaptations to food and other resources, and to predation and other hazards. For a startling lack of relationships between social, ecological, and life-history variables in primates, see Harvey et al.

Harvey, P. H., R. D. Martin, and T. H. Clutton-Brock. 1987. Life histories in comparative perspective. In *Primate Societies,* ref. *1.*

Marx, K. 1859 (reprinted 1904). *A Contribution to the Critique of Political Economy.* Chicago: Kerr.

40. C. Darwin. 1838. Notebook M, p. 84. In *Charles Darwin's Notebooks, 1836–1844,* ed. P. H. Barrett, P. J. Gautrey, S. Herbert, D. Kohn, and S. Smith. Brit. Mus. (Nat. Hist.).

The following *American Scientist* staff artists contributed illustrations to the articles in this collection.

Elyse Carter

Robin M. Gowen

Brian Hayes

Susan Hochgraf

Linda K. Huff

Rebecca Lehmann-Sprouse

Edward D. Roberts III

Linda Price Thomson

In addition, the work of the following freelance artists appears on the pages cited.

Beverly Benner Fig. 3, p. 6 (with V. Kask); Fig. 5, p. 7; Fig. 9, p. 9; Fig. 10, p. 10; Fig. 11, p. 11; Fig. 7, p. 49; Fig. 2, p. 154; Fig. 3, p. 155; Figs. 5 and 6, p. 157; Fig. 7, p. 158; Fig. 4, p. 194.

Sally Black Fig. 1, pp. 278-279.

Aaron Cox Fig. 8, p. 34 and Fig. 13, p. 36 (with L. Huff); Fig. 14, p. 37; Fig. 15, p. 38 (with L. Huff).

Virge Kask Fig. 3, p. 6 (with B. Benner); Fig. 11, p. 35; Fig. 12, p. 36; Fig. 3, p. 46; Fig. 6, p. 145; Fig. 7, p. 146; Fig. 9, p. 148; Fig. 1, p. 153; Fig. 2, p. 192.